TExES Generalist 4-8
111 Teacher Certification Exam

By: Sharon Wynne, M.S.
Southern Connecticut State University

"And, while there's no reason yet to panic, I think it's only prudent that we make preparations to panic."

XAMonline, INC.
Boston

To obtain permission(s) to use the material from this work for any purpose including workshops or seminars, please submit a written request to:

XAMonline, Inc.
21 Orient Ave.
Melrose, MA 02176
Toll Free 1-800-509-4128
Email: info@xamonline.com
Web www.xamonline.com
Fax: 1-781-662-9268

Library of Congress Cataloging-in-Publication Data
Wynne, Sharon A.
TExES: Generalist 4-8 111 Teacher Certification / Sharon A. Wynne. -2nd ed. ISBN: 978-1-58197-271-9
1. Generalist 4-8 111 2. Study Guides. 3. TExES 4. Teachers' Certification & Licensure. 5. Careers

Managing Editor	Dr. Harte Weiner, Ph. D.
Copy Editor	Deborah Harbin, M.A.
Assistant Editor	Anna Wong
Production Coordinator	David Aronson

Disclaimer:
The opinions expressed in this publication are the sole works of XAMonline and were created independently from the National Education Association, Educational Testing Service, or any State Department of Education, National Evaluation Systems or other testing affiliates. Between the time of publication and printing, state specific standards as well as testing formats and website information may change that is not included in part or in whole within this product. Sample test questions are developed by XAMonline and reflect similar content as on real tests; however, they are not former tests. XAMonline assembles content that aligns with state standards but makes no claims nor guarantees teacher candidates a passing score. Numerical scores are determined by testing companies such as NES or ETS and then are compared with individual state standards. A passing score varies from state to state.

Printed in the United States of America   œ-1

TExES: Generalist 4-8 111
ISBN: 978-1-58197-271-9

Table of Contents

DOMAIN IV.   SCIENCE

Great Study and Testing Tips!

What to study in order to prepare for the subject assessments is the focus of this study guide but equally important is *how* you study.

You can increase your chances of truly mastering the information by taking some simple, but effective steps.

Study Tips:

1. Some foods aid the learning process. Foods such as milk, nuts, seeds, rice, and oats help your study efforts by releasing natural memory enhancers called CCKs (*cholecystokinin*) composed of *tryptopha*n, *choline*, and *phenylalanine*. All of these chemicals enhance the neurotransmitters associated with memory. Before studying, try a light, protein-rich meal of eggs, turkey, and fish. All of these foods release the memory enhancing chemicals. The better the connections, the more you comprehend.

Likewise, before you take a test, stick to a light snack of energy boosting and relaxing foods. A glass of milk, a piece of fruit, or some peanuts all release various memory-boosting chemicals and help you to relax and focus on the subject at hand.

2. Learn to take great notes. A by-product of our modern culture is that we have grown accustomed to getting our information in short doses (i.e. TV news sound bites or USA Today style newspaper articles.)

Consequently, we've subconsciously trained ourselves to assimilate information better in neat little packages. If your notes are scrawled all over the paper, it fragments the flow of the information. Strive for clarity. Newspapers use a standard format to achieve clarity. Your notes can be much clearer through use of proper formatting. A very effective format is called the *"Cornell Method."*

> Take a sheet of loose-leaf lined notebook paper and draw a line all the way down the paper about 1-2" from the left-hand edge.

> Draw another line across the width of the paper about 1-2" up from the bottom. Repeat this process on the reverse side of the page.

Look at the highly effective result. You have ample room for notes, a left hand margin for special emphasis items or inserting supplementary data from the textbook, a large area at the bottom for a brief summary, and a little rectangular space for just about anything you want.

3. Get the concept then the details. Too often we focus on the details and don't gather an understanding of the concept. However, if you simply memorize only dates, places, or names, you may well miss the whole point of the subject.

A key way to understand things is to put them in your own words. If you are working from a textbook, automatically summarize each paragraph in your mind. If you are outlining text, don't simply copy the author's words.

Rephrase them in your own words. You remember your own thoughts and words much better than someone else's, and subconsciously tend to associate the important details to the core concepts.

4. Ask Why? Pull apart written material paragraph by paragraph and don't forget the captions under the illustrations.

Example: If the heading is "Stream Erosion", flip it around to read "Why do streams erode?" Then answer the questions.

If you train your mind to think in a series of questions and answers, not only will you learn more, but it also helps to lessen the test anxiety because you are used to answering questions.

5. Read for reinforcement and future needs. Even if you only have 10 minutes, put your notes or a book in your hand. Your mind is similar to a computer; you have to input data in order to have it processed. *By reading, you are creating the neural connections for future retrieval.* The more times you read something, the more you reinforce the learning of ideas.

Even if you don't fully understand something on the first pass, *your mind stores much of the material for later recall.*

6. Relax to learn so go into exile. Our bodies respond to an inner clock called biorhythms. Burning the midnight oil works well for some people, but not everyone.

If possible, set aside a particular place to study that is free of distractions. Shut off the television, cell phone, and pager and exile your friends and family during your study period.

If you really are bothered by silence, try background music. Light classical music at a low volume has been shown to aid in concentration over other types. Music that evokes pleasant emotions without lyrics is highly suggested. Try just about anything by Mozart. It relaxes you.

7. <u>**Use arrows not highlighters.**</u> At best, it's difficult to read a page full of yellow, pink, blue, and green streaks. Try staring at a neon sign for a while and you'll soon see that the horde of colors obscure the message.

A quick note, a brief dash of color, an underline, and an arrow pointing to a particular passage is much clearer than a horde of highlighted words.

8. <u>**Budget your study time.**</u> Although you shouldn't ignore any of the material, *allocate your available study time in the same ratio that topics may appear on the test.*

Testing Tips:

1. Get smart, play dumb. Don't read anything into the question. Don't make an assumption that the test writer is looking for something else than what is asked. Stick to the question as written and don't read extra things into it.

2. Read the question and all the choices *twice* before answering the question. You may miss something by not carefully reading, and then re-reading both the question and the answers.

If you really don't have a clue as to the right answer, leave it blank on the first time through. Go on to the other questions, as they may provide a clue as to how to answer the skipped questions.

If later on, you still can't answer the skipped ones . . . ***Guess.*** The only penalty for guessing is that you *might* get it wrong. Only one thing is certain; if you don't put anything down, you will get it wrong!

3. Turn the question into a statement. Look at the way the questions are worded. The syntax of the question usually provides a clue. Does it seem more familiar as a statement rather than as a question? Does it sound strange?

By turning a question into a statement, you may be able to spot if an answer sounds right, and it may also trigger memories of material you have read.

4. Look for hidden clues. It's actually very difficult to compose multiple-foil (choice) questions without giving away part of the answer in the options presented.

In most multiple-choice questions you can often readily eliminate one or two of the potential answers. This leaves you with only two real possibilities and automatically your odds go to Fifty-Fifty for very little work.

5. Trust your instincts. For every fact that you have read, you subconsciously retain something of that knowledge. On questions that you aren't really certain about, go with your basic instincts. **Your first impression on how to answer a question is usually correct.**

6. Mark your answers directly on the test booklet. Don't bother trying to fill in the optical scan sheet on the first pass through the test.

Just be very careful not to miss-mark your answers when you eventually transcribe them to the scan sheet.

7. Watch the clock! You have a set amount of time to answer the questions. Don't get bogged down trying to answer a single question at the expense of 10 questions you can more readily answer.

COMPETENCY 1.0 ORAL LANGUAGE

Skill 1.1   Knows basic linguistic concepts and developmental stages in acquiring oral language, including stages in phonology, semantics, syntax, and pragmatics, and recognizes that individual variations occur.

Learning approach

Early theories of language development were formulated from learning theory research. The assumption was language development evolved by learning the rules of language structures and applying them through imitation and reinforcement. This approach also assumed language, cognitive, and social developments were independent of each other. Thus, children were expected to learn language from patterning after adults who spoke and wrote standard English. No allowance was made for communication through child jargon, idiomatic expressions, grammatical and mechanical errors resulting from too strict adherence to the rules of inflection (*childs* instead of *children*) or conjugation (*runned* instead of *ran*). No association was made between physical and operational development and language mastery.

Linguistic approach

Studies spearheaded by Noam Chomsky in the 1950s formulated the theory that language ability is innate and develops through natural human maturation as environmental stimuli trigger acquisition of syntactical structures appropriate to each exposure level. The assumption of a hierarchy of syntax downplayed the significance of semantics. Because of the complexity of syntax and the relative speed with which children acquire language, linguists attributed language development to biology rather than cognitive or social influences.

Cognitive approach

Some researchers in the 1970s proposed that language knowledge derives from both syntactic and semantic structures. Drawing on the studies of Piaget and other cognitive learning theorists (see Skill 4.7), supporters of the cognitive approach maintained children acquire knowledge of linguistic structures after they have acquired the cognitive structures necessary to process language. For example, joining words for specific meaning necessitates sensory motor intelligence. The child must be able to coordinate movement and recognize objects before she can identify words to name the objects or word groups to describe the actions performed with those objects.

Adolescents must have developed the mental abilities for <u>organizing concepts as well as concrete operations</u>, <u>predicting outcomes</u>, and <u>theorizing</u> before they can assimilate and verbalize complex sentence structures, choose vocabulary for particular nuances of meaning, and examine semantic structures for tone and manipulative effect.

Sociocognitive approach

Other theorists in the 1970s proposed language development results from sociolinguistic competence. Language, cognitive, and social knowledge are interactive elements of total human development. Emphasis on verbal communication as the medium for language expression resulted in the inclusion of speech activities in most language arts curricula.

Unlike previous approaches, the sociocognitive allowed that determining the appropriateness of language in given situations for specific listeners is as important as understanding semantic and syntactic structures. By engaging in conversation, children at all stages of development have opportunities to test their language skills, receive feedback, and make modifications. As a social activity, conversation is as structured by social order as grammar is structured by the rules of syntax. Conversation satisfies the learner's need to be heard and understood and to influence others. Thus, his choices of vocabulary, tone, and content are dictated by his ability to assess the language knowledge of his listeners. He is constantly applying his cognitive skills to using language in a social interaction. If the capacity to acquire language is inborn, without an environment in which to practice language, a child would not pass beyond the grunts and gestures used by primitive man.

Of course, the varying degrees of environmental stimuli to which children are exposed at all age levels creates a slower or faster development of language. Some children are prepared to articulate concepts and recognize symbolism by the time they enter fifth grade because they have been exposed to challenging reading and conversations with well-spoken adults at home or in their social groups. Others are still trying to master the sight recognition skills and are not yet ready to combine words in complex patterns.

Concerns for the teacher

Because teachers must, by virtue of tradition and the mandates of the curriculum, teach grammar, usage, and writing as well as reading and later literature, the problem becomes when to teach what to whom. The profusion of approaches to teaching grammar alone are mind-boggling. In the universities, other forms of grammar are taught including: transformational grammar, stratificational grammar, sectoral grammar, etc. In practice, most teachers supported by presentations in textbooks and by the methods they themselves learned, return to the same traditional prescriptive approach - read and imitate - structural approach - learn the parts of speech, the parts of sentence, punctuation rules, sentence patterns.

After enough of the terminology and rules are stored in the brain, children learn to write and speak. For some educators, the best solution is the worst - they do not teach grammar.

The same problems occur in teaching usage. How much can we demand students communicate in only standard English? Different schools of thought suggest a study of dialect, idioms, and recognition of various jargons is a vital part of language development. Social pressures, especially on students in middle and junior high schools, to be accepted within their peer groups and to speak the non-standard language spoken outside the school setting make adolescents resistant to the corrective, remedial approach. In many communities where the immigrant populations are high, new words are entering English from other languages even as words and expressions that were previously common have become rare or obsolete.

Regardless of differences of opinion concerning language development, it is safe to say a language arts teacher will be most effective using the styles and approaches with which she is most comfortable. In a student-centered approach, the teacher may find that the students have much to teach her and each other. Moffett and Wagner in the Fourth Edition of *Student-centered Language Arts K-12* stress the three I's: individualization, interaction, and integration. Essentially, this supports the socio-cognitive approach to language development. By providing an opportunity for the student to select his own activities and resources, his instruction is individualized. By centering on and teaching each other, students are interactive. Finally, by allowing students to synthesize a variety of knowledge structures, they integrate them. The teacher's role becomes that of a facilitator.

Benefits of the socio-cognitive approach

This approach tended to guide the whole language movement within reading. Most basal readers utilize an integrated, cross-curricular approach to successful grammar, language, and usage. Reinforcement becomes an intradepartmental responsibility. Language incorporates diction and terminology across the curriculum. Standard usage is encouraged and supported by both the core classroom textbooks and current software for technology. Teachers need to acquaint themselves with the computer capabilities in their school district and at their individual school sites. Advances in technologies require the teacher to familiarize herself with programs that would best serve her students' needs. Students respond enthusiastically to technology. Several highly effective programs are available in various formats to assist students with initial instruction or remediation. Grammar texts, such as the Warriner's series, employ various methods to reach individual learning styles. The school library media center should become a focal point for individual exploration.

Skill 1.2 **Knows characteristics and uses of informal and formal oral language assessments and uses multiple, ongoing assessments to monitor and evaluate students' oral language skills.**

Language Skills to Evaluate:

- The ability to talk at length with few pauses and fill time with speech
- The ability to call up appropriate thing to say in a wide range of contexts
- The size and range of a student's vocabulary and syntax skills
- The coherence of their sentences, the ability to speak in reasoned and semantically dense sentences
- Knowledge of the various forms of interaction and conversation for various situations
- Knowledge of the standard rules of conversation
- The ability to be creative and imaginative with language, and express oneself in original ways
- The ability to invent and entertain, and take risks in linguistic expression

Methods of Evaluation:

- Commercially designed language assessment products
- Instructor observation using a rating scale from 1 to 5 (where 1=limited proficiency and 5=native speaker equivalency)
- Informal observation of students' behaviors

Skill 1.3 **Provides language instruction that acknowledges students' current oral language skills and that builds on these skills to increase students' oral language proficiency.**

See Skills 1.4, 1.5, and 1.6.

Skill 1.4 **Plans, implements, and adapts instruction that is based on informal and formal assessment of students' progress in oral language development and that addresses the needs, strengths, and interests of individual students, including English Language Learners.**

Second Language Learners

Students who are raised in homes where English is not the first language and/or where standard English is not spoken, may have difficulty hearing the difference between similar sounding words like "send" and "sent." Any student who is not in an environment where they are regularly exposed to English phonology, may have difficulty perceiving and demonstrating the differences between the many English language phonemes.

If students can not hear the difference between words that "sound similar" like "grow" and "glow," they may be confused when these words appear in a print context. This confusion will of course, sadly, impact their comprehension.

Considerations for teaching to English Language Learners (ELL) include recognition by the teacher that there will be differences in teaching strategies for students for whom English is the primary language and those for whom it is not.

Research recommends that ELL students learn to read initially in their first language. It has been found to be a priority for ELL students to learn to speak English before being taught to read it. Research supports oral language development, since it lays the foundation for phonological awareness a foundational skill for reading skill development.

Skill 1.5 Recognizes when oral language delays or differences warrant in-depth evaluation and additional help or intervention.

Without immediate, consistent, and appropriate intervention, children who begin their formal education with cultural/language differences or other delays in literacy development may quickly fall behind, and typically, they do not "catch up." By the time they reach middle school, they may have already repeated several grades and/or have been assigned to numerous transition classes.

By the time students are in middle school, they are expected to use reading as a primary method of learning and to be able to communicate effectively orally and in writing. Students who have fallen behind in the early grades fail to meet these expectations and are forced to develop coping strategies to compensate for their perceived failures. These coping strategies, which often include inappropriate, problematic, and disruptive behavior, serve to further isolate and remove the students from the mainstream educational process and from effective interventional efforts.

Middle school students with delays in literacy development can be identified in a number of ways: they avoid reading as much as possible; when reading out loud, they read everything at the same rate, slowly; they do not read outside of school; they demonstrate a limited vocabulary, they rely on teachers or classmates for information; they resist participation in classroom discussions; they have limited attention spans; they demonstrate a lack of comprehension of material they have read; they are unfamiliar with and do not exhibit reading strategies; they are poor listeners; their writing is unstructured and contains a high rate of misspellings and grammatical and mechanical errors; they "give up" quickly when given a reading or writing task; they do not ask relevant questions; they do not know what to do when they encounter material they do not understand; and they read and write without a sense of purpose.

In addition to students with delayed literacy development, non-English-speaking students may also be in need of in-depth evaluation and intervention. Because command of the spoken language serves as a basis for understanding and learning alphabetic principles, as well as the structure and content of the language, oral proficiency precedes proficiency in reading and writing. Thus children without strong oral skills are in need of special consideration—assisting them in gaining oral proficiency must become the primary task.

Skill 1.6   **Knows how to provide explicit, systematic oral language instruction and supports students' learning and use of oral language through meaningful and purposeful activities implemented one-to-one and in a group.**

Have students break into groups and ask them to prepare a plan for how to best communicate to their audience (the other members of their group). Tell them to keep these guidelines in mind:

- **Values**- What is important to this group of people? What is their background and how will that affect their perception of your speech?
- **Needs**- Find out in advance what the audience's needs are. Why are they listening to you? Find a way to satisfy their needs.
- **Constraints**- What might hold the audience back from being fully engaged in what you are saying, or agreeing with your point of view, or processing what you are trying to say? These could be political reasons, which make them wary of your presentation's ideology from the start, or knowledge reasons, in which the audience lacks the appropriate background information to grasp your ideas. Avoid this last constraint by staying away from technical terminology, slang, or abbreviations that may be unclear to your audience.
- **Demographic Information**- Take the audience's size into account, as well as the location of the presentation.

Start where the listeners are, and then take them where you want to go!

Skill 1.7   **Selects and uses instructional materials and strategies that promote students' oral language development; that respond to students' individual strengths, needs and interests; that reflect cultural diversity; and that build on students' cultural, linguistic, and home backgrounds to enhance their oral language development.**

"Political correctness" is a new concept tossed around frequently in the 21st century. It has always existed, of course. The successful speaker of the 19th century understood and was sensitive to audiences. However due to societal norms of the time, that person was typically a man, and the only audience that was important was a male audience, and more often than not, the only important audience was a white one.

Many things have changed since the 19th century. Just as the society the speaker lives in and addresses has changed, the speaker who disregards the existing conventions for "political correctness" usually finds himself/herself in trouble. Rap music makes a point of ignoring those conventions, particularly with regard to gender, and is often the target of very hostile attacks. On the other hand, rap performers often intend to be revolutionary, have developed their own audiences, and have become outrageously wealthy by exploiting those newly-developed audiences based primarily by thumbing their noses at establishment conventions.

Even so, the successful speaker must understand and be sensitive to what is current in "political correctness." The "n word" is a case in point. There was a time when that term was thrown about at will by politicians and other public speakers, but no more. Nothing could spell the end of a politician's career more certainly than using that term in his campaign or public addresses.

These terms are called "pejorative"—a word or phrase that expresses contempt or disapproval. Such terms as *redneck*, *queer*, or *cripple* may only be considered pejorative if used by a non-member of the group they apply to. For example, the "n word," which became very inflammatory in the 1960s, is now being used sometimes by African-American artists to refer to themselves, especially in their music, with the intention of underscoring their protest of the establishment.

References to gender have became particularly sensitive in the 20th century as a result of the women's rights movement, and the speaker who disregards these sensitivities does so at his/her own peril. The generic "he" is no longer acceptable, and this requires a strategy to deal with pronominal references without repetitive he/she, his/her, etc. Several ways to approach this: switch to a passive construction that does not require a subject; switch back and forth, using the male pronoun in one reference and the female pronoun in another one, being sure to sprinkle them reasonably evenly; or switch to the plural. The last alternative is the one most often chosen. This requires some care, and the speaker should spend time developing these skills before speaking in front of an audience.

Skill 1.8 **Understands relationships between the development of oral language and the development of reading and provides instruction that interrelated oral and written language to promote students' reading proficiency and learning.**

English is an Indo-European language that evolved through several periods. The origin of English dates to the settlement of the British Isles in the fifth and sixth centuries by Germanic tribes called the Angles, Saxons, and Jutes. The original Britons spoke a Celtic tongue while the Angles spoke a Germanic dialect. Modern English derives from the speech of the Anglo-Saxons who imposed not only their language but also their social customs and laws on their new land. From the fifth to the tenth century, Britain's language was the tongue we now refer to as Old English. During the next four centuries, the many French attempts at English conquest introduced many of the French words to English. However, the grammar and syntax of the language remained Germanic.

Middle English, most evident in the writings of Geoffrey Chaucer, dates loosely from 1066 to 1509. William Caxton brought the printing press to England in 1474 and increased literacy. Old English words required numerous inflections to indicate noun cases and plurals as well as verb conjugations. Middle English continued the use of many inflections and pronunciations which treated these inflections as separately pronounced syllables. English in 1300 would have been written "Olde Anglishe" with the e's at the ends of the words pronounced as our short a vowel. Even adjectives had plural inflections: "long day" became "longe daies" pronounced "long-a day-as." Spelling was phonetic, thus every vowel had multiple pronunciations, a fact that continues to affect the language.

Modern English dates from the introduction of The Great Vowels Shift because it created guidelines for spelling and pronunciation. Before the printing press, books were copied laboriously by hand; the language was subject to the individual interpretation of the scribes. Printers and subsequently lexicographers, like Samuel Johnson and America's Noah Webster, influenced the guidelines. As reading matter was mass produced, the reading public was forced to adopt the speech and writing habits developed by those who wrote and printed books.

Despite many students' insistence to the contrary, Shakespeare's writings are in Modern English. It is important to stress to students that language, like customs, morals, and other social factors, is constantly subject to change. Immigration, inventions, and cataclysmic events change language as much as any other facet of life affected by these changes. The domination of one race or nation over others can change a language significantly. Beginning with the colonization of the New World, English and Spanish became dominant languages in the Western hemisphere. American English today is somewhat different in pronunciation and sometimes vocabulary from British English. The British call a truck a "lorry;" baby carriages a "pram," short for "perambulator;" and an elevator a "lift."

There are very few syntactical differences, and even the tonal qualities that were once so clearly different are converging.

Though Modern English is less complex than Middle English, having lost many unnecessary inflections, it is still considered difficult to learn because of its many exceptions to the rules. It has, however, become the world's dominant language due to the great political, military, and social power of England from the fifteenth to the nineteenth century and of America in the twentieth century.

Modern inventions - the telephone, phonograph, radio, television, and motion pictures - have especially affected English pronunciation. Regional dialects, once a hindrance to clear understanding, have fewer distinct characteristics. The speakers from different parts of the United States of America can be identified by their accents, but more and more as educators and media personalities stress uniform pronunciations and proper grammar, the differences are diminishing.

The English language has a more extensive vocabulary than any other language. Ours is a language of synonyms, words borrowed from other languages, and coined words/phrases - many of them introduced by the rapid expansion of technology. *—dropping an -e*

It is important for students to understand language is in constant flux. Emphasis should be placed on learning and using language for specific purposes and audiences. Negative criticism of a student's errors in word choice or sentence structures will inhibit creativity. Positive criticism that suggests ways to enhance communication skills will encourage exploration.

Skill 1.9 Knows similarities and differences between oral and written language and how to promote students' awareness of these similarities and differences.

Although widely different in many aspects, written and spoken English share a common basic structure or syntax (subject, verb, object) and the common purpose of fulfilling the need to communicate—but there, the similarities end.

Spoken English does follow the basic word order mentioned above (subject, verb object) as does written English. We would write as we would speak, "I sang a song." It is usually only in poetry or music that that word order or syntax is altered: "Sang I a song." However, beyond that, spoken English is freed from the constraints and expectations imposed upon the written word.

Because of these restraints, in the form of rules of grammar and punctuation, learning to read and write occupy years of formal schooling, whereas learning to speak is a natural developmental stage, much like walking, that is accomplished before the tedious process of learning to write what has been spoken is endured.

These rules are imposed upon the written language, in part, because of necessity. Written English is an isolated event. The writer must use an expected, ordered structure, complete with proper spacing and punctuation in order to be understood by an audience that he or she may never see.

In contrast, the speaker of English can rely on hand gestures, facial expressions, and tone of voice to convey information and emotions beyond that which is conveyed in his or her words alone. In addition, speaking is not usually an isolated event. A speaker has a listener who can interrupt, ask questions, or provide additional information, ensuring the communication is understood.

Thus, spoken English is a much more fluid form of communication and is more directly suited to meeting the needs of the particular audience. This gives rise to regional dialects and forms of expressions that with time and usage may find their way into formal written English.

However, with technology, there are new avenues for communication that are resulting in a synthesis of these two forms of communication: text messaging and chat room dialogues. In these forms, written English is not bound by the formal rules of spelling, grammar, and punctuation—rather it is free to more closely mimic its spoken counterpart.

Want to shout your answer? USE ALL CAPS! Saying something with a smile? Then show it! ☺ The limited space on cell phones and the immediacy of Internet chat rooms has also led to adaptations in spelling, where, for example, "text message" becomes "txt msg." Other abbreviated spellings and expressions have gained reached such popular usage that in 2005, the world's first dxNRE & glosRE (dictionary and glossary), "transl8it!" (Translate!) was published to help in the translation of standard English into text speak. Although these unorthodox forms of communication may frighten formal grammarians, this brave new world of communicating, as employed online and via cell phones, is far from being the death knell for "proper" English. Rather it is just one more indication of the versatility of our language and the ingenuity and creativity of the individuals who employ it.

Skill 1.10 **Selects and uses instructional strategies, materials, activities, and models to strengthen students' oral vocabulary and narrative skills in spoken language and teaches students to connect spoken and printed language.**

See Skill 1.3.

Skill 1.11 **Selects and uses instructional strategies, materials, activities, and models to teach students skills for speaking to different audiences for various purposes and for adapting spoken language for various audiences, purposes, and occasions.**

The content in material to be presented orally plays a big role in how it is organized and delivered. For example, a literary analysis or a book report will be organized inductively, laying out the details and then presenting a conclusion, which will usually be what the author's purpose, message, and intent are. If the analysis is focusing on multiple layers in a story, it will probably follow the preliminary conclusion. On the other hand, keeping in mind that the speaker will want to keep the audience's attention, if the content has to do with difficult-to-follow facts and statistics, slides (or PowerPoint) may be used as a guide to the presentation, and the speaker will intersperse interesting anecdotes, jokes, or humor from time to time so the listeners don't fall asleep.

It's also important to take the consistency of the audience into account when organizing a presentation. If the audience can be counted on to have a high level of interest in what is being presented, little would need to be done in the way of organizing and presenting to hold interest. On the other hand, if many of those in the audience are there because they have to be, or if the level of interest can be counted on not to be very high, something like a PowerPoint presentation can be very helpful. Also the lead-in and introduction need to be structured not only to be entertaining and interest-grabbing, it should create an interest in the topic. If the audience is senior citizens, it's important to keep the presentation lively and to be careful not to "speak down" to them. Carefully written introductions aimed specifically at this audience will go a long way to attract their interest in the topic.

No speaker should stand up to make a presentation if the purpose has not been carefully determined ahead of time. If the speaker is not focused on the purpose, the audience will quickly lose interest. As to organizing for a particular purpose, there are some decisions to be made, including : where to place key pieces of information about the purpose, whether displaying the purpose on a chart, PowerPoint, or banner will enhance the presentation and other more general organization items such as outlining the entire presentation or just providing a brief overview. The purpose might be the lead-in for a presentation if it can be counted on to grab the interest of the listeners, in which case, the organization will be deductive. If it seems better to save the purpose until the end, the organization, of course, will be inductive.

The occasion, of course, plays an important role in the development and delivery of a presentation. A celebration speech when the company has achieved an important accomplishment will be organized around congratulating those who were most responsible for the accomplishment and giving some details about how it was achieved and probably something about the competition for the achievement. The presentation will be upbeat and not too long.

On the other hand, if bad news is being presented, it will probably be the CEO who is making the presentation and the bad-news announcement will come first followed with details about the news itself, how it came about, and probably end with a pep talk or encouragement to do better the next time.

Skill 1.12 Selects and uses instructional strategies, materials, and models to teach students listening skills for various purposes and provides students with opportunities to engage in active, purposeful listening in a variety of contexts.

Facilitating. It is quite acceptable to use standard opening lines to facilitate a conversation. Don't agonize over trying to come up with witty "one-liners," as the main obstacle in initiating conversation is just getting started. After that, the real substance begins. A useful technique may be to make a comment or ask a question about a shared situation. This may be anything from the weather, the food you are eating, to a new policy at work. Use an opener you are comfortable with, because most likely, your partner in conversation will be comfortable with it as well.

Stimulating Higher Level Critical Thinking Through Inquiry. Many people rely on questions to communicate with others. However, most fall back on simple clarifying questions rather than open-ended inquiries. Try to ask open-ended, deeper-level questions, since those tend to have the greatest reward and lead to a greater understanding. In answering those questions, more complex connections are made and more significant realizations are achieved.

Skill 1.13 Selects and uses instructional strategies, materials, activities, and models to teach students to evaluate the content and effectiveness of their own spoken messages and the messages of others.

Different from the basic writing forms of discourse is the art of debating, discussion, and conversation. The ability to use language and logic to convince the audience to accept your reasoning and to side with you is an art. This form of writing/speaking is extremely confined/structured, logically sequenced, with supporting reasons and evidence. At its best, it is the highest form of propaganda. A position statement, evidence, reason, evaluation and refutation are integral parts of this schema.

Interviewing provides opportunities for students to apply expository and informative communication. It teaches them how to structure questions to evoke fact-filled responses. Compiling the information from an interview into a biographical essay or speech helps students to list, sort, and arrange details in an orderly fashion.

Speeches encourage them to describe persons, places, or events in their own lives or oral interpretations of literature help them sense the creativity and effort used by professional writers.

Useful resources

Price, Brent - *Basic Composition Activities Kit* - provides practical suggestions and student guide sheets for use in the development of student writing.

Simmons, John S., R.E. Shafer, and Gail B. West. (1976). *Decisions About The Teaching of English - "Advertising, or Buy It, You'll Like It."* Allyn & Bacon.

Skill 1.14   Knows how to promote students' development of oral communication skills through the use of technology.

Instructors are obligated to become familiar with and competent in the use of available technologies (computer, Internet, video cameras, tape recorders, digital cameras, etc.). Such technologies can serve to greatly enhance the development of students' oral communication skills. Whether it is encouraging and assisting students in preparing a PowerPoint presentation for their oral presentations or videotaping an interpretive reading, the use of technology can serve to increase the students' interest and participation in developing these critical skills. For example, video-taped presentations can be saved, so students can view, for themselves, the progress they are making in utilizing facial expressions, hand gestures, and tone in conveying their messages. As proficiency in spoken English is enhanced, so is a student's personal confidence and self-image. In addition, increased proficiency in oral communication skills often translates to an increased proficiency in reading and writing.

COMPETENCY 2.0 EARLY LITERACY DEVELOPMENT

Skill 2.1   Understands the signification of phonological and phonemic awareness for reading and typical patterns in the development of phonological and phonemic awareness and recognizes that individual variations occur.

Just as countries and families have histories, so do words. Knowing and understanding the origin of a word, where it has been used, and the history of its meaning as it has changed is an important component of the writing and language teacher's tool kit. Never in the history of the English language, or any other language for that matter, have the forms and meanings of words changed so rapidly. When America was settled originally, immigration from many countries made it a "melting pot." Immigration accelerated rapidly within the first hundred years, resulting in pockets of language throughout the country. When trains began to make transportation available and affordable, individuals from those various pockets came in contact with each other, shared vocabularies, and attempted to converse. From that time forward, every generation brought the introduction of a technology which made language interchange not only more possible, but more important.

Radio began the trend to standardize dialects. A Bostonian might not be understood by a native of Louisiana, who therefore might not be interested in turning the dial to hear the news or a drama or the advertisements of the vendors that had a vested interest in being heard and understood. Soap and soup producers recognized a goldmine when they saw it and created a market for radio announcers and actors who spoke without a pronounced dialect. In return, listeners began to hear the English language in a dialect very different from the one they spoke, and as it settled into their thinking processes, it eventually made its way to their tongues, and spoken English began to lose some of its local peculiarities. It has been a slow process, but most Americans can easily understand other Americans, no matter where they come from. They can even converse with a native of Great Britain with little difficulty. The introduction of television carried the evolution further as did the explosion of electronic communicating devices over the past fifty years.

An excellent example of the changes that have occurred in English is a comparison of Shakespeare's original works with modern translations. Without help, twenty-first-century Americans are unable to read the *Folio*. On the other hand, teachers must constantly be mindful of the vocabularies and etymologies of their students, who are on the receiving end of the escalation brought about by technology and increased global influence and contact.

Skill 2.2 Understands elements of the alphabetic principle and typical patterns of students' alphabetic skills development, and recognizes that individual variations occur.

The alphabetic principle can be defined as the use of letters to represent sounds, (i.e., speech can be turned into print, and print can be turned into speech). Typically, there are four stages or levels in the development of students' alphabetic skills:

1. **Pre-alphabetic Level** –At this level, students become aware of the relationship between sounds and letters. Phonemes are the smallest sounds in a spoken word; thus, changing a phoneme can change the meaning of the word. For example, the first sound or phoneme in "hat" is /h/. Change the sound /h/ to the phoneme /p/, and you change "hat" to "pat." Recognizing initial and final phonemes in words and matching them with their alphabetic representatives (graphemes, i.e., the letter "h" represents the sound /h/)) and playing rhyming games ("/p/ig" to "/b/ig" to "/f/ig")are examples of activities at this level.

2. **Early Alphabetic Reading**—Students at this level begin blending single sounds into words. Most programs begin with printed words that have a limited set of sounds, (i.e., a few consonants and one or two vowels). Decoding strategies are implemented. Students may finger-point and sound out the words, becoming more and more fluent as they read: My "cat," "Pat," likes to wear a "hat."

3. **Mature Alphabetic Level**—Now, students should know and be able to decipher simple words. As they progress, students readily recognize often repeated initial letter groupings (ch, th, sh, sl, gr) and word endings (-ing, -ed, and –est) in orthography (written language).

4. **Orthographic Stage**—Students continue to practice reading and are becoming familiar with larger and more complex words and sentence structures. They move from sounding out words, letter by letter, to learning new words by their analogy to known words.

Students who do not come from a print-rich environment, who are not familiar with the alphabet, and who have not fully mastered oral skills will need additional encouragement and opportunities to develop their awareness of this sound-to-letter relationship. *Reading is good.*

Skill 2.3   Understands that comprehension is an integral part of early literacy.

Comprehension is important to literacy because it is the reason and purpose behind reading (i.e., we learn to read, so we can read to learn).

Research in the area of comprehension, especially in early literacy, indicates that comprehension can be taught, developed and that the following six strategies are particularly useful for teaching comprehension:

1. Monitor comprehension—Make sure students are aware of what they understand and of what they do not understand in their readings. Good readers are active, purposeful readers who use metacognition (thinking about thinking) strategies, namely, they have a purpose in mind before they read, whether it is to learn about 18th century England or why the Beastie Boys have left the country; they adjust their reading speed as the text becomes easier or more difficult; they clarify information they do not understand; they anticipate what they will read next; and they review what they have read and what they have learned from their readings.

2. Use graphic or semantic organizers—Graphs, word maps, and diagrams can help students identify their comprehension goals and illustrate the relationship between various concepts presented in the text.

3. Answer questions—Knowing that there are questions to answer following reading a text helps direct the purpose of reading to specific knowledge areas, and it helps students to actively think while they read.

4. Generate questions—When student create their own questions from material read, they are clarifying their own understanding of the material, as well as becoming even more active in their reading, integrating material from all sections of the text.

5. Recognize story structure—Helping students recognize basic story structure (introduction, plot development, character development, and plot resolution) increases a student's appreciation of the story, as well as his or her memory of the story.

6. Summarize—Have students identify the main or most important points of a text and then restate those points in their own words. This activity helps students to focus on the important information, to integrate elements in the text, and, most of all, to remember what they read.

Skill 2.4   Understands that not all written languages are alphabetic and that many alphabetic languages are more phonetically regular than English and knows the significance of this for students' literacy development in English.

The English language utilizes a Roman alphabetic script, which has letters that represent individual sounds (phonemes). Groupings of these letters then form words—decoding these groupings is the basis of reading. Other languages that employ a Roman alphabetic script include French, German, and Spanish.

Speakers of these languages will be familiar with the relationship between the letter(s) and the sounds of words, and they will find many similarities between the sound-symbols in both languages.

However, not all languages employ a Roman alphabetic script. Examples of such non-Roman alphabetic languages are Arabic, Greek, Russian, and Thai. Although these languages employ alphabets, the symbols for their letters are different, as may be the directionality of the writing (Arabic is written from right to left). These students will need extra time in practicing writing, and they may have difficulty in immediately correlating sounds with the alphabetic symbols.

Finally, some languages, such as Chinese or Japanese, have non-alphabetic scripts. These languages, when written, have symbols that represent entire words, rather than separate sounds. These students will need to establish an "alphabetic strategy" to be able to learn to read and write in English.

For students with a primary alphabetic language, studies have shown that reading and teaching phonemic awareness tend to reinforce each other. At the same time, research shows that for students with a non-alphabetic background, there is still a strong correlation between reading ability and phonological awareness, making the phonological principle in reading independent of the writing system employed.

Skill 2.5 Understands that literacy acquisition generally develops in a predictable pattern from pre-reading (emergent literacy) to conventional literacy and recognizes that individual variations occur.

The process of moving from emergent literacy to conventional literacy is influenced by many things: a child's physical and mental capabilities and/or handicaps; primary language differences; home environment, involvement and capabilities of primary caregivers, and the commitment of these caregivers, as well as classroom teachers and school administrators to promote literacy.

While understanding that deficits in one or more of the areas listed above can hinder and delay literacy development, by the time children enter kindergarten and begin formal literacy instruction, they have reached the stage of emergent literacy. To be successful at this stage, children should already have strong oral skills and be familiar with books, often imitating reading by telling stories from pictures. The tone of voice they use when "reading" from their favorite books is similar to that of adult readers, and the vocabulary employed by emergent readers is taken from the stories and materials that they have repeatedly heard.

Children at this level also continue their experimentation with writing, which typically begins between the ages of three and four. While their earliest attempts involve squiggles and curvy lines, in imitation of script, students at the emergent level will now add strings of letters to their scribbles, regardless of the sounds associated with the letters. As they advance, they employ invented or phonetic spellings, bringing their writing efforts closer and closer to that which they are imitating.

Between first and third grade, most students move from emergent to conventional literacy. This is a gradual process, with no set time limit on arriving at the conventional literacy level. During this transitional stage, students become more and more adept at identifying and remembering words in print, at decoding words and using known words to decipher new words. Their spelling becomes more recognizable, as they are now able to apply spelling rules and are remembering the correct spelling of frequently used and seen words. At the conventional literacy level, students are spending less and less time decoding printed words and are focusing more on reading for meaning.

That final point is critical for understanding middle school literacy problems. Most middle school age students have reached the conventional level of literacy and are ready to read for meaning. Unfortunately, students who have fallen behind in the early grades are often lumped together in single-purpose remedial classrooms, where not enough attention is paid to developing advanced strategies for enhancing the comprehension capabilities of the students.

Skill 2.6   Understands that literacy development occurs in multiple contexts through reading, writing, and the use of oral language.

See Skill 6.14.

Skill 2.7   Knows characteristics of informal and formal literacy assessments.

Skills to Evaluate:

- Ability to use syntactic cues when encountering an unknown word. A good reader will expect the word to fit the syntax he/she is familiar with. A poor reader may substitute a word that does not fit the syntax, and will not correct him/herself.
- Ability to use semantic cues to determine the meaning of an unknown word. A good reader will consider the meanings of all the known words in the sentence. A poor reader may read one word at a time with no regard for the other words.
- Ability to use schematic cues to connect words read with prior knowledge. A good reader will incorporate what he/she knows with what the text says or implies. A poor reader may think only of the word he/she is reading without associating it with prior knowledge.

- Ability to use phonics cues to improve ease and efficiency in reading. A good reader will apply letter and sound associations almost subconsciously. A poor reader may have one of two kinds of problems. He/she may have underdeveloped phonics/skills, and use only an initial clue without analyzing vowel patterns before quickly guessing the word. Or he/she may use phonics skills in isolation, becoming so absorbed in the word "noises" that he/she ignores or forgets the message of the text.
- Ability to process information from text. A student should be able to take in information from the text, as well as store, retrieve and integrate it for later use.
- Ability to use interpretive thinking to make logical predictions and inferences.
- Ability to use critical thinking to make decisions and insights about the text.
- Ability to use appreciative thinking to respond to the text, whether emotionally, mentally, ideologically, etc.

Methods of Evaluation:

- Assess students at the beginning of each year and regularly throughout the year to determine grouping for instruction.
- Judge whether a student recognizes when a word does not make sense.
- Monitor whether the student corrects him/herself, if they know when to ignore and read on or when to reread a sentence.
- Looks for skill such as recognizing cause and effect, finding main ideas, and using comparison and contrast techniques.
- Use oral reading to assess reading skills. Pay attention to word recognition skills rather than the reader's ability to communicate the author's message. Strong oral reading sounds like natural speech, utilizes phrasing and pace that match the meaning of the text, and uses pitch and tone to interpret the text (fluency and prosody).
- Keep dated records to follow individual progress. Focus on a few students each day. Grade them on a scale of 1-5 according to how well they perform certain reading abilities (e.g. logically predicts coming events). Also include informal observations, such as "Ed was able to determine the meaning of the word 'immigrant' by examining the other words in the sentence."
- Remember that evaluation is important, but enjoyment of reading is the most important thing to emphasize. Keep reading as a pressure-free, fun activity so students do not become intimidated by reading. Even if the student is not meeting excellent standards, if they continue wanting to read each day, that is a success!

Skill 2.8 Knows how to select, administer, and use results from informal and formal assessments of literary acquisition.

See Skill 2.7.

Skill 2.9   **Knows how to use ongoing assessment to determine when a students needs additional help or intervention to bring the student's performance to grade level, based on state content and performance standards for reading in the Texas Essential Knowledge and Skills (TEKS).**

If students take turns reading aloud in your classroom, those who read word to word and haltingly have probably not developed reading fluency, and could use some special help to improve their reading skills. Readers who are not fluent must intentionally decode a majority of the words they encounter in a text. Fluent readers are able to read texts with expression or prosody, the combination that makes oral reading sound like spoken language.

If students don't read aloud in your classroom but have reading assignments that call for written reports, those reports will have clues to reading ability also. If sentences are poorly-organized structurally, if words are left out, and if the student is using a vocabulary he/she does not have control of, these are signs that the student's reading level is below-par.

There are a number of reliable reading tests that can be administered to provide empirical data to let you know where your students' reading skills lie. Your school or your district can probably recommend one. Some of these can be given at the beginning of the school year and at the end to let you know what impact your teaching is having.

For slow, immature readers, special activities designed to improve reading may be in order, making as certain as possible that it isn't seen as criticism or judgment. Some of the activities that might be useful for that separate section:

- Repeated readings: Using short passages, the group will read it several times, trying to improve with each reading.
- Echo reading: Teacher reads a sentence and students read after her. Once a story has been completed, use the same text and do the exercise one more time.
- Wide reading: Teacher reads a sentence and students read after her, but they move on to a new reading once the first one is finished.
- Choosing a story that the students like, such as a Harry Potter story, have each student read a page, going around the group, until the book is completed. Discuss what the story is about, then give an exam on the content of the story. When the focus of an assignment is on meaning, students tend to make greater gains in comprehension than when the focus is on word analysis and accurate reading.
- Sometimes watching a dramatization of a story played on a television set or a screen will encourage an interest in reading a particular story and provide variety as well as an opportunity to think about language in spoken as well as written form.

Some causes which can make reading a struggle include auditory trauma and ear infections that affect the ability to hear speech. Such a student will need one-on-one support with articulation and perception of different sounds. It might be necessary to consult with a speech therapist or audiologist. As a teacher educator, you need to take time to identify those children who may be struggling due to a hearing difficulty. Some students may also have vision problems that call for treatment. Inquiring about a vision examination is in order if you suspect that a child is not reading well because of visual difficulties.

Students who are using English as a second language may need special consideration. If they are not able to comprehend at a passing level in your class, they might be referred to an ELL specialist within your building.

If you conclude a student is not prepared to participate successfully in your classroom, then a formal referral may be the best choice. Guidance counselors, speech pathologists, and school psychologist are available in most schools.

Skill 2.10 Analyzes students' errors in reading and responds to individual students' needs by providing focused instruction to promote literacy acquisition.

The responsibility for student literacy falls heavily on the shoulders of the elementary teacher. If children do not learn to read at this stage in their education, it's unlikely that they will ever become readers. For that reason, it becomes more and more important for the kindergarten and first grade teacher to have strong skills in assessing student reading levels and an effective tool-kit for developing literacy skills.

Assessment

There is more and more attention being directed to the development of literacy in the elementary classroom; for this reason, there are many reliable standardized instruments available for measuring student performance. Formal assessment will involve standardized tests and procedures carried out under circumscribed conditions and may include state tests, standardized achievement tests, NAEP tests, etc. However, informal assessment is at least as important, probably more so, in the day-to-day management of the reading classroom.

Effective assessment should have the following characteristics:
1. It should be an ongoing process with the teacher making some kind of informal or formal assessment almost every time the students speaks, listens, reads, writes, or views something in the classroom. The assessment should be a natural part of the instruction and not intrusive.
2. The most effective assessment is integrated into the ongoing instruction. Throughout the teaching and learning day, the child's written, spoken and reading contributions to the class or lack thereof need to be continually assessed.

3. Assessment should reflect the actual reading and writing experiences that classroom learning has prepared the student for.
4. Assessment needs to be a collaborative and reflective process. Teachers can learn from what the students reveal about their own individual assessments. Students should be supported by their teacher to continually and routinely ask themselves questions to assess their reading progress.
5. Quality valid assessment is multidimensional and may include samples of writing, student retellings, running records, anecdotal teacher observations, self-evaluations, etc. This not only enables the teacher to derive a consistent level of performance but also to design additional instruction that will enhance that level of performance.
6. Assessment must take into account the student's age and ethnic/cultural patterns of learning.
7. Assess to teach students from their strengths, not their weaknesses. Find out what reading behaviors students demonstrate well and then design instruction to support those behaviors.

Given this, the teacher should also be alert and sensitive to special circumstances that may interfere with a child's learning to read such as auditory trauma and ear infections that interfere with the ability to hear speech. These students will require one-on-one instruction in the articulation and perception of different sounds. The services of a speech therapist or audiologist may also be required. Vision problems may also be a factor for some students. It's appropriate to inquire about an eye exam if you suspect that a child may not be reading as well as he or she could because of a vision deficiency.

Also, students who are using English as a second language may need special consideration. If they are not able to comprehend at a passing level in your class, they should be referred to an ELL class.

Instruction

The five areas that need to be addressed in the Reading classroom are phonemic awareness, phonics, fluency, vocabulary, and text comprehension.

Phonemic Awareness:
Key findings from the scientific research on phonemic awareness instruction tell us that phonemic awareness *can* be taught and learned. Effective phonemic awareness instruction teaches children to notice, think about, and work with (manipulate) sounds in spoken language. Also, phonemic awareness instruction helps children learn to read and to spell. Phonemic awareness instruction is most effective when children are taught to manipulate phonemes by using the letters of the alphabet and when it focuses on only one or two types of phoneme manipulation rather than several types.

Phonics

A program of phonics instruction that is systematic and consistent has been demonstrated to improve significantly kindergarten and first-grade children's abilities to recognize and spell words. It will also significantly impact reading comprehension. Dealing with children from a range of social and economic levels creates special problems in the reading curriculum; however, phonics instruction is an important tool in covering all the students in a diverse classroom. There will be some children in a classroom who have less need for extensive phonics instruction; however, for those who struggle to develop reading skills (those who could be defined as the at-risk group), systematic phonics is crucial. Given all of the above, it's important to remember that the time for phonics instruction is kindergarten or first grade. It has steadily decreasing value in the reading classroom as the children grow older and move into higher grades. Also, phonics should never be the only reading instruction going on in the classroom, a mistake that has sometimes been made in the past.

Fluency

Oral reading is a useful tool for improving fluency; however, repetition and monitoring should be a part of the program. At this time, it appears from the research results available that silent, independent reading programs such as Silent Sustained Reading (SSR) or Drop Everything and Read (DEAR) improve fluency even with guidance and feedback. While it's true that the students who becomes a voluntary avid reader benefits enormously academically in the long run, it appears that the programs being used to achieve that are not particularly successful (Center for the Improvement of Early Reading Achievement).

Vocabulary

The fact is, direct teaching of vocabulary is not the most effective way to expand the numbers of words children recognize and/or are able to use in conversation or writing. Meanings of most words are learned indirectly by experiencing them either orally or in writing. For this reason, children who read more have larger vocabularies. Children who come from homes where there is more vocal interaction also have larger vocabularies. This is not to say that vocabulary lists should not be a part of the reading curriculum; however, the time devoted to them should be realistic in light of the value derived. Also, when vocabulary lists are included in a reading lesson, the words should come from actual material that is being read and experienced in the classroom.

Comprehension

Strategies for comprehending text make up an important component in any successful reading classroom. For example, awareness of what *is* understood as well as what is not and developing appropriate means for resolving problems in comprehension are important tools. Also, learning to recognize story structure and practicing summarizing are useful. Teachers should be aware that cooperative learning is very useful and effective in developing comprehension skills. These skills may be more appropriate for post-primary grades; however, even in the earlier grades, the foundation can be laid for reading comprehension.

A valuable resource for the elementary-grades reading teacher can be downloaded free at

www.nifl.gov/partnershipfor**reading**/publications/**reading**_first1.html

Skill 2.11 **Selects and uses instructional materials that build on the current language skills of individual students, including English Language Learners, to promote development from emergent literacy to conventional literacy.**

Academic literacy, which encompasses ways of knowing particular content and refers to strategies for understanding, discussing, organizing, and producing texts, is key to success in school. To be literate in an academic sense, one should be able to understand and to articulate conceptual relationships within, between, and among disciplines. Academic literacy also encompasses critical literacy, that is, the ability to evaluate the credibility and validity of informational sources. In a practical sense, when a student is academically literate, s/he should be able to read and understand interdisciplinary texts, to articulate comprehension through expository written pieces, and to further knowledge through sustained and focused research.

Developing academic literacy is especially difficult for ELL students who are struggling to acquire and improve the language and critical thinking skills they need to become full members of the academic mainstream community. The needs of these ELL students may be met through the creation of a functional language learning environment that engages them in meaningful and authentic language processing through planned, purposeful, and academically-based activities, teaching them how to extract, question, and evaluate the central points and methodology of a range of material, and construct responses using the conventions of academic/expository writing. Effective academic writing requires that the student be able to choose appropriate patterns of discourse, which in turn involves knowing sociolinguistic conventions relating to audience and purpose. These skills, acquired through students' attempts to process and produce texts, can be refined over time by having students complete a range of assignments of progressive complexity which derive from the sustained and focused study of one or more academic disciplines.

Sustained content area study is more effectively carried out when an extensive body of instructional and informational resources, such as is found on the internet, is available. Through its extensive collection of reading materials and numerous contexts for meaningful written communication and analysis of issues, the internet creates a highly motivating learning environment that encourages ELL students to interact with language in new and varied ways. Used as a resource for focus discipline research, the internet is highly effective in helping these students develop and refine the academic literacy so necessary for a successful educational experience.

Used as a tool for sustained content study, the internet is a powerful resource that offers easier, wider, and more rapid access to interdisciplinary information than do traditional libraries. Using the internet allows ELL students to control the direction of their reading and research, teaches them to think creatively, and increases motivation for learning as students work individually and collaboratively to gather focus discipline information. By allowing easy access to cross-referenced documents and screens, internet hypertext encourages students to read widely on interdisciplinary topics. This type of reading presents cognitively demanding language, a wide range of linguistic forms, and enables ELL students to build a wider range of schemata and a broader base of knowledge, which may help them grasp future texts. Additionally, hypermedia provides the benefit of immediate visual reinforcement through pictures and/or slideshows, facilitating comprehension of the often-abstract concepts presented in academic readings.

Academic research skills are often underdeveloped in the ELL student population making research reports especially frightening and enormously challenging. The research skills students need to complete focus discipline projects are the same skills they need to succeed in classes.

Instruction that targets the development of research skills teaches ELL students the rhetorical conventions of term papers, which subsequently leads to better writing and hence improved performance in class. Moreover, the research skills acquired through sustained content study and focus discipline research enable students to manage information more effectively, which serves them throughout their academic years and into the workforce.

COMPETENCY 3.0 WORD IDENTIFICATION SKILLS AND READING FLUENCY

Skill 3.1   Understands that many students develop word analysis skills and reading fluency in a predictable sequence and recognizes that individual variations occur.

See Skill 1.1.

Skill 3.2   Understands differences in students' development of word identification skills and reading fluency and knows instructional practices for meeting students' individual needs in these areas.

What are word identification skills?

Word identification skills help individuals recognize unknown words accurately and rapidly. These skills include phonetic analysis, structural analysis, and contextual analysis.

Why are word identification skills important for secondary struggling readers?

- In content-area classes, students are required to read large amounts of text that often contain multisyllabic words the students may not know. Students need well developed word identification skills to be able to identify these unknown words.
- The ability to decode unknown words rapidly and accurately is necessary for effective and efficient comprehension.
- When students do not recognize words with automaticity, they spend time on decoding that could be devoted to comprehending text.

What is the goal of word identification instruction for secondary struggling readers?

The goal of word identification instruction for secondary students is to help students develop and apply strategies for tackling unfamiliar or difficult words accurately, effortlessly, and rapidly.

What are some instructional guidelines for teaching word identification skills?

- Explicit, systematic instruction is an effective procedure for teaching students word identification skills and strategies.
- Words should be taken from the content-area materials that students have difficulty reading in the context of their classes.

- Students should possess basic word identification skills, including the following:

    1. Sound-symbol correspondence,
    2. Recognition of phonetically regular consonant-vowel-consonant words,
    3. Recognition of some sight or high frequency words.

- Word identification skills include phonetic analysis, structural analysis, and contextual analysis to read multisyllabic words.

What are some research-based interventions for teaching word identification skills to secondary struggling readers?

Word Identification Strategy: Students learn how to break words into parts to facilitate decoding. It is helpful if students recognize prefixes and suffixes and have some knowledge of phonics.

Overt Word Parts Strategy: Student circle parts at the beginning and end of the word and underline letters representing the vowel sounds in the remaining part of the word. Students pronounce the parts fast to say the word.

Making Words: Students use their knowledge of sound/letter correspondences, orthographic patterns, structural analysis, and content-specific vocabulary to build words.

What are some guidelines for English-language learners?

- Teach words with vowel combinations because these words may be difficult for English-language learners.
- Correct differences in speech sounds judiciously because some speech sounds in English may be different from those of the students' first language.

What materials can be used to develop word identification skills?

- Syllable puzzles
- Letters to form words
- Lists of words from content-area text
- Lists of prefixes and suffixes

What are some examples of publishers that offer age-appropriate materials for word identification skills?

- Curriculum Associates
- Good Apple
- Sopris West

Skill 3.3   Understands the connection of word identification skills and reading fluency to reading comprehension.

In the past, the Oxford English Dictionary has been the most reliable source for etymologies. Some of the collegiate dictionaries are also useful. *Merriam-Webster's 3rd Unabridged Dictionary* is useful in tracing the sources of words in American English. *Merriam-Webster's Unabridged Dictionary* may be out of date, so a teacher should also have a *Merriam-Webster's Collegiate Dictionary*, which is updated regularly.

However, there are many up-to-date sources for keeping up and keeping track of the changes that have occurred and are occurring constantly. Google "etymology," for instance, or even the word you're unsure of, and you can find a multitude of sources. Don't trust a single one. The information should be validated by at least three sources. Wikipedia is very useful, but it can be changed by anyone who chooses, so any information on it should be backed up by other sources. If you go to http://www.etymonline.com/sources.php, you will find a long list of resources on etymology.

In order to know when to label a usage "jargon" or "colloquial" nowadays, the teacher must be aware of the possibility that it's a word that is now accepted as standard. In order to remain current, the teacher must continually keep up with the etymological aids available, particularly online.

Spelling in English is complicated by the fact that it is not phonetic—that is, it is not based on the one-sound/one letter formula used by many other languages. The reason for this is that it is based on the Latin alphabet, which originally had twenty letters, consisting of the present English alphabet minus J, K, V, W, Y, and Z. The Romans added K to be used in abbreviations and Y and Z in words that came from the Greek. This twenty-three-letter alphabet was adopted by the English, who developed W as a ligatured doubling of U and later J and V as consonantal variants of I and U. The result was our alphabet of twenty-six letters with upper case (capital) and lower case forms.

Spelling is based primarily on 15th century English. The problem is that pronunciation has changed drastically since then, especially long vowels and diphthongs. This Great Vowel Shift affected the seven long vowels. For a long time, spelling was erratic—there were no standards. As long as the meaning was clear, spelling was not considered very important. Samuel Johnson tackled this problem, and his *Dictionary of the English Language* (1755) brought standards to spelling, which became very important once printing presses were invented. There have been some changes, of course, through the years; but spelling is still not strictly phonetic. There have been many attempts to nudge the spelling into a more phonetic representation of the sounds, but for the most part, all have failed. A good example is Noah Webster's *Spelling Book* (1783), which was a precursor to the first edition (1828) of his *American Dictionary of the English Language*.

While there are rules for spelling, and it's important that students learn the rules, there are many exceptions; and memorizing exceptions and giving plenty of opportunities for practicing them seems the only solution for the teacher of English.

Skill 3.4   Knows the continuum of word analysis skills in the statewide curriculum and grade-level expectations for attainment of these skills.

According to the Texas Essential Knowledge and Skills (TEKS), expectations for word analysis skills are as follows:

- The student is expected to rely on context to determine meanings of words and phrases such as figurative language, idioms, multiple-meaning words, and technical vocabulary.
- Apply meanings of prefixes, roots, and suffixes in order to comprehend.
- Use reference materials such as glossaries, dictionaries, thesauruses, and available technology to determine precise meanings and usage.

Skill 3.5   Knows how students develop fluency in oral and silent reading.

When children begin to learn to read, they bring to the task a set of well-developed oral language comprehension skills. These skills, remarkably developed in a short period of time, are relative and important to the task of learning to read. Learning to read is not learning the language but learning to decode *symbols* for the language they already know. A child's language skills continue to develop as he/she grows, and learning to read plays a role in that development.

Previous experience has been in conversations where the child plays both speaker and listener roles. The conversationalists are together and share a space, time, and situation context. Their speech to each other is facilitated by intonation, facial expression, and gestures.

In reading, that is, in visually decoding the written words, aspects of the spoken word play a role: stress, intonation, and other prosodic features. Temporal characteristics of speech such as pauses and changes in speed often provide clues for the chunking of words into larger constituents. Also, pauses and breaths occur at the ends of sentences. Actually, pauses at phrase and clause boundaries increases comprehension. We rely on stress in spoken language to communicate those boundaries and convey the meanings they contribute. A good example is the restrictive versus the nonrestrictive clause: "John's dogs that are of mixed breed often make good pets" (nonrestrictive). "John's dogs, which are of mixed breed, often make good pets" (restrictive). The difference is clearly understood in speech. Punctuation provides a code for communicating even some of those aspects of spoken language. However, there are many more of those devices available in spoken language than in written.

Even so, written language does have some compensatory aspects. Paragraph demarcations, for example, are an organizational aid not available in oral language. Also, the ability to look back over passages that have been previously read and making corrections the second time around is only available in writing. A major strategy a student must develop is a method for using the permanence of text, for example, keeping some structure of the text in mind to facilitate looking back and checking a fact. In oral language, of course, the listener may just ask for clarification.

For the English teacher, the implication of all of this is that students need to read aloud in order to strengthen the link between their superior understanding of the structure of the language and their decoding skills with regard to written language. They need to be encouraged to use facial expressions, intonation, pauses, etc. as they read aloud to other students, and they need to practice these skills as frequently as possible. They also need to develop skills for using the advantages of written language in their silent reading.

Skill 3.6 **Understands that fluency involves rate, accuracy, and intonation and knows the norms for reading fluency that have been established in the Texas Essential Knowledge and Skills (TEKS) for various age and grade levels.**

See Skill 2.7.

Skill 3.7 **Knows factors affecting students' word identification skills and reading fluency.**

Language, though an innate human ability, must be learned. Thus, the acquisition and use of language is subject to many influences on the learner. Linguists agree that language is first a vocal system of word symbols that enable a human to communicate his feelings, thoughts, and desires to other human beings. Language was instrumental in the development of all cultures and is influenced by the changes in these societies.

See Skill 1.8 for the historical influences

Geographical influences

Dialect differences are basically in pronunciation. Bostonians say "potty" for party" and Southerners blend words like "you all" into "y'all." Besides the dialect differences already mentioned, the biggest geographical factors in American English stem from minor word choice variances. Depending on the region where you live, when you order a carbonated, syrupy beverage most generically called a soft drink, you might ask for a "soda" in the South, or a "pop" in the Midwest. If you order a soda in New York, then you will get a scoop of ice cream in your soft drink, while in other areas you would have to ask for a "float."

Social influences

Social influences are mostly those imposed by family, peer groups, and mass media. The economic and educational levels of families determine the properness of language use. Exposure to adults who encourage and assist children to speak well enhances readiness for other areas of learning and contributes to a child's ability to communicate his needs. Historically, children learned language, speech patterns, and grammar from members of the extended family just as they learned the rules of conduct within their family unit and community. In modern times, the mother in a nuclear family became the dominant force in influencing the child's development. With increasing social changes, many children are not receiving the proper guidance in all areas of development, especially language.

Those who are fortunate to be in educational day care programs like Head Start or in certified preschools develop better language skills than those whose care is entrusted to untrained care providers. Once a child enters elementary school, he is also greatly influenced by peer language. This peer influence becomes significant in adolescence as the use of teen jargon gives teenagers a sense of identity within his chosen group(s) and independence from the influence of adults. In some lower socio-economic groups, children use Standard English in school and street language outside the school. Some children of immigrant families become bilingual by necessity if no English is spoken in the home.

Research has shown a strong correlation between socio-economic characteristics and all areas of intellectual development. Traditional paper measurement instruments rely on verbal ability to establish intelligence. Research findings and test scores reflect that children, reared in nuclear families who provide cultural experiences and individual attention, become more language proficient than those who are denied that security and stimulation.

Personal influences

The rate of physical development and identifiable language disabilities also influence language development. Nutritional deficiencies, poor eyesight, and conditions such as stuttering or dyslexia can inhibit a child's ability to master language. Unless diagnosed early they can hamper communication into adulthood. These conditions also stymie the development of self-confidence and, therefore, the willingness to learn or to overcome the handicap. Children should receive proper diagnosis and positive corrective instruction.

In adolescence, the child's choice of role models and his decision about his future determine the growth of identity. Rapid physical and emotional changes and the stress of coping with the pressure of sexual awareness make concentration on any educational pursuits difficult. The easier the transition from childhood to adulthood, the better the competence will be in all learning areas.

Middle school and junior high school teachers are confronted by a student body ranging from fifth graders who are still childish to eighth or ninth graders who, if not in fact, at least in their minds, are young adults. Teachers must approach language instruction as a social development tool with more emphasis on vocabulary acquisition, reading improvement, and speaking/writing skills. High school teachers can deal with the more formalized instruction of grammar, usage, and literature for older adolescents whose social development allows them to pay more attention to studies that will improve their chances for a better adult life.

As a tool, language must have relevance to the student's real environment. Many high schools have developed practical English classes for business/ vocational students whose specific needs are determined by their desire to enter the workforce upon graduation. More emphasis is placed upon accuracy of mechanics and understanding verbal and written directions because these are skills desired by employers. Writing résumés, completing forms, reading policy and operations manuals, and generating reports are some of the desired skills. Emphasis is placed on higher level thinking skills, including inferential thinking and literary interpretation, in literature classes for college-bound students.

Skill 3.8   Understands important phonetic elements and conventions of the English language.

See Skill 3.13.

Skill 3.9   Knows a variety of informal and formal procedures for assessing students' word identification skills and reading fluency on an ongoing basis and uses appropriate assessments to monitor students' performance in these areas and to plan instruction for individual students, including English Language Learners.

See Skill 2.7.

Skill 3.10   Analyzes students' errors in word analysis and uses the results of this analysis to inform future instruction.

Common Language Errors:

- Application of rules that apply in a student's first language but not in the second
- Using pronunciation that applies to a student's first language but not in the second
- Applying a general rule to all cases even when there are exceptions
- Trying to cut corners by using an incorrect word or syntactic form
- Avoiding use of precise vocabulary or idiomatic expressions
- Using incorrect verb tense

Uses of Language Assessment:

- Diagnosis of language strengths and weaknesses
- Detection of patterns of systematic errors
- Appropriate bilingual/ELL program placement if necessary

Skill 3.11   Applies norms and expectations for word identification skills and reading fluency, as specified in the Texas Essential Knowledge and Skills (TEKS), to evaluate students' reading performance.

See Skills 2.7 and 3.13.

Skill 3.12   Knows how to use ongoing assessment of word identification skills and reading fluency to determine when a student needs additional help or intervention to bring the student's performance to grade level, based on state content and performance standards for reading in the Texas Essential Knowledge and Skills (TEKS).

See Skill 2.9.

Skill 3.13   Knows strategies for decoding increasingly complex words, including using the alphabetic principle, structural cues, and syllables, and for using syntax and semantics to support word identification and confirm word meaning.

Phonological Awareness

Phonological awareness is the ability of the reader to recognize the sound of spoken language. This recognition includes how these sounds can be blended together, segmented (divided up), and manipulated (switched around). This awareness then leads to phonics, a method for teaching students to read. It helps them "sound out words."

Instructional methods to teach phonological awareness may include any or all of the following: auditory games and drills during which students recognize and manipulate the sounds of words, separate or segment the sounds of words, take out sounds, blend sounds, add in new sounds, or take apart sound to recombine them in new formations are good way to foster phonological awareness.

Identification of common morphemes, prefixes, and suffixes

This aspect of vocabulary development is to help students identify structural elements within words which they can use independently to help them determine meaning.

The terms listed below are generally recognized as the key structural analysis components.

Root words: A root word is a word from which another word is developed. The second word can be said to have its "root" in the first. This structural component nicely lends itself to a tree with roots illustration which can concretize the meaning for students. Students may also want to literally construct root words using cardboard trees and/or actual roots from plants to create word family models. This is a lovely way to help students own their root words.

Base words: A stand-alone linguistic unit which cannot be deconstructed or broken down into smaller words. For example, in the word "re-tell," the base word is "tell."

Contractions: These are shortened forms of two words in which a letter or letters have been deleted. These deleted letter have been replaced by an apostrophe.

Prefixes: These are beginning units of meaning which can be added (the vocabulary word for this type of structural adding is "affixed") to a base word or root word. They can not stand alone. They are also sometimes known as "bound morphemes," meaning that they can not stand alone as a base word.

Suffixes: These are ending units of meaning which can be "affixed" or added on to the ends of root or base words. Suffixes transform the original meanings of base and root words. Like prefixes, they are also known as "bound morphemes," because they can not stand alone as words.

Compound words: Occur when two or more base words are connected to form a new word. The meaning of the new word is in some way connected with that of the base word.

Inflectional endings: Are types are suffixes that impart a new meaning to the base or root word. These endings in particular change the gender, number, tense, or form of the base or root words. Just like other suffixes, these are also termed "bound morphemes."

To effectively teach language, it is necessary to understand that, as human beings acquire language, they realize that words have <u>denotative</u> and <u>connotative</u> meanings. Generally, denotative words point to things and connotative words deal with mental suggestions that the words convey. The word *skunk* has a denotative meaning if the speaker can point to the actual animal as he speaks the word and intends the word to identify the animal. *Skunk* has connotative meaning depending upon the tone of delivery, the socially acceptable attitudes about the animal, and the speaker's personal feelings about the animal.

Informative connotations

Informative connotations are definitions agreed upon by the society in which the learner operates. A *skunk* is "a black and white mammal of the weasel family with a pair of perineal glands which secrete a pungent odor." The *Merriam Webster Collegiate Dictionary* adds "...and offensive" odor. Identification of the color, species, and glandular characteristics are informative. The interpretation of the odor as *offensive* is affective.

Affective connotations

Affective connotations are the personal feelings a word arouses. A child who has no personal experience with a skunk and its odor or has had a pet skunk will feel differently about the word *skunk* than a child who has smelled the spray or been conditioned vicariously to associate offensiveness with the animal denoted *skunk*. The very fact that our society views a skunk as an animal to be avoided will affect the child's interpretation of the word.

In fact, it is not necessary for one to have actually seen a skunk (that is, have a denotative understanding) to use the word in either connotative expression. For example, one child might call another child a skunk, connoting an unpleasant reaction (affective use) or, seeing another small black and white animal, call it a skunk based on the definition (informative use).

Using connotations

In everyday language, we attach affective meanings to words unconsciously; we exercise more conscious control of informative connotations. In the process of language development, the leaner must come not only to grasp the definitions of words but also to become more conscious of the affective connotations and how his listeners process these connotations. Gaining this conscious control over language makes it possible to use language appropriately in various situations and to evaluate its uses in literature and other forms of communication.

The manipulation of language for a variety of purposes is the goal of language instruction. Advertisers and satirists are especially conscious of the effect word choice has on their audiences. By evoking the proper responses from readers/listeners, we can prompt them to take action.

Choice of the medium through which the message is delivered to the receiver is a significant factor in controlling language. Spoken language relies as much on the gestures, facial expression, and tone of voice of the speaker as on the words he speaks. Slapstick comics can evoke laughter without speaking a word. Young children use body language overtly and older children more subtly to convey messages. These refinings of body language are paralleled by an ability to recognize and apply the nuances of spoken language. To work strictly with the written work, the writer must use words to imply the body language.

Skill 3.14   **Selects and uses instructional strategies, materials, activities, and models to teach students to recognize high-frequency irregular words, to promote students' ability to decode increasingly complex words, and to enhance word identification skills for students reading at different levels.**

Students frequently encounter problems with homonyms—words that are spelled and pronounced the same as another but that have different meanings such as *mean*, a verb, "to intend"; *mean* an adjective, "unkind"; and *mean* a noun or adjective, "average." These words are actually both homonyms and homographs (written the same way).

A similar phenomenon that causes trouble is heteronyms (also sometimes called heterophones), words that are spelled the same but have different pronunciations and meanings (in other words, they are homographs that differ in pronunciation or, technically, homographs that are not homophones).

For example, the homographs *desert* (abandon) and *desert* (arid region) are heteronyms (pronounced differently); but *mean* (intend) and *mean* (average) are not. They are pronounced the same, or are homonyms.

Another similar occurrence in English is the capitonym, a word that is spelled the same but has different meanings when it is capitalized and may or may not have different pronunciations. Example: *polish* (to make shiny) and *Polish* (from Poland).

Some of the most troubling homonyms are those that are spelled differently but sound the same. Examples: *its* (3d person singular neuter pronoun) and *it's* ("it is"); *there*, *their* (3d person plural pronoun) and *they're* ("they are").

Others: *to, too, two;*

Some homonyms/homographs are particularly complicated and troubling. Fluke, *for instance is a fish, a flatworm, the end parts of an anchor, the fins on a whale's tail, and a stroke of luck.*

Common ones that are troubling to student writers:

accept: tolerate; *except*: everything but.
add: put together with; *ad*: short for advertisement.
allowed: permitted; *aloud*: audibly.
allot: to distribute, allocate; *a lot* (often "*alot*"): much, many (a lot of).
allusion: indirect reference; *illusion*: a distortion of sensory perception.
bare: naked, exposed or very little (bare necessities); *bear*: as a noun, a large mammal and as a verb, to carry.
boy: a male adolescent or child; *buoy*: (noun) a floating marker in the sea.
bridal: pertaining to a bride (bridal gown, bridal suite); *bridle*: (noun) part of a horse's tack.
capital: punishable by death, with an upper-case letter, principal town or city, or wealth and money; *Capitol*: the home of the Congress of the United States and some other legislatures.
chord: group of musical notes; *cord*: rope, long electrical line.
compliment: a praising or flattering remark; *complement*: something that completes.
discreet: tactful or diplomatic; *discrete*: separate or distinct.
dyeing: artificially coloring; *dying*: passing away.
effect: outcome; *affect*: have an effect on.
gorilla: the largest of the great apes; *guerrilla*: a small combat group.
hair: an outgrowth of the epidermis in mammals; *hare*: rabbit.
hoard: to accumulate and store up; *horde*: large group of warriors, mob.
lam: US slang, "on the lam" means "on the run"; *lamb*: a young sheep.
lead: pronounced to rhyme with "seed", to guide or serve as the head of; *lead*: pronounced to rhyme with "head," a heavy metal; *led*: the past tense of "lead."

medal: an award to be strung around the neck; *meddle*: stick one's nose into others' affairs; *metal*: shiny, malleable element or alloy like silver or gold; *mettle*: toughness, guts.

morning: the time between midnight and midday; *mourning*: period of grieving after a death.

past: time before now (past, present and future); *passed*: past tense of "to pass."

piece: portion; *peace*: opposite of war.

peak: tip, height, to reach its highest point; *peek*: to take a brief look; *pique*: fit of anger; to incite (pique one's interest).

Strategies to help students conquer these demons: Practice using them in sentences. Context is useful in understanding the difference. Drill is necessary to overcome the misuses.

Skill 3.15   Selects and uses appropriate instructional strategies, materials, activities, and models to improve reading fluency for students reading at different levels.

If a student is reading a story he/she is familiar with, attention can be given to developing fluency since it will not be necessary to concentrate on the content as much. The teacher can concentrate on teaching oral reading skills more easily if the story is already known.

Students who have not achieved fluency tend to read word-by-word or by creating unnatural groupings, and their reading is usually monotonous, reflecting their inability to transfer prosodic elements that occur naturally in speech onto written text. A repeated-reading strategy has been demonstrated to be successful in developing fluency. Echo-reading text twice, followed by the students' reading without the echo has been demonstrated to promote fluency. A variation of genres is useful in these exercises because students need to learn to reflect in their oral reading phrasing, pitch, and emphasis, typical of fluent readers. Reading poetry in addition to prose has been shown to be advantageous in these exercises.

COMPETENCY 4.0 READING COMPREHENSION AND ASSESSMENT

Skill 4.1   Understands reading comprehension as an active process of constructing meaning.

Children become curious about printed symbols once they recognize that print, like talk, conveys meaningful messages that direct, inform or entertain people. By school age, many children are eager to continue their exploration of print.

One goal is to develop fluent and proficient readers who are knowledgeable about the reading process. Effective reading instruction should enable students to eventually become self-directed readers who can:

- Construct meaning from various types of print material
- Recognize that there are different kinds of reading materials and different purposes for reading
- Select strategies appropriate for different reading activities
- Develop a life-long interest and enjoyment in reading a variety of material for different purposes.

To assist teachers in achieving these goals, apply the use of a wide variety of fiction and non-fiction resources including:

- environmental signs and labels
- rhymes, chants, songs
- poetry
- wordless picture books
- predictable books
- cumulative stories
- maps, charts
- novels
- print resources from all subject areas
- notes, messages, letters
- folktales
- myths and legends
- writing by students and teachers
- newspapers, magazines, pamphlets
- mysteries

The resources shared with students should stimulate their imaginations and kindle their curiosity. Familiarization with narrative and expository materials, and frequent opportunities to write in all subject areas, facilitate the reading process. By becoming authors themselves, students increase their awareness of the organization and structures of printed language.

To read for meaning, students must simultaneously utilize clues from all cueing systems. Readers bring knowledge and past experiences to the reading task in order to construct interpretations and determine if the print makes sense to them. It is easier for readers to understand print when the content is relevant to their personal experiences. Familiar content and topics convey meaning or clues through the semantic cueing system. When students are comfortable and familiar with the content of a passage, they can predict upcoming text and take greater risks in reading. Research has repeatedly shown fluent readers take more guesses when interacting with unfamiliar print than poorer readers. They derive more meaning from passages than readers who frequently stop to sound or decode words by individual phonemes or letters.

Knowledge of word order and the rules of grammar which structure oral language guide readers' predictions for printed language. Such language-pattern clues comprise the syntactic cueing system. Readers should constantly question the text to ensure what they are reading makes sense and sounds like language patterns they are used to hearing.

Reading experiences that focus on relevant and familiar content, vocabulary and language patterns increase students' chances of constructing meaning and being successful readers. At the middle school level, successful reading experiences reaffirm students' confidence as language users and learners. The holistic approach to the reading process stresses the importance of presenting students with whole and meaningful reading passages. This approach is based on the principle that the readers' understanding of an entire sentence, passage or story facilitates the reading and comprehension of individual words within those passages.

Skill 4.2   Understand the continuum of reading comprehension skills in the statewide curriculum and grade-level expectations for these skills.

5th Grade Reading Expectations

1. Determine the definition, various meanings, and structure of content-specific vocabulary by using syntax (parts of speech), context clues, and phonetics.
2. Demonstrate the ability to use glossaries, dictionaries, and indexes.
3. Distinguish between statements of fact and opinion.
4. Sequence events.
5. Follow a series of written directions in a written text.
6. Determine the stated or implied main idea and supporting details in text.
7. Read for literal comprehension.
8. Paraphrase and summarize information from a variety of written works.
9. Identify cause and effect .

10. Interpret visual information, for example: maps, lists, flowcharts, graphs, tables, charts, diagrams, and timelines.
11. Identify literary elements such as character, plot, and setting.

6th Grade Reading Expectations

1. Determine the definition, various meanings, and structure of content-specific vocabulary by using syntax (parts of speech), context clues, and phonetics.
2. Demonstrate the ability to use glossaries, dictionaries, and indexes.
3. Distinguish between statements of fact and opinion.
4. Sequence events.
5. Follow a series of written directions in a written text.
6. Determine the stated or implied main idea and supporting details in text.
7. Read for literal comprehension.
8. Paraphrase and summarize information from a variety of written works.
9. Identify cause and effect.
10. Interpret visual information, for example: maps, lists, flowcharts, graphs, tables, charts, diagrams, and timelines.
11. Identify literary elements such as character, plot, and setting.

7th Grade Reading Expectations

1. Determine the definition, various meanings, and structure of content-specific vocabulary by using syntax (parts of speech), context clues, and phonetics.
2. Demonstrate the ability to use glossaries, dictionaries, and indexes.
3. Distinguish between statements of fact and opinion.
4. Sequence events.
5. Follow a series of written directions in a written text.
6. Determine the stated or implied main idea and supporting details in text.
7. Read for literal comprehension.
8. Paraphrase and summarize information from a variety of written works.
9. Identify cause and effect.
10. Interpret visual information, for example: maps, lists, flowcharts, graphs, tables, charts, diagrams, and timelines.
11. Identify literary elements such as character, plot, and setting.
12. Identify conflict.

8th Grade Reading Expectations

1. Determine the definition, various meanings, and structure of content-specific vocabulary by using syntax (parts of speech), context clues, and phonetics.
2. Demonstrate the ability to use glossaries, dictionaries, and indexes.
3. Demonstrate the ability to use a thesaurus.
4. Distinguish between statements of fact and opinion.
5. Sequence events.
6. Follow a series of written directions in a written text.
7. Determine the stated or implied main idea and supporting details in text.

8.   Read for literal comprehension.
9.   Paraphrase and summarize information from a variety of written works.
10. Identify cause and effect.
11. Interpret visual information, for example: maps, lists, flowcharts, graphs, tables, charts, diagrams, and timelines.
12. Identify point of view.
13. Identify literary elements such as character, plot, and setting.
14. Identify literary devices (such as similes and metaphors).

Skill 4.3   Understands factors affecting students' reading comprehension.

See Skill 3.7.

Skill 4.4   Knows characteristics of informal and formal reading comprehension assessments.

Skills to evaluate:

- Ability to understand what is happening in a story.
- Ability to use more than one example or piece of information when responding to the reading.
- Ability to ask questions regarding the reading to show analytical thinking.
- Ability to make predictions based on information from the story or from personal experiences that are similar to events in the story.
- Ability to make clear and understandable connections between the literature and personal experiences, as well as other literature the student has read.

Methods of Evaluation:

- Have students keep reading journals that document their reactions to the literature they are reading.
- Assign both free writing exercises, in which they respond to any element of the story, as well as prompt-driven responses, in which they respond to a specified topic you assign. Make sure the prompts are created to get the students thinking deeply about the reading. An example might be, "Write about the main conflict in the story. Tell why it is so important and how it is solved."
- Ask that students back up any assertions or assumptions they make with evidence from the text. This clearly demonstrates their mental comprehension processes.

Skill 4.5 Selects and uses appropriate informal and formal assessments to monitor and evaluate students' reading comprehension.

See Skill 4.4.

Skill 4.6 Analyzes student errors and provides focused instruction in reading comprehension based on the strengths and needs of individual students, including English Language Learners.

See Skill 2.10.

Skill 4.7 Knows how to use ongoing assessment to determine when a student needs additional help or intervention to bring the student's performance to grade level, based on state content and performance standards for reading in the Texas Essential Knowledge and Skills (TEKS).

See Skill 2.9.

Skill 4.8 Understands metacognitive skills, including self-evaluation and self-monitoring skills, and teaches students to use these skills to enhance their own reading comprehension.

Metacognition refers to the ability of students to be aware of and monitor their learning processes. In other words, it is the process of "thinking about thinking." Provide students with a mental checklist of factors to keep in mind while reading:

- Am I understanding what I read?
- Am I reading words by sounding them out?
- Am I paying attention to what I read?
- Am I reading fast enough to keep up?
- Does what I'm reading make sense?
- Am I constructing the meaning of words I don't know?

Skill 4.9 Knows how to determine students' independent, instructional, and frustration reading levels and uses this information to select and adapt reading materials for individual students, as well as to guide their selection of independent reading materials.

Students who have access to books and who read regularly learn to read more easily and more quickly, keep improving their reading skills throughout their school years, perform better on language tests, are better writers, develop oral skills and literacy in a second language more easily, have better levels of reading comprehension, have a higher vocabulary, and have a better general knowledge. So how can we encourage reading and an enjoyment of reading?

Tips to Encourage Independent Reading for Pleasure

Remember, books won't work by themselves. As a teacher, you have to make sure books are read by setting aside time regularly for reading. For example:

Have a DEAR period - Drop Everything and Read:
Everyone can participate in a DEAR period and read for 15 minutes. This often works well right at the beginning of the school day, every day.

SSR period: Sustained silent reading:
Have everyone choose a book and read without interruption for 20 to 30 minutes. Ideally this should take place daily but even twice a week will show results

Independent reading sessions:
Set aside one day a week for learners to select new books, read independently or in pairs, and have time to respond to the books they have read. This should take place weekly. Break time, after school and free periods are good opportunities to read.

Read with children:
Taking books home is a very good option as learners can read to and with other family members. Even if children can read alone, they will still benefit from being read to.

Encourage reading of any suitable and relevant written material if books are not accessible: Try newspaper or magazine articles; street signs; food packaging labels; posters etc. Anything can be used, provided it is at the correct level.

Encourage readers to make their own material and/or bring additional material to school for to read.

Having books in a classroom is one of the easiest and most effective ways of increasing reading, linguistic and cognitive development. No other single variable can be shown to carry the same significance.

Once regular reading habits have been established, independent reading should be encouraged. Reading independently:

- Allows a learner to read, re-read and engage with a text at their own pace
- Allows learners to choose what they want to read about and so motivates them to read
- Impacts on language development in the areas of vocabulary and syntax
- Impacts on knowledge of sight words and phonics

Is important for second language learners as it provides a wealth of real language input

Reading for pleasure should be encouraged synonymously with teaching reading and basic literacy. Reading for pleasure is therapeutic and enlightening, and paves the way for developing a culture of reading and of life-long learning.

Skill 4.10   Uses various instructional strategies to enhance students' reading comprehension.

In order to discover multiple layers of meaning in a literary work, the first step is a thorough analysis, examining such things as setting, characters and characterization, plot (focusing particularly on conflicts and pattern of action), theme, tone, figures of speech, and symbolism. It's useful in looking for underlying themes to consider the author's biography, particularly with regard to setting and theme, and the date and time of the writing, paying particular attention to literary undercurrents at the time as well as political and social milieu.

Once the analysis is complete and data accumulated on the historical background, determine the overt meaning. What does the story say about the characters and their conflicts, where does the climax occur, and is there a denouement? Once the forthright, overt meaning is determined, then begin to look for undercurrents, subthemes that are related to the author's life and to what is going on in the literary, political, and social background at the time of writing.

In organization of the presentation, it's usually best to begin with an explication of the overt level of meaning and then follow up with the other messages that emerge from the text.

Skill 4.11   Knows how to provide students with direct, explicit instruction in the use of strategies to improve their reading comprehension.

Reading emphasis in middle school

Reading for comprehension of factual material - content area textbooks, reference books, and newspapers - is closely related to study strategies in the middle/junior high. Organized study models, such as the SQ3R method, a technique that makes it possible and feasible to learn the content of even large amounts of text (Survey, Question, Read, Recite, and Review Studying), teach students to locate main ideas and supporting details, to recognize sequential order, to distinguish fact from opinion, and to determine cause/ effect relationships.

Strategies

1. Teacher-guided activities that require students to organize and to summarize information based on the author's explicit intent are pertinent strategies in middle grades. Evaluation techniques include oral and written responses to standardized or teacher-made worksheets.

2. Reading of fiction introduces and reinforces skills in inferring meaning from narration and description. Teaching-guided activities in the process of reading for meaning should be followed by cooperative planning of the skills to be studied and of the selection of reading resources. Many printed reading for comprehension instruments as well as individualized computer software programs exist to monitor the progress of acquiring comprehension skills.

3. Older middle school students should be given opportunities for more student-centered activities - individual and collaborative selection of reading choices based on student interest, small group discussions of selected works, and greater written expression. Evaluation techniques include teacher monitoring and observation of discussions and written work samples.

4. Certain students may begin some fundamental critical interpretation - recognizing fallacious reasoning in news media, examining the accuracy of news reports and advertising, explaining their reasons for preferring one author's writing to another's. Development of these skills may require a more learning-centered approach in which the teacher identifies a number of objectives and suggested resources from which the student may choose his course of study. Self-evaluation through a reading diary should be stressed. Teacher and peer evaluation of creative projects resulting from such study is encouraged.

5. Reading aloud before the entire class as a formal means of teacher evaluation should be phased out in favor of one-to-one tutoring or peer-assisted reading. Occasional sharing of favored selections by both teacher and willing students is a good oral interpretation basic.

Reading emphasis in high school

Students in high school literature classes should focus on interpretive and critical reading. Teachers should guide the study of the elements of inferential (interpretive) reading - drawing conclusions, predicting outcomes, and recognizing examples of specific genre characteristics, for example - and critical reading to judge the quality of the writer's work against recognized standards. At this level students should understand the skills of language and reading that they are expected to master and be able to evaluate their own progress.

Strategies

1. The teacher becomes more facilitator than instructor - helping the student to make a diagnosis of his own strengths and weaknesses, keeping a record of progress, and interacting with other students and the teacher in practicing skills.

2. Despite the requisites and prerequisites of most literature courses, students should be encouraged to pursue independent study and enrichment reading.

3. Ample opportunities should be provided for oral interpretation of literature, special projects in creative dramatics, writing for publication in school literary magazines or newspapers, and speech/debate activities. A student portfolio provides for teacher and peer evaluation.

Skill 4.12   Uses various communication modes to promote students' reading comprehension.

When preparing to present a book analysis orally, the analyst should become acquainted with the elements of the story such as setting, characterization, style (language, both technically with regard to dialect but also structurally with regard to use of description, length of sentences, phrases, etc.), plot (particularly conflicts and pattern), tone (what is the *attitude* of the writer toward characters, theme, etc.) and particularly theme (the message or point the story conveys). It's not essential to know the writer's biography, but it is often helpful, especially in responding to questions where it is necessary to consider things from the analyst's point of view.

Literature is written to evoke a personal response in readers. This is why so many books are sold. Once the analyst has a grip on the story—a thorough understanding of the story—then an analysis of one's own response to it is in order.

The following questions are useful:

1. Do you respond emotionally to one of the characters? Why? Is a character similar to someone you know or have known?
2. Is the setting evocative for you because of a place, situation, or milieu that you have experienced and that had meaning for you? Why?
3. Did the vocabulary, descriptions, or short or long sentences have impact on you? Why? For example, short, simple sentence after short, simple sentence may be used deliberately, but do you find it annoying?
4. Do you agree with the author's attitude toward the characters, setting, story, etc.? For example, has a character been written unsympathetically that you felt deserved more consideration? Does the author demonstrate a distaste for the setting he has chosen, and do you feel he is being unjust? Or do you experience the same distaste? Etc.

Reading is personal. Responding to it personally adds important dimensions to an analysis for others.

Skill 4.13 **Understands levels of reading comprehension and how to model and teach literal, inferential, and evaluative comprehension skills.**

Literal Comprehension

From general to specific is a continuum. In other words, a term or phrase may be more specific than one term or more general than another one. For example, car is about the middle of the continuum; however, if I mention John Smith's car, it has become more specific. The most specific is a unique item: John Smith's 2007 Lexus, serial #000000000. Cars is a general term that can be narrowed and narrowed and narrowed to suit whatever purposes the writer has for the term. For instance, it would be possible to make a statement about all the cars in the United States, which has been narrowed somewhat from cars. It is, however, a very general term. A thesis statement is typically a generality: All the cars in the United States run on gasoline. Then specifics would be needed to prove that generalization.

In developing a line of reasoning, the choice will be either inductive, going from the specific to the general, or deductive, going from the general to the specific. Inductive reasoning might be as follows: "I tasted a green apple from my grandfather's yard when I was five years old, and it was sour. I also tasted a green apple my friend brought to school in his lunchbox when I was eight years old, and it was sour. I was in Browns' roadside market and bought some green Granny Smith apples last week, and they were sour." This is a series of specifics. From those specifics, I might draw a conclusion—a generalization—all apples are sour, and I would have reasoned inductively to arrive at that generalization.

The same simplistic argument developed deductively would begin with the generalization: all apples are sour. Then specifics would be offered to support that generalization: the sour green apple I tasted in my grandfather's orchard, the sour green apple in my friend's lunchbox, the Granny Smith apples from the market.

When reasoning is this simple and straightforward, it's easy to follow, but it's also easy to see fallacies. For example, this person hasn't tasted all the green apples in the world; and, in fact, some green apples are not sour. However, it's rarely that easy to see the generalizations and the specifics. In determining whether a point has been proven, it's necessary to do that.

Sometimes generalizations are cited on the assumption that they are commonly accepted and do not need to be supported. An example: all men die sooner or later. Examples wouldn't be needed because that is commonly accepted. Now, some people might require that "die" be defined, but even the definition of "die" is assumed in this generalization.

Some current generalizations that may assume common acceptance: Providing healthcare for all citizens is the responsibility of the government. All true patriots will support any war the government declares.

Flaws in argument, either intended or unintended, frequently have to do with generalizations and specifics. Are the specifics sufficient to prove the truth of the generality? Does a particular specific actually apply to this generalization? Many times it will depend on definitions. The question can always be asked: has the writer (or speaker) established the generalization?

Inferential Comprehension

A common fallacy in reasoning is the *post hoc ergo propter hoc* ("after this, therefore because of this") or the false-cause fallacy. These occur in cause/effect reasoning, which may either go from cause to effect or effect to cause. They happen when an inadequate cause is offered for a particular effect; when the possibility of more than one cause is ignored; and when a connection between a particular cause and a particular effect is not made.

An example of a *post hoc*: Our sales shot up thirty-five percent after we ran that television campaign; therefore the campaign caused the increase in sales. It might have been a cause, of course, but more evidence is needed to prove it.

An example of an inadequate cause for a particular effect: An Iraqi truck driver reported that Saddam Hussein had nuclear weapons; therefore, Saddam Hussein is a threat to world security. More causes are needed to prove the conclusion.

An example of ignoring the possibility of more than one possible cause: John Brown was caught out in a thunderstorm and his clothes were wet before he was rescued; therefore, he developed influenza the next day was because he got wet. Being chilled may have played a role in the illness, but Brown would have had to contract the influenza virus before he would come down with it whether or not he had gotten wet.

An example of failing to make a connection between a particular cause and an effect assigned to it. Anna fell into a putrid pond on Saturday; on Monday she came down with polio; therefore, the polio was caused by the pond. This, of course, is not acceptable unless the polio virus is found in a sample of water from the pond. A connection must be proven.

Critical Comprehension

Facts are statements that are verifiable. Opinions are statements that must be supported in order to be accepted. Facts are used to support opinions.

For example, "Jane is a bad girl" is an opinion. However, "Jane hit her sister with a baseball bat" is a *fact* upon which the opinion is based. Judgments are opinions—decisions or declarations based on observation or reasoning that express approval or disapproval. Facts report what has happened or exists and come from observation, measurement, or calculation. Facts can be tested and verified whereas opinions and judgments cannot. They can only be supported with facts.

Most statements cannot be so clearly distinguished. "I believe that Jane is a bad girl" is a fact. The speaker knows what he/she believes. However, it obviously includes a judgment that could be disputed by another person who might believe otherwise. Judgments are not usually so firm. They are, rather, plausible opinions that provoke thought or lead to factual development.

An inference is drawn from an inductive line of reasoning. The most famous one is "all men are mortal," which is drawn from the observation that everyone a person knows has died or will die and that everyone else concurs in that judgment. It is assumed to be true and for that reason can be used as proof of another conclusion: "Socrates is a man; therefore, he will die."

Sometimes the inference is assumed to be proven when it is not reliably true in all cases, such as "aging brings physical and mental infirmity." Reasoning from that *inference*, many companies will not hire anyone above a certain age. Actually, being old does not necessarily imply physical and/or mental impairment. There are many instances where elderly people have made important contributions that require exceptional ability.

An argument is a generalization that is proven or supported with facts. If the facts are not accurate, the generalization remains unproven. Using inaccurate "facts" to support an argument is called a *fallacy* in reasoning.

Some factors to consider in judging whether the facts used to support an argument are accurate are as follow:
1. Are the facts current or are they out of date? For example, if the proposition "birth defects in babies born to drug-using mothers are increasing," then the data must include the latest that is available.
2. Another important factor to consider in judging the accuracy of a fact is its source. Where was the data obtained, and is that source reliable?
3. The calculations on which the facts are based may be unreliable. It's a good idea to run one's own calculations before using a piece of derived information.

Even facts that are true and have a sharp impact on the argument may not be relevant to the case at hand.

1. Health statistics from an entire state may have no relevance, or little relevance, to a particular county or zip code. Statistics from an entire country cannot be used to prove very much about a particular state or county.
2. An analogy can be useful in making a point, but the comparison must match up in all characteristics or it will not be relevant. Analogy should be used very carefully. It is often just as likely to destroy an argument as it is to strengthen it.

The importance or significance of a fact may not be sufficient to strengthen an argument. For example, of the millions of immigrants in the U.S., using a single family to support a solution to the immigration problem will not make much difference overall even though those single-example arguments are often used to support one approach or another. They may achieve a positive reaction, but they will not prove that one solution is better than another. If enough cases were cited from a variety of geographical locations, the information might be significant.

How much is enough? Generally speaking, three strong supporting facts are sufficient to establish the thesis of an argument. For example:

Conclusion: All green apples are sour.

- When I was a child, I bit into a green apple from my grandfather's orchard, and it was sour.
- I once bought green apples from a roadside vendor, and when I bit into one, it was sour.
- My grocery store had a sale on green Granny Smith apples last week, and I bought several only to find that they were sour when I bit into one.

The fallacy in the above argument is that the sample was insufficient. A more exhaustive search of literature, etc., will probably turn up some green apples that are not sour.

Sometimes more than three arguments are too many. On the other hand, it's not unusual to hear public speakers, particularly politicians, who will cite a long litany of facts to support their positions.

A very good example of the omission of facts in an argument is the resumé of an applicant for a job. The applicant is arguing that he/she should be chosen to be awarded a particular job. The application form will ask for information about past employment, and unfavorable dismissals from jobs in the past may just be omitted. Employers are usually suspicious of periods of time when the applicant has not listed an employer.

A writer makes choices about which facts will be used and which will be discarded in developing an argument. Those choices may exclude anything that is not supportive of the point of view the arguer is taking. It's always a good idea for the reader to do some research to spot the omissions and to ask whether they have impact on acceptance of the point of view presented in the argument.

No judgment is either black or white. If the argument seems too neat or too compelling, there are probably facts that might be relevant that have not been included.

A piece of writing is an integrated whole. It's not enough to just look at the various parts; the total entity must be examined. It should be considered in two ways:
- As an emotional expression of the author
- As an artistic embodiment of a meaning or set of meanings.

This is what is sometimes called "**tone**" in literary criticism.

It's important to remember the writer is a human being with his/her own individual bents, prejudices, and emotions. A writer is telling the readers about the world as he/she sees it and will give voice to certain phases of his/her own personality. By reading a writer's works, we can know the personal qualities and emotions of the writer embodied in the work itself. However, it's important to remember that not all the writer's characteristics will be revealed in a single work. People change and may have very different attitudes at different times in their lives. Sometimes, a writer will be influenced by a desire to have a piece of work accepted or to appear to be current or by the interests and desires of the readers he/she hopes to attract. It can destroy a work or make it less than it might be. Sometimes the best works are not commercial successes in the generation when they were written but are discovered at a later time by another generation.

There are three places to look for tone:
- Choice of form: tragedy or comedy; melodrama or farce; parody or sober lyric.
- Choice of materials: characters that have human qualities that are attractive; others that are repugnant. What an author shows in a setting will often indicate what his/her interests are.
- The writer's interpretation: it may be explicit—telling us how he/she feels.
- The writer's implicit interpretations: the author's feelings for a character come through in the description. For example, the use of "smirked" instead of "laughed"; "minced," "stalked," "marched," instead of walked.

The reader is asked to join the writer in the feelings expressed about the world and the things that happen in it. The tone of a piece of writing is important in a critical review of it.

Style, in literature, means a distinctive manner of expression and applies to all levels of language, beginning at the phonemic level—word choices, alliteration, assonance, etc.; the syntactic level—length of sentences, choice of structure and phraseology, patterns, etc.; and extends even beyond the sentence to paragraphs and chapters. What is distinctive about this writer's use of these elements?

In Steinbeck's *Grapes of Wrath*, for instance, the style is quite simple in the narrative sections and the dialogue is dialectal. Because the emphasis is on the story—the narrative—his style is straightforward, for the most part. He just tells the story.

However, there are chapters where he varies his style. He uses symbols and combines them with description that are realistic. He sometimes shifts to a crisp, repetitive pattern to underscore the beeping and speeding of cars. By contrast, some of those inter chapters are lyrical, almost poetic.

These shifts in style reflect the attitude of the author toward the subject matter. He intends to make a statement, and he uses a variety of styles to strengthen the point.

Skill 4.14   Knows how to provide instruction to help students increase their reading vocabulary.

See Skill 1.10.

Skill 4.15   Understands reading comprehension issues for students with different needs and knows effective reading strategies for those students.

See Skill 5.5.

Skill 4.16   Knows the difference between guided and independent practice in reading and provides students with frequent opportunities for both.

See Skill 5.16.

Skill 4.17   Knows how to promote students' development of an extensive reading and writing vocabulary by providing them with many opportunities to read and write.

News reporters generally become excellent writers because they get a lot of practice, which is a principle most writing teachers try to employ with their students. Also, news writing is instructive in skills for writing clearly and coherently. Reporters generally write in two modes: straight reporting and feature writing. In both modes, the writer must be concerned with accuracy and objectivity. The reporter does not write his opinions. S/he does not write persuasive discourse. The topic is typically assigned, although some experienced reporters have the opportunity to seek out and develop their own stories.

Investigative reporting is sometimes seen as a distinct class although, technically, all reporters are "investigative." That is, they research the background of the story they're reporting, using as many means as are available. For example, the wife of a conservative, model minister murders him premeditatively and in cold blood. The reporter reports the murder and the arrest of the wife, but the story is far from complete until some questions are answered, the most obvious one being "why?" The reporter is obligated to try to answer that question and to do so will interview as many people as will talk to him about the lives of both minister and wife, their parents, members of the church, their neighbors, etc. The reporter will also look at newspaper archives in the town where the murder took place as well as in newspapers in any town the husband and/or wife has lived in previously. High-school yearbooks are a source that are often explored in these cases.

When Bob Woodward and Carl Bernstein, reporters for *The Washington Post,* began to break the Watergate story in 1972 and 1973, they set new standards for investigative reporting and had a strong influence on journalistic writing. Most reporters wanted to be Woodward and Bernstein and became more aggressive than reporters had been in the past. Even so, the basic techniques and principles still apply. The reporting of these two talented journalists demonstrated that while newspapers keep communities aware of what's going on, they also have the power to influence it.

A good news story is written as an "inverted pyramid." That is, the reasoning is deductive. The "thesis" or point is stated first and is supported with details. It reasons from general to specific.

The lead sentence might be, "The body of John Smith was found in the street in front of his home with a bullet wound through his skull." The headline will be a trimmed-down version of that sentence and shaped to grab attention. It might read: "Murdered man found on Spruce Street." The news article might fill several columns, the first details having to do with the finding of the body, the next the role of the police; the third will spread out and include details about the victim's life, then the scope will broaden to details about his family, friends, neighbors, etc. If he held a position of prominence in the community, those details will broaden further and include information about his relationships to fellow-workers and his day-to-day contacts in the community. The successful reporter's skills include the ability to do thorough research, to maintain an objective stance (not to become involved personally in the story), and to write an effective "inverted pyramid."

Feature writing is more like an informative essay although it may also follow the inverted pyramid model. This form of reporting focuses on a topic designed to be interesting to at least one segment of the readership—possible sports enthusiasts, travelers, vacationers, families, women, food lovers, etc. The article will focus on one aspect of the area of interest such as a particular experience for the vacationing family. The first sentence might read something like this: "Lake Lure offers a close-to-home relaxing weekend getaway for families in East Tennessee." The development can be an ever-widening pyramid of details focused particularly on what the family can experience at Lake Lure but also directions for how to get there.

While the headline is intended to contain in capsule form the point that an article makes, it is rarely written by the reporter. This can sometimes result in a disconnection between headline and article. Well-written headlines will provide a guide for the reader as to what is in the article; they will also be attention-grabbers. This requires a special kind of writing, quite different from the inverted pyramid that distinguishes these writers from the investigative or feature reporter.

COMPETENCY 5.0 READING APPLICATIONS

Skill 5.1   **Understands skills and strategies for understanding, interpreting, and evaluating different types of written materials, including narratives, expository texts, technical writing, and content-area textbooks.**

To *interpret* means essentially to read with understanding and appreciation. It is not as daunting as it is made out to be. Simple techniques for interpreting literature are as follows:

- **Context:** This includes the author's feelings, beliefs, past experiences, goals, needs, and physical environment. Incorporate an understanding of how these elements may have affected the writing to enrich an interpretation of it.
- **Symbols:** Also referred to as a sign, a symbol designates something which stands for something else. In most cases, it is standing for something that has a deeper meaning than its literal denotation. Symbols can have personal, cultural, or universal associations. Use an understanding of symbols to unearth a meaning the author might have intended but not expressed, or even something the author never intended at all.
- **Questions:** Asking questions, such as "How would I react in this situation?" may shed further light on how you feel about the work.

It's no accident that **plot** is sometimes called action. If the plot does not *move*, the story quickly dies. Therefore, the successful writer of stories uses a wide variety of active verbs in creative and unusual ways. If a reader is kept on his/her toes by the movement of the story, the experience of reading it will be pleasurable. That reader will probably want to read more of this author's work. Careful, unique, and unusual choices of active verbs will bring about that effect. William Faulkner is a good example of a successful writer whose stories are lively and memorable because of his use of unusual active verbs. In analyzing the development of plot, it's wise to look at the verbs. However, the development of believable conflicts is also vital. If there is no conflict, there is no story. What devices does a writer use to develop the conflicts, and are they real and believable?

Character is portrayed in many ways: description of physical characteristics, dialogue, interior monologue, the thoughts of the character, the attitudes of other characters toward this one, etc. Descriptive language depends on the ability to recreate a sensory experience for the reader. If the description of the character's appearance is a visual one, then the reader must be able to *see* the character. What's the shape of the nose? What color are the eyes? How tall or how short is this character? Thin or chubby? How does the character move? How does the character walk? Terms must be chosen that will create a picture for the reader. It's not enough to say the eyes are blue, for example. What blue?

Often the color of eyes is compared to something else to enhance the readers' ability to visualize the character. A good test of characterization is the level of emotional involvement of the reader in the character. If the reader is to become involved, the description must provide an actual experience—seeing, smelling, hearing, tasting, or feeling.

Dialogue will reflect characteristics. Is it clipped? Is it highly dialectal? Does a character use a lot of colloquialisms? The ability to portray the speech of a character can make or break a story. The kind of person the character is in the mind of the reader is dependent on impressions created by description and dialogue. How do other characters feel about this one as revealed by their treatment of him/her, their discussions of him/her with each other, or their overt descriptions of the character. For example, "John, of course, can't be trusted with another person's possessions." In analyzing a story, it's useful to discuss the devices used to produce character.

Setting may be visual, temporal, psychological, or social. Descriptive words are often used here also. In Edgar Allan Poe's description of the house in "The Fall of the House of Usher" as the protagonist/narrator approaches it, the air of dread and gloom that pervades the story is caught in the setting and sets the stage for the story. A setting may also be symbolic, as it is in Poe's story, where the house is a symbol of the family that lives in it. As the house disintegrates, so does the family.

The language used in all of these aspects of a story—plot, character, and setting—work together to create the **mood** of a story. Poe's first sentence establishes the mood of the story: "During the whole of a dull, dark, and soundless day in the autumn of the year, when the clouds hung oppressively low in the heavens, I had been passing alone, on horseback, through a singularly dreary tract of country; and at length found myself, as the shades of the evening drew on, within view of the melancholy House of Usher."

Skill 5.2   Understands different purposes for reading and related reading strategies.

The question to be asked first when approaching a reading task is what is my objective? What do I want to achieve from this reading? How will I use the information I gain from this reading? Do I only need to grasp the gist of the piece? Do I need to know the line of reasoning—not only the thesis but the subpoints? Will I be reporting important and significant details orally or in a written document?

A written document can be expected to have a thesis—either expressed or derived. To discover the thesis, the reader needs to ask what point the writer intended to make?

The writing can also be expected to be organized in some logical way and to have subpoints that support or establish the thesis is valid. It is also reasonable to expect there will be details or examples that will support the subpoints. Knowing this, the reader can make a decision about reading techniques required for the purpose that has already been established.

If the reader only needs to know the gist of a written document, speed-reading skimming techniques may be sufficient by using the forefinger, moving the eyes down the page, picking up the important statements in each paragraph and deducing mentally that this piece is about such-and-such. If the reader needs to a little better grasp of how the writer achieved his/her purpose in the document, a quick and cursory glance—a skimming—of each paragraph will yield what the subpoints are, the topic sentences of the paragraphs, and how the thesis is developed, yielding a greater understanding of the author's purpose and method of development.

In-depth reading requires the scrutiny of each phrase and sentence with care, looking for the thesis first of all and then the topic sentences in the paragraphs that provide the development of the thesis, also looking for connections such as transitional devices that provide clues to the direction the reasoning is taking.

Sometimes rereading is necessary in order to make use of a piece of writing for an oral or written report upon a document. If this is the purpose of reading the document, the first reading should provide a map for the rereading or second reading. The second time through should follow this map, and those points that are going to be used in a report or analysis will be focused upon on more carefully. Some new understandings may occur in this rereading, and it may become apparent that the "map" that was derived from the first reading will need to be adjusted. If this rereading is for the purpose of writing an analysis or using material for a report, either highlighting or note-taking is advisable.

Skill 5.3   Knows and teaches strategies to facilitate comprehension of different types of text before, during, and after reading.

See Skill 4.13.

Skill 5.4   Provides instruction in comprehension skills that support students' transition from "learning to read" to "reading to learn."

Writers, from the time of the invention of the printing press, have played important roles in shaping public opinion, not only in their own countries but also around the world. Worldwide philosophical trends can be traced to the literature that was popular in a particular period of time. America has always been a nation of readers. With the development of theaters and ultimately movies and television that often dramatized popular novels, the power of the written word has increased.

John Steinbeck's *Grapes of Wrath* focused the attention of Americans on the plight of the common people who suffered more than anyone else because of the Great Depression. His revelation that Americans were starving to death in a land of great abundance still resonates with the public. Members of the "establishment" in the farms and towns of California are revealed as callous and greedy. Church members, particularly clergy and leaders, don't come off much better in his revealing story. Steinbeck lived with some of the migrants so he could write authentically and with first-hand knowledge. Many of the writers who have influenced public opinion write from personal experience.

The feminist movement has virtually been fueled by literature going back several hundred years. Although the organized movement began with the first women's rights convention at Seneca Falls, New York, in 1948, in 1869, John Stuart Mill had already published *The Subjection of Women* to demonstrate that the legal subordination of one sex to the other is wrong. Virginia Woolf's essay, *A Room of One's Own*, first published in 1929, had a strong influence on how women were beginning to see their roles.

However, in the crusade that was ignited by the Civil Rights movement of the 1960s, Betty Friedan's book, *The Feminine Mystique*, published in 1963, was very popular and influenced many women to become involved, both in changes in their own outlooks and behaviors, but also in the movement at large as activists. Feminism has been so much a part of the thinking throughout the world that it should always be included in the potential themes one looks for when writing a critique of a literary work.

Uncle Tom's Cabin broke new ground in literature on social injustice and was very powerful in influencing the thinking of American people about slavery. It was the best-selling novel of the 19th century and is credited with helping to fuel the abolitionist cause prior to the American Civil War. Written by Harriet Beecher Stowe and published in 1852, slavery is its central theme.

The Vietnam War inspired many novels although most were written after the war was over. However, the attitudes of Americans about the war have been influenced by these novels, and for many, they have formed the concept they carry with them about the conflict.

Some examples of novels about the Vietnam War:
- *Apocalypse Now*
- *Full Metal Jacket*
- *Platoon*
- *Good Morning Vietnam*
- *The Deer Hunter*
- *Born on the Fourth of July*
- *Hamburger Hill*

Skill 5.5   Understand the importance of reading as a skill in all content areas.

Content areas such as science, mathematics, history and social studies rely on textbooks and other printed materials that use primarily expository text to introduce, explain, and illustrate new subject matter. From a reading perspective, students face several challenges when approaching these texts, such as deciphering unfamiliar vocabulary, and adapting to new structures of content organization, that directly impact their ability to understand, synthesize, and apply the information contained therein.

Students lacking a solid foundation of reading strategies will likely experience difficulties in developing the competencies needed to master a subject area's academic requirements. At the secondary level, reading and understanding is only the beginning. Students are expected to absorb, evaluate, and form opinions and theories about topics within the subject matter, and then discuss, write about, and apply what they've learned on high level.

Metacognitive reading development strategies can help students engage effectively with their reading materials across the curriculum. The sample strategies below can be employed through structured activities that occur before reading, during reading, and after reading.

Before reading
- Incorporate prior knowledge: Draw a connection between students' previous experiences – both personal and educational – and the topic at hand. A student who has helped out in the family garden, for example, will have a visual and basic vocabulary starting point for the study of plant physiology.
- Make predictions about what will be learned: Encourage students to identify what they think they will learn from the text, based on cues in the material (e.g., book titles, chapter headings, pictures, etc.)
- Prepare questions: Write specific questions to be answered during reading.

During reading:
- Use context cues: Utilize other words and concepts in same the sentence or paragraph to determine the meaning of an unfamiliar word.
- Reread challenging text: Practice rereading a selection of text to check for understanding.
- Use visualizing techniques: Mental pictures formed during the reading of text can aid in comprehension and retention of information. Read alouds, followed by a discussion of how these mental pictures factually reflect the text, provide opportunity for practicing and reinforcing this technique at all grade levels.

- <u>Make inferences:</u> Much of human communication relies on our ability to "read between the lines" of explicit statements and make logical guesses that fill in the blanks of information not provided. Similarly, for textbooks, making inferences means making connections to information extending beyond the text and subject matter at hand. For example, a geography book making the simple declaration that Brazil has a tropical climate can allow the student to deduce a wealth of information not stated in the text (e.g., tropical climates have warm year-round temperatures and high precipitation levels, therefore certain crops will grow quite successfully and can positively impact the local economy, etc.)

- <u>Check the predictions made before reading:</u> Use the text to confirm earlier predictions about content, and answer the questions posed prior to reading.

After reading:

- <u>Summarize information:</u> Students who understand the information they have read should be able to restate what they have learned in an organized manner. This activity can be practiced in both written and oral forms.

- <u>Make critical evaluations:</u> Encourage students to respond to the text with the ideas and opinions they've formed during reading. Facilitate discussions by devising questions that lead students to make qualitative and evaluative judgments about the content they've read.

Skill 5.6	Understands the value of using dictionaries, glossaries, and other sources to determine the meanings, pronunciations, and derivation of unfamiliar words and teaches students to use these sources.

Explore the distribution of letters

It's not always easy to find a word in the dictionary, but there are a number of strategies which can be used to help your students. To familiarize students with the distribution of letters and to save them time and frustration when they look words up, you can do the following exercise:

Hold a dictionary in front of you so that all the class can see it. Open it, and ask them to guess which letter the book is open at. Try this a few times, then get them to do it in pairs.

You can also ask questions such as:

- What do you think the first word in the dictionary is?

- What is the last word?

- Which letter starts the most words in English?

- How many pages do you think it takes up in the dictionary?

- This again helps them to locate more easily where they will find words.

Remind students of guide words

Students can often ignore the two guide words at the top of each dictionary page. It is worth pointing out to them that these words are there to tell them which is the first and which the last word on the page. Practice using the help these words offer with the following short exercises:

- On the page *lilac* to *limit*, which of the following words would you find?
  limb, like, lime-green, lily, limp

- Suggest two other words that should be on that page.

- On the page *smell* to *smoke*, which of the following words would not be there?
  smart, smile, smoked, smog, smoker

- When students are ready, ask them to compare their answers with the dictionary.

Focus on pronunciation

It's important for students to understand the way pronunciation is shown in the dictionary. Practice using the phonetics symbols in a playful way. Here are a couple of exercises to show you what you can do in class:

- Ask the class to work in teams and give each team three different words that they probably don't know. Ask each team to choose a word and write the word in three phonetic spellings, two of which are incorrect. When they are ready, ask each team to say and write its word as if they all could be correct. The other teams try to deduce or guess the correct pronunciation without using the dictionary.

- Do the same activity but this time ask the teams to find three stress patterns for their word. Ask students to find a word of three or more syllables. When they are ready, they write the word on the board, in normal spelling, and then say each of the three pronunciations aloud. The other teams try to guess which stress pattern is most probable, and check with their dictionaries.

Learn about phrases and idioms

Point out to students that words rarely appear in isolation and that dictionaries are a valuable source of phrases and idioms. Make sure students know where these phrases and idioms are listed in an entry and encourage them to use them appropriately. You can practice with this exercise:

- In the entry for the noun *name*, find the following:
- A phrase that means 'to remember the name of someone you recognize'

- A phrase that means 'to do something that shows that someone is not guilty of something wrong or illegal that they have been accused of'

- A phrase that means 'to use a particular name, especially when it is not your real name'

Explore phrasal verbs

Phrasal verbs are often difficult for students. They do not always realize how many different meanings they have. Look at an entry for a common verb (e.g. *come*, *give*), spend some time exploring it, ensuring that students discover in which part of the entry they can find phrasal verbs. Do the following exercise to help students practice finding the phrasal verb they are looking for:

- Get students to look up the phrasal verbs for *stand* in their dictionaries and ask questions such as:
- How many different phrasal verbs does *stand* have?
- How many senses are there for *stand for*?
- Which sense of *stand out* means 'to be much more impressive or important than others'?

Use the examples

The examples in modern dictionaries are taken from natural written or spoken English. Use these as your source for grammar or vocabulary work in the classroom. For example, take a frequent word you want your class to study, and find the examples that are given for each meaning of that word in the dictionary. Remove the word itself from the examples leaving a blank. Where there is more than one meaning, provide examples for each meaning, with the word itself taken out. Read or show the examples with blanks to the class and invite students to discuss them and guess the blank word, explaining their choice.

Focus on frequent words

Most modern dictionaries provide extra information on aspects of English such as correct usage, common errors, synonyms, metaphors, differences between American and British English, and information on what the most frequent words are. Explore the dictionary drawing students' attention to these types of information and create classroom activities around them. To focus on frequent words, you can do the following activities:

- Choose the three words from the page *operetta* to *opportunity* that are used the most frequently: *opinion, opinionated, opportunist, opportunity, ophthalmologist*
- List three words you think are marked as the most frequent ones on the page *reach* to *read*. Then check your answers in the dictionary.

Skill 5.7   Knows how to teach students to interpret information presented in various formats and how to locate, retrieve, and retain information from a range of texts and technologies.

Visual representations of information which simply store descriptive information in a form available for general use are called repository **tables**. They usually contain primary data, which simply summarize raw data. They are not intended to analyze the data, so any analysis is left to the reader or user of the table. A good example of a repository table would be a report of birth statistics by the federal Health and Human Services Department. An analytical table, on the other hand, is constructed from some sort of analysis of primary or secondary data, possibly from a repository table or from the raw data itself. An example of an analytical table would be one that compares birth statistics in 1980 to birth statistics in 2005 for the country at large. It might also break the data down into comparisons by state.

Graphs also present data in visual form. Whereas tables are useful for showing large numbers of specific, related facts or statistics in a brief space, trends, movements, distributions and cycles are more readily apparent in a graph. However, although graphs can present statistics in a more interesting and comprehensible form than tables, they are less accurate. For this reason, the two will often be shown together.

While the most obvious use for **maps** is to locate places geographically, they can also show specific geographic features such as roads, mountains, rivers, etc. The can also show information according to geographic distribution such as population, housing, manufacturing centers, etc.

A wide range of **illustrations** may be used to illuminate the text in a document. They may also be a part of a graphic layout designed to make the page more attractive.

Some possibilities for the analysis of data whether presented in tables, charts, graphs, maps, or other illustrations are as follow:
- Qualitative descriptions—drawing conclusions about the quality of a particular treatment, course of action as revealed by the illustration.
- Quantitative descriptions—how much do the results of one particular treatment or course of action differ from another one, and is that variation significant?
- Classification—is worthwhile information derived from breaking the information down into classifications?
- Estimations—is it possible to estimate future performance on the basis of the information in the illustration?
- Comparisons—is it useful to make comparisons based on the data?
- Relationships—are relationships between components revealed by the scrutiny of the data?

- Cause-and-effect relationships—is it suggested by the data that there were cause-and-effect relationships that were not previously apparent?
- Mapping and modeling—if the data were mapped and a model drawn up, would the point of the document be demonstrated or refuted?

Questions to ask regarding an illustration: Why is it in this document? What was the writer's purpose in putting it in the document and why at this particular place? Does it make a point clearer? What implications are inherent in a table that shows birth statistics in all states or even in some selected states? What does that have to do with the point and purpose of this piece of writing? Is there adequate preparation in the text for the inclusion of the illustration? Does the illustration underscore or clarify any of the points made in the text? Is there a clear connection between the illustration and the subject matter of the text?

Skill 5.8   **Knows how to help students comprehend abstract content and ideas in written materials.**

See Skill 5.5.

Skill 5.9   **Knows literary genres and their characteristics.**

The major literary genres include allegory, ballad, drama, epic, epistle, essay, fable, novel, poem, romance, and the short story.

Allegory: A story in verse or prose with characters representing virtues and vices. There are two meanings, symbolic and literal. John Bunyan's *The Pilgrim's Progress* is the most renowned of this genre.

Autobiography: A form of biography, but it is written by the subject him/herself. Autobiographies can range from the very formal to intimate writings made during one's life that were not intended for publication. These include letters, diaries, journals, memoirs, and reminiscences. Autobiography, generally speaking, began in the 15th century; one of the first examples is one written in England by Margery Kempe. There are four kinds of autobiography: thematic, religious, intellectual, and fictionalized. Some "novels" may be thinly disguised autobiography, such as the novels of Thomas Wolfe.

Ballad: An *in medias res* story told or sung, usually in verse and accompanied by music. Literary devices found in ballads include the refrain, or repeated section, and incremental repetition, or anaphora, for effect. Earliest forms were anonymous folk ballads. Later forms include Coleridge's Romantic masterpiece, "The Rime of the Ancient Mariner."

Biography: A form of nonfictional literature, the subject of which is the life of an individual. The earliest biographical writings were probably funeral speeches and inscriptions, usually praising the life and example of the deceased. Early biographies evolved from this and were almost invariably uncritical, even distorted, and always laudatory.

Beginning in the 18th century, this form of literature saw major development; an eminent example is James Boswell's *Life of Johnson*, which is very detailed and even records conversations. Eventually, the antithesis of the grossly exaggerated tomes praising an individual, usually a person of circumstance, developed. This form is denunciatory, debunking, and often inflammatory. A famous modern example is Lytton Strachey's *Eminent Victorians* (1918).

Drama: Plays – comedy, modern, or tragedy - typically in five acts. Traditionalists and neoclassicists adhere to Aristotle's unities of time, place and action. Plot development is advanced via dialogue. Literary devices include asides, soliloquies and the chorus representing public opinion. Greatest of all dramatists/playwrights is William Shakespeare. Other dramaturges include Ibsen, Williams, Miller, Shaw, Stoppard, Racine, Moliére, Sophocles, Aeschylus, Euripides, and Aristophanes.

Epic: Long poem usually of book length reflecting values inherent in the generative society. Epic devices include an invocation to a Muse for inspiration, purpose for writing, universal setting, protagonist and antagonist who possess supernatural strength and acumen, and interventions of a God or the gods. Understandably, there are very few epics: Homer's *Iliad* and *Odyssey*, Virgil's *Aeneid*, Milton's *Paradise Lost*, Spenser's *The Fairie Queene*, Barrett Browning's *Aurora Leigh*, and Pope's mock-epic, *The Rape of the Lock*.

Epistle: A letter that is not always originally intended for public distribution, but due to the fame of the sender and/or recipient, becomes public domain. Paul wrote epistles that were later placed in the Bible.

Essay: Typically a limited length prose work focusing on a topic and propounding a definite point of view and authoritative tone. Great essayists include Carlyle, Lamb, DeQuincy, Emerson and Montaigne, who is credited with defining this genre.

Fable: Terse tale offering up a moral or exemplum. Chaucer's "The Nun's Priest's Tale" is a fine example of a *bete fabliau* or beast fable in which animals speak and act characteristically human, illustrating human foibles.

Informational books and articles: Make up much of the reading of modern Americans. Magazines began to be popular in the 19th century in this country, and while many of the contributors to those publications intended to influence the political/social/religious convictions of their readers, many also simply intended to pass on information. A book or article whose purpose is simply to be informative, that is, not to persuade, is called exposition (adjectival form: expository). An example of an expository book is the *MLA Style Manual*. The writers do not intend to persuade their readers to use the recommended stylistic features in their writing; they are simply making them available in case a reader needs such a guide.

Articles in magazines such as *Time* may be persuasive in purpose, such as Joe Klein's regular column, but for the most part they are expository, giving information that television coverage of a news story might not have time to include.

Legend: A traditional narrative or collection of related narratives, popularly regarded as historically factual but actually a mixture of fact and fiction.

Myth: Stories that are more or less universally shared within a culture to explain its history and traditions.

Newspaper accounts of events: Expository in nature, of course, a reporting of a happening. That happening might be a school board meeting, an automobile accident that sent several people to a hospital and accounted for the death of a passenger, or the election of the mayor. They are not intended to be persuasive although the bias of a reporter or of an editor must be factored in. A newspapers' editorial stance is often openly declared, and it may be reflected in such things as news reports. Reporters are expected to be unbiased in their coverage and most of them will defend their disinterest fiercely, but what a writer *sees* in an event is inevitably shaped to some extent by the writer's beliefs and experiences.

Novel: The longest form of fictional prose containing a variety of characterizations, settings, local color and regionalism. Most have complex plots, expanded description, and attention to detail. Some of the great novelists include Austin, the Brontes, Twain, Tolstoy, Hugo, Hardy, Dickens, Hawthorne, Forster, and Flaubert.

Poem: The only requirement is rhythm. Sub-genres include fixed types of literature such as the sonnet, elegy, ode, pastoral, and villanelle. Unfixed types of literature include blank verse and dramatic monologue.

Romance: A highly imaginative tale set in a fantastical realm dealing with the conflicts between heroes, villains and/or monsters. "The Knight's Tale" from Chaucer's *Canterbury Tales*, *Sir Gawain and the Green Knight* and Keats' "The Eve of St. Agnes" are prime representatives.

Short Story: Typically a terse narrative, with less developmental background about characters. May include description, author's point of view, and tone. Poe emphasized that a successful short story should create one focused impact. Considered to be great short story writers are Hemingway, Faulkner, Twain, Joyce, Shirley Jackson, Flannery O'Connor, de Maupassant, Saki, Edgar Allen Poe, and Pushkin.

Dramatic Texts:

Comedy: The comedic form of dramatic literature is meant to amuse, and often ends happily. It uses techniques such as satire or parody, and can take many forms, from farce to burlesque.

Examples include Dante Alighieri's *The Divine Comedy,* Noel Coward's play *Private Lives,* and some of Geoffrey Chaucer's *Canterbury Tales* and William Shakespeare's plays.

Tragedy: Tragedy is comedy's other half. It is defined as a work of drama written in either prose or poetry, telling the story of a brave, noble hero who, because of some tragic character flaw, brings ruin upon himself. It is characterized by serious, poetic language that evokes pity and fear. In modern times, dramatists have tried to update its image by drawing its main characters from the middle class and showing their nobility through their nature instead of their standing. The classic example of tragedy is Sophocles' *Oedipus Rex*, while Henrik Ibsen and Arthur Miller epitomize modern tragedy.

Drama: In its most general sense, a drama is any work that is designed to be performed by actors onstage. It can also refer to the broad literary genre that includes comedy and tragedy. Contemporary usage, however, denotes drama as a work that treats serious subjects and themes but does not aim for the same grandeur as tragedy. Drama usually deals with characters of a less stately nature than tragedy. A classical example is Sophocles' tragedy *Oedipus Rex,* while Eugene O'Neill's *The Iceman Cometh* represents modern drama.

Dramatic Monologue: A dramatic monologue is a speech given by an actor, usually intended for themselves, but with the intended audience in mind. It reveals key aspects of the character's psyche and sheds insight on the situation at hand. The audience takes the part of the silent listener, passing judgment and giving sympathy at the same time. This form was invented and used predominantly by Victorian poet Robert Browning.

Tempo: Interpretation of dialogue must be connected to motivation and detail. During this time, the director is also concerned with pace and seeks a variation of tempo. If the overall pace is too slow, then the action becomes dull and dragging. If the overall pace is too fast, then the audience will not be able to understand what is going on, for they are being hit with too much information to process.

Dramatic Arc: Good drama is built on conflict of some kind — an opposition of forces or desires that must be resolved by the end of the story. The conflict can be internal, involving emotional and psychological pressures, or it can be external, drawing the characters into tumultuous events. These themes are presented to the audience in a narrative arc that looks roughly like this:

Climax

Intro | Conflict Development | Resolution

Following the Arc: Although any performance may have a series of rising and falling levels of intensity, in general the opening should set in motion the events which will generate an emotional high toward the middle or end of the story. Then, regardless of whether the ending is happy, sad, bittersweet, or despairing, the resolution eases the audience down from those heights and establishes some sense of closure. Reaching the climax too soon undermines the dramatic impact of the remaining portion of the performance, whereas reaching it too late rushes the ending and creates a jarringly abrupt end to events.

Skill 5.10   **Recognizes a wide range of literature and other texts appropriate for students.**

Adolescent literature, because of the age range of readers, is extremely diverse. Fiction for the middle group, usually ages ten/eleven to fourteen/fifteen, deals with issues of coping with internal and external changes in their lives. Because children's writers in the twentieth century have produced increasingly realistic fiction, adolescents can now find problems dealt with honestly in novels.

Teachers of middle/junior high school students see the greatest change in interests and reading abilities. Fifth and sixth graders, included in elementary grades in many schools, are viewed as older children while seventh and eighth graders are preadolescent. Ninth graders, included sometimes as top dogs in junior high school and sometimes as underlings in high school, definitely view themselves as teenagers. Their literature choices will often be governed more by interest than by ability; thus, the wealth of high-interest, low readability books that have flooded the market in recent years. Tenth through twelfth graders will still select high-interest books for pleasure reading but are also easily encouraged to stretch their literature muscles by reading more classics.

Because of the rapid social changes, topics that once did not interest young people until they reached their teens - suicide, gangs, homosexuality - are now subjects of books for even younger readers. The plethora of high-interest books reveals how desperately schools have failed to produce on-level readers and how the market has adapted to that need. However, these high-interest books are now readable for younger children whose reading levels are at or above normal. No matter how tastefully written, some contents are inappropriate for younger readers.

The problem becomes not so much steering them toward books that they have the reading ability to handle but encouraging them toward books whose content is appropriate to their levels of cognitive and social development. A fifth-grader may be able to read V.C. Andrews book *Flowers in the Attic* but not possess the social/moral development to handle the deviant behavior of the characters. At the same time, because of the complex changes affecting adolescents, the teacher must be well versed in learning theory and child development as well as competent to teach the subject matter of language and literature.

These classic and contemporary works combine the characteristics of multiple theories. Functioning at the concrete operations stage (Piaget), being of the "good person," orientation (Kohlberg), still highly dependent on external rewards (Bandura), and exhibiting all five needs previously discussed from Maslow's hierarchy, these eleven to twelve year olds should appreciate the following titles, grouped by reading level. These titles are also cited for interest at that grade level and do not reflect high-interest titles for older readers who do not read at grade level. Some high interest titles will be cited later.

For Sixth Grades

>Barrett, William. *Lilies of the Field*
>Cormier, Robert. *Other Bells for Us to Ring*
>Dahl, Roald. *Danny, Champion of the World; Charlie and the Chocolate Factory*
>Lindgren, Astrid. *Pippi Longstocking*
>Lindbergh, Anne. *Three Lives to Live*
>Lowry, Lois. *Rabble Starkey*
>Naylor, Phyllis. *The Year of the Gopher, Reluctantly Alice*
>Peck, Robert Newton. *Arly*
>Speare, Elizabeth. *The Witch of Blackbird Pond*
>Sleator, William. *The Boy Who Reversed Himself*

For seventh and eighth grades

Most seventh and eight grade students, according to learning theory, are still functioning cognitively, psychologically, and morally as sixth graders. As these are not inflexible standards, there are some twelve and thirteen year olds who are much more mature socially, intellectually, and physically than the younger children who share the same school. They are becoming concerned with establishing individual and peer group identities that presents conflicts with breaking from authority and the rigidity of rules. Some at this age are still tied firmly to the family and its expectations while others identify more with those their own age or older. Enrichment reading for this group must help them cope with life's rapid changes or provide escape and thus must be either realistic or fantastic depending on the child's needs. Adventures and mysteries (the Hardy Boys and Nancy Drew series) are still popular today.

These preteens also become more interested in biographies of contemporary figures rather than legendary figures of the past.

Reading level 7.0 to 7.9

Armstrong, William. *Sounder*
Bagnold, Enid. *National Velvet*
Barrie, James. *Peter Pan*
London, Jack. *White Fang, Call of the Wild*
Lowry, Lois. *Taking Care of Terrific*
McCaffrey, Anne. The *Dragonsinger* series
Montgomery, L. M. *Anne of Green Gables* and sequels
Steinbeck, John. *The Pearl*
Tolkien, J. R. R. *The Hobbit*
Zindel, Paul. *The Pigman*

Reading level 8.0 to 8.9

Cormier, Robert. *I Am the Cheese*
McCullers, Carson. *The Member of the Wedding*
North, Sterling. *Rascal*
Twain, Mark. *The Adventures of Tom Sawyer*
Zindel, Paul. *My Darling , My Hamburger*

Skill 5.11   **Provides multiple opportunities for students to listen and respond to a wide variety of children's and young people's literature, both fiction and nonfiction, and to recognize characteristics of various types of narrative and expository texts.**

Prior to twentieth century research on child development and child/adolescent literature's relationship to that development, books for adolescents were primarily didactic. They were designed to be instructive of history, manners, and morals.

Middle Ages

As early as the eleventh century, Anselm, the Archbishop of Canterbury, wrote an encyclopedia designed to instill in children the beliefs and principles of conduct acceptable to adults in medieval society. Early monastic translations of the *Bible* and other religious writings were written in Latin, for the edification of the upper class. Fifteenth century hornbooks were designed to teach reading and religious lessons. William Caxton printed English versions of *Aesop's Fables*, Malory's *Le Morte d'Arthur* and stories from Greek and Roman mythology. Though printed for adults, tales of adventures of Odysseus and the Arthurian knights were also popular with literate adolescents.

Renaissance

The Renaissance saw the introduction of the inexpensive chapbooks, small in size and 16-64 pages in length. Chapbooks were condensed versions of mythology and fairy tales. Designed for the common people, chapbooks were imperfect grammatically but were immensely popular because of their adventurous contents. Though most of the serious, educated adults frowned on the sometimes-vulgar little books, they received praise from Richard Steele of *Tatler* fame for inspiring his grandson's interest in reading and pursuing his other studies.

Meanwhile, the Puritans' three most popular reads were the *Bible*, John Foxe's *Book of Martyrs*, and John Bunyan's *Pilgrim's Progress*. Though venerating religious martyrs and preaching the moral propriety which was to lead to eternal happiness, the stories of the *Book of Martyrs* were often lurid in their descriptions of the fate of the damned. Not written for children and difficult reading even for adults, *Pilgrim's Progress* was as attractive to adolescents for its adventurous plot as for its moral outcome. In Puritan America, the *New England Primer* set forth the prayers, catechisms, *Bible* verses, and illustrations meant to instruct children in the Puritan ethic. The seventeenth-century French used fables and fairy tales to entertain adults, but children found them enjoyable as well.

Seventeenth century CHILDREN'S LIT

The late seventeenth century brought the first concern with providing literature that specifically targeted the young. Pierre Perrault's *Fairy Tales*, Jean de la Fontaine's retellings of famous fables, Mme. d'Aulnoy's novels based on old folktales, and Mme. de Beaumont's "Beauty and the Beast" were written to delight as well as instruct young people. In England, publisher John Newbury was the first to publish a line for children. These include a translation of Perrault's *Tales of Mother Goose; A Little Pretty Pocket-Book*, "intended for instruction and amusement" but decidedly moralistic and bland in comparison to the previous century's chapbooks; and *The Renowned History of Little Goody Two Shoes*, allegedly written by Oliver Goldsmith for a juvenile audience.

Eighteenth century

By and large, however, into the eighteenth century adolescents were finding their reading pleasure in adult books: Daniel Defoe's *Robinson Crusoe*, Jonathan Swift's *Gulliver's Travels*, and Johann Wyss's *Swiss Family Robinson*. More books were being written for children, but the moral didacticism, though less religious, was nevertheless ever present. The short stories of Maria Edgeworth, the four-volume *The History of Sandford and Merton* by Thomas Day, and Martha Farquharson's twenty-six volume *Elsie Dinsmore* series dealt with pious protagonists who learned restraint, repentance, and rehabilitation from sin.

Two bright spots in this period of didacticism were Jean Jacques Rousseau's *Emile* and *The Tales of Shakespear*, Charles and Mary Lamb's simplified versions of Shakespeare's plays. Rousseau believed that a child's abilities were enhanced by a free, happy life, and the Lambs subscribed to the notion that children were entitled to more entertaining literature in language comprehensible to them.

Nineteenth century

Child/adolescent literature truly began its modern rise in nineteenth century Europe. Hans Christian Andersen's *Fairy Tales* were fanciful adaptations of the somber revisions of the Grimm brothers in the previous century. Andrew Lang's series of colorful fairy books contain the folklores of many nations and are still part of the collections of many modern libraries. Clement Moore's "A Visit from St. Nicholas" is a cheery, non-threatening child's view of the "night before Christmas." The humor of Lewis Carroll's books about Alice's adventures, Edward Lear's poems with caricatures, Lucretia Nole's stories of the Philadelphia Peterkin family, were full of fancy and not a smidgen of morality. Other popular Victorian novels introduced the modern fantasy and science fiction genres: William Makepeace Thackeray's *The Rose and the Ring*, Charles Dickens' *The Magic Fishbone*, and Jules Verne's *Twenty Thousand Leagues Under the Sea*. Adventure to exotic places became a popular topic: Rudyard Kipling's *Jungle Books*, Verne's *Around the World in Eighty Days*, and Robert Louis Stevenson's *Treasure Island* and *Kidnapped*. In 1884, the first English translation Johanna Spyre's *Heidi* appeared.

North America was also finding its voices for adolescent readers. American Louisa May Alcott's *Little Women* and Canadian L.M. Montgomery's *Anne of Green Gables* ushered in the modern age of realistic fiction. American youth were enjoying the articles of Tom Sawyer and Huckleberry Finn. For the first time children were able to read books about real people just like themselves.

Twentieth century

The literature of the twentieth century is extensive and diverse, and as in previous centuries much influenced by the adults who write, edit, and select books for youth consumption. In the first third of the century, suitable adolescent literature dealt with children from good homes with large families. These books projected an image of a peaceful, rural existence. Though the characters and plots were more realistic, the stories maintained focus on topics that were considered emotionally and intellectually proper. Popular at this time were Laura Ingalls Wilder's Little House on the Prairie Series and Carl Sandburg's biography *Abe Lincoln Grows Up*. English author J.R.R. Tolkien's fantasy *The Hobbit* prefaced modern adolescent readers' fascination with the works of Piers Antony, Madelaine L'Engle, and Anne McCaffery.

Fiction and Nonfiction

Fiction is the opposite of fact, and, simple as that may seem, it's the major distinction between fictional works and nonfictional works. The earliest nonfiction came in the form of cave-paintings, the record of what prehistoric man caught on hunting trips.

On the other hand, we don't know that some of it might be fiction—that is, what they would like to catch on future hunting trips. Cuneiform inscriptions, which hold the earliest writings, are probably nonfiction, about conveying goods such as oxen and barley and dealing with the buying and selling of these items. It's easy to assume that nonfiction, then, is pretty boring, since it simply serves the purpose of recording everyday facts. Fiction, on the other hand, is the result of imagination and is recorded for the purpose of entertainment. If a work of nonfiction endures beyond its original time, it tends to be viewed as either exceptionally well made or perfectly embodying the ideas, manners, and attitudes of the time when it was produced.

Some (not all) types of nonfiction:
- Almanac
- Autobiography
- Biography
- Blueprint
- Book report
- Diary
- Dictionary
- Documentary film
- Encyclopedia

- Essay
- History
- Journal
- Letter
- Philosophy
- Science book
- Textbook
- User manual

These can also be called genres of nonfiction—divisions of a particular art according to criteria particular to that form. How these divisions are formed is vague. There are actually no fixed boundaries for either fiction or nonfiction. They are formed by sets of conventions and many works cross into multiple genres by way of borrowing and recombining these conventions.

Some genres of fiction (not all):
- Action-adventure
- Crime
- Detective
- Erotica
- Fantasy
- Horror
- Mystery
- Romance
- Science fiction
- Thriller
- Western

A *bildungsroman* (from the German) means "novel of education" or "novel of formation" and is a novel that traces the spiritual, moral, psychological, or social development and growth of the main character from childhood to maturity. Dickens' *David Copperfield* (1850) represents this genre as does Thomas Wolfe's *Look Homeward Angel* (1929).

A work of fiction typically has a central character, called the protagonist, and a character that stands in opposition, called the antagonist. The antagonist might be something other than a person. In Stephen Crane's short story, *The Open Boat*, for example, the antagonist is a hostile environment, a stormy sea. Conflicts between protagonist and antagonist are typical of a work of fiction, and climax is the point at which those conflicts are resolved. The plot has to do with the form or shape that the conflicts take as they move toward resolution. A fiction writer artistically uses devices labeled characterization to reveal character. Characterization can depend on dialogue, description, or the attitude or attitudes of one or more characters toward another.

Enjoying fiction depends upon the ability of the reader to suspend belief, to some extent. The reader makes a deal with the writer that for the time it takes to read the story, his/her own belief will be put aside, replaced by the convictions and reality that the writer has written into the story. This is not true in nonfiction. The writer of nonfiction declares in the choice of that genre that the work is reliably based upon reality. The *MLA Style Manual*, for instance, can be relied upon because it is not the result of someone's imagination.

Skill 5.12 **Understands and promotes students' development of literary response and analysis, including teaching students elements of literary analysis and providing students with opportunities to apply comprehension skills to literature.**

There are many ways to talk about the merit of a particular piece of literature. Making the New York Times best-seller list is a pinnacle that most novel writers hope to achieve although those that make the list are not necessarily very highly rated by literary critics. Longevity may be the only true test of the merit of a writer's works. The Nobel Prize for Literature is coveted by serious writers and the recipients are usually considered to be writing valuable and worthwhile works. However, in looking at a particular work and making judgments about its merit, genre must be taken into account. A list of all the possible genres is very long and will include not only romance novels but a long list of subgenres under it, which is indicative of the complications involved in determining the genre a particular piece might fit into and what other works it can reasonably be compared to.

Encyclopedia Britannica points out that even in the oral literature of preliterate people, the important literary genres all existed: heroic epic; songs in praise of priests and kings; stories of mystery and the supernatural; love lyrics; personal songs; love stories; tales of adventure and heroism; satire; satirical combats; ballads; folktales of tragedy and murder; folk stories; animal fables; riddles, proverbs, and philosophical observations; hymns, incantations, and mysterious songs of priests; and mythology.

It's inevitable with all of the writing and publishing going on now that subdivisions have developed in all of these major genres, so for an individual critic to determine exactly what subgenre a particular work appears in can be difficult. Even so, works must be judged against the standards for their genres. Comparing a mystery novel to a romantic novel is not very useful.

At the most basic level, all poetry can be measured by certain standards: A bad poem tends to be stereotyped; an excellent poem unique. What is it trying to do and be and does it succeed? Before judging a poem, one must understand it, although an obscure poem that demands much from the reader may be worthwhile for that very reason. Thomas Aquinas' definition of beauty, "wholeness, harmony, and radiance," is useful in determining whether a poem is successful, valuable, and worthwhile. A good poem should have a significant theme although that is not enough to make it great. Even not-so-good poems can have admirable themes. A great poem shocks us into another order of perception, helps us know ourselves, and points beyond words to something still more essential. The best poem ushers us into an experience so profoundly moving that we feel changed. A bad or indifferent poem fails to do so. Different periods will judge the same poem differently. It's useful to read what earlier critics have said about a poem and measure their conclusions against those of a different era and of the current understanding of what is valuable and what is not.

Much of the same can be said of the novel. While the novel existed before the 18th century, it was during that period that it came into its own. Pierre Daniel Huet published a treatise on the analysis of the novel in 1670 in which he recommended the following questions:

What did the fictional work of a foreign culture or distant period tell us about those who constructed the fiction? What were the cultural needs such stories answered? Are there fundamental anthropological premises which make us create fictional worlds? Did these fictions entertain, divert and instruct? Did they—as one could assume when reading ancient and medieval myths—just provide a substitute for better, more scientific knowledge, or did they add to the luxuries of life a particular culture enjoyed?

Suddenly, reading a novel became more than just getting lost in a dream world of romance; the potential for adding to the readers' store of knowledge about earlier and foreign cultures was an acceptable reason for reading. Literary criticism, critical discussions of poetry and fiction did not come into being until the second half of the eighteenth century. This threw a whole new light on writing. Now novelists could write to be criticized, and the public could observe the interaction between critics and authors. The result was a division into popular fictions and literary production, the latter deemed worthy of discussion and criticism. The Romantic Movement, which began in the 1770s ushered in the *avant garde* novel, where emotions found their test cases. The *Bildungsroman*, a novel of personal development, emerged during this time. For the most part, these novels are too sentimental to pass muster with a 21st century reader or reviewer.

Toward the end of the 18th century, the gothic novel was born. In these novels the sublime (or awful) was juxtaposed with the beautiful. The beautiful heroine's susceptibility to supernatural elements is featured in these novels, designed to scare and terrify readers. By the beginning of the 19th century, the gothic novel had run its course. Jane Austen's *Northanger Abbey* (1803) parodied the gothic novel, reflecting its death. Austen introduced the comedy of manners—novels that were funny but also scathingly critical of the restrictive rural culture of the early 19th century. Before the end of the 19th century, novels had begun to be separated into high and low forms, which continues into the 21st century. The high forms are those that are worthy of criticism; the low forms do not achieve that distinction.

The "low" novelist is usually preoccupied with plot whereas the writer of novels that are adjudged to be "high" enough for criticism are usually concerned with the convolutions of the human personality. The experiences that are the basis for the conflicts in the story are carefully crafted and are the chief preoccupation. A character may or may not be a human being. In some novels, the conflicts are between non-human elements—the setting or even an animal as in Jack London's *Call of the Wild*. If the characters claim readers' interest, they may be willing to put up with other elements that may be less than perfect. If the character or characters are memorable, the reader tends to see the novel as a good one. If the character seems to have a life beyond the book, the author tends to be better regarded than others.

A novel must be adjudged by the period in which it was created. The sentimentalism of an earlier period might not be appealing to a 21st century reader or critic; nevertheless, they were probably appropriate in the period in which they were written. If they have endured and have continued to be read and enjoyed, then time has proven their worth.

Skill 5.13   Selects and uses a variety of materials to teach students about authors and about different purposes for writing.

Teachers should select a variety of texts to give students a broad experience in the writing process. Exposure to both narrative and expository texts allows them to build and expand their knowledge base, identify and distinguish genres, learn how different texts are structured, and experience a variety of authors' writing styles, ideas and language usage across eras.

Fiction: Students should read an assortment of fiction works to provide opportunity to learn about character and plot development in the various genres, the role of setting and dialog, themes and narrative story structure, as well as the ability to define and identify elements of fiction (e.g., tone, mood, foreshadowing, irony, symbolism). Types of texts to be included in the reading curriculum are folktales, myths, legends, short stories, mysteries, historical fiction, science fiction, plays and general-interest novels.

Nonfiction: Appropriate selection of nonfiction materials provides the opportunity to practice and reinforce the complex reading comprehension skills necessary to succeed across the curriculum. Topics should contain a high level of detail, covering diverse topics which encourage active discussion, questioning, synthesizing and evaluation of the information presented. Readers should be exposed to complex content structures and be required to apply critical reading skills to evaluate the quality of information. Text selection should include textbooks, autobiographies/biographies, informational books, Web sites, newspapers, magazines, encyclopedias, and brochures.

Skill 5.14   Provides students with opportunities to engage in silent reading and extended reading of a wide range of materials, including expository texts and various literary genres.

See Skill 5.9.

Skill 5.15   Engages students in varied reading experiences and encourages students to interact with others about their reading.

Reading literature involves a reciprocal interaction between the reader and the text.

Types of responses

Emotional

The reader can identify with the characters and situations so as to project himself into the story. The reader feels a sense of satisfaction by associating aspects of his own life with the people, places, and events in the literature. Emotional responses are observed in a reader's verbal and non-verbal reactions - laughter, comments on its effects, and retelling or dramatizing the action.

Interpretive

Interpretive responses result in inferences about character development, setting, or plot; analysis of style elements - metaphor, simile, allusion, rhythm, tone; outcomes derivable from information provided in the narrative; and assessment of the author's intent. Interpretive responses are made verbally or in writing.

Critical

Critical responses involve making value judgments about the quality of a piece of literature. Reactions to the effectiveness of the writer's style and language use are observed through discussion and written reactions.

Evaluative

Some reading response theory researchers also add a response that considers the readers considerations of such factors as how well the piece of literature represents its genre, how well it reflects the social/ethical mores of society, and how well the author has approached the subject for freshness and slant.

Middle school readers will exhibit both emotional and interpretive responses. Naturally, making interpretive responses depends on the degree of knowledge the student has of literary elements. A child's being able to say why a particular book was boring or why a particular poem made him sad evidences critical reactions on a fundamental level. Adolescents in ninth and tenth grades should begin to make critical responses by addressing the specific language and genre characteristics of literature. Evaluative responses are harder to detect and are rarely made by any but a few advanced high school students. However, if the teacher knows what to listen for, she can recognize evaluative responses and incorporate them into discussions.

For example, if a student says, "I don't understand why that character is doing that," he is making an interpretive response to character motivation. However, if he goes on to say, "What good is that action?" he is giving an evaluative response that should be explored in terms of "What good should it do and why isn't that positive action happening?"

At the emotional level, the student says, "I almost broke into a sweat when he was describing the heat in the burning house." An interpretive response says, "The author used descriptive adjectives to bring his setting to life." Critically, the student adds, "The author's use of descriptive language contributes to the success of the narrative and maintains reader interest through the whole story." If he goes on to wonder why the author allowed the grandmother in the story to die in the fire, he is making an evaluative response.

Levels of response

The levels of reader response will depend largely on the reader's level of social, psychological, and intellectual development. Most middle school students have progressed beyond merely involving themselves in the story enough to be able to retell the events in some logical sequence or describe the feeling that the story evoked. They are aware to some degree that the feeling evoked was the result of a careful manipulation of good elements of fiction writing. They may not explain that awareness as successfully as a high school student, but they are beginning to grasp the concepts and not just the personal reactions. They are beginning to differentiate between responding to the story itself and responding a literary creation.

Fostering self-esteem and empathy for others and the world in which one lives

All-important is the use of literature as bibliotherapy that allows the reader to identify with others and become aware of alternatives, while not feeling directly betrayed or threatened. For the high school student the ability to empathize is an evaluative response, a much desired outcome of literature studies. Use of these books either individually or as a thematic unit of study allows for discussion or writing. The titles are grouped by theme, not by reading level.

ABUSE:

Blair, Maury and Brendel, Doug. *Maury, Wednesday's Child*

Dizenzo, Patricia. *Why Me?*

Parrot, Andrea. *Coping with Date Rape and Acquaintance Rape*

NATURAL WORLD CONCERNS:

Caduto, M. and Bruchac, J. *Keeper's of Earth*

Gay, Kathlyn. *Greenhouse Effect*

Johnson, Daenis. *Fiskadaro*

Madison, Arnold. *It Can't Happen to Me*

EATING DISORDERS:

Arnold, Caroline. *Too Fat, Too Thin, Do I Have a Choice?*

DeClements, Barthe. *Nothing's Fair in Fifth Grade*

Snyder, Anne. *Goodbye, Paper Doll*

FAMILY

Chopin, Kate. *The Runner*

Cormier, Robert. *Tunes for Bears to Dance to*

Danzinger, Paula. *The Divorce Express*

Neufield, John. *Sunday Father*

Okimoto, Jean Davies. *Molly by any Other Name*

Peck, Richard. *Don't Look and It Won't Hurt*

Zindel, Paul. *I Never Loved Your Mind*

STEREOTYPING:

Baklanov, Grigory. (Trans. by Antonina W. Bouis) *Forever Nineteen*

Kerr, M.E. *Gentle Hands*

Greene, Betty. *Summer of My German Soldier*

Reiss, Johanna. *The Upstairs Room*

Taylor, Mildred D. *Roll of Thunder, Hear Me Cry*

Wakatsuki-Houston, Jeanne and Houston, James D. *Farewell to Manzanar*

SUICIDE AND DEATH:

Blume, Judy. *Tiger Eyes*

Bunting, Eve. *If I Asked You, Would You Stay?*

Gunther, John. *Death Be Not Proud*

Mazer, Harry. *When the Phone Rings*

Peck, Richard. *Remembering the Good Times*

Richter, Elizabeth. *Losing Someone You Love*

Strasser, Todd. *Friends Till the End*

Cautions

There is always a caution when reading materials of a sensitive or controversial nature. The teacher must be cognizant of the happenings in the school and outside community to spare students undue suffering. A child who has known a recent death in his family or circle of friends may need to distance himself from classroom discussion. Whenever open discussion of a topic brings pain or embarrassment, the child should not be further subjected. Older children and young adults will be able to discuss issues with greater objectivity and without making blurted, insensitive comments. The teacher must be able to gauge the level of emotional development of her students when selecting subject matter and the strategies for studying it. The student or his parents may consider some material objectionable. Should a student choose not to read an assigned material, it is the teacher's responsibility to allow the student to select an alternate title. It is always advisable to notify parents if a particularly sensitive piece is to be studied.

Skill 5.16   Uses strategies to encourage reading for pleasure and lifelong learning.

Reading for enjoyment makes it possible to go to places in the world we will never be able to visit, or perhaps when we learn about the enchantments of a particular place, we will set a goal of someday visiting. When *Under the Tuscan Sun* by Frances Mayes was published, it became a best seller. It also increased tourism to Italy. Many of the readers of that book visited Italy for the first time in their lives.

In fiction, we can live through experiences we will never encounter. We delve into feelings that are similar to our own or are so far removed from our own that we are filled with wonder and curiosity. In fact, we read because we're curious—curious to visit, experience, and know new and different things. The reader lives with a crowd of people and a vast landscape.

Life is constantly being enriched by the reading, and the mind is constantly being expanded. To read is to grow. Sometimes the experience of reading a particular book or story is so delicious that we go back and read it again and again, such as the works of Jane Austen. We keep track of what is truly happening in the world when we read current best-sellers because they not only reflect what everyone else is interested in right now, they can influence trends. We can know in-depth what television news cannot cram in by reading publications like *Time* and *Newsweek*.

How do we model this wonderful gift for our students? We can bring those interesting stories into our classrooms and share the excitement we feel when we discover them. We can relate things that make us laugh so students may see the humor and laugh with us. We can vary the established curriculum to include something we are reading that we want to share. The tendency of students nowadays is to receive all of their information from television or the internet. It's important for the teacher to help students understand that television and the internet are not substitutes for reading. They should be an accessory, an extension, a springboard for reading.

Another thing teachers can do to inspire students to become readers is to assign a book that you have never read before and read along with them, chapter by chapter. Run a contest and the winner gets to pick a book that you and they will read chapter by chapter. If you are excited about it and are experiencing satisfaction from the reading, that excitement will be contagious. Be sure that the discussion sessions allow for students to relate what they are thinking and feeling about what they are reading. Lively discussions and the opportunity to express their own feelings will lead to more spontaneous reading.

You can also hand out a reading list of your favorite books and spend some time telling the students what you liked about each. Make sure the list is diverse. It's good to include nonfiction along with fiction. Don't forget that a good biography or autobiography may encourage students to read beyond thrillers and detective stories.

When the class is discussing the latest movie, whether formally as a part of the curriculum or informally and incidentally, if the movie is based on a book, this is a good opportunity to demonstrate how much more can be derived from the reading than from the watching. Or how the two combined make the experience more satisfying and worthwhile.

Share with your students the excitement you have for reading. Successful writers are usually good readers. The two go hand-in-hand.

Skill 5.17   Knows how to teach students strategies for selecting their own books for independent reading.

See Skill 4.9.

Skill 5.18   Uses technology to promote students' literacy and teaches students to use technology to access a wide range of appropriate narrative and expository texts.

Multimedia refers to a technology for presenting material in both visual and verbal forms. This format is especially conducive to the classroom, since it reaches both visual and auditory learners.

Knowing how to select effective teaching software is the first step in efficient multi-media education. First, decide what you need the software for (creating spreadsheets, making diagrams, creating slideshows, etc.) Consult magazines such as *Popular Computing, PC World, MacWorld,* and *Multimedia World* to learn about the newest programs available. Go to a local computer store and ask a customer service representative to help you find the exact equipment you need. If possible, test the programs you are interested in. Check reviews in magazines such as *Consumer Reports, PCWorld, Electronic Learning* or *MultiMedia Schools* to ensure the software's quality.

Software programs useful for producing teaching material
- Adobe
- Aldus Freehand
- CorelDRAW!
- DrawPerfect
- Claris Works
- PC Paintbrush
- Harvard Graphics
- Visio
- Microsoft Word
- Microsoft Power Point

COMPTENCY 6.0 WRITTEN LANGUAGE—WRITING CONVENTIONS

Skill 6.1   Knows predictable stages in the development of writing conventions and recognizes that individual variations occur.

Types of Clauses

Clauses are connected word groups that are composed of *at least* one subject and one verb. (A subject is the doer of an action or the element that is being joined. A verb conveys either the action or the link.)

Students are waiting for the start of the assembly.
Subject   Verb

At the end of the play, students wait for the curtain to come down.
                          Subject   Verb

Clauses can be independent or dependent.

Independent clauses can stand alone or can be joined to other clauses.

Independent clause	for and nor	
Independent clause,	but or yet so	Independent clause
Independent clause	;	Independent clause
Dependent clause	,	Independent clause

Dependent clauses, by definition, contain at least one subject and one verb. However, they cannot stand alone as a complete sentence. They are structurally dependent on the main clause.

There are two types of dependent clauses: (1) those with a subordinating conjunction, and (2) those with a relative pronoun

Sample coordinating conjunctions:
Although
When
If
Unless
Because

Unless a cure is discovered, many more people will die of the disease.
      Dependent clause   +   Independent clause

Sample relative pronouns:
Who
Whom
Which
That

The White House has an official website, which contains press releases, news updates, and biographies of the President and Vice-President.
(Independent clause + relative pronoun + relative dependent clause)

Misplaced and Dangling Modifiers
Particular phrases that are not placed near the word they modify often result in misplaced modifiers. Particular phrases that do not relate to the subject being modified result in dangling modifiers.

Error: Weighing the options carefully, a decision was made regarding the punishment of the convicted murderer.

Problem: Who is weighing the options? No one capable of weighing is named in the sentence; thus, the participle phrase weighing the options carefully dangles. This problem can be corrected by adding a subject of the sentence capable of doing the action.

Correction: Weighing the options carefully, the judge made a decision regarding the punishment of the convicted murderer.

Error: Returning to my favorite watering hole, brought back many fond memories.

Problem: The person who returned is never indicated, and the participle phrase dangles. This problem can be corrected by creating a dependent clause from the modifying phrase.

Correction: When I returned to my favorite watering hole, many fond memories came back to me.

Error: One damaged house stood only to remind townspeople of the hurricane.

Problem: The placement of the misplaced modifier *only* suggests that the sole reason the house remained was to serve as a reminder. The faulty modifier creates ambiguity.

Correction: Only one damaged house stood, reminding townspeople of the hurricane.

Spelling

Concentration in this section will be on spelling plurals and possessives. The multiplicity and complexity of spelling rules based on phonics, letter doubling, and exceptions to rules - not mastered by adulthood - should be replaced by a good dictionary. As spelling mastery is also difficult for adolescents, our recommendation is the same. Learning the use of a dictionary and thesaurus will be a more rewarding use of time.

Most plurals of nouns that end in hard consonants or hard consonant sounds followed by a silent *e* are made by adding *s*. Some words ending in vowels only add *s*.

fingers, numerals, banks, bugs, riots, homes, gates, radios, bananas

Nouns that end in soft consonant sounds *s, j, x, z, ch,* and *sh*, add *es*. Some nouns ending in *o* add es.

dresses, waxes, churches, brushes, tomatoes, potatoes

Nouns ending in *y* preceded by a vowel just add *s*.

boys, alleys

Nouns ending in *y* preceded by a consonant change the *y* to *i* and add *es*.

babies, corollaries, frugalities, poppies

Some nouns plurals are formed irregularly or remain the same.

sheep, deer, children, leaves, oxen

Some nouns derived from foreign words, especially Latin, may make their plurals in two different ways - one of them Anglicized. Sometimes, the meanings are the same; other times, the two plurals are used in slightly different contexts. It is always wise to consult the dictionary.

appendices, appendixes   criterion, criteria
indexes, indices   crisis, crises

Make the plurals of closed (solid) compound words in the usual way except for words ending in *ful* which make their plurals on the root word.

timelines, hairpins, cupsful

Make the plurals of open or hyphenated compounds by adding the change in inflection to the word that changes in number.

fathers-in-law, courts-martial, masters of art, doctors of medicine

Make the plurals of letters, numbers, and abbreviations by adding *s*.

fives and tens, IBMs, 1990s, *p*s and *q*s (Note that letters are italicized.)

Capitalization
Capitalize all proper names of persons (including specific organizations or agencies of government); places (countries, states, cities, parks, and specific geographical areas); and things (political parties, structures, historical and cultural terms, and calendar and time designations); and religious terms (any deity, revered person or group, sacred writings).

Percy Bysshe Shelley, Argentina, Mount Rainier National Park, Grand Canyon, League of Nations, the Sears Tower, Birmingham, Lyric Theater, Americans, Midwesterners, Democrats, Renaissance, Boy Scouts of America, Easter, God, Bible, Dead Sea Scrolls, Koran

Capitalize proper adjectives and titles used with proper names.

California gold rush, President John Adams, French fries, Homeric epic, Romanesque architecture, Senator John Glenn

Note: Some words that represent titles and offices are not capitalized unless used with a proper name.

Capitalized	Not Capitalized
Congressman McKay	the congressman from Florida
Commander Alger	commander of the Pacific Fleet
Queen Elizabeth	the queen of England

Capitalize all main words in titles of works of literature, art, and music. (See "Using Italics" in the Punctuation section.)

The candidate should be cognizant of proper rules and conventions of punctuation, capitalization, and spelling.

Competency exams will generally test the ability to apply the more advanced skills; thus, a limited number of more frustrating rules is presented here. Rules should be applied according to the American style of English (i.e. spelling *theater* instead of *theatre* and placing terminal marks of punctuation almost exclusively within other marks of punctuation).

Punctuation

Using terminal punctuation in relation to quotation marks
In a quoted statement that is either declarative or imperative, place the period inside the closing quotation marks.

> "The airplane crashed on the runway during takeoff."

If the quotation is followed by other words in the sentence, place a comma inside the closing quotations marks and a period at the end of the sentence.

> "The airplane crashed on the runway during takeoff," said the announcer.

In most instances in which a quoted title or expression occurs at the end of a sentence, the period is placed before either the single or double quotation marks.

> "The middle school readers were unprepared to understand Bryant's poem 'Thanatopsis.'"

> Early book-length adventure stories like *Don Quixote* and *The Three Musketeers* were known as "picaresque novels."

There is an instance in which the final quotation mark would precede the period - if the content of the sentence were about a speech or quote so that the understanding of the meaning would be confused by the placement of the period.

> The first thing out of his mouth was "Hi, I'm home."
> *but*
> The first line of his speech began "I arrived home to an empty house".

In sentences that are interrogatory or exclamatory, the question mark or exclamation point should be positioned outside the closing quotation marks if the quote itself is a statement or command or cited title.

> Who decided to lead us in the recitation of the "Pledge of Allegiance"?
> Why was Tillie shaking as she began her recitation, "Once upon a midnight dreary..."?
> I was embarrassed when Mrs. White said, "Your slip is showing"!

In sentences that are declarative but the quotation is a question or an exclamation, place the question mark or exclamation point inside the quotation marks.

The hall monitor yelled, "Fire! Fire!"

"Fire! Fire!" yelled the hall monitor.

Cory shrieked, "Is there a mouse in the room?" (In this instance, the question supersedes the exclamation.)

Using periods with parentheses or brackets

Place the period inside the parentheses or brackets if they enclose a complete sentence, independent of the other sentences around it.

Stephen Crane was a confirmed alcohol and drug addict. (He admitted as much to other journalists in Cuba.)

If the parenthetical expression is a statement inserted within another statement, the period in the enclosure is omitted.

Mark Twain used the character Indian Joe (He also appeared in *The Adventures of Tom Sawyer*) as a foil for Jim in *The Adventures of Huckleberry Finn*.

When enclosed matter comes at the end of a sentence requiring quotation marks, place the period outside the parentheses or brackets.

"The secretary of state consulted with the ambassador [Albright]."

Using commas

Separate two or more coordinate adjectives, modifying the same word and three or more nouns, phrases, or clauses in a list.

Maggie's hair was dull, dirty, and lice-ridden.

Dickens portrayed the Artful Dodger as skillful pickpocket, loyal follower of Fagin, and defendant of Oliver Twist.

Ellen daydreamed about getting out of the rain, taking a shower, and eating a hot dinner.

In Elizabethan England, Ben Johnson wrote comedy, Christopher Marlowe wrote tragedies, and William Shakespeare composed both.

Use commas to separate antithetical or complimentary expressions from the rest of the sentence.

The veterinarian, not his assistant, would perform the delicate surgery.

The more he knew about her, the less he wished he had known.

Randy hopes to, and probably will, get an appointment to the Naval Academy.

His thorough, though esoteric, scientific research could not easily be understood by high school students.

Using double quotation marks with other punctuation
Quotations - whether words, phrases, or clauses - should be punctuated according to the rules of the grammatical function they serve in the sentence.

The works of Shakespeare, "the bard of Avon," have been contested as originating with other authors.

"You'll get my money," the old man warned, "when 'Hell freezes over'."

Sheila cited the passage that began "Four score and seven years ago...." (Note the ellipsis followed by an enclosed period.)

"Old Ironsides" inspired the preservation of the U.S.S. Constitution. Use quotation marks to enclose the titles of shorter works: songs, short poems, short stories, essays, and chapters of books. (See "Using Italics" for punctuating longer titles.)

"The Tell-Tale Heart"   "Casey at the Bat"   "America the Beautiful"

Using semicolons
Use semicolons to separate independent clauses when the second clause is introduced by a transitional adverb. (These clauses may also be written as separate sentences, preferably by placing the adverb within the second sentence.)

The Elizabethans modified the rhyme scheme of the sonnet; thus, it was called the English sonnet.
or
The Elizabethans modified the rhyme scheme of the sonnet. It thus was called the English sonnet.

Use semicolons to separate items in a series that are long and complex or have internal punctuation.

> The Italian Renaissance produced masters in the fine arts: Dante Alighieri, author of the *Divine Comedy;* Leonardo da Vinci, painter of *The Last Supper;* and Donatello, sculptor of the *Quattro Coronati,* the four saints.

> The leading scorers in the WNBA were Haizhaw Zheng, averaging 23.9 points per game; Lisa Leslie, 22; and Cynthia Cooper, 19.5.

Using colons

Place a colon at the beginning of a list of items. (Note its use in the sentence about Renaissance Italians on the previous page.)

> The teacher directed us to compare Faulkner's three symbolic novels: *Absalom, Absalom; As I Lay Dying;* and *Light in August.*

Do **not** use a comma if the list is preceded by a verb.

> Three of Faulkner's symbolic novels are *Absalom, Absalom; As I Lay Dying,* and *Light in August.*

Using dashes

Place dashes to denote sudden breaks in thought.

> Some periods in literature - the Romantic Age, for example - spanned different time periods in different countries.

Use dashes instead of commas if commas are already used elsewhere in the sentence for amplification or explanation.

> The Fireside Poets included three Brahmans - James Russell Lowell, Henry David Wadsworth, Oliver Wendell Holmes - and John Greenleaf Whittier.

Use italics to punctuate the titles of long works of literature, names of periodical publications, musical scores, works of art and motion picture television, and radio programs. (When unable to write in italics, students should be instructed to underline in their own writing where italics would be appropriate.)

The Idylls of the King	*Hiawatha*	*The Sound and the Fury*
Mary Poppins	*Newsweek*	*The Nutcracker Suite*

Skill 6.2 **Knows and applies appropriate instructional strategies and sequences to teach writing conventions and their applications to all students, including English Language Learners.**

Syntax

Sentence completeness

Avoid fragments and run-on sentences. Recognition of sentence elements necessary to make a complete thought, proper use of independent and dependent clauses (see *Use correct coordination and subordination*), and proper punctuation will correct such errors.

Sentence structure

Recognize simple, compound, complex, and compound-complex sentences. Use dependent (subordinate) and independent clauses correctly to create these sentence structures.

Simple	Joyce wrote a letter.
Compound	Joyce wrote a letter, and Dot drew a picture.
Complex	While Joyce wrote a letter, Dot drew a picture.
Compound/Complex	When Mother asked the girls to demonstrate their new-found skills, Joyce wrote a letter, and Dot drew a picture.

Note: Do **not** confuse compound sentence elements with compound sentences.

Simple sentence with compound subject
    <u>Joyce</u> and <u>Dot</u> wrote letters.
    The <u>girl</u> in row three and the <u>boy</u> next to her were passing notes across the aisle.

Simple sentence with compound predicate
    Joyce <u>wrote letters</u> and <u>drew pictures</u>.
    The captain of the high school debate team <u>graduated with honors</u> and <u>studied broadcast journalism in college</u>.

Simple sentence with compound object of preposition
    Coleen graded the students' essays for <u>style</u> and <u>mechanical accuracy</u>.

Skill 6.3 **Knows informal and formal procedures for assessing students' use of writing conventions and uses multiple, ongoing assessments to monitor and evaluate students' development in this area.**

- Have students write a short story, essay or other specified genre of writing
- Assess their ability to write about a given body of knowledge in a logical and critical way
- Observe their ability to use language resources appropriate for the required task.
- Use a rating system. For example, a scale from 1 to 4 (where 1=unsatisfactory and 4=excellent).
- Monitor their use of source material
- Evaluate the structure and development of their writing
- Ensure that their writing style is appropriate for the task assigned
- Check for grammatical correctness
- Provide follow-up support for any weaknesses detected

Skill 6.4 **Uses ongoing assessment of writing conventions to determine when a student needs additional help or intervention to bring the student's performance to grade level, based on state content and performance standards for writing in the Texas Essential Knowledge and Skills (TEKS).**

See Skill 1.5.

Skill 6.5 **Analyzes students' errors in applying writing conventions and uses the results of this analysis as a basis for future instruction.**

See Skill 6.2.

Skill 6.6 **Knows writing conventions and appropriate grammar and usage and provides students with direct instruction and guided practice in these areas.**

See Skill 6.1.

Skill 6.7 **Understands the contribution of conventional spelling towards success in reading and writing.**

See Skills 3.3 and 6.1.

Skill 6.8   Understands stages of spelling development and how and when to support students' development from one stage to the next.

Semi-Phonetic Phase

- Realization that there is a relationship between letters and sounds. Students tend to spell by sound, often using consonants. Teachers should emphasize phonetic strategies (sounding the word out).

Phonetic Phase

- Students write one letter or letter cluster for every sound in a word. Teachers should emphasize visual strategies (looking for predictable letter sequences and patterns).

Transitional Phase

- The beginning stage of using visual memory. Students have learned about letter patterns but often use them incorrectly. During this stage, teachers should implement visual and morphemic strategies.

Skill 6.9   Provides systematic spelling instruction and gives students opportunities to use and develop spelling skills in the context of meaningful written expression.

Spelling skills should develop as part of an overall language arts phonemic awareness, phonics , reading comprehension, vocabulary and reading fluency, grammar, reading and writing program. Students should (with help from their teacher) develop their foundational spelling skills through an interest in words, regular writing, constant reading, a study of spelling rules, and playing of spelling games. Skilled, fluent readers are the culmination of the successful learning of a broad array of pre-reading and reading skills. Irrespective of family background, learning to be a skilled speller is often not a trouble-free process. Spelling programs, personalized tutoring, reading workbooks, spelling games, and structured computer spelling programs can help teach or reinforce these skills.

Some children need spelling practice, while others need more intensive remedial spelling programs. Teachers can help their students with the spelling process by providing high-quality educational materials, establishing a pattern of daily spelling and reading, instructing through guided spelling activity, creating a rich language environment, and discussing a child's progress with parents.

COMPETENCY 7.0 WRITTEN LANGUAGE—COMPOSITION

Skill 7.1   **Knows predictable stages in the development of written language and recognizes that individual variations occur.**

Introductions:

It's important to remember that in the writing process, the introduction should be written last. Until the body of the paper has been determined—thesis, development—it's difficult to make strategic decisions regarding the introduction. The Greek rhetoricians called this part of a discourse *exordium*, a "leading into." The basic purpose of the introduction, then, is to lead the audience into the discourse. It can let the reader know what the purpose of the discourse is and it can condition the audience to be receptive to what the writer wants to say. It can be very brief or it can take up a large percentage of the total word count. Aristotle said that the introduction could be compared to the flourishes that flute players make before their performance—an overture in which the musicians display what they can play best in order to gain the favor and attention of the audience for the main performance.

In order to do this, we must first of all know what we are going to say; who the readership is likely to be; what the social, political, economic, etc., climate is; what preconceived notions the audience is likely to have regarding the subject; and how long the discourse is going to be.

There are many ways to do this:
- Show that the subject is important.
- Show that although the points we are presenting may seem improbable, they are true.
- Show that the subject has been neglected, misunderstood, or misrepresented.
- Explain an unusual mode of development.
- Forestall any misconception of the purpose.
- Apologize for a deficiency.
- Arouse interest in the subject with an anecdotal lead-in.
- Ingratiate oneself with the readership.
- Establish one's own credibility.

The introduction often ends with the thesis, the point or purpose of the paper. However, this is not set in stone. The thesis may open the body of the discussion, or it may conclude the discourse. The most important thing to remember is that the purpose and structure of the introduction should be deliberate if it is to serve the purpose of "leading the reader into the discussion."

Conclusions:

It's easier to write a conclusion after the decisions regarding the introduction have been made. Aristotle taught that the conclusion should strive to do five things:

1. Inspire the reader with a favorable opinion of the writer.
2. Amplify the force of the points made in the body of the paper.
3. Reinforce the points made in the body.
4. Rouse appropriate emotions in the reader.
5. Restate in a summary way what has been said.

The conclusion may be short or it may be long depending on its purpose in the paper. Recapitulation, a brief restatement of the main points or certainly of the thesis is the most common form of effective conclusions. A good example is the closing argument in a court trial.

Text Organization:

In studies of professional writers and how they produce their successful works, it has been revealed writing is a process that can be clearly defined although in practice it must have enough flexibility to allow for creativity. The teacher must be able to define the various stages that a successful writer goes through in order to make a statement that has value. There must be a discovery stage when ideas, materials, supporting details, etc., are deliberately collected. These may come from many possible sources: the writer's own experience and observations, deliberate research of written sources, interviews of live persons, television presentations, or the internet.

The next stage is organization where the purpose, thesis, and supporting points are determined. Most writers will put forth more than one possible thesis and in the next stage, the writing of the paper, settle on one as the result of trial and error. Once the paper is written, the editing stage is necessary and is probably the most important stage. This is not just the polishing stage. At this point, decisions must be made regarding whether the reasoning is cohesive—does it hold together? Is the arrangement the best possible one or should the points be rearranged? Are there holes that need to be filled in? What form will the introduction take? Does the conclusion lead the reader out of the discourse or is it inadequate or too abrupt, etc.

It's important to remember that the best writers engage in all of these stages recursively. They may go back to discovery at any point in the process. They may go back and rethink the organization, etc. To help students become effective writers, the teacher needs to give them adequate practice in the various stages and encourage them to engage deliberately in the creative thinking that makes writers successful.

Techniques to Maintain Focus:

- **Focus on a main point.** The point should be clear to readers, and all sentences in the paragraph should relate to it.
- **Start the paragraph with a topic sentence.** This should be a general, one-sentence summary of the paragraph's main point, relating both back towards the thesis and toward the content of the paragraph. (A topic sentence is sometimes unnecessary if the paragraph continues a developing idea clearly introduced in a preceding paragraph, or if the paragraph appears in a narrative of events where generalizations might interrupt the flow of the story.)
- **Stick to the point.** Eliminate sentences that do not support the topic sentence.

Be flexible. If there is not enough evidence to support the claim your topic sentence is making, do not fall into the trap of wandering or introducing new ideas within the paragraph. Either find more evidence, or adjust the topic sentence to collaborate with the evidence that is available.

Enhancing Interest:
- Start out with an attention-grabbing introduction. This sets an engaging tone for the entire piece and will be more likely to pull the reader in.
- Use dynamic vocabulary and varied sentence beginnings. Keep the reader on their toes. If they can predict what you are going to say next, make changes.
- Avoid using clichés (as cold as ice, the best thing since sliced bread, nip it in the bud). These are easy shortcuts, but they are not interesting, memorable, or convincing.

Ensuring Understanding:
- Avoid using the words, "clearly," "obviously," and "undoubtedly." Often, things that are clear or obvious to the author are not as apparent to the reader. Instead of using these words, make your point so strongly that it is clear on its own.
- Use the word that best fits the meaning you intend for, even if they are longer or a little less common. Try to find a balance, a go with a familiar yet precise word.
- When in doubt, explain further.

Skill 7.2   Promotes student recognition of the practical uses of writing, creates an environment in which students are motivated to express ideas in writing, and models writing as an enjoyable activity and a tool for lifelong learning.

Writing, however academic it may seem, is one of life's most basic skills. The practical uses are endless: thank you letters, wedding day toasts, keeping a journal, to-do lists, etc. Therefore, a teacher should foster that practicality in the classroom by calling attention to writing in its most basic and enjoyable forms. Remind students writing can allow them to express thoughts they might not otherwise put forth. Furthermore, when those thoughts are put down on paper, the choice is up to them whether they want to share them with their peers or keep them as private notes. Allow students to have occasional free-writing periods, and inform them that they need not turn in their work. This breaks down the inhibitions that most students have when writing in a classroom setting. Encourage students to save their writing, describing the enjoyment they will have when looking back on it at an older age.

Many students see writing as a painful task, but they should be reminded writing is not used solely for essays and reports. Think about signing yearbooks, writing screen plays, writing to pen pals, or writing an angry note to vent frustration (whether it is ever sent or not). Finally, stress the idea that the more you write, you can only get better.

Skill 7.3   Knows and applies appropriate instructional strategies and sequences to develop students' writing skills.

It seems simplistic, yet it's an often-overlooked truism: the first and most important measure of a story is the story itself. *The story's the thing.* However, a good story must have certain characteristics. Without conflict there is no story, so determining what the conflicts are should be a priority for the writer. Once the conflicts are determined, the outcome of the story must be decided. Who wins? Who loses? And what factors go into making one side of the equation win out over the other one? The pattern of the plot is also an important consideration. Where is the climax going to occur? Is denouement necessary? Does the reader need to see the unwinding of all the strands? Many stories fail because a denouement is needed but not supplied.

Characterization, the choice the writer makes about the devices he/she will use to reveal character, requires an understanding of human nature and the artistic skill to convey a personality to the reader. This is usually accomplished subtly through dialogue, interior monologue, description, and the character's actions and behavior. In some successful stories, the writer comes right out and tells the reader what this character is like.

However, sometimes there will be discrepancies between what the narrator tells the reader about the character and what is revealed to be actual, in which case the narrator is unreliable, and that unreliability of the voice the reader must depend on becomes an important and significant device for understanding the story.

Point of view is a powerful tool not only for the writer but for the enjoyment and understanding of the reader. The writer must choose among several possibilities: first-person narrator objective, first-person narrator omniscient, third-person objective, third-person omniscient, and third-person limited omniscient. The most successful story-writers use point of view very creatively to accomplish their purposes. If a writer wishes to be successful, he/she must develop point-of-view skills.

Style—the unique way a writer uses language—is often the writer's signature. The reader does not need to be told that William Faulkner wrote a story to know it because his style is so distinctive that it is immediately recognizable. Even the writing of Toni Morrison, which could be said to be Faulknerian, cannot be mistaken for the work of Faulkner, himself. The writer must be cognizant of his/her own strengths and weaknesses and continually work to hone the way sentences are written, words are chosen, and descriptions are crafted until they are razor-sharp. The best advice to the aspiring writer: read the works of successful writers. If a writer wants to write a best-seller, then that writer needs to be reading best-sellers.

Poetry. Writing poetry in the 21st century is quite different from writing it in earlier periods. There was a time when a poem was required to fit a certain pattern or scheme. Poetry was once defined as a piece of writing made up of end-rhymes. No more. The rhymed poem makes up only a small percentage of worthwhile and successful poems nowadays.

The first skill to work on for the budding poet is descriptive writing, defined as language that appeals to one or more of the five senses. A good poem makes it possible for the reader to experience an emotional event—seeing a mountain range as the sun dawns, watching small children on a playground, smelling the fragrance of a rose, hearing a carillon peal a religious tune at sunset, feeling fine silk under one's fingers. Creating language that makes that experience available to the readers is only the first step, however, because the ultimate goal is to evoke an emotional response. Feeling the horror of the battleground, weeping with the mother whose child was drowned, exulting with a winning soccer team. It's not enough to tell the reader what it's like. It's the *showing* that is necessary.

The aspiring poet should know the possibilities as well as the limitations of this genre. A poem can tell a story, for instance, but the emotional response is more important than the story itself.

Edgar Allen Poe, in an 1842 review of Hawthorne's *Twice-Told Tales* in *Graham's Magazine* had important advice for the writer of poetry: " . . . the unity of effect or impression is a point of the greatest importance." Even though he considered the tale or short story the best way to achieve this, he wrote several memorable poems and much of his prose writing is considered to be as close to poetry as to prose by most critics. He also wrote in 1847, in an expansion of his critique of Hawthorne's works, that ". . .true originality . . .is that which, in bringing out the half-formed, the reluctant, or the unexpressed fancies of mankind, or in exciting the more delicate pulses of the heart's passion, or in giving birth to some universal sentiment or instinct in embryo, thus combines with the pleasurable effect of *apparent* novelty, a real egoistic delight."

Play writing. Play writing uses many of the same skills that are necessary to successful story writing. However, in addition to those skills, there are many more required of the writer who wishes his/her story to be told on stage or on film. The point of view, of course, is always objective unless the writers uses the Shakespearean device of the soliloquy, where a player steps forward and gives information about what's going on. The audience must figure out the meaning of the play on the basis of the actions and speeches of the actors.

A successful playwright is expert in characterization as described above under **story**. What a character is like is determined by dialogue, appearance (costume, etc.), behavior, actions. A successful playwright also understands motivation. If a character's behavior cannot be traced to motivating circumstances, the audience will probably find the action incoherent—a major barrier to positive reception of the play.

The writing must be very carefully honed. Absolutely no excess of words can be found in a successful play. It takes very little time to lose an audience; every word counts. The playwright should concentrate on saying the most possible with the fewest words possible.

Setting is an important feature of the play. Most plays have only one because changing settings in the middle is difficult and disrupting. This calls for a very special kind of writing. The entire action of the play must either take place within the setting or be brought forth in that setting by the reporting or recounting of what is going on outside of the setting by one or more of the characters. The writer must determine what the setting will be. The actual building and creation of the set is in the hands of another kind of artist—one who specializes in settings.

The plot of most plays is rising; that is, the conflicts are introduced early in the play and continue to develop and intensify over the life of the play. As a general rule, the climax is the last thing that happens before the final curtain falls, but not necessarily. Plots of plays demonstrate the same breadth of patterns that are true of stories. For example, a play may end with nothing resolved.

Denouement is less likely to follow a climax in a play than in a story, but epilogues do sometimes occur.

Skill 7.4   Knows characteristics and uses of informal and formal written language assessments, and uses multiple, ongoing assessments to monitor and evaluate students' writing development.

See Skill 6.3.

Skill 7.5   Uses assessment results to plan focused instruction to address the writing strengths, needs, and interests of all individuals and groups, including English Language Learners.

1. Keep an idea book so that they can jot down ideas that come to mind.
2. Write in a daily journal.
3. Write down whatever comes to mind; this is called free writing. Students do not stop to make corrections or interrupt the flow of ideas. A variation of this technique is focused free writing - writing on a specific topic - to prepare for an essay.
4. Make a list of all ideas connected with their topic; this is called brainstorming. Make sure students know that this technique works best when they let their mind work freely. After completing the list, students should analyze the list to see if a pattern or way to group the ideas.
5. Ask the questions Who? What? When? Where? When? and How? Help the writer approach a topic from several perspectives
6. Create a visual map on paper to gather ideas. Cluster circles and lines to show connections between ideas. Students should try to identify the relationship that exists between their ideas. If they cannot see the relationships, have them pair up, exchange papers and have their partners look for some related ideas.
7. Observe details of sight, hearing, taste, touch, and taste.
8. Visualize by making mental images of something and write down the details in a list

After they have practiced with each of these writing strategies, ask them to pick out the ones they prefer and ask them to discuss how they might use the techniques to help them with future writing assignments. It is important to remember that they can use more than one writing strategy at a time. Also they may find that different writing situations may suggest certain techniques.

Skill 7.6   Uses ongoing assessment of written language to determine when a student needs additional help or intervention to bring the student's performance to grade level, based on state content and performance standards for writing in the Texas Essential Knowledge and Skills (TEKS).

See Skill 6.4.

Skill 7.7   Understands the use of self-assessment in writing and provides opportunities for students to self-assess their writings and their development as writers.

Viewing writing as a process allows teachers and students to see the writing classroom as a cooperative workshop where students and teachers encourage and support each other in each writing endeavor. Listed below are some techniques that help teachers to facilitate and create a supportive classroom environment.

1.   Create peer response/support groups that are working on similar writing assignments. The members help each other in all stages of the writing process-from prewriting, writing, revising, editing, and publishing.

2.   Provide several prompts to give students the freedom to write on a topic of their own. Writing should be generated out of personal experience and students should be introduced to in-class journals. One effective way to get into writing is to let them write often and freely about their own lives, without having to worry about grades or evaluation.

3.   Respond in the form of a question whenever possible. Teacher/facilitator should respond noncritically and use positive, supportive language.

4.   Respond to formal writing acknowledging the student's strengths and focusing on the composition skills demonstrated by the writing. A response should encourage the student by offering praise for what the student has done well. Give the student a focus for revision and demonstrate that the process of revision has applications in many other writing situations.

5.   Provide students with readers' checklists so that students can write observational critiques of others' drafts, and then they can revise their own papers at home using the checklists as a guide.

6.   Pair students so that they can give and receive responses. Pairing students keeps them aware of the role of an audience in the composing process and in evaluating stylistic effects.

7.   Focus critical comments on aspects of the writing that can be observed in the writing. Comments like "I noticed you use the word 'is' frequently" will be more helpful than "Your introduction is dull" and will not demoralize the writer.

8.   Provide the group with a series of questions to guide them through the group writing sessions.

Sometimes this exercise is seen by students as simply catching errors in spelling or word use. Students need to reframe their thinking about revising and editing. Some questions that need to be asked:

- Is the reasoning coherent?
- Is the point established?
- Does the introduction make the reader want to read this discourse?
- What is the thesis? Is it proven?
- What is the purpose? Is it clear? Is it useful, valuable, interesting?
- Is the style of writing so wordy that it exhausts the reader and interferes with engagement?
- Is the writing so spare that it is boring?
- Are the sentences too uniform in structure?
- Are there too many simple sentences?
- Are too many of the complex sentences the same structure?
- Are the compounds truly compounds or are they unbalanced?
- Are parallel structures truly parallel?
- If there are characters, are they believable?
- If there is dialogue, is it natural or stilted?
- Is the title appropriate?
- Does the writing show creativity or is it boring?
- Is the language appropriate? Is it too formal? Too informal? If jargon is used, is it appropriate?

Studies have clearly demonstrated the most fertile area in teaching writing is this one. If students can learn to revise their own work effectively, they are well on their way to becoming effective, mature writers. Word processing is an important tool for teaching this stage in the writing process. Microsoft Word has tracking features that make the revision exchanges between teachers and students more effective than ever before.

Skill 7.8   **Understands differences between first-draft writing and writing for publication, and provides instruction in various stages of writing, including prewriting, drafting, editing, and revising.**

Prior to writing, you will need to prewrite for ideas and details as well as decide how the essay will be organized. In the hour you have to write, you should spend no more than five to ten minutes prewriting and organizing your ideas. As you prewrite, it might be helpful to remember you should have at least three main points and at least two to three details to support your main ideas. There are several types of graphic organizers you should practice using as you prepare for the essay portion of the test.

PREWRITE TO EXPLAIN HOW OR WHY

Reread a question from the chart on the previous referenced page that asks you to explain how a poet creates tone and mood use imagery and word choice. Then fill out the organizer on the following page that identifies how the poet effectively creates tone and mood. Support with examples from the poem.

VISUAL ORGANIZER: GIVING REASONS

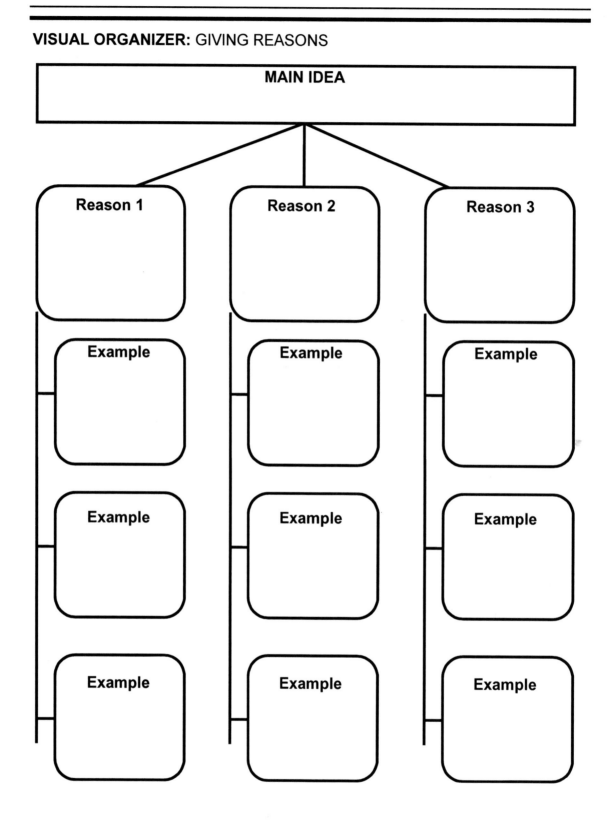

STEP 3: PREWRITE TO ORGANIZE IDEAS

After you have completed a graphic organizer, you need to decide how you will organize your essay. To organize your essay, you might consider one of the following patterns to structure your essay.

1. Examine individual elements such as **plot**, **setting**, **theme**, **character**, **point of view**, **tone**, **mood**, or **style**.

   SINGLE ELEMENT OUTLINE
   Intro - main idea statement
   Main point 1 with at least two supporting details
   Main point 2 with at least two supporting details
   Main point 3 with at least two supporting details
   Conclusion (restates main ideas and summary of main pts)

2. **Compare and contrast two elements.**

POINT-BY-POINT	BLOCK
Introduction Statement of main idea about A and B	Introduction Statement of main idea about A and B
Main Point 1 Discussion of A Discussion of B	Discussion of A Main Point 1 Main Point 2 Main point 3
Main Point 2 Discussion of A Discussion of B	Discussion of B Main Point 1 Main Point 2 Main Point 3
Main Point 3 Discussion of A Discussion of B	Conclusion Restate main idea
Conclusion Restatement or summary of main idea	

PRACTICE:
Using the cluster on the next page, choose an organizing chart and complete for your topic.

VISUAL ORGANIZER: GIVING INFORMATION

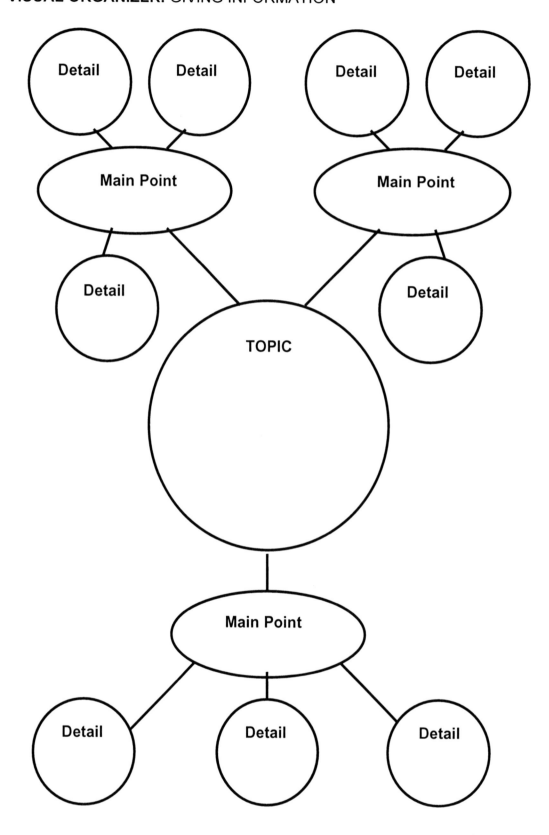

Seeing writing as a process is very helpful in saving preparation time, particularly in the taking of notes and the development of drafts. Once a decision is made about the topic to be developed, some preliminary review of literature is helpful in thinking about the next step, which is to determine what the purpose of the written document will be. For example, if the topic is immigration, a cursory review of the various points of view in the debate going on in the country will help the writer decide what this particular written piece will try to accomplish. The purpose could just be a review of the various points of view, which would be an informative purpose. On the other hand, the writer might want to take a point of view and provide proof and support with the purpose of changing the reader's mind. The writer might even want the reader to take some action as the result of reading. Another possible purpose might be simply to write a description of a family of immigrants.

Once that cursory review has been completed, it's time to begin research in earnest and to prepare to take notes. If the thesis has been clearly defined, and some thought has been given to what will be used to prove or support it, a tentative outline can be developed. A thesis plus three points is typical. Decisions about introduction and conclusion should be deferred until the body of the paper is written. Note-taking is much more effective if the notes are being taken to provide information for an outline. There is much less danger that the writer will go off on time-consuming tangents.

Formal outlines inhibit effective writing. However, a loosely constructed outline can be an effective device for note-taking that will yield the information for a worthwhile statement about a topic. Sentence outlines are better than topic outlines because they require the writer to do some thinking about the direction a subtopic will take.

Once this preliminary note-taking phase is over, the first draft can be developed. The writing at this stage is likely to be highly individualistic. However, successful writers tend to just write, keeping in mind the purpose of the paper, the point that is going to be made in it, and the information that has been turned up in the research. Student writers need to understand that this first draft is just that—the first one. It takes more than one draft to write a worthwhile statement about a topic. This is what successful writers do. It's sometimes helpful to have students read the various drafts of a story by a well-known writer.

Once the draft is on paper, a stage that is sometimes called editing occurs. With word processors, this is much more easily achieved than in the past. Sections can be deleted, words can be changed, and additions can be made without completing the entire project over a second time.

What to look for: mechanics, of course, spelling, punctuation, etc., but it's important that student writers not mistake that for editing. Editing is rereading objectively, testing the effectiveness on a reader of the arrangement and the line of reasoning. The kinds of changes that will need to be made are: rearranging the parts, adding information that is missing and needed, and deleting information that doesn't fit or contribute to the accomplishment of the purpose.

Once the body of the paper has been shaped to the writer's satisfaction, the introduction and conclusion should be fashioned. An introduction should grab the reader's interest and, perhaps, announce the purpose and thesis of the paper unless the reasoning is inductive, in which case, purpose and thesis may come later in the paper. The conclusion is to reaffirm the purpose in some way.

Skill 7.9   Understands the development of writing in relation to the other language arts, and uses instructional strategies that connect these various aspects of language.

The last twenty years have seen great change in instruction in the English classroom. Gone are the days when literature is taught on Monday, Wednesday is grammar day and Friday you assign writing. Integrating reading, writing, speaking, listening and viewing allow students to make connections between each aspect of language development during each class.

Suggestions for Integrating Language Arts:
- Use prereading activities such as discussion, writing, research, and journals. Use writing to tap into prior knowledge before students read; engage students in class discussions about themes, issues, and ideas explored in journals, predicting the outcome and exploring related information.
- Use prewriting activities such as reading model essays, researching, interviewing others, combining sentences and other prewriting activities. Remember that developing language proficiency is a recursive process and involves practice in reading, writing, thinking, speaking, listening and viewing.
- Create writing activities that are relevant to students by having them write and share with real audiences.
- Connect correctness - including developing skills of conventional usage, spelling, grammar, and punctuation - to the revision and editing stage of writing. Review of mechanics and punctuation can be done with mini-lessons that use sentences from student papers, sentence combining strategies, and modeling passages of skilled writers.
- Connect reading, writing, listening, speaking, and viewing by using literature read as a springboard for a variety of activities.

Skill 7.10 **Understands similarities and differences between language used in spoken and written English and helps students use knowledge of these similarities and differences to enhance their own writing.**

See Skill 1.9.

Skill 7.11 **Understands writing for a variety of audiences, purposes, and settings, and provides students with opportunities to write for various audiences, purposes, and settings.**

In the past teachers have assigned reports, paragraphs and essays that focused on the teacher as the audience with the purpose of explaining information. However, for students to be meaningfully engaged in their writing, they must write for a variety of reasons. Writing for different audiences and aims allows students to be more involved in their writing. If they write for the same audience and purpose, they will continue to see writing as just another assignment. Listed below are suggestions that give students an opportunity to write in more creative and critical ways.

- Write letters to the editor, to a college, to a friend, to another student that would be sent to the intended audience.
- Write stories that would be read aloud to a group (the class, another group of students, to a group of elementary school students) or published in a literary magazine or class anthology.
- Write plays that would be performed.
- Have students discuss the parallels between the different speech styles we use and writing styles for different readers or audiences.
- Allow students to write a particular piece for different audiences.
- Make sure students consider the following when analyzing the needs of their audience.

  1. Why is the audience reading my writing? Do they expect to be informed, amused or persuaded?
  2. What does my audience already know about my topic?
  3. What does the audience want or need to know? What will interest them?
  4. What type of language suits my readers?

- As part of the prewriting have students identify the audience.
- Expose students to writing that is on the same topic but with a different audience and have them identify the variations in sentence structure and style.
- Remind your students that it is not necessary to identify all the specifics of the audience in the initial stage of the writing process but that at some point they must make some determinations about audience.

It may seem sometimes the **business letter** is a thing of the past. Although much business-letter writing has been relegated to email communications, letters are still a valuable and potentially valuable form of communication. A carefully-written letter can be powerful. It can alienate, convince, persuade, entice, motivate, and/or create good-will.

As with any other communication, it's worthwhile to learn as much as possible about the receiver. This may be complicated if there will be more than one receiver of the message; in these cases, it's best to aim for the lowest common denominator if that can be achieved without "writing down" to any of those who will read and be affected or influenced by the letter. It may be better to send more than one form of the letter to the various receivers in some cases.

Purpose is the most powerful factor in writing a business letter. What is the letter expected to accomplish? Is it intended to get the receiver to act or to act in a specific manner? Are you hoping to see some action take place as the result of the letter? If so, you should clearly define for yourself what the purpose is before you craft the letter, and it's good to include a time deadline for the response.

Reasons for choosing the letter as the channel of communication include the following:
1. It's easy to keep a record of the transaction.
2. The message can be edited and perfected before it is transmitted.
3. It facilitates the handling of details.
4. It's ideal for communicating complex information.
5. It's a good way to disseminate mass messages at a relatively low cost.

The parts of a business letter are as follow: date line, inside address, salutation, subject line*, body, complimentary close, company name*, signature block, reference initials*, enclosure notation*, copy notation*, and postscript*.

Business letters typically use formal language. They should be straightforward and courteous. The writing should be concise, and special care should be taken to leave no important information out. Clarity is very important; otherwise, it may take more than one exchange of letters or phone calls to get the message across.

A complaint is a different kind of business letter. It can come under the classification of a "bad news" business letter, and there are some guidelines that are helpful when writing this kind of letter. A positive writing style can overcome much of the inherent negativity of a letter of complaint. No matter how much in the right you may be, maintaining self-control and courtesy and avoiding demeaning or blaming language is more likely to be effective. Abruptness, condescension, or harshness of tone will not help achieve your purpose, particularly if you are requesting a positive response such as reimbursement for a bad product or some help in righting a wrong that may have been done to you. It's important to remember that you want to solve the specific problem and to retain the good will of the receiver if possible.

Induction is better than deduction for this type of communication. Beginning with the details and building to the statement of the problem generally has the effect of softening the bad news. It's also useful to begin with an opening that will serve as a buffer. The same is true for the closing. It's good to leave the reader with a favorable impression by writing a closing paragraph that will generate good will rather than bad.

News articles are written in the "inverted pyramid" format—they are deductive in nature: the opening statement is the point of the article; everything else is details. "Who, what, why, when, and where" are usually the questions to be answered in a news article.

A formal essay, on the other hand, may be persuasive, informative, descriptive, or narrative in nature. The purpose should be clearly defined, and development must be coherent and easy to follow.

Email has revolutionized business communications. It has most of the advantages of business letters and the added ones of immediacy, lower costs, and convenience. Even very long reports can be attached to an email. On the other hand, a two-line message can be sent and a response received immediately bringing together the features of a postal system and the telephone. Instant messaging goes even one step further. It can do all of the above—send messages, attach reports, etc.—and still have many of the advantages of a telephone conversation. Email has an unwritten code of behavior that includes restrictions on how informal the writing can be. The level of accepted business conversation is usually also acceptable in emails. Capital letters and bolding are considered shouting and are usually frowned on.

*not required but sometimes useful.

Skill 7.12   Knows how to write using voices and styles appropriate for different audiences and purposes, and provides students with opportunities to write using various voices and styles.

Listening to students sitting on the steps that lead into the building which houses their classrooms, teachers will hear dialogue that may not even be understandable to them. The student who is writing to his peers will need to know and understand the peculiarities of that discourse in order to be very effective with them. This is a good example for students of what it means to tailor language for a particular audience and for a particular person.

This is a good time to teach the concept of jargon. Writing to be read by a lawyer is a different thing from writing to be read by a medical doctor. Writing to be read by parents is different from writing to be read by the administrator of the school. Not only are the vocabularies different, but the formality/informality of the discourse will need to be adjusted.

The things to be aware of in determining what the language should be for a particular audience, then, hinges on two things: vocabulary and formality/informality. The most formal language does not use contractions or slang. The most informal language will certainly use contractions and the slang that is appropriate for the particular audience. Formal language will use longer sentences and will not sound like a conversation. The most informal language will use shorter sentences—not necessarily simple sentences—but shorter constructions and will sound like a conversation.

Novels use formal language only when it is in the mouth of a character who would speak that way, such as a lawyer or a school superintendent. It's jarring to read a novel that has a construction worker using formal language. Using examples of various characters and their dialogues from fiction is useful in helping students understand this crucial aspect of writing.

Skill 7.13   Understands the benefits of technology for teaching writing and writing for publication, and provides instruction in the use of technology to facilitate written communication.

The Internet has transformed all kinds of communications all over the world. Very few people write letters in the 21st century that will be delivered physically to an individual's mailbox. However, there are still important reasons for writing letters. For one thing, they are more personal and convey a quite different message from an e-mail, especially if they are handwritten. For another, not everybody has and uses e-mail regularly.

An electronic mailbox will retain what has been sent and received, sometimes to the writer's regret; even so, those messages and exchanges will not endure in the way that paper letters sometimes do over long periods.

A husband and wife who married in 1954 always corresponded with his parents by mail approximately once a week in the first thirty years of their marriage. The three children often included a note of their own. It was before the long-distance call became routine and affordable. After the grandmother and grandfather had died, the family discovered that they had kept all of those letters. It's a priceless record of a period in the family's life. If that correspondence had occurred via e-mail, it would be lost to history.

Sometimes there's a business reason for a paper letter. It may contain a receipt or legal information that needs to be retained. For those people who do not yet have a computer or access to e-mail, paper letters are necessary. Sometimes a company or organization wishes to advertise a product or even issue invitations to an event when not all e-mail addresses are known. Mass-mailings can be sent quite easily to make sure that everyone on the list can be reached. Advertisers, of course, use mass-mail more than anyone else because they do not even need to know the addresses to get their literature into all the mailboxes in a zip code.

Sometimes courtesy requires a personally written letter either typed or handwritten. If a person in high office has taken the time to do something for an individual, certainly a handwritten letter of thanks would be in order. In the U.S., the form of the letter can be full block (all lines blocked at the left margin); modified block (all lines blocked at the left margin except the date and closing lines, which begin at the center point); and semi-block (same as modified block except that the first lines of paragraphs are indented by five points). Microsoft Word's letter wizard will automatically format a business letter according to these three styles.

Social notes should be handwritten on note paper, which varies in size but is smaller than letter-sized paper. They should be courteous and brief and should be specific about what is intended. For example, if the note is to say thank you, then the gift or favor should be specifically acknowledged in the note. If the note is an invitation, the same rule applies: the language should be courteous, the place and time specified, and any useful information such as "casual dress" or parking recommendations should be included.

A high percentage of communications between individuals, groups, and businesses is conducted nowadays over the Internet. It has even replaced many telephone calls. Internet language should be courteous, free of words that might be offensive, and clear. In the early days of e-mail, a writer was censured for using bold or capital letters. That has relaxed somewhat. Nowadays, almost anything goes although it's generally accepted that restrained language is assumed for business people and personal communications. The blog, where a person has his/her own website and uses it to send messages, is a new wrinkle. Chat is available on most blogs as well as other Internet sites. The language and the messages tend to be unrestrained there.

Some people use the same styles for letters via e-mail that are recommended for paper letters; however, the formatting has tended to become less and less formal. It is not uncommon for thank-you letters and invitations to be sent via e-mail. One important feature of the Internet that makes it so valuable is that it reaches everywhere—to small communities, all the way across the country, and overseas. It's possible to dash off an e-mail note to a person or business or several persons or businesses in Europe as quickly as to a person in the next office, and it costs no extra money beyond the cost of equipment and Internet services.

The fax machine is yet another dimension of electronic communications. At first, it was used primarily by businesses, but it has become so affordable that many people have them in their homes. The fax makes possible an actual picture of a document. This may be preferable to retyping it or sending it by paper mail because it can go immediately. Sometimes people who are exchanging contracts will use the fax to cut down on the time it takes to get them signed and sent back and forth. The scanner will do the same thing but will produce a document that can be e-mailed.

COMPETENCY 8.0 VIEWING AND REPRESENTING

Skill 8.1   Knows grade-level expectations in the Texas Essential Knowledge and Skills (TEKS) and procedures for assessing students' skills in interpreting, analyzing, evaluating, and producing visual images, messages, and meanings.

Let's face it. The day of the handwritten essay is past. We have been suddenly projected into a world where many of the activities of the writing classroom of the past have vanished. It's important to remember that the students sitting in your writing class are going to be required to have the skills to write clearly and succinctly and to think critically in the world they will soon be entering. Even those who will not be going on to college will be required to use technological tools to deal with their worlds. They will be filling out forms on a computer and communicating with many people via website and e-mail that they have dealt with face-to-face or via telephone in the past. The demands on the writing teacher are no longer simply teaching thinking/writing skills, but also teaching students skills that will connect them to the technological world of the 21st century.

Students need to know how to get on the Internet, where to find e-mail (there are more than one mail programs, Microsoft Outlook, for example; how to compose an e-mail in order to be understood; and some of the etiquette required for effective e-mail communications. Job applications are often filled out on a website. Students need to know how to interact on Acrobat, which includes finding the icon that permits text insertion. They also need to know how to conduct searches, so they need to be aware of what "search" means, what Boolean terms are, what the major search engines are, and how to use them.

In most colleges nowadays, themes are exchanged on a website set up specifically for the school. The students need to be prepared to present their themes electronically and exchange messages with their teachers in this way, so they need to understand Microsoft Word well enough to be able to read and respond to comments on Word's tracking function and to create a "clean version" of a paper while retaining the one from the teacher with edits and comments.

Skill 8.2   Uses ongoing assessment and knowledge of grade-level expectations in the Texas Essential Knowledge and Skills (TEKS) to identify students' needs regarding the interpretation, analysis, evaluation, and production of visual images, messages, and meanings and to plan instruction.

See 8.1

Skill 8.3   Understands characteristics and functions of different types of media and knows how different types of media influence and inform.

Media's impact on today's society is immense and ever-increasing. As children, we watch programs on television that are amazingly fast-paced and visually rich. Parent's roles as verbal and moral teachers are diminishing in response to the much more stimulating guidance of the television set. Adolescence, which used to be the time for going out and exploring the world first hand, is now consumed by the allure of MTV, popular music, and video games. Young adults are exposed to uncensored sex and violence.

But media's affect on society is beneficial and progressive at the same time. Its affect on education in particular provides special challenges and opportunities for teachers and students.

Thanks to satellite technology, instructional radio and television programs can be received by urban classrooms and rural villages. CD-ROMs can allow students to learn information through a virtual reality experience. The internet allows instant access to unlimited data and connects people across all cultures through shared interests. Educational media, when used in a productive way, enriches instruction and makes it more individualized, accessible, and economical.

Skill 8.4   Compares and contrasts print, visual, and electronic media.

Tips for using print media and visual aids
- Use pictures over words whenever possible.
- Present one key point per visual.
- Use no more than 3-4 colors per visual to avoid clutter and confusion.
- Use contrasting colors such as dark blue and bright yellow.
- Use a maximum of 25-35 numbers per visual aid.
- Use bullets instead of paragraphs when possible.
- Make sure it is student-centered, not media-centered. Delivery is just as important as the media presented.

Tips for using film and television
- Study programs in advance.
- Obtain supplementary materials such as printed transcripts of the narrative or study guides.
- Provide your students with background information, explain unfamiliar concepts, and anticipate outcomes.
- Assign outside readings based on their viewing.
- Ask cuing questions.
- Watch along with students.
- Observe students' reactions.
- Follow up viewing with discussions and related activities.

Skill 8.5 **Evaluates how visual image makers represent messages and meanings and provides students with varied opportunities to interpret and evaluate visual images in various media.**

More money is spent each year on advertising towards children than educating them. Thus, the media's strategies are considerably well thought out and effective. They employ large, clear letters, bold colors, simple line drawings, and popular symbols to announce upcoming events, push ideas and advertise products. By using attractive photographs, brightly colored cartoon characters or instructive messages, they increase sales, win votes or stimulate learning. The graphics are designed to communicate messages clearly, precisely, and efficiently. Some even target subconscious yearnings for sex and status.

Because so much effort is being spent on influencing students through media tactics, just as much effort should be devoted to educating those students about media awareness. A teacher should explain that artists and the aspect they choose to portray, as well as the ways in which they portray them, reflect their attitude and understanding of those aspects. The artistic choices they make are not entirely based on creative license—they also reflect an imbedded meaning the artist wants to represent. Colors, shapes, and positions are meant to arouse basic instincts for food, sex, and status, and are often used to sell cars, clothing, or liquor.

To stimulate analysis of media strategies, ask students such questions as:

- Where/when do you think this picture was taken/film was shot/piece was written?
- Would you like to have lived at this time in history, or in this place?
- What objects are present?
- What do the people presented look like? Are they happy or sad?
- Who is being targeted?
- What can you learn from this piece of media?
- Is it telling you something is good or bad?
- What message is being broadcasted?

Skill 8.6 **Knows how to teach students to analyze visual image makers' choices and evaluate how these choices help to represent or extend meaning.**

See Skill 8.5.

Skill 8.7 **Provides students with opportunities to interpret events and ideas based on information from maps, charts, graphics, video segments, and technology presentations and to use media to compare ideas and points of view.**

See Skill 5.7.

Skill 8.8 **Knows steps and procedures for producing visual images, messages, and meaning to communicate with others.**

The old adage that a picture is worth a thousand words is never more evident than in the use of charts, graphs, and tables in expository writing. It's one thing to say that the GDP of the United States rose fifteen percentage points in the last five years, it's an entirely different thing to show a graph that depicts that rapid rise. If the point being made is that the increase in the GDP is better than it has ever been in the past fifty years, then a graph showing that growth cinches the point. If the point being made is that the growth in the GDP corresponds to the growth of the stock market for the same period, then that also can be graphed.

It's important data in charts and graphs be simple and comprehensive. Also, it should only be used if it does, in fact, display the information more effectively than words alone can. However, it should also be able to stand alone. It should make the point by itself. If two or more charts or tables are used within a work, they should be consistent in style. Whatever graphic is used, elements of the same kind must always be represented in the same way. This is not a time to be artistic graphically; visual effects should be used only for the purpose of making the point, not for variety.

In graphs, both the horizontal and vertical axes should be labeled. In a column, both column heads and stubs should be labeled. In a graph, the vertical axis is always read from the bottom up and curves or bars should be graphically distinct (color or dotted lines, for example) and all elements should be clearly identified in a key. The title appears in a caption rather than as a title and is lowercased except for names that would normally be capitalized in the text. If abbreviations are used, care should be taken to make them easily recognizable unless they are explained in the key or in the caption.

A table can often give information that would take several paragraphs to present and can do so more clearly. Tables should be as simple as the material allows and should be understandable without explanation even to a reader who might be unfamiliar with the subject matter. Only necessary explanations should be presented in the text; the table should be able to stand alone.

The advent of word processing makes the creation and insertion of charts, graphs, and tables much more practical than ever before. It takes very little knowledge or skill to create these illustrative devices, and helping students develop those skills is a valuable enhancement to a writing course.

Skill 8.9 **Teaches students how to select, organize, and produce visuals to complement and extend meanings.**

Tips for creating visual media
- Limit your graph to just one idea or concept
- Keep the content simple and concise (avoid too many lines, words, or pictures)
- Balance substance and visual appeal
- Make sure the text is large enough for the class to read
- Match the information to the format that will fit it best

Skill 8.10 **Provides students with opportunities to use technology to produce various types of communications and helps students analyze how language, medium, and presentation contribute to the message.**

See Skill 6.18.

COMPETENCY 9.0 STUDY AND INQUIRY SKILLS

Skill 9.1   Understands study and inquiry skills and knows the significance of these skills for student learning and achievement.

The best place to start research is usually at your local library. Not only does it have numerous books, videos, and periodicals to use for references, the librarian is always a valuable resource for information, or where to get that information.

"Those who declared librarians obsolete when the internet rage first appeared are now red-faced. We need them more than ever. The internet is full of 'stuff' but its value and readability is often questionable. 'Stuff' doesn't give you a competitive edge, high-quality related information does."
        -Patricia Schroeder, President of the Association of American Publishers

The internet is a multi-faceted goldmine of information, but you must be careful to discriminate between reliable and unreliable sources. Stick to sites that are associated with an academic institution, whether it be a college or university or a scholarly organization.

Keep **content** and **context** in mind when researching. Don't be so wrapped up how you are going to apply your resource to your project that you miss the author's entire purpose or message. Remember that there are multiple ways to get the information you need. Read an encyclopedia article about your topic to get a general overview, and then focus in from there. Note important names of people associated with your subject, time periods, and geographic areas. Make a list of key words and their synonyms to use while searching for information. And finally, don't forget about articles in magazines and newspapers, or even personal interviews with experts related to your field of interest!

Skill 9.2   Knows grade-level expectations for study and inquiry skills in the Texas Essential Knowledge and Skills (TEKS) and procedures for assessing students' development and use of these skills.

According to the Texas Essential Knowledge and Skills, expectations for study and inquiry are as follows:

- The student is expected to read in varied sources such as diaries, journals, textbooks, maps, newspapers, letters, speeches, memoranda, electronic texts, and other media.
- Analyze the characteristics of clearly written texts, including the patterns of organization, syntax, and word choice.
- Evaluate the credibility of information sources, including how the writer's motivation may affect that credibility.
- Recognize logical, deceptive, and/or faulty modes of persuasion in texts.

Skill 9.3 **Knows and applies instructional practices that promote the acquisition and use of study and inquiry skills across the curriculum by all students, including English Language Learners.**

An easy and effective way of organizing information to be used in a work of nonfiction is by asking specific questions that are geared towards a particular mode of presentation. An example of these questions follows:

Useful research questions:

What is it?

It is the process of thinking up and writing down a set of questions that you want to answer about the research topic you have selected.

Why should I do it?

It will keep you from getting lost or off-track when looking for information. You will try to find the answers to these questions when you do your research.

When do I do it?

After you have written your statement of purpose, and have a focused topic to ask questions about, begin research.

How do I do it?

Make two lists of questions. Label one "factual" questions and one "interpretive" questions. The answers to factual questions will give your reader the basic background information they need to understand your topic. The answers to interpretive questions show your creative thinking in your project and can become the basis for your thesis statement.

Asking factual questions:

Assume your reader knows nothing about your subject. Make an effort to tell them everything they need to know to understand what you will say in your project.

Make a list of specific questions that ask: Who? What? When? Where?

Example: For a report about President Abraham Lincoln's attitude and policies towards slavery, people will have to know; Who was Abraham Lincoln? Where and when was he born? What political party did he belong to? When was he elected president? What were the attitudes and laws about slavery during his lifetime? How did his actions affect slavery?

Asking Interpretive Questions:

These kinds of questions are the result of your own original thinking. They can be based on the preliminary research you have done on your chosen topic. Select one or two to answer in your presentation. They can be the basis of forming a thesis statement.

- **Hypothetical**: How would things be different today if something in the past had been different?

Example: How would our lives be different today if the Confederate (southern) states had won the United States Civil War? What would have happened to the course of World War Two if the Atomic Bomb hadn't been dropped on Hiroshima and Nagasaki?

- **Prediction**: How will something look or be in the future, based on the way it is now?

Example: What will happen to sea levels if global warming due to ozone layer depletion continues and the polar caps melt significantly? If the population of China continues to grow at the current rate for the next fifty years, how will that impact its role in world politics?

- **Solution**: What solutions can be offered to a problem that exists today?

Example: How could global warming be stopped? What can be done to stop the spread of sexually transmitted diseases among teenagers?

- **Comparison or Analogy**: Find the similarities and differences between your main subject and a similar subject, or with another subject in the same time period or place.

Example: In what ways is the Civil War in the former Yugoslavia similar to (or different from) the United States Civil War?
What is the difference in performance between a Porsche and a Lamborghini?

- **Judgment**: Based on the information you find, what can you say as your informed opinion about the subject?

Example: How does tobacco advertising affect teen cigarette smoking? What are the major causes of eating disorders among young women? How does teen parenthood affect the future lives of young women and men?

Skill 9.4   **Knows how to provide students with varied and meaningful opportunities to learn and apply study and inquiry skills to enhance their achievement across the curriculum.**

See Skill 9.3.

Skill 9.5   **Uses ongoing assessment and knowledge of grade-level expectations in the Texas Essential Knowledge and Skills (TEKS) to identify students' needs regarding study and inquiry skills, to determine when a student requires additional help of intervention, and to plan instruction.**

See Skill 1.5.

Skill 9.6   **Responds to students' needs by providing direct, explicit instruction to promote the acquisition and use of study and inquiry skills.**

See Skills 9.1 and 9.3.

Sample Test: Language Arts

Directions: Select the best answer in each group of multiple choices.

1. **If a student has a poor vocabulary the teacher should recommend that (Skill 1.10) (Rigorous)**

   A. The student read newspapers, magazines and books on a regular basis.
   B. The student enroll in a Latin class.
   C. The student write the words repetitively after looking them up in the dictionary.
   D. The student use a thesaurus to locate synonyms and incorporate them into his/her vocabulary.

2. **The arrangement and relationship of words in sentences or sentence structure best describes (Skill 1.1, 3.13, 7.10) (Average)**

   A. Style.

   B. Discourse.

   C. Thesis.

   D. Syntax.

3. **Which of the following is a formal reading level assessment? (Skill 2.8) (Easy)**

   A. A standardized reading test

   B. A teacher-made reading test

   C. An interview

   D. A reading diary.

4. **The literary device of personification is used in which example below? (Skill 4.2) (Average)**

   A. "Beg me no beggary by soul or parents, whining dog!"

   B. "Happiness sped through the halls cajoling as it went."

   C. "O wind thy horn, thou proud fellow."

   D. "And that one talent which is death to hide."

5. Which teaching method would be most effective for interesting underachievers in the required senior English class?
(Skill 4.11) (Rigorous)

A. Assign use of glossary work and extensively footnoted excerpts of great works.

B. Have students take turns reading aloud the anthology selection.

C. Let students choose which readings they'll study and write about.

D. Use a chronologically arranged, traditional text, but assigning group work, panel presentations, and portfolio management.

6. Which definition below is the best for defining diction?
(Skill 5.1) (Rigorous)

A. The specific word choices of an author to create a particular mood or feeling in the reader.

B. Writing which explains something thoroughly.

C. The background, or exposition, for a short story or drama.

D. Word choices which help teach a truth or moral.

7. Which is not a true statement concerning an author's literary tone?
(Skill 4.13) (Rigorous)

A. Tone is partly revealed through the selection of details.

B. Tone is the expression of the author's attitude toward his/her subject.

C. Tone in literature is usually satiric or angry.

D. Tone in literature corresponds to the tone of voice a speaker uses.

8. What were two major characteristics of the first American literature?
(Skill 5.4 and 5.12) (Rigorous)

A. Vengefulness and arrogance

B. Bellicosity and derision

C. Oral delivery and reverence for the land

D. Maudlin and self-pitying geocentricism

9. Which of the following is an example of the subject of a tall-tale?
(Skill 5.9) (Rigorous)

A. John Henry.

B. Paul Bunyan.

C. George Washington.

D. Rip Van Winkle.

10. Which term best describes the form of the following poetic excerpts?
(Skill 5.9 and 7.3) (Rigorous)

And more to lulle him in his slumber soft,
A trickling streame from high rock tumbling downe,
And ever-drizzling raine upon the loft.
Mixt with a murmuring winde, much like a swowne
No other noyse, nor peoples troubles cryes.
As still we wont t'annoy the walle'd towne,
Might there be heard: but careless Quiet lyes,
Wrapt in eternall silence farre from enemyes.

A. Ballad

B. Elegy

C. Spenserian stanza

D. Octava rima

11. Which sonnet form describes the following?
(Skill 5.9) (Rigorous)

My galley charg'ed with forgetfulness
Through sharp seas, in winter night doth pass
'Tween rock and rock; and eke mine enemy, alas,
That is my lord steereth with cruelness.
And every oar a thought in readiness,
As though that death were light in such a case.
An endless wind doth tear the sail apace
Or forc'ed sighs and trusty fearfulness.
A rain of tears, a cloud of dark disdain,
Hath done the wearied cords great hinderance,
Wreathed with error and eke with ignorance.
The stars be hid that led me to this pain
Drowned is reason that should me consort,
And I remain despairing of the poet.

A. Petrarchan or Italian sonnet

B. Shakespearean or Elizabethan sonnet

C. Romantic sonnet

D. Spenserian sonnet

12. A figure of speech in which someone absent or something inhuman is addressed as though present and able to respond describes
(Skill 5.11) (Average)

    A. Personification.

    B. Synecdoche.

    C. Metonymy.

    D. Apostrophe.

See competency 5 for further clarification

13. The quality in a work of literature which evokes feelings of pity or compassion is called
(Skill 5.12) (Easy)

    A. Colloquy.

    B. Irony.

    C. Pathos.

    D. Paradox.

14. An extended metaphor which compares two very dissimilar things - one lofty, one lowly, is a definition of a/an
(Skill 5.15) (Average)

    A. antithesis.

    B. Aphorism.

    C. Apostrophe.

    D. Conceit.

15. Which of the following is a complex sentence?
(Skill 6.2) (Easy)

    A. Anna and Margaret read a total of fifty-four books during summer vacation.

    B. The youngest boy on the team had the best earned run average, which mystifies the coaching staff.

    C. Earl decided to attend Princeton; his twin brother Roy, who aced the ASVAB test, will be going to Annapolis.

    D. "Easy come, easy go," Marcia moaned.

16. **Middle and high school students are more receptive to studying grammar and syntax**
(Skill 6.2 and 6.6) (Rigorous)

   A. Through worksheets and end-of-lesson practices in textbooks.

   B. Through independent, homework assignments.

   C. Through analytical examination of the writings of famous authors.

   D. Though application to their own writing.

17. **A punctuation mark indicating omission, interrupted thought, or an incomplete statement is a/an**
(Skill 6.2 and 6.6) (Rigorous)

   A. Ellipsis.

   B. Anachronism

   C. Colloquy.

   D. Idiom.

18. **Which of the following contains an error in possessive inflection?**
(Skill 6.5 and 6.6) (Easy)

   A. Doris's shawl

   B. Mother's-in-law frown

   C. Children's lunches

   D. Ambassador's briefcase

19. **Wally groaned, "Why do I have to do an oral interpretation of "The Raven."**
(Skill 6.6) (Average)

   A. Groaned, "Why ... of 'The Raven' ?"

   B. Groaned "Why ... of "The Raven" ?

   C. Groaned ",Why ... of "The Raven?"

   D. Groaned, "Why ... of "The Raven."

20. Mr. Smith <u>respectfully submitted his resignation and had</u> a new job.
    (Skill 6.6) (Average)

    A. Respectively submitted his resignation and has

    B. Respectively submitted his resignation before accepting

    C. Respectfully submitted his resignation because of

    D. Respectfully submitted his resignation and has

21. There were <u>fewer pieces</u> of evidence presented during the second trial.
    (Skill 6.6) (Average)

    A. Fewer peaces

    B. Less peaces

    C. Less pieces

    D. Fewer pieces

22. The teacher <u>implied</u> from our angry words that there was conflict <u>between</u> <u>you and me</u>.
    (Skill 6.6)(Easy)

    A. Implied ... between you and I

    B. Inferred... between you and I

    C. Inferred...between you and me

    D. Implied ... between you and me

23. Which of the following is not one of the four forms of discourse?
    (Skill 6.6)(Average)

    A. Exposition

    B. Description

    C. Rhetoric

    D. Persuasion

24. "Clean as a whistle" or "Easy as falling off a log" are examples of
    (Skill 7.1) (Average)

    A. Semantics.

    B. Parody.

    C. Irony.

    D. Clichés.

25. **What is the figure of speech present in line one below in which the dead body of Caesar is addressed as though he were still a living being?**
(Skill 7.1) (Average)

"O, pardon me, thou bleeding piece of earth
That I am meek and gentle with these butchers."
Marc Antony from Julius *Caesar*

A. Apostrophe

B. Allusion

C. Antithesis

D. Anachronism

26. **A sixth-grade science teacher has given her class a paper to read on the relationship between food and weight gain. The writing contains signal words such as "because," "consequently," "this is how," and "due to." This paper has which text structure?**
(Skill 7.1) (Rigorous)

A. Cause & effect
B. Compare & contrast
C. Description
D. Sequencing

27. **A form of discourse which explains or informs is**
(Skill 7.1) (Average)

A. Exposition

B. Narration.

C. Persuasion.

D. Description.

28. **The following passage is written from which point of view?**
(Skill 7.3) (Rigorous)

As she mused the pitiful vision of her mother's life laid its spell on the very quick of her being - that life of commonplace sacrifices closing in final craziness. She trembled as she heard again her mother's voice saying constantly with foolish insistence: Derevaun Seraun! Derevaun Seraun !*
* "The end of pleasure is pain!" (Gaelic)

A. First person, narrator

B. Second person, direct address

C. Third person, omniscient

D. First person, omniscient

29. **Which of the following should not be included in the opening paragraph of an informative essay?**
(Skill 7.8) (Average)

    A. Thesis sentence

    B. Details and examples supporting the main idea

    C. A broad general introduction to the topic

    D. A style and tone that grab the reader's attention

30. **Which of the following is not a technique of prewriting?**
(Skill 7.8) (Average)

    A. Clustering

    B. Listing

    C. Brainstorming

    D. Proofreading

31. **Which of the following is not an approach to keep students ever conscious of the need to write for audience appeal?**
(Skill 7.3) (Rigorous)

    A. Pairing students during the writing process

    B. Reading all rough drafts before the students write the final copies

    C. Having students compose stories or articles for publication in school literary magazines or newspapers

    D. Writing letters to friends or relatives

Answer Key: Language Arts

1. A	9. B	17. A	25. B
2. D	10. D	18. B	26. A
3. A	11. A	19. A	27. A
4. C	12. D	20. C	28. C
5. C	13. C	21. D	29. B
6. A	14. D	22. C	30. D
7. C	15. B	23. C	31. A
8. D	16. D	24. D	

Rigor Table: Language Arts

Easy (20%)	Average (40%)	Rigorous(40%)
3,13,15,17,18,22	2,4,12,14,19,20,21,23,24,25,27,29,30	1,5,6,7,8,9,10,11,16,26,28,31

Rationales with Sample Questions: Language Arts

1. **If a student has a poor vocabulary the teacher should recommend that:**
   (Skill 1.10) (Rigorous)

   A.   The student read newspapers, magazines and books on a regular basis.

   B.   The student enroll in a Latin class.

   C.   The student write the words repetitively after looking them up in the dictionary.

   D.   The student use a thesaurus to locate synonyms and incorporate them into his/her vocabulary

The answer is A. It is up to the teacher to help the student choose reading material, but the student must be able to choose where s/he will search for the reading pleasure indispensable for enriching vocabulary.

2. **The arrangement and relationship of words in sentences or sentence structure best describes**
   (Skill 1.10) (Rigorous)

   A.   Style.

   B.   Discourse.

   C.   Thesis.

   D.   Syntax.

The answer is D. Syntax is the grammatical structure of sentences.

3. **Which of the following is a formal reading assessment? (Skill 1.10) (Rigorous)**

    A.   A standardized reading test

    B.   A teacher-made reading test

    C.   An interview

    D.   A reading diary

The answer is A. If assessment is standardized, it has to be objective, whereas B, C and D are all subjective assessments

4. **The literary device of personification is used in which example below? (Skill 4.2) (Average)**

    a.   "Beg me no beggary by soul or parents, whining dog!"

    b.   "Happiness sped through the halls cajoling as it went."

    c.   "O wind thy horn, thou proud fellow."

    d.   "And that one talent which is death to hide."

The answer is C. It gives human characteristics to an inanimate object

5. **Which teaching method would be most effective for interesting underachievers in the required senior English class? (Skill 4.11) (Rigorous)**

    A.   Assign use of glossary work and extensively footnoted excerpts of great works.

    B.   Have students take turns reading aloud the anthology selection

    C.   Let students choose which readings they'll study and write about.

    D.   Use a chronologically arranged, traditional text, but assigning group work, panel presentations, and portfolio management

The answer is C. It will encourage students to react honestly to literature. Students should take notes on what they're reading so they will be able to discuss the material. They should not only react to literature, but also experience it. Small-group work is a good way to encourage them. The other answers are not fit for junior-high or high school students. They should be encouraged, however, to read critics of works in order to understand criteria work.

6. **Which definition is the best for defining diction? (Skill 5.1) (Rigorous)**

    A.   The specific word choices of an author to create a particular mood or feeling in the reader.

    B.   Writing which explains something thoroughly.

    C.   The background, or exposition, for a short story or drama.

    D.   Word choices which help teach a truth or moral.

The answer is A. Diction refers to an author's choice of words, expressions and style to convey his/her meaning.

7. **Which is <u>not</u> a true statement concerning an author's literary tone? (Skill 4.13) (Rigorous)**

      A.   Tone is partly revealed through the selection of details.

      B.   Tone is the expression of the author's attitude towards his/her subject.

      C.   Tone in literature is usually satiric or angry.

      D.   Tone in literature corresponds to the tone of voice a speaker uses.

The answer is C. Tone in literature conveys a mood and can be as varied as the tone of voice of a speaker (see D), e.g. sad, nostalgic, whimsical, angry, formal, intimate, satirical, sentimental, etc.

8. **What were two major characteristics of the first American literature? (Skill 5.4 and 5.12) (Rigorous)**

      A.   Vengefulness and arrogance

      B.   Bellicosity and derision

      C.   Oral delivery and reverence for the land

      D.   Maudlin and self-pitying egocentricism

The answer is D. This characteristic can be seen in Captain John Smith's work. as well as William Bradford's, and Michael Wigglesworth's works.

9. An example of the subject a tall tale is
(Skill 5.9) (Rigorous)

    A.   John Henry

    B.   Paul Bunyan

    C.   George Washington

    D.   Rip Van Winkle

The answer is B. A tall tale is a Folklore genre, originating on the American frontier, in which the physical attributes, capabilities, and exploits of characters are wildly exaggerated. This is the case of giant logger Paul Bunyan of the American Northwestern forests. James Stevens traced Paul Bunyan to a French Canadian logger named Paul Bunyon. He won a reputation as a great fighter in the Papineau Rebellion against England in 1837 and later became famous as the boss of a logging camp. Paul Bunyan's first appearance in print seems to be in an advertising pamphlet, *Paul Bunyan and His Big Blue Ox*, published by the Red River Company. It immediately became very popular and was reissued many times.

10. **Which term best describes the form of the following poetic excerpt? (Skill 5.9 and 7.3) (Rigorous)**

> And more to lulle him in his
> slumber soft,
> A trickling streake from high rock
> tumbling downe,
> And ever-drizzling raine upon
> the loft.
> Mixt with a murmuring winde,
> much like a swowne
> No other noyse, nor peoples
> troubles cryes.
> As still we wont t'annoy the
> walle'd towne,
> Might there be heard: but
> careless Quiet lyes,
> Wrapt in eternall silence farre
> from enemyes.

    A.   Ballad

    B.   Elegy

    C.   Spenserian stanza

    D.   Octava rima

The answer is D. The Octava Rima is a specific eight-line stanza whose rhyme scheme is abababcc.

11. Which sonnet form describes the following?
(Skill 5.9) (Rigorous)

My galley charg'd with
    forgetfulness,

Through sharp seas, in
    winter night doth pass

'Tween rock and rock; and
    eke mine enemy, alas,

That is my lord steereth with
    cruelness.

And every oar a thought with
    readiness,

As though that death were
    light in such a case.

An endless wind doth tear
    the sail apace

Or forc'ed sighs and trusty
    fearfulness.

A rain of tears, a cloud of dark
    disdain,

Hath done the wearied
    cords great hinderance,

Wreathed with error and eke
    with ignorance.

The stars be hid that led me
    to this pain

Drowned is reason that
    should me consort,

And I remain despairing
    of the poet

A. Petrarchan or Italian sonnet

B. Shakespearian or Elizabethan sonnet

C. Romantic sonnet

D. Spenserian sonnet

The answer is A. The Petrarchan Sonnet, also known as Italian sonnet, is named after the Italian poet Petrarch (1304-74). It is divided into an octave rhyming *abbaabba* and a sestet normally rhyming *cdecde*.

12. A figure of speech in which someone absent or something inhuman is addressed as though as though present and able to respond describes (Skill 5.11) (Average)

      A.   Personification.

      B.   Synechdoche.

      C.   Metonymy

      D.   Apostrophe.

The answer is D. Apostrophe gives human reactions and thoughts to animals, things and abstract ideas alike. This figure of speech is often present in allegory: for instance, the Giant Despair in John Bunyon's *Pilgrim's Progress*. Also, fables use personification to make animals able to speak.

13. The quality in a work of literature which evokes feelings of pity or compassion is called
(Skill 5.12) (Easy)

      A.   Colloquy.

      B.   Irony.

      C.   Pathos.

      D.   Paradox

The answer is C. A very well known example of pathos is Desdemona's death in Othello, but there are many other examples of pathos.

14. An extended metaphor which compares two very dissimilar things—one lofty, one lowly, is a definition of a/an
(Skill 5.15) (Average)

      A.   antithesis.

      B.   aphorism.

      C.   apostrophe.

      D.   Conceit.

The answer is D. A conceit is an unusually far-fetched metaphor in which an object, person or situation is presented in a parallel and simpler analogue between two apparently very different things or feelings, one very sophisticated and one very ordinary, usually taken either from nature or a well known every day concept familiar to both reader and author alike. The conceit was first developed by Petrarch and spread to England in the sixteenth century.

15. Which of the following is a complex sentence?
(Skill 6.2) (Easy)

      A.   Anna and Margaret read a total of fifty-four books during summer vacation.

      B.   The youngest boy on the team had the best earned run average which mystifies the coaching staff.

      C.   Earl decided to attend Princeton; his twin brother Roy, who aced the ASVAB test, will be going to Annapolis.

      D.   "Easy come, easy go," Marcia moaned.

The answer is B. Here, the use of the relative pronoun "which", whose antecedent is "the best run average, introduces a clause that is dependent on the independent clause "The youngest boy on the team had the best run average". The idea expressed in the subordinate clause is subordinate to the one expressed in the independent clause.

16. Middle and high school students are more receptive to studying grammar and syntax
(Skill 6.2 and 6.6) (Rigorous)

      A.   Through worksheets and end of lessons practices in textbooks.

      B.   Through independent, homework assignment.

      C.   Through analytical examination of the writings of famous authors.

      D.   Through application to their own writing.

The answer is D. At this age, students learn grammatical concepts best through practical application in their own writing.

17. **A punctuation mark indicating omission, interrupted thought, or an incomplete statement is a/an**
    (Skill 6.5 and 6.6) (Easy)

    A. Ellipsis.

    B. Anachronism.

    C. Colloquy.

    D. Idiom.

The answer is A. In an ellipsis, a word or words that would clarify the sentence's message are missing, yet it is still possible to understand them from the context. **See competency 6 for further clarification**

18. **Which of the following contains an error in possessive inflection?**
    (Skill 6.5 and 6.6) (Easy)

    A.   Doris's shawl

    B.   mother's-in-law frown

    C.   children's lunches

    D.   ambassador's briefcase

The answer is B. Mother-in-Law is a compound common noun and the inflection should be at the end of the word, according to the rule.

19. Wally <u>groaned, "Why</u> do I have to do an oral interpretation of "The Raven."
(Skill 6.6) (Average)

    A.   Groaned "Why... of 'The Raven'?"

    B.   Groaned "Why... of "The Raven"?

    C.   Groaned ", Why... of "The Raven?"

    D.   Groaned, "Why... of "The Raven."

The answer is A. The question mark in a quotation that is an interrogation should be within the quotation marks. Also, when quoting a work of literature within another quotation, one should use single quotation marks ('...') for the title of this work, and they should close before the final quotation mark.

20. Mr Smith <u>respectfully submitted his resignation and</u> <u>had</u> a new job.
(Skill 6.6) (Average)

    A.   Respectfully submitted his resignation and has

    B.   Respectfully submitted his resignation before accepting

    C.   Respectfully submitted his resignation because of

    D.   Respectfully submitted his resignation and had

The answer is C. A eliminates any relationship of causality between submitting the resignation and having the new job. B just changes the sentence and does not indicate the fact that Mr Smith had a new job before submitting his resignation. D means that Mr Smith first submitted his resignation, then got a new job.

21. There were <u>fewer pieces</u> of evidence presented during the second trial
(Skill 6.6) (Average)

      A.   Fewer peaces

      B.   Less peaces

      C.   Less pieces

      D.   Fewer pieces

The answer is D. "Less" is impossible is the plural, and "peace" is the opposite of war, not a "piece" of evidence.

22. The teacher <u>implied</u> from our angry words that there was conflict
<u>between</u> <u>you and me</u>
(Skill 6.6) (Easy)

      A.   Implied... between you and I

      B.   Inferred... between you and I

      C.   Inferred... between you and me

      D.   Implied... between you and me

The answer is C: the difference between the verb "to imply" and the verb "to infer" is that implying is directing an interpretation toward other people; to infer is to deduce an interpretation from someone else's discourse. Moreover, "between you and I" is grammatically incorrect: after a preposition here "and"), a disjunctive pronoun (me, you, him, her, us, you, them) is needed. **See Competency 6 for further clarification**

23. **Which of the following is not one of the four forms of discourse?**
    (Skill 6.6)(Average)

     A.   Exposition

     B.   Description

     C.   Rhetoric

     D.   Persuasion

The answer is C. Exposition, description and persuasion are styles of writing and ways of influencing a reader or a listener. Rhetoric, on the other hand, is theoretical. It is the theory of expressive and effective speech. Rhetorical figures are ornaments of speech such as anaphora, antithesis, metaphor, etc

24. **"Clean as a whistle or "Easy as falling of a log" are examples of**
    (Skill 7.1) (Average)

     A.   Semantics.

     B.   Parody.

     C.   Irony.

     D.   Clichés.

The answer is D. A cliché is a phrase or expression that has become dull due to overuse.

25. What is the figure of speech present in line one below in which the dead body of Caesar is addressed as though he were still a living being?
(Skill 7.1) (Average)

O, pardon me, though Bleeding piece of earth

That I am meek and gentle with

These butchers.

Marc Antony from *Julius Caesar*

A. Apostrophe

B. Allusion

C. Antithesis

D. Anachronism

The answer is B. This rhetorical figure addresses personified things, absent people or gods. An antithesis is a contrast between two opposing viewpoints, ideas, or presentation of characters. An anachronism is the placing of an object or person out of its time with the time of the text. The best known example is the clock in Shakespeare's *Julius Caesar*

26. **A sixth-grade science teacher has given her class a paper to read on the relationship between food and weight gain. The writing contains signal words such as "because," "consequently," "this is how," and "due to." This paper has which text structure?**
(Skill 7.1) (Rigorous)

    A.   Cause & effect
    B.   Compare & contrast
    C.   Description
    D.   Sequencing

The answer is **A**. Cause and effect is the relationship between two things when one thing makes something else happen. Writers use this text structure to show order, inform, speculate, and change behavior. This text structure uses the process of identifying potential causes of a problem or issue in an orderly way. It is often used to teach social studies and science concepts. It is characterized by signal words such as because, so, so that, if... then, consequently, thus, since, for, for this reason, as a result of, therefore, due to, this is how, nevertheless, and accordingly.

27. **A form or discourse which explains or informs is**
(Skill 7.1) (Average)

    A.   Exposition.

    B.   Narration.

    C.   Persuasion.

    D.   Description.

The answer is A. Exposition sets forth a systematic explanation of any subject. It can also introduce the characters of a literary work, and their situations in the story.

28. The following passage is written from which point of view?
(Skill 7.3) (Rigorous)

> As she mused the pitiful vision of her mother's life laid its spell on the very quick of her being –that life of commonplace sacrifices closing in final craziness. She trembled as she heard again her mother's voice saying constantly with foolish insistence: Dearevaun Seraun! Dearevaun Seraun!* * "The end of pleasure is pain!" (Gaelic)

    A. First person, narrator

    B. Second person, direct address

    C. Third person, omniscient

    D. First person, omniscient

The answer is C. The passage is clearly in the third person (the subject is "she"), and it is omniscient since it gives the characters' inner thoughts.

29. Which of the following should not be included in the opening paragraph of an informative essay?
(Skill 7.8) (Average)

    A. Thesis sentence

    B. Details and examples supporting the main idea

    C. broad general introduction to the topic

    D. A style and tone that grabs the reader's attention

The answer is B. The introductory paragraph should introduce the topic, capture the reader's interest, state the thesis and prepare the reader for the main points in the essay. Details and examples, however, should be given in the second part of the essay, so as to help develop the thesis presented at the end of the introductory paragraph, following the inverted triangle method consisting of a broad general statement followed by some information, and then the thesis at the end of the paragraph.

30. Which of the following is not a technique of prewriting? (Skill 7.8) (Average)

    A.   Clustering

    B.   Listing

    C.   Brainstorming

    D.   Proofreading

The answer is D. Proofreading should be reserved for the final draft.

31. Which of the following is not an approach to keep students ever conscious of the need to write for audience appeal? (Skill 7.10 and 7.11) (Rigorous)

    A.   Pairing students during the writing process

    B.   Reading all rough drafts before the Students write the final copies

    C.   Having students compose stories or articles for publication in school literary magazines or newspaper

    D.   Writing letters to friends or relatives

The answer is A. Reading all rough drafts will not encourage the students to take control of their text and might even inhibit their creativity. On the contrary, pairing students will foster their sense of responsibility, and having them compose stories for literary magazines will boost their self esteem as well as their organization skills. As far as writing letters is concerned, the work of authors such as Madame de Sevigne in the seventeenth century is a good example of epistolary literary work.

COMPETENCY 10.0 UNDERSTAND THE STRUCTURE OF NUMBER SYSTEMS, THE DEVELOPMENT OF A SENSE OF QUANTITY, AND THE RELATIONSHIP BETWEEN QUANTITY AND SYMBOLIC REPRESENTATIONS.

Skill 10.1   Analyze the structure of numeration systems and the roles of place value and zero in the base ten system.

Whole Number Place Value

Consider the number 792. We can assign a place value to each digit.

Reading from left to right, the first digit (7) represents the hundreds' place. The hundreds' place tells us how many sets of one hundred the number contains. Thus, there are 7 sets of one hundred in the number 792.

The second digit (9) represents the tens' place. The tens' place tells us how many sets of ten the number contains. Thus, there are 9 sets of ten in the number 792.

The last digit (2) represents the ones' place. The ones' place tells us how many ones the number contains. Thus, there are 2 sets of one in the number 792.

Therefore, there are 7 sets of 100, plus 9 sets of 10, plus 2 ones in the number 792.

Decimal Place Value

More complex numbers have additional place values to both the left and right of the decimal point. Consider the number 374.8.

Reading from left to right, the first digit (3) is in the hundreds' place and tells us the number contains 3 sets of one hundred.

The second digit (7) is in the tens' place and tells us the number contains 7 sets of ten.

The third digit, 4, is in the ones' place and tells us the number contains 4 ones.

Finally, the number after the decimal (8) is in the tenths' place and tells us the number contains 8 tenths.

Place Value for Older Students

Each digit to the left of the decimal point increases progressively in powers of ten. Each digit to the right of the decimal point decreases progressively in powers of ten.

Example: 12345.6789   occupies the following powers of ten positions:

10^4	10^3	10^2	10^1	10^0	0	10^{-1}	10^{-2}	10^{-3}	10^{-4}
1	2	3	4	5	.	6	7	8	9

Names of power-of-ten positions:

10^0 = ones (note that any non-zero base raised to power zero is 1).   *pos exp = whole*

10^1 = tens   (number 1 and 1 zero or 10)

10^2 = hundred   (number 1 and 2 zeros or 100)

10^3 = thousand   (number 1 and 3 zeros or 1000)

10^4 = ten thousand   (number 1 and 4 zeros or 10000)

$10^{-1} = \dfrac{1}{10^1} = \dfrac{1}{10}$ = tenths   (1st digit after decimal point or 0.1)   *neg exp = decimals*

$10^{-2} = \dfrac{1}{10^2} = \dfrac{1}{100}$ = hundredth   (2nd digit after decimal point or 0.01)

$10^{-3} = \dfrac{1}{10^3} = \dfrac{1}{1000}$ = thousandth   (3rd digit after decimal point or 0.001)

$10^{-4} = \dfrac{1}{10^4} = \dfrac{1}{10000}$ = ten thousandth   (4th digit after decimal point or 0.0001)

Example: Write 73169.00537 in expanded form.

We start by listing all the powers of ten positions.

7	3	1	0	9		0	0	5	3	7
10^4	10^3	10^2	10^1	10^0	.	10^{-1}	10^{-2}	10^{-3}	10^{-4}	10^{-5}

Multiply each digit by its power of ten. Add all the results.

Thus $73169.00537 = (7 \times 10^4) + (3 \times 10^3) + (1 \times 10^2) + (6 \times 10^1)$

$$+ (9 \times 10^0) + (0 \times 10^{-1}) + (0 \times 10^{-2}) + (5 \times 10^{-3})$$

$$+ (3 \times 10^{-4}) + (7 \times 10^{-5})$$

Example: Determine the place value associated with the underlined digit in 3.16$\underline{9}$5.

10^0	.	10^{-1}	10^{-2}	10^{-3}	10^{-4}
3	.	1	6	9	5

The place value for the digit 9 is 10^{-3} or $\dfrac{1}{1000}$.

Example: Write 21×10^3 in standard form.

$$= 21\times1000 = 21,000$$

Example: Write 739×10^{-4} in standard form.

$$= 739\times\frac{1}{10000} = \frac{739}{10000} = 0.0739$$

Skill 10.2   Understand the relative magnitude of whole numbers, integers, rational numbers, and real numbers.

Rational numbers can be expressed as the ratio of two integers, $\frac{a}{b}$ where b ≠ 0, for example $\frac{2}{3}$, $-\frac{4}{5}$, $5 = \frac{5}{1}$.

The rational numbers include integers, fractions and mixed numbers, terminating and repeating decimals. Every rational number can be expressed as a repeating or terminating decimal and can be shown on a number line.

Integers are positive and negative whole numbers and zero.
      ...-6, -5, -4, -3, -2, -1, 0, 1, 2, 3, 4, 5, 6, ...

Whole numbers are natural numbers and zero.
      0, 1, 2, 3, ,4 ,5 ,6 ...

Natural numbers are the counting numbers.
      1, 2, 3, 4, 5, 6, ...

Irrational numbers are real numbers that cannot be written as the ratio of two integers. These are infinite non-repeating decimals.

      Examples: $\sqrt{5}$ = 2.2360.., pi =∏ = 3.1415927...

A **fraction** is an expression of numbers in the form of x/y, where **x** is the numerator and **y** is the denominator, which cannot be zero.

Example: $\dfrac{3}{7}$ 3 is the numerator; 7 is the denominator

If the fraction has common factors for the numerator and denominator, divide both by the common factor to reduce the fraction to its lowest form.

Example:

$$\dfrac{13}{39} = \dfrac{1 \times 13}{3 \times 13} = \dfrac{1}{3}$$ Divide by the common factor 13

A **mixed** number has an integer part and a fractional part.

Example: $2\dfrac{1}{4}, \ ^-5\dfrac{1}{6}, \ 7\dfrac{1}{3}$

Percent = per 100 (written with the symbol %). Thus 10% $= \dfrac{10}{100} = \dfrac{1}{10}$.

Decimals = deci = part of ten. To find the decimal equivalent of a fraction, use the denominator to divide the numerator as shown in the following example.

Example: Find the decimal equivalent of $\dfrac{7}{10}$.

Since 10 cannot divide into 7 evenly

$$\dfrac{7}{10} = 0.7$$

The **exponent form** is a shortcut method to write repeated multiplication. Basic form: b^n, where b is called the base and n is the exponent. b and n are both real numbers. b^n implies that the base b is multiplied by itself n times.

Examples: $3^4 = 3 \times 3 \times 3 \times 3 = 81$

$2^3 = 2 \times 2 \times 2 = 8$

$(^-2)^4 = (^-2) \times (^-2) \times (^-2) \times (^-2) = 16$

$^-2^4 = ^-(2 \times 2 \times 2 \times 2) = ^-16$

Key exponent rules:

For '*a*' nonzero, and '*m*' and '*n*' real numbers:

1) $a^m \cdot a^n = a^{(m+n)}$ Product rule

2) $\dfrac{a^m}{a^n} = a^{(m-n)}$ Quotient rule

3) $\dfrac{a^{-m}}{a^{-n}} = \dfrac{a^n}{a^m}$

When 10 is raised to any power, the exponent tells the numbers of zeroes in the product.

Example: $10^7 = 10,000,000$

Caution: Unless the negative sign is inside the parentheses and the exponent is outside the parentheses, the sign is not affected by the exponent.

$(^-2)^4$ implies that -2 is multiplied by itself 4 times.

$^-2^4$ implies that 2 is multiplied by itself 4 times, then the answer is negated.

Scientific notation is a more convenient method for writing very large and very small numbers. It employs two factors. The first factor is a number between 1 and 10. The second factor is a power of 10. This notation is a "shorthand" for expressing large numbers (like the weight of 100 elephants) or small numbers (like the weight of an atom in pounds).

Recall that:

$10^n = (10)^n$ Ten multiplied by itself *n* times.

$10^0 = 1$ Any nonzero number raised to power of zero is 1.
$10^1 = 10$
$10^2 = 10 \times 10 = 100$
$10^3 = 10 \times 10 \times 10 = 1000$ (kilo)
$10^{-1} = 1/10$ (deci)
$10^{-2} = 1/100$ (centi)
$10^{-3} = 1/1000$ (milli)
$10^{-6} = 1/1,000,000$ (micro)

Example: Write 46,368,000 in scientific notation.

1)   Introduce a decimal point and decimal places.
46,368,000 = 46,368,000.0000

2)   Make a mark between the two digits that give a number between -9.9 and 9.9.
4 ∧ 6,368,000 .0000

3)   Count the number of digit places between the decimal point and the ∧ mark. This number is the 'n'-the power of ten.

So, $46,368,000 = 4.6368 \times 10^{7}$

Example: Write 0.00397 in scientific notation.

1)   Decimal place is already in place.

2)   Make a mark between 3 and 9 to get a one number between -9.9 and 9.9.

3)   Move decimal place to the mark (3 hops).

0.003 ∧ 97

Motion is to the right, so n of 10^{n} is negative.

Therefore, $0.00397 = 3.97 \times 10^{-3}$.

Skill 10.3 **Demonstrate an understanding of a variety of models for representing numbers (e.g., fraction strips, diagrams, patterns, shaded regions, number lines).**

MANIPULATIVES

Example: Using tiles to demonstrate both geometric ideas and number theory.

Give each group of students 12 tiles and instruct them to build rectangles. Students draw their rectangles on paper.

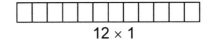
12 × 1

1 × 12

3 × 4

4 × 3

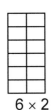
6 × 2

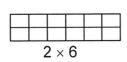
2 × 6

Encourage students to describe their reactions. Extend to 16 tiles. Ask students to form additional problems.

The shaded region represents 47 out of 100 or 0.47 or $\frac{47}{100}$ or 47%.

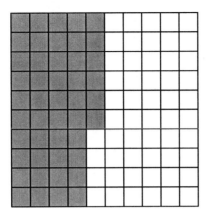

Fraction Strips:

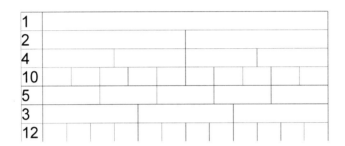

Number Lines:

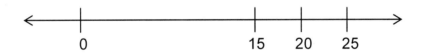

Diagrams:

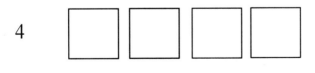

Skill 10.4   Demonstrate an understanding of equivalency among different representations of rational numbers.

See Skill 10.1.

Skill 10.5   Select appropriate representations of real numbers (e.g., fractions, decimals, percents, roots, exponents, scientific notation) for particular situations.

Fractions are used to represent smaller portions of a larger quantity. They are often used in measuring physical quantities and in dividing whole quantities into equal parts.

Examples of situations where fractions are appropriate are:

Cooks measuring for recipes: 1/2 of a cup of flour
Carpenters measuring boards: 2 ¾" x 4 ¼" x 36 ¼"
Architects creating models and drafts of rooms and structures: drawn to ¼ scale
Builders apportioning land into lots: ¾ acre for each lot
Serving foods such as pizza or pie: each person will get 1/8 of the pie

Decimals are based on the number 10 and are used to represent quantities between 0 and 1. Sometimes, they are more appropriate than fractions.

Examples of situations where decimals are appropriate are:

Using the metric system
Expressing U.S. money
Taking body temperatures
Measuring distances, time, and gasoline mileage

Percent is used to denote how large one quantity is in relation to another.

Examples of situations where percents are appropriate:

Commissions
Discounts
Taxes
Tips
Interest on credit cards, loans, investments
Sales mark-up
Nutrition (RDA)
Sports statistics
Portions of populations for statistical purposes

Roots and **exponents** are frequently used in finance and science.

Examples of situations where roots and exponents are used:

Amortization of loans
Describing acid rain, measuring pH
Earthquakes (Richter scale)
The decibel level of sound
Brightness of stars

Scientific notation uses exponents to express very large numbers easily.

Example: $3,725,000,000,000 = 3.725 \times 10^{12}$

Skill 10.6   Understand the characteristics of the set of whole numbers, integers, rational numbers, real numbers, and complex numbers (e.g., commutativity, order, closure, identity elements, inverse elements, density).

Properties are rules that apply for addition, subtraction, multiplication, or division of real numbers. These properties are:

Commutative: You can change the order of the terms or factors as follows.

For addition: $a + b = b + a$
For multiplication: $ab = ba$

Since addition is the inverse operation of subtraction and multiplication is the inverse operation of division, no separate laws are needed for subtraction and division.

<u>Example</u>: $5 + {}^-8 = {}^-8 + 5 = {}^-3$

<u>Example</u>: ${}^-2 \times 6 = 6 \times {}^-2 = {}^-12$

Associative: You can regroup the terms as you like.

For addition: $a + (b + c) = (a + b) + c$
For multiplication: $a(bc) = (ab)c$

This rule does not apply for division and subtraction.

<u>Example</u>: $({}^-2 + 7) + 5 = {}^-2 + (7 + 5)$
                        $5 + 5 = {}^-2 + 12 = 10$

<u>Example</u>: $(3 \times {}^-7) \times 5 = 3 \times ({}^-7 \times 5)$
                        ${}^-21 \times 5 = 3 \times {}^-35 = {}^-105$

Identity: Finding a number so that when added to a term results in that number (additive identity); finding a number such that when multiplied by a term results in that number (multiplicative identity).

For addition: $a + 0 = a$ (zero is additive identity)
For multiplication: $a \cdot 1 = a$ (one is multiplicative)

Example: $17 + 0 = 17$

Example: $^-34 \times 1 = {^-}34$
The product of any number and one is that number.

Inverse: Finding a number such that when added to the number it results in zero; or when multiplied by the number results in 1.

For addition: $a + (-a) = 0$
For multiplication: $a \cdot (1/a) = 1$

$(-a)$ is the additive inverse of a; $(1/a)$, also called the reciprocal, is the multiplicative inverse of a.

Example: $25 + {^-}25 = 0$

Example: $5 \times \frac{1}{5} = 1$ The product of any number and its reciprocal is one.

Distributive: This technique allows us to operate on terms within a parentheses without first performing operations within the parentheses. This is especially helpful when terms within the parentheses cannot be combined.

$a (b + c) = ab + ac$

Example: $6 \times ({^-}4 + 9) = (6 \times {^-}4) + (6 \times 9)$
                $6 \times 5 = {^-}24 + 54 = 30$

To multiply a sum by a number, multiply each addend by the number, then add the products.

Complex numbers can be written in the form $a + bi$ where i represents $\sqrt{-1}$ and a and b are real numbers. a is the real part of the complex number and b is the imaginary part.

If $b = 0$, then the number has no imaginary part and it is a real number.

If $b \neq 0$, then the number is imaginary.

Complex numbers are found when trying to solve equations with negative square roots.

Example: If $x^2 + 9 = 0$
then $x^2 = -9$
and $x = \sqrt{-9}$ or +3i and -3i

When dividing 2 complex numbers, you must eliminate the complex number in the denominator. If the complex number in the denominator is of the form $b\,i$, multiply both the numerator and denominator by **i**. Remember to replace i^2 with $a = -1$ and then continue simplifying the fraction.

Example:

$$\frac{2+3i}{5i} \qquad \text{Multiply this by } \frac{i}{i}$$

$$\frac{2+3i}{5i} \times \frac{i}{i} = \frac{(2+3i)\,i}{5i \cdot i} = \frac{2i+3i^2}{5i^2} = \frac{2i+3(^-1)}{^-5} = \frac{^-3+2i}{^-5} = \frac{3-2i}{5}$$

If the complex number in the denominator is of the form $a + b\,i$, multiply both the numerator and denominator by **the conjugate of the denominator. The conjugate of the denominator** is the same 2 terms with the opposite sign between the 2 terms (the real term does not change signs). The conjugate of 2 – 3i is 2 + 3i. The conjugate of –6 + 11i is –6 – 11i. Multiply together the factors on the top and bottom of the fraction. Remember to replace i^2 with $a = -1$, combine like terms, and then continue simplifying the fraction.

Example:

$$\frac{4+7i}{6-5i} \qquad \text{Multiply by } \frac{6+5i}{6+5i} \text{, the conjugate.}$$

$$\frac{(4+7i)}{(6-5i)} \times \frac{(6+5i)}{(6+5i)} = \frac{24+20i+42i+35i^2}{36+30i-30i-25i^2} = \frac{24+62i+35(^-1)}{36-25(^-1)} = \frac{^-11+62i}{61}$$

Example:

$$\frac{24}{^-3-5i} \qquad \text{Multiply by } \frac{^-3+5i}{^-3+5i} \text{, the conjugate.}$$

$$\frac{24}{^-3-5i} \times \frac{^-3+5i}{^-3+5i} = \frac{^-72+120i}{9-25i^2} = \frac{^-72+120i}{9+25} = \frac{^-72+120i}{34} = \frac{^-36+60i}{17}$$

Divided everything by 2.

Skill 10.7 **Demonstrates an understanding of how some situations that have no solution in one number system (e.g., whole numbers, integers, rational numbers) have solutions in another number system (e.g., real numbers, complex numbers)**

See Skills 10.6, 11.1 and 15.1

COMPETENCY 11.0 UNDERSTAND NUMBER OPERATIONS AND COMPUTATIONAL ALGORITHMS.

Skill 11.1 **Work proficiently with real and complex numbers and their operations.**

Addition of whole numbers

Example: At the end of a day of shopping, a shopper had $24 remaining in his wallet. He spent $45 on various goods. How much money did the shopper have at the beginning of the day?

The total amount of money the shopper started with is the sum of the amount spent and the amount remaining at the end of the day.

$$\begin{array}{r} 24 \\ +\ 45 \\ \hline 69 \end{array}$$ ⟶ The original total was $69.

Example: A race took the winner 1 hr. 58 min. 12 sec. on the first half of the race and 2 hr. 9 min. 57 sec. on the second half of the race. How much time did the entire race take?

$$\begin{array}{l} \quad 1 \text{ hr. } 58 \text{ min. } 12 \text{ sec.} \\ +\ 2 \text{ hr. } \ 9 \text{ min. } 57 \text{ sec.} \\ \hline \quad 3 \text{ hr. } 67 \text{ min. } 69 \text{ sec.} \end{array}$$ Add these numbers

$$+\ 1 \text{ min } {-}60 \text{ sec.}$$ Change 60 seconds to 1 min.

$$\begin{array}{l} \quad 3 \text{ hr. } 68 \text{ min. } \ 9 \text{ sec.} \\ +\ 1 \text{ hr.} {-}60 \text{ min.} \end{array}$$ Change 60 minutes to 1 hr.

$$\begin{array}{l} \hline 4 \text{ hr. } \ 8 \text{ min. } \ 9 \text{ sec.} \end{array}$$ ←final answer

Subtraction of Whole Numbers

Example: At the end of his shift, a cashier has $96 in the cash register. At the beginning of his shift, he had $15. How much money did the cashier collect during his shift?

The total collected is the difference of the ending amount and the starting amount.

$$\begin{array}{r} 96 \\ -\ 15 \\ \hline 81 \end{array}$$ ⟶ The total collected was $81.

Multiplication of whole numbers

Multiplication is one of the four basic number operations. In simple terms, multiplication is the addition of a number to itself a certain number of times. For example, 4 multiplied by 3 is the equal to 4 + 4 + 4 or 3 + 3 + 3 +3. Another way of conceptualizing multiplication is to think in terms of groups. For example, if we have 4 groups of 3 students, the total number of students is 4 multiplied by 3. We call the solution to a multiplication problem the product.

The basic algorithm for whole number multiplication begins with aligning the numbers by place value with the number containing more places on top.

$$\begin{array}{r} 172 \\ \times\ \ 43 \end{array}$$ → Note that we placed 122 on top because it has more places than 43 does.

Next, we multiply the ones' place of the second number by each place value of the top number sequentially.

$$\begin{array}{r} (2) \\ 172 \\ \times\ \ 43 \\ \hline 516 \end{array}$$ → {3 x 2 = 6, 3 x 7 = 21, 3 x 1 = 3}
Note that we had to carry a 2 to the hundreds' column because 3 x 7 = 21. Note also that we add, not multiply, carried numbers to the product.

Next, we multiply the number in the tens' place of the second number by each place value of the top number sequentially. Because we are multiplying by a number in the tens' place, we place a zero at the end of this product.

$$\begin{array}{r} (2) \\ 172 \\ \times\ \ 43 \\ \hline 516 \\ 6880 \end{array}$$ → {4 x 2 = 8, 4 x 7 = 28, 4 x 1 = 4}

Finally, to determine the final product we add the two partial products.

$$\begin{array}{r} 172 \\ \times\ \ 43 \\ \hline 516 \\ +\ 6880 \\ \hline 7396 \end{array}$$ → The product of 172 and 43 is 7396.

Example: A student buys 4 boxes of crayons. Each box contains 16 crayons. How many total crayons does the student have?

The total number of crayons is 16 x 4.

$$\begin{array}{r} 16 \\ \times\ 4 \\ \hline 64 \end{array}$$ → Total number of crayons equals 64.

Division of whole numbers

Division, the inverse of multiplication, is another of the four basic number operations. When we divide one number by another, we determine how many times we can multiply the divisor (number divided by) before we exceed the number we are dividing (dividend). For example, 8 divided by 2 equals 4 because we can multiply 2 four times to reach 8 (2 x 4 = 8 or 2 + 2 + 2 + 2 = 8). Using the grouping conceptualization we used with multiplication, we can divide 8 into 4 groups of 2 or 2 groups of 4. We call the answer to a division problem the quotient.

If the divisor does not divide evenly into the dividend, we express the leftover amount either as a remainder or as a fraction with the divisor as the denominator. For example, 9 divided by 2 equals 4 with a remainder of 1 or 4 ½.

The basic algorithm for division is long division. We start by representing the quotient as follows.

$14\overline{)293}$ → 14 is the divisor and 293 is the dividend.
This represents 293 ÷ 14.

Next, we divide the divisor into the dividend starting from the left.

$14\overline{)293}^{\,2}$ → 14 divides into 29 two times with a remainder.

Next, we multiply the partial quotient by the divisor, subtract this value from the first digits of the dividend, and bring down the remaining dividend digits to complete the number.

$$\begin{array}{r} 2 \\ 14\overline{)293} \\ -28 \\ \hline 13 \end{array}$$ → 2 x 14 = 28, 29 – 28 = 1, and bringing down the 3 yields 13.

Finally, we divide again (the divisor into the remaining value) and repeat the preceding process. The number left after the subtraction represents the remainder.

$$
\begin{array}{r}
20 \\
14\overline{)293} \\
-28 \\
\hline
13 \\
-0 \\
\hline
13 \\
\end{array}
$$

→ The final quotient is 20 with a remainder of 13. We can also represent this quotient as 20 13/14.

Example: Each box of apples contains 24 apples. How many boxes must a grocer purchase to supply a group of 252 people with one apple each?

The grocer needs 252 apples. Because he must buy apples in groups of 24, we divide 252 by 24 to determine how many boxes he needs to buy.

$$
\begin{array}{r}
10 \\
24\overline{)252} \\
-24 \\
\hline
12 \\
-0 \\
\hline
12 \\
\end{array}
$$

→ The quotient is 10 with a remainder of 12.

Thus, the grocer needs 10 boxes plus 12 more apples. Therefore, the minimum number of boxes the grocer can purchase is 11.

Example: At his job, John gets paid $20 for every hour he works. If John made $940 in a week, how many hours did he work?

This is a division problem. To determine the number of hours John worked, we divide the total amount made ($940) by the hourly rate of pay ($20). Thus, the number of hours worked equals 940 divided by 20.

$$
\begin{array}{r}
47 \\
20\overline{)940} \\
-80 \\
\hline
140 \\
-140 \\
\hline
0 \\
\end{array}
$$

→ 20 divides into 940, 47 times with no remainder.

John worked 47 hours.

Addition and Subtraction of Decimals

When adding and subtracting decimals, we align the numbers by place value as we do with whole numbers. After adding or subtracting each column, we bring the decimal down, placing it in the same location as in the numbers added or subtracted.

Example: Find the sum of 152.3 and 36.342.

$$\begin{array}{r} 152.300 \\ +\quad 36.342 \\ \hline 188.642 \end{array}$$

Note that we placed two zeroes after the final place value in 152.3 to clarify the column addition.

Example: Find the difference of 152.3 and 36.342.

$$\begin{array}{r} 2\ 9\ 10 \\ 152.300 \\ -\quad 36.342 \\ \hline 58 \end{array} \longrightarrow \begin{array}{r} (4)11(12) \\ 152.300 \\ -\quad 36.342 \\ \hline 115.958 \end{array}$$

Note how we borrowed to subtract from the zeroes in the hundredths' and thousandths' place of 152.300.

Multiplication of Decimals

When multiplying decimal numbers, we multiply exactly as with whole numbers and place the decimal moving in from the left the total number of decimal places contained in the two numbers multiplied. For example, when multiplying 1.5 and 2.35, we place the decimal in the product 3 places in from the left (3.525).

Example: Find the product of 3.52 and 4.1.

$$\begin{array}{r} 3.52 \\ \times\quad 4.1 \\ \hline 352 \\ +\ 14080 \\ \hline 14432 \end{array}$$

→ Note that there are 3 total decimal places in the two numbers.

→ We place the decimal 3 places in from the left.

Thus, the final product is 14.432.

Example: A shopper has 5 one-dollar bills, 6 quarters, 3 nickels, and 4
            pennies in his pocket. How much money does he have?

                                3
    5 x $1.00 = $5.00 $0.25 $0.05 $0.01
                          x   6   x   3   x   4
                          $1.50 $0.15 $0.04

Note the placement of the decimals in the multiplication products.
Thus, the total amount of money in the shopper's pocket is:

                    $5.00
                     1.50
                     0.15
                  + 0.04
                    $6.69

Division of Decimals

When dividing decimal numbers, we first remove the decimal in the divisor by
moving the decimal in the dividend the same number of spaces to the right. For
example, when dividing 1.45 into 5.3 we convert the numbers to 145 and 530
and perform normal whole number division.

Example: Find the quotient of 5.3 divided by 1.45.
            Convert to 145 and 530.

    Divide.

$$
\begin{array}{r} 3 \\ 145\overline{)530} \end{array}
\quad\longrightarrow\quad
\begin{array}{r} 3.65 \\ 145\overline{)530.00} \end{array}
\quad\longrightarrow\quad
$$
Note that we insert
the decimal to continue
division.

$$
\begin{array}{r} -435 \\ \hline 95 \end{array}
\qquad
\begin{array}{r} -435 \\ \hline 950 \\ -870 \\ \hline 800 \end{array}
$$

Because one of the numbers divided contained one decimal place,
we round the quotient to one decimal place. Thus, the final quotient
is 3.7.

Operating with Percents

Example: 5 is what percent of 20?

            This is the same as converting $\dfrac{5}{20}$ to % form.

            $\dfrac{5}{20} \times \dfrac{100}{1} = \dfrac{5}{1} \times \dfrac{5}{1} = 25\%$

Example: There are 64 dogs in the kennel. 48 are collies. What percent are collies?

Restate the problem.   48 is what percent of 64?
Write an equation. $48 = n \times 64$
Solve. $\frac{48}{64} = n$

$n = \frac{3}{4} = 75\%$

75% of the dogs are collies.

Example: The auditorium was filled to 90% capacity. There were 558 seats occupied. What is the capacity of the auditorium?

Restate the problem.   90% of what number is 558?
Write an equation. $0.9n = 558$
Solve. $n = \frac{558}{.9}$
                         $n = 620$

The capacity of the auditorium is 620 people.

Example: A pair of shoes costs $42.00. Sales tax is 6%. What is the total cost of the shoes?

Restate the problem.   What is 6% of 42?
Write an equation. $n = 0.06 \times 42$
Solve. $n = 2.52$

Add the sales tax to the cost. $42.00 + $2.52 = $44.52

The total cost of the shoes, including sales tax, is $44.52.

Addition and subtraction of fractions

Key Points

1.   You need a common denominator in order to add and subtract reduced and improper fractions.

Example: $\frac{1}{3} + \frac{7}{3} = \frac{1+7}{3} = \frac{8}{3} = 2\frac{2}{3}$

Example: $\frac{4}{12} + \frac{6}{12} - \frac{3}{12} = \frac{4+6-3}{12} = \frac{7}{12}$

2. Adding an integer and a fraction of the <u>same</u> sign results directly in a mixed fraction.

Example: $2 + \dfrac{2}{3} = 2\dfrac{2}{3}$

Example: $^-2 - \dfrac{3}{4} = ^-2\dfrac{3}{4}$

3. Adding an integer and a fraction with different signs involves the following steps.

-get a common denominator
-add or subtract as needed
-change to a mixed fraction if possible

Example: $2 - \dfrac{1}{3} = \dfrac{2 \times 3 - 1}{3} = \dfrac{6 - 1}{3} = \dfrac{5}{3} = 1\dfrac{2}{3}$

Example: Add $7\dfrac{3}{8} + 5\dfrac{2}{7}$

Add the whole numbers; add the fractions and combine the two results:

$$7\dfrac{3}{8} + 5\dfrac{2}{7} = (7 + 5) + (\dfrac{3}{8} + \dfrac{2}{7})$$

$$= 12 + \dfrac{(7 \times 3) + (8 \times 2)}{56} \quad \text{(LCM of 8 and 7)}$$

$$= 12 + \dfrac{21 + 16}{56} = 12 + \dfrac{37}{56} = 12\dfrac{37}{56}$$

Example: Perform the operation.

$$\dfrac{2}{3} - \dfrac{5}{6}$$

We first find the LCM of 3 and 6 which is 6.

$$\dfrac{2 \times 2}{3 \times 2} - \dfrac{5}{6} \rightarrow \dfrac{4 - 5}{6} = \dfrac{^-1}{6} \quad \text{(Using method A)}$$

Example: $^-7\dfrac{1}{4}+2\dfrac{7}{8}$

$$^-7\dfrac{1}{4}+2\dfrac{7}{8}=(^-7+2)+(\dfrac{^-1}{4}+\dfrac{7}{8})$$

$$=(^-5)+\dfrac{(^-2+7)}{8}=(^-5)+(\dfrac{5}{8})$$

$$=(^-5)+\dfrac{5}{8}=\dfrac{^-5\times8}{1\times8}+\dfrac{5}{8}=\dfrac{^-40+5}{8}$$

$$=\dfrac{^-35}{8}=^-4\dfrac{3}{8}$$

Divide 35 by 8 to get 4, remainder 3.

Caution: Common error would be

$$^-7\dfrac{1}{4}+2\dfrac{7}{8}=^-7\dfrac{2}{8}+2\dfrac{7}{8}=^-5\dfrac{9}{8}$$ Wrong.

It is correct to add -7 and 2 to get -5, but adding $\dfrac{2}{8}+\dfrac{7}{8}=\dfrac{9}{8}$

is wrong. It should have been $\dfrac{^-2}{8}+\dfrac{7}{8}=\dfrac{5}{8}$. Then,

$$^-5+\dfrac{5}{8}=^-4\dfrac{3}{8}$$ as before.

Multiplication of fractions

Using the following example: $3\dfrac{1}{4}\times\dfrac{5}{6}$

1. Convert each number to an improper fraction.

$3\dfrac{1}{4}=\dfrac{(12+1)}{4}=\dfrac{13}{4}$ $\dfrac{5}{6}$ is already in reduced form.

2. Reduce (cancel) common factors of the numerator and denominator if they exist.

$\dfrac{13}{4}\times\dfrac{5}{6}$ No common factors exist.

3. Multiply the numerators by each other and the denominators by each other.

$$\frac{13}{4} \times \frac{5}{6} = \frac{65}{24}$$

4. If possible, reduce the fraction back to its lowest term.

$\frac{65}{24}$ Cannot be reduced further.

5. Convert the improper fraction back to a mixed fraction by using long division.

$$\frac{65}{24} = 24\overline{)65} \qquad = 2\frac{17}{24}$$
$$\underline{48}$$
$$17$$

Summary of sign changes for multiplication:

a. $(+) \times (+) = (+)$

b. $(-) \times (+) = (-)$

c. $(+) \times (-) = (-)$

d. $(-) \times (-) = (+)$

Example: $\quad 7\frac{1}{3} \times \frac{5}{11} = \frac{22}{3} \times \frac{5}{11}$ Reduce like terms (22 and 11)

$$= \frac{2}{3} \times \frac{5}{1} = \frac{10}{3} = 3\frac{1}{3}$$

Example: $\quad {}^-6\frac{1}{4} \times \frac{5}{9} = \frac{{}^-25}{4} \times \frac{5}{9}$

$$= \frac{{}^-125}{36} = {}^-3\frac{17}{36}$$

Example: $\quad \frac{{}^-1}{4} \times \frac{{}^-3}{7}$ Negative times a negative equals positive.

$$= \frac{1}{4} \times \frac{3}{7} = \frac{3}{28}$$

Division of fractions:

1. Change mixed fractions to improper fraction.

2. Change the division problem to a multiplication problem by using the reciprocal of the number after the division sign.
3. Find the sign of the final product.

4. Cancel if common factors exist between the numerator and the denominator.

5. Multiply the numerators together and the denominators together.

6. Change the improper fraction to a mixed number.

Example: $3\dfrac{1}{5} \div 2\dfrac{1}{4} = \dfrac{16}{5} \div \dfrac{9}{4}$

$= \dfrac{16}{5} \times \dfrac{4}{9}$ Reciprocal of $\dfrac{9}{4}$ is $\dfrac{4}{9}$.

$= \dfrac{64}{45} = 1\dfrac{19}{45}$

Example: $7\dfrac{3}{4} \div 11\dfrac{5}{8} = \dfrac{31}{4} \div \dfrac{93}{8}$

$= \dfrac{31}{4} \times \dfrac{8}{93}$ Reduce like terms.

$= \dfrac{1}{1} \times \dfrac{2}{3} = \dfrac{2}{3}$

Example: $\left(-2\dfrac{1}{2}\right) \div 4\dfrac{1}{6} = \dfrac{^-5}{2} \div \dfrac{25}{6}$

$= \dfrac{^-5}{2} \times \dfrac{6}{25}$ Reduce like terms.

$= \dfrac{^-1}{1} \times \dfrac{3}{5} = \dfrac{^-3}{5}$

Example:　　$\left(-5\dfrac{3}{8}\right)\div\left(\dfrac{-7}{16}\right)=\dfrac{-43}{8}\div\dfrac{-7}{16}$

$=\dfrac{-43}{8}\times\dfrac{-16}{7}$　　　　Reduce like terms.

$=\dfrac{43}{1}\times\dfrac{2}{7}$　　　　Negative times a negative equals a positive.

$=\dfrac{86}{7}=12\dfrac{2}{7}$

Converting decimals, fractions and percents

A **decimal** can be converted to a **percent** by multiplying by 100, or merely moving the decimal point two places to the right. A **percent** can be converted to a **decimal** by dividing by 100, or moving the decimal point two places to the left.

Examples:　0.375 = 37.5%
0.7 = 70%
0.04 =　4 %
3.15 = 315 %
84% = 0.84
3 % = 0.03
60% = 0.6
110% = 1.1
$\frac{1}{2}$ % = 0.5% = 0.005

A **percent** can be converted to a **fraction** by placing it over 100 and reducing to simplest terms.

Example:　　Convert 0.056 to a fraction.

Multiplying 0.056 by $\dfrac{1000}{1000}$ to get rid of the decimal point:

$$0.056\times\dfrac{1000}{1000}=\dfrac{56}{1000}=\dfrac{7}{125}$$

Example:　　Find 23% of 1000.

$$=\dfrac{23}{100}\times\dfrac{1000}{1}=23\times10=230$$

Example: Convert 6.25% to a decimal and to a fraction.

$$6.25\% = 0.0625 = 0.0625 \times \frac{10000}{10000} = \frac{625}{10000} = \frac{1}{16}$$

An example of a type of problem involving fractions is the conversion of recipes. For example, if a recipe serves 8 people and we want to make enough to serve only 4, we must determine how much of each ingredient to use. The conversion factor, the number we multiply each ingredient by, is:

$$\text{Conversion Factor} = \frac{\text{Number of Servings Needed}}{\text{Number of Servings in Recipe}}$$

Example: Consider the following recipe.

3 cups flour
½ tsp. baking powder
2/3 cups butter
2 cups sugar
2 eggs

If the above recipe serves 8, how much of each ingredient do we need to serve only 4 people?

First, determine the conversion factor.

$$\text{Conversion Factor} = \frac{4}{8} = \frac{1}{2}$$

Next, multiply each ingredient by the conversion factor.

3 x ½ =   1 ½ cups flour
½ x ½ =   ¼ tsp. baking powder
2/3 x ½ = 2/6 =   1/3 cups butter
2 x ½ =   1 cup sugar
2 x ½ =   1 egg

Skill 11.2   Analyze and describe relationships between number properties, operations, and algorithms for the four basic operations involving integers, rational numbers, and real numbers.

Algorithms are methods or strategies for solving problems. There are several different algorithms for solving addition, subtraction, multiplication and division problems involving integers, rational numbers and real numbers.

In general, algorithms make use of number properties to simplify mathematical operations.

Integer algorithms

Addition

Three common algorithms for addition of integers are the partial sums method, column addition method and fast method. The partial sums method is a two-stage process. First, we sum the columns from left to right. To complete the operation we add the column values.

```
        125
      +  89
      + 376     Step 1 – column addition
        400
      + 170
      +  20     Step 2 – final sum
        590
```

The column addition method is also a two-stage process. First, we add the digits in each column. To complete the operation we perform the place carries from right to left.

```
      1 |  2|  5
    + |   8|  9     Stage 1 – column addition
    + 3|  7|  6
      4| 17| 20
      4| 19|  0          ←──────  First carry
      5|  9|  0 = 590    ←──────  Second carry = final answer
```

The fast method of addition is the traditional method of right to left addition. We sum the columns from left to right, performing carries mentally or writing them down.

```
        12   ←──  Carries
        125
      +  89
      + 376
        590
```

All of the integer addition algorithms rely on the commutative and associative properties of addition, allowing re-grouping and re-ordering of numbers.

Subtraction

Three common algorithms of integer subtraction are left to right subtraction, partial differences and the same change rule. In left to right subtraction, we decompose the second number into smaller values and perform the individual subtractions. For example, to solve 335 – 78, we break 78 down into 70 + 8.

```
  335
-  70
  265
-   8
  257
```

The partial differences method is a two-stage process. First, we operate on each column individually, being careful to record the sign of each result. Then, we sum the results to yield the final answer.

```
  335
-  78
+300
- 40
-  3
  257
```

The same change rule takes advantage of the knowledge that subtraction is easier if the smaller number ends in zero. Thus, we change each number by the same amount to produce a smaller number ending in zero.

```
  335  →  333
-  78  → - 80
          257
```

Like the addition algorithms, the subtraction algorithms rely on the commutative and associative properties of addition (because subtraction is addition of a negative number).

Multiplication

Two common multiplication algorithms are the partial products method and the short method. In the partial products method, we decompose each term into base-ten forms and multiply each pair of terms.

```
        84
      x 26

80 x 20  →   1600
80 x 6   →    480
20 x 4   →     80
6 x 4    →     24
             2184
```

The short method is a traditional multiplication algorithm. In the short method, we only decompose the second term.

$$
\begin{array}{r}
84 \\
\times\ 26 \\
\hline
\end{array}
$$

84 x 20 → 1680
84 x 6 → 504
2184

The multiplication algorithms rely on the associative and commutative properties of multiplication and the distribution of multiplication over addition.

Division

A common division algorithm is the partial quotients method. In this method, we make note of two, simple products and estimate our way toward a final answer. For example, to find the quotient of 1440 divided by 18 we first make note that 5 x 18 = 90 and 2 x 18 = 32.

```
18)  1440 |
    - 900 | 50
      540 |
    - 360 | 20
      180 |
    -  90 | 5
       90 |
    -  90 | 5
        0   80  ——→ final quotient = 80 with no remainder
```

Rational and real number algorithms

Operations involving rational numbers represented as fractions require unique algorithms. For example, when adding or subtracting fractions we use the distributive property of multiplication over division to find common denominators.

When completing operations involving real numbers in decimal form we use similar algorithms to those used with integers. We use the associative, commutative and distributive properties of numbers to generate algorithms.

Skill 11.3 Use a variety of concrete and visual representations to demonstrate the connections between operations and algorithms.

Concrete and visual representations can help demonstrate the logic behind operational algorithms. Blocks or other objects modeled on the base ten system are useful concrete tools. Base ten blocks represent ones, tens and hundreds. For example, modeling the partial sums algorithm with base ten blocks helps clarify the thought process. Consider the sum of 242 and 193. We represent 242 with two one hundred blocks, four ten blocks and 2 one blocks. We represent 193 with one one hundred block, nine ten blocks and 3 one blocks. In the partial sums algorithm, we manipulate each place value separately and total the results. Thus, we group the hundred blocks, ten blocks and one blocks and derive a total for each place value. We combine the place values to complete the sum.

An example of a visual representation of an operational algorithm is the modeling of a two-term multiplication as the area of a rectangle. For example, consider the product of 24 and 39. We can represent the product in geometric form. Note that the four sections of the rectangle equate to the four products of the partial products method.

	30	9
20	A = 600	A = 180
4	A = 120	A = 36

Thus, the final product is the sum of the areas or 600 + 180 + 120 + 36 = 936.

Skill 11.4   Justify procedures used in algorithms for the four basic operations with integers, rational numbers, and real numbers, and analyze error patterns that may occur in their application.

Teachers must justify the procedures used in operational algorithms to ensure student understanding. Algorithms of the basic operations make use of number properties to simplify addition, subtraction, multiplication and division. The following are examples of operational algorithms, their justifications and common errors in implementation.

Addition

The partial sums method of integer addition relies on the associative property of addition. Consider the partial sum algorithm of the addition of 125 and 89. We first sum the columns from left to right and then add the results.

```
    125
  +  89
    100  →  Hundreds column sum
  + 100  →  Tens column sum
  +  14  →  Ones column sum
    214
```

The associative property of addition shows why this method works. We can rewrite 125 plus 89 as follows:

$(100 + 20 + 5) + (80 + 9)$

Using the associative property to group the terms:

$(100) + (20 + 80) + (5 + 9) = 100 + 100 + 14 = 214$

Note the final form is the same as the second step of the partial sums algorithm. When evaluating addition by partial sums, teachers should look for errors in assigning place values of the partial sums; for example, in the problem above, recording the sum of eight and two in the tens column as 10 instead of 100.

Rational number addition relies on the distributive property of multiplication over addition and the understanding that multiplication by any number by one yields the same number. Consider the addition of 1/4 to 1/3 by means of common denominator.

$$\frac{1}{4} + \frac{1}{3} = \frac{3}{3}(\frac{1}{4}) + \frac{4}{4}(\frac{1}{3}) = (\frac{3}{12}) + (\frac{4}{12}) = \frac{7}{12}$$ ⟶ Recognize that $\frac{3}{3}$ and $\frac{4}{4}$ both equal 1.

A common error in rational number addition is the failure to find a common denominator and adding both numerators and denominators.

Subtraction

The same change rule of substitution takes advantage of the property of addition of zero. The addition of zero does not change the value of a quantity.

$289 - 97 = 292 - 100$ because
$289 - 97 = (289 + 3) - (97 + 3) = (289 - 97) + (3 - 3) = 289 - 97 + 0$

Note the use of the distributive property of multiplication over addition, the associative property of addition and the property of addition of zero in proving the accuracy of the same change algorithm. A common mistake when using the same change rule is adding from one number and subtracting from the other. This is an error in reasoning resulting from misapplication of the distributive property (e.g. failing to distribute -1).

The same procedure, justification and error pattern applies to the subtraction of rational and real numbers.

$$13 - 2\frac{1}{3} = 13\frac{2}{3} - 3 \text{ because}$$

$$13 - 2\frac{1}{3} = (13 + \frac{2}{3}) - (2\frac{1}{3} + \frac{2}{3}) = (13 - 2\frac{1}{3}) + (\frac{2}{3} - \frac{2}{3}) = 13 - 2\frac{1}{3} + 0$$

or

$13 - 2.456 = 13.544 - 3$ because
$13 - 2.456 = (13 + 0.544) - (2.456 + 0.544) = (13 - 2.456) + (0.544 - 0.544) = 13 - 2.456 + 0$

Multiplication

The partial products algorithm of multiplication decomposes each term into simpler numbers and sums the products of the simpler terms.

$$84 = 80 + 4$$
$$\underline{\times\ 26} = 20 + 6$$

80 x 20 ➤	1600
80 x 6 ➤	480
20 x 4 ➤	80
6 x 4 ➤	24
	2184

We can justify this algorithm by using the "FOIL" method of binomial multiplication and the distributive property of multiplication over addition.

$$(80 + 4)(20 + 6) = (80)(20) + (4)(20) + (6)(80) + (6)(4)$$

Common errors in partial product multiplication result from mistakes in binomial multiplication and mistakes in pairing terms of the partial products (e.g. multiplying incorrect terms).

Division

We can justify the partial quotients algorithm for division by using the distributive property of multiplication over division. Because multiplication is the reverse of division, we check the result by multiplying the divisor by the partial sums.

```
18)   1440 |
    -  900 | 50
       540 |
    -  360 | 20
       180 |
    -   90 | 5
        90 |
    -   90 | 5
         0   80  ──→ final quotient = 80 with no remainder
```

Check:

18 (50 + 20 + 5 + 5) = (18)(50) + (18)(20) + (18)(5) + (18)(5) = 1440

Common errors in division often result from mistakes in translating words to symbols. For example, misinterpreting 10 divided by 5 as 5/10. In addition, when using the partial quotients algorithm errors in subtraction and addition can produce incorrect results.

The main algorithm of rational number division is multiplication by the reciprocal. Thus,

$$\frac{\frac{1}{3}}{\frac{1}{4}} = (\frac{1}{3})(\frac{4}{1}) = \frac{4}{3}.$$

The definition of multiplication and division as inverse operations justifies the use of reciprocal multiplication.

Skill 11.5   Relate operations and algorithms involving numbers to algebraic procedures (e.g., adding fractions to adding rational expressions, division of integers to division of polynomials).

Many algebraic procedures are similar to and rely upon number operations and algorithms. Two examples of this similarity are the adding of rational expressions and division of polynomials.

Addition of rational expressions is similar to fraction addition. The basic algorithm of addition for both fractions and rational expressions is the common denominator method. Consider an example of the addition of numerical fractions.

$$\frac{3}{5} + \frac{2}{3} = \frac{3(3)}{3(5)} + \frac{5(2)}{5(3)} = \frac{9}{15} + \frac{10}{15} = \frac{19}{15}$$

To complete the sum, we first find the least common denominator

Now, consider an example of rational expression addition.

$$\frac{(x+5)}{(x+1)} + \frac{2x}{(x+3)} = \frac{(x+3)(x+5)}{(x+3)(x+1)} + \frac{(x+1)2x}{(x+1)(x+3)}$$
$$= \frac{x^2 + 8x + 15}{(x+3)(x+1)} + \frac{2x^2 + 2x}{(x+3)(x+1)} = \frac{3x^2 + 10x + 15}{(x+3)(x+1)}$$

Note the similarity to fractional addition. The basic algorithm, finding a common denominator and adding numerators, is the same.

Division of polynomials follows the same algorithm as numerical long division. Consider an example of numerical long division.

$$\begin{array}{r} 720 \\ 6\overline{)4321} \\ \underline{42} \\ 12 \\ \underline{12} \\ 01 \end{array}$$

→ 720 1/6 = final quotient

Compare the process of numerical long division to polynomial division.

$$\begin{array}{r} x - 9 \\ x+1\overline{)x^2 - 8x - 9} \\ \underline{-x^2 - x} \\ -9x - 9 \\ \underline{+9x + 9} \\ 0 + 0 \end{array}$$

→ x – 9 = final quotient

Note that the step-by-step process is identical in both cases.

Real numbers: Include two types of numbers, rational and irrational. Rational means fractional. These numbers, when converted to decimals, are either terminating or repeating.

Examples of rational numbers are:

a) $\frac{1}{4} = 0.2500$ (terminating decimal).

b) $\frac{10101}{40000} = 0.252525 = 0.25$ (repeating decimal).

Irrational numbers, on the other hand, when converted to decimal values are neither repeating nor terminating. Examples of irrational numbers are:

a) $\pi = 3.14159...$

b) $\sqrt{7} = 2.645751311...$

Notation: Radicals ($\sqrt{}$) are inverse operators of exponents and are represented by the following form:

$$\sqrt[n]{a^x} \quad \text{where:}$$

n is called the index or root,
a^x is called to radicand,
x is the exponent or power of 'a'.

In the notation above, we are finding the nth root of a^x. In other words, we want to find the number, when multiplied by itself n times, gives a^x.

Example: $\sqrt{16} = \sqrt[2]{16}$ (when the index or root is omitted, it is always assumed to be 2).

$\sqrt{16} = +4$ or $^-4$ since $(+4)(+4) = 16$ and $(-4)(-4) = 16$.

So we can write $\sqrt{16} = \pm 4$ to show the two results. +4 is called the principal square root of 16. This is because the principal square root is the only one that makes since (example: for measurements).

1)   We can only add or subtract radicals that have the same index and the same radicand.

     Example: $2\sqrt{5} + 3\sqrt{5} = 5\sqrt{5}$
     Example: $5\sqrt[3]{2} - 3\sqrt[3]{2} = 2\sqrt[3]{2}$

2)   If the radicand is raised to a power that is equal to the index then the root operation will cancel out the power operation.

Example: Perform the indicated operations.

a) $\sqrt[3]{2^3} = 2$ The power and the index are equal to each other.

b) $2\sqrt{32}$

$32 = 2 \times 16 = 2 \times 4 \times 4 = 2 \times 4^2$ so,

$2\sqrt{32} = 2\sqrt{2 \times 4^2} = 2 \times 4\sqrt[2]{2}$ or $8\sqrt{2}$

3)   If the radicand is raised to a power different from the index, convert the radical to its exponential form and apply laws of exponents.

Skill 11.6   **Extend and generalize the operations of rationals and integers to include exponents, their properties, and their applications to the real numbers.**

Review of Law of Exponents: If a and b are real numbers and m and n are rational numbers, then,

1. $a^m \times a^n = a^{(m+n)}$

2. $\dfrac{a^m}{a^n} = a^{(m-n)}$

3. $(a^m)^n = a^{(mn)}$

4. $(ab)^m = a^m b^m$

5. $a^{-n} = \dfrac{1}{a^n} = (1/a)^n$

6.   If a is any nonzero number, then $a^0 = 1$.

7. $a^{m/n} = \left(a^{1/n}\right)^m = \left(a^m\right)^{1/n}$

8. $\sqrt[n]{a^m}$ (radical form) $= a^{m/n}$ in exponential form.

COMPETENCY 12.0 UNDERSTAND IDEAS OF NUMBER THEORY AND USE NUMBERS TO MODEL AND SOLVE PROBLEMS WITHIN AND OUTSIDE OF MATHEMATICS.

Skill 12.1 **Demonstrate an understanding of ideas from number theory (e.g., prime factorization, greatest common divisor) as they apply to whole numbers, integers, and rational numbers, and use these ideas in problem situations.**

GCF is the abbreviation for the **greatest common factor**. The GCF is the largest number that is a factor of all the numbers given in a problem. The GCF can be no larger than the smallest number given in the problem. If no other number is a common factor, then the GCF will be the number 1. To find the GCF, list all possible factors of the smallest number given (include the number itself). Starting with the largest factor (which is the number itself), determine if it is also a factor of all the other given numbers. If so, that is the GCF. If that factor doesn't work, try the same method on the next smaller factor. Continue until a common factor is found. That is the GCF. Note: There can be other common factors besides the GCF.

Example: Find the GCF of 12, 20, and 36.

The smallest number in the problem is 12. The factors of 12 are 1,2,3,4,6 and 12. 12 is the largest factor, but it does not divide evenly into 20. Neither does 6, but 4 will divide into both 20 and 36 evenly.

Therefore, 4 is the GCF.

Example: Find the GCF of 14 and 15.

Factors of 14 are 1,2,7 and 14. 14 is the largest factor, but it does not divide evenly into 15. Neither does 7 or 2. Therefore, the only factor common to both 14 and 15 is the number 1, the GCF.

LCM is the abbreviation for **least common multiple**. The least common multiple of a group of numbers is the smallest number that all of the given numbers will divide into. The least common multiple will always be the largest of the given numbers or a multiple of the largest number.

Example: Find the LCM of 20, 30 and 40.

The largest number given is 40, but 30 will not divide evenly into 40. The next multiple of 40 is 80 (2 x 40), but 30 will not divide evenly into 80 either. The next multiple of 40 is 120. 120 is divisible by both 20 and 30, so 120 is the LCM (least common multiple).

Example: Find the LCM of 96, 16 and 24.

The largest number is 96. 96 is divisible by both 16 and 24, so 96 is the LCM.

Example: Elly Mae can feed the animals in 15 minutes. Jethro can feed them in 10 minutes. How long will it take them if they work together?

If Elly Mae can feed the animals in 15 minutes, then she could feed 1/15 of them in 1 minute, 2/15 of them in 2 minutes, x/15 of them in x minutes. In the same fashion Jethro could feed x/10 of them in x minutes. Together they complete 1 job. The equation is:

$$\frac{x}{15} + \frac{x}{10} = 1$$

Multiply each term by the LCD of 30:

$$2x + 3x = 30$$
$$x = 6 \text{ minutes}$$

Composite numbers are whole numbers that have more than 2 different factors. For example 9 is composite because besides factors of 1 and 9, 3 is also a factor. 70 is also composite because besides the factors of 1 and 70, the numbers 2,5,7,10,14, and 35 are also all factors.

Prime numbers are numbers that can only be factored into 1 and the number itself. When factoring into prime factors, all the factors must be numbers that cannot be factored again (without using 1). Initially numbers can be factored into any 2 factors. Check each resulting factor to see if it can be factored again. Continue factoring until all remaining factors are prime. This is the list of prime factors. Regardless of what way the original number was factored, the final list of prime factors will always be the same.

Example: Factor 30 into prime factors.

Factor 30 into any 2 factors.

$5 \cdot 6$ Now factor the 6.
$5 \cdot 2 \cdot 3$ These are all prime factors.

Factor 30 into any 2 factors.

$3 \cdot 10$ Now factor the 10.
$3 \cdot 2 \cdot 5$ These are the same prime factors even though the original factors were different.

Example: Factor 240 into prime factors.

Factor 240 into any 2 factors.

$24 \cdot 10$ Now factor both 24 and 10.

$4 \cdot 6 \cdot 2 \cdot 5$ Now factor both 4 and 6.

$2 \cdot 2 \cdot 2 \cdot 3 \cdot 2 \cdot 5$ These are prime factors.

This can also be written as $2^4 \cdot 3 \cdot 5$.

Skill 12.2   **Use integers, rational numbers, and real numbers to describe and quantify phenomena such as money, length, area, volume, and density.**

Weight

Example: Kathy has a bag of potatoes that weighs 5 lbs., 10 oz. She uses one third of the bag to make mashed potatoes. How much does the bag weigh now?

1 lb. = 16 oz.

5(16 oz.) + 10 oz.

= 80 oz + 10 oz = 90 oz.

$90 - (\frac{1}{3})90$ oz.

= 90 oz. − 30 oz.

= 60 oz.

$60 \div 16 = 3.75$ lbs.

.75 = 75%

$75\% = \frac{75}{100} = \frac{3}{4}$

The **perimeter** of any polygon is the sum of the lengths of the sides.

The **area** of a polygon is the number of square units covered by the figure.

FIGURE	AREA FORMULA	PERIMETER FORMULA
Rectangle	LW	$2(L + W)$
Triangle	$\frac{1}{2}bh$	$a + b + c$
Parallelogram	bh	sum of lengths of sides
Trapezoid	$\frac{1}{2}h(a + b)$	sum of lengths of sides

Perimeter

Example: A farmer has a piece of land shaped as shown below. He wishes to fence this land at an estimated cost of $25 per linear foot. What is the total cost of fencing this property to the nearest foot.

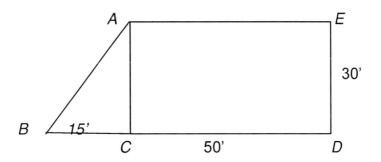

From the right triangle ABC, AC = 30 and BC = 15.

Since (AB) = (AC)^2 + (BC)^2
       (AB) = (30)^2 + (15)^2

So $\sqrt{(AB)^2} = AB = \sqrt{1125} = 33.5410$ feet

To the nearest foot AB = 34 feet.

Perimeter of the piece of land is = $AB + BC + CD + DE + EA$

= 34 + 15 + 50 + 30 + 50 = 179 feet

cost of fencing = $25 x 179 = $4, 475.00

Area

Area is the space that a figure occupies. Example:

Example: What will be the cost of carpeting a rectangular office that measures 12 feet by 15 feet if the carpet costs $12.50 per square yard?

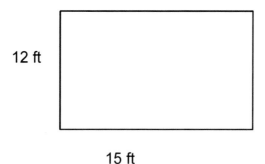

12 ft

15 ft

The problem is asking you to determine the area of the office. The area of a rectangle is *length x width = A*

Substitute the given values in the equation $A = lw$

$A = (12$ ft.$)(15$ ft.$)$

$A = 180$ ft.

The problem asked you to determine the cost of carpet at $12.50 per square yard.

First, you need to convert 180 ft.^{2} into yards^2.

$$1 \text{ yd.} = 3 \text{ ft.}$$
$$(1 \text{ yard})(1 \text{ yard}) = (3 \text{ feet})(3 \text{ feet})$$
$$1 \text{ yd}^2 = 9 \text{ ft 2}$$

Hence, $\dfrac{180 \text{ ft}^2}{1} = \dfrac{1 \text{ yd}^2}{9 \text{ ft}^2} = \dfrac{20}{1} = 20 \text{ yd}^2$

The carpet cost $12.50 per square yard; thus the cost of carpeting the office described is $12.50 x 20 = $250.00.

Example: Find the area of a parallelogram whose base is 6.5 cm and the height of the altitude to that base is 3.7 cm.

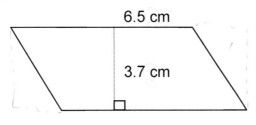

6.5 cm

3.7 cm

$A_{parallelogram}$ = bh

= (3.7)(6.5)
= 24.05 cm^2

Example: Find the area of this triangle.

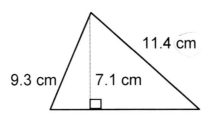

11.4 cm

9.3 cm   7.1 cm

16.8 cm

$A_{triangle}$ = $\frac{1}{2}$bh
= 0.5 (16.8) (7.1)
= 59.64 cm^2

Example: Find the area of this trapezoid.

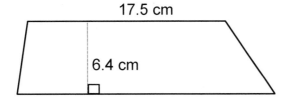

17.5 cm

6.4 cm

23.7 cm

The area of a trapezoid equals one-half the sum of the bases times the altitude.

$A_{trapezoid}$ = $\frac{1}{2}$h(b$_1$ + b$_2$)
= 0.5 (6.4) (17.5 + 23.7)
= 131.84 cm^2

The distance around a circle is the **circumference**. The ratio of the circumference to the diameter is represented by the Greek letter pi. Π ~ 3.14 ~ $\frac{22}{7}$.

The **circumference** of a circle is found by the formula $C = 2\Pi r$ or $C = \Pi d$ where r is the radius of the circle and d is the diameter.

The **area** of a circle is found by the formula $A = \Pi r^2$.

Example: Find the circumference and area of a circle whose radius is 7 meters.

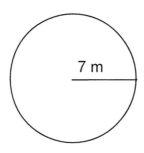

$C = 2\Pi r$ 　　　　　　　 $A = \Pi r^2$
$= 2(3.14)(7)$ 　　　　　 $= 3.14(7)(7)$
$= 43.96 \text{ m}$ 　　　　　 $= 153.86 \text{ m}^2$

Weight

Example: The weight limit of a playground merry-go-round is 1000 pounds. There are 11 children on the merry-go-round.
3 children weigh 100 pounds.
6 children weigh 75 pounds
2 children weigh 60 pounds

George weighs 80 pounds. Can he get on the merry-go-round?

$3(100) + 6(75) + 2(60)$
$= 300 + 450 + 120$
$= 870$
$1000 - 870$
$= 130$

Since 80 is less than 130, George can get on the merry-go-round.

Volume and **Surface area** are computed using the following formulas:

FIGURE	VOLUME	TOTAL SURFACE AREA
Right Cylinder	$\pi r^2 h$	$2\pi rh + 2\pi r^2$
Right Cone	$\dfrac{\pi r^2 h}{3}$	$\pi r\sqrt{r^2 + h^2} + \pi r^2$
Sphere	$\dfrac{4}{3}\pi r^3$	$4\pi r^2$
Rectangular Solid	LWH	$2LW + 2WH + 2LH$

FIGURE	LATERAL AREA	TOTAL AREA	VOLUME
Regular Pyramid	1/2Pl	1/2Pl+B	1/3Bh

P = Perimeter
h = height
B = Area of Base
l = slant height

Example: What is the volume of a shoe box with a length of 35 cms, a width of
              20 cms and a height of 15 cms?

              Volume of a rectangular solid
              = Length x Width x Height
              = 35 x 20 x 15
              = 10500 cm^3

Example: A water company is trying to decide whether to use traditional cylindrical paper cups or to offer conical paper cups since both cost the same. The traditional cups are 8 cm wide and 14 cm high. The conical cups are 12 cm wide and 19 cm high. The company will use the cup that holds the most water.

Draw and label a sketch of each.

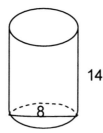 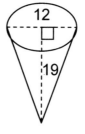

$V = \pi r^2 h$	$V = \dfrac{\pi r^2 h}{3}$	1. write formula
$V = \pi(4)^2(14)$	$V = \dfrac{1}{3}\pi(6)^2(19)$	2. substitute
$V = 703.717$ cm^3	$V = 716.283$ cm^3	3. solve

The choice should be the conical cup since its volume is more.

Example: How much material is needed to make a basketball that has a diameter of 15 inches? How much air is needed to fill the basketball?

Draw and label a sketch:

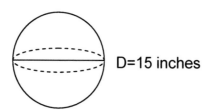

D=15 inches

Total surface area   Volume

$TSA = 4\pi r^2$	$V = \dfrac{4}{3}\pi r^3$	1. write formula
$= 4\pi(7.5)^2$	$= \dfrac{4}{3}\pi(7.5)^3$	2. substitute
$= 706.9$ in^2	$= 1767.1$ in^3	3. solve

Skill 12.3 **Apply knowledge of place value and other number properties to develop techniques of mental mathematics and computational estimation.**

To estimate measurement of familiar objects, it is first necessary to determine the units to be used.

Examples:
Length
1. The coastline of Florida
2. The width of a ribbon
3. The thickness of a book
4. The depth of water in a pool

Weight or mass
1. A bag of sugar
2. A school bus
3. A dime

Capacity or volume
1. Paint to paint a bedroom
2. Glass of milk

Money
1. Cost of a house
2. Cost of a cup of coffee
3. Exchange rate

Perimeter
1. The edge of a backyard
2. The edge of a football field

Area
1. The size of a carpet
2. The size of a state

Example: Estimate the measurements of the following objects:

Length of a dollar bill	6 inches
Weight of a baseball	1 pound
Distance from New York to Florida	1100 km
Volume of water to fill a medicine dropper	1 milliliter
Length of a desk	2 meters
Temperature of water in a swimming pool	80° F

Depending on the degree of accuracy needed, an object may be measured to different units. For example, a pencil may be 6 inches to the nearest inch, or 6 3 8 inches to the

nearest eighth of an inch. Similarly, it might be 15 cm to the nearest cm or 154 mm to the nearest mm.

Given a set of objects and their measurements, the use of rounding procedures is helpful when attempting to round to the nearest given unit. When rounding to a given place value, it is necessary to look at the number in the next smaller place. If this number is 5 or more, the number in the place we are rounding to is increased by one and all numbers to the right are changed to zero. If the number is less than 5, the number in the place we are rounding to stays the same and all numbers to the right are changed to zero.

One method of rounding measurements can require an additional step. First, the measurement must be converted to a decimal number. Then the rules for rounding applied.

Example: Round the measurements to the given units.

MEASUREMENT	ROUND TO NEAREST	ANSWER
1 foot 7 inches	foot	2 ft
5 pound 6 ounces	pound	5 pounds
5 9/16 inches	inch	6 inches

Convert each measurement to a decimal number. Then apply the rules for rounding.

1 foot 7 inches = $1\dfrac{7}{12}$ ft = 1.58333 ft, round up to 2 ft

5 pounds 6 ounces = $5\dfrac{6}{16}$ pounds = 5.375 pound, round to 5 pounds

$5\dfrac{9}{16}$ inches = 5.5625 inches, round up to 6 inches

Example: Janet goes into a store to purchase a CD on sale for $13.95. While shopping, she sees two pairs of shoes, prices $19.95 and $14.50. She only has $50. Can she purchase everything?

Solve by rounding:

$19.95 → $20.00
$14.50 → $15.00
$13.95 → $14.00
$49.00   Yes, she can purchase the CD and the shoes.

Skill 12.4 **Apply knowledge of counting techniques such as permutations and combinations to quantify situations and solve problems.**

See Skill 22.4.

Skill 12.5 **Apply properties of the real numbers to solve a variety of theoretical and applied problems.**

See Skill 10.6.

COMPETENCY 13.0 UNDERSTAND AND USE MATHEMATICAL REASONING TO IDENTIFY, EXTEND, AND ANALYZE PATTERNS AND UNDERSTAND THE RELATIONSHIPS AMONG VARIABLES, EXPRESSIONS, EQUATIONS, INEQUALITIES, RELATIONS, AND FUNCTIONS.

Skill 13.1   Use inductive reasoning to identify, extend, and create patterns using concrete models, figures, numbers, and algebraic expressions.

See Skill 24.2 & 24.3

Skill 13.2   Formulate implicit and explicit rules to describe and construct sequences verbally, numerically, graphically, and symbolically.

Arithmetic Sequences

When given a set of numbers where the common difference between the terms is constant, use the following formula:

$$a_n = a_1 + (n-1)d$$

where a_1 = the first term
n = the nth term (general term)
d = the common difference

Example: Find the 8th term of the arithmetic sequence 5, 8, 11, 14, ...
$a_n = a_1 + (n-1)d$
$a_n = 5$ identify the 1st term
$d = 8 - 5 = 3$ find d
$a_n = 5 + (8-1)3$ substitute
$a_n = 26$

Example: Given two terms of an arithmetic sequence, find a_1 and d.

$a_4 = 21$ $a_6 = 32$

$a_n = a + (n-1)d$ $a_4 = 21, n = 4$

$21 = a_1 + (4-1)d$ $a_6 = 32, n = 6$

$32 = a_1 + (6-1)d$

$21 = a_1 + 3d$ solve the system of equations

$32 = a_1 + 5d$

$21 = a_1 + 3d$

$\underline{-32 = -a_1 - 5d}$ multiply by -1

$-11 = \quad -2d$ add the equations

$5.5 = d$

$21 = a_1 + 3(5.5)$ substitute d = 5.5, into one of the equations

$21 = a_1 + 16.5$

$a_1 = 4.5$

The sequence begins with 4.5 and has a common difference of 5.5 between numbers.

Geometric Sequences

When using geometric sequences, consecutive numbers are compared to find the common ratio.

$$r = \frac{a_{n+1}}{a_n}$$

where r = common ratio

a = the nth term

The ratio is then used in the geometric sequence formula:

$a_n = a_1 r^{n-1}$

Example: Find the 8th term of the geometric sequence 2, 8, 32, 128 ...

$r = \frac{a_{n+1}}{a_n}$ use common ratio formula to find ratio

$r = \frac{8}{2}$ substitute $a_n = 2$ $a_{n+1} = 8$

$r = 4$

$a_n = a_1 \bullet r^{n-1}$ use r = 4 to solve for the 8th term

$a_n = 2 \bullet 4^{8-1}$

$a_n = 32,768$

Skill 13.3   Make, test, validate, and use conjectures about patterns and relationships in data presented in tables, sequences, or graphs.

The following table represents the number of problems Mr. Rodgers is assigning his math students for homework each day, starting with the first day of class.

Day	1	2	3	4	5	6	7	8	9	10	11
Number of Problems	1	1	2	3	5	8	13				

If Mr. Rodgers continues this pattern, how many problems will he assign on the eleventh day?

If we look for a pattern, it appears that the number of problems assigned each day is equal to the sum of the problems assigned for the previous two days. We test this as follows:

Day 2 = 1 + 0 = 1
Day 3 = 1 + 1 = 2
Day 4 = 2 + 1 = 3
Day 5 = 3 + 2 = 5
Day 6 = 5 + 3 = 8
Day 7 = 8 + 5 = 13

Therefore, Day 8 would have 21 problems; Day 9, 34 problems; Day 10, 55 problems; and Day 11, 89 problems.

A sequence is a pattern of numbers arranged in a particular order. When a list of numbers is in a sequence, a pattern may be expressed in terms of variables. Suppose we have the sequence 8, 12, 16…. If we assign the variable a to the initial term, 8, and assign the variable d to the difference between the first two terms, we can formulate a pattern of $a, a + d, a + 2d … a + (n-1)d$. With this formula, we can determine any number in the sequence. For example, let's say we want to know what the 400th term would be. Using the formula,

$$a + (n - 1)d =$$
$$8 + (400 - 1)4 =$$
$$8 + 399(4) =$$
$$8 + 1596 = 1604$$

we determine that the 400th term would be 1604.

Suppose we have an equation $y = 2x + 1$. We construct a table of values in order to graph the equation to see if we can find a pattern.

x	y
-2	-3
-1	-1
0	1
1	3
2	5

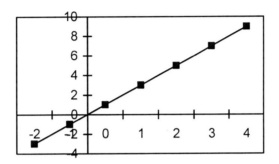

The pattern formed by the points is that they all lie on a line. We, therefore, can determine any solution of y by picking an x-coordinate and finding the corresponding point on the line. For example, if we want to know the solution of y when x is equal to 4, we find the corresponding point and see that y is equal to 9.

Skill 13.4   Give appropriate justification of the manipulation of algebraic expressions.

An algebraic formula is an equation that describes a relationship among variables. While it is not often necessary to derive the formula, one must know how to rewrite a given formula in terms of a desired variable.

Example: Given that the relationship of voltage, V, applied across a material with electrical resistance, R, when a current, I, is flowing through the material is given by the formula V = IR. Find the resistance of the material when a current of 10 milliamps is flowing, when the applied voltage is 2 volts.

$$V = IR. \text{ Solve for R.}$$

$$IR = V; \quad R = V/I \qquad \text{Divide both sides by I.}$$

When V = 2 volts; I = 10×10^{-3} amps; find R.

$$R = \frac{2}{10^1 \times 10^{-3}}$$

$$R = \frac{2}{10^{-2}} \qquad \text{Substituting in R = V/I, we get,}$$

$$R = 2 \times 10^2$$

$$R = 200 \text{ ohms}$$

Example: Given the formula I = PRT, where I is the simple interest to be paid or realized when an amount P, the principal is to be deposited at simple interest rate of R (in %) and T is the time expressed in years, find what principal must be deposited to yield an interest of $586.00 over a period of 2 years at interest of 23.5%.

$$I = PRT \qquad \text{Solve for P} \rightarrow P = \frac{I}{RT} \text{(Divide both sides by RT)}$$

I = 586; R = 23.5% = 0.235; T = 2

$$P = \frac{586}{0.235 \times 2} = \frac{586}{0.47} \qquad \text{Substitute.}$$

$$P = \frac{586}{0.47} = 1246.80 = \$1246.80$$

Check; I = PRT; $1246.8 \times 0.235 \times 2 = 586$

Loosely speaking, an equation like $y = 3x + 5$ describes a relationship between the independent variable x and the dependent variable y. Thus, y is written as $f(x)$ "function of x." But y may not be a "true" function. For a "true" function to exist, there is a relationship between a set of all independent variables (domain) and a set of all outputs or dependent variables (range) such that each element of the domain corresponds to one element of the range. (For any input we get exactly one output).

Example:

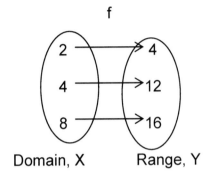

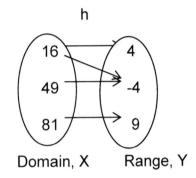

Domain, X   Range, Y   Domain, X   Range, Y

This is a "true" function.   This is not a "true" function.

Example: Given a function $f(x) = 3x + 5$, find $f(2)$; $f(0)$; $f(^-10)$

       $f(2)$ means find the value of the function value at $x = 2$.

$$f(2) = 3(2) + 5 = 6 + 5 = 11$$
$$f(0) = 3(0) + 5 = 0 + 5 = 5 \qquad \text{Substitute for } x.$$
$$f(^-10) = 3(^-10) + 5 =^- 30 + 5 =^- 25$$

Example: Given $h(t) = 3t^2 + t - 9$, find $h(^-4)$.

$$h(^-4) = 3(^-4)^2 - 4 - 9$$
$$h(^-4) = 3(16) - 13 \qquad \text{Substitute for } t.$$
$$h(^-4) = 48 - 13$$
$$h(^-4) = 35$$

Skill 13.5 **Illustrate the concept of a function using concrete models, tables, graphs, and symbolic and verbal representations.**

A relationship between two quantities can be shown using a table, graph or rule. In this example, the rule y= 9x describes the relationship between the total amount earned, y, and the total amount of $9 sunglasses sold, x.

A table using this data would appear as:

number of sunglasses sold	1	5	10	15
total dollars earned	9	45	90	135

Each *(x,y)* relationship between a pair of values is called the coordinate pair and can be plotted on a graph. The coordinate pairs *(1,9), (5,45), (10,90),* and *(15,135),* are plotted on the graph below.

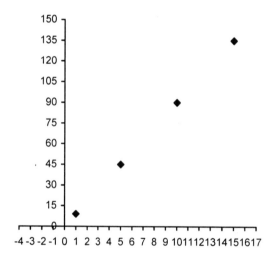

The graph above shows a linear relationship. A linear relationship is one in which two quantities are proportional to each other. Doubling *x* also doubles *y*. On a graph, a straight line depicts a linear relationship.

The function or relationship between two quantities may be analyzed to determine how one quantity depends on the other. For example, the function below shows a relationship between y and x: y=2x+1

The relationship between two or more variables can be analyzed using a table, graph, written description or symbolic rule. The function, y=2x+1, is written as a symbolic rule. The same relationship is also shown in the table below:

x	0	2	3	6	9
y	1	5	7	13	19

A relationship could be written in words by saying the value of y is equal to two times the value of x, plus one. This relationship could be shown on a graph by plotting given points such as the ones shown in the table above.

Another way to describe a function is as a process in which one or more numbers are input into an imaginary machine that produces another number as the output. If 5 is input, (x), into a machine with a process of x +1, the output, (y), will equal 6.

In real situations, relationships can be described mathematically. The function, y=x+1, can be used to describe the idea that people age one year on their birthday. To describe the relationship in which a person's monthly medical costs are 6 times a person's age, we could write y=6x. The monthly cost of medical care could be predicted using this function. A 20 year-old person would spend $120 per month (120=20*6). An 80 year-old person would spend $480 per month (480=80*6). Therefore, one could analyze the relationship to say: as you get older, medical costs increase $6.00 each year.

Skill 13.6   Use transformations to illustrate properties of functions and relations and to solve problems.

See Skill 15.2

COMPETENCY 14.0 UNDERSTAND AND USE LINEAR FUNCTIONS TO MODEL AND SOLVE PROBLEMS.

Skill 14.1 **Demonstrate an understanding of the concept of linear function using concrete models, tables, graphs, and symbolic and verbal representations.**

-A **function** is a relation in which different ordered pairs have different first coordinates. (No x values are repeated.)

- A **relation** is any set of ordered pairs.

- The **domain** of a relation is the set made of all the first coordinates of the ordered pairs.

- The **range** of a relation is the set made of all the second coordinates of the ordered pairs.

- A **mapping** is a diagram with arrows drawn from each element of the domain to the corresponding elements of the range. If 2 arrows are drawn from the same element of the domain, then it is not a function.

- On a graph, use the **vertical line test** to look for a function. If any vertical line intersects the graph of a relation in more than one point, then the relation is not a function.

1. Determine the domain and range
   of this mapping.

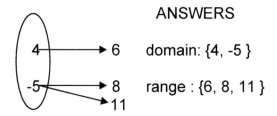

ANSWERS

domain: {4, -5 }

range : {6, 8, 11 }

See Skill 13.5 for more information.

Skill 14.2   Demonstrate an understanding of the connections among linear functions, proportions, and direct variation.

If two things vary directly, as one gets larger, the other also gets larger. If one gets smaller, then the other gets smaller too. If x and y vary directly, there should be a constant, c, such that $y = cx$. Something can also vary directly with the square of something else, $y = cx^2$.

If two things vary inversely, as one gets larger, the other one gets smaller instead. If x and y vary inversely, there should be a constant, c, such that $xy = c$ or $y = c/x$. Something can also vary inversely with the square of something else, $y = c/x^2$.

Example: If $30 is paid for 5 hours work, how much would be paid for 19 hours work?

This is direct variation and $30 = 5c, so the constant is 6 ($6/hour). So $y = 6(19)$ or y = $114.

This could also be done as a proportion:

$$\frac{\$30}{5} = \frac{y}{19}$$

$$5y = 570$$
$$y = 114$$

Example: On a 546 mile trip from Miami to Charlotte, one car drove 65 mph while another car drove 70 mph. How does this affect the driving time for the trip?

This is an inverse variation, since increasing your speed should decrease your driving time. Using the equation: rate × time = distance, rt = d.

65t = 546   and   70t = 546
   t = 8.4   and   t = 7.8

slower speed, more time   faster speed, less time

Example: Consider the average monthly temperatures for a hypothetical
            location.

Month	Avg. Temp. (F)
Jan	40
March	48
May	65
July	81
Sept	80
Nov	60

Note that the graph of the average temperatures resembles the
graph of a trigonometric function with a period of one year. We can
use the periodic nature of seasonal temperature fluctuation to
predict weather patterns.

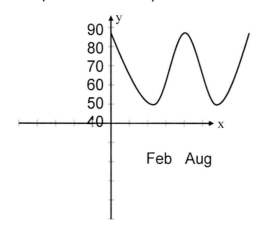

Skill 14.3   Determine the linear function that best models a set of data.

A linear function is a function whose graph is a line. It has the algebraic form $f(x) = ax + b$. The variables a and b are constants. In order to determine the linear function that best models a set of data, we need to figure out a and b.

Example: Johnny delivers flyers for ABC Hardware after school. He is paid a weekly salary of $25 plus a 1% commission on any sales resulting from the flyers. The table of data would look like this:

sales, s	earnings, E(s)
100	26
200	27
300	28
400	29
500	30

The linear function would be $E(s) = (0.01)s + 25$, where E(s) represents total earnings, 0.01 substitutes for a, s represents sales, and 25 substitutes for b.

Skill 14.4   Analyze the relationship between a linear equation and its graph.

A first degree equation has an equation of the form $ax + by = c$. To find the slope of a line, solve the equation for y. This gets the equation into **slope intercept form, $y = mx + b$. The value m is the line's slope.**

The y intercept is the coordinate of the point where a line crosses the y axis. To find the y intercept, substitute 0 for x and solve for y. This is the y intercept. In slope intercept form, $y = mx + b$, b is the y intercept.

To find the x intercept, substitute 0 for y and solve for x. This is the x intercept.

If the equation solves to **x = any number**, then the graph is a **vertical line**. It only has an x intercept. Its slope is **undefined**.

If the equation solves to **y = any number**, then the graph is a **horizontal line**. It only has a y intercept. Its slope is 0 (zero).

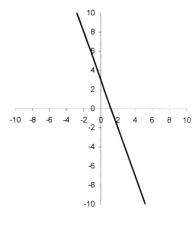

$$5x + 2y = 6$$
$$y = -5/2\,x + 3$$

The equation of a line from its graph can be found by finding its slope and its *y* intercept.

$$Y - y_a = m\left(X - x_a\right)$$

$\left(x_a, y_a\right)$ can be $\left(x_1, y_1\right)$ or $\left(x_2, y_2\right)$ If **m**, the value of the slope, is distributed through the parentheses, the equation can be rewritten into other forms of the equation of a line.

Example: Find the equation of a line through $(9, {}^-6)$ and $({}^-1, 2)$.

$$\text{slope} = \frac{y_2 - y_1}{x_2 - x_1} = \frac{2 - {}^-6}{{}^-1 - 9} = \frac{8}{{}^-10} = -\frac{4}{5}$$

$$Y - y_a = m(X - x_a) \rightarrow Y - 2 = {}^-4/5\,(X - {}^-1) \rightarrow$$
$$Y - 2 = {}^-4/5\,(X + 1) \rightarrow Y - 2 = {}^-4/5\,X - 4/5 \rightarrow$$
$$Y = {}^-4/5\,X + 6/5 \quad \text{This is the slope-intercept form.}$$

Multiplying by 5 to eliminate fractions, it is:

$$5Y = {}^-4X + 6 \rightarrow 4X + 5Y = 6 \quad \text{Standard form.}$$

Example: Find the slope and intercepts of $3x + 2y = 14$.

$$3x + 2y = 14$$
$$2y = {}^-3x + 14$$
$$y = {}^-3/2\ x + 7$$

The slope of the line is $^-3/2$. The y intercept of the line is 7.

The intercepts can also be found by substituting 0 in place of the other variable in the equation.

To find the y intercept:
let $x = 0$; $3(0) + 2y = 14$
$0 + 2y = 14$
$2y = 14$
$y = 7$
$(0,7)$ is the y intercept.

To find the x intercept:
let $y = 0$; $3x + 2(0) = 14$
$3x + 0 = 14$
$3x = 14$
$x = 14/3$
$(14/3, 0)$ is the x intercept.

Example: Sketch the graph of the line represented by $2x + 3y = 6$.

Let $x = 0 \rightarrow 2(0) + 3y = 6$
$\rightarrow 3y = 6$
$\rightarrow y = 2$
$\rightarrow (0,2)$ is the y intercept.

Let $y = 0 \rightarrow 2x + 3(0) = 6$
$\rightarrow 2x = 6$
$\rightarrow x = 3$
$\rightarrow (3,0)$ is the x intercept.

Let $x = 1 \rightarrow 2(1) + 3y = 6$
$\rightarrow 2 + 3y = 6$
$\rightarrow 3y = 4$
$\rightarrow y = \dfrac{4}{3}$
$\rightarrow \left(1, \dfrac{4}{3}\right)$ is the third point.

Plotting the three points on the coordinate system, we get the following:

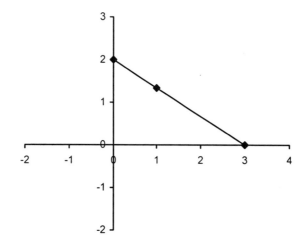

Skill 14.5 Use linear functions, inequalities, and systems to model problems.

See Skill 14.5

Skill 14.6 Use a variety of representations and methods (e.g., numerical methods, tables, graphs, algebraic techniques) to solve systems of linear equations and inequalities.

Example: Mrs. Winters bought 4 dresses and 6 pairs of shoes for $340. Mrs. Summers went to the same store and bought 3 dresses and 8 pairs of shoes for $360. If all the dresses were the same price and all the shoes were the same price, find the price charged for a dress and for a pair of shoes.

Let x = price of a dress
Let y = price of a pair of shoes

Then Mrs. Winters' equation would be: $4x + 6y = 340$
Mrs. Summers' equation would be: $3x + 8y = 360$

To solve by addition-subtraction:

Multiply the first equation by 4: $4(4x + 6y = 340)$

Multiply the other equation by $^-3$: $^-3(3x + 8y = 360)$
By doing this, the equations can be added to each other to eliminate one variable and solve for the other variable.

$$16x + 24y = 1360$$
$$-9x - 24y = {}^-1080$$
$$7x = 280$$
$$x = 40 \leftarrow \text{the price of a dress was \$40}$$

solving for y, $y = 30$ ← the price of a pair of shoes,$30

Example: Aardvark Taxi charges $4 initially plus $1 for every mile traveled. Baboon Taxi charges $6 initially plus $.75 for every mile traveled. Determine when it is cheaper to ride with Aardvark Taxi or to ride with Baboon Taxi.

Aardvark Taxi's equation: $y = 1x + 4$
Baboon Taxi's equation : $y = .75x + 6$

Using substitution: $.75x + 6 = x + 4$
Multiplying by 4: $3x + 24 = 4x + 16$
Solving for x : $8 = x$

This tells you that at 8 miles the total charge for the 2 companies is the same. If you compare the charge for 1 mile, Aardvark charges $5 and Baboon charges $6.75. Clearly Aardvark is cheaper for distances up to 8 miles, but Baboon Taxi is cheaper for distances greater than 8 miles.

This problem can also be solved by graphing the 2 equations.

$$y = 1x + 4 \qquad y = .75x + 6$$

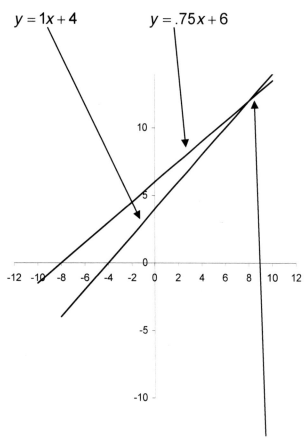

The lines intersect at (8, 12), therefore at 8 miles both companies charge $12. At values less than 8 miles, Aardvark Taxi charges less (the graph is below Baboon). Greater than 8 miles, Aardvark charges more (the graph is above Baboon).

The solution **set of linear equations** is all the ordered pairs of real numbers that satisfy both equations, thus the intersection of the lines There are two methods for solving linear equations: **linear combinations** and **substitution**.

In the **substitution** method, an equation is solved for either variable. Then, that solution is substituted in the other equation to find the remaining variable.

Example: (1) $2x + 8y = 4$
           (2) $x - 3y = 5$

       (2a) $x = 3y + 5$ Solve equation (2) for x

       (1a) $2(3y + 5) + 8y = 4$ Substitute x in equation (1)
               $6y + 10 + 8y = 4$ Solve.
               $14y = -6$
               $y = \frac{-3}{7}$ Solution

       (2) $x - 3y = 5$
           $x - 3(\frac{-3}{7}) = 5$ Substitute the value of y.
           $x = \frac{26}{7} = 3\frac{5}{7}$ Solution

Thus the solution set of the system of equations is $(3\frac{5}{7}, \frac{-3}{7})$.

In the **linear combinations** method, one or both of the equations are replaced with an equivalent equation in order that the two equations can be combined (added or subtracted) to eliminate one variable.

Example: (1) $4x + 3y = -2$
           (2) $5x - y = 7$

       (1) $4x + 3y = -2$
       (2a) $15x - 3y = 21$ Multiply equation (2) by 3

           $19x = 19$ Combining (1) and (2a)
            $x = 1$ Solve.

To find y, substitute the value of x in equation 1 (or 2).

       (1) $4x + 3y = -2$
           $4(1) + 3y = -2$
           $4 + 3y = -2$
               $3y = -2$
                $y = -2$

Thus the solution is $x = 1$ and $y = -2$ or the order pair (1, -2).

Some word problems can be solved using a system (group) of equations or inequalities. Watch for words like greater than, less than, at least, or no more than which indicate the need for inequalities.

Example: Farmer Greenjeans bought 4 cows and 6 sheep for $1700. Mr. Ziffel bought 3 cows and 12 sheep for $2400. If all the cows were the same price and all the sheep were another price, find the price charged for a cow or for a sheep.

Let x = price of a cow
Let y = price of a sheep

Then Farmer Greenjeans' equation would be: $4x + 6y = 1700$
Mr. Ziffel's equation would be: $3x + 12y = 2400$

To solve by **addition-subtraction**:
Multiply the first equation by $^-2$: $^-2(4x + 6y = 1700)$
Keep the other equation the same : $(3x + 12y = 2400)$

By doing this, the equations can be added to each other to eliminate one variable and solve for the other variable.

$$^-8x - 12y = {}^-3400$$
$$\underline{3x + 12y = 2400} \qquad \text{Add these equations.}$$
$$^-5x \qquad = {}^-1000$$

$x = 200 \leftarrow$ the price of a cow was $200.
Solving for y, $y = 150 \leftarrow$ the price of a sheep, $150.

To solve by **substitution**:

Solve one of the equations for a variable. (Try to make an equation without fractions if possible.) Substitute this expression into the equation that you have not yet used. Solve the resulting equation for the value of the remaining variable.

$$4x + 6y = 1700$$
$$3x + 12y = 2400 \leftarrow \text{Solve this equation for } x.$$

It becomes $x = 800 - 4y$. Now substitute $800 - 4y$ in place of x in the OTHER equation. $4x + 6y = 1700$ now becomes:

$$4(800 - 4y) + 6y = 1700$$
$$3200 - 16y + 6y = 1700$$
$$3200 - 10y = 1700$$
$$^{-}10y = ^{-}1500$$
$$y = 150, \text{ or } \$150 \text{ for a sheep.}$$

Substituting 150 back into an equation for y, find x.
$$4x + 6(150) = 1700$$
$$4x + 900 = 1700$$
$$4x = 800 \text{ so } x = 200 \text{ for a cow.}$$

Example: Sharon's Bike Shoppe can assemble a 3 speed bike in 30 minutes or a 10 speed bike in 60 minutes. The profit on each bike sold is $60 for a 3 speed or $75 for a 10 speed bike. How many of each type of bike should they assemble during an 8 hour day (480 minutes) to make the maximum profit? Total daily profit must be at least $300.

Let $x =$ number of 3 speed bikes.
$y =$ number of 10 speed bikes.

Since there are only 480 minutes to use each day,

$30x + 60y \leq 480$ is the first inequality.

Since the total daily profit must be at least $300,

$60x + 75y \geq 300$ is the second inequality.

$30x + 60y \leq 480$ solves to $y \leq 8 - 1/2\,x$

$$60y \leq -30x + 480$$

$$y \leq -\frac{1}{2}x + 8$$

$60x + 75y \geq 300$ solves to $y \geq 4 - 4/5\,x$

$$75y + 60x \geq 300$$

$$75y \geq -60x + 300$$

$$y \geq -\frac{4}{5}x + 4$$

Graph these 2 inequalities:

$$y \leq 8 - 1/2\,x$$

$$y \geq 4 - 4/5\,x$$

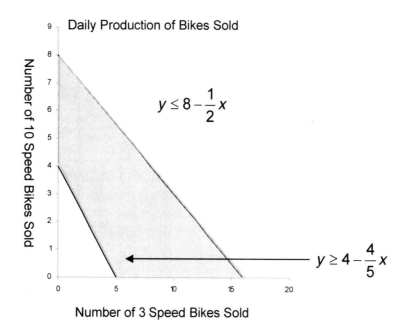

Number of 3 Speed Bikes Sold

Realize that $x \geq 0$ and $y \geq 0$, since the number of bikes assembled can not be a negative number. Graph these as additional constraints on the problem. The number of bikes assembled must always be an integer value, so points within the shaded area of the graph must have integer values. The maximum profit will occur at or near a corner of the shaded portion of this graph. Those points occur at (0,4), (0,8), (16,0), or (5,0).

Since profits are $60/3-speed or $75/10-speed, the profit would be :

$$(0,4) \quad 60(0)+75(4)=300$$
$$(0,8) \quad 60(0)+75(8)=600$$
$$(16,0) \quad 60(16)+75(0)=960 \leftarrow \text{Maximum profit}$$
$$(5,0) \quad 60(5)+75(0)=300$$

The maximum profit would occur if 16 3-speed bikes are made daily.

Example: The YMCA wants to sell raffle tickets to raise at least $32,000. If they must pay $7,250 in expenses and prizes out of the money collected from the tickets, how many tickets worth $25 each must they sell?

Since they want to raise **at least $32,000**, that means they would be happy to get 32,000 **or more**. This requires an inequality.

Let $x =$ number of tickets sold
Then $25x =$ total money collected for x tickets

Total money minus expenses is greater than $32,000.

$$25x - 7250 \geq 32000$$
$$25x \geq 39250$$
$$x \geq 1570$$

If they sell **1,570 tickets or more**, they will raise AT LEAST $32,000.

Example: The Simpsons went out for dinner. All 4 of them ordered the aardvark steak dinner. Bert paid for the 4 meals and included a tip of $12 for a total of $84.60. How much was an aardvark steak dinner?

Let $x =$ the price of one aardvark dinner.
So $4x =$ the price of 4 aardvark dinners.

$$4x + 12 = 84.60$$
$$4x = 72.60$$
$$x = \$18.15 \text{ for each dinner.}$$

Skill 14.7   Demonstrate an understanding of the characteristics of linear models and the advantages and disadvantages of using a linear model in a given situation.

The individual data points on the graph of a linear relationship cluster around a line of best fit. In other words, a relationship is linear if we can sketch a straight line that roughly fits the data points. Thus, in linear relationships the y variable varies by a fixed, absolute amount for each change in x (e.g. 3 units each time). Consider the following examples of linear and non-linear relationships.

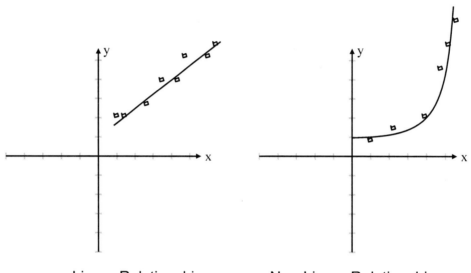

Linear Relationship   Non-Linear Relationship

Note that the non-linear relationship, an exponential relationship in this case, appears linear in parts of the curve. In addition, contrast the preceding graphs to the graph of a data set that shows no relationship between variables.

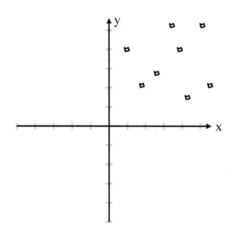

Extrapolation is the process of estimating data points outside a known set of data points. When extrapolating data of a linear relationship, we extend the line of best fit beyond the known values. The extension of the line represents the estimated data points. Extrapolating data is only appropriate if we are relatively certain that the relationship is indeed linear. For example, the death rate of an emerging disease may increase rapidly at first and level off as time goes on. Thus, extrapolating the death rate as if it were linear would yield inappropriately high values at later times. Similarly, extrapolating certain data in a strictly linear fashion, with no restrictions, may yield obviously inappropriate results. For instance, if the number of plant species in a forest were decreasing with time in a linear fashion, extrapolating the data set to infinity would eventually yield a negative number of species, which is clearly unreasonable.

Thus, linear models, when applied appropriately, can simplify the process of trend identification and prediction. Researchers must ensure, however, that the observed data indeed indicates a linear relationship, as creating a linear model when not appropriate can yield aberrant results.

COMPETENCY 15.0 UNDERSTAND AND USE NONLINEAR FUNCTIONS AND RELATIONS TO MODEL AND SOLVE PROBLEMS.

Skill 15.1 **Use a variety of methods to investigate the roots (real and complex), vertex, and symmetry of a quadratic function or relation.**

The discriminant of a quadratic equation is the part of the quadratic formula that is usually inside the radical sign, $b^2 - 4ac$.

$$x = \frac{-b \pm \sqrt{b^2 - 4ac}}{2a}$$

The radical sign is NOT part of the discriminant!! Determine the value of the discriminant by substituting the values of a, b, and c from $ax^2 + bx + c = 0$.

-If the value of the discriminant is **any negative number**, then there are **two complex roots** including "i."
-If the value of the discriminant is **zero**, then there is only **1 real rational root**. This would be a double root.
-If the value of the discriminant is **any positive number that is also a perfect square**, then there are **two real rational roots.** (There are no longer any radical signs.)
-If the value of the discriminant is **any positive number that is NOT a perfect square**, then there are **two real irrational roots.** (There are still unsimplified radical signs.)

Example:

Find the value of the discriminant for the following equations. Then determine the number and nature of the solutions of that quadratic equation.

A) $$2x^2 - 5x + 6 = 0$$

$a = 2$, $b = {}^-5$, $c = 6$ so $b^2 - 4ac = ({}^-5)^2 - 4(2)(6) = 25 - 48 = {}^-23$.

Since ${}^-23$ is a negative number, there are **two complex roots** including "i".

$$x = \frac{5}{4} + \frac{i\sqrt{23}}{4}, \quad x = \frac{5}{4} - \frac{i\sqrt{23}}{4}$$

B) $$3x^2 - 12x + 12 = 0$$

$a = 3$, $b = {}^-12$, $c = 12$ so $b^2 - 4ac = ({}^-12)^2 - 4(3)(12) = 144 - 144 = 0$

Since 0 is the value of the discriminant, there is only **1 real rational root.**

$$x=2$$

C) $$6x^2 - x - 2 = 0$$

$a = 6$, $b = {}^-1$, $c = {}^-2$ so $b^2 - 4ac = ({}^-1)^2 - 4(6)({}^-2) = 1 + 48 = 49$.

Since 49 is positive and is also a perfect square $(\sqrt{49}) = 7$, then there are **two real rational roots.**

$$x = \frac{2}{3}, \quad x = -\frac{1}{2}$$

A **quadratic equation** is written in the form $ax^2 + bx + c = 0$. To solve a quadratic equation by factoring, at least one of the factors must equal zero.

Example: $3x^2 - 20x - 7$ has two factors.

$(3x + 1)$ and $(x - 7)$

To confirm, we use the FOIL method.

$$(3x + 1)(x - 7)$$
$$\text{a} \quad \text{b} \quad \text{c} \quad \text{d}$$

1. F= multiply the First terms (a and c) $\rightarrow 3x \cdot x = 3x^2$

2. O=multiply the Outside terms (a and d) $\rightarrow 3x \cdot {}^-7 = {}^- 21x$

3. I=multiply the Inside terms (b and c) $\rightarrow 1 \cdot x = x$
   Add the inside and outside answers $\rightarrow {}^- 21x + x = {}^- 20x$

4. L=multiply the Last terms $\rightarrow 1 \cdot {}^- 7 = {}^- 7$

   Corresponding to $3x^2 - 20x - 7$

Example: Solve the equation.

$$x^2 + 10x - 24 = 0$$
$$(x + 12)(x - 2) = 0 \qquad \text{Factor.}$$
$$x + 12 = 0 \text{ or } x - 2 = 0 \qquad \text{Set each factor equal to 0.}$$
$$x = {}^{-}12 \qquad x = 2 \qquad \text{Solve.}$$

Check:
$$x^2 + 10x - 24 = 0$$

$$({}^{-}12)^2 + 10({}^{-}12) - 24 = 0 \qquad (2)^2 + 10(2) - 24 = 0$$
$$144 - 120 - 24 = 0 \qquad\qquad 4 + 20 - 24 = 0$$
$$0 = 0 \qquad\qquad\qquad\qquad 0 = 0$$

A quadratic equation that cannot be solved by factoring can be solved by completing the square.

Example: Solve the equation.

$$x^2 - 6x + 8 = 0$$
$$x^2 - 6x = {}^{-}8 \qquad \text{Move the constant to the right side.}$$
$$x^2 - 6x + 9 = {}^{-}8 + 9 \qquad \text{Add the square of half the coefficient of } x \text{ to both sides.}$$

$$(x - 3)^2 = 1 \qquad \text{Write the left side as a perfect square.}$$
$$x - 3 = \pm\sqrt{1} \qquad \text{Take the square root of both sides.}$$

$$x - 3 = 1 \qquad x - 3 = {}^{-}1 \qquad \text{Solve.}$$
$$x = 4 \qquad\quad x = 2$$

Check:

$$x^2 - 6x + 8 = 0$$
$$4^2 - 6(4) + 8 = 0 \qquad 2^2 - 6(2) + 8 = 0$$
$$16 - 24 + 8 = 0 \qquad 4 - 12 + 8 = 0$$
$$0 = 0 \qquad\qquad\quad 0 = 0$$

The general technique for graphing quadratics is the same as for graphing linear equations. Graphing quadratic equations, however, results in a parabola instead of a straight line.

Example: Graph $y = 3x^2 + x - 2$.

x	$y = 3x^2 + x - 2$
$^-2$	8
$^-1$	0
0	$^-2$
1	2
2	12

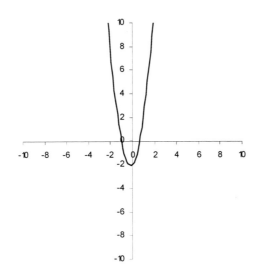

To solve a quadratic equation using the quadratic formula, be sure that your equation is in the form $ax^2 + bx + c = 0$. Substitute these values into the formula:

$$x = \frac{-b \pm \sqrt{b^2 - 4ac}}{2a}$$

Example: Solve the equation.

$$3x^2 = 7 + 2x \rightarrow 3x^2 - 2x - 7 = 0$$

$$a = 3 \quad b = {}^-2 \quad c = {}^-7$$

$$x = \frac{-({}^-2) \pm \sqrt{({}^-2)^2 - 4(3)({}^-7)}}{2(3)}$$

$$x = \frac{2 \pm \sqrt{4 + 84}}{6}$$

$$x = \frac{2 \pm \sqrt{88}}{6}$$

$$x = \frac{2 \pm 2\sqrt{22}}{6}$$

$$x = \frac{1 \pm \sqrt{22}}{3}$$

Skill 15.2   Demonstrate an understanding of the connections among geometric, graphic, numeric, and symbolic representations of quadratic functions.

Quadratic functions are functions of the form $f(x) = ax^2 + bx + c$. A common tool used to solve quadratic equations in scientific problems is the quadratic formula. The quadratic formula produces the solutions of a standard form quadratic equation.

$$x = \frac{-b \pm \sqrt{b^2 - 4ac}}{2a} \quad \{\text{Quadratic Formula}\}$$

GRAPHS OF QUADRATIC FUNCTIONS

The graphs of quadratic functions are parabolas. Parabolas are u-shaped curves that may open upward or downward and vary in height and steepness. To graph quadratic functions, it is best to first convert the function to standard form. Standard form for quadratic functions is $f(x) = a(x - h)^2 + k$. Working from standard form, the vertical axis of symmetry is the line $x = h$. The vertex is the point (h, k). Finally, the parabola opens up if a is positive and down if a is negative.

TRANSFORMATIONS OF QUADRATIC GRAPHS

Different types of function transformations affect the graph and characteristics of a function in predictable ways. The basic types of transformation are horizontal and vertical shift, horizontal and vertical scaling, and reflection. As an example of the types of transformations, we will consider transformations of the functions $f(x) = x^2$.

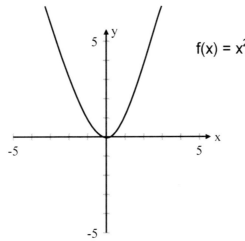

$f(x) = x^2$

Horizontal shifts take the form g(x) = f(x $\pm$ c). For example, we obtain the graph of the function g(x) = (x + 2)^2 by shifting the graph of f(x) = x^2 two units to the left. The graph of the function h(x) = (x – 2)^2 is the graph of f(x) = x^2 shifted two units to the right.

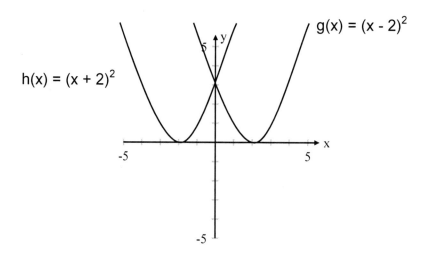

Vertical shifts take the form g(x) = f(x) $\pm$ c. For example, we obtain the graph of the function g(x) = (x^2) – 2 by shifting the graph of f(x) = x^2 two units down. The graph of the function h(x) = (x^2) + 2 is the graph of f(x) = x^2 shifted two units up.

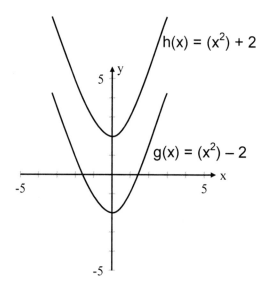

Horizontal scaling takes the form $g(x) = f(cx)$. For example, we obtain the graph of the function $g(x) = (2x)^2$ by compressing the graph of $f(x) = x^2$ in the x-direction by a factor of two. If $c > 1$ the graph is compressed in the x-direction, while if $1 > c > 0$ the graph is stretched in the x-direction.

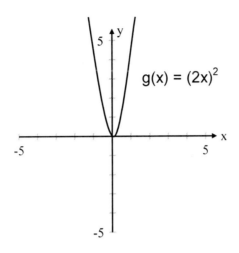

$$g(x) = (2x)^2$$

Vertical scaling takes the form $g(x) = cf(x)$. For example, we obtain the graph of $g(x) = 1/2(x^2)$ by compressing the graph of $f(x) = x^2$ in the y-direction by a factor of 1/2. If $c > 1$ the graph is stretched in the y-direction while if $1 > c > 0$ the graph is compressed in the y-direction.

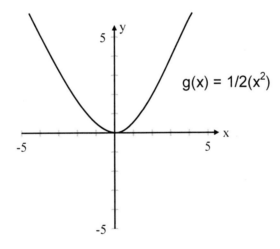

$$g(x) = 1/2(x^2)$$

Related to scaling is reflection, in which the graph of a function flips across either the x or y-axis. Reflections take the form of g(x) = f(-x), horizontal reflection, and g(x) = -f(x), vertical reflection. For example, we obtain the graph of g(x) = -(x²) by reflecting the graph of f(x) = x² across the x-axis. Note that in the case of f(x) = x², horizontal reflection produces the same graph because the function is horizontally symmetrical.

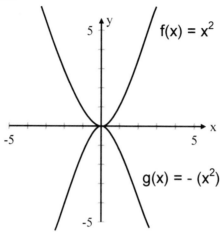

Skill 15.3   Analyze data, represent and solve problems involving exponential growth and decay.

An **exponential function** is a function defined by the equation $y = ab^x$, where a is the starting value, b is the growth factor, and x tells how many times to multiply by the growth factor.

Example: $y = 100(1.5)^x$

x	y
0	100
1	150
2	225
3	337.5
4	506.25

This is an **exponential** or multiplicative pattern of growth.

Two or more quantities can vary directly or inversely to each other. To convert the statements to equations, we introduce another quantity which is constant, called the constant of proportionality.

1)   If x varies directly as y, then $x = k\,y$, where k is the constant of proportionality, or, just a constant.

2)   If x varies inversely as y, then $x = \dfrac{k}{y}$, where k is the constant.

Procedure to solve proportionality problems:

1)   Translate the problem into a mathematical equation.

       Note: k is always in the numerator.
             -the variable that follows the word directly is also in the numerator.
             -the variable that follows the word inversely is in the denominator.

2)   Substitute the given complete set of values in the equation to find k.

       Note: Since k is constant, it will stay the same for any values associated with the other variables.

3)   Substitute the known values of the variables in the equation and solve for the missing variable.

Example: If x varies directly as y, and $x = 6$ when $y = 8$, find y when $x = 48$.

       x varies directly as $y \rightarrow x = ky$ (equation 1)

       Substitute $x = 6$ and $y = 8$ into equation 1 to get

$$6 = 8k \rightarrow k = \frac{6}{8} \rightarrow k = \frac{3}{4}$$

       Substitute $k = \dfrac{3}{4}$ into equation 1 for $x = 48$, we get:

$$48 = \frac{3}{4}y \qquad \text{Multiply both sides by } \frac{4}{3}.$$

$$\frac{4}{3}(48) = y$$

$$y = 64$$

Example: A varies inversely as the square of R. When $A = 2$, $R = 4$. Find A if $R = 10$.

A varies inversely as the square of R.

$$A = \frac{k}{R^2}$$ (equation 1), k is a constant.

Use equation 1 to find k when $A = 2$ and $R = 4$.

$$2 = \frac{k}{4^2} \rightarrow 2 = \frac{k}{16} \rightarrow k = 32 \text{ .}$$

Substituting $k = 32$ into equation 1 with $R = 10$, we get:

$$A = \frac{32}{10^2} \rightarrow A = \frac{32}{100} \rightarrow A = 0.32$$

Example: x varies directly as the cube root of y and inversely as the square of z. When $x = 2$, $y = 27$ and $z = 1$. Find y when $z = 2$ and $x = 1$.

x varies directly as the cube root of y and inversely as the square of z.

$$x = k \cdot \frac{\sqrt[3]{y}}{z^2}$$ (equation 1), k is constant.

Substituting in equation 1 to solve for k when $x = 2$, $y = 27$, and $z = 1$ we get:

$$2 = k \cdot \frac{\sqrt[3]{27}}{1^2} \rightarrow 2 = k \cdot \frac{3}{1} \rightarrow 2 = 3k$$

$$k = \frac{2}{3}$$

To solve for y when $z = 2$ and $x = 1$, we substitute in equation 1 using the value we found for k to get:

$$1 = \frac{2}{3} \cdot \frac{\sqrt[3]{y}}{2^2} \rightarrow 1 = \frac{2 \cdot \sqrt[3]{y}}{3(4)} \rightarrow 1 = \frac{2 \cdot \sqrt[3]{y}}{12}$$

$$1 = \frac{\sqrt[3]{y}}{6} \rightarrow 6 = \sqrt[3]{y} \quad \text{Cube both sides.}$$

$$6^3 = \left(\sqrt[3]{y}\right)^3$$

$$y = 216$$

Exponential Functions

The inverse of a logarithmic function is an exponential function. Exponential functions of base *a* take the basic form

$$f(x) = a^x, \text{ where } a > 0 \text{ and not equal to } 1.$$

The domain of the function, *f*, is (-inf., +inf.). The range is the set of all positive real numbers. If a < 1, *f* is a decreasing function and if a > 1 *f* is an increasing function. The y-intercept of f(x) is (0,1) because any base raised to the power of 0 equals 1. Finally, f(x) has a horizontal asymptote at y = 0.

Example: Graph the function $f(x) = 2^x - 4$.

The domain of the function is the set of all real numbers and the range is y > -4. Because the base is greater than 1, the function is increasing. The y-intercept of f(x) is (0,-3). The x-intercept of f(x) is (2,0). The horizontal asymptote of f(x) is y = -4.

Finally, to construct the graph of f(x) we find two additional values for the function. For example, f(-2) = -3.75 and f(3) = 4.

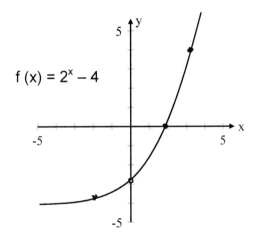

$f(x) = 2^x - 4$

Note that the horizontal asymptote of any exponential function of the form g(x) = a^x + b is y = b. Note also that the graph of such exponential functions is the graph of h(x) = a^x shifted b units up or down. Finally, the graph of exponential functions of the form g(x) = $a^{(x + b)}$ is the graph of h(x) = a^x shifted b units left or right.

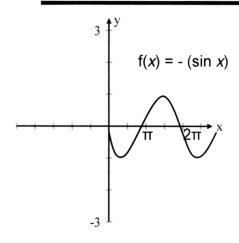

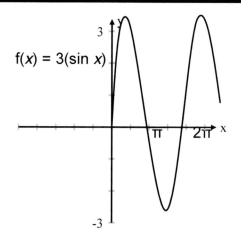

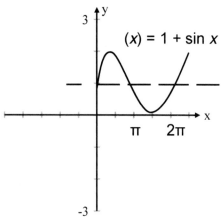

Note the graph of f(x) = - (sin x) is a reflection of f(x) = sin x about the x -axis. The graph of f(x) = 3 (sin x) is a vertical stretch of f(x) = sin x by a factor of 3 that produces an increase in amplitude or range. The graph of f(x) = 1 + sin x is a 1 unit vertical shift of f(x) = sin x. In all cases, the period of the graph is 2π, the same as the period of f(x) = sin x.

Skill 15.4   **Demonstrate an understanding of the connections among proportions, inverse variation, and rational functions.**

Proportions are comparisons of ratios. A proportion is an equation that shows two ratios are equal. For example,

$$\frac{1}{3} = \frac{2}{6} \text{ or } 1:3 = 2:6$$

is a proportion that shows the ratios $\frac{1}{3}$ and $\frac{2}{6}$ are equal. One type of proportions is direct proportions. In direct proportions, each portion of the ratio changes by the same factor. Thus, the preceding example is a direct proportion as both portions of the ratio increase by a factor of two.

Inverse variations (or indirect proportions) are another type of proportion. In inverse proportions, one portion of the ratio gets larger as the other portion gets smaller. In other words, each if one portion of a ratio changes by a factor of x, the other portion of the ratio changes by a factor of $\frac{1}{x}$. For example, if B is indirectly proportional to A, the equation takes the form B $= \frac{k}{A}$ where k is the variation constant. Thus, as one part of the proportion varies by a given quantity, the other part varies by the reciprocal of the quantity.

Rational functions are functions that we can represent as a ratio of two polynomials. For example,

$$\frac{x^2 + 3x - 5}{2x^2 + 5x - 2}$$

is a rational function. The standard form equations of direct proportions (y = kx) and indirect proportions (xy = k) are rational functions.

Skill 15.5   **Understand the effects of transformations such as f(x = c) on the graph of a nonlinear function f(x).**

See Skill 15.2.

Skill 15.6   **Apply properties, graphs, and applications of nonlinear functions to analyze, model, and solve problems.**

Commonly used nonlinear functions include logarithmic functions, exponential functions, quadratic functions, and trigonometric functions.

LOGARITHMIC AND EXPONENTIAL FUNCTIONS

Logarithmic and exponential functions have distinctive characteristics and properties that aid in the identification of unknown graphs and the derivation of symbolic equations from known graphs.

Logarithmic Functions

Logarithmic functions of base a are of the basic form

$f(x) = \log_a x$, where a > 0 and not equal to 1.

The domain of the function, f, is (0, + inf.) and the range is (- inf., + inf.). The x-intercept of the logarithmic function is (1,0) because any number raised to the power of 0 is equal to one. The graph of the function, f, has a vertical asymptote at x = 0. As the value of f(x) approaches negative infinity, x becomes closer and closer to 0.

Example:

Graph the function $f(x) = \log_2 (x + 1)$.

The domain of the function is all values of x such that x + 1 > 0.
Thus, the domain of f(x) is x > -1.

The range of f(x) is (-inf., +inf.).

The vertical asymptote of f(x) is the value of x that satisfies the equation x + 1 = 0. Thus, the vertical asymptote is x = -1. Note that we can find the vertical asymptote of a logarithmic function by setting the product of the logarithm (containing the variable) equal to 0.

The x-intercept of f(x) is the value of x that satisfies the equation x + 1 = 1 because $2^0 = 1$. Thus, the x-intercept of f(x) is (0,0). Note that we can find the x-intercept of a logarithmic function by setting the product of the logarithm equal to 1.

Finally, we find two additional values of f(x), one between the vertical asymptote and the x-intercept and the other to the right of the x-intercept. For example, f(-0.5) = -1 and f(3) = 2.

$f(x) = \log_2 (x + 1)$

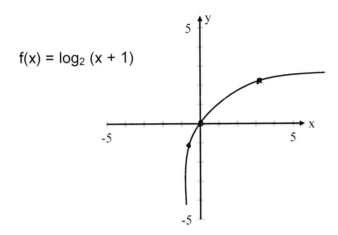

Exponential Functions

The inverse of a logarithmic function is an exponential function. Exponential functions of base a take the basic form

$f(x) = a^x$, where a > 0 and not equal to 1.

The domain of the function, f, is (-inf., +inf.). The range is the set of all positive real numbers. If a < 1, f is a decreasing function and if a > 1 f is an increasing function. The y-intercept of f(x) is (0,1) because any base raised to the power of 0 equals 1. Finally, f(x) has a horizontal asymptote at y = 0.

Example:

Graph the function $f(x) = 2^x - 4$.

The domain of the function is the set of all real numbers and the range is y > -4. Because the base is greater than 1, the function is increasing. The y-intercept of f(x) is (0,-3). The x-intercept of f(x) is (2,0). The horizontal asymptote of f(x) is y = -4.

Finally, to construct the graph of f(x) we find two additional values for the function. For example, f(-2) = -3.75 and f(3) = 4.

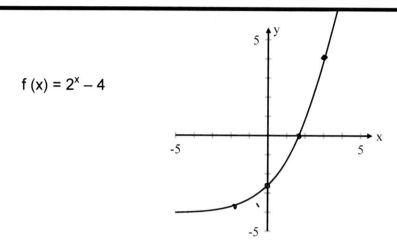

$f(x) = 2^x - 4$

Note that the horizontal asymptote of any exponential function of the form $g(x) = a^x + b$ is $y = b$. Note also that the graph of such exponential functions is the graph of $h(x) = a^x$ shifted b units up or down. Finally, the graph of exponential functions of the form $g(x) = a^{(x + b)}$ is the graph of $h(x) = a^x$ shifted b units left or right.

APPLICATIONS OF EXPONENTIAL AND LOGARITHMIC FUNCTIONS

In finance, the value of a sum of money with compounded interest increases at a rate proportional to the original value. We use an exponential function to determine the growth of an investment accumulating compounded interest. The formula for calculating the value of an investment after a given compounding period is

$$A(t) = A_0(1 + \frac{i}{n})^{nt}.$$

A_0 is the principle, the original value of the investment. The rate of interest is i, the time in years is t, and the number of times the interest is compounded per year is n.

We can solve the compound interest formula for any of the variables by utilizing the properties of exponents and logarithms.

Examples:

1. Determine how long it will take $100 to amount to $1000 at 8% interest compounded 4 times annually.

In this problem we are given the principle ($A_0 = 100$), the final value ($A(t) = 1000$), the interest rate ($i = .08$), and the number of compounding periods per year ($n = 4$). Thus, we solve the compound interest formula for t. Solving for t involves the use logarithms, the inverse function of exponents. To simplify calculations, we use the natural logarithm, ln.

$$A(t) = A_0(1 + \frac{i}{n})^{nt}$$

$$\frac{A(t)}{A_0} = (1 + \frac{i}{n})^{nt}$$

$$\ln\frac{A(t)}{A_0} = \ln(1 + \frac{i}{n})^{nt}$$ Take the ln of both sides.

$$\ln\frac{A(t)}{A_0} = (nt)\ln(1 + \frac{i}{n})$$

Use the properties of logarithms with exponents.

$$\ln\frac{1000}{100} = (4t)\ln(1 + \frac{0.08}{4})$$

Substitute and solve for time (t).

$$t = \frac{\ln 10}{4(\ln 1.02)} = 29.07\,years$$

2. Find the principle (A_0) that yields $500 with an interest rate of 7.5% compounded semiannually for 20 years.

In this problem $A(t) = 500$, the interest rate (i) is 0.075, $n = 2$, and $t = 20$. To find the principle value, we solve for A_0.

$$A(t) = A_0(1 + \frac{i}{n})^{nt}$$

$$500 = A_0(1 + \frac{0.075}{2})^{2(20)}$$

Substitute and solve for A_0.

$$A_0 = \frac{500}{1.0375^{40}} = \$114.67$$

TRIGONOMETRIC FUNCTIONS

Mathematicians use trigonometric functions to model and solve problems involving naturally occurring periodic phenomena. Examples of periodic phenomena found in nature include all forms of radiation (ultraviolet rays, visible light, microwaves, etc.), sound waves, and pendulums. Additionally, trigonometric functions often approximate fluctuations in temperature, employment, and consumer behavior (business models).The following are examples of the use of the sine function to model problems.

Example:

The general form of the sine function that is useful in modeling problems involving time is

$$y = A[\sin \omega(t - \alpha)] + C = A[\sin(\omega t - \alpha\omega) + C$$

where A is the amplitude, C is the vertical offset, ω is the angular frequency $(\frac{2\pi}{P}$, P is period), t is the time in years, and α is the horizontal offset or phase shift.

Consider the following situation. An economist at a temporary employment agency reports that the demand for temporary employment (as measured by thousands of applications for week) varies according to the following model where t is the time in years starting with January 2002.

Demand (d) = 4.7sin(0.75t + 0.4) + 7.7

From this model, we can calculate the characteristics of the sine function and interpret the cyclical nature of demand for temporary employment. Applying the general sine function formula to the model:

A = 4.7
C = 7.7
ω = 0.75
$\omega\alpha$ = 0.4 ⟶ α = 0.4/0.75 = 0.53
P (period) = $\frac{2\pi}{\omega}$ = 8.4

Thus, we interpret the model as follows.

The demand for temporary employment fluctuates in cycles of 8.4 years (period) about a baseline of 7,700 job applications per week (vertical offset). The peak of each cycle is approximately 12,400 job applications per week and the low point of each cycle is 3,000 (vertical offset ± amplitude).

- http://people.hofstra.edu/faculty/Stefan_Waner/trig/trig1.html
derived Example 2 from this website

Scientists use mathematical tools and equations to model and solve scientific problems. Solving scientific problems often involves the use of quadratic, trigonometric, exponential, and logarithmic functions.

Quadratic equations take the standard form $ax^2 + bx + c = 0$. The most appropriate method of solving quadratic equations in scientific problems is the use of the quadratic formula. The quadratic formula produces the solutions of a standard form quadratic equation.

$$x = \frac{-b \pm \sqrt{b^2 - 4ac}}{2a}$$ {Quadratic Formula}

One common application of quadratic equations is the description of biochemical reaction equilibriums. Consider the following problem.

Example 1

80.0 g of ethanoic acid (MW = 60g) reacts with 85.0 g of ethanol (MW = 46g) until equilibrium. The equilibrium constant is 4.00. Determine the amounts of ethyl acetate and water produced at equilibrium.

$$CH_3COOH + CH_3CH_2OH = CH_3CO_2C_2H_5 + H_2O$$

The equilibrium constant, K, describes equilibrium of the reaction, relating the concentrations of products to reactants.

$$K = \frac{[CH_3CO_2C_2H_5][H_2O]}{[CH_3CO_2H][CH_3CH_2OH]} = 4.00$$

The equilibrium values of reactants and products are listed in the following table.

	CH_3COOH	CH_3CH_2OH	$CH_3CO_2C_2H_5$	H_2O
Initial	80/60 = 1.33 mol	85/46 = 1.85 mol	0	0
Equilibrium	1.33 – x	1.85 – x	x	x

Thus, $K = \dfrac{[x][x]}{[1.33-x][1.85-x]} = \dfrac{x^2}{2.46 - 3.18x + x^2} = 4.00$.

Rearrange the equation to produce a standard form quadratic equation.

$$\frac{x^2}{2.46 - 3.18x + x^2} = 4.00$$

$$x^2 = 4.00(2.46 - 3.18x + x^2) = 9.84 - 12.72x + 4x^2$$

$$0 = 3x^2 - 12.72x + 9.84$$

Use the quadratic formula to solve for x.

$$x = \frac{-(-12.72) \pm \sqrt{(-12.72)^2 - 4(3)(9.84)}}{2(3)} = 3.22 \text{ or } 1.02$$

3.22 is not an appropriate answer, because we started with only 3.18 moles of reactants. Thus, the amount of each product produced at equilibrium is 1.02 moles.

Scientists use trigonometric functions to define angles and lengths. For example, field biologists can use trigonometric functions to estimate distances and directions. The basic trigonometric functions are sine, cosine, and tangent. Consider the following triangle describing these relationships.

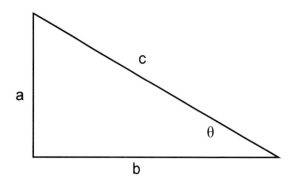

$$\sin \theta = \frac{a}{c}, \cos \theta = \frac{b}{c}, \tan \theta = \frac{a}{b}$$

Exponential functions are useful in modeling many scientific phenomena. For example, scientists use exponential functions to describe bacterial growth and radioactive decay. The general form of exponential equations is $f(x) = Ca^x$ (C is a constant). Consider the following problem involving bacterial growth.

Example 2

Determine the number of bacteria present in a culture inoculated with a single bacterium after 24 hours if the bacterial population doubles every 2 hours. Use $N(t) = N_0 e^{kt}$ as a model of bacterial growth where N(t) is the size of the population at time t, N_0 is the initial population size, and k is the growth constant.

We must first determine the growth constant, k. At t = 2, the size of the population doubles from 1 to 2. Thus, we substitute and solve for k.

$$2 = 1(e^{2k})$$

$\ln 2 = \ln e^{2k}$ Take the natural log of each side.

$\ln 2 = 2k(\ln e) = 2k$ ln e = 1

$k = \dfrac{\ln 2}{2}$ Solve for k.

Thus, the population size at t = 24 is

$$N(24) = e^{(\frac{\ln 2}{2})24} = e^{12\ln 2} = 4096.$$

Finally, logarithmic functions have many applications to science and biology. One simple example of a logarithmic application is the pH scale. Scientists define pH as follows.

pH = - $\log_{10}$ [H+], where [H+] is the concentration of hydrogen ions

Thus, we can determine the pH of a solution with a [H+] value of 0.0005 mol/L by using the logarithmic formula.

pH = - $\log_{10}$ [0.0005] = 3.3

Skill 15.7 **Use a variety of representations and methods (e.g., numerical methods, tables, graphs, algebraic techniques) to solve systems of quadratic equations and inequalities.**

See Skill 14.

Skill 15.8 **Understand how to use properties, graphs, and applications of non-linear relations including polynomial, rational, radical, absolute value, exponential, logarithmic, trigonometric, and piecewise functions and relations to analyze, model, and solve problems.**

To graph an inequality, graph the quadratic as if it was an equation; however, if the inequality has just a $>$ or $<$ sign, then make the curve itself dotted. Shade above the curve for $>$ or $\geq$. Shade below the curve for $<$ or $\leq$.

Examples:

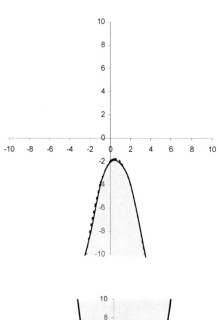

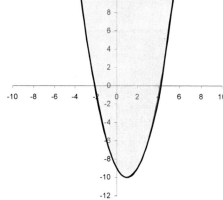

The **absolute value function** for a 1st degree equation is of the form:

$y = m(x - h) + k$. Its graph is in the shape of a $\vee$. The point (h, k) is the location of the maximum/minimum point on the graph. "$\pm m$" are the slopes of the 2 sides of the $\vee$. The graph opens up if m is positive and down if m is negative.

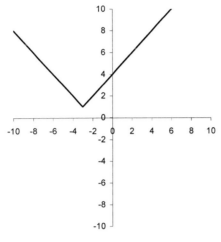

$$y = |x + 3| + 1$$

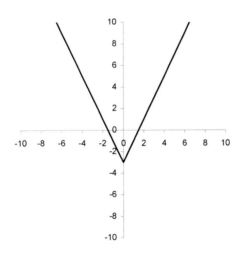

$$y = 2|x| - 3$$

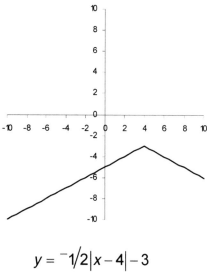

$$y = {}^-1/2|x-4|-3$$

Note that on the first graph above, the graph opens up since m is positive 1. It has $(^-3,1)$ as its minimum point. The slopes of the 2 upward rays are ± 1.

The second graph also opens up since m is positive. Its minimum point is $(0,-3)$. The slopes of the 2 upward rays are ± 2.

The third graph is a downward $\wedge$ because m is $^-1/2$. The maximum point on the graph is at $(4,^-3)$. The slopes of the 2 downward rays are $\pm 1/2$.

The **identity function** is the linear equation $y = x$. Its graph is a line going through the origin $(0,0)$ and through the first and third quadrants at a $45°$ degree angle.

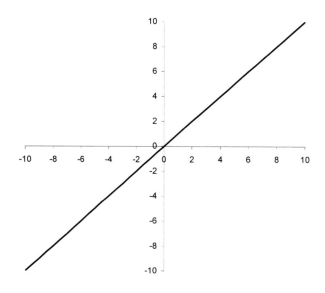

The **greatest integer function** or **step function** has the equation:

$f(x) = j[rx - h] + k$ or $y = j[rx - h] + k$. (h,k) is the location of the left endpoint of one step. j is the vertical jump from step to step. r is the reciprocal of the length of each step. If (x, y) is a point of the function, then when x is an integer, its y value is the same integer. If (x, y) is a point of the function, then when x is not an integer, its y value is the first integer less than x. Points on $y = [x]$ would include: $(3,3)$, $(^-2, ^-2)$, $(0,0)$, $(1.5,1)$, $(2.83,2)$, $(^-3.2, ^-4)$, $(^-.4, ^-1)$.

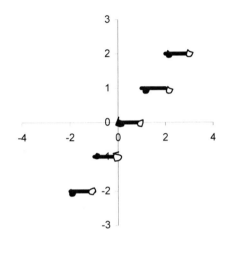

$$y = [x]$$

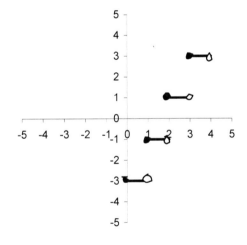

$$y = 2[x] - 3$$

Note that in the graph of the first equation, the steps are going up as they move to the right. Each step is one space wide (inverse of r) with a solid dot on the left and a hollow dot on the right where the jump to the next step occurs. Each step is one square higher (j = 1) than the previous step. One step of the graph starts at $(0,0) \leftarrow$ values of (h,k).

In the second graph, the graph goes up to the right. One step starts at the point $(0,\bar{}3) \leftarrow$ values of (h,k). Each step is one square wide (r = 1) and each step is 2 squares higher than the previous step (j = 2).

A **rational function** is given in the form $f(x) = p(x)/q(x)$. In the equation, $p(x)$ and $q(x)$ both represent polynomial functions where $q(x)$ does not equal zero. The branches of rational functions approach asymptotes. Setting the denominator equal to zero and solving will give the value(s) of the vertical asymptotes(s) since the function will be undefined at this point. If the value of $f(x)$ approaches b as the $|x|$ increases, the equation $y = b$ is a horizontal asymptote. To find the horizontal asymptote it is necessary to make a table of value for x that are to the right and left of the vertical asymptotes. The pattern for the horizontal asymptotes will become apparent as the $|x|$ increases.

If there are more than one vertical asymptotes, remember to choose numbers to the right and left of each one in order to find the horizontal asymptotes and have sufficient points to graph the function.

Example: Graph $f(x) = \dfrac{3x+1}{x-2}$.

$x - 2 = 0$
$x = 2$

1. Set denominator $= 0$ to find the vertical asymptote.

x	f(x)
3	10
10	3.875
100	3.07
1000	3.007
1	$^-4$
$^-10$	2.417
$^-100$	2.93
$^-1000$	2.99

2. Make table choosing numbers to the right and left of the vertical asymptote.

3. The pattern shows that as the $|x|$ increases $f(x)$ approaches the value 3, therefore a horizontal asymptote exists at $y = 3$

Sketch the graph.

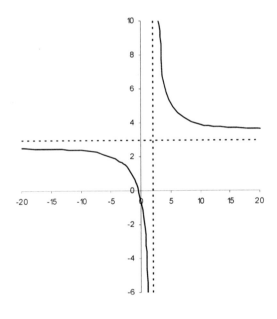

Functions defined by two or more formulas are **piecewise functions**. The formula used to evaluate piecewise functions varies depending on the value of x. The graphs of piecewise functions consist of two or more pieces, or intervals, and are often discontinuous.

Example:

Example:

$$f(x) = \begin{array}{l} x + 1 \quad \text{if } x > 2 \\ x - 2 \quad \text{if } x \le 2 \end{array}$$

$$f(x) = \begin{array}{l} x \quad \text{if } x \ge 1 \\ x^2 \quad \text{if } x < 1 \end{array}$$

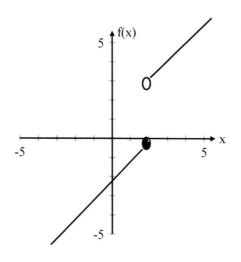

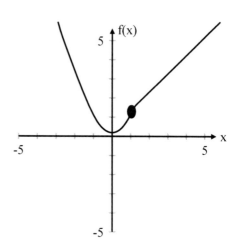

When graphing or interpreting the graph of piecewise functions it is important to note the points at the beginning and end of each interval because the graph must clearly indicate what happens at the end of each interval. Note that in the graph of Example 1, point (2, 3) is not part of the graph and is represented by an empty circle. On the other hand, point (2, 0) is part of the graph and is represented as a solid circle. Note also that the graph of Example 2 is continuous despite representing a piecewise function.

COMPETENCY 16.0 USE AND UNDERSTAND THE CONCEPTUAL FOUNDATIONS OF CALCULUS RELATED TO TOPICS IN MIDDLE SCHOOL MATHEMATICS.

Skill 16.1 Relates topics in middle school mathematics to the concept of limit in sequences and series.

When teaching sequences and series, middle school teachers should introduce the concept of limit because understanding of limits is essential to the understanding of topics in pre-calculus and calculus.

A sequence is a list of numbers that follow a specific pattern. For example, the following list of numbers represents a sequence defined by the formula $\dfrac{n}{n+1}$.

$$\frac{1}{2}, \frac{2}{3}, \frac{3}{4}, \frac{4}{5}, \frac{5}{6}, \dots \frac{99}{100}, \dots$$

We say the limit of the sequence is 1, because as n approaches infinity, the sequence approaches 1. Thus, a limit is the upper or lower boundary of a sequence; the value that the sequence will never pass.

A series is a sum of numbers. Convergent series possess a numerical limit. For example, the sum of the series $\dfrac{1}{2^n}$ starting with n = 1, has a limit of 1. We represent the series as follows:

$$\sum_{n=1}^{\infty} \frac{1}{2^n} = \frac{1}{2} + \frac{1}{4} + \frac{1}{8} + \frac{1}{16} + \frac{1}{32} + \dots$$

The symbol $\sum$ (sigma) represents summation and the numbers to the right of the sigma symbol are the beginning and end values of the series. Note, that no matter how many values we add in the series, the total sum approaches, but never reaches 1.

Skill 16.2 **Relates the concept of average rate of change to the slope of the secant line and instantaneous rate of change to the slope of the tangent line.**

The **difference quotient** is the average rate of change over an interval. For a function f, the **difference quotient** is represented by the formula:

$$\frac{f(x+h)-f(x)}{h}.$$

This formula computes the slope of the secant line through two points on the graph of f. These are the points with x-coordinates x and $x+h$.

Example: Find the difference quotient for the function $f(x)=2x^2+3x-5$.

$$\frac{f(x+h)-f(x)}{h}=\frac{2(x+h)^2+3(x+h)-5-(2x^2+3x-5)}{h}$$

$$=\frac{2(x^2+2hx+h^2)+3x+3h-5-2x^2-3x+5}{h}$$

$$=\frac{2x^2+4hx+2h^2+3x+3h-5-2x^2-3x+5}{h}$$

$$=\frac{4hx+2h^2+3h}{h}$$

$$=4x+2h+3$$

The **derivative** is the slope of a tangent line to a graph $f(x)$, and is usually denoted $f'(x)$. This is also referred to as the instantaneous rate of change.

The derivative of $f(x)$ at $x=a$ is given by taking the limit of the average rates of change (computed by the difference quotient) as h approaches 0.

$$f'(a)=\lim_{h\to 0}\frac{f(a+h)-f(a)}{h}$$

Example: Suppose a company's annual profit (in millions of dollars) is represented by the above function $f(x) = 2x^2 + 3x - 5$ and x represents the number of years in the interval. Compute the rate at which the annual profit was changing over a period of 2 years.

$$f'(a) = \lim_{h \to 0} \frac{f(a+h) - f(a)}{h}$$

$$= f'(2) = \lim_{h \to 0} \frac{f(2+h) - f(2)}{h}$$

Using the difference quotient we computed above, $4x + 2h + 3$, we get

$$f'(2) = \lim_{h \to 0} (4(2) + 2h + 3)$$
$$= 8 + 3$$
$$= 11.$$

We have, therefore, determined that the annual profit for the company has increased at the average rate of $11 million per year over the two-year period.

Skill 16.3 **Relates topics in middle school mathematics to the area under a curve.**

Taking the integral of a function and evaluating it from one x value to another provides the total **area under the curve** (i.e. between the curve and the x axis). Remember, though, that regions above the x axis have "positive" area and regions below the x axis have "negative" area. You must account for these positive and negative values when finding the area under curves. Follow these steps.

1. Determine the x values that will serve as the left and right boundaries of the region.
2. Find all x values between the boundaries that are either solutions to the function or are values which are not in the domain of the function. These numbers are the interval numbers.
3. Integrate the function.
4. Evaluate the integral once for each of the intervals using the boundary numbers.
5. If any of the intervals evaluates to a negative number, make it positive (the negative simply tells you that the region is below the x axis).
6. Add the value of each integral to arrive at the area under the curve.

Example:

Find the area under the following function on the given intervals.
$f(x) = \sin x$; $(0, 2\pi)$

$\sin x = 0$

Find any roots to f(x) on $(0, 2\pi)$.

$x = \pi$

$(0, \pi)$ $(\pi, 2\pi)$

Determine the intervals using the boundary numbers and the roots.

$\int \sin x\,dx = {}^- \cos x$

Integrate f(x). We can ignore the constant c because we have numbers to use to evaluate the integral.

$\left. {}^- \cos x \right]_{x=0}^{x=\pi} = {}^- \cos \pi - ({}^- \cos 0)$

$\left. {}^- \cos x \right]_{x=0}^{x=\pi} = {}^- (-1) + (1) = 2$

$\left. {}^- \cos x \right]_{x=\pi}^{x=2\pi} = {}^- \cos 2\pi - ({}^- \cos \pi)$

$\left. {}^- \cos x \right]_{x=\pi}^{x=2\pi} = {}^- 1 + ({}^- 1) = {}^- 2$

The $^-2$ means that for $(\pi, 2\pi)$, the region is below the x axis, but the area is still 2.

Area $= 2 + 2 = 4$

Add the 2 integrals together to get the area.

The derivative of a function has two basic interpretations.

    I.   Instantaneous rate of change
    II.   Slope of a tangent line at a given point

If a question asks for the rate of change of a function, take the derivative to find the equation for the rate of change. Then plug in for the variable to find the instantaneous rate of change.

The following is a list summarizing some of the more common quantities referred to in rate of change problems.

area	height	profit
decay	population growth	sales
distance	position	temperature
frequency	pressure	volume

Pick a point, say $x = {}^-3$, on the graph of a function. Draw a tangent line at that point. Find the derivative of the function and plug in $x = {}^-3$. The result will be the slope of the tangent line.

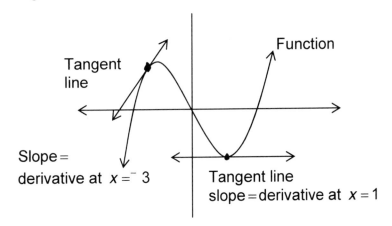

Tangent line

Function

Slope =
derivative at $x = {}^-3$

Tangent line
slope = derivative at $x = 1$

A function is said to be **increasing** if it is rising from left to right and **decreasing** if it is falling from left to right. Lines with positive slopes are increasing, and lines with negative slopes are decreasing. If the function in question is something other than a line, simply refer to the slopes of the tangent lines as the test for increasing or decreasing. Take the derivative of the function and plug in an x value to get the slope of the tangent line; a positive slope means the function is increasing and a negative slope means it is decreasing. If an interval for x values is given, just pick any point between the two values to substitute.

Sample tangent line on $(^-2,0)$

On the interval $(^-2,0)$, $f(x)$ is increasing. The tangent lines on this part of the graph have positive slopes.

Example:

The growth of a certain bacteria is given by $f(x) = x + \dfrac{1}{x}$. Determine if the rate of growth is increasing or decreasing on the time interval $(^-1,0)$.

$f'(x) = 1 + \dfrac{^-1}{x^2}$

$f'\left(\dfrac{^-1}{2}\right) = 1 + \dfrac{^-1}{(^-1/2)^2}$

To test for increasing or decreasing, find the slope of the tangent line by taking the derivative.

$f'\left(\dfrac{^-1}{2}\right) = 1 + \dfrac{^-1}{1/4}$

$= 1 - 4$

$= {}^-3$

Pick any point on $(^-1,0)$ and substitute into the derivative.

The slope of the tangent line at $x = \dfrac{^-1}{2}$ is $^-3$. The exact value of the slope is not important. The important fact is that the slope is negative.

Substituting an x value into a function produces a corresponding y value. The coordinates of the point (x, y), where y is the largest of all the y values, is said to be a **maximum point**. The coordinates of the point (x, y), where y is the smallest of all the y values, is said to be a **minimum point**. To find these points, only a few x values must be tested. First, find all of the x values that make the derivative either zero or undefined. Substitute these values into the original function to obtain the corresponding y values. Compare the y values. The largest y value is a maximum; the smallest y value is a minimum. If the question asks for the maxima or minima on an interval, be certain to also find the y values that correspond to the numbers at either end of the interval.

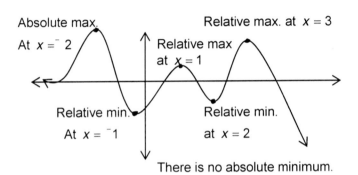

Example:

Find the maxima and minima of $f(x) = 2x^4 - 4x^2$ at the interval $(^-2, 1)$.

$f'(x) = 8x^3 - 8x$	Take the derivative first. Find all the x values (critical values)
$8x^3 - 8x = 0$	that make the derivative zero
$8x(x^2 - 1) = 0$	or undefined. In this case,
$8x(x - 1)(x + 1) = 0$	there are no x values that make
$x = 0,\ x = 1,$ or $x = ^-1$	the derivative undefined.
$f(0) = 2(0)^4 - 4(0)^2 = 0$	Substitute the critical values into the original function. Also,
$f(1) = 2(1)^4 - 4(1)^2 = ^-2$	plug in the endpoint of the
$f(^-1) = 2(^-1)^4 - 4(^-1)^2 = ^-2$	interval. Note that 1 is
$f(^-2) = 2(^-2)^4 - 4(^-2)^2 = 16$	a critical point and an endpoint.

The maximum is at $(^-2, 16)$ and there are minima at $(1, ^-2)$ and $(^-1, ^-2)$. $(0,0)$ is neither the maximum or minimum on $(^-2, 1)$ but it is still considered a relative extra point.

The first derivative reveals whether a curve is rising or falling (increasing or decreasing) from the left to the right. In much the same way, the second derivative relates whether the curve is concave up or concave down. Curves which are concave up are said to "collect water;" curves which are concave down are said to "dump water." To find the intervals where a curve is concave up or concave down, follow the following steps.

1. Take the second derivative (i.e. the derivative of the first derivative).
2. Find the critical x values.
    -Set the second derivative equal to zero and solve for critical x values.
    -Find the x values that make the second derivative undefined (i.e. make the denominator of the second derivative equal to zero).
    Such values may not always exist.
3. Pick sample values which are both less than and greater than each of the critical values.
4. Substitute each of these sample values into the second derivative and determine whether the result is positive or negative.
    -If the sample value yields a positive number for the second derivative, the curve is concave up on the interval where the sample value originated.
    -If the sample value yields a negative number for the second derivative, the curve is concave down on the interval where the sample value originated.

Example:

Find the intervals where the curve is concave up and concave down for
$f(x) = x^4 - 4x^3 + 16x - 16$.

$f'(x) = 4x^3 - 12x^2 + 16$	Take the second derivative.
$f''(x) = 12x^2 - 24x$	Find the critical values by setting the second derivative equal
$12x^2 - 24x = 0$	to zero.
$12x(x-2) = 0$	There are no values that make the second derivative undefined.
$x = 0$ or $x = 2$	

Set up a number line with the critical values.

Sample values: $^-1, 1, 3$

Pick sample values in each of the 3 intervals. If the sample value produces a negative number, the function is concave down.

$f''(^-1) = 12(^-1)^2 - 24(^-1) = 36$

$f''(1) = 12(1)^2 - 24(1) = {}^-12$

$f''(3) = 12(3)^2 - 24(3) = 36$

If the value produces a positive number, the curve is concave up. If the value produces a zero, the function is linear.

A **point of inflection** is a point where a curve changes from being concave up to concave down or vice versa. To find these points, follow the steps for finding the intervals where a curve is concave up or concave down. A critical value is part of an inflection point if the curve is concave up on one side of the value and concave down on the other. The critical value is the x coordinate of the inflection point. To get the y coordinate, plug the critical value into the **original** function.

Example: Find the inflection points of $f(x) = 2x - \tan x$ where $\dfrac{^-\pi}{2} < x < \dfrac{\pi}{2}$.

$(x) = 2x - \tan x \qquad \dfrac{^-\pi}{2} < x < \dfrac{\pi}{2}$ \hspace{2em} Note the restriction on x.

$f'(x) = 2 - \sec^2 x$ \hspace{4em} Take the second derivative.

$f''(x) = 0 - 2 \bullet \sec x \bullet (\sec x \tan x)$ \hspace{2em} Use the Power rule.

$= {}^-2 \bullet \dfrac{1}{\cos x} \bullet \dfrac{1}{\cos x} \bullet \dfrac{\sin x}{\cos x}$ \hspace{2em} The derivative of $\sec x$ is $(\sec x \tan x)$.

$f''(x) = \dfrac{^-2\sin x}{\cos^3 x}$ \hspace{4em} Find critical values by solving for the second derivative equal to zero.

$0 = \dfrac{^-2\sin x}{\cos^3 x}$ \hspace{4em} No x values on $\left(\dfrac{^-\pi}{2}, \dfrac{\pi}{2}\right)$ make the denominator zero.

${}^-2\sin x = 0$
$\sin x = 0$
$x = 0$ \hspace{6em} Pick sample values on each side of the critical value $x = 0$.

$\xleftarrow{\hspace{2em}} \overset{0}{|} \xrightarrow{\hspace{2em}}$

Sample values: \hspace{6em} $x = \dfrac{^-\pi}{4}$ and $x = \dfrac{\pi}{4}$

$f''\left(\dfrac{^-\pi}{4}\right) = \dfrac{^-2\sin(^-\pi/4)}{\cos^3(\pi/4)} = \dfrac{^-2(^-\sqrt{2}/2)}{(\sqrt{2}/2)^3} = \dfrac{\sqrt{2}}{(\sqrt{8}/8)} = \dfrac{8\sqrt{2}}{\sqrt{8}} = \dfrac{8\sqrt{2}}{\sqrt{8}} \bullet \dfrac{\sqrt{8}}{\sqrt{8}}$

$\hspace{10em} = \dfrac{8\sqrt{16}}{8} = 4$

$f''\left(\dfrac{\pi}{4}\right) = \dfrac{^-2\sin(\pi/4)}{\cos^3(\pi/4)} = \dfrac{^-2(\sqrt{2}/2)}{(\sqrt{2}/2)^3} = \dfrac{^-\sqrt{2}}{(\sqrt{8}/8)} = \dfrac{^-8\sqrt{2}}{\sqrt{8}} = -4$

The second derivative is positive on $(0, \infty)$ and negative on $(-\infty, 0)$. So the curve changes concavity at $x = 0$. Use the original equation to find the y value that inflection occurs at.

$$f(0) = 2(0) - \tan 0 = 0 - 0 = 0$$

The inflection point is $(0,0)$.

Skill 16.4 **Demonstrate an understanding of the use of calculus concepts to answer questions about rates of change, areas, volumes, and properties of functions and their graphs.**

Extreme value problems are also known as max-min problems. Extreme value problems require using the first derivative to find values which either maximize or minimize some quantity such as area, profit, or volume. Follow these steps to solve an extreme value problem.

1. Write an equation for the quantity to be maximized or minimized.
2. Use the other information in the problem to write secondary equations.
3. Use the secondary equations for substitutions, and rewrite the original equation in terms of only one variable.
4. Find the derivative of the primary equation (step 1) and the critical values of this derivative.
5. Substitute these critical values into the primary equation. The value which produces either the largest or smallest value is used to find the solution.

Example:

A manufacturer wishes to construct an open box from the piece of metal shown below by cutting squares from each corner and folding up the sides. The square piece of metal is 12 feet on a side. What are the dimensions of the squares to be cut out which will maximize the volume?

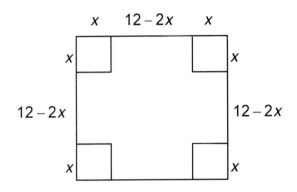

Volume $= lwh$	Primary equation.
$l = 12 - 2x$	
$w = 12 - 2x$	Secondary equations.
$h = x$	
$V = (12 - 2x)(12 - 2x)(x)$	Make substitutions.
$V = (144x - 48x^2 + 4x^3)$	Take the derivative.
$\dfrac{dV}{dx} = 144 - 96x + 12x^2$	
	Find critical values by setting the
$0 = 12(x^2 - 8x + 12)$	derivative equal to zero.
$0 = 12(x - 6)(x - 2)$	
$x = 6$ and $x = 2$	Substitute critical values into volume equation.

$V = 144(6) - 48(6)^2 + 4(6)^3 \qquad V = 144(2) - 48(2)^2 + 4(2)^3$

$\quad V = 0$ ft^3 when $x = 6 \qquad\qquad V = 128$ ft^3 when $x = 2$

Therefore, the manufacturer can maximize the volume if the squares to be cut out are 2 feet by 2 feet ($x = 2$).

If a particle (or a car, a bullet, etc.) is moving along a line, then the **distance that the particle travels** can be expressed by a function in terms of time.

1. The first derivative of the distance function will provide the velocity function for the particle. Substituting a value for time into this expression will provide the instantaneous velocity of the particle at the time. Velocity is the rate of change of the distance traveled by the particle. Taking the absolute value of the derivative provides the speed of the particle. A positive value for the velocity indicates that the particle is moving forward, and a negative value indicates the particle is moving backwards.

2. The second derivative of the distance function (which would also be the first derivative of the velocity function) provides the acceleration function. The acceleration of the particle is the rate of change of the velocity. If a value for time produces a positive acceleration, the particle is speeding up; if it produces a negative value, the particle is slowing down. If the acceleration is zero, the particle is moving at a constant speed.

To find the time when a particle stops, set the first derivative (i.e. the velocity function) equal to zero and solve for time. This time value is also the instant when the particle changes direction.

Example:

The motion of a particle moving along a line is according to the equation:

$s(t) = 20 + 3t - 5t^2$ where s is in meters and t is in seconds. Find the position, velocity, and acceleration of a particle at $t = 2$ seconds.

$s(2) = 20 + 3(2) - 5(2)^2$ $\quad = 6$ meters	Plug $t = 2$ into the original equation to find the position.
$s'(t) = v(t) = 3 - 10t$	The derivative of the first function gives the velocity.
$v(2) = 3 - 10(2) = {}^-17$ m/s	Plug $t = 2$ into the velocity function to find the velocity. ${}^-17$ m/s indicates the particle is moving backwards.
$s''(t) = a(t) = {}^-10$	The second derivation of position gives the acceleration.
$a(2) = {}^-10$ m/s²	Substitute $t = 2$, yields an acceleration of ${}^-10$ m/s², which indicates the particle is slowing down.

Finding the rate of change of one quantity (for example distance, volume, etc.) with respect to time it is often referred to as a rate of change problem. To find an instantaneous rate of change of a particular quantity, write a function in terms of time for that quantity; then take the derivative of the function. Substitute in the values at which the instantaneous rate of change is sought.

Functions which are in terms of more than one variable may be used to find related rates of change. These functions are often not written in terms of time. To find a related rate of change, follow these steps.

1. Write an equation which relates all the quantities referred to in the problem.

2. Take the derivative of both sides of the equation with respect to time.

    Follow the same steps as used in implicit differentiation. This means take the derivative of each part of the equation remembering to multiply each term by the derivative of the variable involved with respect to time. For example, if a term includes the variable v for volume, take the derivative of the term remembering to multiply by dv/dt for the derivative of volume with respect to time. dv/dt is the rate of change of the volume.

3. Substitute the known rates of change and quantities, and solve for the desired rate of change.

Example:

1. What is the instantaneous rate of change of the area of a circle where the radius is 3 cm?

$A(r) = \pi r^2$ Write an equation for area.

$A'(r) = 2\pi r$ Take the derivative to find the rate of change.

$A'(3) = 2\pi(3) = 6\pi$ Substitute in $r = 3$ to arrive at the instantaneous rate of change.

COMPETENCY 17.0 UNDERSTAND MEASUREMENT AS A PROCESS.

Skill 17.1 **Select and use appropriate units of measurement (e.g., temperature, money, mass, weight, area, capacity, density, percents, speed, acceleration) to quantify, compare, and communicate information.**

Measurements of length (English system)

12 inches (in)	=	1 foot (ft)
3 feet (ft)	=	1 yard (yd)
1760 yards (yd)	=	1 mile (mi)

Measurements of length (Metric system)

kilometer (km)	=	1000 meters (m)
hectometer (hm)	=	100 meters (m)
decameter (dam)	=	10 meters (m)
meter (m)	=	1 meter (m)
decimeter (dm)	=	1/10 meter (m)
centimeter (cm)	=	1/100 meter (m)
millimeter (mm)	=	1/1000 meter (m)

Conversion of length from English to Metric

1 inch	=	2.54 centimeters
1 foot	≈	30.48 centimeters
1 yard	≈	0.91 meters
1 mile	≈	1.61 kilometers

Measurements of weight (English system)

28.35 grams (g)	=	1 ounce (oz)
16 ounces (oz)	=	1 pound (lb)
2000 pounds (lb)	=	1 ton (t) (short ton)
1.1 ton (t)	=	1 metric ton (t)

Measurements of weight (Metric system)

kilogram (kg)	=	1000 grams (g)
gram (g)	=	1 gram (g)
milligram (mg)	=	1/1000 gram (g)

Conversion of weight from English to metric

1 ounce	≈	28.35 grams
1 pound	≈	0.454 kilogram
1.1 ton	=	1 metric ton

Measurement of volume (English system)

8 fluid ounces (oz)	=	1 cup (c)
2 cups (c)	=	1 pint (pt)
2 pints (pt)	=	1 quart (qt)
4 quarts (qt)	=	1 gallon (gal)

Measurement of volume (Metric system)

kiloliter (kl)	=	1000 liters (l)
liter (l)	=	1 liter (l)
milliliter (ml)	=	1/1000 liter (ml)

Conversion of volume from English to metric

1 teaspoon (tsp)	≈	5 milliliters
1 fluid ounce	≈	29.56 milliliters
1 cup	≈	0.24 liters
1 pint	≈	0.47 liters
1 quart	≈	0.95 liters

Note: (') represents feet and (") represents inches.

Square units can be derived with knowledge of basic units of length by squaring the equivalent measurements.

> 1 square foot (sq. ft.) = 144 sq. in.
> 1 sq. yd. = 9 sq. ft.
> 1 sq. yd. = 1296 sq. in.

Example:
14 sq. yd. = _____ sq. ft.
14 × 9 = 126 sq. ft.

Skill 17.2   Develop, justify, and use conversions within measurement systems.

Length

Example: A car skidded 170 yards on an icy road before coming to a stop. How long is the skid distance in kilometers?

Since 1 yard ≈ 0.9 meters, multiply 170 yards by 0.9.

$$170 \times 0.9 = 153 \text{ meters}$$

Since 1000 meters = 1 kilometer, divide 153 by 1000.

$$\frac{153}{1000} = 0.153 \text{ kilometers}$$

Example: The distance around a race course is exactly 1 mile, 17 feet, and $9\frac{1}{4}$ inches. Approximate this distance to the nearest tenth of a foot.

Convert the distance to feet.

$$1 \text{ mile} = 1760 \text{ yards} = 1760 \times 3 \text{ feet} = 5280 \text{ feet.}$$
$$9\frac{1}{4} \text{ inches} = \frac{37}{4} \times \frac{1}{12} = \frac{37}{48} \approx 0.77083 \text{ feet}$$

So 1 mile, 17 feet and $9\frac{1}{4}$ inches = $5280 + 17 + 0.77083$ feet
$$= 5297.\underline{7}7083 \text{ feet.}$$

Now, we need to round to the nearest tenth digit. The underlined 7 is in the tenth place. The digit in the hundredth place, also a 7, is greater than 5, the 7 in the tenths place needs to be rounded up to 8 to get a final answer of 5297.8 feet.

Weight

Example: Zachary weighs 150 pounds. Tom weighs 153 pounds. What is the difference in their weights in grams?

153 pounds − 150 pounds = 3 pounds
1 pound = 454 grams
3(454 grams) = 1362 grams

Capacity

Example: Students in a fourth grade class want to fill a 3 gallon jug using cups of water. How many cups of water are needed?

1 gallon = 16 cups of water
3 gallons x 16 cups = 48 cups of water are needed.

Time
Example: It takes Cynthia 45 minutes to get ready each morning. How many hours does she spend getting ready each week?

45 minutes X 7 days = 315 minutes

$$\frac{315 \text{ minutes}}{60 \text{ minutes in an hour}} = 5.25 \text{ hours}$$

Skill 17.3 **Apply dimensional analysis to derive units and formulas in a variety of situations (e.g., rates of change of one variable with respect to another) and to find and evaluate solutions to problems.**

Example: A class wants to take a field trip from New York City to Albany to visit the capital. The trip is approximately 160 miles. If they will be traveling at 50 miles per hour, how long will it take for them to get there (assuming traveling at a steady rate)?

Set up the equation as a proportion and solve:

$$\frac{160 \text{ miles}}{x \text{ hours}} = \frac{50 \text{ miles}}{1 \text{ hour}}$$

(160 miles)(1 hour) = (50 miles) (x hours)

160 = 50x

x = 3.2 hours

Example: A salesman drove 480 miles from Pittsburgh to Hartford. The next day he returned the same distance to Pittsburgh in half an hour less time than his original trip took, because he increased his average speed by 4 mph. Find his original speed.

Since distance = rate x time then time = $\dfrac{distance}{rate}$

original time $- 1/2$ hour $=$ shorter return time

$$\frac{480}{x} - \frac{1}{2} = \frac{480}{x+4}$$

Multiplying by the LCD of $2x(x+4)$, the equation becomes:

$480\left[2(x+4)\right] - 1\left[x(x+4)\right] = 480(2x)$

$960x + 3840 - x^2 - 4x = 960x$

$x^2 + 4x - 3840 = 0$

$(x+64)(x-60) = 0$

$x = 60$ 60 mph is the original speed

                  64 mph is the faster return speed

Cost per unit

The unit rate for purchasing an item is its price divided by the number of pounds/ounces, etc. in the item. The item with the lower unit rate is the lower price. See Skill 3.2 for further information.

Example: Find the item with the best unit price:

          $1.79 for 10 ounces
          $1.89 for 12 ounces
          $5.49 for 32 ounces

$\dfrac{1.79}{10} = .179$ per ounce $\dfrac{1.89}{12} = .1575$ per ounce $\dfrac{5.49}{32} = .172$ per ounce

          $1.89 for 12 ounces is the best price.

Skill 17.4   Describe the precision of measurement and the effects of error on measurement.

When reading an instrument, students should first determine the interval of scale on the instrument. To achieve the greatest accuracy, they should read the scale to the nearest measurement mark.

If you are using a scale with a needle that has a mirrored plate behind it, view the scale so that the needle's reflection is hidden behind the needle itself. Do not look at it from an angle. In order to read a balance scale accurately, place the scale on a level surface and make sure that the hand points precisely at 0. Place objects on the plate gently and take them away gently. Face the dial straight on to read the graduation accurately. Students should read from the large graduation to smaller graduation. If the dial hand points between two graduations, they should choose the number that is closest to the hand.

When reading inches on a ruler, the student needs to understand that each inch is divided into halves by the longest mark in the middle; into fourths by the next longest marks; into eighths by the next; and into sixteenths by the shortest. When the measurement falls between two inch marks, they can give the whole number of inches, count the additional fractional marks, and give the answer as the number and fraction of inches. Remind students that the convention is always to express a fraction by its lowest possible denominator.

If students are using the metric system on a ruler, have them focus on the marks between the whole numbers (centimeters). Point out that each centimeter is broken into tenths, with the mark in the middle being longer to indicate a halfway mark. Students should learn to measure things accurately to the nearest tenth of a centimeter, then the nearest hundredth, and finally the nearest thousandth. Measurements using the metric system should always be written using the decimal system, for ex., 3.756 centimeters.

When reading a thermometer, hold it vertically at eye level. Students should check the scale of the thermometer to make certain they read it as many significant digits as possible. Thermometers with heavy or extended lines that are marked 10, 20, 30 ... should be read to the nearest 0.1 degree. Thermometers with fine lines every two degrees may be read to the nearest 0.5 degree.

In order to get an accurate reading in a liquid measuring cup, set the cup on a level surface and read it at eye level. Read the measurement at the bottom of the concave arc at the liquid's surface (the meniscus line). When measuring dry ingredients, dip the appropriate size measuring cup into the ingredient and sweep away the excess across the top with a straight-edged object.

Protractors measure angles in degrees. To measure accurately, find the center hole on the straight edge of the protractor and place it over the vertex of the angle you wish to measure. Line up the zero on the straight edge with one of the sides of the angle. Find the point where the second side of the angle intersects the curved edge of the protractor and read the number that is written at the point of intersection.

When reading an instrument such as a rain gauge, it is again important to read at eye level and at the base of the meniscus. The measuring tube is divided, marked, and labeled in tenths and hundredths. The greatest number of decimal places you will have is two.

Skill 17.5   Apply the Pythagorean theorem, proportional reasoning, and right triangle trigonometry to solve measurement problems.

The Pythagorean Theorem

Given any right-angles triangle, $\triangle ABC$, the square of the hypotenuse is equal to the sum of the squares of the other two sides.

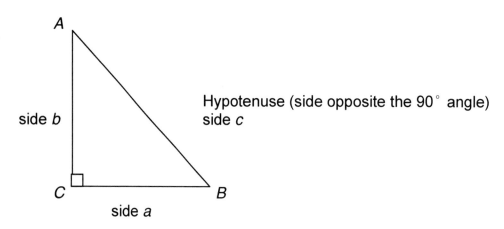

This theorem says that $(AB)^2 = (BC)^2 + (AC)^2$

or

$$c^2 = a^2 + b^2$$

Example: Find the area and perimeter of a rectangle if its length is 12 inches and its diagonal is 15 inches.

1. Draw and label sketch.

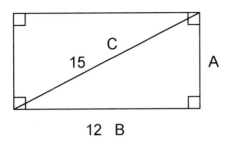

2. Since the height is still needed use Pythagorean formula to find missing leg of the triangle.

$$A^2 + B^2 = C^2$$
$$A^2 + 12^2 = 15^2$$
$$A^2 = 15^2 - 12^2$$
$$A^2 = 81$$
$$A = 9$$

Now use this information to find the area and perimeter.

$A = LW$	$P = 2(L + W)$	1. write formula
$A = (12)(9)$	$P = 2(12 + 9)$	2. substitute
$A = 108 \text{ in}^2$	$P = 42$ inches	3. solve

Example: Two cars leave a road intersection at the same time. One car travels due north at 55 mph while the other car travels due east. After 3 hours, the cars are 180 miles apart. Find the speed of the second car.

Using a right triangle to represent the problem we get the figure:

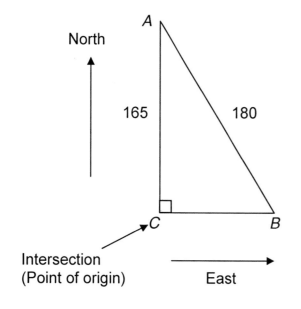

Traveling at 55 mph for 3 hours, the northbound car has driven (55)(3)=165 miles. This is the side *AC*.

We are given that the cars are 180 miles apart. This is side *AB*.

Since △*ABC* is a right triangle, then, by Pythagorean Theorem, we get:

$$(AB)^2 = (BC)^2 + (AC)^2 \text{ or}$$
$$(BC)^2 = (AB)^2 - (AC)^2$$

$$(BC)^2 = 180^2 - 165^2$$
$$(BC)^2 = 32400 - 27225$$
$$(BC)^2 = 5175$$

Take the square root of (BC^2) to get:

$$\sqrt{(BC)^2} = \sqrt{5175} \approx 71.937 \text{ miles}$$

Since the east bound car has traveled 71.935 miles in 3 hours, then the average speed is:

$$\frac{71.937}{3} \approx 23.97 \text{ mph}$$

COMPETENCY 18.0 UNDERSTAND THE GEOMETRIC RELATIONSHIPS AND AXIOMATIC STRUCTURE OF EUCLIDEAN GEOMETRY.

Skill 18.1 Understand concepts and properties of points, lines, planes, angles, lengths, and distances.

A point, a line and a plane are actually undefined terms since we cannot give a satisfactory definition using simple defined terms. However, their properties and characteristics give a clear understanding of what they are.

A **point** indicates place or position. It has no length, width or thickness.

       point A

A **line** is considered a set of points. Lines may be straight or curved, but the term line commonly denotes a straight line. Lines extend indefinitely.

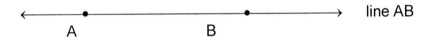

line AB

A **plane** is a set of points composing a flat surface. A plane also has no boundaries.

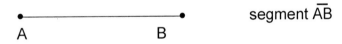

plane A

A **line segment** has two endpoints.

segment $\overline{AB}$

A **ray** has exactly one endpoint. It extend indefinitely in one direction.

ray $\overrightarrow{AB}$

An **angle** is formed by the intersection of two rays.

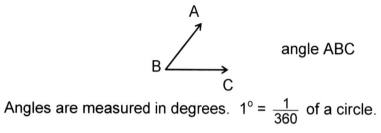

angle ABC

Angles are measured in degrees. $1° = \frac{1}{360}$ of a circle.

A **right angle** measures 90°.

An **acute angle** measures more than 0° and less than 90°.

An **obtuse angle** measures more than 90° and less than 180°.

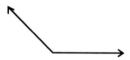

A **straight angle** measures 180°.

A **reflexive angle** measures more than 180° and less than 360°.

An infinite number of lines can be drawn through any point.

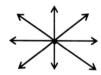

Exactly one line can be drawn through two points.

Skill 18.2   Analyze and apply the properties of parallel and perpendicular lines.

Two lines intersect at exactly one point. Two lines are **perpendicular** if their intersection forms right angles.

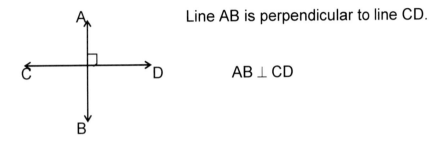

Line AB is perpendicular to line CD.

AB ⊥ CD

Two lines in the same plane that do not intersect are **parallel**. Parallel lines are everywhere equidistant.

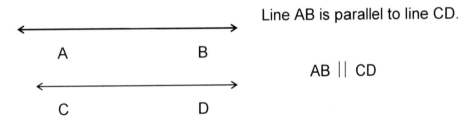

Line AB is parallel to line CD.

AB ∥ CD

Intersecting lines share a common point and intersecting planes share a common set of points or line.

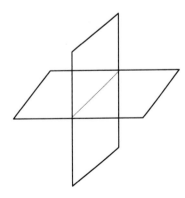

Skew lines do not intersect and do not lie on the same plane.

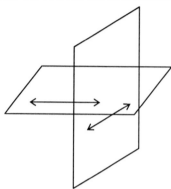

Example: One line passes through the points (-4, -6) and (4, 6); another line passes through the points (-5, -4) and (3, 8). Are these lines parallel, perpendicular or neither?

Find the slopes.

$$m = \frac{y_2 - y_1}{x_2 - x_1}$$

$$m_1 = \frac{6-(-6)}{4-(-4)} = \frac{6+6}{4+4} = \frac{12}{8} = \frac{3}{2}$$

$$m_2 = \frac{8-(-4)}{3-(-5)} = \frac{8+4}{3+5} = \frac{12}{8} = \frac{3}{2}$$

Since the slopes are the same, the lines are parallel.

Example: One line passes through the points (1, -3) and (0, -6); another line passes through the points (4, 1) and (-2, 3). Are these lines parallel, perpendicular or neither?

Find the slopes.

$$m = \frac{y_2 - y_1}{x_2 - x_1}$$

$$m_1 = \frac{-6-(-3)}{0-1} = \frac{-6+3}{-1} = \frac{-3}{-1} = 3$$

$$m_2 = \frac{3-1}{-2-4} = \frac{2}{-6} = -\frac{1}{3}$$

The slopes are negative reciprocals, so the lines are perpendicular.

Example: One line passes through the points (-2, 4) and (2, 5); another line passes through the points (-1, 0) and (5, 4). Are these lines parallel, perpendicular or neither?

Find the slopes.

$$m = \frac{y_2 - y_1}{x_2 - x_1}$$

$$m_1 = \frac{5-4}{2-(-2)} = \frac{1}{2+2} = \frac{1}{4}$$

$$m_2 = \frac{4-0}{5-(-1)} = \frac{4}{5+1} = \frac{4}{6} = \frac{2}{3}$$

Since the slopes are not the same, the lines are not parallel. Since they are not negative reciprocals, they are not perpendicular, either. Therefore, the answer is "neither."

Skill 18.3   Use the properties of congruent triangles to explore geometric relationships and prove theorems.

Two triangles are congruent if each of the three angles and three sides of one triangle match up in a one-to-one fashion with congruent angles and sides of the second triangle. In order to see how the sides and angles match up, it is sometimes necessary to imagine rotating or reflecting one of the triangles so the two figures are oriented in the same position.

There are shortcuts to the above procedure for proving two triangles congruent.

Side-Side-Side (SSS) Congruence--If the three sides of one triangle match up in a one-to-one congruent fashion with the three sides of the other triangle, then the two triangles are congruent. With SSS it is not necessary to even compare the angles; they will automatically be congruent.

Angle-Side-Angle (ASA) Congruence--If two angles of one triangle match up in a one-to-one congruent fashion with two angles in the other triangle and if the sides between the two angles are also congruent, then the two triangles are congruent. With ASA the sides that are used for congruence must be located between the two angles used in the first part of the proof.

Side-Angle-Side (SAS) Congruence--If two sides of one triangle match up in a one-to-one congruent fashion with two sides in the other triangle and if the angles between the two sides are also congruent, then the two triangles are congruent. With SAS the angles that are used for congruence must be located between the two sides used in the first part of the proof.

Angle-Angle-Side (AAS) - if two angles of one triangle match up in a one-to-one congruent fashion with two angle in the other triangle and if two sides that are not between the aforementioned sets of angles are also congruent, then the triangles are congruent. ASA and AAS are very similar; the only difference is where the congruent sides are located. If the sides are between the congruent sets of angles, use ASA. If the sides are not located between the congruent sets of angles, use AAS.

Hypotenuse-Leg (HL) is a congruence shortcut which can only be used with right triangles. If the hypotenuse and leg of one right triangle are congruent to the hypotenuse and leg of the other right triangle, then the two triangles are congruent.

Two triangles are overlapping if a portion of the interior region of one triangle is shared in common with all or a part of the interior region of the second triangle.

The most effective method for proving two overlapping triangles congruent is to draw the two triangles separated. Separate the two triangles and label all of the vertices using the labels from the original overlapping figures. Once the separation is complete, apply one of the congruence shortcuts: SSS, ASA, SAS, AAS, or HL.

Skill 18.4 **Describe and justify geometric constructions made using a compass and straight edge and other appropriate technologies.**

A **geometric construction** is a drawing made using only a compass and straightedge. A construction consists of only segments, arcs, and points. The easiest construction to make is to duplicate a given line segment. Given segment *AB*, construct a segment equal in length to segment AB by following these steps.

The easiest construction to make is to duplicate a given line segment. Given segment *AB*, construct a segment equal in length to segment AB by following these steps.

1. Place a point anywhere in the plane to anchor the duplicate segment. Call this point S.

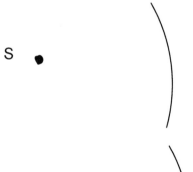

2. Open the compass to match the length of segment *AB*. Keeping the compass rigid, swing an arc from S.

3. Draw a segment from S to any point on the arc. This segment will be the same length as *AB*.

Given a line such as line $\overline{AB}$ and a point K on the line, follow these steps to construct a perpendicular line to line l through K.

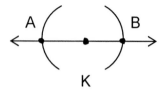

1. Swing an arc of any radius from point K so that it intersects line $\overline{AB}$ in two points, A and B.

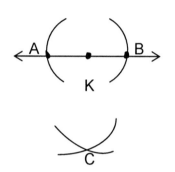

2. Open the compass to any length and swing one arc from B and another from A so that the two arcs intersect at point C.

3. Connect K and C to form line KC which is perpendicular to line $\overline{AB}$.

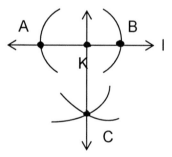

Given a line segment with two endpoints such as A and B, follow these steps to construct the line which both bisects and is perpendicular to the line given segment.

1. Swing an arc of any radius from point A. Swing another arc of the same radius from B. The arcs will intersect at two points. Label these points C and D.

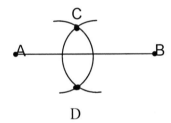

2. Connect C and D to form the perpendicular bisector of segment *AB*

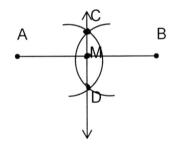

3. The point M where line $\overline{CD}$ and segment $\overline{AB}$ intersect is the midpoint of segment $\overline{AB}$.

Skill 18.5 Apply knowledge of the axiomatic structure of Euclidean geometry to justify and prove theorems.

Euclid wrote a set of 13 books around 330 B.C. called the Elements. He outlined ten axioms and then deduced 465 theorems. Euclidean geometry is based on the undefined concept of the point, line and plane.

The fifth of Euclid's axioms (referred to as the parallel postulate) was not as readily accepted as the other nine axioms. Many mathematicians throughout the years have attempted to prove that this axiom is not necessary because it could be proved by the other nine. Among the many who attempted to prove this was Carl Friedrich Gauss. His works led to the development of hyperbolic geometry. Elliptical or Reimannian geometry was suggested by G.F. Berhard Riemann. He based his work on the theory of surfaces and used models as physical interpretations of the undefined terms that satisfy the axioms.

The chart below lists the fifth axiom (parallel postulate) as it is given in each of the three geometries.

EUCLIDEAN	ELLIPTICAL	HYPERBOLIC
Given a line and a point not on that line, one and only one line can be drawn through the given point parallel to the given line.	Given a line and a point not on that line, no line can be drawn through the given point parallel to the given line.	Given a line and a point not on that line, two or more lines can be drawn through the point parallel to the given line.

COMPETENCY 19.0 ANALYZE THE PROPERTIES OF TWO- AND THREE-DIMENSIONAL FIGURES.

Skill 19.1 Use and understand the development of formulas to find lengths, perimeters, areas, and volumes of basic geometric figures.

Polygons, simple closed **two-dimensional figures** composed of line segments, are named according to the number of sides they have.

A **quadrilateral** is a polygon with four sides.
The sum of the measures of the angles of a quadrilateral is 360°.

A **trapezoid** is a quadrilateral with exactly <u>one</u> pair of parallel sides.

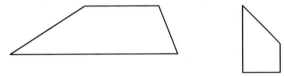

In an **isosceles trapezoid**, the non-parallel sides are congruent.

A **parallelogram** is a quadrilateral with <u>two</u> pairs of parallel sides.

In a parallelogram:
The diagonals bisect each other.
Each diagonal divides the parallelogram into two congruent triangles.
Both pairs of opposite sides are congruent.
Both pairs of opposite angles are congruent.
Two adjacent angles are supplementary.

A **rectangle** is a parallelogram with a right angle.

A **rhombus** is a parallelogram with all sides equal length.

A **square** is a rectangle with all sides equal length.

Example: True or false?

All squares are rhombuses.	True
All parallelograms are rectangles.	False - some parallelograms are rectangles
All rectangles are parallelograms.	True
Some rhombuses are squares.	True
Some rectangles are trapezoids.	False - only one pair of parallel sides
All quadrilaterals are parallelograms.	False -some quadrilaterals are parallelograms
Some squares are rectangles.	False - all squares are rectangles
Some parallelograms are rhombuses.	True

A **triangle** is a polygon with three sides.

Triangles can be classified by the types of angles or the lengths of their sides.

An **acute** triangle has exactly three *acute* angles.
A **right** triangle has one *right* angle.
An **obtuse** triangle has one *obtuse* angle.

        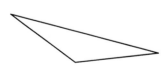

acute   right   obtuse

All *three* sides of an **equilateral** triangle are the same length.
Two sides of an **isosceles** triangle are the same length.
None of the sides of a **scalene** triangle are the same length.

  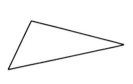

equilateral   isosceles   scalene

Example: Can a triangle have two right angles?
No. A right angle measures 90°, therefore the sum of two right angles would be 180° and there could not be third angle.

Example: Can a triangle have two obtuse angles?
No. Since an obtuse angle measures more than 90° the sum of two obtuse angles would be greater than 180°.

A **cylinder** has two congruent circular bases that are parallel.

A **sphere** is a space figure having all its points the same distance from the center.

A **cone** is a space figure having a circular base and a single vertex.

A **pyramid** is a space figure with a square base and 4 triangle-shaped sides.

A **tetrahedron** is a 4-sided space triangle. Each face is a triangle.

A **prism** is a space figure with two congruent, parallel bases that are polygons.

Skill 19.2   Apply relationships among similar figures, scale, and proportion and analyze how changes in scale affect area and volume measurements.

Similarity

Two figures that have the same shape are **similar**. Polygons are similar if and only if corresponding angles are congruent and corresponding sides are in proportion. Corresponding parts of similar polygons are proportional.

Example: Given the rectangles below, compare the area and perimeter.

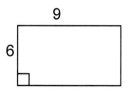
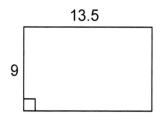

$A = LW$	$A = LW$	1. write formula
$A = (6)(9)$	$A = (9)(13.5)$	2. substitute known values
$A = 54$ sq. units	$A = 121.5$ sq. units	3. compute
$P = 2(L + W)$	$P = 2(L + W)$	1. write formula
$P = 2(6 + 9)$	$P = 2(9 + 13.5)$	2. substitute known values
$P = 30$ units	$P = 45$ units	3. compute

Notice that the areas relate to each other in the following manner:

Ratio of sides $9/13.5 = 2/3$

Multiply the first area by the square of the reciprocal $(3/2)^2$ to get the second area.
$$54 \times (3/2)^2 = 121.5$$
The perimeters relate to each other in the following manner:

Ratio of sides $9/13.5 = 2/3$

Multiply the perimeter of the first by the reciprocal of the ratio to get the perimeter of the second.

$$30 \times 3/2 = 45$$

Example: Tommy draws and cuts out 2 triangles for a school project. One of them has sides of 3, 6, and 9 inches. The other triangle has sides of 2, 4, and 6. Is there a relationship between the two triangles?

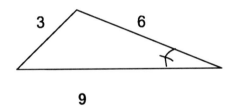

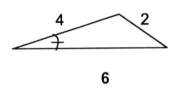

9   6

Take the proportion of the corresponding sides.

$$\frac{2}{3} \qquad \frac{4}{6} = \frac{2}{3} \qquad \frac{6}{9} = \frac{2}{3}$$

The smaller triangle is 2/3 the size of the large triangle.

Similar solids share the same shape but are not necessarily the same size. The ratio of any two corresponding measurements of similar solids is the scale factor. For example, the scale factor for two square pyramids, one with a side measuring 2 inches and the other with a side measuring 4 inches, is 2:4.

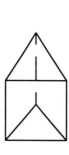

2

4

The base perimeter, the surface area, and the volume of similar solids are directly related to the scale factor. If the scale factor of two similar solids is a:b, then the...

ratio of base perimeters = a:b
ratio of areas = $a^2:b^2$
ratio of volumes = $a^3:b^3$

Thus, for the above example the...

ratio of base perimeters = 2:4
ratio of areas = $2^2:4^2$ = 4:16
ratio of volumes = $2^3:4^3$ = 8:64

Example: What happens to the volume of a square pyramid when the length of the sides of the base are doubled?

scale factor = a:b = 1:2
ratio of volume = $1^3:2^3$ = 1:8 (The volume is increased 8 times.)

2. Given the following measurements for two similar cylinders with a scale factor of 2:5 (Cylinders A to Cylinder B), determine the height, radius, and volume of each cylinder.

Cylinder A: r = 2
Cylinder B: h = 10

Solution:

Cylinder A −

$$\frac{h_a}{10} = \frac{2}{5}$$
$5h_a = 20$ Solve for h_a
$h_a = 4$

Volume of Cylinder a = $\pi r^2 h = \pi (2)^2 4 = 16\pi$

Cylinder B −

$$\frac{2}{r_b} = \frac{2}{5}$$
$2r_b = 10$ Solve for r_b
$r_b = 5$

Volume of Cylinder b = $\pi r^2 h = \pi (5)^2 10 = 250\pi$

Skill 19.3 **Use a variety of representations (e.g., numeric, verbal, graphic, symbolic) to analyze and solve problems involving two- and three-dimensional figures such as circles, triangles, polygons, cylinders, prisms, and spheres.**

See Skill 19.1

Skill 19.4 **Analyze the relationship among three-dimensional figures and related two-dimensional representations (e.g., projections, cross-sections, nets) and use these representations to solve problems.**

We refer to three-dimensional figures in geometry as **solids**. A solid is the union of all points on a simple closed surface and all points in its interior. A **polyhedron** is a simple closed surface formed from planar polygonal regions. Each polygonal region is called a **face** of the polyhedron. The vertices and edges of the polygonal regions are called the **vertices** and **edges** of the polyhedron.

We may form a cube from three congruent squares. However, if we tried to put four squares about a single vertex, their interior angle measures would add up to 360°; i.e., four edge-to-edge squares with a common vertex lie in a common plane and therefore cannot form a corner figure of a regular polyhedron.

There are five ways to form corner figures with congruent regular polygons:

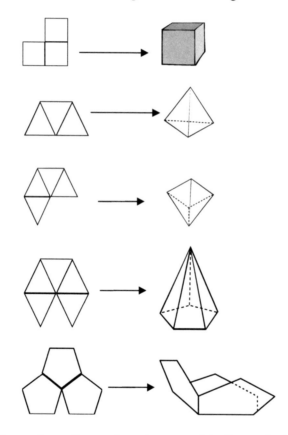

We can represent any two-dimensional geometric figure in the **Cartesian** or **rectangular coordinate system**. The Cartesian or rectangular coordinate system is formed by two perpendicular axes (coordinate axes): the X-axis and the Y-axis. If we know the dimensions of a two-dimensional, or planar, figure, we can use this coordinate system to visualize the shape of the figure.

COMPETENCY 20.0 UNDERSTAND TRANSFORMATIONAL GEOMETRY AND RELATES ALGEBRA TO GEOMETRY AND TRIGONOMETRY USING THE CARTESIAN COORDINATE SYSTEM.

Skill 20.1 Describe and justify geometric constructions made using a reflection device and other appropriate technologies.

Reflection devices and other technologies, like overhead projectors, transform geometric constructions in predictable ways. Students should have the ability to recognize the patterns and properties of geometric constructions made with these technologies.

The most common reflection device is a mirror. Mirrors reflect geometric constructions across a given axis. For example, if we place a mirror on the side AC of the triangle (below) the composite image created by the original figure and the reflection is a square.

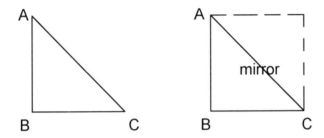

Projection devices, like overhead projectors, often expand geometric figures. These expansions are proportional, meaning the ratio of the measures of the figure remains the same. Consider the following projection of the rectangle ABCD.

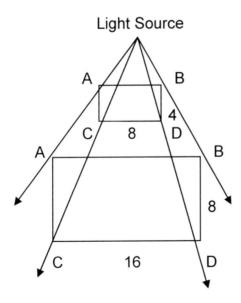

Skill 20.2 **Use translations, reflections, glide-reflections, and rotations to demonstrate congruence and to explore the symmetries of figures.**

A **transformation** is a change in the position, shape, or size of a geometric figure. **Transformational geometry** is the study of manipulating objects by flipping, twisting, turning and scaling. **Symmetry** is exact similarity between two parts or halves, as if one were a mirror image of the other.

There are four basic **transformational symmetries** that can be used: **translation, rotation, reflection,** and **glide reflection**. The transformation of an object is called its image. If the original object was labeled with letters, such as *ABCD*, the image may be labeled with the same letters followed by a prime symbol, *A'B'C'D'*.

A **translation** is a transformation that "slides" an object a fixed distance in a given direction. The original object and its translation have the same shape and size, and they face in the same direction.

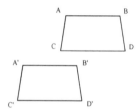

An example of a translation in architecture would be stadium seating. The seats are the same size and the same shape and face in the same direction.

A **rotation** is a transformation that turns a figure about a fixed point called the center of rotation. An object and its rotation are the same shape and size, but the figures may be turned in different directions. Rotations can occur in either a clockwise or a counterclockwise direction.

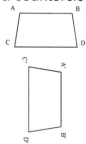

Rotations can be seen in wallpaper and art, and a Ferris wheel is an example of rotation.

An object and its **reflection** have the same shape and size, but the figures face in opposite directions.

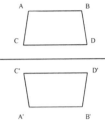

The line (where a mirror may be placed) is called the **line of reflection**. The distance from a point to the line of reflection is the same as the distance from the point's image to the line of reflection.

A **glide reflection** is a combination of a reflection and a translation.

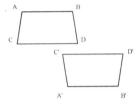

Objects that are **tangent** make contact at a single point or along a line without crossing. Understanding tangency is critical in the construction industry where architects and engineers must figure out how various elements will fit together. An example would be the building of a stair railing. The architect must determine the points of tangency between the banisters, which might even be curved, and the posts supporting the banisters.

Many types of flooring found in our homes are examples of **symmetry**: Oriental carpets, tiling, patterned carpet, etc. The human body is an example of symmetry, even though it is not usually perfect. If you split the torso down the middle, on each half, you will find one ear, one eye, one nostril, one shoulder, one arm, one leg, and so on, in approximately the same place.

Skill 20.3   Use dilations (expansions and contractions) to illustrate similar figures and proportionality.

Another type of transformation is **dilation**. Dilation is a transformation that "shrinks" or "makes it bigger."

Example: Using dilation to transform a diagram.

Starting with a triangle whose center of dilation is point P,

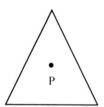

we dilate the lengths of the sides by the same factor to create a new triangle.

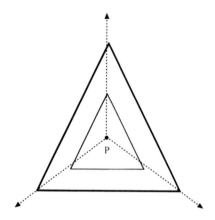

Skill 20.4   Use symmetry to describe tessellations and shows how they can be used to illustrate geometric concepts, properties, and relationships.

A **Tessellation** is an arrangement of closed shapes that completely covers the plane without overlapping or leaving gaps. Unlike **tilings**, tessellations do not require the use of regular polygons. In art the term is used to refer to pictures or tiles mostly in the form of animals and other life forms, which cover the surface of a plane in a symmetrical way without overlapping or leaving gaps. M. C. Escher is known as the "Father" of modern tessellations. Tessellations are used for tiling, mosaics, quilts and art.

If you look at a completed tessellation, you will see the original motif repeats in a pattern. There are 17 possible ways that a pattern can be used to tile a flat surface or "wallpaper."

The tessellation below is a combination of the four types of transformational symmetry we have discussed:

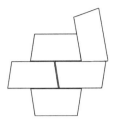

Skill 20.5 **Apply concepts and properties of slope, midpoint, parallelism, and distance in the coordinate plane to explore properties of geometric figures and solve problems.**

Coordinate plane - A plane with a point selected as an origin, some length selected as a unit of distance, and two perpendicular lines that intersect at the origin, with positive and negative direction selected on each line. Traditionally, the lines are called x (drawn from left to right, with positive direction to the right of the origin) and y (drawn from bottom to top, with positive direction upward of the origin). Coordinates of a point are determined by the distance of this point from the lines, and the signs of the coordinates are determined by whether the point is in the positive or in the negative direction from the origin. The standard coordinate plane consists of a plane divided into 4 quadrants by the intersection of two axis, the x-axis (horizontal axis), and the y-axis (vertical axis).

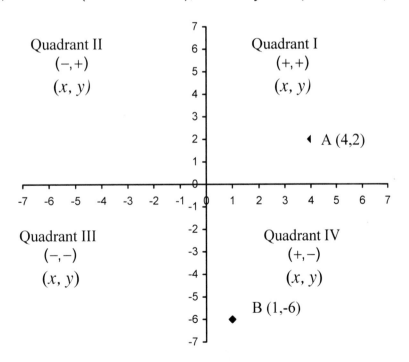

Coordinates - A unique **ordered pair** of numbers that identifies a point on the coordinate plane. The first number in the ordered pair identifies the position with regard to the x-axis while the second number identifies the position on the y-axis (x, y)

In the coordinate plane shown above, point A has the ordered pair (4,2); point B has the ordered pair (1,-6).

Slope – The slope of a line is the "slant" of a line. A downward left to right slant means a negative slope. An upward slant is a positive slope.
The formula for calculating the slope of a line with coordinates $(x_1, y_1) and (x_2, y_2)$ is:

$$slope = \frac{y_2 - y_1}{x_2 - x_1}$$

The top of the fraction represents the change in the y coordinates; it is called the **rise**.

The bottom of the fraction represents the change in the x coordinates, it is called the **run.**

Example: Find the slope of a line with points at (2,2) and (7,8).

$\dfrac{(8)-(2)}{(7)-(2)}$ plug the values into the formula

$\dfrac{6}{5}$ solve the rise over run

$= 1.2$ solve for the slope

The length of a line segment is the **distance** between two different points, A and B. The formula for the length of a line is:

$$length = \sqrt{(x_1 - x_2)^2 + (y_1 - y_2)^2}$$

Example: Find the length between the points (2,2) and (7,8)

$= \sqrt{(2-7)^2 + (2-8)^2}$ plug the values into the formula

$= \sqrt{(-5)^2 + (-6)^2}$ calculate the x and y differences

$= \sqrt{25 + 36}$ square the values

$= \sqrt{61}$ add the two values

$= 7.81$ calculate the square root

Midpoint Definition:

If a line segment has endpoints of (x_1, y_1) and (x_2, y_2), then the midpoint can be found using:

$$\left(\frac{x_1 + x_2}{2}, \frac{y_1 + y_2}{2} \right)$$

Sample problems:

1. Find the center of a circle with a diameter whose endpoints are (3,7) and ($^-4, ^-5$).

$$\text{Midpoint} = \left(\frac{3 + (^-4)}{2}, \frac{7 + (^-5)}{2} \right)$$

$$\text{Midpoint} = \left(\frac{^-1}{2}, 1 \right)$$

2. Find the midpoint given the two points $\left(5, 8\sqrt{6} \right)$ and $\left(9, ^-4\sqrt{6} \right)$.

$$\text{Midpoint} = \left(\frac{5 + 9}{2}, \frac{8\sqrt{6} + (^-4\sqrt{6})}{2} \right)$$

$$\text{Midpoint} = \left(7, 2\sqrt{6} \right)$$

To graph an inequality, solve the inequality for y. This gets the inequality in **slope intercept form**, (for example: $y < mx + b$). The point (0,b) is the y-intercept and m is the line's slope.

If the inequality solves to $x \geq$ **any number**, then the graph includes a **vertical line**.

If the inequality solves to $y \leq$ **any number**, then the graph includes a **horizontal line**.

When graphing a linear inequality, the line will be dotted if the inequality sign is $<$ or $>$. If the inequality signs are either $\geq$ or $\leq$, the line on the graph will be a solid line. Shade above the line when the inequality sign is $\geq$ or $>$. Shade below the line when the inequality sign is $<$ or $\leq$. For inequalities of the forms $x >$ number, $x \leq$ number , $x <$ number ,or $x \geq$ number, draw a vertical line (solid or dotted). Shade to the right for $>$ or $\geq$. Shade to the left for $<$ or $\leq$.

Remember: **Dividing or multiplying by a negative number will reverse the direction of the inequality sign.**

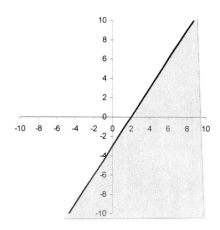

$$3x - 2y \geq 6$$
$$y \leq 3/2\,x - 3$$

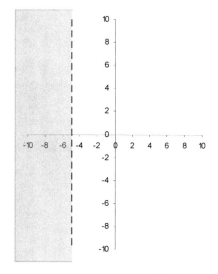

$$3x + 12 < -3$$

$$x < {}^{-}5$$

Example: Solve by graphing:

$$x + y \leq 6$$
$$x - 2y \leq 6$$

Solving the inequalities for y, they become:

$y \leq {}^-x + 6$ (y intercept of 6 and slope = $^-1$)

$y \geq 1/2\,x - 3$ (y intercept of $^-3$ and slope = $1/2$)

A graph with shading is shown below:

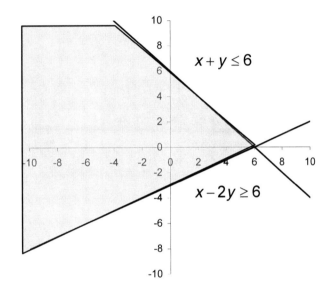

See Skill 14.4 for more information

Skill 20.6   Apply transformations in the coordinate plane.

Plot the given ordered pairs on a coordinate plane and join them in the given order, then join the first and last points.

(-3, -2), (3, -2), (5, -4), (5, -6), (2, -4), (-2, -4), (-5, -6), (-5, -4)

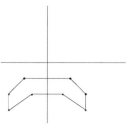

Increase all y-coordinates by 6.

(-3, 4), (3, 4), (5, 2), (5, 0), (2, 2), (-2, 2), (-5, 0), (-5, 2)

Plot the points and join them to form a second figure.

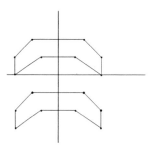

A figure on a coordinate plane can be translated by changing the ordered pairs.

Skill 20.7   Use the unit circle in the coordinate plane to explore properties of trigonometric functions.

The unit circle is a circle with a radius of one centered at (0,0) on the coordinate plane. Thus, any ray from the origin to a point on the circle forms an angle, t, with the positive x-axis. In addition, the ray from the origin to a point on the circle in the first quadrant forms a right triangle with a hypotenuse measuring one unit. Applying the Pythagorean theorem, $x^2 + y^2 = 1$. Because the reflections of the triangle about both the x- and y-axis are on the unit circle and $x^2 = (-x)^2$ for all x values, the formula holds for all points on the unit circle.

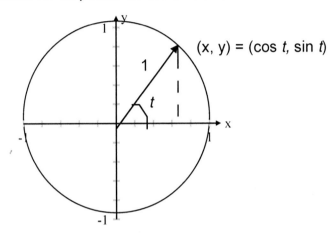

Note that because the length of the hypotenuse of the right triangles formed in the unit circle is one, the point on the unit circle that forms the triangle is (cos t, sin t). In other words, for any point on the unit circle, the x value represents the cosine of t, the y value represents the sine of t, and the ratio of the y-coordinate to the x-coordinate is the tangent of t.

The unit circle illustrates several properties of trigonometric functions. For example, applying the Pythagorean theorem to the unit circle yields the equation $\cos^2(t) + \sin^2(t) = 1$. In addition, the unit circle reveals the periodic nature of trigonometric functions. When we increase the angle t beyond 2π radians or 360 degrees, the values of x and y coordinates on the unit circle remain the same. Thus, the sine and cosine values repeat with each revolution. The unit circle also reveals the range of the sine and cosine functions. The values of sine and cosine are always between one and negative one. Finally, the unit circle shows that when the x coordinate of a point on the circle is zero, the tangent function is undefined. Thus, tangent is undefined at the angles $\dfrac{\pi}{2}, \dfrac{3\pi}{2}$ and the corresponding angles in all subsequent revolutions.

COMPETENCY 21.0 UNDERSTAND HOW TO USE GRAPHICAL AND NUMERICAL TECHNIQUES TO EXPLORE DATA, CHARACTERIZE PATTERNS, AND DESCRIBE DEPARTURES FROM PATTERNS.

Skill 21.1   Organize and display data in a variety of formats (e.g., tables, frequency distributions, stem-and-leaf plots, box-and-whisker plots, histograms, pie charts).

Stem and leaf plots are visually similar to line plots. The **stems** are the digits in the greatest place value of the data values, and the **leaves** are the digits in the next greatest place values. Stem and leaf plots are best suited for small sets of data and are especially useful for comparing two sets of data. The following is an example using test scores:

4	9
5	4 9
6	1 2 3 4 6 7 8 8
7	0 3 4 6 6 6 7 7 7 8 8 8 8
8	3 5 5 7 8
9	0 0 3 4 5
10	0 0

To make a **bar graph** or a **pictograph**, determine the scale to be used for the graph. Then determine the length of each bar on the graph or determine the number of pictures needed to represent each item of information. Be sure to include an explanation of the scale in the legend.

Example: A class had the following grades:
4 A's, 9 B's, 8 C's, 1 D, 3 F's.
Graph these on a bar graph and a pictograph.

Pictograph

Bar graph

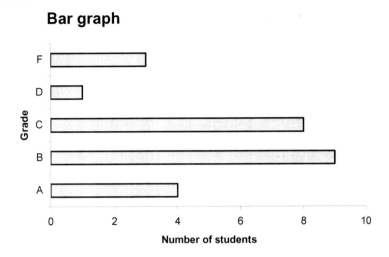

To make a **line graph**, determine appropriate scales for both the vertical and horizontal axes (based on the information to be graphed). Describe what each axis represents and mark the scale periodically on each axis. Graph the individual points of the graph and connect the points on the graph from left to right.

Example: Graph the following information using a line graph.

The number of National Merit finalists/school year

	90-91	91-92	92-93	93-94	94-95	95-96
Central	3	5	1	4	6	8
Wilson	4	2	3	2	3	2

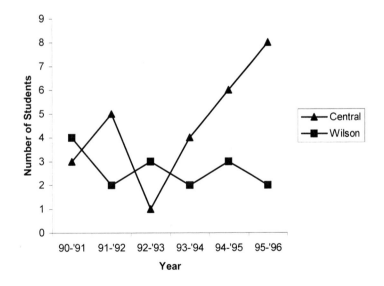

To make a **circle graph**, total all the information that is to be included on the graph. Determine the central angle to be used for each sector of the graph using the following formula:

$$\frac{\text{information}}{\text{total information}} \times 360° = \text{degrees in central} \measuredangle$$

Lay out the central angles to these sizes, label each section and include its percent.

Example: Graph this information on a circle graph:

Monthly expenses:

Rent, $400

Food, $150
Utilities, $75
Clothes, $75
Church, $100
Misc., $200

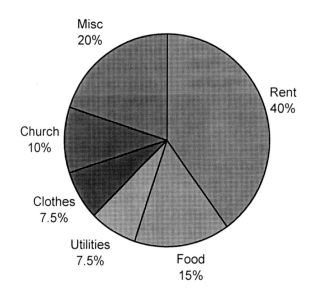

Histograms are used to summarize information from large sets of data that can be naturally grouped into intervals. The vertical axis indicates **frequency** (the number of times any particular data value occurs), and the horizontal axis indicates data values or ranges of data values. The number of data values in any interval is the **frequency of the interval**.

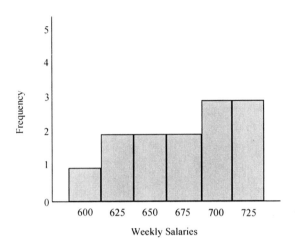

Skill 21.2   Apply concepts of center, spread, shape, and skewness to describe a data distribution.

The shape of a data distribution is described as symmetrical or asymmetrical. In a symmetrical distribution, Mean = Mode = Median. The opposite of a symmetrical distribution is one that demonstrates **skewness**, meaning the distribution is asymmetrical.

Center and spread are concepts that describe the characteristics of a data set. Measures of central tendency define the center of a data set and measures of dispersion define the amount of spread. Wide dispersion in a data set indicates the presence of data gaps and narrow dispersion indicates data clusters. Graphical representations of center and spread, like box-and-whisker plots, allow identification of data outliers.

The most common measures of central tendency that define the center of a data set are mean, median and mode. Mean is the average value of a data set; Median is the middle value of a data set; Mode is the value that appears the most in a data set. The mean is the most descriptive value for tightly clustered data with few outliers. Outlier data, values in a data set that are unusually high or low, can greatly distort the mean of a data set. Median, on the other hand, may better describe widely dispersed data and data sets with outliers because outliers and dispersion have little effect on the median value.

The most common measures of spread that define the dispersion of a data set are range, variance, standard deviation and quantiles. Range is the difference between the highest and lowest values in a data set. The variance is the average squared distance from each value of a data set to the mean. The standard deviation is the square root of the variance. A data set clustered around the center has a small variance and standard deviation, while a disperse data set with many gaps has a large variance and standard deviation. Quantiles or percentiles, divide a data set into equal sections. For example, the 50th quantile is the median value of a data set.

Finally, graphical representations of data sets, like box-and-whisker plots, help relate the measures of central tendency to data outliers, clusters and gaps. Consider the hypothetical box-and-whisker plot with one outlier value on each end of the distribution.

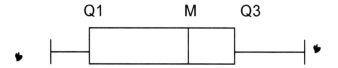

Note the beginning of the box is the value of the first quartile of the data set and the end is the value of the third quartile. We represent the median as a vertical line in the box. The "whiskers" extend to the last point that is not an outlier (i.e. within 3/2 times the range between Q1 and Q3). The points beyond the figure represent outlier values.

Skill 21.3   Supports arguments, make predictions, and draw conclusions using summary statistics and graphs to analyze and interpret one-variable data.

A **trend** line on a line graph shows the correlation between two sets of data. A trend may show positive correlation (both sets of data get bigger together) negative correlation (one set of data gets bigger while the other gets smaller), or no correlation.

An **inference** is a statement which is derived from reasoning. When reading a graph, inferences help with interpretation of the data that is being presented. From this information, a **conclusion** and even **predictions** about what the data actually means is possible.

Example: Katherine and Tom were both doing poorly in math class. Their teacher had a conference with each of them in November. The following graph shows their math test scores during the school year.

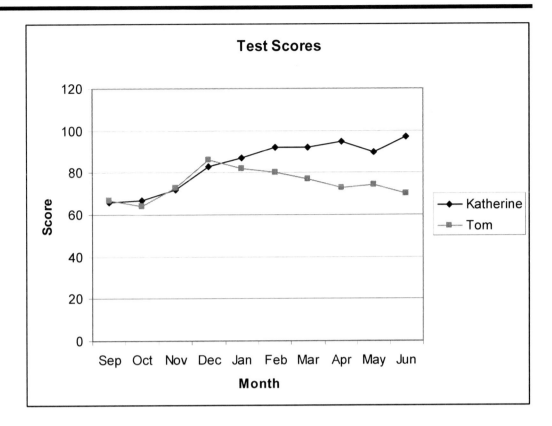

What kind of trend does this graph show?

This graph shows that there is a positive trend in Katherine's test scores and a negative trend in Tom's test scores.

What inferences can you make from this graph?

We can infer that Katherine's test scores rose steadily after November. Tom's test scores spiked in December but then began to fall again and became negatively trended.

What conclusion can you draw based upon this graph?

We can conclude that Katherine took her teacher's meeting seriously and began to study in order to do better on the exams. It seems as though Tom tried harder for a bit, but his test scores eventually slipped back down to the level where he began.

Skill 21.4 **Demonstrate an understanding of measures of central tendency (e.g., mean, median, mode) and dispersion (e.g., range, variance, standard deviation).**

The arithmetic **mean** (or average) of a set of numbers is the *sum* of the numbers given, *divided* by the number of items being averaged.

Example: Find the mean. Round to the nearest tenth.
24.6, 57.3, 44.1, 39.8, 64.5
The sum is 230.3 ~ 5
= 46.06, rounded to 46.1

The **median** of a set is the middle number. To calculate the median, the terms must be arranged in order. If there are an even number of terms, the median is the mean of the two middle terms.

Example 1:   Find the median.

12, 14, 27, 3, 13, 7, 17,   12, 22, 6,   16
Rearrange the terms.
3, 6, 7, 12, 12, 13, 14,   16, 17, 22, 27

Since there are 11 numbers, the middle would be the sixth number or 13.

The **mode** of a set of numbers is the number that occurs with the greatest frequency. A set can have no mode if each term appears exactly one time. Similarly, there can also be more than one mode.

Example: Find the mode.

26, 15, 37, **26,** 35, **26,** 15

15 appears twice, but 26 appears 3 times, therefore the mode is 26.

The **range** is the difference between the highest and lowest value of data items.

The **variance** is the sum of the squares quantity divided by the number of items. (the lower case Greek letter sigma squared (σ^2)represents variance).

$$\frac{Sx^2}{N} = \sigma^2$$

The larger the value of the variance the larger the spread

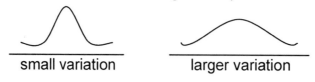

small variation   larger variation

Standard deviation means the square root of the variance. The lower case Greek letter sigma (σ) is used to represent standard deviation.

$$\sigma = \sqrt{\sigma^2}$$

Most statistical calculators have standard deviation keys on them and should be used when asked to calculate statistical functions. It is important to become familiar with the calculator and the location of the keys needed.

Example: Given the ungrouped data below, calculate the mean, range, standard deviation and the variance.

15	22	28	25	34	38
18	25	30	33	19	23

Mean (X) = 25.8333333
Range: $38 - 15 = 23$
Standard Deviation (σ) $= 6.699137$
Variance (σ^2) $= 48.87879$

Skill 21.5 **Analyze connections among concepts of center and spread, data clusters and gaps, data outliers, and measures of central tendency and dispersion.**

See Skill 2.2

Skill 21.6 **Calculate and interpret percentiles and quartiles.**

Percentiles divide data into 100 equal parts. A person whose score falls in the 65th percentile has outperformed 65 percent of all those who took the test. This does not mean that the score was 65 percent out of 100 nor does it mean that 65 percent of the questions answered were correct. It means that the grade was higher than 65 percent of all those who took the test.

Stanine "standard nine" scores combine the understandability of percentages with the properties of the normal curve of probability. Stanines divide the bell curve into nine sections, the largest of which stretches from the 40th to the 60th percentile and is the "Fifth Stanine" (the average of taking into account error possibilities).

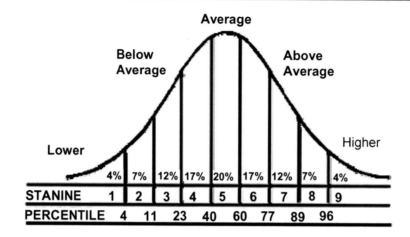

Quartiles divide the data into 4 parts. First find the median of the data set (Q2), then find the median of the upper (Q3) and lower (Q1) halves of the data set. If there are an odd number of values in the data set, include the median value in both halves when finding quartile values. For example, given the data set: {1, 4, 9, 16, 25, 36, 49, 64, 81} first find the median value, which is 25 this is the second quartile. Since there are an odd number of values in the data set (9), we include the median in both halves. To find the quartile values, we much find the medians of: {1, 4, 9, 16, 25} and {25, 36, 49, 64, 81}. Since each of these subsets had an odd number of elements (5), we use the middle value. Thus the first quartile value is 9 and the third quartile value is 49. If the data set had an even number of elements, average the middle two values. The quartile values are always either one of the data points, or exactly half way between two data points.

Example: Given the following set of data, find the percentile of the score 104.

70, 72, 82, 83, 84, 87, 100, 104, 108, 109, 110, 115

Find the percentage of scores below 104.

7/12 of the scores are less than 104. This is 58.333%; therefore, the score of 104 is in the 58th percentile.

2. Find the first, second and third quartile for the data listed.
6, 7, 8, 9, 10, 12, 13, 14, 15, 16, 18, 23, 24, 25, 27, 29, 30, 33, 34, 37

Quartile 1: The 1st Quartile is the median of the lower half of the data set, which is 11.

Quartile 2: The median of the data set is the 2nd Quartile, which is 17.

Quartile 3: The 3rd Quartile is the median of the upper half of the data set, which is 28.

COMPETENCY 22.0 UNDERSTAND THE THEORY OF PROBABILITY.

Skill 22.1   Explore concepts of probability through data collection, experiments, and simulations.

In probability, the **sample space** is a list of all possible outcomes of an experiment. For example, the sample space of tossing two coins is the set {HH, HT, TT, TH}, the sample space of rolling a six-sided die is the set {1, 2, 3, 4, 5, 6}, and the sample space of measuring the height of students in a class is the set of all real numbers {R}. **Probability** measures the chances of an event occurring. The probability of an event that *must* occur, a certain event, is **one**. When no outcome is favorable, the probability of an impossible event is **zero**

$$P(event) = \frac{\text{number of favorable outcomes}}{\text{number of possible outcomes}}$$

Skill 22.2   Use the concepts and principles of probability to describe the outcome of simple and compound events.

Example: Given one die with faces numbered 1 - 6, the probability of tossing an even number on one throw of the die is 3/6 or ½ since there are 3 favorable outcomes (even faces) and a total of 6 possible outcomes (faces).

Example: If a fair die is rolled.

a)Find the probability of rolling an even number
b)Find the probability of rolling a number less than three.

a)The sample space is

S = {1, 2, 3, 4, 5, 6} and the event representing even numbers is

E = {2, 4, 6}

Hence, the probability of rolling an even number is

$$p(E) = \frac{n(E)}{n(S)} = \frac{3}{6} = \frac{1}{2} \text{ or } 0.5$$

b)The event of rolling a number less than three is represented by

A = {1, 2}

Hence, the probability of rolling a number less than three is

$$p(A) = \frac{n(A)}{n(S)} = \frac{2}{6} = \frac{1}{3} \text{ or } 0.33$$

Example: A class has thirty students. Out of the thirty students, twenty-four are males. Assuming all the students have the same chance of being selected, find the probability of selecting a female. (Only one person is selected.)

The number of females in the class is

$$30 - 24 = 6$$

Hence, the probability of selecting a female is

$$p(female) = \frac{6}{30} = \frac{1}{5} \text{ or } 0.2$$

If A and B are **independent** events then the outcome of event A does not affect the outcome of event B or vice versa. The multiplication rule is used to find joint probability.

$$P(A \text{ and } B) = P(A) \times P(B)$$

Example: The probability that a patient is allergic to aspirin is .30. If the probability of a patient having a window in his/her room is .40, find the probability that the patient is allergic to aspirin and has a window in his/her room.

Defining the events: A = The patient being allergic to aspirin.
B = The patient has a window in his/her room.

Events A and B are independent, hence
$p(A \text{ and } B) = p(A) \cdot p(B)$
$= (.30)(.40)$
$= .12 \text{ or } 12\%$

Example: A jar contains 10 marbles: 3 red, 5 black, and 2 white. What is the probability of drawing a red marble and then a white marble if the first marble is returned to the jar after choosing?

$$3/10 \times 2/10 = 6/100 = 3/50$$

When the outcome of the first event affects the outcome of the second event, the events are **dependent**. Any two events that are not independent are dependent. This is also known as conditional probability.

$$\text{Probability of } (A \text{ and } B) = P(A) \times P(B \text{ given } A)$$

Example: Two cards are drawn from a deck of 52 cards, without replacement; that is, the first card is not returned to the deck before the second card is drawn. What is the probability of drawing a diamond?

A = drawing a diamond first
B = drawing a diamond second

P(A) = drawing a diamond first
P(B) = drawing a diamond second

P(A) = 13/52 = ¼   P(B) =   12/52 = 4/17

(PA+B) = ¼ X 14/17 = 1/17

Example: A class of ten students has six males and four females. If two students are selected to represent the class, find the probability that

a) the first is a male and the second is a female.
b) the first is a female and the second is a male.
c) both are females.
d) both are males.

Defining the events: F = a female is selected to represent the class.
          M = a male is selected to represent the class.

F/M = a female is selected after a male has been selected.
M/F = a male is selected after a female has been selected.

a)   Since F and M are dependent events, it follows that
      P(M and F) = P(M) · P(F/M)
$$= \frac{6}{10} \times \frac{4}{9} = \frac{3}{5} \times \frac{4}{9} = \frac{12}{45}$$

$P(F/M) = \dfrac{4}{9}$ instead of , $\dfrac{4}{10}$ since the selection of a male first changed the Sample Space from ten to nine students.

b)   P(F and M) = P(F) · P(M/F)
$$= \frac{4}{10} \times \frac{6}{9} = \frac{2}{5} \times \frac{2}{3} = \frac{4}{15}$$

c)   P(F and F) = p(F) · p(F/F)
$$= \frac{4}{10} \times \frac{3}{9} = \frac{2}{5} \times \frac{1}{3} = \frac{2}{15}$$

d)   P(both are males) = p(M and M)

$$= \frac{6}{10} \times \frac{5}{9} = \frac{30}{90} = \frac{1}{3}$$

Odds are defined as the ratio of the number of favorable outcomes to the number of unfavorable outcomes. The sum of the favorable outcomes and the unfavorable outcomes should always equal the total possible outcomes.

For example, given a bag of 12 red and 7 green marbles compute the odds of randomly selecting a red marble.

$$\text{Odds of red} = \frac{12}{19}$$

$$\text{Odds of not getting red} = \frac{7}{19}$$

In the case of flipping a coin, it is equally likely that a head or a tail will be tossed. The odds of tossing a head are 1:1. This is called even odds.

Skill 22.3   Generate, simulate, and use probability models to represent a situation.

See Skills 22.1 and 22.2.

Skill 22.4   Determine probabilities by constructing sample spaces to model situations.

A sample space is the set of all possible outcomes of an event. When conducting an experiment, we construct sample spaces to simplify the process of modeling and the determination of probability. The probability of an event is the number of outcomes that satisfy the event's criteria divided by the total possible outcomes in the sample space.

Example 1:

Determine the sample space of tossing two coins and rolling two 6-sided dices.

Step 1 – Determine the elements of each event.

Coin 1 = {H, T}
Coin 2 = {H, T}
Die 1 = {1, 2, 3, 4, 5, 6}
Die 2 = {1, 2, 3, 4, 5, 6}

Step 2 – Find the sample space.

In this case, the sample space is the product of the possible outcomes of each event. There are two possible outcomes for each tossed coin, heads and tails. There are six possible outcomes for each dice rolled. Because we are tossing two coins and rolling two dice, the sample space is:

2 x 2 x 6 x 6 = 144

Example 2:

We roll one 6-sided die and toss two coins. Find the probability that at least one coin will land on tails and the value of the rolled die is greater than 4.

Step 1 – Determine the elements of each event.

Coin 1 = {H, T}
Coin 2 = {H, T}
Die 1 = {1, 2, 3, 4, 5, 6}

Step 2 – Determine the sample space.

2 x 2 x 6 = 24

Step 3 – Find the number of outcomes that satisfy our criteria.
Possible Outcomes:

HH1, HH2, HH3, HH4, HH5, HH6, TT 1, TT2, TT3, TT4, **TT5**, **TT6**, HT1, HT2, HT3, HT4, **HT5**, **HT6**, TH 1, TH2, TH3, TH4, **TH5**, **TH6**

The outcomes in bold satisfy the criteria of at least one "tails" and a die value of greater than 4. 6 outcomes satisfy the criteria.

Step 4 – Find the probability.

The probability that an event will occur is the number of possible outcomes that satisfy the criteria divided by the total number of outcomes in the sample space. Thus, the probability of our event is:

6/24 = 1/4

Skill 22.5   Solve a variety of probability problems using combinations and permutations

Counting Procedures

So far, in all the problems we dealt with, the Sample Space was given or can be easily obtained. In many real life situations, the Sample Space and events within it are very large and difficult to find.

There are three techniques to help find the number of elements in one event or a Sample Space: counting principle, permutations, and combinations.

The Counting Principle: In a sequence of two distinct events in which the first one has n number of outcomes or possibilities, the second one has m number of outcomes or possibilities, the total number or possibilities of the sequence will be

$$n \cdot m$$

Example: A car dealership has three Mazda models and each model comes in a choice of four colors. How many Mazda cars are available at the dealership.

Number of available Mazda cars = (3)(4) = 12

Example: If a license plate consists of three digits followed by three letters, find the possible number of licenses if

a) repetition of letters and digits are **not** allowed.

b) repetition of letters and digits are allowed.

a)   Since we have twenty-six letters and ten digits, using the counting principle, we get

possible # of licenses = (26)(25)(24)(10)(9)(8)
                                        = 11,232,000

b)   Since repetitions are allowed, we get

possible # of licenses = (26)(26)(26)(10)(10)(10)
                                        = 17,576,000

The Addition Principle of Counting states:

If A and B are events, $n(AorB) = n(A) + n(B) - n(A \cap B)$.

Example: In how many ways can you select a black card or a Jack from an ordinary deck of playing cards?

Let B denote the set of black cards and let J denote the set of Jacks. Then, $n(B) = 26, n(J) = 4, n(B \cap J) = 2$ and
$$n(BorJ) = n(B) + n(J) - n(B \cap A)$$
$$= 26 + 4 - 2$$
$$= 28.$$

The Addition Principle of Counting for Mutually Exclusive Events states:

If A and B are mutually exclusive events, $n(AorB) = n(A) + n(B)$.

Example: A travel agency offers 40 possible trips: 14 to Asia, 16 to Europe and 10 to South America. In how many ways can you select a trip to Asia or Europe through this agency?

Let A denote trips to Asia and let E denote trips to Europe. Then, $A \cap E = \varnothing$ and $n(AorE) = 14 + 16 = 30$.

Therefore, the number of ways you can select a trip to Asia or Europe is 30.

The Multiplication Principle of Counting for Dependent Events states:

Let A be a set of outcomes of Stage 1 and B a set of outcomes of Stage 2. Then the number of ways $n(AandB)$, that A and B can occur in a two-stage experiment is given by:
$$n(AandB) = n(A)n(B|A),$$

where $n(B|A)$ denotes the number of ways B can occur given that A has already occurred.

Example: How many ways from an ordinary deck of 52 cards can two Jacks be drawn in succession if the first card is drawn but not replaced in the deck and then the second card is drawn?

This is a two-stage experiment for which we wish to compute $n(AandB)$, where A is the set of outcomes for which a Jack is obtained on the first draw and B is the set of outcomes for which a Jack is obtained on the second draw.

If the first card drawn is a Jack, then there are only three remaining Jacks left to choose from on the second draw. Thus, drawing two cards without replacement means the events A and B are dependent. $n(AandB) = n(A)n(B|A) = 4 \cdot 3 = 12$

The Multiplication Principle of Counting for Independent Events states:

Let A be a set of outcomes of Stage 1 and B a set of outcomes of Stage 2. If A and B are independent events then the number of ways $n(A \text{ and } B)$, that A and B can occur in a two-stage experiment is given by: $n(A \text{ and } B) = n(A)n(B)$.

Example: How many six-letter code "words" can be formed if repetition of letters is not allowed?

Since these are code words, a word does not have to look like a word; for example, abcdef could be a code word. Since we must choose a first letter *and* a second letter *and* a third letter *and* a fourth letter *and* a fifth letter *and* a sixth letter, this experiment has six stages.

Since repetition is not allowed there are 26 choices for the first letter; 25 for the second; 24 for the third; 23 for the fourth; 22 for the fifth; and 21 for the sixth. Therefore, we have:

n(six-letter code words without repetition of letters)

$$= 26 \cdot 25 \cdot 24 \cdot 23 \cdot 22 \cdot 21$$

$$= 165,765,600$$

Permutations

In order to understand **Permutations**, the concept of factorials must be addressed.

n factorial, written n!, is represented by n ! = n(n-1)(n-2) . . . . . (2)(1)

5! = (5)(4)(3)(2)(1) = 120

3! = 3(2)(1) = 6

By definition: 0! = 1
1! = 1

$\frac{6!}{6!} = 1$ but $\frac{6!}{2!} \neq 3!$

$\frac{6!}{2!} = \frac{6 \cdot 5 \cdot 4 \cdot 3 \cdot 2!}{2!} = 6 \cdot 5 \cdot 4 \cdot 3 = 360$

The number of Permutations represents the number of ways r items can be selected from n items and arranged in a specific order. It is written as $_nP_r$ and is calculated using the following relationship.

$$_nP_r = \frac{n!}{(n-r)!}$$

When calculating permutations order counts. For example, 2, 3, 4 and 4, 3, 2 are counted as two different permutations. Calculating the number of permutations is not valid with experiments where replacement is allowed.

Example: How many different ways can a president and a vice president be selected from a math class if seven students are available?

We know we are looking for the number of Permutations, since the positions of president and vice president are not equal.

$$_7P_2 = \frac{7!}{(7-2)!} = \frac{7!}{5!} = \frac{7 \cdot 6 \cdot 5!}{5!} = 7 \cdot 6 = 42$$

It is important to recognize that the number of Permutations is a special case of the Counting Principle. Unless we are specifically asked to use the Permutation relationship, we use the Counting Principle to solve problems dealing with the number of Permutations. For instance, in this example we have seven available students to choose a president from. After a president is chosen, we have six available students to choose a vice president.

Hence, using the Counting Principle
the ways a president and a vice president can be chosen = 7.6 = 42

Combinations

When dealing with the number of **combinations,** the order in which elements are selected is not important. For instance,

2, 3, 4 and 4, 2, 3 are considered one combination.

The numbers of combinations represents the number of ways r elements are selected from n elements (in no particular order). The number of combinations is represented by $_nC_r$ and can be calculated using the following relationship.

$$_nC_r = \frac{n!}{(n-r)r!}$$

Example: In how many ways can two students be selected from a class of seven students to represent the class?

Since both representatives have the same position, the order is not important and we are dealing with the number of combinations.

$$_nC_r = \frac{7!}{(7-2)!2!} = \frac{7 \cdot 6 \cdot 5!}{5!2 \cdot 1} = 21$$

Example: In a club there are six women and four men. A committee of two women and one man is to be selected. How many different committees can be selected.

This problem has a sequence of two events. The first event involves selecting two women out of six women and the second event involves selecting one man out of four men. We use the Combination relationship to find the number of ways in events 1 and 2 and the Counting Principle to find the number of ways the sequence can happen.

$$\text{\# of Committees} = {_6C_2} \cdot {_4C_1}$$
$$\frac{6!}{(6-2)!2!} x \frac{4!}{(4-1)!1!}$$
$$= \frac{6 \cdot 5 \cdot 4!}{4! \cdot 2 \cdot 1} x \frac{4 \cdot 3!}{3! \cdot 1}$$
$$= (15)x(4) = 60$$

Using tables

Example: The results of a survey of 47 students are summarized in the table below.

	Black Hair	Blonde Hair	Red Hair	Total
Male	10	8	6	24
Female	6	12	5	23
Total	16	20	11	47

Use the table to answer questions a - c.

a)   If one student is selected at random, find the probability of selecting a male student.

$$\frac{\text{Number of male students}}{\text{Number of students}} = \frac{24}{47}$$

b)   If one student is selected at random, find the probability of selecting a female with red hair.

$$\frac{\text{Number of red hair females}}{\text{Number of students}} = \frac{5}{47}$$

c)   If one student is selected at random, find the probability of selecting a student that does not have red hair.

$$\frac{\text{Red hair students}}{\text{Number of students}} = \frac{11}{47}$$

$$1 - \frac{11}{47} = \frac{36}{47}$$

Skill 22.6   **Use the binomial, geometric, and normal distributions to solve problems.**

The **binomial distribution** is a sequence of probabilities with each probability corresponding to the likelihood of a particular event occurring. It is called a binomial distribution because each trial has precisely two possible outcomes. An **event** is defined as a sequence of Bernoulli trials that has within it a specific number of successes. The order of success is not important.

Note: There are two parameters to consider in a binomial distribution:
1. p = the probability of a success
2. n = the number of Bernoulli trials (i.e., the length of the sequence).

Example: Toss a coin two times. Each toss is a Bernoulli trial as discussed above. Consider heads to be success. One event is one sequence of two coin tosses. Order does not matter.

There are two possibilities for each coin toss. Therefore, there are four (2·2) possible subevents: 00, 01, 10, 11 (where 0 = tail and 1 = head).

According to the multiplication rule, each subevent has a probability of $\frac{1}{4}\left(\frac{1}{2}\cdot\frac{1}{2}\right)$.

One subevent has zero heads, so the event of zero heads in two tosses is $p(h=0)=\frac{1}{4}$.

Two subevents have one head, so the event of one head in two tosses is $p(h=1)=\frac{2}{4}$.

One subevent has two heads, so the event of two heads in two tosses is $p(h=2)=\frac{1}{4}$.

So the binomial distribution for two tosses of a fair coin is:

$$p(h=0)=\frac{1}{4},\ p(h=1)=\frac{2}{4},\ p(h=2)=\frac{1}{4}.$$

A **normal distribution** is the distribution associated with most sets of real-world data. It is frequently called a **bell curve**. A normal distribution has a **random variable** X with mean μ and variance σ^2.

Example: Albert's Bagel Shop's morning customer load follows a normal distribution, with **mean** (average) 50 and **standard deviation** 10. The standard deviation is the measure of the variation in the distribution. Determine the probability that the number of customers tomorrow will be less than 42.

First convert the raw score to a **z-score**. A z-score is a measure of the distance in standard deviations of a sample from the mean.

The z-score $=\dfrac{X_i=\bar{X}}{s}=\dfrac{42-50}{10}=\dfrac{-8}{10}=-.8$

Next, use a table to find the probability corresponding to the z-score. The table gives us .2881. Since our raw score is negative, we subtract the table value from .5.

$$.5 - .2881 = .2119$$

We can conclude that $P(x < 42) = .2119$. This means that there is about a 21% chance that there will be fewer than 42 customers tomorrow morning.

Example: The scores on Mr. Rogers' statistics exam follow a normal distribution with mean 85 and standard deviation 5. A student is wondering what the probability is that she will score between a 90 and a 95 on her exam.

We wish to compute $P(90 < x < 95)$.

Compute the z-scores for each raw score.

$$\frac{90 - 85}{5} = \frac{5}{5} = 1 \quad \text{and} \quad \frac{95 - 85}{5} = \frac{10}{5} = 2.$$

Now we want $P(1 < z < 2)$.

Since we are looking for an occurrence between two values, we subtract:

$$P(1 < z < 2) = P(z < 2) - P(z < 1).$$

We use a table to get :

$P(1 < z < 2) = .9772 - .8413 = .1359.$ (Remember that since the z-scores are positive, we add .5 to each probability.)

We can then conclude that there is a 13.6% chance that the student will score between a 90 and a 95 on her exam.

COMPETENCY 23.0 UNDERSTAND THE RELATIONSHIP AMONG PROBABILITY THEORY, SAMPLING AND STATISTICAL INFERENCE, AND HOW STATISTICAL INFERENCE IS USED IN MAKING AND EVALUATING PREDICTIONS.

Skill 23.1 Apply knowledge of designing, conducting, analyzing, and interpreting statistical experiments to investigate real-world problems.

The four main types of measurement scales used in statistical analysis are nominal, ordinal, interval, and ratio. The type of variable measured and the research questions asked determine the appropriate measurement scale. The different measurement scales have distinctive qualities and attributes.

The nominal measurement scale is the most basic measurement scale. When measuring using the nominal scale, we simply label or classify responses into categories. Examples of variables measured on the nominal scale are gender, religion, ethnicity, and marital status. The essential attribute of the nominal scale is that the classifications have no numerical or comparative value. For example, when classifying people by marital status, there is no sense in which "single" is greater or less than "married". The only measure of central tendency applicable to the nominal scale is mode and the only applicable arithmetic operation is counting.

The ordinal measurement scale is more descriptive than the nominal scale in that the ordinal scale allows comparison between categories. Examples of variables measured on the ordinal scale are movie ratings, consumer satisfaction surveys, and the rank or order of anything. While we can compare categories of responses on the ordinal scale (e.g. "highly satisfied" indicates a higher level of satisfaction than "somewhat satisfied"), we cannot determine anything about the difference between the categories. In other words, we cannot presume that the difference between two categories is the same as the distance between two other categories. Even if the responses are in numeric form (e.g. 1 = good, 2 = fair, 3 = poor), we can presume nothing about the intervals separating the groups. Ordinal scales allow greater or less-than comparisons and the applicable measures of central tendency are range and median.

The next measurement scale is the interval scale. Interval scales are numeric scales where intervals have a fixed, uniform value throughout the scale. An example of an interval scale is the Fahrenheit temperature scale. On the Fahrenheit scale, the difference between 40 degrees and 50 degrees is the same as the difference between 70 degrees and 80 degrees. The major limitation of interval scales is that there is no fixed zero point.

For example, while the Fahrenheit scale has a value of zero degrees, this assignment is arbitrary because the measurement does not represent the absence of temperature. Because interval scales lack a true zero point, ratio comparison of values has no meaning. Thus, the arithmetic operations addition and subtraction are applicable to interval scales while multiplication and division are not. The measures of central tendency applicable to interval scales are mode, median, and arithmetic mean.

The final, and most informative, measurement scale is the ratio scale. The ratio scale is essentially an interval scale with a true zero point. Examples of ratio scales are measurement of length (meters, inches, etc.), monetary systems, and degrees Kelvin. The zero value of each of these scales represents the absence of length, money, and temperature, respectively. The presence of a true zero point allows proportional comparisons. For example, we can say that someone with one dollar has twice as much money as someone with fifty cents. Because ratios have meaning on ratio scales, we can apply the arithmetic operations of multiplication and division to the data sets.

Skill 23.2   Demonstrate an understanding of random samples, sample statistics, and the relationship between sample size and confidence intervals.

Random sampling is the process of studying an aspect of a population by selecting and gathering data from a segment of the population and making inferences and generalizations based on the results. Two main types of random sampling are simple and stratified. With simple random sampling, each member of the population has an equal chance of selection to the sample group. With stratified random sampling, each member of the population has a known but unequal chance of selection to the sample group, as the study selects a random sample from each population demographic. In general, stratified random sampling is more accurate because it provides a more representative sample group. Sample statistics are important generalizations about the entire sample such as mean, median, mode, range, and sampling error (standard deviation). Various factors affect the accuracy of sample statistics and the generalizations made from them about the larger population.

Sample size is one important factor in the accuracy and reliability of sample statistics. As sample size increases, sampling error (standard deviation) decreases. Sampling error is the main determinant of the size of the confidence interval. Confidence intervals decrease in size as sample size increases.

A confidence interval gives an estimated range of values, which is likely to include a particular population parameter. The confidence level associated with a confidence interval is the probability that the interval contains the population parameter. For example, a poll reports 60% of a sample group prefers candidate A with a margin of error of $\pm$ 3% and a confidence level of 95%. In this poll, there is a 95% chance that the preference for candidate A in the whole population is between 57% and 63%.

The ultimate goal of sampling is to make generalizations about a population based on the characteristics of a random sample. Estimators are sample statistics used to make such generalizations. For example, the mean value of a sample is the estimator of the population mean. Unbiased estimators, on average, accurately predict the corresponding population characteristic. Biased estimators, on the other hand, do not exactly mirror the corresponding population characteristic. While most estimators contain some level of bias, limiting bias to achieve accurate projections is the goal of statisticians.

Skill 23.3   Apply knowledge of the use of probability to make observations and draw conclusions from single variable data and to describe the level of confidence in the conclusion.

The law of large numbers and the central limit theorem are two fundamental concepts in statistics. The law of large numbers states that the larger the sample size, or the more times we measure a variable in a population, the closer the sample mean will be to the population mean. For example, the average weight of 40 apples out of a population of 100 will more closely approximate the population average weight than will a sample of 5 apples. The central limit theorem expands on the law of large numbers. The central limit theorem states that as the number of samples increases, the distribution of sample means (averages) approaches a normal distribution. This holds true regardless of the distribution of the population. Thus, as the number of samples taken increases the sample mean becomes closer to the population mean. This property of statistics allows us to analyze the properties of populations of unknown distribution.

In conclusion, the law of large numbers and central limit theorem show the importance of large sample size and large number of samples to the process of statistical inference. As sample size and the number of samples taken increase, the accuracy of conclusions about the population drawn from the sample data increases.

Correlation is a measure of association between two variables. It varies from -1 to 1, with 0 being a random relationship, 1 being a perfect positive linear relationship, and -1 being a perfect negative linear relationship.

The **correlation coefficient** (r) is used to describe the strength of the association between the variables and the direction of the association.

Example:

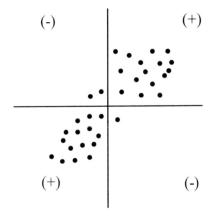

Horizontal and vertical lines are drawn through the point of averages which is the point on the averages of the x and y values. This divides the scatter plot into four quadrants. If a point is in the lower left quadrant, the product of two negatives is positive; in the upper right, the product of two positives is positive. The positive quadrants are depicted with the positive sign (+). In the two remaining quadrants (upper left and lower right), the product of a negative and a positive is negative. The negative quadrants are depicted with the negative sign (-). If r is positive, then there are more points in the positive quadrants and if r is negative, then there are more points in the two negative quadrants.

Regression is a form of statistical analysis used to predict a dependent variable (y) from values of an independent variable (x). A regression equation is derived from a known set of data.

The simplest regression analysis models the relationship between two variables using the following equation: $y = a + bx$, where y is the dependent variable and x is the independent variable. This simple equation denotes a linear relationship between x and y. This form would be appropriate if, when you plotted a graph of x and y, you tended to see the points roughly form along a straight line.

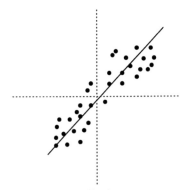

The line can then be used to make predictions.

If all of the data points fell on the line, there would be a perfect correlation ($r = 1.0$) between the x and y data points. These cases represent the best scenarios for prediction. A positive or negative r value represents how y varies with x. When r is positive, y increases as x increases. When r is negative y decreases as x increases.

Skill 23.4 **Make inferences about a population using binomial, normal, and geometric distributions.**

See Skill 23.3.

Skill 23.5 **Demonstrate an understanding of the use of techniques such as scatter plots, regression lines, correlation coefficients, and residual analysis to explore bivariate data and to make and evaluate predictions.**

See Skill 23.3.

COMPETENCY 24.0 UNDERSTAND MATHEMATICAL REASONING AND PROBLEM SOLVING.

Skill 24.1 **Demonstrate an understanding of proof, including indirect proof, in mathematics.**

In a 2 column proof, the left side of the proof should be the given information, or statements that could be proved by deductive reasoning. The right column of the proof consists of the reasons used to determine that each statement to the left was verifiably true. The right side can identify given information, or state theorems, postulates, definitions or algebraic properties used to prove that particular line of the proof is true.

Skill 24.2 **Apply correct mathematical reasoning to derive valid conclusions from a set of premises.**

A simple statement represents a simple idea, that can be described as either "true" or "false", but not both. A simple statement is represented by a small letter of the alphabet.

Example: "Today is Monday." This is a simple statement since it can be determine that this statement is either true or false. We can write p = "Today is Monday".

Example: "John, please be quite". This is not considered a simple statement in our study of logic, since we cannot assign a truth value to it.

Simple statements joined together by **connectives** ("and", "or", "not", "if then", and "if and only if") result in compound statements. Note that compound statements can also be formed using "but", "however", or "never the less". A compound statement can be assigned a truth value.

Conditional statements are frequently written in "if-then" form. The "if" clause of the conditional is known as the **hypothesis**, and the "then" clause is called the **conclusion**. In a proof, the hypothesis is the information that is assumed to be true, while the conclusion is what is to be proven true. A conditional is considered to be of the form: **If p, then q** where p is the hypothesis and q is the conclusion.

$p \rightarrow q$ is read "if p then q".
$\sim$ (statement) is read "it is not true that (statement)".

Quantifiers are words describing a quantity under discussion. These include words like "all', "none" (or "no"), and "some".

Negation of a Statement- If a statement is true, then its negation must be false (and vice versa).

A Summary of Negation Rules:

statement	negation
(1) q	(1) <u>not</u> q
(2) <u>not</u> q	(2) q
(3) π <u>and</u> s	(3) (not π) <u>or</u> (not s)
(4) π <u>or</u> s	(4) (not π) <u>and</u> (not s)
(5) if p, then q	(5) (p) <u>and</u> (not q)

Example: Select the statement that is the negation of "some winter nights are not cold".

   A. All winter nights are not cold.
   B. Some winter nights are cold.
   C. All winter nights are cold.
   D. None of the winter nights are cold.

   Negation of "some are" is "none are". So the negation statement is "none of the winter night is cold". So the answer is D.

Example: Select the statement that is the negation of "if it rains, then the beach party will not be held".

   A. If it does not rain, then the beach party will be held.
   B. If the beach party is held, then it will not rain.
   C. It does not rain and the beach party will be held.
   D. It rains and the beach party will be held.

   Negation of "if p, then q" is "p and (not q)". So the negation of the given statement is "it rains and the beach party will be held". So select D.

Example: Select the negation of the statement "If they get elected, then all politicians go back on election promises".

   A. If they get elected, then many politicians go back on election promises.
   B. They get elected and some politicians go back on election promises.
   C. If they do not get elected, some politicians do not go back on election promises.
   D. None of the above statements is the negation of the given statement.

Identify the key words of "if...then" and "all...go back". The negation of the given statement is "they get elected and none of the politicians go back on election promises". So select response D, since A, B, and C, statements are not the negations.

Example: Select the statement that is the negation of "the sun is shining bright <u>and</u> I feel great".

A. If the sun is not shining bright. I do not feel great.
B. The sun is not shining bright and I do not feel great.
C. The sun is not shining bring or I do not feel great.
D. the sun is shining bright and I do not feel great.

The negation of "r and s" is "(not r) or (not s)". So the negation of the given statement is "the sun is <u>not</u> shining bright <u>or</u> I do not feel great". We select response C.

Conditional statements can be diagrammed using a **Venn diagram**. A diagram can be drawn with one circle inside another circle. The inner circle represents the hypothesis. The outer circle represents the conclusion. If the hypothesis is taken to be true, then you are located inside the inner circle. If you are located in the inner circle then you are also inside the outer circle, so that proves the conclusion is true.

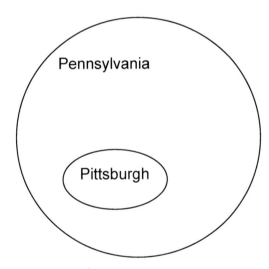

Example: If an angle has a measure of 90 degrees, then it is a right angle.

In this statement "an angle has a measure of 90 degrees" is the hypothesis. In this statement "it is a right angle" is the conclusion.

Example: If you are in Pittsburgh, then you are in Pennsylvania.
In this statement "you are in Pittsburgh" is the hypothesis.
In this statement "you are in Pennsylvania" is the conclusion.

Skill 24.3 **Demonstrate an understanding of the use of inductive reasoning to make conjectures and deductive methods to evaluate the validity of conjectures.**

Inductive thinking is the process of finding a pattern from a group of examples. That pattern is the conclusion that this set of examples seemed to indicate. It may be a correct conclusion or it may be an incorrect conclusion because other examples may not follow the predicted pattern.

Deductive reasoning is the process of arriving at a conclusion based on other statements that are all known to be true.

A symbolic argument consists of a set of premises and a conclusion in the format of of if [Premise 1 and premise 2] then [conclusion].

An argument is **valid** when the conclusion follows necessarily from the premises. An argument is **invalid** or a fallacy when the conclusion does not follow from the premises.

There are 4 standard forms of valid arguments which must be remembered.

1. Law of Detachment	If p, then q	(premise 1)
	p,	(premise 2)
	Therefore, q	
2. Law of Contraposition	If p, then q	
	not q,	
	Therefore not p	
3. Law of Syllogism	If p, then q	
	If q, then r	
	Therefore if p, then r	
4. Disjunctive Syllogism	p or q	
	not p	
	Therefore, q	

Example: Can a conclusion be reached from these two statements?

    A.   All swimmers are athletes.
          All athletes are scholars.

In "if-then" form, these would be:
    If you are a swimmer, then you are an athlete.
    If you are an athlete, then you are a scholar.

Clearly, if you are a swimmer, then you are also an athlete. This includes you in the group of scholars.

    B.   All swimmers are athletes.
          All wrestlers are athletes.

In "if-then" form, these would be:
    If you are a swimmer, then you are an athlete.
    If you are a wrestler, then you are an athlete.

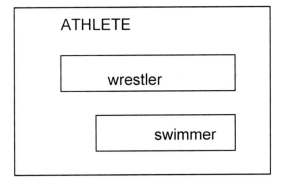

Clearly, if you are a swimmer or a wrestler, then you are also an athlete. This does NOT allow you to come to any other conclusions.

A swimmer may or may NOT also be a wrestler. Therefore, NO CONCLUSION IS POSSIBLE.

Suppose that these statements were given to you, and you are asked to try to reach a conclusion. The statements are:

Example: Determine whether statement A, B, C, or D can be deduced from the following:

(i)If John drives the big truck, then the shipment will be delivered.

(ii)The shipment will not be delivered.

a.John does not drive the big truck.
b.John drives the big truck.
c.The shipment will not be delivered.
d.None of the above conclusion is true.

Let p: John drives the big truck.
    q: The shipment is delivered.

statement (i) gives p → q, statement (ii) gives ~ q. This is the Law of Contraposition.

Therefore, the logical conclusion is ~p or "John does not drive the big truck". So the answer is response A.

Example: Given that:
(i)Peter is a Jet Pilot or Peter is a Navigator.
(ii)Peter is not a Jet Pilot

Determine which conclusion can be logically deduced.

a.Peter is not a Navigator.
b.Peter is a Navigator.
c.Peter is neither a Jet Pilot nor a Navigator.
d.None of the above is true.

Let p: Peter is a Jet Pilot
    q: Peter is a Navigator.

So we have p ∨ q from statement (i)
           ~p   from statement (ii)

So choose response B.

Try These:

What conclusion, if any, can be reached? Assume each statement is true, regardless of any personal beliefs.

1. If the Red Sox win the World Series, I will die.
   I died.

2. If an angle's measure is between 0° and 90°, then the angle is acute. Angle B is not acute.

3. Students who do well in geometry will succeed in college.
   Annie is doing extremely well in geometry.

4. Left-handed people are witty and charming.
   You are left-handed.

Answers:

Question #1   The Red Sox won the World Series.
Question #2   Angle B is not between 0 and 90 degrees.
Question #3   Annie will do well in college.
Question #4   You are witty and charming.

Skill 24.4   Apply knowledge of the use of formal and informal reasoning to explore, investigate, and justify mathematical ideas.

See Skill 24.1.

Skill 24.5   Recognize that a mathematical problem can be solved in a variety of ways and selects an appropriate strategy for a given problem.

The **questioning technique** is a mathematic process skill in which students devise questions to clarify the problem, eliminate possible solutions, and simplify the problem solving process. By developing and attempting to answer simple questions, students can tackle difficult and complex problems.

Observation-inference is another mathematic process skill that used regularly in statistics. We can use the data gathered or observed from a sample of the population to make inferences about traits and qualities of the population as a whole. For example, if we observe that 40% of voters in our sample favors Candidate A, then we can infer that 40% of the entire voting population favors Candidate A. Successful use of observation-inference depends on accurate observation and representative sampling.

Skill 24.6 Demonstrate an understanding of estimation and evaluates its appropriate use and evaluate the reasonableness of a solution to a given problem.

Estimation and testing for **reasonableness** are related skills students should employ prior to and after solving a problem. These skills are particularly important when students use calculators to find answers.

Example: Find the sum of 4387 + 7226 + 5893.
  4300 + 7200 + 5800 = 17300   Estimation.
  4387 + 7226 + 5893 = 17506   Actual sum.

By comparing the estimate to the actual sum, students can determine that their answer is reasonable.

Successful math teachers introduce their students to multiple problem solving strategies and create a classroom environment where free thought and experimentation are encouraged. Teachers can promote problem solving by allowing multiple attempts at problems, giving credit for reworking test or homework problems, and encouraging the sharing of ideas through class discussion. There are several specific problem solving skills with which teachers should be familiar.

The **guess-and-check** strategy calls for students to make an initial guess at the solution, check the answer, and use the outcome of to guide the next guess. With each successive guess, the student should get closer to the correct answer. Constructing a table from the guesses can help organize the data.

Example: There are 100 coins in a jar. 10 are dimes. The rest are pennies and nickels. There are twice as many pennies as nickels. How many pennies and nickels are in the jar?

There are 90 total nickels and pennies in the jar (100 coins – 10 dimes).

There are twice as many pennies as nickels. Make guesses that fulfill the criteria and adjust based on the answer found. Continue until we find the correct answer, 60 pennies and 30 nickels.

Number of Pennies	Number of Nickels	Total Number of Pennies and Nickels
40	20	60
80	40	120
70	35	105
60	30	90

When solving a problem where the final result and the steps to reach the result are given, students must **work backwards** to determine what the starting point must have been.

Example: John subtracted seven from his age, and divided the result by 3. The final result was 4. What is John's age?

Work backward by reversing the operations.
$4 \times 3 = 12$;
$12 + 7 = 19$
John is 19 years old.

Skill 24.7   Applies content knowledge to develop a mathematical model of a real-world situation and analyzes and evaluates how well the model presents the situation

See Skill 14.3

Skill 24.8   Demonstrates an understanding of estimation and evaluates its appropriate uses

See Skill 24.6

COMPETENCY 25.0 UNDERSTAND MATHEMATICAL CONNECTIONS WITHIN AND OUTSIDE OF MATHEMATICS AND HOW TO COMMUNICATE MATHEMATICAL IDEAS AND CONCEPTS.

Skill 25.1   Recognize and use multiple representations of a mathematical concept (e.g., a point and its coordinates, the area of circle as a quadratic function in *r*, probability as the ratio of two areas).

See other skills.

Skill 25.2   Use mathematics to model and solve problems in other disciplines, such as art, music, science, social science, and business.

Artists, musicians, scientists, social scientists, and business people use mathematical modeling to solve problems in their disciplines. These disciplines rely on the tools and symbology of mathematics to model natural events and manipulate data. Mathematics is a key aspect of visual art.

Artists use the geometric properties of shapes, ratios, and proportions in creating paintings and sculptures. For example, mathematics is essential to the concept of perspective. Artists must determine the appropriate lengths and heights of objects to portray three-dimensional distance in two dimensions.

Mathematics is also an important part of music. Many musical terms have mathematical connections. For example, the musical octave contains twelve notes and spans a factor of two in frequency. In other words, the frequency, the speed of vibration that determines tone and sound quality, doubles from the first note in an octave to the last. Thus, starting from any note we can determine the frequency of any other note with the following formula.

$$\text{Freq} = \text{note} \times 2^{N/12}$$

Where N is the number of notes from the starting point and note is the frequency of the starting note. Mathematical understanding of frequency plays an important role in the tuning of musical instruments.

In addition to the visual and auditory arts, mathematics is an integral part of most scientific disciplines. The uses of mathematics in science are almost endless. The following are but a few examples of how scientists use mathematics. Physical scientists use vectors, functions, derivatives, and integrals to describe and model the movement of objects. Biologists and ecologists use mathematics to model ecosystems and study DNA. Finally, chemists use mathematics to study the interaction of molecules and to determine proper amounts and proportions of reactants.

Many social science disciplines use mathematics to model and solve problems. Economists, for example, use functions, graphs, and matrices to model the activities of producers, consumers, and firms. Political scientists use mathematics to model the behavior and opinions of the electorate. Finally, sociologists use mathematical functions to model the behavior of humans and human populations.

Finally, mathematical problem solving and modeling is essential to business planning and execution. For example, businesses rely on mathematical projections to plan business strategy. Additionally, stock market analysis and accounting rely on mathematical concepts.

Mathematical concepts and procedures can take many different forms. Students of mathematics must be able to recognize different forms of equivalent concepts.

For example, we can represent the slope of a line graphically, algebraically, verbally, and numerically. A line drawn on a coordinate plane will show the slope. In the equation of a line, $y = mx + b$, the term m represents the slope. We can define the slope of a line several different ways. The slope of a line is the change in the value of the y divided by the change in the value of x over a given interval. Alternatively, the slope of a line is the ratio of "rise" to "run" between two points. Finally, we can calculate the numeric value of the slope by using the verbal definitions and the algebraic representation of the line.

Skill 25.3 Communicate mathematical ideas using a variety of representations (e.g., numeric, verbal, graphic, pictorial, symbolic, concrete).

Examples, illustrations, and symbolic representations are useful tools in explaining and understanding mathematical concepts. The ability to create examples and alternative methods of expression allows students to solve real world problems and better communicate their thoughts.

Concrete examples are real world applications of mathematical concepts. For example, measuring the shadow produced by a tree or building is a real world application of trigonometric functions, acceleration or velocity of a car is an application of derivatives, and finding the volume or area of a swimming pool is a real world application of geometric principles.

Pictorial illustrations of mathematic concepts help clarify difficult ideas and simplify problem solving.

Example: Rectangle R represents the 300 students in School A. Circle represents the 150 students that participated in band. Circle Q represents the 170 students that participated in a sport. 70 students participated in both band and a sport.

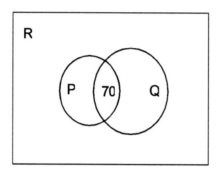

Pictorial representation of above situation.

Example: A ball rolls up an incline and rolls back to its original position. Create a graph of the velocity of the ball.

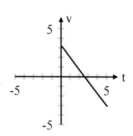

Velocity starts out at its maximum as the ball begins to roll, decreases to zero at the top of the incline, and returns to the maximum in the opposite direction at the bottom of the incline.

Symbolic representation is the basic language of mathematics. Converting data to symbols allows for easy manipulation and problem solving. Students should have the ability to recognize what the symbolic notation represents and convert information into symbolic form. For example, from the graph of a line, students should have the ability to determine the slope and intercepts and derive the line's equation from the observed data. Another possible application of symbolic representation is the formulation of algebraic expressions and relations from data presented in word problem form.

Examples, illustrations, and symbolic representations are useful tools in explaining and understanding mathematical concepts. The ability to create examples and alternative methods of expression allows students to solve real world problems and better communicate their thoughts.

Pictorial illustrations of mathematic concepts help clarify difficult ideas and simplify problem solving.

Skill 25.4   Demonstrate an understanding of the use of visual media such as graphs, tables, diagrams, and animations to communicate mathematical information.

See Skill 21.1.

Skill 25.5   Use the language of mathematics as a precise means of expressing mathematical ideas.

In order to understand mathematics and solve problems, one must know the definitions of basic mathematic terms and concepts. For a list of definitions and explanations of basic math terms, visit the following website:
http://home.blarg.net/~math/deflist.html

Additionally, one must use the language of mathematics correctly and precisely to accurately communicate concepts and ideas.

For example, the statement "minus ten times minus five equals plus fifty" is incorrect because minus and plus are arithmetic operations not numerical modifiers. The statement should read "negative ten times negative five equals positive 50".

Students need to use the proper mathematical terms and expressions. When reading decimals, they need to read 0.4 as "four tenths" to promote better understanding of the concepts. They should do their work in a neat and organized manner. Students need to be encouraged to verbalize their strategies, both in computation and word problems. Additionally, writing original word problems fosters understanding of math language. Another idea is requiring students to develop their own glossary of mathematical glossary. Knowing the answers and being able to communicate them are equally important.

Skill 25.6   Uses the language of mathematics as a precise means of expressing mathematical ideas

See previous Skills

Skill 25.7   Understands the structural properties common to the mathematical disciplines

See previous Skills

COMPETENCY 26.0 UNDERSTAND HOW CHILDREN LEARN AND DEVELOP MATHEMATICAL SKILLS, PROCEDURES, AND CONCEPTS.

Skill 26.1 Apply theories and principles of learning mathematics to plan appropriate instructional activities for all students.

Teachers can use theories of learning to plan curriculum and instructional activities. Research indicates that students learn math more easily in an applied, project-based setting. In addition, prior knowledge, learning, and self-taught understanding are important factors that dictate a student's ability to learn and preferred method of learning.

Many educators believe that the best method of teaching math is situated learning. Proponents of situated learning argue that learning is largely a function of the activity, context, and environment in which learning occurs. According to situated learning theory, students learn more easily from instruction involving relevant, real-world situations and applications rather than abstract thoughts and ideas. Research or project-based learning is a product of situated learning theory. Open-ended research tasks and projects promote learning by engaging students on multiple levels. Such tasks require the use of multiple skills and reasoning strategies and help keep students focused and attentive. Additionally, projects promote active learning by encouraging the sharing of thoughts and ideas and teacher-student and student-student interaction.

Skill 26.2 Understand how students differ in their approaches to learning mathematics with regards to diversity.

The cultural and ethnic background of a student greatly affects his or her approach to learning mathematics. In addition, factors such as socioeconomic status can affect student learning styles. Teachers must have the ability to tailor their teaching style, methods, and curriculum to the varying learning styles present in a diverse classroom.

Students of certain ethnic and racial groups that emphasize expressiveness and communication may benefit from a more interactive learning environment. For example, such students may benefit from lessons involving discussion, group work and hands-on projects. Conversely, students of ethnic groups that emphasize personal learning and discipline may benefit from a more structured, traditional learning environment. As is always the case when considering ethnic differences, however, we must be careful to avoid making inappropriate generalizations.

We must remember that ethnicity is only one form of diversity and that there is great diversity within ethnic and racial groups.

Socioeconomic status is another source of classroom diversity. Low-income students may not have the same early educational background and exposure to traditional educational reasoning strategies and techniques. Thus, low-income students may initially require a more application-based curriculum until they develop sufficient abstract reasoning skills.

A popular theory of math learning is constructivism. Constructivism argues that prior knowledge greatly influences the learning of math and learning is cumulative and vertically structured. Thus, it is important for teachers to recognize the knowledge and ideas about a subject that students already possess. Instruction must build on the innate knowledge of students and address any common misconceptions. Teachers can gain insight into the prior knowledge of students by beginning each lesson with open questions that allow students to share their thoughts and ideas on the subject or topic.

Skill 26.3 Use students' prior mathematical knowledge to build conceptual links to new knowledge and plan instruction that builds on students' strengths and addresses students' needs.

Middle school mathematics lays the groundwork for the progression of concrete ideas mastered in the elementary years to less concrete, more algebraic understandings of mathematical ideas. As students progress to later grades the concepts are developed deeper and connections between the various skills become more apparent. Skills developed in middle school are part of the progression of skills that begins formally in the primary grades and continues afterwards into high school and beyond.

In middle school, students are developing their number sense, focusing mainly on decimals, fractions, proportion, roots and negative numbers. A clear understanding of these ideas is essential, as their task in high school years is to understand how numeration concepts relate to each other. Estimation is largely a rote, pen and paper skill in middle school years, but in high school and beyond, estimation is strongly geared around evaluating the reasonableness of answers that uses the understanding developed in middle school. Sophisticated calculators are utilized in high school in ways that involve calculated rounding, either user-defined or part of the calculator's programming. For this reason, the high school student needs to be able to recognize the reasonableness of the outcomes of functions when calculated on a calculator.

The analysis of relationships or functions progresses to more algebraic forms in middle school, but the skill of developing models to demonstrate patterns and functions is also maintained. In high school and beyond students extend their understanding of functions to include the symbolic ideas of domain, range and $f(x)$ notation. Both the concrete and symbolic understandings of functions are used in advanced mathematics. Many careers including engineering, architects and other professionals rely on the use and analysis of concrete working models.

Calculus mainly involves the study of limit, rate of change, area under a curve and slope of a tangent line. In middle school, the base work for these concepts is developed. Students develop an understanding for infinity, linear growth, exponential growth, slope and change over time. High school level pre-calculus is generally aimed at developing understanding of main calculus concepts. More specific calculus techniques such as differentiation and convergence testing are generally reserved for college-level mathematics.

Trigonometry is a branch of mathematics dealing with the angles, triangles and the functions sine, cosine and tangent. Two aspects of trigonometry developed in middle school are geometrical knowledge (eg. similar triangles, the Pythagorean Theorem) and algebraic skills (solving equations and using algebraic expressions). Trigonometry is adapted into careers involving astronomy, land surveying and acoustics, among a wide array of others.

Skill 26.4   Understand how learning may be assisted through the use of mathematics manipulatives and technological tools.

The use of supplementary materials in the classroom can greatly enhance the learning experience by stimulating student interest and satisfying different learning styles. Manipulatives, models, and technology are examples of tools available to teachers.

Manipulatives are materials that students can physically handle and move. Manipulatives allow students to understand mathematic concepts by allowing them to see concrete examples of abstract processes. Manipulatives are attractive to students because they appeal to the students' visual and tactile senses. Available for all levels of math, manipulatives are useful tools for reinforcing operations and concepts. They are not, however, a substitute for the development of sound computational skills.

Models are another means of representing mathematical concepts by relating the concepts to real-world situations. Teachers must choose wisely when devising and selecting models because, to be effective, models must be applied properly. For example, a building with floors above and below ground is a good model for introducing the concept of negative numbers. It would be difficult, however, to use the building model in teaching subtraction of negative numbers.

Finally, there are many forms of **technology** available to math teachers. For example, students can test their understanding of math concepts by working on skill specific computer programs and websites. Graphing calculators can help students visualize the graphs of functions. Teachers can also enhance their lectures and classroom presentations by creating multimedia presentations.

Skill 26.5 **Understand how to motivate students and actively engage them in the learning process by using a variety of interesting, challenging, and worthwhile mathematical tasks in individual, small-group, and large-group settings.**

Successful teachers select and implement instructional delivery methods that best fit the needs of a particular classroom format. Individual, small-group and large-group classroom formats require different techniques and methods of instruction.

Individual instruction allows the teacher to interact closely with the student. Teachers may use a variety of methods in an individual setting that are not practical when working with a large number of students. For example, teachers can use manipulatives to illustrate a mathematical concept.

In addition, teachers can observe and evaluate the student's reasoning and problem solving skills through verbal questioning and by checking the student's written work. Finally, individual instruction allows the teacher to work problems with the student, thus familiarizing the student with the problem-solving process.

Small-group formats require the teacher to provide instruction to multiple students at the same time. Because the size of the group is small, instructional methods that encourage student interaction and cooperative learning are particularly effective. For example, group projects, discussion, and question-and-answer sessions promote cooperative learning and maintain student interest. In addition, working problems as a group or in pairs can help students learn problem-solving strategies from each other.

Large-group formats require instructional methods that can effectively deliver information to a large number of students. Lecture is a common instructional method for large groups. In addition, demonstrating methods of problem solving and allowing students to ask questions about homework and test problems is an effective strategy for teaching large-groups.

Skill 26.6 **Understand how to provide instruction along a continuum from concrete to abstract.**

When introducing a new mathematical concept to students, teachers should utilize the concrete-to-representational-to-abstract sequence of instruction. The first step of the instructional progression is the introduction of a concept modeled with concrete materials. The second step is the translation of concrete models into representational diagrams or pictures. The third and final step is the translation of representational models into abstract models using only numbers and symbols.

Teachers should first use concrete models to introduce a mathematical concept because they are easiest to understand. For example, teachers can allow students to use counting blocks to learn basic arithmetic. Teachers should give students ample time and many opportunities to experiment, practice, and demonstrate mastery with the concrete materials.

Skill 26.7   Recognizes the implications of current trends and research in mathematics and mathematics education.

See Previous Skills

COMPETENCY 27.0 UNDERSTAND HOW TO PLAN, ORGANIZE, AND IMPLEMENT INSTRUCTION USING KNOWLEDGE OF STUDENTS, SUBJECT MATTER, AND STATEWIDE CURRICULUM (TEXAS ESSENTIAL KNOWLEDGE AND SKILLS [TEKS]) TO TEACH ALL STUDENTS TO USE MATHEMATICS.

Skill 27.1 Demonstrate an understanding of a variety of instructional methods, tools, and tasks that promote students' ability to do mathematics described in the TEKS.

The Texas Essential Knowledge and Skills (TEKS) are a comprehensive list of standards for subject matter learning. TEKS provide teachers with a framework for curriculum design and instructional method selection. The different skills described in TEKS require different teaching strategies and techniques.

The primary goals of middle school math instruction, as defined by TEKS, are the building of a strong foundation in mathematical concepts and the development of problem-solving and analytical skills. Direct teaching methods, including lecture and demonstration, are particularly effective in teaching basic mathematical concepts. To stimulate interest, accommodate different learning styles and enhance understanding, teachers should incorporate manipulatives and technology into their lectures and demonstrations. Indirect teaching methods, including cooperative learning, discussion and projects, promote the development of problem solving skills. Cooperative learning and discussion allow students to share ideas and strategies with their peers. In addition, projects require students to apply knowledge and develop and implement problem-solving strategies.

Skill 27.2 Understand planning strategies for developing mathematical instruction as a discipline of interconnected concepts and procedures.

The TEKS provide teachers with a comprehensive list of skills that the state requires students to master. Utilizing the learning goals presented in TEKS, teachers can plan instruction to promote student understanding. In addition, teachers can deliver instruction in ways that are appropriate to the specific skill, classroom environment and student population. To assess the effectiveness of instruction, teachers can design tests that evaluate student mastery of specific skills. In grading such tests, teachers should look for patterns in student mistakes and errors that may indicate a deficiency in the instructional plan. In reevaluating instruction, teachers can attempt to use different instructional methods or shift areas of emphasis to meet the needs of the students.

Skill 27.3 Understand procedures for developing instruction that establishes transitions between concrete, symbolic, and abstract representations of mathematical knowledge.

The second step in the learning process is the translation of concrete materials to representational models. For example, students may use tally marks or pictures to represent the counting blocks they used in the previous stage. Once again, teachers should give students ample time to master the concept on the representational level.

The final step in the learning process is the translation of representational models into abstract numbers and symbols. For example, students represent the processes carried out in the previous stages using only numbers and arithmetic symbols.

To ease the transition, teachers should associate numbers and symbols with the concrete and representational models throughout the learning progression.

Skill 27.4 Apply knowledge of a variety of instructional delivery methods, such as individual, structured small-group, and large-group formats.

See Skill 26.5.

Skill 27.5 Demonstrate an understanding of a variety of questioning strategies to encourage mathematical discourse and to help students analyze and evaluate their mathematical thinking.

As the teacher's role in the classroom changes from lecturer to facilitator, the questions need to further stimulate students in various ways.

- Helping students work together
    - What do you think about what John said?
    - Do you agree? Disagree?
    - Can anyone explain that differently?

- Helping students determine for themselves if an answer is correct
    - Why do you think that is true?
    - How did you get that answer?
    - Do you think that is reasonable? Why?

- Helping students learn to reason mathematically
    - Will that method always work?
    - Can you think of a case where it is not true?
    - How can you prove that?
    - Is that answer true in all cases?

- Helping student brainstorm and problem solve

    Is there a pattern?
    What else can you do?
    Can you predict the answer?
    What if...?

- Helping students connect mathematical ideas

    What did we learn before that is like this?
    Can you give an example?
    What math did you see on television last night? in the newspaper?

Skill 27.6 **Understand how technological tools and manipulatives can be used appropriately to assist students in developing, comprehending, and applying mathematical concepts.**

See Skill 26.4

Skill 27.7 **Understand how to relate mathematics to students' lives and a variety of careers and professions.**

Teachers can increase student interest in math and promote learning and understanding by relating mathematical concepts to the lives of students. Instead of using only abstract presentations and examples, teachers should relate concepts to real-world situations to shift the emphasis from memorization and abstract application to understanding and applied problem solving. In addition, relating math to careers and professions helps illustrate the relevance of math and aids in the career exploration process.

For example, when teaching a unit on the geometry of certain shapes, teachers can ask students to design a structure of interest to the student using the shapes in question. This exercise serves the dual purpose of teaching students to learn and apply the properties (e.g. area, volume) of shapes while demonstrating the relevance of geometry to architectural and engineering professions.

Skill 27.8 **Understands how technological tools and manipulatives can be used appropriately to assist students in developing, comprehending, and applying mathematical concepts**

See Skill 26.4

Skill 27.9 **Understands how to relate mathematics to students' lives and a variety of careers and professions**

See Skill 25.2

COMPETENCY 28.0 UNDERSTAND ASSESSMENT AND USE A VARIETY OF FORMAL AND INFORMAL ASSESSMENT TECHNIQUES TO MONITOR AND GUIDE MATHEMATICS INSTRUCTION AND TO EVALUATE STUDENT PROGRESS.

Skill 28.1   Demonstrates an understanding of the purpose, characteristics, and uses of various assessments in mathematics, including formative and summative assessments.

❖

Skill 28.2   Understands how to select and develop assessments that are consistent with what is taught and how it is taught.

❖

Skill 28.3   Demonstrates an understanding of how to develop a variety of assessments and scoring procedures consisting of worthwhile tasks that assess mathematical understanding, common misconceptions, and error patterns.

❖

Skill 28.4   Understands how to evaluate a variety of assessment methods and materials for reliability, validity, absence of bias, clarity of language, and appropriateness of mathematical level.

❖

Skill 28.5   Understands the relationship between assessment and instruction and knows how to evaluate assessment results to design, monitor, and modify instruction to improve mathematical learning for all students, including English Language Learners.

❖

➤   *For Skills 28.1-28.5 see content in pages 353-354*

In addition to the traditional methods of performance assessment like multiple choice, true/false, and matching tests, there are many other methods of student assessment available to teachers. Alternative assessment is any type of assessment in which students create a response rather than choose an answer. It is sometimes know as formative assessment, due to the emphasis placed on feedback and the flow of communication between teacher and student. It is the opposite of summative assessment, which occurs periodically and consists of temporary interaction between teacher and student.

Short response and **essay** questions are alternative methods of performance assessment. In responding to such questions, students must utilize verbal, graphical, and mathematical skills to construct answers to problems. These multi-faceted responses allow the teacher to examine more closely a student's problem solving and reasoning skills.

Student **portfolios** are another method of alternative assessment. In creating a portfolio, students collect samples and drafts of their work, self-assessments, and teacher evaluations over a period of time. Such a collection allows students, parents, and teachers to evaluate student progress and achievements. In addition, portfolios provide insight into a student's thought process and learning style.

Projects, **demonstrations**, and **oral presentations** are means of alternative assessment that require students to use different skills than those used on traditional tests. Such assessments require higher order thinking, creativity, and the integration of reasoning and communication skills. The use of predetermined rubrics, with specific criteria for performance assessment, is the accepted method of evaluation for projects, demonstrations, and presentations.

Student assessment is an important part of the educational process. High quality assessment methods are necessary for the development and maintenance of a successful learning environment. Teachers must develop and implement assessment procedures that accurately evaluate student progress, test content areas of greatest importance, and enhance and improve learning. To enhance learning and accurately evaluate student progress, teachers should use a variety of assessment tasks to gain a better understanding a student's strengths and weaknesses. Finally, teachers should implement scoring patterns that fairly and accurately evaluate student performance.

Teachers should use a variety of assessment procedures to evaluate student knowledge and understanding. One type of alternative assessment is bundled testing. Bundled testing is the grouping of different question formats for the same skill or competency. For example, a bundled test of exponential functions may include multiple choice questions, short response questions, word problems, and essay questions. The variety of questions tests different levels of reasoning and expression. Another type of alternative assessment is projects. Projects are longer term, creative tasks that require many levels of reasoning and expression.

Projects are often a good indicator of understanding because they require high-level thinking. A final type of alternative assessment is student portfolios.

Portfolios are collections of student work over a period of time. Portfolios aid in the evaluation of student growth and progress.

Scoring methods are an important, and often overlooked, part of effective assessment. Teachers can use a simple three-point scale for evaluating student responses. No answer or an inappropriate answer that shows no understanding scores zero points. A partial response showing a lack of understanding, a lack of explanation, or major computational errors scores one point. A somewhat satisfactory answer that answers most of the question correctly but contains simple computational errors or minor flaws in reasoning receives two points. Finally, a satisfactory response displaying full understanding, adequate explanation, and appropriate reasoning receives three points. When evaluating student responses, teachers should look for common error patterns and mistakes in computation. Teachers should also incorporate questions and scoring procedures that address common error patterns and misconceptions into their methods of assessment.

The primary purpose of student assessment is to evaluate the effectiveness of the curriculum and instruction by measuring student performance. Teachers and school officials use the results of student assessments to monitor student progress and modify and design curriculum to meet the needs of the students. Teachers and school officials carefully assess the results of tests to determine the parts of the curriculum that need altering. For example, the results of a test may indicate that the majority of the students in a class struggle with problems involving logarithmic functions. In response to such findings, the teacher would evaluate the method of logarithmic function instruction and make the necessary changes to increase student understanding.

A special type of student assessment, state standardized testing, is an important tool for curriculum design and modification. Most states have stated curriculum standards that mandate what students should know. Teachers can use the standards to focus their instruction and curriculum planning. State tests evaluate and report student performance on the specific curriculum standards. Thus, teachers can easily determine the areas that require greater attention.

Finally, teachers and school officials must understand the special needs of English Language Learners. Mathematic assessments may understate the abilities of English Language Learners because poor test scores may stem from difficulty in reading comprehension, not a lack of understanding of mathematic principles. Uncharacteristically poor performance on word problems by English Language Learners is a sign that reading comprehension, not mathematic understanding, is the underlying problem.

Sample Test: Mathematics

1. $\dfrac{2^{10}}{2^5} =$

(Moderate Rigorous)(Skill 10.2)

   A. 2^2

   B. 2^5

   C. 2^{50}

   D. $2^{\frac{1}{2}}$

2. $\left(\dfrac{^-4}{9}\right) + \left(\dfrac{^-7}{10}\right) =$

(Moderate Rigorous)(Skill 11.1)

   A. $\dfrac{23}{90}$

   B. $\dfrac{^-23}{90}$

   C. $\dfrac{103}{90}$

   D. $\dfrac{^-103}{90}$

3. $0.74 =$

(Easy Rigorous)(Skill 11.1)

   A. $\dfrac{74}{100}$

   B. 7.4%

   C. $\dfrac{33}{50}$

   D. $\dfrac{74}{10}$

4. $(5.6) \times \left(^-0.11\right) =$

(Moderate Rigorous) (Skill 11.1)

   A. $^-0.616$

   B. 0.616

   C. $^-6.110$

   D. 6.110

5. An item that sells for $375 is put on sale at $120. What is the percent of decrease? (Easy Rigorous)(Skill 11.1)

   A.   25%

   B.   28%

   C.   68%

   D.   34%

6. Which denotes an irrational number? (Easy Rigorous)(Skill 11.5)

   A)   4.2500000

   B) $\sqrt{16}$

   C.   0.25252525

   D. $\Pi = 3.141592\ldots$

7. What is the greatest common factor of 16, 28, and 36? (Moderate Rigorous)(Skill 12.1)

   A.   2

   B.   4

   C.   8

   D.   16

8. Compute the surface area of the prism. (Moderate Rigorous)(Skill 12.2)

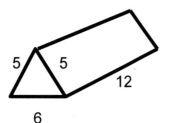

   A. 204

   B. 216

   C. 360

   D. 180

9. What is the area of a square whose side is 13 feet? (Easy Rigorous)(Skill 12.2)

   A. 169 feet

   B. 169 square feet

   C. 52 feet

   D. 52 square feet

10. The owner of a rectangular piece of land 40 yards in length and 30 yards in width wants to divide it into two parts. She plans to join two opposite corners with a fence as shown in the diagram below. The cost of the fence will be approximately $25 per linear foot. What is the estimated cost for the fence needed by the owner? (Rigorous)(Skill 12.2)

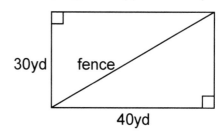

   A. $1,250

   B. $62,500

   C. $5,250

   D. $3,750

11. Find the surface area of a box which is 3 feet wide, 5 feet tall, and 4 feet deep. (Moderate Rigorous)(Skill 12.2)

   A. 47 sq. ft.

   B. 60 sq. ft.

   C. 94 sq. ft

   D. 188 sq. ft.

12. The trunk of a tree has a 2.1 meter radius. What is its circumference? (Moderate Rigorous)(Skill 12.2)

A. 2.1π square meters

B. 4.2π meters

C. 2.1π meters

D. 4.2π square meters

13. Set A, B, C, and U are related as shown in the diagram.

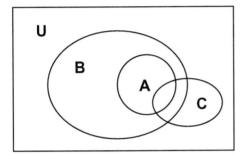

Which of the following is true, assuming not one of the six regions is empty? (Moderate Rigorous)(Skill 13.1)

A. Any element that is a member of set B is also a member of set A.

B. No element is a member of all three sets A, B, and C.

C. Any element that is a member of set U is also a member of set B.

D. None of the above statements is true.

14. If $4x - (3 - x) = 7(x - 3) + 10$, then

(Rigorous)(Skill 13.4)

A. $x = 8$

B. $x = -8$

C. $x = 4$

D. $x = -4$

15. It takes 5 equally skilled people 9 hours to shingle Mr. Joe's roof. Let t be the time required for only 3 of these men to do the same job. Select the correct statement of the given condition.(Rigorous)(Skill 14.2)

A. $\dfrac{3}{5} = \dfrac{9}{t}$

B. $\dfrac{9}{5} = \dfrac{3}{t}$

C. $\dfrac{5}{9} = \dfrac{3}{t}$

D. $\dfrac{14}{9} = \dfrac{t}{5}$

16. Find the equation of a line through (5,6) and (-1,-2) in standard form.(Rigorous) (Skill 14.3)

   A.   3y=4x-2

   B. $-2y = \dfrac{4}{3}x - 1$

   C.   6y + 5x – 1

   D.   y = 4x -6

17. Find the real roots of the equation $3x^2 - 45 + 22x$. (Rigorous)(Skill 15.1)

   A. $\dfrac{^-5}{3}$ and 9

   B. $\dfrac{5}{3}$ and $^-9$

   C.   5 and 9

   D.   -5 and -9

18. {1,4,7,10, . . .}

   What is the 40th term in this sequence?(Rigorous) (Skill 16.1)

   A. 43

   B. 121

   C. 118

   D. 120

19. Which term most accurately describes two coplanar lines without any common points? (Moderate Rigorous)(Skill 18.2)

   A. perpendicular

   B. parallel

   C. intersecting

   D. skew

20. Given similar polygons with corresponding sides 6 and 8, what is the area of the smaller if the area of the larger is 64? (Rigorous)(Skill 19.2)

   A. 48

   B. 36

   C. 144

   D. 78

21. Study figures A, B, C, and D. Select the letter in which all triangles are similar. (Easy Rigorous)(Skill 19.2)

A.

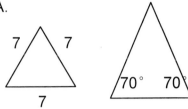

B.

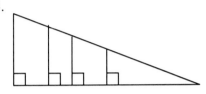

C.

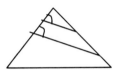

D.

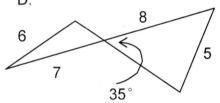

22. Find the midpoint of (2,5) and (7,-4). (Rigorous)(Skill 20.5)

A. (9,-1)

B. (5,9)

C. (9/2 , -1/2)

D. (9/2, 1/2)

23. The following chart shows the yearly average number of international tourists visiting Palm Beach for 1990-1994. How may more international tourists visited Palm Beach in 1994 than in 1991? (Moderate Rigorous)(Skill 21.1)

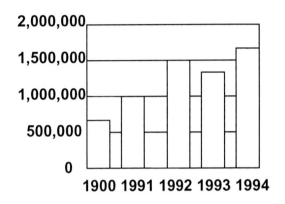

A. 100,000

B. 600,000

C. 1,600,000

D. 8,000,000

24. What conclusion can be drawn from the graph below?(Moderate Rigorous) (Skill 21.3)

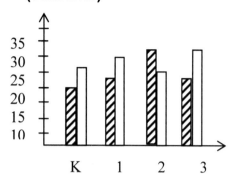

MLK Elementary ▨ ☐
Student Enrollment Girls Boys

A. The number of students in first grade
   exceeds the number in second grade.
B. There are more boys than girls in the
   entire school.
C. There are more girls than boys in the
   first grade.
D. Third grade has the largest number of
   students.

25. Mary did comparison shopping on her favorite brand of coffee. Over half of the stores priced the coffee at $1.70. Most of the remaining stores priced the coffee at $1.80, except for a few who charged $1.90. Which of the following statements is true about the distribution of prices? (Rigorous)(Skill 21.4)

A. The mean and the mode are the same.
B. The mean is greater than the mode.
C. The mean is less than the mode.
D. The mean is less than the median.

26. What is the mode of the data in the following sample? (Easy Rigorous)(Skill 21.4)

9, 10, 11, 9, 10, 11, 9, 13

A. 9

B. 9.5

C. 10

D. 11

27. A coin is tossed and a die is rolled. What is the probability of landing on the head side of the coin and rolling a 3 on the dice? *die?* (Rigorous)(Skill 22.2)

A. $\dfrac{1}{2}$

B. $\dfrac{1}{6}$

C. $\dfrac{1}{12}$

D. $\dfrac{1}{15}$

28. What is the probability of drawing 2 consecutive aces from a standard deck of cards? (Rigorous)(Skill 22.2)

A. $\dfrac{3}{51}$

B. $\dfrac{1}{221}$

C. $\dfrac{2}{104}$

D. $\dfrac{2}{52}$

Answer Key: Mathematics

1.	B	8.	B	15.	B	22.	D
2.	D	9.	B	16.	A	23.	B
3.	A	10.	D	17.	B	24.	B
4.	A	11.	C	18.	C	25.	B
5.	C	12.	B	19.	B	26.	A
6.	D	13.	D	20.	B	27.	C
7.	B	14.	C	21.	B	28.	B

Rigor Table: Mathematics

Easy Rigorous (20%)	Moderate Rigorous (40%)	Rigorous (40%)
3,5,6,9,21,26	1,2,4,7,8,11,12,13,19,23,24	10,14,15,16,17,18,20,22,25,27,28

Rationales with Sample Questions: Mathematics

1. $\dfrac{2^{10}}{2^{5}} =$

   (Moderate Rigorous)(Skill 10.2)

   A. 2^2

   B. 2^5

   C. 2^{50}

   D. $2^{\frac{1}{2}}$

The quotient rule of exponents says $\dfrac{a^m}{a^n} = a^{(m-n)}$ so $\dfrac{2^{10}}{2^{5}} = 2^{(10-5)} = 2^5$ which is answer **B**.

2. $\left(\dfrac{^{-}4}{9}\right) + \left(\dfrac{^{-}7}{10}\right) =$

   (Moderate Rigorous)(Skill 11.1)

   A. $\dfrac{23}{90}$

   B. $\dfrac{^{-}23}{90}$

   C. $\dfrac{103}{90}$

   D. $\dfrac{^{-}103}{90}$

Find the LCD of $\dfrac{^{-}4}{9}$ and $\dfrac{^{-}7}{10}$. The LCD is 90, so you get $\dfrac{^{-}40}{90} + \dfrac{^{-}63}{90} = \dfrac{^{-}103}{90}$, which is answer **D**. **(Skill 11.1)**

3.   **0.74 =**

   (Easy Rigorous)(Skill 11.1)

   A. $\dfrac{74}{100}$

   B.   7.4%

   C. $\dfrac{33}{50}$

   D. $\dfrac{74}{10}$

0.74→the 4 is in the hundredths place, so the answer is $\dfrac{74}{100}$, which is **A.**

4. $(5.6) \times (^-0.11) =$

   (Moderate Rigorous) (Skill 11.1)

   A. $^-0.616$

   B. 0.616

   C. $^-6.110$

   D. 6.110

Simple multiplication. The answer will be negative because a positive times a negative is a negative number. $5.6 \times^- 0.11 =^- 0.616$, which is answer **A.**

5.   **An item that sells for $375 is put on sale at $120. What is the percent of decrease?**
   (Easy Rigorous)(Skill 11.1)

   A.   25%

   B.   28%

   C.   68%

   D.   34%

Use $(1 - x)$ as the discount. $375x = 120$.
$375(1 - x) = 120 \rightarrow 375 - 375x = 120 \rightarrow 375x = 255 \rightarrow x = 0.68 = 68\%$
which is answer **C.**

6. **Which denotes an irrational number? (Easy Rigorous)(Skill 11.5)**

   A) 4.2500000

   B) $\sqrt{16}$

   C. 0.25252525

   D. Π=3.141592...

An irrational number is neither terminal or repeating. Rational numbers either terminal or repeating. Only the value of pi is an irrational number. The answer is **D.**

7. **What is the greatest common factor of 16, 28, and 36? (Moderate Rigorous)(Skill 12.1)**

   A.   2

   B.   4

   C.   8

   D.   16

The smallest number in this set is 16; its factors are 1, 2, 4, 8 and 16. 16 in the largest factor, but it does not divide into 28 or 36. Neither does 8. 4 does factor into both 28 and 36. The answer is **B.**

8.   **Compute the surface area of the prism. (Moderate Rigorous)(Skill 12.2)**

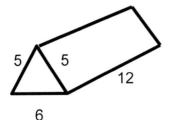

    A. 204

    B. 216

    C. 360

    D. 180

There are five surfaces which make up the prism. The bottom rectangle has area 6 x 12 = 72. The sloping sides are two rectangles each with an area of 5 x 12 = 60. The height of the and triangles is determined to be 4 using the Pythagorean theorem. Therefore each triangle has area 1/2bh = 1/2(6)(4) -12. Thus, the surface area is 72 + 60 + 60 + 12 + 12 = 216. The answer is **B.**

9.   **What is the area of a square whose side is 13 feet? (Easy Rigorous)(Skill 12.2)**

    A.   169 feet

    B.   169 square feet

    C.   52 feet

    D.   52 square feet

Area = length times width (*lw*).
Length = 13 feet
Width = 13 feet (square, so length and width are the same).
Area = $13 \times 13 = 169$ square feet.
Area is measured in square feet. So the answer is **B.**

10. The owner of a rectangular piece of land 40 yards in length and 30 yards in width wants to divide it into two parts. She plans to join two opposite corners with a fence as shown in the diagram below. The cost of the fence will be approximately $25 per linear foot. What is the estimated cost for the fence needed by the owner? (Rigorous)(Skill 12.2)

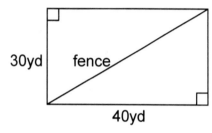

40yd

A. $1,250

B. $62,500

C. $5,250

D. $3,750

Find the length of the diagonal by using the Pythagorean theorem. Let x be the length of the diagonal.

$$30^2 + 40^2 = x^2 \rightarrow 900 + 1600 = x^2$$
$$2500 = x^2 \rightarrow \sqrt{2500} = \sqrt{x^2}$$
$$x = 50 \text{ yards}$$

Convert to feet. $\dfrac{50 \text{ yards}}{x \text{ feet}} = \dfrac{1 \text{ yard}}{3 \text{ feet}} \rightarrow 1500 \text{ feet}$

It cost $25.00 per linear foot, so the cost is (1500 ft)($25) = $3750, which is answer **D**.

11. **Find the surface area of a box which is 3 feet wide, 5 feet tall, and 4 feet deep. (Moderate Rigorous)(Skill 12.2)**

   A. 47 sq. ft.

   B. 60 sq. ft.

   C. 94 sq. ft

   D. 188 sq. ft.

Let's assume the base of the rectangular solid (box) is 3 by 4, and the height is 5. Then the surface area of the top and bottom together is 2(12) = 24. The sum of the areas of the front and back are 2(15) = 30, while the sum of the areas of the sides are 2(20)=40. The total surface area is therefore 94 square feet. Answer is **C**.

12. **The trunk of a tree has a 2.1 meter radius. What is its circumference? (Moderate Rigorous)(Skill 12.2)**

   A. 2.1π square meters

   B. 4.2π meters

   C. $2.1\ \pi$ meters

   D. 4.2π square meters

Circumference is $2\pi r$, where r is the radius. The circumference is $2\pi 2.1 = 4.2\pi$ meters (not square meters because not measuring area), which is answer **B.**

13. **Set A, B, C, and U are related as shown in the diagram.**

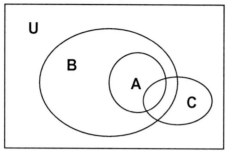

Which of the following is true, assuming not one of the six regions is empty? (Moderate Rigorous)(Skill 13.1)

A. Any element that is a member of set B is also a member of set A.

B. No element is a member of all three sets A, B, and C.

C. Any element that is a member of set U is also a member of set B.

D. None of the above statements is true.

Answer A is incorrect because not all members of set B are also in set A. Answer B is incorrect because there are elements that are members of all three sets A, B, and C. Answer C is incorrect because not all members of set U is a member of set B. This leaves answer **D**, which states that none of the above choices are true.

14. If $4x - (3 - x) = 7(x - 3) + 10$, then
(Rigorous)(Skill 13.4)

   A. $x = 8$

   B. $x = -8$

   C. $x = 4$

   D. $x = -4$

The answer is **C.** Solve for x.
$4x - (3 - x) = 7(x - 3) + 10$
$4x - 3 + x = 7x - 21 + 10$
$5x - 3 = 7x - 11$
$5x = 7x - 11 + 3$
$5x - 7x = ^- 8$
$^-2x = ^- 8$
$x = 4$

15. It takes 5 equally skilled people 9 hours to shingle Mr. Joe's roof. Let t be the time required for only 3 of these men to do the same job. Select the correct statement of the given condition.(Rigorous)(Skill 14.2)

   A. $\dfrac{3}{5} = \dfrac{9}{t}$

   B. $\dfrac{9}{5} = \dfrac{3}{t}$

   C. $\dfrac{5}{9} = \dfrac{3}{t}$

   D. $\dfrac{14}{9} = \dfrac{t}{5}$

The answer is **A** .

$$\dfrac{3 \text{ people}}{5 \text{ people}} = \dfrac{9 \text{ hours}}{t \text{ hours}}$$

16. **Find the equation of a line through (5,6) and (-1,-2) in standard form.(Rigorous)(Skill 14.3)**

A. $3y=4x-2$

B. $-2y = \dfrac{4}{3}x - 1$

C. $6y + 5x - 1$

D. $y = 4x - 6$

The answer is **A**.

$$\text{slope} = \frac{y_2 - y_1}{x_2 - x_1} = \frac{-2-6}{-1-5} = \frac{-8}{-6} = \frac{4}{3}$$

$$Y - y_a = m(X - x_a) \rightarrow Y + 2 = \frac{4}{3}(X + 1) \rightarrow$$

$$Y + 2 = \frac{4}{3}x + \frac{4}{3}$$

$$Y = \frac{4}{3}x - \frac{2}{3} \qquad \text{This is the slope-intercept form.}$$

Multiply by 3 to eliminate fractions

$$3y = 4x - 2 \qquad \text{This is the standard form.}$$

17.   Find the real roots of the equation $3x^2 - 45 + 22x$.
       (Rigorous)(Skill 15.1)

       A. $\dfrac{^-5}{3}$ and 9

       B. $\dfrac{5}{3}$ and $^-9$

       C.   5 and 9

       D.   -5 and -9

The answer is **B.**
Factor.
$(\ -\ )(\ +\ )$
$(3x - 5)(x + 9)$ Set each part equal to 0 and solve for x.
$3x - 5 = 0$
$3x = 5$ $x + 9 = 0$
$x = \dfrac{5}{3}$ $x = ^- 9$

18.   {1,4,7,10, . . .}
       What is the 40th term in
       this sequence?(Rigorous) (Skill 16.1)

       A. 43

       B. 121

       C. 118

       D. 120

The answer is **C.**

19. **Which term most accurately describes two coplanar lines without any common points? (Moderate Rigorous)(Skill 18.2)**

    A. perpendicular

    B. parallel

    C. intersecting

    D. skew

By definition, parallel lines are coplanar lines without any common points. Answer is **B.**

20. **Given similar polygons with corresponding sides 6 and 8, what is the area of the smaller if the area of the larger is 64? (Rigorous)(Skill 19.2)**

    A. 48

    B. 36

    C. 144

    D. 78

In similar polygons, the areas are proportional to the squares of the sides. 36/64 = x/64. Answer is B.

21.   Study figures A, B, C, and
       D. Select the letter in which
       all triangles are similar.
       (Easy Rigorous)(Skill 19.2)

A.

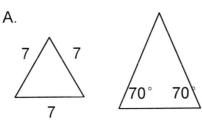

B.

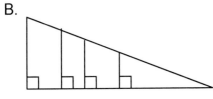

C.

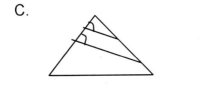

D.

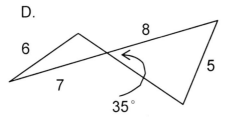

Choice A is not correct because one triangle is equilateral and the other is isosceles. Choice C is not correct because the two smaller triangles are similar, but the large triangle is not. Choice D is not correct because the lengths and angles are not proportional to each other. Therefore, the correct answer is **B** because all the triangles have the same angles.

22. **Find the midpoint of (2,5) and (7,-4). (Rigorous)(Skill 20.5)**

   A. (9,-1)

   B. (5,9)

   C. (9/2 , -1/2)

   D. (9/2, 1/2)

The answer is **D.** Using the midpoint formula

$x = (2 + 7)/2 \quad y = (5 + -4)/2$

23. The following chart shows the yearly average number of international tourists visiting Palm Beach for 1990-1994. How may more international tourists visited Palm Beach in 1994 than in 1991? (Moderate Rigorous)(Skill 21.1)

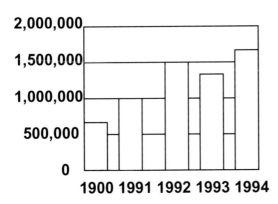

A.   100,000

B.   600,000

C.   1,600,000

D.   8,000,000

The number of tourists in 1991 was 1,000,000 and the number in 1994 was 1,600,000. Subtract to get a difference of 600,000, which is answer **B.**

24. **What conclusion can be drawn from the graph below?(Moderate Rigorous) (Skill 21.3).**

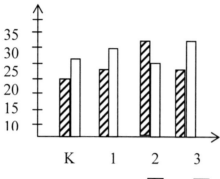

MLK Elementary
Student Enrollment   Girls Boys

  A. The number of students in first grade exceeds the number in second grade.

  B. There are more boys than girls in the entire school.

  C. There are more girls than boys in the first grade.

  D. Third grade has the largest number of students.

In Kindergarten, first grade, and third grade, there are more boys than girls. The number of extra girls in grade two is more than made up for by the extra boys in all the other grades put together. Answer is **B**.

25. Mary did comparison shopping on her favorite brand of coffee. Over half of the stores priced the coffee at $1.70. Most of the remaining stores priced the coffee at $1.80, except for a few who charged $1.90. Which of the following statements is true about the distribution of prices?
(Rigorous)(Skill 21.4)

   A.   The mean and the mode are the same.

   B.   The mean is greaterthan the mode.

   C.   The mean is less than the mode.

   D.   The mean is less than the median.

Over half the stores priced the coffee at $1.70, so this means that this is the mode. The mean would be slightly over $1.70 because other stores priced the coffee at over $1.70. Therefore, the answer is **B**.

26. What is the mode of the data in the following sample? (Easy Rigorous)(Skill 21.4)

   9, 10, 11, 9, 10, 11, 9, 13

   A.   9

   B.   9.5

   C.   10

   D.   11

The mode is the number that appears most frequently. 9 appears 3 times, which is more than the other numbers. Therefore the answer is **A**.

27. **A coin is tossed and a die is rolled. What is the probability of landing on the head side of the coin and rolling a 3 on the dice? (Rigorous)(Skill 22.2)**

    A. $\dfrac{1}{2}$

    B. $\dfrac{1}{6}$

    C. $\dfrac{1}{12}$

    D. $\dfrac{1}{15}$

$P(\text{head}) = \dfrac{1}{2}. \quad P(3) = \dfrac{1}{6}$

$P(\text{head and 3}) = P(\text{head}) \times P(3)$

$= \dfrac{1}{2} \times \dfrac{1}{6} = \dfrac{1}{12}$

The answer is **C.**

28. **What is the probability of drawing 2 consecutive aces from a standard deck of cards? (Rigorous)(Skill 22.2)**

    A. $\dfrac{3}{51}$

    B. $\dfrac{1}{221}$

    C. $\dfrac{2}{104}$

    D. $\dfrac{2}{52}$

There are 4 aces in the 52 card deck. $P(\text{first ace}) = \dfrac{4}{52}$. $P(\text{second ace}) = \dfrac{3}{51}$.

$P(\text{first ace and second ace}) = P(\text{one ace}) \times P(\text{second ace}|\text{first ace})$

$= \dfrac{4}{52} \times \dfrac{3}{51} = \dfrac{1}{221}$. This is answer **B.**

COMPETENCY 29.0 HISTORY

Skill 29.1   Understand traditional historical points of reference in the history of Texas, the United States, and the world.

Key points of reference in the history of Texas include the following:

Settlement and culture of Native American Tribes before European contact
1529: Spanish explorer Alonso Alvarez de Pineda maps the Texas coast
1528-34: Alvar Nunez Cabeza de Vaca (Spanish explorer) explores Texas for trade
1685: LaSalle established Fort St. Louis at Matagorda Bay, providing the basis of the French claim to Texas territory
1688: The French colony is massacred
1689: The French continue to claim Texas but no longer physically occupy any part of the territory
1690: Alonso de Leon establishes San Francisco de los Tejas Mission in East Texas, opening the Old San Antonio Road portion of the Camino Real
1700-1799: Spain establishes Catholic missions throughout Texas
1762: the French give up their claims to Texas and cede Louisiana to Spain until 1800
1800: Much of north Texas is returned to France and later sold to the U.S. in the Louisiana Purchase
1823: Stephen Austin begins a colony known as the Old Three Hundred along the Brazos River
1832: Battle of Velasco – first casualties of the Texas Revolution
1832-33: The "Conventions" responded to unrest over the policies of the Mexican government
1835: The Texas Revolution officially began in an effort to obtain freedom from Mexico
1836: The "Convention of 1836" signed the Texas Declaration of Independence
     The Battle of the Alamo
     Santa Anna executed nearly 400 Texans in the Massacre at Goliad
     Santa Anna is believed to have ended the Texas rebellion
     Sam Houston leads an army of 800 to victory by capturing the entire Mexican army at the Battle of San Jacinto
     The Treaty of Velasco is signed by Santa Anna and Republic of Texas officials
1837: Sam Houston moves the capital of Texas five times, ending in Houston in 1837
1839: Austin becomes the capital of the Republic of Texas
1842: Mexican forces twice capture San Antonio and retreat
1845: Texas admitted to the Union as a state

1850: The Compromise of 1850 adjusts the state boundary and assumes Texas'
     debts

1861: Texas secedes from the Union and joins the Confederacy
     A government is organized, replacing Houston because he refused to
     swear allegiance to the Confederacy

1865: Union troops landed in Galveston and put the Emancipation Proclamation
     into effect in Texas, thus ending slavery

1870: Texas is readmitted to the Union

1900: Galveston is destroyed and 8000 people are killed by a category 4
     hurricane

1901: The Lucas Gusher comes in, starting the Texas oil boom

The **Age of Exploration** actually had its beginnings centuries before exploration took place. The rise and spread of Islam in the seventh century and its subsequent control over the holy city of Jerusalem led to the European so-called holy wars, the Crusades, to free Jerusalem and the Holy Land from this control. Even though the Crusades were not a success, those who survived and returned to their homes and countries in Western Europe brought back with them new products such as silks, spices, perfumes, new and different foods. Luxuries that were unheard of that gave new meaning to colorless, drab, dull lives.

New ideas, new inventions, and new methods also went to Western Europe with the returning Crusaders, and from these new influences came the intellectual stimulation that led to the period known as the Renaissance. The revival of interest in classical Greek art, architecture, literature, science, astronomy, medicine, increased trade between Europe and Asia and the invention of the printing press helped to push the spread of knowledge and start exploration.

The rise of Christianity in early modern Europe was due as much to the iron hand of feudalism as it was to the Church itself. **Feudalism**, more than any other factor, helped the Church get its grip on Europe. Like the caste system in India, feudalism kept people in strict control according to their social class. If you were a peasant, you had been born that way and you had an excellent chance of staying that way for your entire life. The rich and powerful were the highest class in society, and the friends of the rich and powerful were the clergy.

The purpose of the **Crusades** was to rid Jerusalem of Muslim control and this series of violent, bloody conflicts did affect trade and stimulated later explorations seeking the new, exotic products such as silks and spices. The Crusaders came into contact with other religions and cultures and learned and spread many new ideas.

Also coming into importance at this time was the era of knighthood and its code of chivalry as well as the tremendous influence of the Church (Roman Catholic). Until the period of the Renaissance, the Church was the only place where people could be educated. The Bible and other books were hand-copied by monks in the monasteries. Cathedrals were built and were decorated with art depicting religious subjects.

The period from the 1700s to the 1800s was characterized in Western countries by opposing political ideas of democracy and nationalism. This resulted in strong nationalistic feelings and people of common cultures asserting their belief in the right to have a part in their government.

The **American Revolution** resulted in the successful efforts of the English colonists in America to win their freedom from Great Britain. After more than one hundred years of mostly self-government, the colonists resented the increased British meddling and control, they declared their freedom, won the Revolutionary War with aid from France, and formed a new independent nation.

The **French Revolution** was the revolt of the middle and lower classes against the gross political and economic excesses of the rulers and the supporting nobility. It ended with the establishment of the First in a series of French Republics. Conditions leading to revolt included extreme taxation, inflation, lack of food, and the total disregard for the impossible, degrading, and unacceptable condition of the people on the part of the rulers, nobility, and the Church.

The American Revolution and the French Revolution were similar yet different, liberating their people from unwanted government interference and installing a different kind of government. They were both fought for the liberty of the common people, and they both were built on writings and ideas that embraced such an outcome. Both Revolutions proved that people could expect more from their government and that such rights as self-determination were worth fighting—and dying—for. Several important differences should be emphasized:
- The British colonists were striking back against unwanted taxation and other sorts of "government interference." The French people were starving and, in many cases, destitute and were striking back against an autocratic regime that cared more for high fashion and courtly love than bread and circuses.
- The American Revolution involved a years-long campaign, of often bloody battles, skirmishes, and stalemates. The French Revolution was bloody to a degree but mainly an overthrow of society and its outdated traditions.
- The American Revolution resulted in a representative government, which marketed itself as a beacon of democracy for the rest of the world. The French Revolution resulted in a consulship, a generalship, and then an emperor—probably not what the perpetrators of the Revolution had in mind when they first struck back at the king and queen.

Still, both Revolutions are looked back upon as turning points in history, as times when the governed stood up to the governors and said, "Enough."

The **Reformation** period consisted of two phases: the **Protestant Reformation** and the **Catholic Counter-Reformation**. The Protestant Reformation came about because of religious, political, and economic reasons. The religious reasons stemmed from abuses in the Catholic Church including fraudulent clergy with their scandalous immoral lifestyles; the sale of religious offices, indulgences, and dispensations; different theologies within the Church; and frauds involving sacred relics.

In Europe, Italy and Germany each were totally united into one nation from many smaller states. There were revolutions in Austria and Hungary, the Franco-Prussian War, the dividing of Africa among the strong European nations, interference and intervention of Western nations in Asia, and the breakup of Turkish dominance in the Balkans.

In Africa, France, Great Britain, Italy, Portugal, Spain, Germany, and Belgium controlled the entire continent except Liberia and Ethiopia. In Asia and the Pacific Islands, only China, Japan, and present-day Thailand (Siam) kept their independence. The others were controlled by the strong European nations. An additional reason for **European imperialism** was the harsh, urgent demand for the raw materials needed to fuel and feed the great Industrial Revolution. These resources were not available in the huge quantity so desperately needed which necessitated (and rationalized) the partitioning of the continent of Africa and parts of Asia. In turn, these colonial areas would purchase the finished manufactured goods. Europe in the nineteenth century was a crowded place. Populations were growing but resources were not. The peoples of many European countries were also agitating for rights. To address these concerns, European powers began to look elsewhere for relief.

One of the main places for European imperialist expansion was Africa. Britain, France, Germany, and Belgium took over countries in Africa and claimed them as their own. The resources were then shipped back to the mainland and claimed as colonial gains. The Europeans made a big deal about "civilizing the savages," reasoning that their technological superiority gave them the right to rule and "educate" the peoples of Africa.

Southeast Asia was another area of European expansion at this time, mainly by France. So, too, was India, colonized by Great Britain. These two nations combined with Spain to occupy countries in Latin America. Spain also seized the rich lands of the Philippines.

In the United States, **territorial expansion** occurred in the expansion westward under the banner of **Manifest Destiny.** In addition, the U.S. was involved in the War with Mexico, the Spanish-American War, and support of the Latin American colonies of Spain in their revolt for independence. In Latin America, the Spanish colonies were successful in their fight for independence and self-government.

World War I - 1914 to 1918

The origins of World War I are complex. Divisions were drawn mainly along the lines of various alliances and treaties that existed between the world powers. Imperialism, nationalism and economic conditions of the time led to a series of sometimes shaky alliances among the powerful nations, each wishing to protect its holdings and provide mutual defense from smaller powers.

On June 28, 1914, Serbian Gavrilo Princip assassinated Archduke Ferdinand of Austria-Hungary, while on a visit to Sarajevo, Serbia. Serbian nationalism had led the country to seek dominance on the Balkan Peninsula, a movement that had been opposed by Austria-Hungary. Seeing an opportunity to move on Serbia, Austria-Hungary issued an ultimatum after the assassination, demanding that they be allowed to perform a complete investigation. Serbia refused, and in July, Austria-Hungary, with the backing of its ally Germany, declared war on Serbia. Serbia called on its ally Russia to come to its defense, and Russia began to move troops into the area.

Germany, allied with Austria-Hungary, viewed the Russian mobilization as an act of war, and declared war on Russia. A few days afterwards, Germany declared war on France, which was allied with Russia by treaty. Germany invaded Belgium, a neutral country, to be closer to Paris. Britain, bound by treaty to defend both Belgium and France, subsequently declared war on Germany.

The United States, under President Woodrow Wilson, declared neutrality in the affair, and did not enter the war immediately. Not until Germany threatened commercial shipping with submarine warfare did the US join the fray, in 1917. Fighting continued until November 1918, when Germany petitioned for armistice. Peace negotiations began in early 1919, and the Treaty of Versailles was signed in June of that year. Also growing out of the peace negotiations was the League of Nations, a group of countries agreeing to avoid armed conflict through disarmament and diplomacy.

World War II - 1939 to 1945

An extreme form of patriotism called nationalism, a contributing cause at the start of World War 1, grew even stronger in 1918, as that war drew to a close. Political, social, and economic unrest ensued. In Germany in particular, the economic sanctions imposed in the wake of the first war caused crippling day-to-day hardship. Adolf Hitler came to power in Germany in 1933 under the banner of the Nazi party. Hitler promised prosperity, self-respect, and Aryan ascendancy, asking nothing but blind loyalty. Vulnerable and desperate for relief, people fell into step. There seemed great appeal to his glamour, power and promises. He swayed his people against their sense of common humanity, by an artful and highly orchestrated rhetoric. Leading the Axis powers, Hitler nearly succeeded in his campaign to conquer, in however cruel a fashion, first the sovereign states of Europe, then the entire free world. Proclaiming racist and homophobic views, and a specific hatred toward the people of Jewish descent, Hitler systematically deported and exterminated Jews, Gypsies and homosexuals in what he called the "Final Solution." Six million people died in a network of "concentration camps" constructed for the purpose of exterminated racially "inferior" of sexually aberrant human beings, during this war.

The Nazi Party in Germany, which came to power in the 1930's, maintained power to the end of World War II in 1945. In the Soviet Union, Joseph Stalin succeeded in gaining political control and establishing a strong harsh dictatorship. Benito Mussolini and the Fascist party, promising prosperity and order in Italy, gained national support and set up a strong government. In Japan, although the ruler was considered Emperor Hirohito, actual control and administration of government came under military officers.

Germany, Italy, and Japan initiated a policy of aggressive territorial expansion; Japan was the first to initiate. In 1931, the Japanese forces seized control of Manchuria, a part of China containing rich natural resources, and in 1937 began an attack on China, occupying most of its eastern part by 1938. Italy invaded Ethiopia in Africa in 1935, having it totally under its control by 1936. The Soviet Union did not invade or take over any territory but along with Italy and Germany, actively participated in the Spanish Civil War, using it as a proving ground to test tactics and weapons setting the stage for World War II.

In Germany, almost immediately after taking power, in direct violation of the World War I peace treaty, Hitler began the buildup of the armed forces. He sent troops into the Rhineland in 1936, invaded Austria in 1938 and united it with Germany. Hitler then seized control of the Sudetenland in 1938 (part of western Czechoslovakia and containing mostly Germans), the rest of Czechoslovakia in March 1939, and, on September 1, 1939, began World War II in Europe by invading Poland. In 1940, Germany invaded and controlled Norway, Denmark, Belgium, Luxembourg, the Netherlands, and France.

After the war began in Europe, U.S. President Franklin D. Roosevelt announced that the United States was neutral. Most Americans, although hoping for an Allied victory, wanted the U.S. to stay out of the war. President Roosevelt and his supporters, called "interventionists," favored all aid except war to the Allied nations fighting Axis aggression. They were fearful that an Axis victory would seriously threaten and endanger all democracies. On the other hand, the "isolationists" were against any U.S. aid being given to the warring nations, accusing President Roosevelt of leading the U.S. into a war very much unprepared to fight. Roosevelt's plan was to defeat the Axis nations by sending the Allied nations the equipment needed to fight; ships, aircraft, tanks, and other war materials.

In Asia, the U.S. had opposed Japan's invasion of Southeast Asia, an effort to gain Japanese control of that region's rich resources. Consequently, the U.S. stopped all important exports to Japan, whose industries depended heavily on petroleum, scrap metal, and other raw materials. Later Roosevelt refused the Japanese withdrawal of its funds from American banks. General Tojo became the Japanese premier in October 1941 and quickly realized that the U.S. Navy was powerful enough to block Japanese expansion into Asia. Deciding to cripple the Pacific Fleet, the Japanese aircraft, without warning, bombed the Fleet December 7, 1941, while at anchor in Pearl Harbor in Hawaii. Temporarily, it was a success. It destroyed many aircraft and disabled much of the U.S. Pacific Fleet. In the end, it was a costly mistake. The bombing of U.S. naval ships at Pearl Harbor quickly jolted Americans into preparedness for war. We joined to fight alongside the Allied nations in Europe and Asia.

Military strategy in the European theater of war as developed by Roosevelt, Churchill, and Stalin was to concentrate on Germany's defeat first, then Japan's. The start was made in North Africa, pushing Germans and Italians off the continent, beginning in the summer of 1942 and ending successfully in May 1943. Before the war, Hitler and Stalin had signed a non-aggression pact in 1939, which Hitler violated in 1941 by invading the Soviet Union. The German defeat at Stalingrad, marked a turning point in the war, was brought about by a combination of entrapment by Soviet troops and death of German troops by starvation and freezing due to the horrendous winter conditions. This occurred at the same time that the Allies were driving them out of North Africa.

The liberation of Italy began in July 1943 and ended May 2, 1945. The third part of the strategy was D-Day, June 6, 1944, with the Allied invasion of France at Normandy. At the same time, starting in January 1943, the Soviets began pushing the German troops back into Europe and they were greatly assisted by supplies from Britain and the United States. By April 1945, Allies occupied positions beyond the Rhine and the Soviets moved on to Berlin, surrounding it by April 25. Germany surrendered May 7 and the war in Europe was finally over.

Meanwhile, in the Pacific, in the six months after the attack on Pearl Harbor, Japanese forces moved across Southeast Asia and the western Pacific Ocean. By August 1942, the Japanese Empire was at its largest size and stretched northeast to Alaska's Aleutian Islands, west to Burma, south to what is now Indonesia. Invaded and controlled areas included Hong Kong, Guam, Wake Island, Thailand, part of Malaysia, Singapore, the Philippines, and bombed Darwin on the north coast of Australia.

The raid of General Doolittle's bombers on Japanese cities and the American naval victory at Midway along with the fighting in the Battle of the Coral Sea helped turn the tide against Japan. Island-hopping by U.S. Seabees and Marines and the grueling bloody battles fought resulted in gradually pushing the Japanese back towards Japan.

After victory was attained in Europe, concentrated efforts were made to secure Japan's surrender, but it took dropping two atomic bombs on the cities of Hiroshima and Nagasaki to finally end the war in the Pacific. Japan formally surrendered on September 2, 1945, aboard the U.S. battleship Missouri, anchored in Tokyo Bay. The war was finally over.

Before war in Europe had ended, the Allies had agreed on a military occupation of Germany. It was divided into four zones, each one occupied by Great Britain, France, the Soviet Union, and the United States and the four powers jointly administering Berlin. After the war, the Allies agreed that Germany's armed forces would be abolished, the Nazi Party outlawed, and the territory east of the Oder and Neisse Rivers taken away. Nazi leaders were accused of war crimes and brought to trial.

After Japan's defeat, the Allies began a military occupation directed by American General Douglas MacArthur, who introduced a number of reforms eventually ridding Japan of its military institutions transforming it into a democracy. A constitution was drawn up in 1947 transferring all political rights from the emperor to the people, granting women the right to vote, and denying Japan the right to declare war. War crimes trials of 25 war leaders and government officials were also conducted. The U.S. did not sign a peace treaty until 1951. The treaty permitted Japan to rearm but took away its overseas empire.

Again, after a major world war came efforts to prevent war from occurring again throughout the world. Preliminary work began in 1943 when the U.S., Great Britain, the Soviet Union, and China sent representatives to Moscow where they agreed to set up an international organization that would work to promote peace around the earth. In 1944, the four Allied powers met again and made the decision to name the organization the United Nations. In 1945, a charter for the U. N. was drawn up and signed, taking effect in October of that year.

Major consequences of the war included horrendous death and destruction, millions of displaced persons, the gaining of strength and spread of Communism and Cold War tensions as a result of the beginning of the nuclear age. World War II ended more lives and caused more devastation than any other war.

Besides the losses of millions of military personnel, the devastation and destruction directly affected civilians, reducing cities, houses, and factories to ruin and rubble and totally wrecking communication and transportation systems. Millions of civilian deaths, especially in China and the Soviet Union, were the results of famine.

More than twelve million people were uprooted by wars end having no place to live. They were prisoners of war, those that survived Nazi concentration camps and slave labor camps, orphans, and people who escaped war-torn areas and invading armies. Changing national boundary lines also caused the mass movement of displaced persons.

Germany and Japan were completely defeated; Great Britain and France were seriously weakened; and the Soviet Union and the United States became the world's leading powers. Although allied during the war, the alliance fell apart as the Soviets pushed Communism in Europe and Asia. In spite of the tremendous destruction it suffered, the Soviet Union was stronger than ever. During the war, it took control of Lithuania, Estonia, and Latvia and by mid-1945 parts of Poland, Czechoslovakia, Finland, and Romania. It helped Communist governments gain power in Bulgaria, Romania, Hungary, Czechoslovakia, Poland, and North Korea. China fell to Mao Zedong's Communist forces in 1949. Before the fall of the Berlin Wall in 1989 and the dissolution of Communist governments in Eastern Europe and the Soviet Union, the United States and the Soviet Union faced off in what was called a "Cold War".

Looming over both countries was the possibility of the terrifying destruction by nuclear weapons.

Korean War - 1950 to 1953

With the surrender of Japan at the end of WWII, its 35-year occupation of Korea came to an end. The Soviet Union and the United States assumed trusteeship of the country, with the Soviets occupying the northern half and the US controlling the south. Elections were ordered by the United Nations to elect a unified government, but with each occupying country backing different candidates, the result was the formation of two separate states divided along the 38th parallel of latitude, each claiming sovereignty over the whole country. These conflicting claims to sovereignty led to occasional military skirmishes along the common border throughout 1949, with each side aiming to unify the country under its own government. In June 1950, North Korea mounted a major attack across the 38th parallel marking what is considered the beginning of the war.

The North Korean faction received military aid and backing from the Soviet Union, which aroused the United States' fear that communism and Soviet influence might spread. In August 1950, American troops arrived in South Korea to join the fight, along with British, Australian and UN forces.

Control of the peninsula see-sawed over the next year, with North Korea capturing the South Korean capital of Seoul, but then being pushed back to the north, with southern forces eventually capturing the North Korean capital, Pyongyang and driving to the border of China. China had already announced its intention to get involved should forces enter North Korea, and the Chinese army mounted a push that reclaimed the North.

In 1953, peace negotiations resulted in a cease-fire and created a buffer zone between the two countries along the 38th parallel. This cease-fire has been in effect for over fifty years. The war has never officially ended. Since the cease-fire, North Korea has become an increasingly isolated communist dictatorship, while South Korea has grown into a major world economy.

The Vietnam War - U.S. Involvement - 1957 to 1973

1955 -1975

Like Korea, Vietnam became a divided country after WWII, with a Soviet and Chinese-backed communist government in the north, led by Ho Chi Minh, and a western-backed government in the south. As the communist-backed north drove out the occupying French and maintained more and more insurgency in the south, the larger powers became increasingly involved, with the United States sending advisors and small numbers of troops between 1955 and 1964.

In 1964, following an attack on US ships by North Vietnamese forces in the Gulf of Tonkin, the United States escalated its military involvement, sending more and more troops over the next four years. As fighting continued with no decisive progress, opposition to the war began to grow among the American public. President Richard Nixon began to make reductions in troops while trying to assist the South Vietnamese Army in building enough strength to fight on its own. In January 1973, the Paris Peace Accords were signed, ending offensive action by the US in Vietnam. Nixon promised defensive assistance, but in 1974 Congress cut off all funding to the South Vietnamese government after Nixon had resigned the presidency following the Watergate scandal.

The withdrawal of the United States left South Vietnam without economic or military support, and the North Vietnamese army was able to overrun and control the entire country. North Vietnamese forces took Saigon, the southern capital, in April 1975. North and South were unified under one socialist government.

Skill 29.2   Analyze how individuals, events, and issues shaped the history of Texas, the United States, and the world.

Native American settlement of the region that is now Texas began during the Upper Paleolithic period approximately 10,000 years ago. Some of the Native tribes that have inhabited the area include the Apache, Comanche, Cherokee and Wichita tribes, among others. In 1529, the Spanish explorer Alonso Alvarez de Pineda first mapped the coast of Texas, while Alvar Nunez Cabeza de Vaca explored inland for potential trade opportunities. It was the French, over 150 years later, who first attempted to establish a colony in the Texas territory.

Fort St. Louis was founded by La Salle at Matagorda Bay in 1685, establishing France's claim on the region. Through mutiny and massacre at the hands of Natives, the colony was eventually destroyed in 1688. France continued to claim Texas for decades following the massacre, even though they had no physical presence in the region.

Meanwhile, the Spanish began to build missions throughout Texas, beginning in 1690 with the San Francisco de los Tejas Mission in East Texas, founded by Alonso de Leon. Spain continued to populate the area with missions through the eighteenth century. France relinquished its claim on Texas in 1762, turning it over to Spain. France also turned over Louisiana, which included northern Texas, until 1800, when it was given back to France and sold to the United States in the Louisiana Purchase.

Spain's effective control over Texas lasted from 1690 until 1821, when Mexico gained independence from Spain. During this time, it had mainly been a thinly populated buffer region between the territories claimed by France and Spain. Mexico, wanting to encourage settlement in the area, invited European and American settlers to the region. In 1823, Stephen Austin began a colony called the Old Three Hundred on the Brazos River, opening the way for further settlement.

As the young nation of Mexico sought to establish its influence over Texas and the new settlers, unrest developed over government policies. Mexico was officially a Catholic country, and expected its citizens to also be Catholic. Many of the white settlers were Protestant, however. Mexico also banned slavery, which was widespread in the southern U.S. at the time. Unrest eventually erupted into conflict in 1832 at the **Battle of Velasco** between a small Mexican force and a militia of Texas colonists. Following the battle Texans held conventions to outline their disagreement with Mexican polices, culminating in the signing of a Texas Declaration of Independence on March 2, 1836. Four days later, a Mexican force of 4,000 to 5,000 besieged a small force of Texans at the Alamo in San Antonio. All the Texan defenders were killed, and the Alamo defeat became a battle cry for Texan independence.

Texas continued to battle against Mexican **General Santa Ana** and his forces. They suffered more setbacks, but eventually emerged victorious at the **Battle of San Jacinto**, where Texan troops led by Sam Houston captured the entire Mexican Army, including Santa Ana. Texas became an independent country with the signing of the Treaty of Velasco on May 15, 1836. Sam Houston was named the first President of the Republic of Texas.

After being moved five times, the capital of the **Republic of Texas** was established at Austin in 1839. Texas' decade as an independent country was marked by division between those who wished to remain independent and expand Texas' borders, and those, like Houston, who wished to become part of the United States. Houston's vision won out, and in 1845, Texas was annexed to the U.S. and made a state at the same time. In 1850, as part of the Compromise of 1850 that ended the Mexican American War, Texas' borders were adjusted to the present boundaries, and the United States assumed Texas' debts incurred while fighting against Mexico.

Approximately a decade later, in 1861, Texas would secede from the United States as part of the Confederacy. **Sam Houston**, then governor of the State of Texas, refused to swear allegiance to the Confederacy and was replaced. The final battle of the Civil War was fought in Texas at Palmito Ranch on May 12, 1865. One month later, Federal troops landed at Galveston to enforce the Emancipation Proclamation, which abolished slavery. Texas was readmitted into the Union in 1870.

The twentieth century began with disaster for Texas when, in 1900, a category 4 hurricane struck the coast at Galveston, completely destroying the city and killing some 8,000 people. The century also started with prosperity, however, when the Spindletop oil range was discovered in early 1901, starting the Texas oil boom and beginning Texas' transformation into an oil-rich state.

Following is a partial list of well-known Americans who contributed their leadership and talents in various fields and reforms:

Lucretia Mott and Elizabeth Cady Stanton for **women's rights**

Emma Hart Willard, Catharine Esther Beecher, and Mary Lyon for **education for women**

Dr. Elizabeth Blackwell, the **first woman doctor**

Antoinette Louisa Blackwell, the **first female minister**
Dorothea Lynde Dix for **reforms in prisons and insane asylums** Elihu Burritt and William Ladd for **peace movements**

Robert Owen for a **Utopian society**

Horace Mann, Henry Barmard, Calvin E. Stowe, Caleb Mills, and John Swett for **public education**

Benjamin Lundy, David Walker, William Lloyd Garrison, Isaac Hooper, Arthur and Lewis Tappan, Theodore Weld, Frederick Douglass, Harriet Tubman, James G. Birney, Henry Highland Garnet, James Forten, Robert Purvis, Harriet Beecher Stowe, Wendell Phillips, and John Brown for **abolition of slavery and the Underground Railroad**

Louisa Mae Alcott, James Fenimore Cooper, Washington Irving, Walt Whitman, Henry David Thoreau, Ralph Waldo Emerson, Herman Melville, Richard Henry Dana, Nathaniel Hawthorne, Henry Wadsworth Longfellow, John Greenleaf Whittier, Edgar Allan Poe, Oliver Wendell Holmes, **famous writers**

John C. Fremont, Zebulon Pike, Kit Carson, **explorers**

Henry Clay, Daniel Webster, Stephen Douglas, John C. Calhoun, American **statesmen**
Robert Fulton, Cyrus McCormick, Eli Whitney, **inventors**

Noah Webster, American **dictionary and spellers**

In 1957 the formation of the **Southern Christian Leadership Conference** by Martin Luther King, Jr., John Duffy, Rev. C. D. Steele, Rev. T. J. Jemison, Rev. Fred Shuttlesworth, Ella Baker, A. Philip Randolph, Bayard Rustin and Stanley Levison provided training and assistance to local efforts to fight segregation. Non-violence was its central doctrine and its major method of fighting segregation and **racism,** a belief or doctrine that biological differences determine success or cultural achievement and that one's own race is superior and has the right to rule over others.

At the turn of the twenty-first century, the world witnessed unprecedented strides in **communications**, a major expansion of international trade, and significant international diplomatic and military activity. The Internet and worldwide web continued to grow and connect people all over the world, opening new routes of communication and providing commercial opportunities. The expansion of **cell phone** usage and Internet access led to a worldwide society that is interconnected like never before. In Asia, new economies matured and the formerly tightly controlled Chinese market became more open to foreign investment, increasing China's influence as a major economic power. In Europe, the European Union made a bold move to a common currency, the Euro, in a successful effort to consolidate the region's economic strength. African nations, many struggling under international debt, appealed to the international community to assist them in building their economies. In South America, countries such as Brazil and Venezuela showed growth despite political unrest, as Argentina suffered a near complete collapse of its economy.

As the technology sector expanded, so did the economy of India, where hi-tech companies found a highly educated work force.

Conflict between the Muslim world and the United States increased during the last decade of the twentieth century, culminating in a **terrorist attack** on New York and Washington, D.C. in 2001. These attacks, sponsored by the radical group Al-Qaida, prompted a military invasion by the US of Afghanistan, where the group is based. Shortly afterwards, the US, England, and several smaller countries addressed further instability in the region by ousting Iraqi dictator Saddam Hussein in a military campaign. In the eastern Mediterranean, tension between Israelis and Palestinians continued to build, regularly erupting into violence.

The threat of the spread of nuclear weapons, largely diminished after the fall of the Soviet Union and the end of the Cold War, reared its head again with the claims of North Korea that it had the ability to arm a nuclear missile, and the suspicion that Iran was working toward the creation of weapons-grade nuclear material. As international conflict and tension increased, the role of international alliances such as NATO and the United Nations grew in importance

Skill 29.3   Analyze the influence of various factors on the development of societies.

Spatial organization is a description of how things are grouped in a given space. In geographical terms, this can describe people, places, and environments anywhere and everywhere on Earth.

The most basic form of spatial organization for people is where they live. The vast majority of people live near other people, in villages and towns and cities and settlements. These people live near others in order to take advantage of the goods and services that naturally arise from cooperation. These villages and towns and cities and settlements are, to varying degrees, near bodies of water, since water is a staple of survival for every person on the planet and is also a good source of energy for factories and other industries as well as a form of transportation for people and goods.

Another way to describe where people live is by the geography and topography around them. The vast majority of people on the planet live in areas that are very hospitable. Yes, people live in the Himalayas and in the Sahara, but the populations in those areas are small indeed when compared to the plains of China, India, Europe, and the United States. People naturally want to live where they won't have to work really hard just to survive, and world population patterns reflect this.

Most places in the world are in some manner close to agricultural land as well. Some cities are more agriculturally inclined than others. Rare is the city, however, that grows absolutely no crops. The kind of food grown is almost entirely dependent on the kind of land available and the climate surrounding that land. Rice doesn't grow well in the desert, for instance, nor do bananas grow well in snowy lands. Certain crops are easier to transport than others as well and the ones that aren't are usually grown nearer ports or other areas of export.

The invention that changed many assumptions is the airplane. Flight has made possible global commerce and goods exchange on a level never before seen. Foods from all around the world can be flown literally around the world and, with the aid of refrigeration techniques, be kept fresh enough to sell in markets nearly everywhere. The same is true of medicine and weapons.

Skill 29.4   Know common characteristics of communities, past and present.

Human communities subsisted initially as gatherers – gathering berries, leaves, etc. With the invention of **tools** it became possible to dig for roots, hunt small animals, and catch fish from rivers and oceans. Humans observed their environments and soon learned to plant seeds and harvest crops. As people migrated to areas in which game and fertile soil were abundant, communities began to develop. When people had the knowledge to grow crops and the skills to hunt game, they began to understand division of labor. Some of the people in the community tended to agricultural needs while others hunted game.

As habitats attracted larger numbers of people, environments became crowded and there was competition. The concept of division of labor and sharing of food soon came, in more heavily populated areas, to be managed. Groups of people focused on growing crops while others concentrated on hunting. Experience led to the development of skills and of knowledge that make the work easier. Farmers began to develop new plant species and hunters began to protect animal species from other predators for their own use. This ability to manage the environment led people to settle down, to guard their resources, and to manage them.

By 8000 BCE, culture was beginning to evolve in villages. **Agriculture** was developed for the production of grain crops, which led to a decreased reliance on wild plants. Domesticating animals for various purposes decreased the need to hunt wild game. Life became more settled. It was then possible to turn attention to such matters as managing water supplies, producing tools, making cloth, etc. There was both the social interaction and the opportunity to reflect upon existence. Mythologies arose and various kinds of belief systems. Rituals arose that re-enacted the mythologies that gave meaning to life.

Two things seem to have come together to produce **cultures and civilizations**: a society and culture based on agriculture and the development of centers of the community with literate social and religious structures. The members of these hierarchies then managed water supply and irrigation, ritual and religious life, and exerted their own right to use a portion of the goods produced by the community for their own subsistence in return for their management.

Sharpened skills, development of more sophisticated tools, commerce with other communities, and increasing knowledge of their environment, the resources available to them, and responses to the needs to share goods, order community life, and protect their possessions from outsiders led to further division of labor and community development.

As **trade** routes developed and travel between cities became easier, trade led to specialization. Trade enables a people to obtain the goods they desire in exchange for the goods they are able to produce. This, in turn, leads to increased attention to refinements of technique and the sharing of ideas. The knowledge of a new discovery or invention provides knowledge and technology that increases the ability to produce goods for trade. As each community learns the value of the goods it produces and improves its ability to produce the goods in greater quantity, industry is born.

Skill 29.5   Apply knowledge of the concept of chronology and its use in understanding history and historical events.

Chronology is the ordering of events through time. Chronologies are often listed along a timeline or in a list by date.

Chronologies allow for easy visualization of a wide expanse of history in one place. This allows a student to quickly get an overview of the major events and changes over time. By including important related events, the causes and effects of major developments can be emphasized. By placing chronologies for different societies parallel to one another, comparisons in relative development can be quickly interpreted, providing material for further historical exploration.

Refer to Skill 29.1.

Skill 29.6   Apply different methods of interpreting the past to understand, evaluate, and support multiple points of view, frames of reference, and the historical context of events and issues.

Research into local history usually requires local sources, such as newspapers, family histories, memoirs and oral interviews with local residents. Local records of births, deaths, land holdings, etc., can often be found at local courthouses and city halls.

Historical events can affect local communities in more significant ways than when a larger viewpoint is taken. A factory closing may not have a large impact on a state's economy, for instance, but might be devastating for the town in which it was located. Interpreting the local historical events, issues and developments of a specific locality requires a sharp focus on how relatively small groups of people are affected by larger historical forces.

Skill 29.7   Understand similarities and differences among Native American groups in Texas, the United States, and the Western Hemisphere before European colonization.

Native American tribes lived throughout what we now call the United States in varying degrees of togetherness. They adopted different customs, pursued different avenues of agriculture and food gathering, and made slightly different weapons. They fought among themselves and with other peoples. To varying degrees, they had established cultures long before Columbus or any other European explorer arrived on the scene.

Archaeologists have discovered evidence of Native American civilization in Texas dating to at least 9,200 BCE. For the most part, these ancient peoples lived in temporary camps along river banks. Their subsistence was based on hunting and gathering. As the resources of an area were exhausted, they moved to another area.   Some of those Native American tribes were "just passing through"; others stayed, in some cases for many years. Among the major settled tribes were the Caddo, Cherokee, Chickasaw, Choctaw, Comanche, Karankawa, Kickapoo, and Tonkawa.

The first known inhabitants of the state date to around 9200 BCE (late ice age) and were connected with the Clovis Complex. The Folsom Complex dates from around 8800-8200 BCE. The Archaic Period of Texas history extended from about 6000 BCE to about 700 CE. The Late Archaic period (1000-300 BCE) continues to be a time of hunting societies. There is abundant evidence that bison have become a vital source of food. The "Transitional Archaic" period (300 BCE – 700 CE) was a time of some development in tool-making, and the time of the first appearance of settled villages. The settlement of villages marks the emergence of agriculture and the beginning of social and political systems.

The Late Prehistoric period extends from 700 CE to historic times. It is during this period that the bow and arrow first appears, as well as new types of stone tools, pottery, and the creation and trade of ornamental items. During this period, as well, the early Caddoan culture begins to emerge and mound building begins. Agriculture spreads and becomes more complex and in some areas pithouse dwellings appear. In particular, the presence of obsidian artifacts demonstrates the participation of these peoples in a north-south system of trade that extended to the Great Plains and to Wyoming and Idaho in particular.

The Caddo, in the east, were good at farming, trading, and making pottery. The Cherokee and Choctaw had advanced political structures, with an elected chief. The Chickasaw didn't stay in Texas long but were known as good hunters and farmers. The Choctaw were also good farmers, hunters, tool-makers, and house-builders. The Comanche were famous horsemen and hunters. The Karankawa were good jewelers and shell-makers. The Tonkawa were famous for hunting bison and for gathering fruits and nuts.

Perhaps the most famous of the Native American tribes is the **Algonquians**. We know so much about this tribe because they were one of the first to interact with the newly arrived English settlers in Plymouth and elsewhere. The Algonquians lived in wigwams and wore clothing made from animal skins. They were proficient hunters, gatherers, and trappers who also knew quite a bit about farming. Beginning with a brave man named Squanto, they shared this agricultural knowledge with the English settlers, including how to plant and cultivate corn, pumpkins, and squash. Other famous Algonquians included Pocahontas and her father, Powhatan, both of whom are immortalized in English literature, and Tecumseh and Black Hawk, known foremost for their fierce fighting ability. To the overall Native American culture, they contributed wampum and dream catchers.

Another group of tribes who lived in the Northeast were the **Iroquois**, who were fierce fighters but also forward thinkers. They lived in long houses and wore clothes made of buckskin. They, too, were expert farmers, growing the "Three Sisters" (corn, squash, and beans). Five of the Iroquois tribes formed a Confederacy which was a shared form of government. The Iroquois also formed the False Face Society, a group of medicine men who shared their medical knowledge with others but kept their identities secret while doing so. These masks are one of the enduring symbols of the Native American era.

Living in the Southeast were the **Seminoles** and **Creeks**, a huge collection of people who lived in chickees (open, bark-covered houses) and wore clothes made from plant fibers. They were expert planters and hunters and were proficient at paddling dugout canoes, which they made. The bead necklaces they created were some of the most beautiful on the continent. They are best known, however, for their struggle against Spanish and English settlers, especially led by the great Osceola.

The **Cherokee** also lived in the Southeast. They were one of the most advanced tribes, living in domed houses and wearing deerskin and rabbit fur. Accomplished hunters, farmers, and fishermen, the Cherokee were known the continent over for their intricate and beautiful basketry and clay pottery. They also played a game called lacrosse, which survives to this day in countries around the world.

In the middle of the continent lived the Plains tribes, such as the **Sioux, Cheyenne, Blackfeet, Comanche, and Pawnee.** These peoples lived in teepees and wore buffalo skins and feather headdresses. (It is this image of the Native American that has made its way into most American movies depicting the period.) They hunted wild animals on the Plains, especially the buffalo. They were well known for their many ceremonies, including the Sun Dance, and for the peace pipes they smoked. Famous Plains people include Crazy Horse and Sitting Bull, authors of the Custer Disaster; Sacagawea, leader of the Lewis & Clark expedition; and Chief Joseph, the famous Nez Perce leader.

Dotting the deserts of the Southwest were a handful of tribes, including the famous **Pueblo**, who lived in houses that bear their tribe's name, wore clothes made of wool and woven cotton, farmed crops in the middle of desert land, created exquisite pottery and Kachina dolls, and had one of the most complex religions of all the tribes. They are perhaps best known for the challenging vista-based villages they constructed from the sheer faces of cliffs and rocks and for their *adobes*, mud-brick buildings that housed their living and meeting quarters. The Pueblos chose their own chiefs. This was perhaps one of the oldest representative governments in the world.

Another well-known Southwestern tribe were the **Apache**, with their famous leader **Geronimo**. The Apache lived in homes called wickiups, which were made of bark, grass, and branches. They wore cotton clothing and were excellent hunters and gatherers. Adept at basketry, the Apache believed that everything in Nature had special powers and that they were honored just to be part of it all.

The **Navajo**, also residents of the Southwest, lived in hogans (round homes built with forked sticks) and wore clothes of rabbit skin. Their major contribution to the overall culture of the continent was in sand painting, weapon-making, silversmithing, and weaving. Some of the most beautiful woven rugs ever were crafted by Navajo hands.

Living in the Northwest were the **Inuit**, who lived in tents made from animal skins or, in some cases, igloos. They wore clothes made of animal skins, usually seals or caribou. They were excellent fishermen and hunters and crafted efficient kayaks and umiaks to take them through waterways and harpoons with which to hunt animals. The Inuit are perhaps best known for the great carvings they left behind. Among these are ivory figures and tall totem poles.

Native Americans have made major contributions to the development of the nation and have been contributors, either directly or indirectly in every area of political and cultural life. In the early years of European settlement, Native Americans were both teachers and neighbors. Even during periods of extermination and relocation, their influence was profound.

Skill 29.8 **Understand the causes and effects of European exploration and colonization of Texas, the United States, and the Western Hemisphere.**

Historic causation is the concept that events in history are linked to one another by an endless chain of cause and effect. The root causes of major historical events cannot always be seen immediately, and are only apparent when looking back from many years later. The advances made during the Renaissance in the areas of astronomy, cartography and shipbuilding opened the possibility of distant travel by sea. As cities grew and trade increased, Europe's monarchs began looking toward new lands to fuel growth. As Islam spread from the east, Christian nations also wished to find routes that bypassed areas of Islamic control. The Age of Exploration was underway.

Portugal led the first wave of exploration by sea in the early fifteenth century, under **Prince Henry the Navigator**. Using ships that borrowed technology from Arab sailing vessels, the Portuguese discovered new islands in the Atlantic and opened sea routes to the west coast of Africa. Over the next several decades, Portuguese explorers pushed farther south along the African coast until, in 1498, Vasco De Gama became the first to navigate the Cape of Good Hope at the southern tip of Africa, opening a new sea route to India. Portugal's control over the African coast troubled the Spanish, who devised a plan to bypass the route entirely by sailing west, around the globe, to the profitable trade lands of Asia.

When Columbus landed in the New World in 1492, the full effect of his discovery could not have been measured at that time. By opening the Western Hemisphere to economic and political development by Europeans, Columbus changed the face of the world. The native populations that had existed before Columbus arrived were quickly decimated by disease and warfare. Over the following century, the Spanish conquered most of South and Central America, and English and French settlers arrived in North America, eventually displacing the native people. This gradual displacement took place over many years and could not have been foreseen by those early explorers. Looking back it can be said that Columbus caused a series of events that greatly impacted world history.

Interaction between cultures, either by exploration and migration or war, often contribute directly to major historical events, but other forces can influence the course of history, as well. Religious movements such as the rise of Catholicism in the Middle Ages created social changes throughout Europe and culminated in the Crusades and the expulsion of Muslims from Spain.

The **Colonial Period** resulted in settlements being established by France, Spain and England; these grew and thrived. Settlers came to America for various reasons, but mostly because it was a chance to own land and to experience freedom of one form or another. The first permanent settlement in North America was by the Spanish in **St. Augustine, Florida** in 1565.

The **English** settlements were along the Eastern seaboard, from Maine to Georgia. The French settled between the Appalachian and Rocky Mountains, from New Orleans to Montreal, giving them control of most of the Great Lakes and the St. Lawrence and Mississippi Rivers. The Spanish settlements included Florida and the West Indies and the land west of the Mississippi. The fact that all three nations claimed the land west of the Mississippi set the stage for later conflicts.

Each of these regions had their own culture as the settlers had brought with them many of the animals and agriculture from the regions they had immigrated from as well as their own customs. Each region had its own characteristics and culture. The New England colonies valued personal and religious freedoms and democratic governments. Their governments were based on the town hall where the adult males met to enact the laws. These British colonists brought British common law heritage with them.

The Middle Atlantic colonies were the considered melting pots of the colonies, since they included the Dutch settlements in New York and the region attracted settlers from all over Europe. They farmed the rich fertile land and produced a surplus of food that they traded with other regions. They also established commercial and manufacturing activities such as shipbuilding, mining, and textile, paper and glass manufacturing. Governmental units based on democracy, with unicameral or bicameral legislative bodies were also established throughout the region.

Further south, the rich fertile land gave rise to large plantations. They also had mines in the South. The labor force was not large enough to staff these mines and plantations on the mainland in the South and in the West Indies so they began to import slaves from Africa. Virginia and the South also established democratic forms of governments. As the plantations grew, they required more and more slave labor. The South also had small family run and operated farms that did not use slaves. Other areas of the South were settled by different groups: Georgia became a haven for debtors from British prisons, North Carolina became settled by Virginia's expansion, and South Carolina was settled by different groups of European nationalities. Agriculture remained the primary form of economic activity for the region even though there was economic activity in lumber and the fur trade.

The common thread throughout all of the regions was a government based on democracy for the settlers. The settlers came to America in search of land ownership and various kinds of freedoms and this is evident in the forms of government they established.

Spain's influence was in Florida, the Gulf Coast from Texas all the way west to California and south to the tip of South America and some of the islands of the West Indies. French control centered from New Orleans north to what is now northern Canada including the entire Mississippi Valley, the St. Lawrence Valley, the Great Lakes, and the land that was part of the Louisiana Territory. A few West Indies islands were also part of France's empire. England settled the eastern seaboard of North America, including parts of Canada and from Maine to Georgia. Some West Indies islands also came under British control. The Dutch had New Amsterdam for a period but later ceded it into British hands. One interesting aspect was each of these three nations, especially in England, the land claims extended partly or all the way across the continent, regardless of the fact that the others claimed the same land. The wars for dominance and control of power and influence in Europe would undoubtedly and eventually extend to the Americas, especially North America.

The part of North America claimed by **France** was called New France and consisted of the land west of the Appalachian Mountains. This area of claims and settlement included the St. Lawrence Valley, the Great Lakes, the Mississippi Valley, and the entire region of land westward to the Rockies. They established the permanent settlements of Montreal and New Orleans, thus giving them control of the two major gateways into the heart of North America, the vast, rich interior. The St. Lawrence River, the Great Lakes, and the Mississippi River along with its tributaries made it possible for the French explorers and traders to roam at will, virtually unhindered in exploring, trapping, trading, and furthering the interests of France.

1685

French and Spanish explorers reached Texas in the sixteenth century, and settlers soon followed. The first important Frenchman to arrive was La Salle, as part of his overall exploration of what became the Mississippi Territory. Other French explorers and settlers came on the scene, but a combination of meager resources and a surge in Spanish explorers eliminated the French from further influence in the majority of Texas. The Spanish were far more successful in colonizing Texas. Spain had a whole colony called the Kingdom of Texas, which was administered by forces of varying sizes. Conflict erupted over Louisiana, but the Spanish missions provided a strong base for settlement and defense and French influence ended with the Louisiana Purchase.

Spanish exploration began with the search for the cities of gold. The failure of the French colony in Texas had become known throughout the world and Spain was quick in moving to destroy the ruins of the French colony and establish a Spanish presence in the area. Spain's interests were both in the resources of Texas, the Catholic missionary zeal to convert native peoples, and expansion of the empire.

Colonization of Texas by Europeans affected the Native peoples in many ways, some of which were undesirable. The Spanish approach to occupation of a new region was to plant Catholic missions that would convert the natives, bring them into conformity with Spanish beliefs and ideas, and teach them subsistence agriculture. One of the negative effects of the arrival of the Spanish was the introduction of a number of diseases to which the native people had not been exposed and to which they had no natural immunities.

The Spanish colonists and missionaries introduced, however, a number of European crops, as well as methods of irrigation that greatly improved the agricultural output of the native people. They also introduced methods of animal husbandry. But throughout the early years of European occupation, Texas was primarily a buffer zone between the French, Spanish, English and Americans as each sought to expand its empire and exploit the native land and people. The greatest influence during this period, however, was that of the Spanish missions and presidios. These colonial institutions had been very successful in Hispanicizing the native people.

Mexican independence from Spain resulted in Mexican control over much of Texas. This control was harsh and dictatorial. In the 1820s, Mexico reached an agreement with **Stephen Austin** to allow several hundred U.S. settlers, called Texians, to move to the area. Mexico wanted to populate and develop the region. In a short period of time, thousands of settlers arrived to populate Texas. Mexico abolished slavery, a move with which many settlers refused to comply, and the Mexican government tried to tighten its control over the political and economic life of the settlers. Further, the government expected good citizens to be members of the Catholic Church. Most of the settlers were Protestant. Emotions were aroused among the settlers and the local Tejanos that led to the Texas Revolution.

Spanish influence continued into the nineteenth century but ended with Mexican independence in 1821. Texas passed into Mexican hands until the end of the Mexican-American War, which handed Texas over to the United States. One prime result of the European occupation was a dedication to Spanish culture, especially in the names of towns and foods, which is still reflected in the state. The French influence has, by and large, disappeared. One prime result of the European occupation was a dedication to Spanish culture, especially in the names of towns and foods, which is still reflected in the state.

Skill 29.9 Understand the foundations of representative government in the United States, significant issues of the revolutionary era, and challenges confronting the U.S. government in the early years of the republic.

The American nation was founded upon a commitment that the people would have a large degree of autonomy and liberty. The famous maxim "no taxation without representation" was a rallying cry for the Revolution, not only because the people didn't want to suffer the increasingly oppressive series of taxes imposed on them by the British Parliament, but also because the people could not in any way influence the lawmakers in Parliament in regard to those taxes. No American colonist had a seat in Parliament and no American colonist could vote for members of Parliament.

Representation, the idea that a people can vote—or even replace—their lawmakers was not a new idea. Residents of other British colonies did not have these rights, of course, and America was only a colony. What the Sons of Liberty and other revolutionaries were asking for was to stand on an equal footing with the Mother Country. Along with the idea of representation comes the notion that key ideas and concepts can be deliberated and discussed, with theoretically everyone having a chance to voice their views. This applied to both lawmakers and the people who elected them. Lawmakers wouldn't just pass bills that became laws; rather, they would debate the particulars and go back and forth on the strengths and weaknesses of proposed laws before voting on them. Members of both houses of Congress had the opportunity to speak out on the issues, as did the people at large, who could contact their lawmakers and express their views. The different branches of government were designed to serve as a mechanism of checks and balances on each other so that no one branch could become too powerful. They each have their own specific powers.

Another key concept in the American ideal is **equality**, the idea that every person has the same rights and responsibilities under the law. The Great Britain the American colonists knew was a stratified society, with social classes firmly in place. The goal of the Declaration of Independence and the Constitution was to provide equality for all governed by them. Due process under law was also a big concern of the founders. Various amendments protect the rights of people. The "American Dream" is that every individual has an equal chance to make his or her fortune in a new land and that the United States welcomes and even encourages that initiative.

Skill 29.10 **Understand westward expansion and analyze its effects on the political, economic, and social development of the United States.**

Westward expansion occurred for a number of reasons, primarily economic. Cotton had become most important in the southern states. The effects of the Industrial Revolution, which began in England, were now being felt in the United States. With the invention of power-driven machines, the demand for cotton fiber greatly increased for the yarn needed in spinning and weaving. Eli Whitney's cotton gin made the separation of the seeds from the cotton much more efficient and faster. This, in turn, increased the demand and more and more farmers became involved in the raising and selling of cotton.

Innovations and developments in long-distance transportation moved the cotton in greater quantities to textile mills in England as well as the areas of New England and Middle Atlantic States in the U.S. As prices increased along with increased demand, southern farmers began expanding by clearing more land to grow more cotton. Movement, settlement, and farming headed west to utilize the fertile soils. This, in turn, increased the need for a large supply of cheap labor. The system of slavery expanded, both in numbers and in the movement to lands west of the South.

Cotton farmers and slave owners were not the only ones heading west. Many, in other fields of economic endeavor began the migration: trappers, miners, merchants, ranchers, and others were all seeking their fortunes. The Lewis and Clark expedition stimulated the westward push. Fur companies hired men, known as "Mountain Men", to go westward, searching for the animal pelts to supply the market and meet the demands of the East and Europe. These men explored and discovered the many passes and trails that would eventually be used by settlers in their trek to the west. The California gold rush also had a very large influence on the movement west.

There were also religious reasons for westward expansion. Increased settlement was encouraged by missionaries who traveled west with the fur traders, then sent word back east for more settlers and the results were tremendous.

The third reason for westward expansion was political. It was the belief of many that the United States was destined to control all of the land between the two oceans or as one newspaper editor termed it, Manifest Destiny. This mass migration westward put the U.S. government on a collision course with the Indians, Great Britain, Spain, and Mexico.

In the American southwest, the results were exactly the opposite. Spain had claimed this area since the 1540s, had spread northward from Mexico City, and, in the 1700s, had established missions, forts, villages, towns, and very large ranches. After the purchase of the Louisiana Territory in 1803, Americans began moving into Spanish territory. A few hundred American families in what is now Texas were allowed to live there but had to agree to become loyal subjects to Spain. In 1821, Mexico successfully revolted against Spanish rule, won independence, and chose to be more tolerant towards the American settlers and traders. The Mexican government encouraged and allowed extensive trade and settlement, especially in Texas. Many of the new settlers were southerners and brought with them their slaves. Slavery was outlawed in Mexico and technically illegal in Texas, although the Mexican government rather looked the other way.

With the influx of so many Americans and the liberal policies of the Mexican government, there came to be concern over the possible growth and development of an American state within Mexico. Settlement restrictions, cancellation of land grants, the forbidding of slavery and increased military activity brought everything to a head. The order of events included the fight for Texas independence, the brief Republic of Texas, eventual annexation of Texas, statehood, and finally war with Mexico. The Texas controversy was not the sole reason for war. Since American settlers had begun pouring into the Southwest cultural differences played a prominent part. Language, religion, law, customs, and government came into conflict.

The impact of the entire westward movement resulted in the completion of the borders of the present-day conterminous United States. These events included the bloody war with Mexico; the ever-growing controversy over slave versus free states affecting the balance of power or influence in the U.S. Congress, especially the Senate; and finally to the Civil War itself.

Skill 29.11   Analyze ways in which political, economic, and social factors led to the growth of sectionalism and the Civil War.

Slavery in the English colonies began in 1619 when 20 Africans arrived in the colony of Virginia at Jamestown. From then on, slavery had a foothold, especially in the agricultural South, where a large amount of slave labor was needed for the extensive plantations. Free men refused to work for wages on the plantations when land was available for settling on the frontier. Therefore, slave labor was the only recourse left. If it had been profitable to use slaves in New England and the Middle Colonies, then without doubt slavery would have been more widespread. However, it came down to whether or not slavery was profitable. It was in the South, but not in the other two colonial regions.

Regionalism can be defined as the political division of an area into partially autonomous regions or to loyalty to the interests of a particular region.

Sectionalism is generally defined as excessive devotion to local interests and customs.

As the young nation grew, territories came to be defined as states. The states began to acquire their own particular cultures and identities. In time regional interests and cultures also began to take shape. Religious interests, economic life, and geography began to be understood as definitive of particular regions. The northeast tended toward industrial development. The south tended to rely upon agriculture. The west was an area of untamed open spaces where people settled and practiced agriculture and animal husbandry.

Each of these regions came to be defined, at least to some extent, on the basis of the way people made their living and the economic and social institutions that supported them. In the industrialized north, the factory system tended to create a division between the tycoons of business and industry and the poor industrial workers. The conditions in which the labor force worked were far from ideal – the hours were long, the conditions bad, and the pay was small.

The south was characterized by cities that were centers of social and commercial life. The agriculture that supported the region was practiced on "plantations" that were owned by the wealthy and worked by slaves or indentured servants.

The west was a vast expanse to be explored and tamed. Life on a western ranch was distinctly different from either life in the industrial north or the agricultural south. The challenges of each region were also distinctly different. The role of children in the economy was different; the role of women was different; the importance of trade was different. And religion was called upon to support each unique regional lifestyle.

The regional differences between North and South came to a head over the issue of slavery. The rise of the abolitionist movement in the North, the publication of ***Uncle Tom's Cabin,*** and issues of trade and efforts by the national government to control trade for the regions coalesced around the issue of slavery in a nation that was founded on the principle of the inalienable right of every person to be free. As the South defended its lifestyle and its economy and the right of the states to be self-determining, the North became stronger in its criticism of slavery. The result was a growing sectionalism.

The North was industrial with towns and factories growing and increasing at a very fast rate. The South had become agricultural, eventually becoming increasingly dependent on the one crop, cotton. In the West, restless pioneers moved into new frontiers seeking land, wealth, and opportunity. Many were from the South and were slave owners, bringing their slaves with them. So between these three different parts of the country, the views on tariffs, public lands, internal improvements at federal expense, banking and currency, and the issue of slavery were decidedly, totally different.

This period of U.S. history was a period of compromises, breakdowns of the compromises, desperate attempts to restore and retain harmony among the three sections, short-lived intervals of the uneasy balance of interests, and ever-increasing conflict.

At the **Constitutional Convention**, one of the slavery compromises concerned counting slaves for deciding the number of representatives for the House and the amount of taxes to be paid. Southerners pushed for counting the slaves for representation but not for taxes. The Northerners pushed for the opposite. The resulting compromise, sometimes referred to as the **"three-fifths compromise,"** was that both groups agreed that three-fifths of the slaves would be counted for both taxes and representation.

The other compromise over slavery was part of the disputes over how much control the central government would have over commercial activities such as trade with other nations and the slave trade. It was agreed that Congress would regulate commerce with other nations, including taxing imports. Southerners were worried about taxing slaves coming into the country and the possibility of Congress prohibiting the slave trade altogether. The agreement reached allowed the states to continue importation of slaves for the next 20 years until 1808, at which time Congress would make the decision as to the future of the slave trade. During the 20-year period, no more than $10 per person could be levied on slaves coming into the country.

These two slavery compromises were a necessary concession to have Southern support and approval for the new document and new government. Many Americans felt that the system of slavery would eventually die out in the U.S., but by 1808, cotton was becoming increasingly important in the primarily agricultural South and the institution of slavery had become firmly entrenched in Southern culture. It is also evident that as early as the Constitutional Convention, active anti-slavery feelings and opinions were very strong, leading to extremely active groups and societies.

The first serious clash between North and South occurred during 1819-1820 when James Monroe was President, concerning admitting Missouri as a state. In 1819, the U.S. consisted of 21 states: 11 free states and 10 slave states. The Missouri Territory allowed slavery and if admitted would cause an imbalance in the number of U.S. Senators. Alabama had already been admitted as a slave state and that had balanced the Senate with the North and South each having 22 senators. The first **Missouri Compromise** resolved the conflict by approving admission of Maine as a free state along with Missouri as a slave state. This continued to keep a balance of power in the Senate with the same number of free and slave states.

An additional provision of this compromise was that with the admission of Missouri, slavery would not be allowed in the rest of the Louisiana Purchase territory north of latitude 36 degrees 30'. This was acceptable to the Southern Congressmen since it was not profitable to grow cotton on land north of this latitude line anyway. It was thought that the crisis had been resolved but in the next year, it was discovered that in its state constitution, Missouri discriminated against the free blacks. Anti-slavery supporters in Congress went into an uproar, determined to exclude Missouri from the Union. Henry Clay, known as the Great Compromiser, then proposed a second Missouri Compromise, which was acceptable to everyone. His proposal stated that the Constitution of the United States guaranteed protections and privileges to citizens of states and Missouri's proposed constitution could not deny these to any of its citizens. The acceptance in 1820 of this second compromise opened the way for Missouri's statehood.

The issue of tariffs also was a divisive factor during this period, especially between 1829 and 1833. The slavery issue was at the root of every problem, crisis, event, decision, and struggle from then on. The next crisis involved the issue concerning Texas. By 1836, Texas was an independent republic with its own constitution. During its fight for independence, Americans were sympathetic to and supportive of the Texans and some recruited volunteers who crossed into Texas to help the struggle. Problems arose when the state petitioned Congress for statehood. Texas wanted to allow slavery but Northerners in Congress opposed admission to the Union because it would disrupt the balance between free and slave states and give Southerners in Congress increased influence. There were others who believed that granting statehood to Texas would lead to a war with Mexico, which had refused to recognize Texas independence. For the time being, statehood was put on hold.

The slavery issue flared again.. It was obvious that the newly acquired territory would be divided up into territories and later become states. In addition to the two factions of Northerners who advocated prohibition of slavery and of Southerners who favored slavery existing there, a third faction arose supporting the doctrine of "**popular sovereignty**". Popular sovereignty stated that people living in territories and states should be allowed to decide for themselves whether or not slavery should be permitted. In 1849, California applied for admittance to the Union and the furor began.

The result was the **Compromise of 1850,** a series of laws designed as a final solution to the issue. Concessions made to the North included the admission of California as a free state and the abolition of slave trading in Washington, D.C. The laws also provided for the creation of the New Mexico and Utah territories. As a concession to Southerners, the residents there would decide whether to permit slavery when these two territories became states. In addition, Congress authorized implementation of stricter measures to capture runaway slaves.

A few years later, Congress took up consideration of new territories between Missouri and present-day Idaho. Again, heated debate over permitting slavery in these areas flared up. Those opposed to slavery used the Missouri Compromise to prove their point showing that the land being considered for territories was part of the area the Compromise had designated as closed to slavery. On May 25, 1854, Congress passed the infamous **Kansas-Nebraska Act**, which nullified this provision, created the territories of Kansas and Nebraska, and provided for the people of these two territories to decide for themselves whether to permit slavery. Feelings were so deep and divided that any further attempts to compromise would meet with little, if any, success. Political and social turmoil swirled everywhere. Kansas was called "Bleeding Kansas" because of the extreme violence and bloodshed throughout the territory because two governments existed there, one pro-slavery and the other anti-slavery.

The Supreme Court in 1857 handed down a decision that caused explosive reactions throughout the country. **Dred Scott** was a slave whose owner had taken him from slave state Missouri, then to free state Illinois, into Minnesota Territory, free under the provisions of the Missouri Compromise, then finally back to slave state Missouri. Abolitionists pursued the dilemma by presenting a court case, stating that since Scott had lived in a free state and free territory, he was in actuality a free man. Two lower courts had ruled before the Supreme Court became involved, one ruling in favor and one against. The Supreme Court decided that residing in a free state and free territory did not make Scott a free man because Scott (and all other slaves) was not a U.S. citizens or state citizen of Missouri. Therefore, he did not have the right to sue in state or federal courts. The Court went a step further and ruled that the old Missouri Compromise was now unconstitutional because Congress did not have the power to prohibit slavery in the Territories.

In 1859, abolitionist **John Brown** and his followers seized the federal arsenal at Harper's Ferry in what is now West Virginia. His purpose was to take the guns stored in the arsenal, give them to slaves nearby, and lead them in a widespread rebellion. Brown and his men were captured by Colonel Robert E. Lee of the United States Army and after a trial with a guilty verdict, Brown was hanged. Most Southerners felt that the majority of Northerners approved of Brown's actions but in actuality, most of them were stunned and shocked. Southern newspapers took great pains to quote a small but well-known minority of abolitionists who applauded and supported Brown's actions. This merely served to widen the gap between the two sections.

The final straw came with the election of Lincoln to the Presidency the next year. Due to a split in the Democratic Party, there were four candidates from four political parties. When Lincoln received a minority of the popular vote and a majority of electoral votes, the Southern states, one by one, voted to secede from the Union as they had promised if Lincoln and the Republicans were victorious. The die was cast.

Skill 29.12 **Know individuals, issues, and events of the Civil War and analyze the effects of Reconstruction on the political, economic, and social life of the nation.**

South Carolina was the first state to secede from the Union and the first shots of the war were fired on Fort Sumter in Charleston Harbor. Both sides quickly prepared for war. The North had more in its favor: a larger population; superiority in finances and transportation facilities; manufacturing, agricultural, and natural resources. The North possessed most of the nation's gold, had about 92% of all industries, and almost all known supplies of copper, coal, iron, and various other minerals. Most of the nation's railroads were in the North and mid-West, men and supplies could be moved wherever needed; food could be transported from the farms of the mid-West to workers in the East and to soldiers on the battlefields. Trade with nations overseas could go on as usual due to control of the navy and the merchant fleet. The Northern states numbered 24 and included western (California and Oregon) and border (Maryland, Delaware, Kentucky, Missouri, and West Virginia) states.

The Southern states numbered 11 and included South Carolina, Georgia, Florida, Alabama, Mississippi, Louisiana, Texas, Virginia, North Carolina, Tennessee, and Arkansas. Although outnumbered in population, the South was completely confident of victory. They knew that all they had to do was fight a defensive war and protect their own territory until the North, who had to invade and defeat an area almost the size of Western Europe, tired of the struggle and gave up. Another advantage of the South was that a number of its best officers had graduated from the U.S. Military Academy at West Point and had had long years of army experience. Some exercised varying degrees of command in the Indian Wars and the War with Mexico.

Men from the South were conditioned to living outdoors and were more familiar with horses and firearms than many men from northeastern cities. Since cotton was such an important crop, Southerners felt that British and French textile mills were so dependent on raw cotton that they would be forced to help the Confederacy in the war.

The South had specific reasons and goals for fighting the war. The major aim of the Confederacy never wavered: to win independence, the right to govern themselves as they wished, and to preserve slavery. The Northerners were not as clear in their reasons for conducting war. At the beginning, most believed, along with Lincoln, that preservation of the Union was paramount. Only a few extremely fanatical abolitionists looked on the war as a way to end slavery. However, by war's end, more and more northerners had come to believe that freeing the slaves was just as important as restoring the Union.

The war strategies for both sides were relatively clear and simple. The South planned a defensive war, wearing down the North until it agreed to peace on Southern terms. One exception was to gain control of Washington, D.C., go North through the Shenandoah Valley into Maryland and Pennsylvania and drive a wedge between the Northeast and mid-West, interrupt the lines of communication, and end the war quickly. The North had three basic strategies:

a.   Blockade the Confederate coastline in order to cripple the South;

b.   Seize control of the Mississippi River and interior railroad lines to split the Confederacy in two; and

c.   Seize the Confederate capital of Richmond, Virginia, driving southward joining up with Union forces coming east from the Mississippi Valley.

The South won decisively until the Battle of Gettysburg, July 1 - 3, 1863. Until Gettysburg, Lincoln's commanders, McDowell and McClellan, were less than desirable, Burnside and Hooker, not what was needed. Lee, on the other hand, had many able officers, Jackson and Stuart depended on heavily by him. Jackson died at Chancellorsville and was replaced by Longstreet. Lee decided to invade the North and depended on J.E.B. Stuart and his cavalry to keep him informed of the location of Union troops and their strengths. Four things worked against Lee at Gettysburg:

1)   The Union troops gained the best positions and the best ground first, making it easier to make a stand there.

2)   Lee's move into Northern territory put him and his army a long way from food and supply lines. They were more or less on their own.

3)   Lee thought that his Army of Northern Virginia was invincible and could fight and win under any conditions or circumstances.

4)   Stuart and his men did not arrive at Gettysburg until the end of the second day of fighting and by then, it was too little too late. He and the men had had to detour around Union soldiers and he was delayed getting the information Lee needed.

Consequently, he made the mistake of failing to listen to Longstreet and following the strategy of regrouping back into Southern territory to the supply lines. Lee felt that regrouping was retreating and almost an admission of defeat. He was convinced the army would be victorious. Longstreet was concerned about the Union troops occupying the best positions and felt that regrouping to a better position would be an advantage. He was also very concerned about the distance from supply lines.

It was not the intention of either side to fight there but the fighting began when a Confederate brigade stumbled into a unit of Union cavalry while looking for shoes. The third and last day Lee launched the final attempt to break Union lines. General George Pickett sent his division of three brigades under Generals Garnet, Kemper, and Armistead against Union troops on Cemetery Ridge under command of General Winfield Scott Hancock. Union lines held and Lee and the defeated Army of Northern Virginia made their way back to Virginia. Although Lincoln's commander George Meade successfully turned back a Confederate charge, he and the Union troops failed to pursue Lee and the Confederates. This battle was the turning point for the North. After this, Lee never again had the troop strength to launch a major offensive.

The day after Gettysburg, on July 4, Vicksburg, Mississippi surrendered to Union General Ulysses Grant, thus severing the western Confederacy from the eastern part. In September 1863, the Confederacy won its last important victory at Chickamauga. In November, the Union victory at Chattanooga made it possible for Union troops to go into Alabama and Georgia, splitting the eastern Confederacy in two. Lincoln gave Grant command of all Northern armies in March of 1864. Grant led his armies into battles in Virginia while Phil Sheridan and his cavalry did as much damage as possible. In a skirmish at a place called Yellow Tavern, Virginia, Sheridan's and Stuart's forces met, with Stuart being fatally wounded. The Union won the Battle of Mobile Bay and in May 1864, William Tecumseh Sherman began his march to successfully demolish Atlanta, then on to Savannah. He and his troops turned northward through the Carolinas to Grant in Virginia. On April 9, 1865, Lee formally surrendered to Grant at Appamattox Courthouse, Virginia.

The Civil War took more American lives than any other war in history, the South losing one-third of its' soldiers in battle compared to about one-sixth for the North. More than half of the deaths were caused by disease and the horrendous conditions of field hospitals. Both sides paid a tremendous economic price but the South suffered more severely from direct damages. Destruction was pervasive with towns, farms, trade, industry, lives destroyed and an entire Southern way of life was lost. The deep resentment, bitterness, and hatred that remained for generations gradually lessened as the years went by but legacies of it surface and remain to this day. The South had no voice in the political, social, and cultural affairs of the nation, lessening to a great degree the influence of the more traditional Southern ideals. The Northern Yankee Protestant ideals of hard work, education, and economic freedom became the standard of the United States and helped influence the development of the nation into a modem, industrial power.

The effects of the Civil War were tremendous. It changed the methods of waging war and has been called the first modern war. It introduced weapons and tactics that, when improved later, were used extensively in wars of the late 1800s and 1900s. Civil War soldiers were the first to fight in trenches, first to fight under a unified command, first to wage a defense called "major cordon defense", a strategy of advance on all fronts. They were also the first to use repeating and breech loading weapons. Observation balloons were first used during the war along with submarines, ironclad ships, and mines. Telegraphy and railroads were put to use first in the Civil War. It was considered a modern war because of the vast destruction and was "total war", involving the use of all resources of the opposing sides. There was probably no *way* it could have ended other than total defeat and unconditional surrender of one side or the other.

By executive proclamation and constitutional amendment, slavery was officially and finally ended, although there remained deep prejudice and racism. Also, the Union was preserved and the states were finally truly united. Sectionalism, especially in the area of politics, remained strong for another 100 years but not to the degree and with the violence as existed before 1861. It has been noted that the Civil War may have been American democracy's greatest failure for, from 1861 to 1865, calm reason, basic to democracy, fell to human passion. Yet, democracy did survive. The victory of the North established that no state has the right to end or leave the Union. Because of unity, the U.S. became a major global power.

Lincoln never proposed to punish the South. He was most concerned with restoring the South to the Union in a program that was flexible and practical rather than rigid and unbending. In fact he never really felt that the states had succeeded in leaving the Union but that they had left the 'family circle" for a short time. His plans consisted of two major steps:

All Southerners taking an oath of allegiance to the Union promising to accept all federal laws and proclamations dealing with slavery would receive a full pardon. The exceptions were men who had resigned from civil and military positions in the federal government to serve in the Confederacy, those who were part of the Confederate government, those in the Confederate army above the rank of lieutenant, and Confederates who were guilty of mistreating prisoners of war and blacks.

A state would be able to write a new constitution, elect new officials, and return to the Union fully equal to all other states on certain conditions. First, a minimum number of persons (at least 10% of those who were qualified voters in their states before secession from the Union who had voted in the 1860 election) must take an oath of allegiance.

As the war dragged on to its bloody, destructive conclusion, Lincoln was very concerned and anxious to get the states restored to the Union. He showed flexibility in his thinking as he made changes to his Reconstruction program to make it as easy and painless as possible. Of course, Congress had final approval of many actions and it would be interesting to know how differently things might have turned out if Lincoln had lived to see some or all of his kind policies, supported by fellow moderates, put into action. Unfortunately, it didn't turn out that way. After Andrew Johnson became President and the radical Republicans gained control of Congress, the harsh measures of radical Reconstruction were implemented.

The economic and social chaos in the South after the war was unbelievable with starvation and disease rampant, especially in the cities. The U.S. Army provided some relief of food and clothing for both white and blacks but the major responsibility fell to the Freedmen's Bureau. Though the bureau agents to a certain extent helped southern whites, their main responsibility was to the freed slaves. They were to assist the freedmen to become self-supporting and protect them from being taken advantage of by others. Northerners looked on it as a real, honest effort to help the South out of the chaos it was in. Most white Southerners charged the bureau with causing racial friction, deliberately encouraging the freedmen to consider former owners as enemies.

As a result, as southern leaders began to be able to restore life as it had once been, they adopted a set of laws known as "black codes", containing many of the provisions of the prewar "slave codes." There were certain improvements in the lives of freedmen, but the codes denied the freedmen their basic civil rights. In short, except for the condition of freedom and a few civil rights, white Southerners made every effort to keep the freedmen in a way of life subordinate to theirs.

Radicals in Congress pointed out these illegal actions by white Southerners as evidence that they were unwilling to recognize, accept, and support the complete freedom of black Americans and could not be trusted. Therefore, Congress drafted its own program of Reconstruction, including laws that would protect and further the rights of blacks. Three amendments were added to the Constitution: the 13th Amendment of 1865 outlawed slavery throughout the entire United States. The 14th Amendment of 1868 made blacks American citizens. The 15th Amendment of 1870 gave black Americans the right to vote and made it illegal to deny anyone the right to vote based on race.

Federal troops were stationed throughout the South and protected Republicans who took control of Southern governments. Bitterly resentful, white Southerners fought the new political system by joining a secret society called the **Ku Klux Klan,** using violence to keep black Americans from voting and getting equality. However, before being allowed to rejoin the Union, the Confederate states were required to agree to all federal laws. Between 1866 and 1870, all of them had returned to the Union, but Northern interest in Reconstruction was fading.

Reconstruction officially ended when the last Federal troops left the South in 1877. It can be said that Reconstruction had a limited success as it set up public school systems and expanded legal rights of black Americans. Nevertheless, white supremacy came to be in control.

Lincoln and Johnson had considered the Civil War a "rebellion of individuals," but Congressional Radicals, such as Charles Sumner in the Senate, considered the Southern states as complete political organizations. He considered them in the same position as any unorganized Territory and should be treated as such. Radical House leader Thaddeus Stevens considered the Confederate States, not as Territories, but as conquered provinces and felt they should be treated that way. President Johnson refused to work with congressional moderates, insisting on having his own way. As a result, the Radicals gained control of both houses of Congress and when Johnson opposed their harsh measures, they came within one vote of impeaching him.

General Grant was elected President in 1868, serving two scandal-ridden terms. He was himself an honest, upright person but he greatly lacked political experience and his greatest weakness was a blind loyalty to his friends. He absolutely refused to believe that his friends were not honest and stubbornly would not admit to their using him to further their own interests.

Skill 29.13 Demonstrate knowledge of major U.S. reform movements of the nineteenth century.

Many **social reform movements** began during this period, including education, women's rights, labor, and working conditions, temperance, prisons and insane asylums. But the most intense and controversial was the abolitionists' efforts to end slavery, an effort alienating and splitting the country, hardening Southern defense of slavery, and leading to four years of bloody war. The abolitionist movement had political fallout, affecting admittance of states into the Union and the government's continued efforts to keep a balance between total numbers of free and slave states. Congressional legislation after 1820 reflected this.

Religion has always been a factor in American life. Many early settlers came to America in search of religious freedom. Religion, particularly Christianity, was an essential element of the value and belief structure shared by the Founding Fathers. Yet the Constitution prescribes a separation of Church and State.

The **First Great Awakening** was a religious movement within American Protestantism in the 1730s and 1740s. This was primarily a movement among Puritans seeking a return to strict interpretation of morality and values as well as emphasizing the importance and power of personal religious or spiritual experience. Many historians believe the First Great Awakening unified the people of the original colonies and supported the independence of the colonists.

The **Second Great Awakening** (the Great Revival) was a broad movement within American Protestantism that led to several kinds of activities that were distinguished by region and denominational tradition. In general terms, the Second Great Awakening, which began in the 1820s, was a time of recognition that "awakened religion" must weed out sin on both a personal and a social level. It inspired a wave of social activism. In New England, the Congregationalists established missionary societies to evangelize the West. Publication and education societies arose, most notably the American Bible Society. This social activism gave rise to the temperance movement, prison reform efforts, help for the handicapped and mentally ill. This period was particularly notable for the abolition movement. In the Appalachian region, the camp meeting was used to revive religion. The camp meeting became a primary method of evangelizing new territory.

The **Third Great Awakening** (the Missionary Awakening) gave rise to the Social Gospel Movement. This period (1858 to 1908) resulted in a massive growth in membership of all major Protestant denominations through their missionary activities. This movement was partly a response to claims that the Bible was fallible. Many churches attempted to reconcile or change biblical teaching to fit scientific theories and discoveries. Colleges associated with Protestant churches began to appear rapidly throughout the nation. In terms of social and political movements, the Third Great Awakening was the most expansive and profound. Coinciding with many changes in production and labor, it won battles against child labor and stopped the exploitation of women in factories. Compulsory elementary education for children came from this movement, as did the establishment of a set work day. Much was also done to protect and rescue children from abandonment and abuse, to improve the care of the sick, to prohibit the use of alcohol and tobacco, as well as numerous other "social ills."

Skilled laborers were organized into a labor union called the **American Federation of Labor**, in an effort to gain better working conditions and wages for its members. Farmers joined organizations such as the National Grange and Farmers Alliances. Farmers were producing more food than people could afford to buy. This was the result of (1) new farmlands rapidly opening on the plains and prairies, and (2) development and availability of new farm machinery and newer and better methods of farming.

American **women** began actively campaigning for the right to vote. Elizabeth Cady Stanton and Susan B. Anthony in 1869 founded the organization called National Women Suffrage Association the same year the Wyoming Territory gave women the right to vote. Soon after, a few states followed by giving women the right to vote, limited to local elections only.

Governmental reform began with the passage of the Civil Service Act, also known as the Pendleton Act. It provided for the Civil Service Commission, a federal agency responsible for giving jobs based on merit rather than as political rewards or favors. Another successful reform was the adoption of the secret ballot in voting, as were such measures as the direct primary, referendum, recall, and direct election of U.S. Senators by the people rather than by their state legislatures. Following the success of reforms made at the national level, the progressives were successful in gaining reforms in government at state and local levels.

Skill 29.14   Understand important issues, events, and individuals of the twentieth century in Texas, the United States, and the world.

In 1900, a category 4 hurricane devastated Galveston, killing 8000 people and destroying the city and its economy.

In 1901 the first major oil well was drilled at Spindletop. This event launched the oil boom and pointed to the size of the East Texas Oil Field, which is the largest in the U.S. This led to great economic expansion and changed the economy of the state.

Texas was hit hard by the Stock Market Crash of 1929 and the ensuing Great Depression. Thousands of city workers lost their jobs and became dependent upon federal relief programs. As cotton and livestock prices fell, farmers and ranchers were devastated. The Dust Bowl phenomenon destroyed agriculture in much of the state, leading to homelessness, hunger and joblessness. Many left Texas to seek new opportunities in the West.

Before and during WWII, the military bases in Texas were expanded and new bases were built to train soldiers and aviators for the war. This allowed an economic recovery and boom.

Since WWII, Texas has modernized, expanded its higher education system, developed new approaches to the distribution of its natural resources, and attracted numerous businesses, particularly in the electronic media sector. There has been a generalized migration from rural areas to the cities, and a general transition from an agricultural economy to a business and industrial economy. The economy later came to be characterized by the high-tech and service industries.

Texas experienced the same struggles with racism and desegregation as the rest of the nation. The political climate of the 1950s was marked by a growing rift between the conservatives and the liberals. Texas politics was essentially dominated by Lyndon Johnson during the 1960s, both in terms of congressional politics, and of his term as John Kennedy's vice president, and then as President of the U.S. The assassination of President Kennedy in 1963 in Dallas scarred the people of Texas in many ways.

The **United States** underwent significant social and economic changes during the twentieth century, and became a **dominant world power** internationally. Economically, the US saw periods of great prosperity as well as severe depression, emerging as a primary economic force. The **industrialization** that had started following the end of the Civil War in the mid nineteenth century continued into the early decades of the twentieth century in America. A wave of immigration at the turn of the century provided industry with a large labor pool and established millions of immigrants and their families in the working class. This prosperity was interrupted by America's entry into the **First World War** in 1917. While reluctant to enter the hostilities, the US played a decisive role in ending the war and in the creation of the League of Nations that followed, establishing its central position in international relations that would increase in importance through the century.

The US resumed its prosperous industrial growth in the years after WWI, but even as industrial profits and stock market investments skyrocketed, farm prices and wages fell creating an unbalanced situation that caused an economic collapse in 1929, when the stock market crashed. The US plummeted into economic depression with high unemployment known as the **Great Depression**. President Franklin Roosevelt proposed that the federal government assist in rebuilding the economy, something his predecessor, President Hoover, thought the government should not do. Roosevelt's "**New Deal**" policies were adopted to wide success, and marked an important shift in the role the US government plays in economic matters and social welfare. The nation's recovery was underway when, in late 1941, it entered the Second World War to fight against Japan and Germany and their allied Axis powers. War industry fueled another period of economic prosperity that lasted through the post war years. The 1950s saw the emergence of a large consumer culture in the US, which has bolstered not only the American economy ever since, but has been an important development for other countries which produce goods for the US.

The US had first established itself as an important world military leader at the turn of the twentieth century during the **Spanish American War**, and cemented this position during the two World Wars. Following WWII, with Europe struggling to recover from the fighting, the US and the Soviet Union emerged as the two dominant world powers. This remained the situation for three decades while the two super powers engaged in a Cold War between the ideals of communism and capitalism.

Poverty remained a serious problem in the central sections of large cities resulting in riots and soaring crime rates, which ultimately found its way to the suburbs. The escalation of the war in Vietnam and the social conflict and upheaval of support versus opposition to U.S. involvement led to antiwar demonstrations. Escalation of drug abuse, weakening of the family unit, homelessness, poverty, mental illness, increasing social, mental, and physical problems experienced by the Vietnam veterans returning to families, marriages, and a country divided and tom apart, contributed to the issues of the time.

The **Watergate** scandal resulting in the first resignation of a sitting American president was the most crucial domestic crisis of the 1970s. The population of the U.S. had greatly increased and along with it the nation's industries and the resulting harmful pollution of the environment.
Factory smoke, automobile exhaust, waste from factories and other sources all combined to create hazardous air, water, and ground pollution which, if not brought under control and significantly diminished, would severely endanger all life on earth. The 1980s was the decade of the horrible Exxon Valdez oil spill off the Alaskan coast and the nuclear accident and melt-down at the Ukrainian nuclear power plant at Chernobyl. The U.S. had a narrow escape with the near disaster at Three Mile Island Nuclear Plant in Pennsylvania.

Inflation increased in the late 1960s, and the 1970s witnessed a period of high unemployment, the result of a severe recession. The decision of the **OPEC** (Organization of Petroleum Exporting Countries) ministers to cut back on oil production thus raising the price of a barrel of oil created a fuel shortage. This made it clear that energy and fuel conservation was necessary in the American economy, especially since fuel shortages created two energy crises during the decade of the 1970s. Americans experienced shortages of fuel oil for heating and gasoline for cars and other vehicles.

The 1980s saw the difficulties of rising inflation, recession, recovery, and the insecurity of long-term employment. Foreign competition and imports, the use of robots and other advanced technology in industries, the opening and operation of American companies and factories in other countries to lower labor costs all contributed to the economic and employment problems.

The nation's farmers experienced economic hardships and October 1987 saw another one-day significant drop in the Dow Jones on the New York Stock Exchange. January 28, 1986 was the day of the loss of seven crewmembers of the NASA space shuttle "**Challenger**". The reliability and soundness of numerous savings and loans institutions were in serious jeopardy when hundreds of these failed and others went into bankruptcy due to customer default on loans and mismanagement. Congressional legislation helped rebuild the industry.

In 1991, the Soviet Union disintegrated into its constituent states as its economy collapsed under the strain of decades of arms spending, marking the end of the Cold War.

Globalization and the global economy surged during the 1990s, as communications advances such as the Internet blurred the lines between markets. The personal computer became a regular household appliance and social and cultural interaction began to transform as more and more people connected "on line." Globalization and communication continue to make great strides in the twenty-first century.

During the twentieth century, the world witnessed unprecedented strides in **communications**, a major expansion of international trade, and significant international diplomatic and military activity, including two world wars.

The rise of **nationalism** in Europe at the end of the nineteenth century led to a series of alliances and agreements among European nations that eventually led to the First World War as nations called on their military allies to provide assistance and defense.

A new model of international relations was proposed following the devastation of WWI, one based on the mission to preserve peace. The **League of Nations** was formed to promote this peace, but it ultimately failed, having no way to enforce its resolutions. When Germany, led by Adolph Hitler, rebelled against the restrictions placed on it following WWI and began a campaign of military expansion through Europe, World War II ensued. Great Britain, the United States and other allied nations combined forces to defeat Germany and the Axis powers.

Taking a lesson from the failure of the League of Nations, the world's nations organized the **United Nations**, an international assembly given the authority to arrange and enforce international resolutions.

World War II left Europe in ruins. As a result, the United States and the Soviet Union emerged as the only two world powers. Although allies in the war, tension arose between the two powers as the US engaged in a policy of halting the spread of communism sponsored by the Soviets and China. The US and Soviet Union never engaged in direct military conflict during this "**Cold War**," but were each involved in protracted conflicts in Korea and Viet Nam. The threat of nuclear war increased as each power produced more and more weapons in an extended arms race. The threat of the spread of nuclear weapons largely diminished after the fall of the Soviet Union in the early 1990s, which ended the Cold War.

In Asia, new economies matured and the formerly tightly controlled Chinese market became more open to foreign investment, increasing China's influence as a major economic power. In Europe, the **European Union** made a bold move to a common currency, the Euro, in a successful effort to consolidate the region's economic strength. In South America, countries such as Brazil and Venezuela showed growth despite political unrest, as Argentina suffered a near complete collapse of its economy. As the technology sector expanded, so did the economy of India, where hi-tech companies found a highly educated work force.

Conflict between the Muslim world and the United States increased during the last decade of the twentieth century, culminating in a terrorist attack on New York City and Washington, D.C. in 2001. These attacks, sponsored by the radical group Al-Qaida, prompted a military invasion by the US of Afghanistan, where the group is based. Shortly afterwards, the US, England, and several smaller countries addressed further instability in the region by ousting Iraqi dictator Saddam Hussein in a military campaign. In the eastern Mediterranean, tension between Israelis and Palestinians continued to build, regularly erupting into violence.

Skill 29.15 Understand the contributions of people of various racial, ethnic, and religious groups in Texas, the United States, and the world.

Among the Native American tribes who made their home in Texas were the Apache, Cherokee, and Comanche. These were by no means the only tribes; numerous tribes roamed the plains of Texas. The Native American peoples of Texas have come from diverse parts of the nation and co-existed with the Spanish, Mexican, American, African American and other immigrants. The early civilization of Spain in Texas was marked by an intentional effort to Hispanicize the native people by converting them to Roman Catholicism, forcing them to give up traditional practices and beliefs, and incorporating them into a new culture marked by a sharing of some beliefs, values and institutions. The influence of Spain, and later Mexico, is apparent at every turn throughout the state.

French and Spanish explorers reached the area in the sixteenth century, and settlers soon followed. The Rio Grande and other rivers provided avenues for transportation, of both goods and people. Americans came in during the late eighteenth and early nineteenth centuries after the **Louisiana Purchase**.

African Americans were brought to Texas first as slaves of the early white settlers. They worked both cattle ranches and cotton fields. After the Civil War, many African American migrated from Southern states in search of greater opportunity. Curtis Graves and Barbara Jordan were the first African Americans elected to the state legislature since 1898. The Mansfield School Desegregation Incident was a notable turning point in school desegregation in Texas.

The nineteenth century saw tremendous change in Texas. At the urging of the Mexican government, which wanted to expand the population possibilities of the newly independent territory, **Stephen F. Austin** and other Americans moved into the area, to stay. Austin soon led a movement to colonize the area as American. This conflict escalated for several years until the United States annexed Texas. This, in part, brought on the **Mexican-American War.**

The American victory in that war brought with it a tremendous influx of American settlers into Texas. The state's population continued to grow at a rapid rate throughout the rest of the nineteenth century and into the twentieth century. Not even the Civil War could stop the tide of new Texas residents. They came for economic and settlement opportunities, working at oil fields and on farms and ranches. They came to start new businesses and new lives. The latter half of the twentieth century saw a boom in high-tech companies and jobs, with **Houston, San Antonio**, and **Dallas** leading the way. These cities—and the state in general—continue to be a driving force in high tech and modern technologies.

In a sort of reverse trend, the number of Mexicans moving into Texas began to grow in the twentieth century, reaching a staggering rate in the latter half of the century and into the twenty-first century (with the exception of the 1930s, when the Dust Bowl drove Texans away in droves). The proximity of the American state and the promise of new opportunity drove immigration to an all-time high. Texas to this day is made up mostly of Americans and Mexican-Americans.

Stretching back through the history of the Mexican Territory, the number of Mexican residents who have migrated to Texas to seek their fortunes is very large indeed. The forecast is that Latinos will outnumber Caucasians in Texas by 2030. These Mexican-Americans serve in a variety of capacities throughout the state—in agriculture, at oil fields, on ranches, and in hundreds of other white collar capacities.

Major cultural regions of the United States

By far, the nation's immigrants were an important reason for America's phenomenal industrial growth from 1865 to 1900. They came seeking work and better opportunities for themselves and their families than what life in their native country could give them. What they found in America was suspicion and distrust because they were competitors with Americans for jobs, housing, and decent wages. Their languages, customs, and ways of living were different, especially between the different national and ethnic groups. Until the early 1880s, most immigrants were from parts of northwestern Europe such as Germany, Scandinavia, the Netherlands, Ireland, and Great Britain. After 1890, the new arrivals increasingly came from eastern and southern Europe. Chinese immigrants on the Pacific coast, so crucial to the construction of the western part of the first transcontinental railroad, were the first to experience this increasing distrust that eventually erupted into violence and bloodshed. From about 1879 to the present time, the U.S. Congress made, repealed, and amended numerous pieces of legislation concerning quotas, restrictions, and other requirements pertaining to immigrants. The immigrant laborers, both skilled and unskilled, were the foundation of the modern labor union movement as a means of gaining recognition, support, respect, rights, fair wages, and better working conditions.

New England is located in the northeastern part of the United States and includes the states of Maine, New Hampshire, Vermont, Massachusetts, Rhode Island and Connecticut. It was the first region of the US to be heavily settled by Europeans, beginning in the seventeenth century. The largest city in the region is Boston. New Englanders, or "Yankees" as they are often called, share a tradition of direct involvement in government through small town meetings where local decisions are made. The Democratic Party is the dominant political group in the region. Education is highly regarded, and several of the nation's top universities are located in New England.

The **Mid-Atlantic** region is located in the central part of the east coast of the US, and includes the states of New York, New Jersey, Pennsylvania, Delaware and Maryland. Virginia and West Virginia are usually included in this region, but are sometimes considered southern states. Some of the country's most densely settled urban areas are in this region, including New York City, Philadelphia, and Washington, D.C. The Mid-Atlantic region has always been more ethnically diverse than other east coast regions, with settlers from a wider range of the world. The political feelings are mainly liberal within the urban areas, but political opinions of all types come together in Washington, D.C., which is the capital of the nation. The Mid-Atlantic area has provided much of the heavy industry and manufacturing for the country, and has a large working class population. From colonial times through the nineteenth century, this region has served as a kind of buffer zone between the northern and southern states, which is one of the reasons it was chosen for the site of the capital.

The **South** is one of the country's most distinctive cultural regions, and includes the states of North Carolina, South Carolina, Tennessee, Georgia, Florida, Alabama, Mississippi, Louisiana, Texas and Arkansas. Also sometimes considered part of the South are the states of Oklahoma, Missouri, Kentucky, Virginia and West Virginia. Major urban centers in the South include Atlanta, Miami, New Orleans, Dallas and Houston.

With the exception of some French and Latin-settled regions such as in Louisiana and Florida, the South is predominantly Protestant Christian in religion, and is the location of the area sometimes called the Bible Belt. Texas, which was one of the Confederate States, extends westward into the Southwest region of the US. Oklahoma, which is sometimes considered part of the South, also has a large population of Native Americans who were moved to the area from other parts of the eastern US. Florida's warm climate has made it a popular retirement area for people from all over the US, and its proximity to Cuba and other Latino-settled islands has contributed a large Hispanic population to the region.

The **Midwest** is located in the northern central part of the United States, and traditionally includes the states of Minnesota, Wisconsin, Iowa, Illinois, Indiana, Ohio and Michigan. North Dakota, South Dakota, Nebraska, Kansas and Missouri are also sometimes thought of as being Midwestern States. Major Midwestern cities include Chicago, Minneapolis, Cincinnati, St. Louis and Detroit. Outside the urban areas, the region is characterized by many small towns that grew around agriculture. Early settlers found rich soil drained by the Ohio, Missouri and Mississippi Rivers. The western portions of the region contain rolling, grassy range land suitable for ranching.

Beginning in the 1790s, the Midwest was settled mainly by pioneers of western European heritage. They found several Native American peoples in the area, who were gradually pushed westward and eventually removed to reservations. European Americans make up most of the population of the central Midwestern states. In the twentieth century, African Americans from the South migrated northwards to industrial areas such as St. Louis, Chicago, Indianapolis and Detroit. Traditionally, Midwesterners are thought of as hard working and stoic, embodying the values of the American pioneer. Religion plays an important role in the social relationships of many Midwesterners, who are mainly Christian. The region extends westward to include what is considered Western cultural areas, and borders on the Mid-Atlantic States to the east, where parts of Ohio are perhaps more closely associated with the industrial East than the more agricultural Midwest.

The **Southwest** cultural region of the US is an area where Native and Latin American culture has had the most influence. Arizona and New Mexico are the two states that make up the main part of the Southwest, with some of the surrounding states of California, Nevada, Utah, Colorado, Oklahoma and Texas extending into the region.

Major cities in the region include Phoenix and Albuquerque. Once a part of Spanish territory, then a part of Mexico, the Southwest has retained its cultural connection to these countries. Native American cultures established settlements in this region thousands of years ago, and their influence is still seen. Arizona has the largest population of Native Americans in the US.

The **West** region extends from the Pacific Coast of the US eastward to the Rocky Mountain States, and includes the states of California, Colorado, Idaho, Montana, Nevada, Oregon, Utah, Washington, and Wyoming. Major western cities include Los Angeles, San Francisco, Denver, Salt Lake City, Portland and Seattle. The West has some of the least densely populated areas in the country, particularly in the desert regions of the southwest and areas of Montana and Wyoming. Immigration from the eastern US began seriously in the 1840s, along the Oregon Trail to the Pacific Northwest region. Mormons also settled in Utah at around this time, and are still prevalent in that state. In 1849, the discovery of gold near San Francisco brought thousands of new people to the area.

Situated along the Pacific Rim, the West has a high concentration of Asian immigrants especially evident in the coastal cities. It is a very diverse region with wide influence on American culture, especially from California, where most American television programs and movies are produced.

Major cultural regions of the world

North America includes the countries of the United States and Canada. Mexico, while geographically part of North America, is often thought of as being closer to Latin and South America culturally. English is the primary language of North America, with large sections of French speakers in Quebec, Canada, and Spanish speakers in the southwestern US. Because of its history of immigration from wide areas, North America contains people of many cultures, with people of western European descent in the majority. Christianity is the primary religion, with significant populations practicing other religions such as Judaism and Islam.

Latin America includes the mainly Spanish and Portuguese speaking countries of Mexico, Central America and South America. Culturally, this area has been heavily influenced by Spain and Portugal, who explored and conquered much of the region in the 16th Century. Catholicism, introduced by the conquistadors and through subsequent missions, is the primary religious observance. Native practices are still observed in many areas, and several groups of indigenous peoples still inhabit the interior of South America.

Europe is a diverse collection of independent countries who have banded together economically. Primarily Christian in observance, Europe contains several significant groups that observe other religions. Turkey, a Muslim nation, is often considered to be part of Europe culturally owing to its long history of interaction with the western countries.

Middle East and North Africa includes the countries of Saudi Arabia, Egypt, Libya, Iran, Iraq, Lebanon, Jordan and Syria. This region is largely Islamic in faith, and once extended well into present day Europe. Arabic is the primary language. Israel is located in this region, but is officially a Jewish state with a sizable Arabic-speaking Palestinian population.

Sub Saharan Africa is that portion of Africa located south of the great Sahara desert and includes the countries of South Africa, Kenya, Rwanda, and Ghana as well as 38 other nations. This is a culturally diverse area, stemming from the widespread colonization of the region by European countries upon whom many African countries still rely for assistance.

The region of **Russia and Central Asia** is made up of many of the former states of the Soviet Union, which was dominated by the Russian language and culture. Russia observes the Eastern Orthodox religion, and is renowned for its contributions to the arts, especially ballet and music. Since the breakup of the Soviet Union, several of the smaller states in Central Asia have re-established cultural connections with the Muslim nations of the Middle East and South Asia.

East Asia includes China, North and South Korea and Japan. Historically, China has dominated this region, with the Korean and Japanese cultures developing independent from the Chinese. Presently China and North Korea are communist countries, however China has developed a hybrid system that allows some free enterprise. Japan and South Korea are democratic countries with thriving economies. Religion is varied within the region, and includes Buddhism, Taoism, Shinto and the philosophy of Confucianism.

South Asia includes the countries of India, Pakistan, Bangladesh, Nepal, and Sri Lanka. This area is the most densely populated region of the world, and contains around 1.6 billion people. The predominant religion is Hinduism, especially in India, although there is a long and rich Muslim culture as well, particularly in Pakistan. India, the largest nation in the region, came under British rule in the 19th Century and gained independence in 1947. British culture has contributed to the region significantly. Movies are a popular form of entertainment, and India is the second largest producer of motion pictures after the US.

Southeast Asia includes the countries of Thailand, Vietnam, Cambodia, and Laos on the mainland of Asia, and Indonesia, the Philippines, Malaysia and Singapore off the shore of Asia. The mainland countries have been heavily influenced by the proximity of China and are mainly Buddhist, with several other faiths observed. Indonesia is the world's most populous Muslim country, and the Philippines is mainly Christian.

Australia and New Zealand are two former British colonies that have much in common with western European and American cultures. Aboriginal culture has influenced the region, but these people are now in the minority.

Skill 29.16 Analyze ways in which particular contemporary societies reflect historical events.

Human characteristics of a place include the architecture, roads, patterns of settlement and land use. These characteristics can be shaped by conditions of the past that affect how humans interact with the geography of their home. The relative wealth and poverty of a person or a community can determine the type of architecture encountered, for example. A formerly poor area that finds prosperity may demolish older, less desirable buildings and replace them with newer ones. Likewise, a formerly prosperous area that falls on hard times may still be living among older buildings, lacking the resources to replace them.

Land use in the past can affect settlement patterns. Small villages often arose among open agricultural areas, and as agriculture gave way to industry, these villages emerged into towns and cities even though their original reason for existing had passed. The narrow, wandering streets of Greenwich Village in Manhattan, for instance, are remnants of the country lanes that existed before New York City expanded into the area, replacing the lanes with paved streets.

Language and religion are also human characteristics that define a place. These social aspects of a place are greatly affected by traditions of the region, but can also be influenced by other regions through colonial settlement or conquest. For example, present day Central and South America are largely Spanish-speaking and Roman Catholic, a result of the region having been conquered and colonized by Spain in the sixteenth century.

COMPETENCY 30.0 GEOGRAPHY

Skill 30.1   Understand and apply the geographic concept of region.

A **landform** comprises a geomorphological unit. Landforms are categorized by characteristics such as elevation, slope, orientation, stratification, rock exposure, and soil type. Landforms include berms, mounds, hills, cliffs, valleys, and others. Oceans and continents exemplify highest-order landforms. Landform elements are parts of a landform that can be further identified. The generic landform elements are: pits, peaks, channels, ridges, passes, pools, planes etc, and can be often extracted from a digital elevation model using some automated or semi-automated techniques.

Elementary landforms (segments, facets, relief units) are the smallest homogeneous divisions of the land surface, at the given scale/resolution. A plateau or a hill can be observed at various scales ranging from few hundred meters to hundreds of kilometers. Hence, the spatial distribution of landforms is often fuzzy and scale-dependent as is the case for soils and geological strata.

A number of factors, ranging from plate tectonics to erosion and deposition can generate and affect landforms. Biological factors can also influence landforms—see for example the role of plants in the development of dune systems and salt marshes, and the work of corals and algae in the formation of coral reefs.

The earth's surface is made up of 70% water and 30% land. Physical features of the land surface include mountains, hills, plateaus, valleys, and plains. Other minor landforms include deserts, deltas, canyons, mesas, basins, foothills, marshes and swamps. Earth's water features include oceans, seas, lakes, rivers, and canals.

Mountains are landforms with rather steep slopes at least 2,000 feet or more above sea level. Mountains are found in groups called mountain chains or mountain ranges. At least one range can be found on six of the earth's seven continents. North America has the Appalachian and Rocky Mountains; South America the Andes; Asia the Himalayas; Australia the Great Dividing Range; Europe the Alps; and Africa the Atlas, Ahaggar, and Drakensburg Mountains. Mountains are commonly formed by volcanic activity, or when land is thrust upward where two tectonic plates collide.

Hills are elevated landforms rising to an elevation of about 500 to 2000 feet. They are found everywhere on earth including Antarctica where they are covered by ice.

Plateaus are elevated landforms usually level on top. Depending on location, they range from being an area that is very cold to one that is cool and healthful. Some plateaus are dry because they are surrounded by mountains that keep out any moisture. Some examples include the Kenya Plateau in East Africa, which is very cool. The plateau extending north from the Himalayas is extremely dry while those in Antarctica and Greenland are covered with ice and snow. Plateaus can be formed by underground volcanic activity, erosion, or colliding tectonic plates.

Plains are described as areas of flat or slightly rolling land, usually lower than the landforms next to them. Sometimes called lowlands (and sometimes located along **seacoasts)** they support the majority of the world's people. Some are found inland and many have been formed by large rivers. This resulted in extremely fertile soil for successful cultivation of crops and numerous large settlements of people. In North America, the vast plains areas extend from the Gulf of Mexico north to the Arctic Ocean and between the Appalachian and Rocky Mountains. In Europe, rich plains extend east from Great Britain into central Europe on into the Siberian region of Russia. Plains in river valleys are found in China (the Yangtze River valley), India (the Ganges River valley), and Southeast Asia (the Mekong River valley).

Valleys are land areas that are found between hills and mountains. Some have gentle slopes containing trees and plants; others have very steep walls and are referred to as canyons. One famous example is Arizona's Grand Canyon of the Colorado River, which was formed by erosion.

Deserts are large dry areas of land receiving ten inches or less of rainfall each year. Among the better known deserts are Africa's large Sahara Desert, the Arabian Desert on the Arabian Peninsula, and the desert Outback covering roughly one third of Australia. Deserts are found mainly in the tropical latitudes, and are formed when surrounding features such as mountain ranges extract most of the moisture from the prevailing winds

Deltas are areas of lowlands formed by soil and sediment deposited at the mouths of rivers. The soil is generally very fertile and most fertile river deltas are important crop-growing areas. One well-known example is the delta of Egypt's Nile River, known for its production of cotton.

Mesas are the flat tops of hills or mountains usually with steep sides. Mesas are similar to plateaus, but smaller.

Basins are considered to be low areas drained by rivers or low spots in mountains.

Foothills are generally considered a low series of hills found between a plain and a mountain range.

Marshes and swamps are wet lowlands providing growth of such plants as rushes and reeds.

Oceans are the largest bodies of water on the planet. The four oceans of the earth are the **Atlantic Ocean**, one-half the size of the Pacific and separating North and South America from Africa and Europe; the **Pacific Ocean**, covering almost one-third of the entire surface of the earth and separating North and South America from Asia and Australia; the **Indian Ocean**, touching Africa, Asia, and Australia; and the ice-filled **Arctic Ocean,** extending from North America and Europe to the North Pole. The waters of the Atlantic, Pacific, and Indian Oceans also touch the shores of Antarctica.

Seas are smaller than oceans and are surrounded by land. Some examples include the Mediterranean Sea found between Europe, Asia, and Africa; and the Caribbean Sea, touching the West Indies, South and Central America. A lake is a body of water surrounded by land. The Great Lakes in North America are a good example.

Rivers, considered a nation's lifeblood, usually begin as very small streams, formed by melting snow and rainfall, flowing from higher to lower land, emptying into a larger body of water, usually a sea or an ocean. Examples of important rivers for the people and countries affected by and/or dependent on them include the Nile, Niger, and Zaire Rivers of Africa; the Rhine, Danube, and Thames Rivers of Europe; the Yangtze, Ganges, Mekong, Hwang He, and Irrawaddy Rivers of Asia; the Murray-Darling in Australia; and the Orinoco in South America. River systems are made up of large rivers and numerous smaller rivers or tributaries flowing into them. Examples include the vast Amazon Rivers system in South America and the Mississippi River system in the United States.

Canals are man-made water passages constructed to connect two larger bodies of water. Famous examples include the **Panama Canal** across Panama's isthmus connecting the Atlantic and Pacific Oceans and the **Suez Canal** in the Middle East between Africa and the Arabian peninsulas connecting the Red and Mediterranean Seas.

Weather is the condition of the air which surrounds the day-to-day atmospheric conditions including temperature, air pressure, wind and moisture or precipitation which includes rain, snow, hail, or sleet. **Climate** is average weather or daily weather conditions for a specific region or location over a long or extended period of time. Studying the climate of an area includes information gathered on the area's monthly and yearly temperatures and its monthly and yearly amounts of precipitation. In addition, a characteristic of an area's climate is the length of its growing season.

Skill 30.2   Know the location and the human and physical characteristics of places and regions in Texas, the United States, and the world.

Refer to Skill 30.8.

Skill 30.3   Analyze ways in which humans adapt to, use, and modify the physical environment.

By nature, people are essentially social creatures. They generally live in communities or settlements of some kind and of some size. Settlements are the cradles of culture, political structure, education, and the management of resources. The relative placement of these settlements or communities is shaped by the proximity to natural resources, the movement of raw materials, the production of finished products, the availability of a work force, and the delivery of finished products. Shared values, language, culture, religion, and subsistence will, at least to some extent, determine the composition of communities.

The theme of human-environmental interaction has three main concepts: humans adapt to the environment (wearing warm clothing in a cold climate, for instance,) humans modify the environment (planting trees to block a prevailing wind, for example,) and humans depend on the environment (for food, water and raw materials.) Environmental and geographic factors have affected the pattern of urban development in Texas and the rest of the US. In turn, urban infrastructure and development patterns are interrelated factors

The growth of suburbs had the effect in many cities of creating a type of economic segregation. Working class people who could not afford new suburban homes and perhaps an automobile to carry them to and from work were relegated to closer, more densely populated areas. Frequently, these areas had to be passed through by those on their way to the suburbs, and rail lines and freeways sometimes bisected these urban communities. Acres of farmland and forest were cleared to make way for growing suburban areas.

Also Refer to Skill 30.10.

Skill 30.4   Know how regional physical characteristics and human modifications to the environment affect people's activities and settlement patterns.

Refer to Skill 30.9.

Skill 30.5 **Analyze ways in which location (absolute and relative) affects people, places, and environments.**

Geography involves studying location and how living things and earth's features are distributed throughout the earth. It includes where animals, people, and plants live and the effects of their relationship with earth's physical features. Geographers also explore the locations of earth's features, how they got there, and why it is so important. Another way to describe where people live is by the **geography** and **topography** around them. The vast majority of people on the planet live in areas that are very hospitable. Yes, people live in the Himalayas and in the Sahara, but the populations in those areas are small indeed when compared to the plains of China, India, Europe, and the United States. People naturally want to live where they won't have to work really hard just to survive, and world population patterns reflect this.

The six themes of geography are:

Location - including relative and absolute location. A relative location refers to the surrounding geography, e.g., "on the banks of the Mississippi River." Absolute location refers to a specific point, such as 41 degrees North latitude, 90 degrees West longitude, or 123 Main Street.

Spatial organization is a description of how things are grouped in a given space. In geographical terms, this can describe people, places, and environments anywhere and everywhere on Earth. The most basic form of spatial organization for people is where they live. The vast majority of people live near other people, in villages and towns and cities and settlements. These people live near others in order to take advantage of the goods and services that naturally arise from cooperation. These villages and towns and cities and settlements are, to varying degrees, near bodies of water.

Place - A place has both human and physical characteristics. Physical characteristics include features such as mountains, rivers, deserts, etc. Human characteristics are the features created by human interaction with their environment such as canals and roads.

Human-Environmental Interaction - The theme of human-environmental interaction has three main concepts: humans adapt to the environment (wearing warm clothing in a cold climate, for instance,) humans modify the environment (planting trees to block a prevailing wind, for example,) and humans depend on the environment (for food, water and raw materials.)

Movement - The theme of movement covers how humans interact with one another through trade, communications, emigration and other forms of interaction.

Regions - A region is an area that has some kind of unifying characteristic, such as a common language, a common government, etc. There are three main types of regions. Formal regions are areas defined by actual political boundaries, such as a city, county, or state. Functional regions are defined by a common function, such as the area covered by a telephone service. Vernacular regions are less formally defined areas that are formed by people's perception, e.g. "the Middle East," and "the South."

Absolute location is the exact whereabouts of a person, place, or thing according to any kind of geographical indicators you want to name. For example, Paris is at 48 degrees north longitude and 2 degrees east latitude.

Relative location, on the other hand, is *always* a description that involves more than one thing. When you describe a relative location, you tell where something is by describing what is around it. The same description of where the nearest post office is in terms of absolute location might be this: "It's down the street from the supermarket, on the right side of the street, next to the dentist's office."

Skill 30.6   Demonstrate knowledge of physical processes and their effects on environmental patterns.

World weather patterns are greatly influenced by ocean surface currents in the upper layer of the ocean. These currents continuously move along the ocean surface in specific directions. Ocean currents that flow deep below the surface are called sub-surface currents. These currents are influenced by such factors as the location of landmasses in the current's path and the earth's rotation.

Climate is average weather or daily weather conditions for a specific region or location over a long or extended period of time. Studying the climate of an area includes information gathered on the area's monthly and yearly temperatures and its monthly and yearly amounts of precipitation. In addition, a characteristic of an area's climate is the length of its growing season.

Natural changes can occur that alter habitats – floods, volcanoes, storms, earthquakes. These changes can affect the species that exist within the habitat, either by causing extinction or by changing the environment in a way that will no longer support the life systems. Climate changes can have similar effects. Inhabiting species can also alter habitats, particularly through migration.

Plate tectonics, is a geological theory that explains **continental drift**, which is the large movements of the solid portions of the Earth's crust floating on the molten mantle. There are ten major tectonic plates, with several smaller plates. There are three types of plate boundaries, convergent, divergent and transform. Convergent boundaries are where plates are moving toward one another. When this happens, the two plates collide and fold up against one another, called **continental collision**, or one plate slides under the other, called **subduction**.

Erosion is the displacement of solid earth surfaces such as rock and soil. Erosion is often a result of wind, water or ice acting on surfaces with loose particles, such as sand, loose soils, or decomposing rock. Gravity can also cause erosion on loose surfaces. Factors such as slope, soil and rock composition, plant cover, and human activity all affect erosion.

Weathering is the natural decomposition of the Earth's surface from contact with the atmosphere. It is not the same as erosion, but can be a factor in erosion. Heat, water, ice and pressure are all factors that can lead to weathering. Chemicals in the atmosphere can also contribute to weathering

Transportation is the movement of eroded material from one place to another by wind, water or ice. Examples of transportation include pebbles rolling down a streambed and boulders being carried by moving glaciers.

Deposition is the result of transportation, and occurs when the material being carried settles on the surface and is deposited. Sand dunes and moraines are formed by transportation and deposition of glacial material.

Skill 30.7   **Understand the characteristics, distribution, and migration of populations in Texas, the United States, and the world.**

Refer to Skill 29.15

Skill 30.8   **Understand the physical environmental characteristics of Texas, the United States, and the world, past and present, and how humans have adapted to and modified the environment.**

The state of Texas has varied geographical features and uses, which have changed over time, depending on who was living where at the time. Among the known settlers have been Native Americans, French, Spanish, and Americans.

The majority of Texas geography is flat farmland. This is very true in West Texas, where the dominant crops are cotton, wheat, and sorghum. The land is semiarid and, for the most part, flat, with the exception of some hills and a mountain range, the Davis Mountains. Oil can be found in West Texas as well, near the Midland-Odessa corridor.

The antebellum and Civil Wartime civilizations in East Texas depended almost entirely on King Cotton, with the various hills and swamps dominated by vast plantations. Cotton's influence can still be felt there, but the dominant crop now is rice. The vast majority of the state's rice comes from this region. Lumber can be found here as well. As in nearly every other part of the state, however, oil is the new king of East Texas.

The Gulf Coast is dominated by Houston, the fourth largest city in the United States. Houston is a port city, capitalizing on an early twentieth century canal to the Gulf of Mexico as a way to ship goods to the world. Indeed, only New York ships more than Houston. The lower Rio Grande area has citrus fruits and winter vegetables in abundance. The rest of the Rio Grande Valley is dotted with cattle ranches, some of them very large indeed.

Further north can be found the blackland prairies, a large range of agriculture and ranch land. Cotton and grain grow here in great numbers, as do cattle. The large cities of Dallas and Fort Worth can be found here. These two cities together form one of the most burgeoning metropolitan areas, with big business in oil refining, grain milling, and cotton processing. The high plains have a somewhat varied landscape, although the semiarid climate falls mostly on flat land. Of note is a dry-farming area near Lubbock, one of the larger cities of the region. Oil, grain, wheat, and cotton are the major industries.

All major cities in Texas play a role in the advancement of modern technology, although Houston, Dallas, and Fort Worth are the leaders in the high-tech arena, as they were during World War II in weapons production. The people who live and have lived in Texas have made the land their own, turning flat, sometimes water-starved lands into vast plantations, ranches, and fields. Large cities have not been confined to waterways (although the state's largest city, Houston, can be found on the Gulf Coast). Dirt roads, railroads, and then paved roads have connected the large state's many, many towns and cities. Nowadays, they are connected by the Information Superhighway.

The most drastic change to the environment wrought by people has been the sheer number of square miles devoted to living space. Texas still maintains vast areas of agricultural and ranch land, but that number is shrinking by the year, as more and more people claim and put stakes down on land designed to be lived on exclusively. The farmers of the past lived on their land but also lived off it. Their houses were part of their farms, and their jobs were working the land. Nowadays, skyscrapers dot the skylines of large cities along with high-rise apartment buildings, which serve no function other than to provide living areas for the people who work on those large cities.

The continental United States is bordered by the Pacific Ocean on the west and the Atlantic Ocean on the east. The country is divided into two main sections by the Rocky Mountains, which extend from New Mexico in the south through the Canadian border on the north. The western portion of the country contains forested, mountainous areas in the Pacific Northwest and Northern California, including Mt. St. Helens, an active volcano in the Cascade Range. Dryer, warmer regions in the south include the Mojave Desert in the Southwest. The Great Salt Lake in Utah is at the foot of the Wasatch Mountains.

The Rocky Mountains slope down in the east to the Great Plains, a large, grassy region drained by the Mississippi River, the nation's largest river, and one of the largest rivers in the world. The Great Plains give way in the east to hilly, forested regions. The Appalachian Mountain chain runs near the eastern coast of the U.S. Along the border with Canada between Minnesota and New York are Lake Huron, Lake Ontario, Lake Michigan, Lake Erie and Lake Superior, known as the Great Lakes.

Alaska is located in northwestern North America and contains Mt. McKinley, also called Denali, which is the highest mountain on the continent. Hawaii is a series of volcanic islands in the South Pacific

Also Refer to Skill 30.1 for further discussion.

Skill 30.9   **Analyze how geographic factors have influenced the settlement patterns, economic development, political relationships, and policies of societies and regions in Texas, the United States, and the world.**

The varied geography of Texas has produced some vastly different settlement patterns, economic developments, and political conflicts over the hundreds of years that people have been migrating to the area
The vast plains of central and western Texas are perfect for agricultural and ranch land, and that's what they have become. Among the areas that are inhabited and/or controlled by humans, wheat, cotton, sorghum, and cattle are the top-producing industries. The farms are big and the ranches bigger. The relative flatness of the land contributes to a sense of shared hardship, since one rancher can usually see the lands of his neighbor, even if they are far away. This also means, of course, that the potential for land disputes is high, even today.

East Texas is similar in a way, in that huge rice fields dot the landscape, with corresponding towns built up around them.

The Gulf Coast is definitely known for its oil and its ports Nearly all of the state's myriad products flow out through one or a handful of the state's Gulf Coast ports. Oil can be found in many places in the state, not just on the Gulf Coast. Texas is known for its oil production and its oil exports, particularly in the west part of the state.

The larger cities of Texas—Houston, Austin, Dallas, and Fort Worth, most noticeably—are known for their dedication to high tech. Many Internet and computer companies make their home in Texas, and the state is a leader in scientific development efforts as well.

Politics throughout the history of the state have been contentious. Early on, it was the Americans versus the Mexicans, as American settlers encroached on previously Mexican-owned territories and settled in for the long haul. After Mexico gave up all claims to Texas, a reverse immigration took place. This people movement is still taking place, some years more than ever. The vast agricultural lands of Texas cry out for cheap labor, and many Mexican residents are only too happy to cross the border and supply it. The question of legal vs. illegal immigrants continues to be a huge policy debate today. (This is the case in other states as well but more so in Texas because it shares such a long border with Mexico.)

Another source of contention is the struggle between the ranch politics of yesteryear and the high-tech politics of today. Farmers and ranchers obviously have different interests than atomic scientists, and these different interests often clash. In a sense, geography is driving all of this, since farmers and ranchers have their concerns largely because of their location and urban parties gain their perspectives from their environments, which are much more metropolitan. Oil continues to be a staggeringly large business in Texas, and oil interests often clash with those of other industries.

Skill 30.10 Analyze interactions between people and the physical environment and the effects of these interactions on the development of places and regions.

Environmental and geographic factors have affected the pattern of urban development in Texas and the rest of the US. In turn, urban infrastructure and development patterns are interrelated factors.

The growth of urban areas is often linked to the advantages provided by its geographic location. Before the advent of efficient overland routes of commerce such as railroads and highways, water provided the primary means of transportation of commercial goods. Most large American cities are situated along bodies of water.

As **transportation** technology advanced, the supporting infrastructure was built to connect cities with one another and to connect remote areas to larger communities. The railroad, for example, allowed for the quick transport of agricultural products from rural areas to urban centers. This newfound efficiency not only further fueled the growth of urban centers, it changed the economy of rural America. Where once farmers had practiced only subsistence farming – growing enough to support one's own family – the new infrastructure meant that one could convert agricultural products into cash by selling them at market.

For urban dwellers, improvements in building technology and advances in transportation allowed for larger cities. Growth brought with it a new set of problems unique to each location. The bodies of water that had made the development of cities possible in their early days also formed natural barriers to growth. Further infrastructure in the form of bridges, tunnels and ferry routes were needed to connect central urban areas with outlying communities.

In the modern age, advancements in **telecommunications** infrastructure may have an impact on urban growth patterns as information can pass instantly and freely between almost any two points on the globe, allowing access to some aspects of urban life to those in remote areas.

Cities are the major hubs of human settlement. Almost half of the population of the world now lives in cities. These percentages are much higher in developed regions. Established cities continue to grow. The fastest growth, however, is occurring in developing areas. While European and North American cities tend to be well linked both by transportation and communication connections, there are other places in the world in which communication between the cities of the country may be inferior to communication with the rest of the world.

Natural resources are naturally occurring substances that are considered valuable in their natural form. A commodity is generally considered a natural resource when the primary activities associated with it are extraction and purification, as opposed to creation. Thus, mining, petroleum extraction, fishing, and forestry are generally considered natural-resource industries, while agriculture is not.

Natural resources are often classified into **renewable** and **non-renewable resources**. Renewable resources are generally living resources (fish, coffee, and forests, for example), which can restock (renew) themselves if they are not over-harvested. Renewable resources can restock themselves and be used indefinitely if they are sustained. Once renewable resources are consumed at a rate that exceeds their natural rate of replacement, the standing stock will diminish and eventually run out. The rate of sustainable use of a renewable resource is determined by the replacement rate and amount of standing stock of that particular resource. Non-living renewable natural resources include soil, as well as water, wind, tides and solar radiation. Natural resources include soil, timber, oil, minerals, and other goods taken more or less as they are from the Earth.

Deforestation or clear cutting is of particular concern in rainforest regions, which hold most of the Earth's natural biodiversity - irreplaceable genetic natural capital. Conservation of natural resources is the major focus of Natural Capitalism, environmentalism, the ecology movement, and Green Parties. Some view this depletion as a major source of social unrest and conflicts in developing nations.

Environmental policy is concerned with the sustainability of the earth, the region under the administration of the governing group or individual or a local habitat. The concern of environmental policy is the preservation of the region, habitat or ecosystem. Because humans, both individually and in community, live upon the earth, draw upon the natural resources of the earth, and affect the environment in many ways, environmental and social policy must be mutually supportive.

COMPETENCY 31.0 ECONOMICS

Skill 31.1   Understand that basic human needs are met in many ways.

Consumer economics refers to how consumers make their decisions and the role consumer decision-making plays in a capitalist economy. Consumers buy the goods and services that give them satisfaction, or utility. They want to obtain the most utility they can for their dollar. The quantity of goods and services that consumers are willing and able to purchase at different prices during a given period of time is referred to as **demand**. Aggregating all of the individual demands yields the market demand for a good or service.

Consumers do not have enough time and money to do everything that they want and to buy everything that they want. **Time** and **money** are scarce resources. If a consumer spends his time doing one activity, he is sacrificing another activity. For example, if the consumer spends the afternoon playing golf, he is sacrificing doing the garden work.

Scarcity is evident in personal financial management. Scarcity here refers to dollars and paying bills. The buying of one good means sacrificing another good. This is the concept of **opportunity cost**. The consumer has to decide which goods give him the most satisfaction for his dollars. There are only so many dollars available. Just as consumers have to choose how to spend their time, they also have to choose how to spend their dollars. Scarcity means that consumers can't have all of the goods that they want. This is true on both a micro and a macro level. Scarcity affects the decision making of all economic agents. Scarcity means that choices have to be made by all. Producing more of one good means that there aren't enough resources to produce other goods. That is the constraint of a fixed supply of resources. This is the relationship given in the Production Possibilities Curve. Every point on the curve represents the different combinations that the economy can have of the two goods, given their supply or resources and that they are producing efficiently. The curve shows the trade-off between the two goods, or the opportunity cost imposed on society by the fact that resources are scarce.

This means that households, businesses and governments, in addition to society as a whole, must make decisions and choices within this framework. There are only so many resources that can be devoted to the production of consumption goods for households. Households have to decide which goods they want within those parameters. A limited budget means they can't afford to buy both a new car and a new house. So which do they buy? Whichever gives them the most satisfaction.

Skill 31.2   Understand and apply knowledge of basic economic concepts.

Economics is the study of how a society allocates its scarce resources to satisfy what are basically unlimited and competing wants. A fundamental fact of economics is that resources are scarce and that wants are infinite. The fact that scarce resources have to satisfy unlimited wants means that choices have to be made. If society uses its resources to produce good A then it doesn't have those resources to produce good B. More of good A means less of good B. This trade-off is referred to as the opportunity cost, or the value of the sacrificed alternative.

Economic systems refer to the arrangements a society has devised to answer what are known as the Three Questions: What goods to produce, How to produce the goods, and For Whom are the goods being produced, or how is the allocation of the output determined. Different economic systems answer these questions in different ways A **market economy** answers these questions in terms of demand and supply and the use of markets. **Demand** is based on consumer preferences and satisfaction and refers to the quantities of a good or service buyers are willing and able to buy at different prices during a given period of time. **Supply** is based on costs of production and refers to the quantities sellers are willing and able to sell at different prices during a given period of time. The determination of market equilibrium price is where the buying decisions of buyers coincide with the selling decision of sellers

Consumers vote for the products they want with their spending. Goods acquiring enough dollar votes are profitable, signaling to the producers that society wants their scarce resources used in this way. This is how the "What" question is answered. The producer then hires inputs in accordance with the goods consumers want, looking for the most efficient or lowest cost method of production. The lower the firm's costs for any given level of revenue, the higher the firm's profits. This is the way in which the "How" question is answered in a market economy.   The "For Whom" question is answered in the marketplace by the determination of the equilibrium price. Price serves to ration the good to those who can and will transact at the market price or better. Those who can't or won't are excluded from the market. This mechanism results in market efficiency or obtaining the most output from the available inputs that are consistent with the preferences of consumers. Society's scarce resources are being used the way society wants them to be used.

Skill 31.3   Demonstrate knowledge of the ways in which people organize economic systems, and similarities and differences among various economic systems around the world.

Economic systems refer to the arrangements a society has devised to answer what are known as the Three Questions: What goods to produce, How to produce the goods, and For Whom are the goods being produced, or how is the allocation of the output determined. Different economic systems answer these questions in different ways. These are the different "isms" that exist that define the method of resource and output allocation.

A market economy answers these questions in terms of demand and supply and the use of markets. Consumers vote for the products they want with their dollar spending. Goods acquiring enough dollar votes are profitable, signaling to the producers that society wants their scarce resources used in this way. This is how the "What" question is answered. The producer then hires inputs in accordance with the goods consumers wants, looking for the most efficient or lowest cost method of production. The lower the firm's costs for any given level of revenue, the higher the firm's profits. This is the way in which the "How" question is answered in a market economy. The "For Whom" question is answered in the marketplace by the determination of the equilibrium price. Price serves to ration the good to those who can and will transact at the market price of better. Those who can't or won't are excluded from the market. The United States has a market economy.

The opposite of the **market economy** is called the **centrally planned economy**. This used to be called Communism, even though the term in not correct in a strict Marxian sense. In a planned economy, the means of production are publicly owned, with little, if any public ownership. Instead of the Three Questions being solved by markets, they have a planning authority that makes the decisions in place of markets. The planning authority decides what will be produced and how. Since most planned economies directed resources into the production of capital and military goods, there was little remaining for consumer goods and the result was chronic shortages. Price functioned as an accounting measure and did not reflect scarcity. The former Soviet Union and most of the Eastern Bloc countries were planned economies of this sort. In between the two extremes is **market socialism.** This is a mixed economic system that uses both markets and planning. Planning is usually used to direct resources at the upper levels of the economy, with markets being used to determine prices of consumer goods and wages. This kind of economic system answers the three questions with planning and markets. The former Yugoslavia was a market socialist economy.

Skill 31.4   Understand the value and importance of work and purposes for spending and saving money.

In the two markets, inputs and outputs are exchanged and paid for by households and businesses. Factor owners sell their factors to employers in the input market. Firms use those factors to produce outputs that are sold in the output market. This is where factors owners spend their incomes on goods and services. Receipts for goods and services flow from households to businesses and factor incomes flow from businesses to households.

The means of payment, whether it is barter, currency or credit do not affect the above flows they are just different ways in which the money can flow through the economy. Barter refers to the exchange of one good for another good. A barter transaction would be a painter painting a mechanic's house in exchange for the mechanic repairing the painter's car. The monetary value of these transactions would be represented by the flows through the circular flow diagram. The goods are the painting and the car repair work, the factor flows are the labor services of the painter and the mechanic. The value of the labor services represents the factor incomes and the value of the painting and repairs represent the receipts for goods and services. If currency were used instead of barter, there would be actual dollars flowing through the input and output markets between the households and the businesses, as portrayed in the first paragraph.

Payment by use of credit does not alter any of the relationships either. Credit cards just allow the consumers to spend beyond their incomes. So there is more output purchased and more dollars flowing to producers from credit card companies with households making their payments to credit card companies. The credit card companies are more or less acting as an intermediary facilitating the flow of money through the economy.

All markets function to effect an efficient allocation of resources, even financial markets. These markets also function on the basis of supply and demand and serve to allocate loanable funds to those who are willing to transact at the market price. The market price of loanable funds is the interest rate. The supply of loanable funds come from savings. Since savings represent dollars of postponed spending, households have to have some form of inducement to save. They have to be compensated in some way to postpone their spending and holding dollars in the form of savings. This inducement or payment for savings dollars is the interest rate. The higher the interest rate is the more dollars households will be willing to save. The interest rate is an opportunity cost. At higher interest rates, the opportunity cost of not saving dollars is higher than at lower interest rates. Thus, the supply of loanable funds curve is upward sloping.

Loanable funds are needed for investment purposes by businesses and by individuals. Borrowers are willing to pay a price for the funds they borrow. This price is the interest rate. Borrowers want more funds at lower interest rates than they do at higher interest rates. This means that the demand for loanable funds curve is downward sloping. We now have the downward sloping demand for loanable funds curve and the upward sloping supply of loanable funds curve. If we put the two curves together, we have market equilibrium at the point of intersection of demand and supply. This gives the equilibrium rate of interest that equates the quantity demanded and quantity supplied of loanable funds. Lenders and borrowers willing and able to transact at that interest rate are included in the market. Lenders and borrowers who can't or won't transact at that interest rate are excluded from the market. The market interest rate performs an allocative function just as a market price does. The interest rate will adjust to guarantee the equality of quantity demanded and quantity supplied, keeping the market in equilibrium.

Since investment is a component of GDP, the financial markets and their stability are an important part of the economy. Economies need investment funds in order to grow. Economies with higher rates of savings have higher rates of investment and therefore higher growth rates. When households save and delay consumption, they are freeing resources for other uses, principally for investment. This is what leads to economic growth. Economies with low rates of savings are economies that don't domestically supply enough funds for investment purposes. These are economies that have lower growth rates because they don't have the investment funds required for growth. The banking sector, with its financial markets is very important for economies. Without a well-developed banking center there is no mechanism for savings and therefore no investment funds for economic growth.

Skill 31.5 Demonstrate knowledge of patterns of work and economic activities in Texas, the United States, and the world, past and present.

Mexico controlled Texas for many years and there were few problems until they began to limit migration into Texas as the U.S. expanded westward. Mexico refused to allow slavery in Texas. Texas entered the Union as a free state in 1845. Cattle and livestock and agriculture were important factors in the development of Texas with its wide open spaces. As the nation developed, so did Texas. Many of the cities began as trading posts and then developed. Railroads and other modes of transportation aided the growth of the cities. Dallas became a focal point for grain and cotton trade and was a stop off point for western migration. Houston was a center for the sugar trade. Texas also became a major oil producing state, which resulted in the creation of many jobs and the infrastructure to support such an industry. In the 1940s major companies began to relocate to Texas providing even more jobs. Houston has its major port and is a center for the oil and aeronautics industry.

The United States and Texas both have a history based on immigration. These immigrants settled in various parts of the country, assimilated, and contributed greatly to the development of the United States and to Texas. Texas's history is rich with settlements by the Spanish. Texas also has a diverse commercial and resource base with the oil and aerospace industries. Its agricultural area extends throughout the state

Each group has different issues that are important to them. Agricultural areas are more concerned with issues pertaining to immigration and farm policy. Industrial workers are concerned mostly with issues of wages and benefits. The state's history is also rich in Spanish and Mexican culture. Understanding the history of Texas illustrates how all of these different cultures and industries came into being and how the state is diverse enough to accommodate all of them.

Skill 31.6   Understand the characteristics, benefits, and development of the free enterprise system in Texas and the United States.

The free enterprise system in Texas developed as it did in the rest of the United States. In a market economy the markets function on the basis of supply and demand and, if markets are free, the result is an efficient allocation of resources. Please refer to **Skills 31.1 and 31.2** for further discussion of supply and demand.

Consumers are basically voting for the goods and services they want with their dollar spending. When a good accumulates enough dollar votes, the producer earns a profit. The existence of profits is the way the market signals the seller that he is using society's resources in a way that society wants them used. Consumers are obtaining the most satisfaction that they can from the way their society's scarce resources are being used. When consumers don't want a good or service, they don't purchase it and the producer doesn't accumulate enough dollar votes to have profits. Losses are the markets' way of signaling that consumers don't want their scarce resources used in the production of that particular good or service. They want their resources used in some other manner. Firms that incur losses eventually go out of business. They either have a product that consumers don't want or they have an inefficient production process that results in higher costs, and therefore higher prices. Higher costs than the competitors' means that there an inefficiency in production. All of this occurs naturally in markets in a market economy.

Skill 31.7   Analyze the roles of producers and consumers in the production of goods and services.

Free enterprise, individual entrepreneurship, competitive markets and consumer sovereignty are all parts of a market economy. Individuals have the right to make their own decisions as to what they want to do as a career. The financial incentives are there for individuals who are willing to take the risk. A successful venture earns profit. It is these financial incentives that motivate inventors and small businesses. The same is true for businesses. They are free to determine what production technique they want to use and what output they want to produce within the confines of the legal system. They can make investments based on their own decisions. Competitive markets, relatively free from government interference are also a manifestation of the freedom that the U.S. economic system is based on. These markets function on the basis of supply and demand to determine output mix and resource allocation. Since consumers buy the goods and services that give them satisfaction, this means that, for the most part, they don't buy the goods and services that they don't want that don't give them satisfaction. Consumers are, in effect, voting for the goods and services they want with the dollars or what is called dollar voting. Consumers are basically signaling firms as to how they want society's scarce resources used with their dollar votes. A good that society wants acquires enough dollar votes for the producer to experience profits – a situation where the firm's revenues exceed the firm's costs. The existence of profits indicate to the firm that it is producing the goods and services consumers want and that society's scarce resources are being used in accordance with consumer preferences. When a firm does not have a profitable product, it is because that product is not tabulating enough dollar votes of consumers. Consumers don't want the good or service and they don't want society's scarce resources being used in its production.

This process where consumers vote with their dollars is called consumer sovereignty. Consumers are basically directing the allocation of scarce resources in the economy with dollar spending. Firms, who are in business to earn profit, then hire resources, or inputs, in accordance with consumer preferences. This is the way resources are allocated in a market economy. This is the way society achieves the output mix that it desires.

Skill 31.8   Demonstrate knowledge of how businesses operate in the U.S. free enterprise system.

The fundamental characteristics of the U.S. economic system are the uses of competition and markets. Profit and competition all go together in the U.S. economic system. Competition is determined by market structure. Since the cost curves are the same for all the firms, the only difference comes from the revenue side. The most competitive of all market structures is perfect competition, characterized by numerous buyers and sellers, all with perfect knowledge. No one seller is big enough to influence price so the firm is a price taker. Products are homogenous so buyers are indifferent as to whom they buy from. The absence of barriers to entry makes it easy for firms to enter and leave the industry.

At the other end of the spectrum is monopoly, the only seller of a unique product. Barriers to entry are significant enough to keep firms from entering or leaving the industry. In monopolistic competition firms sell similar products in an industry with low barriers to entry, making it easy for firms to enter and leave the industry.

Oligopoly is a market structure with a few large firms selling heterogeneous or homogeneous product in a market structure with the strength of barriers to entry varying. Each firm maximizes profit by producing at the point where marginal cost equal marginal revenue. The existence of economic profits, an above-normal rate of return, attracts capital to an industry and result in expansion. Whether or not new firms can enter depends on barriers to entry. Firms can enter easily in perfect competition and the expansion will continue until economic profits are eliminated and firms earn a normal rate of return. The significant barriers to entry in monopoly serve to keep firms out so the monopolist continues to earn an above-normal rate of return. Some firms will be able to enter in monopolistic competition but won't have a monopoly over the existing firm's brand name. The competitiveness of the market structure determines whether new firms or capital can enter in response to profits.

Profit functions as a financial incentive for individuals and firms. The possibility of earning profit is why individuals are willing to undertake entrepreneurial ventures and why firms are willing to spend money on research and development and innovation. Without these kinds of financial incentives, there wouldn't be new product development or technological advancement.

Skill 31.9   Apply knowledge of the effects of supply and demand on consumers and producers in a free-enterprise system.

A market is technically whatever mechanism there is that brings buyers and sellers in contact with each other so they can buy and sell. Buyers and sellers do not have to meet face to face. When the consumer buys a good from a catalog or through the Internet, the buyer never comes face to face with the seller, yet both buyer and seller are part of a bona fide market. Markets exist in both the input and output sides of the economy. The input market is the market in which factors of production, or resources, are bought and sold.
Factors of production, or inputs, fall into four broad categories: land, labor, capital and entrepreneurship.

The supply curve represents the selling and production decisions of the seller and is based on the costs of production. The costs of production of a product are based on the costs of the resources used in its production. The costs of resources are based on the scarcity of the resource. The scarcer a resource is, relatively speaking, the higher its price. A diamond costs more than paper because diamonds are scarcer than paper is. All of these concepts are embodied in the seller's supply curve.   Where the demand and supply curves intersect is where the buying decisions of buyers are equal to the selling decisions of sellers. The quantity that buyers want to buy at a particular price is equal to the quantity that sellers want to sell at that particular price. The market is in equilibrium.

What happens when there is a change? Suppose a new big oil field is found. Also suppose there is a technology that allows its recovery and refining at a fraction of the present costs. The result is a big increase in the supply of oil at lower costs, as reflected by a rightward shifting oil supply curve. Oil is used as an input into almost all production. Firms now have lower costs. This means the firm can produce the same amount of output at a lower cost or can produce a larger amount of output at the same cost. The result is a rightward shift of the firm's, and therefore, the industry supply curve. This means sellers are willing and able to offer for sale larger quantities of output at each price. Assuming buyers buying decisions stay the same, there is a new market equilibrium, or new point of intersection of the shifted supply curve with the buyers' demand curve. The result is a lower price with a larger quantity of output. The market has achieved a new equilibrium based on the increase in the quantity of a resource.

In a market-oriented economy, all of these markets function on the basis of supply and demand, whether they are input or output markets. The equilibrium price is determined where the buying decisions of buyers coincide with the selling decision of sellers. This is true whether the market in an input market with a market rate of wage or an output markets with a market price of the output. This results in the most efficient allocation of resources.

Skill 31.10 Demonstrate knowledge of categories of economic activities and methods used to measure a society's economic level.

Macroeconomics refers to the functioning of the economy on the national level and the functioning of the aggregate units that comprise the national economy. It is concerned with a study of the economy's overall economic performance, or what is called the Gross Domestic Product or GDP. The GDP is a monetary measure of the economy's output during a specified time period. Tabulating the economy's output can be measured in two ways, both of which give the same result: the expenditures approach and the incomes approach. Basically, what is spent on the national output by each sector of the economy is equal to what is earned producing the national output by each of the factors of production. The two methods must be equal.

The macro economy consists of four broad sectors: consumers, businesses, government and the foreign sector. In the expenditures approach, GDP is determined by the amount of spending in each sector. GDP is equal to the consumption expenditures of consumers plus the investment expenditures of businesses plus spending of all three levels of government plus the net export spending in the foreign sector.

$$GDP = C + I + G + (X-M)$$

The above formula is called the *GDP identity*. The computation of GDP includes only final goods and services, not the value of intermediate goods. An intermediate good is a good that is used in the production of other goods. It is an input and its value is included in the price of the final good. If the value of intermediate goods is included, there would be double counting and GDP would be overstated.

What is spent buying the national output must be equal to what is earned in producing the national output. This basically involves computing the incomes of the four factors with several adjustments being made. Labor earns wages, which is called Compensation of Employees. Land earns Rental Income and capital earns Interest Income. Since entrepreneurial ability can be in the form of individual effort or corporations, there are two different categories here. The return to the individual entrepreneur is called Proprietor's Income. The return to the corporation is called Corporate Profit. Corporations do three things with their profits; they pay the corporate profits tax, they pay dividends and the rest is kept as retained earnings. So these are the three components of corporate profits. To complete the tabulation of GDP from the incomes approach, we have to adjust for two non-income charges. First are Indirect Business Taxes, like property taxes and sales taxes. Second is depreciation or the amount of capital that is worn out producing the current term's output. Both Indirect Business Taxes and depreciation are subtracted and the figure remaining is GDP. This figure is identical to the figure computed in the expenditures approach.

Skill 31.11   Use economic indicators to describe and measure levels of economic activity.

Most measures of economic output are expressed in terms of dollars. The purchasing power of the dollar can change due to inflation and economic growth. Therefore, the price level and the purchasing power of the dollar are very important. Comparing output figures like Gross Domestic Product over the years shows fluctuations from year to year. Are these fluctuations due to actual differences in the level of output, or are they due to inflation and changes in the price level? There is no way to know unless the figures are expressed in terms of constant dollars. This is a way of adjusting for inflation or controlling for the changes in the value of the dollar. Real GDP or constant dollar GDP is GDP adjusted for inflation. Nominal, current dollar or unadjusted GDP refers to GDP figures in dollars that have not been adjusted for inflation.

The construction and use of the GDP deflator is rather simple. The first step is to select one year to be the base year and then use that year to construct the price index. It doesn't matter what year is selected as long as the information is stated. The formula is very simple.

$$\text{Price Index} = \frac{\text{Price in any year}}{\text{Price in base year}} \times 100$$

This index number then is used to compute the real GDP figure. The formula is given below:

$$\text{Real GDP} = \frac{\text{Nominal GDP}}{\text{Index Number}}$$

The above formula takes the GDP figure for any year and expresses it in base year dollars. Now perusing a column of GDP figures over any period of time has all of them expressed in dollars that have the same value as the dollar has in the base year. That's why it doesn't matter which year is used as the base year. Any differences in GDP are the result of real changes in the level of output and not due to changes in the dollar's value. Now meaningful comparisons can be made between the years. Economists never want to work with raw unadjusted data. You can look at the figures over the years but they are literally meaningless because you don't know if the changes are from actual output levels or changes in the dollar.

You will rarely have to construct your own price index and GDP deflator. Data figures are usually reported both ways and will say so in a footnote or somewhere around the table. The base year used will be reported somewhere near the figures. When you use these output figures, you must state whether they are adjusted or unadjusted, and if the figures are adjusted, what is used as the base year. If you are working with unadjusted figures, you must state that fact and be very careful of any inferences and conclusion you draw.

Real GDP, the unemployment rate and the inflation rate are economic indicators. They are revealing what is happening in the economy, how poorly or how well it is doing. Inflation refers to a rise in the general level of prices which causes a decrease in the purchasing power of the dollar. This basically means that one dollar does not buy as much as it did before. Policy makers need information on inflation because it calls for contractionary policies in an economy that is expanding too rapidly. Any year in the series can be selected as the base year and it is then used to compute the index number for the rest of the years, as given in the above formula.

The index numbers are then used to compute the inflation rate using the formula below:

$$\text{Inflation Rate} = \frac{\text{this year's index \# - last years index \#}}{\text{Last year's index \#}}$$

The unemployment rate refers to the percentage of the labor force that is unemployed, or:

$$\text{Unemployment Rate} = \frac{\text{Number of People Unemployed}}{\text{Number of People in Labor Force}} \times 100$$

The labor force is not one hundred percent of the population. It includes people who are capable of working and are willing to work and are either working or actively seeking employment. Excluded are people who can't work (under age sixteen, institutionalized) or who could work but chose not to work, like stay at home moms, full-time students, and retirees. The labor force is roughly one-half of the population.

Real GDP figures, along with the unemployment figures tell us the state of the economy. An economy in a recession needs to be stimulated with expansionary monetary and fiscal policy; just as an economy that is expanding too rapidly and with inflation needs to be slowed down with contractionary monetary and fiscal policy. Economists and government policy makers can work with the figures and determine the strength of the policy that is needed. They also watch the unemployment, inflation and GDP figures to ascertain whether the policy is working, and, if not, what else needs to be done.

Skill 31.12   Understand major events and trends in economic history.

The Agricultural Revolution, initiated by the invention of the plow, led to a thoroughgoing transformation of human society by making large-scale agricultural production possible and facilitating the development of agrarian societies. During the period during which the plow was invented, the wheel, numbers, and writing were also invented. Coinciding with the shift from hunting wild game to the domestication of animals, this period was one of dramatic social and economic change.

Settled communities that produce the necessities of life are self-supporting. Advances in agricultural technology and the ability to produce a surplus of produce create two opportunities: first, the opportunity to trade the surplus goods for other desired goods, and second, the vulnerability to others who steal those goods. Protecting domesticated livestock and surplus, as well as stored, crops becomes an issue for the community. This, in turn, leads to the construction of walls and other fortifications around the community.

The ability to produce surplus crops creates the opportunity to trade or barter with other communities in exchange for desired goods. Traders and trade routes begin to develop between villages and cities. The domestication of animals expands the range of trade and facilitates an exchange of ideas and knowledge.

The Industrial Revolution of the eighteenth and nineteenth centuries resulted in even greater changes in human civilization and even greater opportunities for trade, increased production, and the exchange of ideas and knowledge.

The first phase of the Industrial Revolution (1750-1830) saw the mechanization of the textile industry, vast improvements in mining, with the invention of the steam engine, and numerous improvements in transportation, with the development and improvement of turnpikes, canals, and the invention of the railroad.

The second phase (1830-1910) resulted in vast improvements in a number of industries that had already been mechanized through such inventions as the Bessemer steel process and the invention of steam ships. New industries arose as a result of the new technological advances, such as photography, electricity, and chemical processes. New sources of power were harnessed and applied, including petroleum and hydroelectric power. Precision instruments were developed and engineering was launched. It was during this second phase that the industrial revolution spread to other European countries, to Japan, and to the United States.

The direct results of the industrial revolution, particularly as they affected industry, commerce, and agriculture, included:

- Enormous increase in productivity
- Huge increase in world trade
- Specialization and division of labor
- Standardization of parts and mass production
- Growth of giant business conglomerates and monopolies
- A new revolution in agriculture facilitated by the steam engine, machinery, chemical fertilizers, processing, canning, and refrigeration

The social results of the Industrial Revolution include:

- Increase of population, especially in industrial centers
- Advances in science applied to agriculture, sanitation and medicine
- Growth of great cities
- Disappearance of the difference between city dwellers and farmers
- Faster tempo of life and increased stress from the monotony of the work routine

Increased mobility produced a rapid diffusion of knowledge and ideas. Increased mobility also resulted in wide-scale immigration to industrialized countries. Cultures clashed and cultures melded. As the economy grew and developed and expanded north, south and westward, the areas developed in different ways. The southern states developed economies based on slave labor as the nation expanded southward. The vast plantations required a cheap source of labor to make the South's exports low priced in world markets. Westward expansion was based on family occupation of farms that didn't need slaves to operate them. The North and the South developed in different ways which brought them into conflict over the issue of slavery. This led to different patterns of economic activity in the different areas of the country.

Skill 31.13   Analyze the interdependence of the Texas economy with the United States and the world.

Texas is a part of the U.S. economy just as other states. Texas interacts with other states and the national government through trade and commerce in the same way that other states do. In today's world, markets are international. Nations are all part of a global economy. No nation exists in isolation or is totally independent of other nations. Isolationism is referred to as autarky or a closed economy. Membership is a global economy means that what one nation does affects other nations because economies are linked through international trade, commerce and finance. They all have open economies. International transactions affect the levels of income, employment and prices in each of the trading economies. The relative importance of trade is based on what percentage of Gross Domestic Product trade constitutes. In a country like the United States, trade represents only a few percent of GDP. In other nations, trade may represent over fifty percent of GDP. For those countries changes in international transactions can cause many economic fluctuations and problems.

Trade barriers are a way in which economic problems are caused in other countries. Suppose the domestic government is confronted with rising unemployment in the domestic industry due to cheaper foreign imports. Consumers are buying the cheaper foreign import instead of the higher priced domestic good. In order to protect domestic labor, government imposes a tariff, thus raising the price of the more efficiently produced foreign good. The result of the tariff is that consumers buy more of the domestic good and less of the foreign good. The problem is that the foreign good is the product of the foreign nation's labor. A decrease in the demand for the foreign good means foreign producers don't need as much labor, so they lay off workers in the foreign country. The result of the trade barrier is that unemployment has been exported from the domestic country to the foreign country. Treaties like NAFTA are a way of lowering or eliminating trade barriers on a regional basis. As trade barriers are lowered or eliminated, this causes changes in labor and output markets. Some grow; some shrink. These adjustments are taking place now for Canada, the United States and Mexico. Membership in a global economy adds another dimension to economics, in terms of aiding developing countries and in terms of national policies that are implemented.

Skill 31.14   Apply knowledge of significant economic events and issues and their effects in Texas, the United States, and the world.

The United States engaged in trade but remained basically isolationist until World War I. The end of the war began a period of prosperity that lasted until 1929. The "Roaring Twenties" wasn't just a period of speakeasies and bootleggers. The economy, freed from its wartime restraints, had to satisfy the pent up demand caused by the war. Mass production satisfied the mass demand and supplied the wages for the people to buy the output.

Manufacturing output doubled during this period. The building sector experienced a boom that eventually faded. The financial sector was making loans for all the building. The stock market was booming with almost unlimited buying and selling on margin. When the stock prices fell, many speculators could not meet their margin calls. This led to the onset of the Great Depression. The New Deal policies of public spending and the onset of World War II bring the economy slowly out of the Great Depression.

The United States, along with the Soviet Union, emerged as the new world powers after World War II. The European economies were shattered by the war, as was their infrastructure. America embarked on a program of massive aid, called the Marshall Plan, to help the war devastated economies rebuild.

The Bretton Woods System is established to provide stable exchange rates. GATT and other trade organizations are established to help lower trade barriers. This system worked well and the world economies recovered from the war. Under the Bretton Woods System, the U.S. dollar was expressed in terms of gold at $35 per ounce, and all other world currencies were expressed in terms of the dollar. Nations were required to keep their currency values within a specified range and nations would settle their Balance of Payments imbalances at the end of the year. This system worked well until the 1960s, when the world kept experiencing exchange rate crises which were resulting in the exchange markets closing. The situation continued until 1973 when world exchange rates began to float. This eliminated the need for the settlement of payments imbalances because the exchange rate adjusts to eliminate and payments disequilibrium. A deficit results in currency depreciation and a surplus results in currency appreciation. As firms and traders became more adept at hedging, currency problems were eliminated and international trade continued to grow. After this time, many industries began to relocate to Texas and the oil and aeronautics industries, as well as others developed. Houston remains a major international shipping center.

In today's world, all nations are members of a global economy. What happens in one nation, affects the other nations because they are all related through international trade and finance. For example, if one nation lowers its interest rates to stimulate its domestic economy, the lower interest rates cause an outflow of dollars to a foreign country with higher interest rates. This results in dollar depreciation and an appreciation of the foreign currency. The cheaper dollar makes U.S. exports more attractive to foreigners because they are cheaper due to the lower priced dollar. The result is foreigners buy more U.S. exports. The higher value of the foreign currency makes foreign imports more expensive to U.S. citizens so they buy fewer foreign imports. The result is higher employment levels in the U.S. and more unemployment in the foreign country. A nation cannot act in isolation in today's world.

COMPETENCY 32.0 GOVERNMENT AND CITIZENSHIP

Skill 32.1 **Understand the purpose of rules and laws; the relationship between rules, rights, and responsibilities; and the individual's role in making and enforcing rules and ensuring the welfare of society.**

Federal laws are passed by the Congress and can originate in either the House of Representatives or the Senate. The first step in the passing of a law is for the proposed law to be introduced in one of the houses of Congress. A proposed law is called a bill while it is under consideration by Congress. A bill can be introduced, or sponsored, by a member of Congress by giving a copy to the clerk or by placing a copy in a special box called a hopper.

Once a bill is introduced, copies are printed and it is assigned to one of several standing committees of the house in which it was introduced. The committee studies the bill and performs research on the issues it would cover. Committees may call experts to testify on the bill and gather public comments. The committee may revise the bill. Finally, the committee votes on whether to release the bill to be voted on by the full body. A committee may also lay aside a bill so that it cannot be voted on. Once a bill is released, it can be debated and amended by the full body before being voted on. If it passes by a simple majority vote, the bill is sent to the other house of Congress, where the process begins again.

Once a bill has passed both the House of Representatives and the Senate, it is assigned to a conference committee that is made up of members of both houses. The conference committee resolves differences between the House and Senate versions of a bill, if any, and then sends it back to both houses for final approval. Once a bill receives final approval, it is signed by the Speaker of the House and the Vice President, who is also the President of the Senate, and sent to the President for consideration. The President may either sign the bill or veto it. If he vetoes the bill, his veto may be overruled if two-thirds of both the Senate and the House vote to do so. Once it is signed by the President, the bill becomes a law.

Federal laws are enforced by the executive branch and its departments. The Department of Justice, led by the United States Attorney General is the primary law enforcement department of the federal government. The Justice Department is aided by other investigative and enforcement departments such as the Federal Bureau of Investigation (FBI) and the U.S. Postal Inspectors.

The U.S. Constitution and Congressional laws provide basic as well as additional rights to American citizens. These civil rights include freedom of religion, assembly, speech, voting, holding public office, and traveling throughout the country. U.S. citizens have the right to live in America and cannot be forced to leave. American citizenship is guaranteed and will not be taken away for any reason, unless one commits certain serious actions. Civil rights have limitations such as minimum age for voting and limited free speech, forbidding the damage to someone's reputation by slander and lying.

Popular sovereignty grants citizens the ability to directly participate in their own government by voting and running for public office. This is based on a belief in equality that holds that all citizens have an equal right to engage in their own governance, as established in the United States Constitution. The Constitution also contains a list of specific rights granted to citizens, upon which the government cannot infringe. Popular sovereignty also allows for citizens to change their government if they feel it is necessary. This was the driving ideal behind the Declaration of Independence and is embodied in the governmental structure laid out in the Constitution.

The **rule of law** is the commitment that the law applies not only to the governed, but to the government as well. This core value gives authority to the justice system, which grants citizens protection from the government by requiring that any accusation of a crime be proved by the government before a person is punished. This is called due process and ensures that any accused person will have an opportunity to confront his accusers and provide a defense. Due process follows from the core value of a right to liberty. The government cannot take away a citizen's liberty without reason or without proof. The correlating ideal is also a core value - that someone who does harm another or breaks a law will receive justice under the democratic system. The ideal of justice holds that a punishment will fit the crime, and that any citizen can appeal to the judicial system if he feels he has been wronged.

Citizens' duties also vary from nation to nation. Duties demanded by law (also considered civic responsibilities) include paying taxes, obeying laws, and defending the country. Citizenship is granted one of two ways: either by birth or by naturalization. Some Americans hold dual citizenship.

Skill 32.2 **Know the basic structure and functions of the U.S. government, the Texas government, and local governments and relationships among national, state, and local governments.**

The American governmental system is a federal system—fifty individual states federated or uniting as one nation. The national and state governments share the powers of government. This federal system requires decentralization which makes it impossible to coexist with totalitarianism. Both national and state governments exist and govern by the will of the people, who are the source of their authority. Local governmental systems operate under the same guidelines.

The American political system is a two-party system, consisting of the Democratic and Republican parties. Political parties in America have approximately five major functions: (1) Choose candidates who will run for public office; (2) assist in organizing the government; (3) formulate political platforms and policies; (4) obtain the funds needed to conduct election campaigns; and (5) take the initiative to make sure voters are aware of issues, problems to be solved, and any other information about public affairs. The two-party system in America operates at the national, state, and local levels.

The government of Texas is modeled upon U.S. Government. Texas has three branches of government: Executive, Legislative, and Judicial. The governor heads up the Executive branch, vetoes or signs bills into law, commands the state militia, and can call special sessions of the Legislature. That Legislature has two houses, a House of Representatives with 150 members and a Senate with 31, and meets in regular session every two years. The Judicial branch has many overlapping courts, of which the Supreme Court (civil cases) and the Texas Court of Criminal Appeals are the highest. Judges are elected, as are many members of the Executive branch.

Powers delegated to the federal government:

1. To tax.
2. To borrow and coin money governments.
3. To establish postal service.
4. To grant patents and copyrights.
5. To regulate interstate and foreign commerce.
6. To establish courts.
7. To declare war.
8. To raise and support the armed forces.
9. To govern territories.
10. To define and punish felonies and piracy on the high seas.
11. To fix standards of weights and measures.
12. To conduct foreign affairs.

Powers reserved to the states:

1. To regulate intrastate trade.
2. To establish local
3. To protect general welfare.
4. To protect life and property.
5. To ratify amendments.
6. To conduct elections.
7. To make state and local laws.

Concurrent powers of the federal government and states.

1. Both Congress and the states may tax.
2. Both may borrow money.
3. Both may charter banks and corporations.
4. Both may establish courts.
5. Both may make and enforce laws.
6. Both may take property for public purposes.
7. Both may spend money to provide for the public welfare.

Implied powers of the federal government.

1. To establish banks or other corporations, implied from delegated powers to tax, borrow, and to regulate commerce.
2. To spend money for roads, schools, health, insurance, etc. implied from powers to establish post roads, to tax to provide for general welfare and defense, and to regulate commerce.
3. To create military academies, implied from powers to raise and support an armed force.
4. To locate and generate sources of power and sell surplus, implied from powers to dispose of government property, commerce, and war powers.
5. To assist and regulate agriculture, implied from power to tax and spend for general welfare and regulate commerce.

Skill 32.3   Demonstrate knowledge of key principles and ideas in major political documents of Texas and the United States and relationships among political documents.

The U.S. Constitution set up a federal system of government, dividing powers between the national and state governments. The national government is balanced by having its authority divided among the three branches.

The **legislative branch** includes Congress and eight administrative agencies. Congress is made up of the House of Representatives and the Senate. It is the responsibility of the U.S. Congress to make, repeal, and amend all federal laws as well as levying federal taxes and distributing funds for the government.

The U.S. Senate consists of 100 members, two from each state regardless of size or population, who serve six-year terms. Its exclusive powers include approval of Presidential nominations for major federal offices, approval of any treaty made, and conducting impeachment cases of federal officials. Charges for impeachment include treason, bribes, high crimes and misdemeanors. The Vice-President presides at all impeachment proceedings except in the case of the President, when the Chief Justice of the Supreme Court presides. Two-thirds of the Senate must agree on the verdict.

The House of Representatives has 435 members who serve two-year terms. The number of representatives from each state is determined by population with a guarantee of at least one representative regardless. The number of representatives is set by law and is not subject to change. Its exclusive powers include initiating all financial bills and bringing impeachment charges against high federal officials.

The **executive branch** includes the Executive Office of the President, various executive departments and independent agencies. The U.S. President is the nation's chief of state, chief executive, and the head of the government of the United States. He or she is responsible for enforcing federal laws, appointing and removing any high federal officials, commanding all the armed forces, conducting foreign affairs, and recommending laws to Congress.

The President is responsible for appointing American representatives to carry out diplomatic missions in foreign lands and to serve in international organizations. The President is also required to perform many ceremonial duties. He or she is elected to a term of four years and is limited constitutionally to no more than two terms.

The **judicial branch** is made up of the Supreme Court and other lower federal courts. Consisting of a chief justice and eight associate justices, the Supreme Court is the highest court in the land. All nine justices are appointed by the president with Senate approval. The lower federal courts consist of district courts, courts of appeal, and a group of courts handling specialized cases. All federal courts hear cases involving the Constitution and federal laws. These judges are also appointed by the President with Senate approval and, along with the Supreme Court justices, hold office for life. Under the process called "judicial review" (as set forth in "Marbury vs. Madison," 1803), the Supreme Court has the authority to declare unconstitutional any executive orders or any legislative acts of both federal and state governments, based on the statement in the U.S. Constitution stating that it and all treaties and federal laws are the supreme law of the land.

The U.S. Constitution created a federal government solidly based on four fundamental principles. The first principle is that of "federalism," a system of government in which powers are divided between the national and state governments. This, in turn, set up four types of governmental powers: (1) delegated or expressed—those listed directly; (2) implied powers—not stated directly but suggested; (3) reserved powers—not given to the national government but reserved for the people or for the states; and (4) concurrent powers—given to both national and state governments at the same time.

The second constitutional principle is the separation of powers with the system of checks and balances. The writers of the Constitution were concerned with protecting the new nation from any form of tyranny, seizure of power by a military dictator, or any one branch of government becoming stronger and more powerful than the others. Therefore it was determined to keep the three branches separate and equal. Additionally a system of checks and balances was written into the Constitution.

This gives each of the three branches some powers that affect the other two. Some examples include: Congress checks the President by having the authority to appropriate funds for running the government. Congress checks the judicial branch due to its power to provide for and set up the courts along with their rules of procedure. The President can check Congress with his power to veto bills it passes. The President checks the courts with his power to appoint judges and justices. The courts can check both Congress and the President by reviewing executive orders and legislative acts and declaring them unconstitutional.

A third principle provides for the protection of individual rights and liberties. These provisions include the following: The Constitution prohibits the passage of "ex post facto laws" (laws passed "after the deed" providing the penalty for an act that was not an illegal act at the time it was committed) and "bills of attainder" (laws that render punishment to someone through fines, imprisonment, and confiscation of property without a court trial first). Individual rights are also protected by granting one a "writ of habeas corpus" which is a legal document requiring release from jail or prison if an individual has not been formally charged with or convicted of a crime.

Special protection is given to those accused of treason as well as their innocent relatives. The accused is entitled to a fair trial and due process of law and would be protected against being accused merely because of criticism against the government. Treason was defined by the Constitution as waging war against the United States or supporting enemies of the U.S. by giving them assistance. It would require at least two witnesses testifying for conviction. Only the guilty would be convicted and punished; no punishment or penalty is allowed against one's family or relatives.

The first ten amendments to the Constitution, known as the **Bill of Rights,** guarantee protection for individuals against any action by the federal government which would threaten the loss of their life, liberty, or property without proper legal procedure. These laws guarantee freedoms such as speech, press, assembly, religion, petition, unreasonable searches and seizures, and protection against arbitrary arrest and punishment.

The fourth constitutional principle is adaptation to changing times and circumstances. One important process is the ability to meet needed changes through amendments. The other is the inclusion of what is known as the "elastic clause." In addition to its specific powers, the writers granted to Congress the power to make any additional laws needed to implement other powers.

The U.S. Constitution is a unique document among national governments today. It has stood the test of time for two reasons: (1) It has set out procedural rules that must be followed, even in extreme and critical circumstances; and (2) due to amending along with customs and practices, it is flexible and adaptable making it possible to meet the demands and changes of a growing nation.

The Texas Constitution is an extremely long document, full of details for nearly every imaginable eventuality. It also has several long stretches of nothing, since wholesale sections of it have been repealed. State and local statutes range from the vital to the trivial, from land sales to road construction, from parks administration to dueling. Seemingly everything is covered by a statute in the Texas Constitution. The Constitution also has an exceedingly large number of amendments, covering many aspects of society. The Constitution has a Bill of Rights, just like the federal document, and other amendments as well.

The overriding idea, though, behind the thrust of the Constitution is the protection of individual rights. Texas was a frontier society for much of its existence. The Constitution, as vibrant today as when it was created in 1876, goes out of its way to protect the individual—the person or the corporation—against encroachment from the government.

Skill 32.4 Know how people organized governments in colonial America and during the early development of Texas.

Government of the colonies differed depending on the type of colony. Each colony had a lower legislative assembly that was elected, and a higher council and governor that were elected or appointed in different ways depending on the how the colony was organized initially. In most colonies, the councils and governors were appointed by the King of England, or by British property owners or agencies. In corporate colonies the council and governors were elected by colonial property owners who maintained a close connection to England.

Thus, while the colonies were allowed to tax themselves and regulate much of their daily lives through representation in the colonial assemblies, Britain maintained control of international affairs and international trade by controlling the upper levels of colonial government. In practice, Britain allowed the colonies to go about their business without interference, largely because the colonies were providing important raw materials to the home country.

The early presidential administrations established much of the form and many of the procedures still present today, including the development of the party system. George Washington, the first US President, established a cabinet form of government, with individual advisors overseeing the various functions of the executive branch and advising the President, who makes a final decision. Divisions within his cabinet and within Congress during his administration eventually led to the development of political parties, which Washington opposed. Washington was also instrumental in establishing the power of the federal government when he rode at the head of militia forces to put down a rebellion in Pennsylvania. Washington was elected to two terms and served from 1789 to 1797.

From its earliest days, Texas was governed by a document of some sort. The Republic of Texas had a Constitution that closely resembled the U.S. Constitution, with a government that had three branches, a tradition of checks and balances, a stipulation for democratic elections of officials, and a bill of rights. The constitution also had certain Spanish and Mexican traditions, such as provisions for community property and debt relief. That tradition has held through to the modern day.

It wasn't always easy, however. Texas was, of course, a Confederate State and had a separate constitution covering that period in its history. A flurry of governmental activity followed the end of the Civil War, and no fewer than three full-fledged constitutions came into existence between 1866 and 1876. The Texas State Constitution was incorporated in 1876 and continues to dominate Texas politics today.

Skill 32.5   Understand the political process in the United States and Texas and how the U.S. political system works.

Many of the core values in the U.S. democratic system can be found in the opening words of the Declaration of Independence, including the belief in equality, and the rights of citizens to "life, liberty and the pursuit of happiness."

The Declaration was a condemnation of the British king's tyrannical government, and these words emphasized the American colonists' belief that a government received its authority to rule from the people, and its function should not be to suppress the governed, but to protect the rights of the governed, including protection from the government itself. These two ideals, **popular sovereignty** and the **rule of law** are basic core values.

Popular sovereignty grants citizens the ability to directly participate in their own government by voting and running for public office. This ideal is based on a belief of **equality** that holds that all citizens have an equal right to engage in their own governance. The ideal of equality has changed over the years, as women and non-white citizens were not always allowed to vote or bring suit in court. Now all U.S citizens above the age of 18 are allowed to vote. This expansion of rights since the adoption of the Constitution demonstrates an American value of **respect for minority rights.**

The democratic system of election and representation is based on **majority rule**. In the case of most public elections, the candidate receiving the most votes is awarded the office. Majority rule is also used to pass legislation in Congress. Majority rule is meant to ensure that authority cannot be concentrated in one small group of people.

Central to the ideal of justice is an expectation that citizens will act in a way that promotes the **common good**, that they will treat one another with **honesty** and respect and will exercise **self-discipline** in their interactions with others. These are among the basic responsibilities of a citizen of a democracy.

Texas has, primarily, two political parties, the Democratic and Republican Parties. The Democratic Party was the dominant party for years, for most of the state's existence, in fact. The Republican Party has enjoyed resurgence in the past few decades and now controls much of the state government. The state Legislature, with its two houses, drafts, writes, and passes laws, which the governor either approves (signs into law) or rejects (vetoes). The state courts can weigh in on matters of dispute or constitutionality regarding laws that the Legislature passes and the governor signs. The Legislature itself meets only every two years but for an extended period of time. A proposed constitutional amendment needs only two-thirds of both houses of the legislature to approve and then approval of a simple majority of the registered state voters.

Skill 32.6 Demonstrate knowledge of types of government and their effectiveness in meeting citizens' needs.

A political system can be explained or defined as the unique way a nation governs itself. There are several different political systems in existence:

(1) **Monarchy**—a government headed by a king or queen. Most monarchies are considered constitutional or limited, meaning that the king or queen does not have sole, absolute authority, but that executive power is usually carried out through a prime minister and cabinet and laws are made in a legislative body, such as a parliament.

(2) **Oligarchy**—a type of modern government in which a small group of people control the government. Some examples are a republic, an aristocracy, even some dictatorships, especially if based on wealth or military authority.

(3) **Democracy**—means "rule by the people." There are two types of democracy: A.) pure or direct democracy—when the citizens themselves meet in one place and make laws for themselves and their community. A familiar example of this form was in ancient Greece practiced by the citizens of Athens. The other type is B.) representative democracy— practiced by most modern democracies. Because it is impossible or inconvenient for all the people to meet in one place to make laws, voters elect representatives to meet and make laws for them. This form of government is also sometimes referred to as republican government or a democratic republic.

(4) **Despotism and Dictatorships**—a form of government where there is unlimited power over the people and no legislative body to limit rulers. This is similar to the definitions for tyranny, autocracy, and totalitarianism.

(5) **Parliamentary system**—a government made up of a legislative body, called a parliament, and a cabinet with a premier or prime minister heading the cabinet. The cabinet is chosen and supported by the majority political party in parliament and stays in power as long as it has this support.

(6) **Presidential system**—a government of separate executive and legislative branches. The executive branch is headed by the president who is elected for a fixed term.

(7) **Federalism**—a single government of limited powers under which two or more sovereign political units, such as states or provinces, are united.

(8) **Constitutionalism**—a political system in which laws and traditions limit the powers of government.

Skill 32.7   Know the formal and informal process of changing the U.S. and Texas constitutions and the impact of changes on society.

An amendment is a change or addition to the United States Constitution. Two-thirds of both houses of Congress must propose and then pass one. Or two-thirds of the state legislatures must call a convention to propose one and then it must be ratified by three-fourths of the state legislatures. To date there are only 27 amendments to the Constitution. An amendment may be used to cancel out a previous one, such as the 18th Amendment (1919) known as Prohibition, canceled by the 21st Amendment (1933). Amending the United States Constitution is an extremely difficult thing to do.

An Amendment must start in Congress. One or more lawmakers propose it, and then each house votes on it in turn. The Amendment must have the support of two-thirds of each house separately in order to progress on its path into law. (It should be noted here that this two-thirds need be only two-thirds of a quorum, which is just a simple majority. Thus, it is theoretically possible for an Amendment to be passed and be legal even though it has been approved by less than half of one or both houses.)

The final and most difficult step for an Amendment is the ratification by state legislature. A total of three-fourths of those must approve the Amendment. Approvals there need be only a simple majority, but the number of states that must approve the Amendment is 38. Hundreds of Amendments have been proposed through the years, but only 27 have become part of the Constitution.

A key element in some of those failures has been the time limit that Congress has the option to put on Amendment proposals. A famous example of an Amendment that got close but didn't reach the threshold before the deadline expired was the Equal Rights Amendment, which was proposed in 1972 but which couldn't muster enough support for passage, even though its deadline was extended from seven to ten years.

Passage of an amendment to the Texas Constitution is easier. A proposed amendment needs only two-thirds of both houses of the legislature to approve and then a simple majority of the registered state voters.

Skill 32.8   Understand the impact of landmark Supreme Court cases.

Marbury v. Madison is perhaps the most famous Supreme Court case of them all. It was the first case to establish what has become the Court's main duty, judicial review.

After George Washington retired, his vice-president, John Adams, succeeded him. Adams ran for election in 1800, and was opposed by his vice-president, Thomas Jefferson. Adams was a Federalist. Jefferson was elected in November 1800. At that time, the new president didn't take office until March 4 of the following year. So Adams had a few months to try to get things done before Jefferson took over. One of the things Adams tried to do was get as many Federalist judges appointed as he could. As March 4 drew near, Adams got more and more concerned with doing this. He kept appointing judges long into the night on March 3. These were known as the "Midnight Judges." One of these "Midnight Judges" was William Marbury, who was named to be justice of the peace for the District of Columbia.

The normal practice of making such appointments was to deliver a "commission," or notice, of appointment. This was normally done by the Secretary of State. Jefferson's Secretary of State at the time was James Madison. Jefferson didn't want all those Federalist judges, so he told Madison not to deliver the commission. Marshall and the rest of the Supreme Court decided that the power to deliver commissions to judges, since it was part of the Judiciary Act of 1789 and *not* part of the Constitution itself, was in conflict with the Constitution and, therefore, illegal. Further, the *entire* Judiciary Act of 1789 was illegal because it gave to the Judicial Branch powers not granted to it by the Constitution.

It appeared that Marshall sided with his political enemies, but this was not the case. Marbury, a Federalist, didn't get to be justice of the peace in the District of Columbia. Adams was probably quite angry because his commission was denied. Jefferson and Madison were probably quite happy because they got to name their own friendly justice of the peace. But Marshall gave to the Supreme Court a whole new power: the power to throw out laws of Congress. So, no matter how many laws Thomas Jefferson and his Democratic-Republicans passed and made into law, the Supreme Court always had the ultimate check on that legislative and executive power. John Marshall, in appearing to lose the political battle, won the political war.

One of the chief political battles of the nineteenth century was between the federal government and state governments. The Supreme Court took this battle to heart and issued a series of decisions that, for the most part, made it clear that any dispute between governments at the state and federal levels would be settled in favor of the federal government. One of the main examples of this was **McCulloch** *v.* **Maryland**, which settled a dispute involving the Bank of the United States.

The United States, at this time (1819) still had a federal bank, the Bank of the United States. The State of Maryland voted to tax all bank business not done with state banks. This was meant to be a tax on people who lived in Maryland but who did business with banks in other states. However, the State of Maryland also sought to tax the federal bank. Andrew McCulloch, who worked in the Baltimore branch of the Bank of the United States, refused to pay the tax. The State of Maryland sued, and the Supreme Court accepted the case.

Writing for the Court, Chief Justice John Marshall wrote that the federal government did indeed have the right and power to set up a federal bank. Further, he wrote, a state did *not* have the power to tax the federal government. "The right to tax is the right to destroy," he wrote, and states should not have that power over the federal government. The Bank of the United States did not survive, but the judicial review of the Supreme Court did.

The Supreme Court reasserted the power of judicial review in this case, one of the most dynamic and divisive of the twentieth century in **United States *v.* Richard Nixon**. The issue was whether the President had the ability to keep certain items secret. In this case, the items were secret recordings that Richard Nixon, the President at the time, had made of conversations he had had with his advisers. The recordings were thought to implicate Nixon in the cover-up of the Watergate break-in, an attempt by a team of thieves to gain information on the activities of George McGovern, Nixon's opponent in the 1972 election. Nixon claimed that the tapes were the property of the Executive Branch and, more to the point, of Nixon himself. Nixon claimed an "executive privilege" that would keep him from having to relinquish the recordings.

Skill 32.9 **Understand components of the democratic process and their significance in a democratic society.**

Refer to Skill 32.11.

Skill 32.10 **Demonstrate knowledge of important customs, symbols, and celebrations that represent American beliefs and principles and contribute to national unity.**

The United States recognizes several national holidays that reflect dominant patriotic views. Presidents' Day honors two of the country's most beloved leaders, George Washington and Abraham Lincoln. Veterans' Day displays the American ideal of military service as an honorable endeavor in defense of the country's ideals. Independence Day celebrates the founding of the country in 1776, when independence from England was declared. These celebrations contribute to the shared experience of all Americans and promote patriotic ideals and unity.

The U.S. flag is perhaps the most important symbol of the country. The flag displays 13 stripes representing the original colonies that gained independence from England as well as 50 stars, one for each state in the union. The flag symbolizes both the independence and unity of the 50 states, an important ideal in the republican form of government.

The bald eagle is another widely used symbol of the United States and appears on the currency and the Presidential Seal. The eagle was chosen by the founding fathers of the country to represent the strength and independence of the new nation.

Skill 32.11 **Analyze the relationship among individual rights, responsibilities, and freedoms in democratic societies.**

Citizenship in a democracy bestows on an individual certain rights, foremost being the right to participate in one's own government. Along with these rights come responsibilities, including the responsibility of a citizen to participate.

The most basic form of participation is the vote. Those who have reached the age of 18 in the US are eligible to vote in public elections. With this right comes the responsibility to be informed before voting, and not to sell or otherwise give away one's vote. Citizens are also eligible to run for public office. Along with the right to run for office comes the responsibility to represent the electors as fairly as possible and to perform the duties expected of a government representative.

In the United States, citizens are guaranteed the right to free speech; the right to express an opinion on public issues. In turn, citizens have the responsibility to allow others to speak freely. At the community level, this might mean speaking at a city council hearing while allowing others with different or opposing viewpoints to have their say without interruption or comment.

The US Constitution also guarantees freedom of religion. This means that the government may not impose an official religion on its citizens, and that people are free to practice their religion. Citizens are also responsible for allowing those of other religions to practice freely without obstruction. Occasionally, religious issues will be put before the public at the state level in the form of ballot measures or initiatives. To what extent it should be acceptable for religious beliefs to be expressed in a public setting, such as a public school, is an issue that has been debated recently.

In making decisions on matters like these, the citizen is expected to take responsibility to become informed of the issues involved and to make his vote based on his own opinion. Being informed of how one's government works and what the effects of new legislation will be is an essential part of being a good citizen.

The US Constitution also guarantees that all citizens be treated equally by the law. In addition, federal and state laws make it a crime to discriminate against citizens based on their sex, race, religion and other factors. To ensure that all people are treated equally, citizens have the responsibility to follow these laws.

These rights and responsibilities are essentially the same whether one is voting in a local school board race, for the passage of a new state law, or for the President of the United States. Being a good citizen means exercising one's own rights while allowing others to do the same.

Almost all representative democracies in the world guarantee similar rights to their citizens and expect them to take similar responsibilities to respect the rights of others. As a citizen of the world one is expected to respect the rights of other nations, and the people of those nations, in the same way.

Skill 32.12 Apply knowledge of the rights and responsibilities of citizens in Texas and the United States, past and present.

People who live in Texas have a host of rights and responsibilities as part of their contract with the state. The state constitution protects them from harm, from unfair government and laws and from violence from outside sources. The state government protects their right to a legal job at a fair wage as well.

Texas residents are expected to obey their state, local, and national laws and to pay their taxes and vote in elections at all three levels of government. They are expected to represent their state well when they travel outside its borders.

Respect is an attitude toward others that recognizes their feelings, interests and beliefs and values both the other (person or group) and their feelings, interests and beliefs, without necessarily agreeing with them. The idea of the rights of individuals and groups is a socially normalized outgrowth of respect.

Obedience is essentially submissive compliance with the orders or instructions, laws or rules of others. Obedience generally involves some recognition of social or legal dominance and submission. It is thus unlike "compliance" which is generally influenced by one's peers, and unlike "conformity" which is generally a willingness to match the behavior of the majority.

Forms of human obedience include obedience to social norms, laws, government, political organizations, religion, church or synagogue, God, self-imposed constraints, philosophical ethical codes, etc.

Dissent is a belief or opinion in opposition to an accepted ideology or to those who hold particular beliefs, powers, or policies. Dissent may be expressed in a number of ways, some of which are socially and politically acceptable while others are not.

Voting is an approach to decision-making that permits each entitled individual to express a view or opinion on a matter or a person seeking political leadership office. It is generally considered a hallmark of democratic government.

Skill 32.13   Understand how the nature, rights, and responsibilities of citizenship vary among societies.

Citizenship is membership in a political state such as a country or state. With citizenship comes the right to participate politically in a society. Citizenship and nationality are closely related, but are not always the same thing. A person can hold citizenship in one country, for instance, but live and work in another country.

Anyone born in the United States can be a citizen of the U.S., regardless of the nationality or citizenship of the parents. Other countries have different rules about obtaining citizenship that may be based on parental heritage or ethnicity. Some countries, such as Switzerland, hold local elections on whether a person may become a citizen.

In the past, many countries required an oath of allegiance to become a citizen, and some still do. Some countries, such as Israel, require all citizens to serve at least one term in the military.

At times, countries that grant individual citizenship may join together and create a combined political group that has citizenship rights and responsibilities of its own. The British Commonwealth and the European Union are examples of this kind of group. Citizens of the member states hold additional rights and share additional responsibilities of the larger group. They may also have the right to move freely within the member states.

In all cases, citizenship also implies a responsibility to participate in the general improvement of one's society.

COMPETENCY 33.0 CULTURE, SCIENCE, TECHNOLOGY, AND SOCIETY

Skill 33.1   Understand basic concepts of culture and the processes of cultural adaptation, diffusion, and exchange.

Innovation is the introduction of new ways of performing work or organizing societies, and can spur drastic changes in a culture. Prior to the innovation of agriculture, for instance, human cultures were largely nomadic and survived by hunting and gathering their food. Agriculture led directly to the development of permanent settlements and a radical change in social organization. Likewise, technological innovations in the Industrial Revolution of the 19th Century changed the way work was performed and transformed the economic institutions of western cultures. Recent innovations in communications are changing the way cultures interact today.

Cultural diffusion is the movement of cultural ideas or materials between populations independent of the movement of those populations. Cultural diffusion can take place when two populations are close to one another, through direct interaction, or across great distances, through mass media and other routes. American movies are popular all over the world, for instance.

Adaptation is the process that individuals and societies go through in changing their behavior and organization to cope with social, economic and environmental pressures.

Acculturation is an exchange or adoption of cultural features when two cultures come into regular direct contact. An example of acculturation is the adoption of Christianity and western dress by many Native Americans in the United States.

Assimilation is the process of a minority ethnic group largely adopting the culture of the larger group it exists within. These groups are typically immigrants moving to a new country, as with the European immigrants who traveled to the United States at the beginning of the twentieth century who assimilated to American culture.

Extinction is the complete disappearance of a culture. Extinction can occur suddenly, from disease, famine or war when the people of a culture are completely destroyed, or slowly over time as a culture adapt, acculturate or assimilate to the point where its original features are lost.

Skill 33.2   Analyze similarities and differences in the ways various peoples at different times in history have lived and met basic human needs.

Food, clothing and shelter are the three basic needs of human beings. As early humans increased in number and moved into new parts of the world, they had to adapt to their new environments by adopting new ways to obtain these needs.

Early humans hunted animals and gathered food from wild sources. Taking their basic support from nature like this required them to move with their food sources. Game animals might migrate, and seasonal food sources might require groups to travel to the regions where the food could be had. To take full advantage of varying areas where food could be found, portable methods of shelter were developed such as the Native American teepee or the Mongolian yurt. These shelters could be carried from place to place, allowing a greater range.

Clothing allowed humans to adapt to the wider range of climates they discovered as they moved from place to place, both in their annual circuit and as they moved into new wilderness areas that had lower average temperatures. Clothing protects the body from cold, sun exposure, and the elements. In very hot climates, little or no clothing was worn by early humans. The advantages of having an extra layer of protection were soon realized, however, and basic coverings were fashioned from animal skin. Foot coverings were developed to protect the feet from rough ground and sharp rocks. In colder climates, clothing was crucial for survival. Animal pelts with the fur attached provided warmth. Foot coverings could also be fur-lined or stuffed with grass. Mittens or gloves kept vulnerable fingers warm and protected.

As humans moved away from hunting and gathering into agricultural pursuits, other materials for clothing became available. Wool-bearing animals were domesticated and plant fibers were woven into cloth. During the Industrial Revolution, cloth weaving methods took a great stride forward, greatly expanding the use of woven cloth clothing.

Agriculture also expanded the types of food that were available, Grains and fruits could be grown in place and meat could be had from domesticated animals. Not all climates are suitable for all crops, however, and humans have had to adapt varieties and methods to successfully produce food.

Just as their environment shaped their needs, so did the environment provide the means to meet those needs. For thousands of years, food and shelter had to be obtained from local resources, or from resources that could be grown locally. Human technology has reached a point now, however, that we are able to supply food to any location on the planet and adapt clothing and shelter to any environment, even outer space.

Skill 33.3   Apply knowledge of the role of families in meeting basic human needs and how families and cultures develop and use customs, traditions, and beliefs to define themselves.

Sociologists have identified three main types of norms, or ways that cultures define behavioral expectations, each associated with different consequences if they are violated. These norms are called folkways, mores and laws.

Folkways are the informal rules of etiquette and behaviors that a society follows in day-to-day practice. Forming a line at a shop counter or holding a door open for an elderly person are examples of folkways in many societies. Someone who violates a folkway - by pushing to the front of a line, for instance - might be seen as rude, but is not thought to have done anything immoral or illegal.

Mores are stronger than folkways in the consequences they carry for not observing them. Examples of mores might include honesty and integrity. Cheating on a test or lying might violate a social more, and a person who does so may be considered immoral.

Laws are formal adoptions of norms by a society with formal punishment for their violation. Laws are usually based on the mores of a society. The more that it is wrong to kill is codified in a law against murder, for example. Laws are the most formal types of social norm, as their enforcement is specifically provided for. Folkways and mores, on the other hand, are primarily enforced informally by the fellow members of a society.

The folkways, mores and laws of a society are based on the prevailing beliefs and values of that society. Beliefs and values are similar and interrelated systems. **Beliefs** are those things that are thought to be true. Beliefs are often associated with religion, but beliefs can also be based on political or ideological philosophies. "All men are created equal," is an example of an ideological belief.

Values are what a society thinks are right and wrong, and are often based on and shaped by beliefs. The value that every member of the society has a right to participate in his government might be considered to be based on the belief that "All mean are created equal," for instance.

The **family** is the primary social unit in most societies. It is through the family that children learn the most essential skills for functioning in their society such as language and appropriate forms of interaction. The size of the family unit varies among cultures, with some including grandparents, aunts, uncles and cousins as part of the basic family, who may all live together. The family is also related to a society's economic institutions, as families often purchase and consume goods as a unit. A family that works to produce its own food and clothing, as was the case historically in many societies, is also a unit of economic production.

Skill 33.4   **Demonstrate knowledge of institutions that exist in all societies and how characteristics of these institutions may vary among societies.**

Sociologists have identified five different types of institutions around which societies are structured: family, education, government, religion and economy. These institutions provide a framework for members of a society to learn about and participate in a society, and allow for a society to perpetuate its beliefs and values to succeeding generations.

The **family** is the primary social unit in most societies. It is through the family that children learn the most essential skills for functioning in their society such as language and appropriate forms of interaction. The family is connected to ethnicity, which is partly defined by a person's heritage.

Education is an important institution in a society, as it allows for the formal passing on of a culture's collected knowledge. The institution of education is connected to the family, as that is where a child's earliest education takes place. The United States has a public school system administered by the states that ensures a basic education and provides a common experience for most children.

A society's **governmental** institutions often embody its beliefs and values. Laws, for instance, reflect a society's values by enforcing its ideas of right and wrong. The structure of a society's government can reflect a society's ideals about the role of an individual in his society. The American form of democracy emphasizes the rights of the individual, but in return expects individuals to respect the rights of others, including those of ethnic or political minorities.

Religion is frequently the institution from which springs a society's primary beliefs and values, and can be closely related to other social institutions. Many religions have definite teachings on the structure and importance of the family, for instance. The U.S. Constitution guarantees the free practice of religion, which has led to a large number of denominations practicing in the U.S. today.
A society's **economic** institutions define how an individual can contribute and receive economic reward from his society. The United States has a capitalist economy motivated by free enterprise. While this system allows for economic advancement for the individual, it can also produce areas of poverty and economic depression.

Skill 33.5   **Understand how people use oral tradition, stories, real and mythical heroes, music, paintings, and sculpture to create and represent culture in communities in Texas, the United States, and the world.**

The traditions and behaviors of a culture are based on the prevailing beliefs and values of that culture. Beliefs and values are similar and interrelated systems.

Beliefs are those things that are thought to be true. Beliefs are often associated with religion, but beliefs can also be based on political or ideological philosophies. "All men are created equal," is an example of an ideological belief.

Values are what a society thinks are right and wrong, and are often based on and shaped by beliefs. The value that every member of the society has a right to participate in his government might be considered to be based on the belief that "All mean are created equal," for instance.

A cultures beliefs and values are reflected in the cultural products it produces, such as literature, the arts, media and architecture. These products become part of the culture and last from generation to generation, becoming one way that culture is transmitted through time. A common language among all members of a culture make this transmission possible.

Skill 33.6   Understand the contributions of people of various racial, ethnic, and religious groups in Texas, the United States, and the world.

Refer to Skill 29.1.

Skill 33.7   Demonstrate knowledge of relationships among world cultures and relationships between and among people from various groups, including racial, ethnic, and religious groups, in the United States and throughout the world.

Race, ethnicity and religion are three lines along which many people group themselves and view themselves as distinct from other groups. Tension between groups can arise for various reasons, leading to longstanding conflict between some groups. Groups that have minority status within a larger group are often disadvantaged in their societies owing to the dominant group favoring its own members in social and political policies and in daily interactions. These kinds of majority/minority relationships can be based on race, ethnicity and religion.

Ethnic and religious tension can also arise from traditional historical relationships between groups. Ethnicity and religion are two frameworks by which social views can be passed from generation to generation, perpetuating tension and conflict between groups. Religion can also play an important role in relationships between groups. Some religious beliefs directly conflict with others, giving rise to disagreement.

Skill 33.8   Analyze relationships among religion, philosophy, and culture, and the impact of religion on ways of life in the United States and world areas.

Race is a term used most generally to describe a population of people from a common geographic area that share certain common physical traits. Skin color and facial features have traditionally been used to categorize individuals by race. The term has generated some controversy among sociologists, anthropologists and biologists as to what if anything, is meant by race and racial variation. Biologically speaking a race of people share a common genetic lineage. Socially, race can be more complicated to define, with many people identifying themselves as part of a racial group that others might not. This self-perception of race, and the perception of race by others, is perhaps more crucial than any genetic variation when trying to understand the social implications of variations in race.

An **ethnic group** is a group of people who identify themselves as having a common social background and set of behaviors, and who perpetuate their culture by traditions of marriage within their own group. Ethnic groups will often share a common language and ancestral background, and frequently exist within larger populations with which they interact. Ethnicity and race are sometimes interlinked, but differ in that many ethnic groups can exist within a population of people thought to be of the same race. Ethnicity is based more on common cultural behaviors and institutions than common physical traits.

Religion can be closely tied to ethnicity, as it is frequently one of the common social institutions shared by an ethnic group. Like ethnicity, religion varies in practices and beliefs even within the large major religions. Some religions and religious sects link their beliefs closely to their ancestry, and so are closely linked to the concept of race.

Variations in race, ethnicity and religion - both real and perceived - are primary ways in which cultures and cultural groups are defined. They are useful in understanding cultures, but can also be the source of cultural biases and prejudices.

Skill 33.9 Understand the concept of diversity within unity.

In the United States many diverse cultures were coming together in a steady stream of immigration to the new world. These cultures were mainly Western European, and the immigrants that came to the U.S., while they were allowed to maintain their language and culture, in practice usually assimilated to American culture within two generations, although their practices and traditions often survived in an Americanized form.

While somewhat tolerant of other European immigrants and cultural practices, Americans treated most non-white cultures as inferior. African-Americans were enslaved for centuries, and even after the end of slavery were officially segregated from European-American society in some parts of the country.

In recent years, a respect for cultural diversity has grown worldwide and within the United States. Texas, with its history of shifting dominant cultures and immigration, has been a leader within the U.S. in promoting cultural diversity. The Hispanic heritage of many Texas citizens is officially honored by the preservation of early settlements and artifacts, such as Ceremonial Cave, Espiritu Santo and Morhiss Mound and ethnic and cultural concentrations of people currently thrive. But overall, we are all American citizens united under one flag.

Skill 33.10   Analyze the effects of race, gender, and socioeconomic class on ways of life in the United States and throughout the world.

Social Stratification is the division of a society into different levels based on factors such as race, religion, economic standing or family heritage. Various types of social stratification may be closely related. For instance stratification by race may result in people of one race being relegated to a certain economic class as well. The pioneering sociologist Max Weber theorized that there are three components of social stratification: **class, status** and **political**. Social class, as Weber defined it, is based on economics and a person's relationship to the economic market, e.g. a factory worker is of a different social class than a factory owner. Social status is based on non-economic factors like honor or religion. Political status is based on the relationships and influence one has in the political domain.

The economic revolutionary Karl Marx identified social stratification as the source of exploitation of one level of society by another, and based his theory of revolution and economic reform on this belief. Mobility between social strata may differ between societies. In some societies, a person may move up or down in social class owing to changes in one personal economic fortunes, for instance. Political status can change when prevailing political thought shifts. Some systems of stratification are quite formal, however, as in the former caste system in India. In these systems lines between strata are more rigid, with employment, marriage and other social activities tightly defined by one's position.

Skill 33.11   Understand the various roles of men, women, children, and families in cultures past and present.

During colonial times, residents of the New England Colonies were primarily small farmers. Each family had its own subsistence farm with supporting livestock. Women were expected to care for the children and take care of the household, while Men tended to the farming and livestock. Families encouraged their sons to continue to farm, and provided them with land and livestock to establish them. Women were expected to marry. New England settlers were primarily from England.

The middle colonies had a more diverse population than New England, with immigrants from Holland, Scotland, Ireland and Germany making up the largest groups. These peoples were also largely farmers, each group bringing its own methods and techniques. Family structure was similar to that in New England, but unlike their Puritan counterparts, German and Dutch women were allowed to hold property and could often be found working in the fields.

Skill 33.12 Understand how the self develops and the dynamic relationship between self and social context.

Socialization is the process by which humans learn the expectations their society has for their behavior, in order that they might successfully function within that society.

Socialization takes place primarily in children as they learn and are taught the rules and norms of their culture. Children grow up eating the common foods of a culture, and develop a "taste" for these foods, for example. By observing adults and older children, they learn about gender roles, and appropriate ways to interact. The family is the primary influence in this kind of socialization, and contributes directly to a person's sense of self-importance and personal identity.

Through socialization, a person gains a sense of belonging to a group of people with common ideals and behaviors. When a person encounters people affiliated with other groups, their own group affiliation can be reinforced in contrast, contributing to their own sense of personal identity.

Skill 33.13 Apply knowledge of the effects of scientific discoveries and technological innovations on political, economic, social, and environmental developments and on everyday life in Texas, the United States, and the world.

The **microscope** first appeared about 1590, and was steadily improved upon. The microscope revealed an entire world of invisible activity by bacteria and fungus, and laid bare the cell structure of complex organisms. Advancements in microscopy led directly to important discoveries concerning germs, viruses and the cause of disease, greatly aiding the field of medicine.

Electrical power is a phenomenon that has been known for centuries, but not until the late nineteenth century had understanding and technology advanced to the point where it could be reliably produced and transmitted. The ability to transmit power by wire over distances changed the nature of industry, which previously had relied on other sources, such as steam plants or water power to move machinery.

The **Theory of Relativity** was proposed by Albert Einstein, and revolutionized physics. Einstein proposed that the measurement of time and space changed relative to the position of the observer, implying that time and space were not fixed but could warp and change. This had radical implications for Newtonian physics, particularly as it related to gravity, and opened new fields of scientific study.

Penicillin was developed in the mid twentieth century, and rapidly became an important drug, saving countless lives. Penicillin is derived from a mold, which, it was discovered, inhibited and even killed many kinds of germs. In drug form, it could be used to fight infections of various kinds in humans. Penicillin and similarly derived drugs are called antibiotics.

The **microchip** was developed in the 1950s as a way to reduce the size of transistor-based electronic equipment. By replacing individual transistors with a single chip of semiconductor material, more capability could be included in less space. This development led directly to the microprocessor, which is at the heart of every modern computer and most modern electronic products.

The religious beliefs and institutions of a culture can greatly influence scientific research and technological innovation. Political factors have affected scientific advancement, as well, especially in cultures that partially support scientific research with public money. Warfare has traditionally been a strong driver of technological advancement as cultures strive to outpace their neighbors with better weapons and defenses. Technologies developed for military purposes often find their way into the mainstream. Significant advances in flight technology, for example, were made during the two World Wars.

Socially, many cultures have come to value innovation and welcome new products and improvements to older products. This desire to always be advancing and obtaining the latest, newest technology creates economic incentive for innovation.

Skill 33.14 Analyze how science and technology relate to political, economic, social, and cultural issues and events.

Science and technology have increasing effects on our daily lives. Also, we can use the scientific method and experiments to more fully understand many of the phenomena around us. In each of the areas listed below, there are several examples of scientific principles at work.

Health care: In this area, we can see many of the fruits of science and technology in nutrition, genetics, and the development of therapeutic agents. We can see an example of the adaptation of organisms in the development of resistant strains of microbes in response to use of antibiotics. Organic chemistry and biochemistry have been exploited to identify therapeutic targets and to screen and develop new medicines. Advances in molecular biology and our understanding of inheritance have led to the development of genetic screening and allowed us to sequence the human genome.

Environment: There are two broad happenings in environmental science and technology. First, there are many studies being conducted to determine the effects of changing environmental conditions and pollutions. New instruments and monitoring systems have increased the accuracy of these results. Second, advances are being made to mitigate the effects of pollution, develop sustainable methods of agriculture and energy production, and improve waste management.

Agriculture: Development of new technology in agriculture is particularly important as we strive to feed more people with less arable land. Again we see the importance of genetics in developing hybrids that have desirable characteristics. New strains of plants and farming techniques may allow the production of more nutrient rich food and/or allow crops to be grown successfully in harsh conditions. However, it is also important to consider the environmental impact of transgenic species and the use of pesticides and fertilizers. Scientific reasoning and experimentation can assist us in ascertaining the real effect of modern agricultural practices and ways to minimize their impact.

Skill 33.15   Demonstrate knowledge of the origins, diffusion, and effects of major scientific, mathematical, and technological discoveries throughout history.

Historic causation is the concept that events in history are linked to one another by an endless chain of cause and effect. The root causes of major historical events cannot always be seen immediately, and are only apparent when looking back from many years later.

In some cases, individual events can have an immediate, clear effect. In 1941, Europe was embroiled in war. On the Pacific Rim, Japan was engaged in military occupation of Korea and other Asian countries. The United States took a position of isolation, choosing not to become directly involved with the conflicts. This position changed rapidly, however, on the morning of December 7, 1941, when Japanese forces launched a surprise attack on a US naval base at Pearl Harbor in Hawaii. The United States immediately declared war on Japan, and became involved in Europe shortly afterwards. The entry of the United States into the Second World War undoubtedly contributed to the eventual victory of the Allied forces in Europe, and the defeat of Japan after two atomic bombs were dropped there by the US. The surprise attack on Pearl Harbor affected the outcome of the war and the shape of the modern world.

Interaction between cultures, either by exploration and migration or war, often contribute directly to major historical events, but other forces can influence the course of history, as well. Religious movements such as the rise of Catholicism in the Middle Ages created social changes throughout Europe and culminated in the Crusades and the expulsion of Muslims from Spain. Technological developments can lead to major historical events, such as the Industrial Revolution, which was driven by the replacement of water power with steam.

Social movements can also cause major historical shifts. Between the Civil War and the early 1960s in the United States, racial segregation was practiced legally in many parts of the country through "Jim Crow" laws. Demonstrations and activism opposing segregation began to escalate during the late 1950s and early 1960s, eventually leading to the passage in the US Congress of the Civil Rights Act of 1964, which ended legal segregation in the United States.

The **Agricultural Revolution**, initiated by the invention of the plow, led to a thoroughgoing transformation of human society by making large-scale agricultural production possible and facilitating the development of agrarian societies. During the period during which the plow was invented, the wheel, numbers, and writing were also invented. Coinciding with the shift from hunting wild game to the domestication of animals, this period was one of dramatic social and economic change.

The **Scientific Revolution** and the Enlightenment were two of the most important movements in the history of civilization, resulting in a new sense of self-examination and a wider view of the world than ever before. The Scientific Revolution was, above all, a shift in focus from belief to evidence. Scientists and philosophers wanted to see the proof, not just believe what other people told them. It was an exciting time, if you were a forward-looking thinker.

The **Industrial Revolution** of the eighteenth and nineteenth centuries resulted in even greater changes in human civilization and even greater opportunities for trade, increased production, and the exchange of ideas and knowledge. The first phase of the Industrial Revolution (1750-1830) saw the mechanization of the textile industry, vast improvements in mining, with the invention of the steam engine, and numerous improvements in transportation, with the development and improvement of turnpikes, canals, and the invention of the railroad.

Refer to Skill 31.12 for results of Industrial Revolution.

The **Information Revolution** refers to the sweeping changes during the latter half of the twentieth century as a result of technological advances and a new respect for the knowledge or information provided by trained, skilled and experienced professionals in a variety of fields. This approach to understanding a number of social and economic changes in global society arose from the ability to make computer technology both accessible and affordable. In particular, the development of the computer chip has led to such technological advances as the Internet, the cell phone, Cybernetics, wireless communication, and the related ability to disseminate and access a massive amount of information quite readily.

In terms of economic theory and segmentation, it is now the norm to think of three basic economic sectors: agriculture and mining, manufacturing, and "services." Indeed, labor is now often divided between manual labor and informational labor. The fact that businesses are involved in the production and distribution, processing and transmission of information has, according to some, created a new business sector.

Skill 33.16 **Know how developments in science and technology have affected the physical environment; the growth of economies and societies; and definitions of, access to, and use of physical and human resources.**

The supply curve represents the selling and production decisions of the seller and is based on the costs of production. The costs of production of a product are based on the costs of the resources used in its production. The costs of resources are based on the scarcity of the resource. The scarcer a resource is, relatively speaking, the higher its price. A diamond costs more than paper because diamonds are scarcer than paper is. All of these concepts are embodied in the seller's supply curve. The same thing is true on the buying side of the market.

The buyer's preferences, tastes, income, etc. – all of his buying decisions – are embodied in the demand curve. Where the demand and supply curves intersect is where the buying decisions of buyers are equal to the selling decisions of sellers. The quantity that buyers want to buy at a particular price is equal to the quantity that sellers want to sell at that particular price. The market is in equilibrium.

What happens when there is a change? Technological developments result in newer and more efficient ways of doing things. Technology means more efficient production techniques that allow for larger output at lower costs. Suppose a new big oil field is found. Also suppose there is a technology that allows its recovery and refining at a fraction of the present costs. The result is a big increase in the supply of oil at lower costs, as reflected by a rightward shifting oil supply curve. Oil is used as an input into almost all production. Firms now have lower costs. This means that the firm can produce the same amount of output at a lower cost or can produce a larger amount of output at the same cost. The result is a rightward shift of the firm's, and therefore, the industry supply curve. This means that sellers are willing and able to offer for sale larger quantities of output at each price. Assuming buyers' buying decisions stay the same, there is a new market equilibrium, or new point of intersection of the shifted supply curve with the buyers' demand curve. The result is a lower price with a larger quantity of output. The market has achieved a new equilibrium based on the increase in the quantity of a resource. Technological progress and innovation allow for the production of more output at lower prices. This leads to increased consumption for consumers. Technology can also result in unemployment by displacing workers. This is referred to as structural unemployment. The displaced workers must be retrained and find jobs in other industries.

Skill 33.17   Know how changes in science and technology affect moral and ethical issues.

Nuclear energy was once hailed as a cheap and relatively clean alternative to fossil fuels, but fell largely out of favor in the US owing to some high-profile accidents at nuclear plants. Nuclear technology has continued to advance, and nuclear energy is gaining attention once again as a potential resource. One of the crucial considerations in the use of nuclear energy is safety. Nuclear fuels are highly radioactive and very dangerous should they enter the environment. The nuclear waste from creating nuclear energy is another important issue, as the dangerous by product must be carefully and safely stored. Internationally, there is concern that nuclear power plants may be outfitted to produce material for nuclear weapons, creating another level of controversy over the spread of nuclear technology.

Biotechnology is another area that shows promise, but also brings controversy. Advances in biotechnology have opened the possibility of cloning and genetically altering organisms. Serious ethical issues have been raised about proceeding with this type of research, especially where it relates to human beings or human tissues.

In the area of **ecology**, scientific research is focused primarily on finding efficient fuel alternatives. Advances in solar and wind power technology have made these options feasible in some areas. Hybrid technology that uses electricity and fuel cells to supplement fossil fuels has found a market niche that expands yearly.

COMPETENCY 34.0 SOCIAL STUDIES FOUNDATIONS AND SKILLS

Skill 34.1   Understand the philosophical foundations of the social science disciplines and know how knowledge generated by the social sciences affects society and people's lives.

The social sciences are built upon the philosophy that human movements and interactions can be measured, studied, and ultimately predicted using a variety of methods and research techniques. By studying how humans act individually and within their societies, the social sciences seek to discover and explain common motivations and reactions among humans.

The body of knowledge generated by the social sciences has great influence on both the individual and societal levels. Methods of individual psychological treatment, for instance, are based on ongoing research in the social science of psychology. In the larger scheme, a country bases its foreign policy largely on the analysis of political scientists and other social research.

Skill 34.2   Understand how social science disciplines relate to each other.

The major disciplines within the social sciences are definitely intertwined and interrelated. Knowledge and expertise in one requires background that involves some or most of the others. **Anthropology** is the field of study of human culture--how different groups of people live, how they have adapted to their physical environment, what they make or produce, and their relationship to other cultures, behavior, differences and similarities. To pursue the study of people, the anthropologist must know the history of the people being studied; their geography--physical environment; their governmental structure, organization, and its impact on the people; sociology is closely related to this field so knowledge and study in this area is helpful; their goods and produce and how they are used tie in with a background of economics.

Archaeology studies human cultures in the past, examining artifacts left behind to determine how certain people or groups lived their daily lives. Certainly, knowledge of history gives a background as a foundation of study. Geography makes its contribution by not only knowing where to look for remains but also how geographic conditions contributed to and affected the people or cultural groups being studied; how physical factors contributed to artifacts left behind.

Civics deals with what is required and expected of a region's citizens, their rights and responsibilities to government and each other. Knowledge of history gives the background and foundation and government or political science explains not only the organization and set-up of the government but also the impact of international relations on the country or area.

Economics is tied in mainly with history, geography, and political science. The different interrelationships include: History of economic theory and principles combined with historical background of areas; economic activities in the different countries, regions of the world and how international trade and relations are affected which leads to political science or government--how political organization and government affect an area's economic activities.

Geography is the study of the earth, its people, and how people adapt to life on earth and how they use its resources. It is undeniably connected to history, economics, political science, sociology, anthropology, and even a bit of archaeology. Geography not only deals with people and the earth today but also with: How did it all begin? What is the background of the people of an area? What kind of government or political system do they have? How does that affect their ways of producing goods and the distribution of them? What kind of relationships do these people have with other groups? How is the way they live their lives affected by their physical environment? In what ways do they effect change in their way of living? All of this is tied in with their physical environment, the earth and its people.

History is without doubt an integral part of every other discipline in the social sciences. Knowing historical background on anything and anyone anywhere goes a long way towards explaining that what happened in the past leads up to and explains the present.

Political Science is the study of government, international relations, political thought and activity, and comparison of governments. It is tied in with history (historical background), anthropology (how government affects a group's culture and relationship with other groups), economics (governmental influence and regulation of producing and distributing goods and products), and sociology (insight into how social developments affect political life). Other disciplines are also affected, as the study of political science is crucial to understanding the political processes and the influence of government, civic duties, and responsibilities of people.

Psychology is defined as scientifically studying mental processes and behavior. It is related to anthropology and sociology, two social sciences that also study people in society. All three closely consider relationships and attitudes of humans within their social settings. Anthropology considers humans within their cultures, how they live, what they make or produce, how different groups or cultures relate to each other. Sociology follows the angle of looking at behaviors, attitudes, conditions, and relationships in human society. Psychology focuses on individual behavior and how actions are influenced by feelings and beliefs.

Sociology studies human society with its attitudes, behaviors, conditions, and relationships with others. It is closely related to anthropology, especially applied to groups outside of one's region, nation, or hemisphere. History puts it in perspective with an historical background. Political Science is tied to sociology with the impact of political and governmental regulation of activities. Awareness of, influence of, and use of the physical environment as studied in geography also contributes to understanding. Economic activities are a part of human society. The field of psychology is also related.

Skill 34.3   Understand practical applications of social studies education.

In measuring the social significance of an event or issue, one of the first questions to ask is how many people are affected. Wide sweeping events such as wars, natural disasters, revolutions, etc., are significant partly because they can change the way of life for many people in a short time.

Sometimes significant changes take place over long periods of time, however, so it is also important to look at long-term effects of an event or phenomenon, following the chain of causes and effects. In this way, sometimes events that seem insignificant at the time they occur, or which affect only a small number of people, can be linked directly to large societal changes.

Participation in self government is one of the United States' core democratic values. By participating in democratic institutions, citizens become better informed of their rights and responsibilities in a democracy, and thus better citizens. While elementary students are too young to participate directly by voting, classroom activities that simulate elections can help develop a sense of the importance of participating. Encouraging structured discussion or debate on issues directly affecting the students can help establish respect for minority viewpoints and the importance of free expression, both core democratic values.

Skill 34.4   Relate philosophical assumptions and ideas to issues and trends in the social sciences.

Human societies can differ in an infinite number of ways, but all are faced with similar problems as they develop and change. Identifying how different peoples cope with and solve these challenges illustrates differences between cultures, as well as the common traits they share.

By identifying and analyzing these different approaches to social challenges, one can draw conclusions about the societal sources and causes of these differences that may be unique to each society. These conclusions can then be examined further by themselves, which may lead to the discovery of other social phenomena.

Skill 34.5 **Know characteristics and uses of various primary and secondary sources and use information from a variety of sources to acquire social science information and answer social science questions.**

Primary sources include the following kinds of materials:

1. Documents that reflect the immediate, everyday concerns of people: and that you understand the context in which it was produced.
2. Do not read history blindly; but be certain that you understand both explicit and implicit referenced in the material.
3. Read the entire text you are reviewing; do not simply extract a few sentences to read.
4. Although anthologies of materials may help you identify primary source materials, the full original text should be consulted.

Secondary sources include the following kinds of materials:

- Books written on the basis of primary materials about the period of time
- Books written on the basis of primary materials about persons who played a major role in the events under consideration
- Books and articles written on the basis of primary materials about the culture, the social norms, the language, and the values of the period
- Quotations from primary sources
- Statistical data on the period
- The conclusions and inferences of other historians
- Multiple interpretations of the ethos of the time

Guidelines for the use of secondary sources:

- Do not rely upon only a single secondary source.
- Check facts and interpretations against primary sources whenever possible.
- Do not accept the conclusions of other historians uncritically.
- Place greatest reliance on secondary sources created by the best and most respected scholars.
- Do not use the inferences of other scholars as if they were facts.
- Ensure that you recognize any bias the writer brings to his/her interpretation of history.
- Understand the primary point of the book as a basis for evaluating the value of the material presented in it to your questions.

We use **illustrations** of various sorts because it is often easier to demonstrate a given idea visually instead of orally. Sometimes it is even easier to do so with an illustration than a description. This is especially true in the areas of education and research because humans are visually stimulated. It is a fact that any idea presented visually in some manner is always easier to understand and to comprehend than simply getting an idea across verbally, by hearing it or reading it. Among the more common illustrations used in political and social sciences are various types of **maps, graphs and charts**.

Photographs and **globes** are useful as well, but as they are limited in what kind of information that they can show, they are rarely used. Unless, as in the case of a photograph, it is of a particular political figure or a time that one wishes to visualize.

Although maps have advantages over globes and photographs, they do have a major disadvantage. This problem must be considered as well. The major problem of all maps comes about because most maps are flat and the Earth is a sphere. It is impossible to reproduce exactly on a flat surface an object shaped like a sphere. In order to put the earth's features onto a map they must be stretched in some way. This stretching is called **distortion.**

Distortion does not mean that maps are wrong it simply means that they are not perfect representations of the Earth or its parts. **Cartographers,** or mapmakers, understand the problems of distortion. They try to design them so that there is as little distortion as possible in the maps.

The process of putting the features of the Earth onto a flat surface is called **projection.** All maps are really map projections. There are many different types. Each one deals in a different way with the problem of distortion. Map projections are made in a number of ways. Some are done using complicated mathematics. However, the basic ideas behind map projections can be understood by looking at the three most common types:

(1) **Cylindrical Projections** - These are done by taking a cylinder of paper and wrapping it around a globe. A light is used to project the globe's features onto the paper. Distortion is least where the paper touches the globe. For example, suppose that the paper was wrapped so that it touched the globe at the equator, the map from this projection would have just a little distortion near the equator. However, in moving north or south of the equator, the distortion would increase as you moved further away from the equator. The best known and most widely used cylindrical projection is the **Mercator Projection.** Gerard Mercator, a Flemish mapmaker, first developed it in 1569.

(2) **Conical Projections** - The name for these maps comes from the fact that the projection is made onto a cone of paper. The cone is made so that it touches a globe at the base of the cone only. It can also be made so that it cuts through part of the globe in two different places. Again, there is the least distortion where the paper touches the globe. If the cone touches at two different points, there is some distortion at both of them. Conical projections are most often used to map areas in the **middle latitudes**. Maps of the United States are most often conical projections. This is because most of the country lies within these latitudes.

(3) **Flat-Plane Projections** - These are made with a flat piece of paper. It touches the globe at one point only. Areas near this point show little distortion. Flat-plane projections are often used to show the areas of the north and south poles. One such flat projection is called a **Gnomonic Projection**. On this kind of map all meridians appear as straight lines, Gnomonic projections are useful because any straight line drawn between points on it forms a **Great-Circle Route**.

Maps have four main properties. They are (1) the size of the areas shown on the map. (2) The shapes of the areas, (3) Consistent scales, and (4) Straight line directions. A map can be drawn so that it is correct in one or more of these properties. No map can be correct in all of them.

Equal areas - In an equal area map, the meridians and parallels are drawn so that the areas shown have the same proportions as they do on the Earth. For example, Greenland is about 118th the size of South America, thus it will be show as 118th the size on an equal area map. The **Mercator projection** is an example of a map that does not have equal areas. In it, Greenland appears to be about the same size of South America. This is because the distortion is very bad at the poles and Greenland lies near the North Pole.

Conformal - A second map property is conformal, or correct shapes. There are no maps that can show very large areas of the earth in their exact shapes. Only globes can really do that, however Conformal Maps are as close as possible to true shapes. The United States is often shown by a Lambert Conformal Conic Projection Map.

Consistent Scales - Many maps attempt to use the same scale on all parts of the map. Generally, this is easier when maps show a relatively small part of the earth's surface. For example, a map of Texas might be a Consistent Scale Map. Often such maps will have two scales noted in the key. One scale, for example, might be accurate to measure distances between points along the Equator. Another might be then used to measure distances between the North Pole and the South Pole.

Maps showing physical features often try to show information about the elevation or **relief** of the land. **Elevation** is the distance above or below sea level. The elevation is usually shown with colors, for instance, all areas on a map which are at a certain level will be shown in the same color.

Relief Maps - Show the shape of the land surface, flat, rugged, or steep. Relief maps usually give more detail than simply showing the overall elevation of the land's surface. Relief is also sometimes shown with colors, but another way to show relief is by using **contour lines**. These lines connect all points of a land surface which are the same height surrounding the particular area of land.

Thematic Maps - These are used to show more specific information, often on a single **theme**, or topic. Thematic maps show the distribution or amount of something over a certain given area for example, things such as population density, climate, economic information, cultural, political information, etc.

Distance is the measurement between two points of location on a map. Measurement can be in terms of feet, yards, miles, meters, or kilometers. Distance is often correct on equidistant maps only in the direction of latitude.

Direction is usually measured relative to the location of North or South Pole. Directions determined from these locations are said to be relative to True North or True South. The magnetic poles can also be used to measure direction. However, these points on the Earth are located in spatially different spots from the geographic North and South Pole. The North Magnetic Pole is located at 78.3° North, 104.0° West. In the Southern Hemisphere, the South Magnetic Pole is located in Commonwealth Day, Antarctica and has a geographical location of 65° South, 139° East. The magnetic poles are also not fixed over time and shift their spatial position over time.

Skill 34.6   Know how to formulate research questions and use appropriate procedures to reach supportable judgments and conclusions in the social sciences.

There are many different ways to find ideas for **research problems**. One of the most common ways is through experiencing and assessing relevant problems in a specific field. Researchers are often involved in the fields in which they choose to study, and thus encounter practical problems related to their areas of expertise on a daily basis. The can use their knowledge, expertise and research ability to examine their selected research problem. For students, all that this entails is being curious about the world around them. Research ideas can come from one's background, culture, education, experiences etc. Another way to get research ideas is by exploring literature in a specific field and coming up with a question that extends or refines previous research.

Once a **topic** is decided, a research question must be formulated. A research question is a relevant, researchable, feasible statement that identifies the information to be studied. Once this initial question is formulated, it is a good idea to think of specific issues related to the topic. This will help to create a hypothesis. A research **hypothesis** is a statement of the researcher's expectations for the outcome of the research problem. It is a summary statement of the problem to be addressed in any research document. A good hypothesis states, clearly and concisely, the researcher's expected relationship between the variables they are investigating. Once a hypothesis is decided, the rest of the research paper should focus on analyzing a set of information or arguing a specific point. Thus, there are two types of research papers: analytical and argumentative.

Analytical papers focus on examining and understanding the various parts of a research topic and reformulating them in a new way to support your initial statement. In this type of research paper, the research question is used as both a basis for investigation as well as a topic for the paper. Once a variety of information is collected on the given topic, it is coalesced into a clear discussion

Argumentative papers focus on supporting the question or claim with evidence or reasoning. Instead of presenting research to provide information, an argumentative paper presents research in order to prove a debatable statement and interpretation.

The scientific method is the process by which researchers over time endeavor to construct an accurate (that is, reliable, consistent and non-arbitrary) representation of the world. Recognizing that personal and cultural beliefs influence both our perceptions and our interpretations of natural phenomena, standard procedures and criteria minimize those influences when developing a theory.

The scientific method has four steps:

1. Observation and description of a phenomenon or group of phenomena.
2. Formulation of a hypothesis to explain the phenomena.
3. Use of the hypothesis to predict the existence of other phenomena or to predict quantitatively the results of new observations.
4. Performance of experimental tests of the predictions by several independent experimenters and properly performed experiments.

While the researcher may bring certain biases to the study, it's important that bias not be permitted to enter into the interpretation. It's also important that data that doesn't fit the hypothesis not be ruled out. This is unlikely to happen if the researcher is open to the possibility that the hypothesis might turn out to be null. Another important caution is to be certain that the methods for analyzing and interpreting are flawless. Abiding by these mandates is important if the discovery is to make a contribution to human understanding.

Skill 34.7 **Understand social science research and know how social scientists locate, gather, organize, analyze, and report information using standard research methodologies.**

Primary sources are works, records, etc. that were created during the period being studied or immediately after it. Secondary sources are works written significantly after the period being studied and based upon primary sources.

Suppose you are preparing for a presentation on the Civil War and you intend to focus on causes, an issue that has often been debated. If you are examining the matter of slavery as a cause, a graph of the increase in the number of slaves by area of the country for the previous 100 years would be very useful in the discussion. If you are focusing on the economic conditions that were driving the politics of the age, graphs of GDP, distribution of wealth geographically and individually, and relationship of wealth to ownership of slaves would be useful.

If you are discussing the war in Iraq, detailed maps with geopolitical elements would help clarify not only the day-to-day happenings but also the historical features that led up to it. A map showing the number of oil fields and where they are situated with regard to the various political factions and charts showing output of those fields historically would be useful. If you are teaching the history of space travel, photos of the most famous astronauts will add interest to the discussion. Graphs showing the growth of the industry and charts showing discoveries and their relationship to the lives of everyday Americans would be helpful.

Skill 34.8 **Evaluate the validity of social science information from primary and secondary sources regarding bias issues, propaganda, point of view, and frame of reference.**

Making a decision based on a set of given information requires a careful interpretation of the information to decide the strength of the evidence supplied and what it means.

A chart showing that the number of people of foreign birth living in the U.S. has increased annually over the last ten years might allow one to make conclusions about population growth and changes in the relative sizes of ethnic groups in the U.S. The chart would not give information about the reason the number of foreign-born citizens increased, or address matters of immigration status. Conclusions in these areas would be invalid based on this information.

Also Refer to Skill 34.5 and Skill 34.9.

Skill 34.9   Understand and evaluate multiple points of view and frames of reference relating to issues in the social sciences.

Analyzing an event or issue from multiple perspectives involves seeking out sources that advocate or express those perspectives, and comparing them with one another. Listening to the speeches of Martin Luther King, Jr. provides insight to the perspective of one group of people concerning the issue of civil rights in the U.S. in the 1950s and 1960s. Public statements of George Wallace, an American governor opposed to desegregation provides another perspective from the same time period. Looking at the legislation that was proposed at the time and how it came into effect offers a window into the thinking of the day.

Comparing these perspectives on the matter of civil rights provides information on the key issues that each group was concerned about, and gives a fuller picture of the societal changes that were occurring at that time. Analysis of any social event, issue, problem or phenomenon requires that various perspectives be taken into account in this way.

One way to analyze historical events, patterns and relationships is to focus on historical themes. There are many themes that run throughout human history, and they can be used to make comparisons between different historical times as well as between nations and peoples. While new themes are always being explored, a few of the widely recognized historical themes are as follows:

Politics and political institutions can provide information of prevailing opinions and beliefs of a group of people and how they change over time. Historically, Texas has produced several important political figures and was a traditional supporter of the Democratic Party for nearly a century. This has changed in recent years, with the Republican Party gaining more influence and control of Texas politics. Looking at the political history of the state can reveal the popular social ideals that have developed in Texas, and how they have changed over time.

Race and ethnicity is another historical theme that runs through the history of Texas and the nation. Texas was formerly part of Spanish territory and then part of Mexico, and Hispanic settlers have been present from the earliest days of settlement. European Americans began moving into the area in the early nineteenth century and soon made up most of the Texas population. This has changed recently, with ethnic minority groups in Texas now outnumbering those calling their selves white. Researching the history of how peoples of different races treated one another reflects on many other social aspects of a society, and can be a fruitful line of historical interpretation.

The study of **gender** issues is a theme that focuses on the relative places men and women hold in a society, and is connected to many other themes such as politics and economics. In the United States, for many years women were not allowed to vote, for example. In economic matters, married women were expected not to hold jobs. For women who did work, a limited number of types of work were available. Investigating the historical theme of gender can reveal changes in public attitudes, economic changes and shifting political attitudes, among other things.

Economic factors drive many social activities such as where people live and work and the relative wealth of nations. As a historical theme, economic history can connect events to their economic causes and explore the results. Mexican immigration is a national political issue currently. Economic imbalances between the U.S. and Mexico are driving many Mexicans to look for work in the United States. As a border state with historic ties to Mexico, Texas receives a large number of these immigrants and has the second largest Hispanic population in the country, which plays a crucial role in Texas' current economy. The subject of immigration in Texas is an example of how the historical themes of politics, economics and race can intersect, each providing a line of historic interpretation into Texas' past.

Historical concepts are movements, belief systems or other phenomena that can be identified and examined individually or as part of a historical theme. Capitalism, communism, democracy, racism and globalization are all examples of historical concepts. Historical concepts can be interpreted as part of larger historical themes and provide insight into historical events by placing them in a larger historical context.

The historic concept of colonialism, for example, is one that is connected to the history of Texas. Colonialism is the concept that a nation should seek to control areas outside of its borders for economic and political gain by establishing settlements and controlling the native inhabitants. Beginning in the seventeenth century, France and Spain were both actively colonizing North America, with the French establishing a colony at the mouth of the Mississippi River. Spain moved into the area to contain the French and keep them away from their settlements in present-day Mexico. These colonial powers eventually clashed, with Spain maintaining its hold over the region. France finally sold its holdings to the United States in the Louisiana Purchase, which positioned the U.S. at New Spain's frontier. The eighteenth and early nineteenth centuries were a time of revolutionary movements in many parts of the world. The American and French Revolutions had altered the balance of world power in the 1770s and 1780s, and by the 1820s Mexicans living under Spanish colonial control won independence and Texas became part of the new independent state of Mexico. Texas would itself declare independence from Mexico and survive as an independent country for a decade before being annexed by the United States as a state.

Skill 34.10   Know how to analyze social science information.

Social studies provide an opportunity for students to broaden their general academic skills in many areas. By encouraging students to ask and investigate questions, they gain skill in making meaningful inquiries into social issues. Providing them with a range of sources requires students to make judgments about the best sources for investigating a line of inquiry and develops the ability to determine authenticity among those sources. Collaboration develops the ability to work as part of a team and to respect the viewpoints of others.

Historic events and social issues cannot be considered only in isolation. People and their actions are connected in many ways, and events are linked through cause and effect over time. Identifying and analyzing these social and historic links is a primary goal of the social sciences. The methods used to analyze social phenomena borrow from several of the social sciences. Interviews, statistical evaluation, observation and experimentation are just some of the ways people's opinions and motivations can be measured. From these opinions, larger social beliefs and movements can be interpreted, and events, issues and social problems can be placed in context to provide a fuller view of their importance.

Skill 34.11   Communicate and interpret social science information in written, oral, and visual forms and translates information from one medium to another.

An **atlas** is a collection of maps usually bound into a book and containing geographic features, political boundaries, and perhaps social, religious and economic statistics.   Atlases can be found at most libraries but they are widely available on the Internet.   .

Statistical **surveys** are used in social sciences to collect information on a sample of the population. With any kind of information, care must be taken to accurately record information so the results are not skewed or distorted.

Opinion Polls are used to represent the opinions of a population by asking a number of people a series of questions about a product, place, person, event or perhaps the president and then using the results to apply the answers to a larger group or population. Polls, like surveys are subject to errors in the process. Errors can occur based on who is asked the question, where they are asked, the time of day or the biases one may hold in relevance to the poll being taken.

Also refer to Skill 34.15.

Skill 34.12 **Know how to use problem-solving processes to identify problems, gather information, list and consider options, consider advantages and disadvantages, choose and implement solutions, and evaluate the effectiveness of solutions.**

A clearly presented description of research results will spell out what question the researchers hoped to answer. Analyzing research results includes comparing the information given as it relates to this initial question. One must also consider the methods used to gather the data, and whether they truly measure what the researchers claim they do.

A research project that set out to measure the effect of a change in average temperature on the feeding habits of birds, for instance, should use appropriate measurements such as weather observations and observations of the birds in question. Measuring rainfall would not be an appropriate method for this research, because it is not related to the primary area of research. If, during the experiment, it appeared that rainfall may be affecting the research, a researcher may design another experiment to investigate this additional question.

Refer to Skill 34.6 for discussion on Scientific Method.

Skill 34.13 **Know how to use decision-making processes to identify situations that require decisions, gather information, identify options, predict consequences, and take action to implement decisions.**

Decision-making can be broken down into methodical steps that will result in sound decisions based on the relevant facts.

The first step in decision-making is to identify situations that require decisions. These situations often present themselves in daily life. One decision that faces many people is whether to buy a home or rent an apartment.

Before making a decision to buy or rent, a person should gather information, which is the second step. Information such as availability of apartments and homes for sale in the city where one lives and the relative monthly costs of each option are important facts that must be taken into account. The third step, identifying options, organizes the facts gathered in the second step into clear potential decisions.

Predicting the consequence of a decision is an important step in the process. In this example, forecasting the effect of buying vs. renting on one's monthly income would be a crucial step. One choice might be less expensive but may be farther from work, increasing commuting expenses, for example. Predicting how a decision will affect other areas of one's life is essential before arriving at a final decision, which is the last step in the process.

Skill 34.14   Know how to create maps and other graphics to present geographic, political, historical, economic, and cultural features, distributions, and relationships.

Please refer to Skill 34.4.

Skill 34.15   Analyze social science data by using basic mathematical and statistical concepts and analytical methods.

Demography is the branch of science of statistics most concerned with the social well being of people. **Demographic tables** may include: (1) Analysis of the population on the basis of age, parentage, physical condition, race, occupation and civil position, giving the actual size and the density of each separate area. (2) Changes in the population as a result of birth, marriage, and death. (3) Statistics on population movements and their effects and their relations to given economic, social and political conditions. (4) Statistics of crime, illegitimacy and suicide. (5) Levels of education and economic and social statistics.

Such information is also similar to that area of science known as **vital statistics** and as such is indispensable in studying social trends and making important legislative, economic, and social decisions. Such demographic information is gathered from census, and registrar reports and the like, and by state laws such information, especially vital statistics, is kept by physicians, attorneys, funeral directors, member of the clergy, and similar professional people.

Social scientists analyze data in a variety of ways from simple construction of charts to complex analysis requiring knowledge of advanced calculus and statistics. Social scientists use statistics to describe a variety of observations that might include the characteristics of a population, the result of a survey, and the testing of a hypothesis.

Measures of central tendency include the common average or **mean** routinely calculated by summing the value of observations and dividing by the number of observations; the **median** or middle score of observations; or the **mode** which is the most repeated observation.

It is typically not possible to secure data on a full **population**. Social Scientists routinely collect data on **samples** that are based on measurements or observations of a portion of a population.   The samples are described using measures of central tendencies but also by its range from the low score to the high score. Samples ideally are collected **randomly** meaning that each observation in a population had an equal chance of being selected.

Hypothesis testing involves analyzing the results of a sample to show support for a particular position. A Social Scientist will establish a hypothesis regarding some pattern in the world. This may be that a particular counseling approach is better than another or that the President has greater support than other candidates running for office. The Scientist will collect data and analyze it against a **null hypothesis** that there is no difference in counseling strategies or no preferred Presidential candidate, etc. Using the standard normal curve, the Scientist is able to evaluate if there is a **significant difference** allowing the acceptance or rejection of the null hypothesis.

More advanced forms of analysis include regression analysis, modeling, and game theory.

Social scientists need to be concerned about **bias** in a sample. Bias can be caused by sample selection problems, ambiguous questions, or simply some people refusing to answer some or all of the questions. An **asymmetrical** distribution is one that is skewed either to the right or the left because of some factor in the distribution.

Social Scientists utilize a variety of ways to present data visually including Pie Charts, Bar Charts, Maps, Scatter plots and Tables presenting results from studies and surveys. Clear labeling is an important part of an effective table, and provides important information to the reviewer.

Skill 34.16 Know how to apply skills for resolving conflict, including persuasion, compromise, debate, and negotiation.

Conflict occurs regularly in today's society. Conflict can be as simple as a difference of opinion or as complex as a divorce or a custody battle. Conflict resolved poorly can lead to violence or one side simply giving up. Much of the work of the legal system deals with resolving conflicts through civil action filed in a Court of Law. Legal action is usually the most costly resolution option.

Two parties can choose to negotiate the conflict either between parties or with the assistance of a third party. Negotiation provides the opportunity for issues to be debated and both sides to attempt to persuade the other side to their position. Often the best solutions are win-win solutions where the solution leaves both parties better off, as opposed to the traditional win-lose solution common to legal procedures. Often in a dispute a compromise is reached where at least one party agrees to a settlement which does not meet all of the criteria but is adequate to resolve the conflict.

Mediation provides a third party who acts as the mediator, listening to both sides and attempting to negotiate a settlement of the dispute. When both parties agree to **arbitrate** a dispute, a third party hears the positions and issues an opinion which may be binding on the parties.

Skill 34.17   Understand and use social studies terminology correctly.

Social sciences, like other fields, have a set of terms utilized within each discipline. Throughout this book, we have focused on the identification of terms and definitions specific to each particular discipline. For instance an economist is concerned with supply, demand and factors of production. Review each area in the social studies section, becoming comfortable with the terms used in that discipline.

COMPETENCY 35.0 SOCIAL STUDIES INSTRUCTION AND ASSESSMENT

Skill 35.1   Know state content and performance standards for social studies that comprise the Texas Essential Knowledge and Skills (TEKS).

The mission of the Texas Education Agency is to provide leadership, guidance, and resources to help schools meet the educational needs of all students. The Texas Essential Knowledge and Skills website contains the information needed for grade level to grade level for knowledge and skills. Please refer to www.tea.state.tx.us and for social studies specifics www.tea.state.tx.us/rules/tac/chapter113/index.html for further details.

Skill 35.2   Understand the vertical alignment of the social sciences in the Texas Essential Knowledge and Skills (TEKS) from grade level to grade level, including prerequisite knowledge and skills.

Please refer to http://www.tea.state.tx.us/rules/tac/chapter113/index.html for the vertical alignment of the social sciences for Texas Essential Knowledge and Skills from grade level to grade level.

Skill 35.3   Understand the implications of stages of child growth and development for designing and implementing effective learning experiences in the social sciences.

The teacher has a broad knowledge and thorough understanding of the development that typically occurs during the students' current period of life. More importantly, the teacher understands how children learn best during each period of development. The most important premise of child development is that all domains of development (physical, social, and academic) are integrated. Development in each dimension is influenced by the other dimensions. Moreover, today's educator must also have knowledge of exceptions and how these exceptions effect all domains of a child's development.

Social and behavioral theories look at the social interactions of students in the classroom that instruct or impact learning opportunities in the classroom. The psychological approaches behind both theories are subject to individual variables that are learned and applied either proactively or negatively in the classroom. The stimulus of the classroom can promote learning or evoke behavior that is counterproductive for both students and teachers. Students are social beings that normally gravitate to action in the classroom, so teachers must be cognizant in planning classroom environments that are provide both focus and engagement in maximizing learning opportunities.

Physical Development

It is important for the teacher to be aware of the physical stage of development and how the child's physical growth and development affect the child's learning. Factors determined by the physical stage of development include: ability to sit and attend, the need for activity, the relationship between physical skills and self-esteem, and the degree to which physical involvement in an activity (as opposed to being able to understand an abstract concept) affects learning.

Cognitive (Academic) Development

Children go through patterns of learning, beginning with pre-operational thought processes and move to concrete operational thoughts. Eventually they begin to acquire the mental ability to think about and solve problems in their head because they can manipulate objects symbolically. Children of most ages can use symbols such as words and numbers to represent objects and relations, but they need concrete reference points. It is essential children be encouraged to use and develop their thinking skills in solving problems that interest them. The content of the curriculum must be relevant, engaging, and meaningful to the students.

Social Development

Children progress through a variety of social stages beginning with an awareness of peers but a lack of concern for their presence. Young children engage in "parallel" activities playing alongside their peers without directly interacting with one another. During the primary years, children develop an intense interest in peers. They establish productive, positive social and working relationships with one another. This stage of social growth continues to increase in importance throughout the child's school years including intermediate, middle school, and high school years. It is necessary for the teacher to recognize the importance of developing positive peer group relationships and to provide opportunities and support for cooperative small group projects that not only develop cognitive ability but promote peer interaction. The ability to work and relate effectively with peers is of major importance and contributes greatly to the child's sense of competence.

In order to develop this sense of competence, children need to be successful in acquiring the knowledge and skills recognized by our culture as important, especially those skills which promote academic achievement.

Elementary age children face many changes during their early school years, and these changes may positively and/or negatively impact how learning occurs. Some cognitive developments (i.e., learning to read) may broaden their areas of interest as students realize the amount of information (i.e., novels, magazines, non-fiction books) that is out there. On the other hand, a young student's limited comprehension may inhibit some of their confidence (emotional) or conflict with values taught at home (moral). Joke telling (linguistic) becomes popular with children age six or seven and children may use this newly discovered "talent" to gain friends or social "stature" in their class (social). Learning within one domain often spills over into other areas for young students.

When we say that development takes place within domains, what we mean is simply that different aspects of a human change. So, for example, physical changes take place (e.g., body growth, sexuality); cognitive changes take place (e.g., better ability to reason); linguistic changes take place (e.g., a child's vocabulary develops further); social changes take place (e.g., figuring out identity); emotional changes take place (e.g., changes in ability to be concerned about other people); and moral changes take place (e.g., testing limits).

Skill 35.4   Understand the appropriate use of technology as a tool for learning and communicating social studies concepts.

The Internet and other research resources provide a wealth of information on thousands of interesting topics for students preparing presentations or projects. Using search engines like Google, Microsoft and Infotrac allow students to search multiple Internet resources or databases on one subject search. Students should have an outline of the purpose of a project or research presentation that includes:

- Purpose - identity the reason for the research information
- Objective - having a clear thesis for a project will allow the students opportunities to be specific on Internet searches
- Preparation - when using resources or collecting data, students should create folders for sorting through the information. Providing labels for the folders will create a system of organization that will make construction of the final project or presentation easier and less time consuming
- Procedure - organized folders and a procedural list of what the project or presentation needs to include will create A+ work for students and A+ grading for teachers
- Visuals or artifacts - choose data or visuals that are specific to the subject content or presentation. Make sure poster boards or Power Point presentations can be visually seen from all areas of the classroom. Teachers can provide laptop computers for Power Point presentations.

Having the school's librarian or technology expert as a guest speaker in classrooms provides another method of sharing and modeling proper presentation preparation using technology. Teachers can also appoint technology experts from the students in a classroom to work with students on projects and presentations. In high schools, technology classes provide students with upper-class teacher assistants who fill the role of technology assistants.

Skill 35.5 **Select and use effective instructional practices, activities, technologies, and materials to promote students' knowledge and skills in the social sciences.**

The interdisciplinary curriculum planning approach to student learning creates a meaningful balance inclusive of curriculum depth and breadth. Take for instance the following scenario: Mrs. Jackson presents her 9A Language Arts class with an assignment for collaborative group work. She provides them with the birth date and death of the infamous author Ernest Hemingway and asks them to figure how old he was when he died. She gives them five minutes as a group to work on the final answer. After five minutes, she asked each group for their answer and wrote the answers on the board. Each group gave a different answer. When Mrs. Jackson came to the last group, a female student stated, "Why do we have to do math in a Language Arts class?"

The application of knowledge learned from a basic math class would have problem-solved the Language Arts' question. Given the date of his birth and the date of his death, all students needed to do was subtract his birth from his death year to come up with a numerical answer = age when he died. Providing students with a constructivist modality of applying knowledge to problem-solve pertinent information for a language arts' class should be an integral part of instructional practice and learning in an interdisciplinary classroom.

Historically, previous centuries of educational research have shown a strong correlation between the need for interdisciplinary instruction and cognitive learning application. Understanding how students process information and create learning was the goal of earlier educators. Earlier researchers looked at how the brain connected information pieces into meaning and found that learning takes place along intricate neural pathways that formulate processing and meaning from data input into the brain. The implications for student learning are vast in that teachers can work with students to break down subject content area into bits of information that can be memorized and applied to a former learning experience and then processed into integral resources of information.

Skill 35.6   Know how to promote students' use of social science skills, vocabulary, and research tools, including technological tools.

Teachers should have a toolkit of instructional strategies, materials and technologies to encourage and teach students how to solve problems and think critically about subject content. With each curriculum chosen by a district for school implementation, comes an expectation that students must master benchmarks and standards of learning skills. There is an established level of academic performance and proficiency in public schools that students are required to master in today's classrooms. Research of national and state standards indicate that there are additional benchmarks and learning objectives in the subject areas of science, foreign language, English language arts, history, art, health, civics, economics, geography, physical education, mathematics, and social studies that students are required to master in state assessments (Marzano & Kendall, 1996).

A critical thinking skill is a skill target that teachers help students develop to sustain learning in specific subject areas that can be applied within other subject areas. For example, when learning to understand algebraic concepts in solving a math word problem on how much fencing material is needed to build a fence around a backyard area that has a 8' x 12," a math student must understand the order of numerical expression in how to simplify algebraic expressions. Teachers can provide instructional strategies that show students how to group the fencing measurements into an algebraic word problem that with minor addition, subtraction and multiplication can produce a simple number equal to the amount of fencing materials needed to build the fence.

Students use basic skills to understand things that are read such as a reading passage or a math word problem or directions for a project. However, students apply additional thinking skills to fully comprehend how what was read could be applied to their own life or how to make comparatisons or choices based on the factual information given. These higher-order thinking skills are called critical thinking skills as students think about thinking and teachers are instrumental in helping students use these skills in everyday activities.

There are many resources available for the teaching of social science concepts. The resources used should be appropriate to the learning objectives specified. The teacher wants to use different kinds of resources in order to make the subject matter more interesting to the student and to appeal to different learning styles. First, a good textbook is required. This gives the student something they can refer to and something to study from. Students generally like to have a text to refer to. The use of audio-video aids is also beneficial in the classroom environment. Most people are visual learners and will retain information better when it is in visual form. Audio-visual presentations, like movies, give them concepts in pictures that they will easily retain.

Library projects are good for students also. The library has an abundance of resources that students should become familiar with at an early age, so they learn to use the library. There are books and magazines that they can look through and read to expand their knowledge beyond the textbooks. Younger children, particularly, like to look at pictures. The computer also offers abundant opportunities as a teaching tool and resource. The Internet provides a wealth of information on all topics and something can be found that is suitable for any age group. Children like to play games, so presenting the material in a game-like format is also a good teaching tool. Making little puzzles for vocabulary or letting them present the information in the form of a story or even a play helps them learn and retain various concepts. Field trips, if possible, are also a good way to expose children to various aspects of social science. Trips to the stock markets, the Federal Reserve, etc. are things children enjoy and remember. Today's world of technology makes a myriad of resources available to the teacher. The teacher should make use of as many of them as possible to keep the material more interesting for the student and to aid in their retention of the material.

Skill 35.7   Know how to communicate the value of social studies education to students, parents/caregivers, colleagues, and the community.

In measuring the social significance of an event or issue, one of the first questions to ask is how many people are affected. Wide sweeping events such as wars, natural disasters, revolutions, etc., are significant partly because they can change the way of life for many people in a short time. By involving parents, caregivers, colleagues and the community in the education of students in the social studies, we are all benefiting by learning about what is going on in our world and how we interact with each other.

Sometimes significant changes take place over long periods of time, however, so it is also important to look at long-term effects of an event or phenomenon, following the chain of causes and effects. In this way, sometimes events that seem insignificant at the time they occur, or which affect only a small number of people, can be linked directly to large societal changes.

Skill 35.8   Know how to provide instruction that relates skills, concepts, and ideas in different social science disciplines.

Refer to Skill 34.2 and Skill 35.9.

Skill 35.9   Provide instruction that makes connections between knowledge and methods in the social sciences and in other content areas.

It is important for teachers to consider students' development and readiness when making instructional decisions. If an educational program is child-centered, then it will surely address the developmental abilities and needs of the students because it will take its cues from students' interests, concerns, and questions. Making an educational program child-centered involves building on the natural curiosity children bring to school, and asking children what they want to learn.

Teachers help students to identify their own questions, puzzles, and goals, and then structure for them widening circles of experience and investigation of those topics. Teachers manage to infuse all the skills, knowledge, and concepts that society mandates into a child-driven curriculum. This does not mean passive teachers who respond only to students' explicit cues. Teachers also draw on their understanding of children's characteristic developmental needs and enthusiasms to design experiences that lead children into areas they might not choose, but that they do enjoy and that engage them. Teachers also bring their own interests and enthusiasms into the classroom to share and to act as a motivational means of guiding children.

Implementing such a child-centered curriculum is the result of very careful and deliberate planning. Planning serves as a means of organizing instruction and influences classroom teaching. Well thought-out planning includes specifying behavioral objectives, specifying students' entry behavior (knowledge and skills), selecting and sequencing learning activities so as to move students from entry behavior to objective, and evaluating the outcomes of instruction in order to improve planning.

Skill 35.10   Demonstrate knowledge of forms of assessment appropriate for evaluating students' progress and needs in the social sciences.

See Skill 35.11.

Skill 35.11 **Use multiple forms of assessment and knowledge of the Texas Essential Knowledge and Skills (TEKS) to determine students' progress and needs and to help plan instruction that addresses the strengths, needs, and interests of all students, including English Language Learners.**

Assessment methods are always important in teaching. Assessment methods are ways to determine if the student has sufficiently learned the required material. There are different ways of accomplishing this. Assessment methods basically mean asking a question in some way and receiving a response in some way from the student, whether it is written or verbal. The test is the usual method where the student answers questions on the material he has studied. Tests, of course, can be written or oral. Tests for younger children can be game-like. They can be asked to draw lines connecting various associated symbols or to pick a picture representing a concept. Other methods involve writing essays on various topics. They don't have to be long, but just long enough for the student to demonstrate that he has adequate knowledge of a subject. Oral reports can accomplish the same goal.

In evaluating school reform improvements for school communities, educators may implement and assess student academic performance using norm-referenced, criterion-referenced, and performance-based assessments. Effective classroom assessment can provide educators with a wealth of information on student performance and teacher instructional practices. Using student assessment can provide teachers with data in analyzing student academic performance and making inferences on student learning planning that can foster increased academic achievement and success for students.

Assessments

The process of collecting, quantifying and qualifying student performance data using multiple assessment information on student learning is called assessment. A comprehensive assessment system must include a diversity of assessment tools such as norm-referenced, criterion-referenced, performance-based, or any student generated alternative assessments that can measure learning outcomes and goals for student achievement and success in school communities.

Norm-referenced Assessments

Norm-referenced tests (NRT) are used to classify student learners for homogenous groupings based on ability levels or basic skills into a ranking category. In many school communities, NRTs are used to classify students into AP (Advanced Placement), honors, regular or remedial classes that can significantly impact student future educational opportunities or success.

NRTs are also used by national testing companies such as Iowa Test of Basic Skills (Riverside), Florida Achievement Test (McGraw-Hill), Texas Assessment of Knowledge and Skills (TAKS) by the Student Assessment Division and other major test publishers to test a national sample of students to norm against standard test-takers. Stiggins (1994) states "Norm-referenced tests (NRT) are designed to highlight achievement differences between and among students to produce a dependable rank order of students across a continuum of achievement from high achievers to low achievers."

Educators may select NRTs to focus on student learners with lower basic skills which could limit the development of curriculum content that needs to provide students with academic learning's that accelerate student skills from basic to higher skill application to address the state assessments and core subject expectations. NRT ranking ranges from 1-99 with 25% of students scoring in the lower ranking of 1-25 and 25% of students scoring in the higher ranking of 76-99. TAKS measures statewide curriculum in reading for Grades 3-9; writing for Grades 4 and 7; English Language Arts in Grades 10 and 11; mathematics for Grades 3-11; science for Grades 5, 10 and 11, and social studies for Grades 8, 10, and 11. The Spanish TAKS is given to Grades 3 through 6. Satisfactory performance on the TAKS at Grade 11 is prerequisite for a high school diploma.

Criterion-referenced Assessments

Criterion-referenced assessments look at specific student learning goals and performance compared to a norm group of student learners. According to Bond (1996) "Educators or policy makers may choose to use a Criterion-referenced test (CRT) when they wish to see how well students have learned the knowledge and skills which they are expected to have mastered." Many school districts and state legislation use CRTs to ascertain whether schools are meeting national and state learning standards. The latest national educational mandate of "No Child Left Behind" (NCLB) and Adequate Yearly Progress (AYP) use CRTs to measure student learning, school performance, and school improvement goals as structured accountability expectations in school communities. CRTs are generally used in learning environments to reflect the effectiveness of curriculum implementation and learning outcomes.

Performance-based Assessments

Performance-based assessments are currently being used in a number of state testing programs to measure the learning outcomes of individual students in subject content areas. Attaching a graduation requirement to passing the required state assessment for the class of 2008 has created a high-stakes testing and educational accountability for both students and teachers in meeting the expected skill based requirements for 10th grade students taking the test.

In today's classrooms, performance-based assessments in core subject areas must have established and specific performance criteria that start with pre-testing in a subject area and maintain daily or weekly testing to gauge student learning goals and objectives. To understand a student's learning is to understand how a student processes information. Effective performance assessments will show the gaps or holes in student learning which allows for an intense concentration on providing fillers to bridge non-sequential learning gaps. Typical performance assessments include oral and written student work in the form of research papers, oral presentations, class projects, journals, student portfolio collections of work, and community service projects.

Summary

With today's emphasis on student learning accountability, the public and legislature demands for school community accountability for effective teaching and assessment of student learning outcomes will remain a constant mandate of educational accountability. In 1994, thirty-one states use NRTs for student assessments, while thirty-three states use CRTs in assessing student learning outcomes (Bond, 1996). Performance-based assessments are being used exclusively for state testing of high school students in ascertaining student learning outcomes based on individual processing and presentation of academic learning. Before a state, district, or school community can determine which type of testing is the most effective, there must be a determination of testing outcome expectation; content learning outcome; and deciding effectiveness of the assessments in meeting the learning goals and objectives of the students.

ESOL

Teaching students who are learning English as a second language poses some unique challenges, particularly in a standards-based environment. The key is realizing that no matter how little English a student knows, the teacher should teach with the student's developmental level in mind. This means that instruction should not be "dumbed-down" for ESOL students. Different approaches should be used, however, to ensure that these students (a) get multiple opportunities to learn and practice English and (b) still learn content.

Many ESOL approaches are based on social learning methods. By being placed in mixed level groups or by being paired with a student of another ability level, students will get a chance to practice English in a natural, non-threatening environment. Students should not be pushed in these groups to use complex language or to experiment with words that are too difficult. They should simply get a chance to practice with simple words and phrases.

In teacher-directed instructional situations, visual aids, such as pictures, objects, and video are particularly effective at helping students make connections between words and items they are already familiar with.

ESOL students may need additional accommodations with assessments, assignments, and projects. For example, teachers may find that written tests provide little to no information about a student's understanding of the content. Therefore, an oral test may be better suited for ESOL students. When students are somewhat comfortable and capable with written tests, a shortened test may actually be preferable; take note that they will need extra time to translate.

From high school and college, most of us think that learning a language strictly involves drills, memorization, and tests. While this is a common method used (some people call it a structural, grammatical, or linguistic approach). While this works for some students, it certainly does not work for all.

Although there are dozens of methods that have been developed to help people learn additional languages, the focus will be on some of the more common approaches used in today's K-12 classrooms. Cognitive approaches to language learning focus on concepts. While words and grammar are important, when teachers use the cognitive approach, they focus on using language for conceptual purposes—rather than learning words and grammar for the sake of simply learning new words and grammatical structures. This approach focuses heavily on students' learning styles, and it cannot necessarily be pinned down as having specific techniques. Rather, it is more of a philosophy of instruction.

There are many approaches that are noted for their motivational purposes. In a general sense, when teachers work to motivate students to learn a language, they do things to help reduce fear and to assist students in identifying with native speakers of the target language. A very common method is often called the functional approach. In this approach, the teacher focuses on communicative elements. For example, a first grade ESOL teacher might help students learn phrases that will assist them in finding a restroom, asking for help on the playground, etc. Many functionally-based adult ESOL programs help learners with travel-related phrases and words.

Another very common motivational approach is Total Physical Response. This is a kinesthetic approach that combines language learning and physical movement. In essence, students learn new vocabulary and grammar by responding with physical motion to verbal commands. Some people say it is particularly effective because the physical actions create good brain connections with the words.

In general, the best methods do not treat students as if they have a Language deficit. Rather, the best methods build upon what students already know, and they help to instill the target language as a communicative process rather than a list of vocabulary words that have to be memorized.

Please refer to www.tea.state.tx.us and for social studies specifics www.tea.state.tx.us/rules/tac/chapter113/index.html for further details.

Sample Test: Social Studies

1. The belief that the United States should control all of North America was called: (Skill 29.1) (Easy)

   A. Westward Expansion
   B. Pan Americanism
   C. Manifest Destiny
   D. Nationalism

2. The area of the United States was effectively double through purchase of the Louisiana Territory under which President? (Skill 29.1) (Average)

   A. John Adams
   B. Thomas Jefferson
   C. James Madison
   D. James Monroe

3. A major quarrel between colonial Americans and the British concerned a series of British Acts of Parliament dealing with: (Skill 29.1) (Easy)

   A. Taxes
   B. Slavery
   C. Native Americans
   D. Shipbuilding

4. The international organization established to work for world peace at the end of the Second World War is the : (Skill 29.1) (Average)

   A. League of Nations
   B. United Federation of Nations
   C. United Nations
   D. United World League

5. Which famous battle fought on Texas soil resulted in Texas independence from Mexico? (Skill 29.2) (Rigorous)

   A. The Battle of the Alamo
   B. The Battle of San Jacinto
   C. The Battle of the Rio Grande
   D. The Battle of Shiloh

6. Why is the system of government in the United States referred to as a federal system? (Skill 29.9) (Rigorous)

   A. There are different levels of government
   B. There is one central authority in which all governmental power is vested
   C. The national government cannot operate except with the consent of the governed
   D. Elections are held at stated periodic times, rather than as called by the head of the government

7. **The U.S. Constitution, adopted in 1789, provided for: (Skill 29.9) (Rigorous)**

   A. Direct election of the President by all citizens
   B. Direct election of the President by citizens meeting a standard of wealth
   C. Indirect election of the President by electors
   D. Indirect election of the President by the U.S. Senate

8. **From about 1870 to 1900 the settlement of America's "last frontier," the West, was completed. One attraction for settlers was free land, but it would have been to no avail without: (Skill 29.10) (Rigorous)**

   A. Better farming methods and technology
   B. Surveying to set boundaries
   C. Immigrants and others to seek new land
   D. The railroad to get them there

9. **Slavery arose in the Southern Colonies partly as a perceived economical way to: (Skill 29.11) (Average)**

   A. Increase the owner's wealth through human beings used as a source of exchange
   B. Cultivate large plantations of cotton, tobacco, rice, indigo, and other crops
   C. Provide Africans with humanitarian aid, such as health care, Christianity, and literacy
   D. Keep ships' holds full of cargo on two out of three legs of the "triangular trade" voyage.

10. **The post-Civil War years were a time of low public morality, a time of greed, graft, and dishonesty. Which one of the reasons listed would not be accurate? (Skill 29.12) (Rigorous)**

    A. The war itself, because of the money and materials needed to conduct the War
    B. The very rapid growth of industry and big business after the War
    C. The personal example set by President Grant
    D. Unscrupulous heads of large impersonal corporations

11. A number of women worked hard in the first half of the 19th century for women's rights, but decisive gains did not come until after 1850. The earliest accomplishments were in: (Skill 29.13) (Average)

    A. Medicine
    B. Education
    C. Writing
    D. Temperance

12. Of all the major causes of both World Wars I and II, the most significant one is considered to be: (Skill 2.14) (Average)

    A. Extreme nationalism
    B. Military buildup and aggression
    C. Political unrest
    D. Agreements and alliances

13. Meridians, or lines of longitude, not only help in pinpointing locations but are also used for: (Skill 30.2) (Rigorous)

    A. Measuring distance from the Poles
    B. Determining direction of ocean currents
    C. Determining the time around the world
    D. Measuring distance on the equator

14. The study of the ways in which different societies around the world deal with the problems of limited resources and unlimited needs and wants is in the area of: (Skill 31.2) (Average)

    A. Economics
    B. Sociology
    C. Anthropology
    D. Political Science

15. Capitalism and communism are alike in that they are both: (Skill 31.3) (Easy)

    A. Organic systems
    B. Political systems
    C. Centrally planned systems
    D. Economic systems

16. The purchase of goods or services on one market for immediate resale on another market is: (Skill 31.3) (Average)

    A. Output
    B. Enterprise
    C. Arbitrage
    D. Mercantile

17. The economic system promoting individual ownership of land, capital, and businesses with minimal governmental regulations is called: (Skill 31.3) (Easy)

    A. Macro-economy
    B. Micro-economy
    C. Laissez-faire
    D. Free enterprise

18. The American labor union movement started gaining new momentum: (Skill 31.5) (Rigorous)

   A. During the building of the railroads
   B. After 1865 with the growth of cities
   C. With the rise of industrial giants such as Carnegie and Vanderbilt
   D. During the war years of 1861-1865

19. **It can be reasonably stated that the change in the United States from primarily an agricultural country into an industrial power was due to all of the following except: (Skill 31.12) (Average)**

   A. Tariffs on foreign imports
   B. Millions of hardworking immigrants
   C. An increase in technological developments
   D. The change from steam to electricity for powering industrial machinery

20. There is no doubt of the vast improvement of the US Constitution over the weak Articles of Confederation. Which one of the four accurate statements below is a unique yet eloquent description of the document? (Skill 32.3) (Rigorous)

   A. The establishment of a strong central government in no way lessened or weakened the individual states.
   B. Individual rights were protected and secured.
   C. The Constitution is the best representation of the results of the American genius for compromise.
   D. Its flexibility and adaptation to change gives it a sense of timelessness.

21. "Marbury vs Madison (1803)" was an important Supreme Court case which set the precedent for: (Skill 32.8) (Rigorous)

   A. The elastic clause
   B. Judicial review
   C. The supreme law of the land
   D. Popular sovereignty in the territories

22. Which one of the following is not a function or responsibility of the US political parties? (Skill 32.9) (Rigorous)

   A. Conducting elections or the voting process
   B. Obtaining funds needed for election campaigns
   C. Choosing candidates to run for public office
   D. Making voters aware of issues and other public affairs information

23. Which of the following lists elements usually considered to be responsibilities of citizenship under the American system of government? (Skill 32.11) (Easy)

   A. Serving in public office, voluntary government service, military duty
   B. Paying taxes, jury duty, upholding the Constitution
   C. Maintaining a job, giving to charity, turning in fugitives
   D. Quartering of soldiers, bearing arms, government service

24. In which of the following disciplines would the study of physical mapping, modern or ancient, and the plotting of points and boundaries be least useful? (Skill 34.1) (Average)

   A. Sociology
   B. Geography
   C. Archaeology
   D. History

25. The study of the exercise of power and political behavior in human society today would be conducted by experts in: (Skill 34.2) (Average)

   A. History
   B. Sociology
   C. Political Science
   D. Anthropology

Answer Key: Social Studies

1.	C	8.	D	15.	D	22.	A
2.	B	9.	B	16.	C	23.	B
3.	A	10.	C	17.	D	24.	A
4.	C	11.	B	18.	B	25.	C
5.	B	12.	A	19.	A		
6.	A	13.	C	20.	C		
7.	C	14.	A	21.	B		

Rigor Table: Social Studies

	Easy %20	Average Rigor %40	Rigorous %40
Question #	1, 3, 15, 17, 23	2, 4, 9, 11, 12, 14, 16, 24, 25	5, 6, 7, 8, 10, 13, 18, 20, 21, 22

Rationales with Sample Questions: Social Studies

1. **The belief that the United States should control all of North America was called: (Skill 29.1)(Easy)**

    A. Westward Expansion
    B. Pan Americanism
    C. Manifest Destiny
    D. Nationalism

C. Manifest Destiny

The belief that the United States should control all of North America was called (C) Manifest Destiny. This idea fueled much of the violence and aggression towards those already occupying the lands such as the Native Americans. Manifest Destiny was certainly driven by sentiments of (D) nationalism, and gave rise to (A) westward expansion.

2. **The area of the United States was effectively double through purchase of the Louisiana Territory under which President? (Skill 29.1) (Average)**

    A. John Adams
    B. Thomas Jefferson
    C. James Madison
    D. James Monroe

B. Thomas Jefferson

The Louisiana Purchase, an acquisition of territory from France in 1803, occurred during the presidency of Thomas Jefferson. (A) John Adams (1735-1826) was president from 1797–1801, before the purchase. (C) James Madison (1751-1836) after the purchase (1809-1817). (D) James Monroe (1758-1831) was actually a signatory on the Purchase, but did not become President until 1817.

3. **A major quarrel between colonial Americans and the British concerned a series of British Acts of Parliament dealing with: (Skill 29.1) (Easy)**

    A. Taxes
    B. Slavery
    C. Native Americans
    D. Shipbuilding

A. Taxes

Acts of Parliament imposing taxes on the colonists always provoked resentment. Because the colonies had no direct representation in Parliament, they felt it unjust that that body should impose taxes on them, with so little knowledge of their very different situation in America and no real concern for the consequences of such taxes. (B) While slavery continued to exist in the colonies long after it had been completely abolished in Britain, it never was a source of serious debate between Britain and the colonies. By the time Britain outlawed slavery in its colonies in 1833, the American Revolution had already occurred and the United States was free of British control. (C) There was no series of British Acts of Parliament passed concerning Native Americans. (D) Colonial shipbuilding was an industry, which received little interference from the British.

4. **The international organization established to work for world peace at the end of the Second World War is the : (Skill 29.1) (Average)**

    A. League of Nations
    B. United Federation of Nations
    C. United Nations
    D. United World League

C. United Nations

The international organization established to work for world peace at the end of the Second World War was the United Nations. From the ashes of the failed League of Nations, established following World War I, the United Nations continues to be a major player in world affairs today.

5. Which famous battle fought on Texas soil resulted in Texas independence from Mexico? (Skill 29.2)(Rigorous)

   A. The Battle of the Alamo
   B. The Battle of San Jacinto
   C. The Battle of the Rio Grande
   D. The Battle of Shiloh

B. The Battle of San Jacinto

It was the battle of San Jacinto in which Sam Houston and the Texicans roundly defeated the Mexican army and captured Mexican General and Commander Santa Anna. The result was the independence of the Republic of Texas from Mexican control. (B) The Battle of the Alamo, despite the defeat of the Texans by Santa Anna's troops was a critical event which enabled Houston to gather troops and prepare for the Battle of San Jacinto. (D) The Battle of Shiloh occurred during the Civil War, and it was not in Texas. (C) There was no major battle called the Battle of the Rio Grande.

6. Why is the system of government in the United States referred to as a federal system? (Skill 29.9) (Rigorous)

   A. There are different levels of government
   B. There is one central authority in which all governmental power is vested
   C. The national government cannot operate except with the consent of the governed
   D. Elections are held at stated periodic times, rather than as called by the head of the government

A. There are different levels of government.

(A) The United States is composed of fifty states, each responsible for its own affairs, but united under a federal government. (B) A centralized system is the opposite of a federal system. (C) That national government cannot operate except with the consent of the governed is a founding principle of American politics. It is not a political system like federalism. A centralized democracy could still be consensual, but would not be federal. (D) This is a description of electoral procedure, not a political system like federalism.

7. **The U.S. Constitution, adopted in 1789, provided for: (Skill 29.9) (Rigorous)**

    A. Direct election of the President by all citizens
    B. Direct election of the President by citizens meeting a standard of wealth
    C. Indirect election of the President by electors
    D. Indirect election of the President by the U.S. Senate

C. Indirect election of the President by electors

The United States Constitution has always arranged for the indirect election of the President by electors. The question, by mentioning the original date of adoption, might mislead someone to choose B, but while standards of citizenship have been changed by amendment, the President has never been directly elected. Nor does the Senate have anything to do with presidential elections. The House of Representatives, not the Senate, settles cases where neither candidate wins in the Electoral College.

8. **From about 1870 to 1900 the settlement of America's "last frontier," the West, was completed. One attraction for settlers was free land, but it would have been to no avail without: (Skill 29.10) (Rigorous)**

    A. Better farming methods and technology
    B. Surveying to set boundaries
    C. Immigrants and others to seek new land
    D. The railroad to get them there

D. The railroad to get them there

From about 1870 to 1900, the settlement of America's "last frontier" in the West was made possible by the building of the railroad. Without the railroad, the settlers never could have traveled such distances in an efficient manner.

9. **Slavery arose in the Southern Colonies partly as a perceived economical way to: (Skill 29.11) (Average)**

   A. Increase the owner's wealth through human beings used as a source of exchange
   B. Cultivate large plantations of cotton, tobacco, rice, indigo, and other crops
   C. Provide Africans with humanitarian aid, such as health care, Christianity, and literacy
   D. Keep ships' holds full of cargo on two out of three legs of the "triangular trade" voyage.

B. Cultivate large plantations of cotton, tobacco, rice, indigo, and other crops.

The Southern states, with their smaller populations, were heavily dependent on slave labor as a means of being able to fulfill their role and remain competitive in the greater U.S. economy. (A) When slaves arrived in the South, the vast majority would become permanent fixtures on plantations, intended for work, not as a source of exchange. (C) While some slave owners instructed their slaves in Christianity, provided health care or some level of educations, such attention were not their primary reasons for owning slaves – a cheap and ready labor force was their reason. (D) Whether or not ships' holds were full on two or three legs of the triangular journey was not the concern of Southerners as the final purchasers of slaves. Such details would have concerned the slave traders.

10. **The post-Civil War years were a time of low public morality, a time of greed, graft, and dishonesty. Which one of the reasons listed would not be accurate? (Skill 29.12) (Rigorous)**

   A. The war itself, because of the money and materials needed to conduct the War
   B. The very rapid growth of industry and big business after the War
   C. The personal example set by President Grant
   D. Unscrupulous heads of large impersonal corporations

C. The personal example set by President Grant

The post-Civil War years were a particularly difficult time for the nation, and public morale was especially low. The war had plunged the country into debt, and ultimately into a recession by the 1890s. Racism was rampant throughout the South and the North, where freed Blacks were taking jobs for low wages. The rapid growth of industry and big business caused a polarization of rich and poor, workers and owners. Many people moved into the urban centers to find work in the new industrial sector. These jobs typically paid low wages, required long hours, and offered poor working conditions. The heads of large impersonal corporations treated their workers inhumanely, letting morale drop to a record low. The heads of corporations tried to prevent and disband labor unions.

11. **A number of women worked hard in the first half of the 19th century for women's rights, but decisive gains did not come until after 1850. The earliest accomplishments were in: (Skill 29.13)(Average)**

   A. Medicine
   B. Education
   C. Writing
   D. Temperance

B. Education

Although women worked hard in the early nineteenth century to make gains in medicine, writing, and temperance movements, the most prestigious accomplishments of the early women's movement were in the field of education. Women such as May Wollstonecraft (1759-1797), Alice Palmer (1855-1902), and, of course, Elizabeth Blackwell (1821-1910) led the way for women, particularly in the area of higher education.

12. **Of all the major causes of both World Wars I and II, the most significant one is considered to be: (Skill 2.14)(Average)**

    A. Extreme nationalism
    B. Military buildup and aggression
    C. Political unrest
    D. Agreements and alliances

A. Extreme nationalism

Although military buildup and aggression, political unrest, and agreements and alliances were all characteristic of the world climate before and during World War I and World War II, the most significant cause of both wars was extreme nationalism. Nationalism is the idea that the interests and needs of a particular nation are of the utmost and primary importance above all else. Some nationalist movements could be liberation movements while others were oppressive regimes, much depends on their degree of nationalism. The nationalism that sparked WWI included a rejection of German, Austro-Hungarian, and Ottoman imperialism by Serbs, Slavs and others culminating in the assassination of Archduke Ferdinand by a Serb nationalist in 1914. Following WWI and the Treaty of Versailles, many Germans and others in the Central Alliance Nations, malcontent at the concessions and reparations of the treaty started a new form of nationalism. Adolf Hitler and the Nazi regime led this extreme nationalism. Hitler's ideas were an example of extreme, oppressive nationalism combined with political, social and economic scapegoating and was the primary cause of WWII.

13. **Meridians, or lines of longitude, not only help in pinpointing locations but are also used for: (Skill 30.2)(Rigorous)**

    A. Measuring distance from the Poles
    B. Determining direction of ocean currents
    C. Determining the time around the world
    D. Measuring distance on the equator

C. Determining the time around the world

Meridians, or lines of longitude, are the determining factor in separating time zones and determining time around the world.

14. **The study of the ways in which different societies around the world deal with the problems of limited resources and unlimited needs and wants is in the area of: (Skill 31.2)(Average)**

    A. Economics
    B. Sociology
    C. Anthropology
    D. Political Science

A. Economics

The study of the ways in which different societies around the world deal with the problems of limited resources and unlimited needs and wants is a study of Economics. Economists consider the law of supply and demand as fundamental to the study of the economy. However, Sociology and Political Science also consider the study of economics and its importance in understanding social and political systems.

15. **Capitalism and communism are alike in that they are both: (Skill 31.3) (Easy)**

    A. Organic systems
    B. Political systems
    C. Centrally planned systems
    D. Economic systems

D. Economic systems

While economic and (B) political systems are often closely connected, capitalism and communism are primarily (D) economic systems. Capitalism is a system of economics that allows the open market to determine the relative value of goods and services. Communism is an economic system where the market is planned by a central state. While communism is a (C) centrally planned system, this is not true of capitalism. (A) organic systems are studied in biology, a natural science.

16. The purchase of goods or services on one market for immediate resale on another market is: (Skill 31.3)(Average)

    A. Output
    B. Enterprise
    C. Arbitrage
    D. Mercantile

C. Arbitrage

Output is an amount produced or manufactured by an industry. Enterprise is simply any business organization. Mercantile is one of the first systems of economics in which goods were exchanged. Therefore, arbitrage is an item or service that an industry produces. The dictionary definition of arbitrage is the purchase of securities on one market for immediate resale on another market in order to profit from a price discrepancy.

17. The economic system promoting individual ownership of land, capital, and businesses with minimal governmental regulations is called: (Skill 31.3) (Easy)

    A. Macro-economy
    B. Micro-economy
    C. Laissez-faire
    D. Free enterprise

D. Free Enterprise

(D) Free enterprise or capitalism is the economic system that promotes private ownership of land, capital, and business with minimal government interference. (C) Laissez-faire is the idea that an "invisible hand" will guide the free enterprise system to the maximum potential efficiency.

18. **The American labor union movement started gaining new momentum: (Skill 31.5) (Rigorous)**

   A. During the building of the railroads
   B. After 1865 with the growth of cities
   C. With the rise of industrial giants such as Carnegie and Vanderbilt
   D. During the war years of 1861-1865

B. After 1865 with the growth of cities

The American Labor Union movement had been around since the late 18th and early 19th centuries. The Labor movement began to first experience persecution by employers in the early 1800s. The American Labor Movement remained relatively ineffective until after the Civil War. In 1866, the National Labor Union was formed, pushing such issues as the eight-hour workday and new policies of immigration. This gave rise to the Knights of Labor and eventually the American Federation of Labor (AFL) in the 1890s and the Industrial Workers of the World (1905). Therefore, it was the period following the Civil War that empowered the labor movement in terms of numbers, militancy, and effectiveness.

19. **It can be reasonably stated that the change in the United States from primarily an agricultural country into an industrial power was due to all of the following except: (Skill 31.12) (Average)**

   A. Tariffs on foreign imports
   B. Millions of hardworking immigrants
   C. An increase in technological developments
   D. The change from steam to electricity for powering industrial machinery

A. Tariffs on foreign imports

It can be reasonably stated that the change in the United States from primarily an agricultural country into an industrial power was due to a great degree of three of the reasons listed above. It was a combination of millions of hard-working immigrants, an increase in technological developments, and the change from steam to electricity for powering industrial machinery. The only reason given that really had little effect was the tariffs on foreign imports.

20. There is no doubt of the vast improvement of the US Constitution over the weak Articles of Confederation. Which one of the four accurate statements below is a unique yet eloquent description of the document? (Skill 32.3) (Rigorous)

   A. The establishment of a strong central government in no way lessened or weakened the individual states.
   B. Individual rights were protected and secured.
   C. The Constitution is the best representation of the results of the American genius for compromise.
   D. Its flexibility and adaptation to change gives it a sense of timelessness.

C. The Constitution is the best representation of the results of the American genius for compromise.

The U.S. Constitution was indeed a vast improvement over the Articles of Confederation and the authors of the document took great care to assure longevity. It clearly stated that the establishment of a strong central government in no way lessened or weakened the individual states. In the Bill of Rights, citizens were assured that individual rights were protected and secured. Possibly the most important feature of the new Constitution was its flexibility and adaptation to change which assured longevity.

21. **"Marbury vs Madison (1803)" was an important Supreme Court case which set the precedent for: (Skill 32.8) (Rigorous)**

    A. The elastic clause
    B. Judicial review
    C. The supreme law of the land
    D. Popular sovereignty in the
       Territories

B. Judicial review

Marbury vs. Madison (1803) was an important case for the Supreme Court as it established judicial review. In that case, the Supreme Court set precedence to declare laws passed by Congress as unconstitutional. Popular sovereignty in the territories was a failed plan pushed by Stephen Davis to allow states to decide the slavery question for themselves. In his attempt to appeal to the masses in the pre-Civil War elections. The supreme law of the land is just that, the law that rules. The elastic clause is not a real term.

22. **Which one of the following is not a function or responsibility of the US political parties? (Skill 32.9) (Rigorous)**

    A. Conducting elections or the voting process
    B. Obtaining funds needed for election campaigns
    C. Choosing candidates to run for public office
    D. Making voters aware of issues and other public affairs information

A. Conducting elections or the voting process

The US political parties have numerous functions and responsibilities. Among them are obtaining funds needed for election campaigns, choosing the candidates to run for office, and making voters aware of the issues. The political parties, however, do not conduct elections or the voting process, as that would be an obvious conflict of interest.

23. **Which of the following lists elements usually considered to be responsibilities of citizenship under the American system of government? (Skill 32.11)(Easy)**

    A. Serving in public office, voluntary government service, military duty
    B. Paying taxes, jury duty, upholding the Constitution
    C. Maintaining a job, giving to charity, turning in fugitives
    D. Quartering of soldiers, bearing arms, government service

B. Paying taxes, jury duty, upholding the Constitution

Only paying taxes, jury duty and upholding the Constitution are responsibilities of citizens as a result of rights and commitments outlined in the Constitution; for example, the right of citizens to a jury trial in the Sixth and Seventh Amendments and the right of the federal government to collect taxes in Article 1, Section 8. (A) Serving in public office, voluntary government service and military duty, (C) maintaining a job, giving to charity and turning in fugitives are all considered purely voluntary actions, even when officially recognized and compensated. The United States has none of the compulsory military or civil service requirements of many other countries. (D) The quartering of soldiers is an act which, according to Amendment III of the Bill of Rights, requires a citizen's consent. Bearing arms is a right guaranteed under Amendment II of the Bill of Rights.

24. **In which of the following disciplines would the study of physical mapping, modern or ancient, and the plotting of points and boundaries be least useful? (Skill 34.1)(Average)**

    A. Sociology
    B. Geography
    C. Archaeology
    D. History

A. Sociology

In geography, archaeology, and history, the study of maps and plotting of points and boundaries is very important as all three of these disciplines hold value in understanding the spatial relations and regional characteristics of people and places. Sociology, however, mostly focuses on the social interactions of people and while location is important, the physical location is not as important as the social location such as the differences between studying people in groups or as individuals.

25. The study of the exercise of power and political behavior in human society today would be conducted by experts in: (Skill 34.2) (Average)

   A. History
   B. Sociology
   C. Political Science
   D. Anthropology

C. Political Science

Experts in the field of political science today would likely conduct the study of exercise of power and political behavior in human society. However, it is also reasonable to suggest that such studies would be important to historians (study of the past, often in an effort to understand the present), sociologists (often concerned with power structure in the social and political worlds), and even some anthropologists (study of culture and their behaviors).

COMPETENCY 36.0 THE TEACHER UNDERSTANDS HOW TO MANAGE LEARNING ACTIVITIES TO ENSURE THE SAFETY OF ALL STUDENTS.

Skill 36.1   Understands safety regulations and guidelines for science facilities and science instruction.

All science labs should contain the following items of safety equipment. The following are requirements by law.

- Fire blanket which is visible and accessible
- Ground Fault Circuit Interrupters (GFCI) within two feet of water supplies
- Emergency shower capable of providing a continuous flow of water
- Signs designating room exits
- Emergency eye wash station which can be activated by the foot or forearm
- Eye protection for every student and a means of sanitizing equipment
- Emergency exhaust fans providing ventilation to the outside of the building
- Master cut-off switches for gas, electric, and compressed air. Switches must have permanently attached handles. Cut-off switches must be clearly labeled.
- An ABC fire extinguisher
- Storage cabinets for flammable materials

Also recommended, but not required by law:

- Chemical spill control kit
- Fume hood with a motor which is spark proof
- Protective laboratory aprons made of flame retardant material
- Signs which will alert people to potential hazardous conditions
- Containers for broken glassware, flammables, corrosives, and waste.
- Containers should be labeled.

It is the responsibility of teachers to provide a safe environment for their students. Proper supervision greatly reduces the risk of injury and a teacher should never leave a class for any reason without providing alternate supervision. After an accident, two factors are considered; foreseeability and negligence. **Foreseeability** is the anticipation that an event may occur under certain circumstances. **Negligence** is the failure to exercise ordinary or reasonable care. It is best for a teacher to meet all special requirements for disabled students, and to be good at supervising large groups. However, if a teacher can prove that s/he has done a reasonable job to ensure a safe and effective learning environment, then it is unlikely that she/he would be found negligent. Safety procedures should be a part of the science curriculum and a well managed classroom is important to avoid potential lawsuits

The **"Right to Know Law" statutes** cover science teachers who work with potentially hazardous chemicals. Briefly, the law states that employees must be informed of potentially toxic chemicals. An inventory must be made available if requested. The inventory must contain information about the hazards and properties of the chemicals. Training must be provided in the safe handling and interpretation of the Material Safety Data Sheet.

Skill 36.2   Knows procedures for and sources of information regarding the appropriate handling, use, disposal, care, and maintenance of chemicals, materials, specimens, and equipment.

Safety goggles are the single most important piece of safety equipment in the laboratory, and should be used any time a scientist is using glassware, heat, or chemicals. Other equipment (e.g. tongs, gloves, or even a buret stand) has its place for various applications. However, the most important is safety goggles.

All laboratory solutions should be prepared as directed in the lab manual. Care should be taken to avoid contamination. All glassware should be rinsed thoroughly with distilled water before using, and cleaned well after use. Safety goggles should be worn while working with glassware in case of an accident. All solutions should be made with distilled water as tap water contains dissolved particles which may affect the results of an experiment. Chemical storage should be located in a secured, dry area. Chemicals should be stored in accordance with reactability. Acids are to be locked in a separate area. Used solutions should be disposed of according to local disposal procedures. Any questions regarding safe disposal or chemical safety may be directed to the local fire department.

The following chemicals are potential carcinogens and are not allowed in school facilities:

Acrylonitriel, Arsenic compounds, Asbestos, Bensidine, Benzene, Cadmium compounds, Chloroform, Chromium compounds, Ethylene oxide, Ortho-toluidine, Nickel powder, Mercury.

Skill 36.3   Knows procedures for the safe handling and ethical care and treatment of organisms and specimens.

Dissections - Animals which are not obtained from recognized sources should not be used. Decaying animals or those of unknown origin may harbor pathogens and/or parasites. Specimens should be rinsed before handling. Latex gloves are desirable. If gloves are not available, students with sores or scratches should be excused from the activity. Formaldehyde is a carcinogen and should be avoided or disposed of according to district regulations. Students objecting to dissections for moral reasons should be given an alternative assignment.

Live specimens - No dissections may be performed on living mammalian vertebrates or birds. Lower order life and invertebrates may be used. Biological experiments may be done with all animals except mammalian vertebrates or birds. No physiological harm may result to the animal. All animals housed and cared for in the school must be handled in a safe and humane manner. Animals are not to remain on school premises during extended vacations unless adequate care is provided. Many state laws stipulate that any instructor who intentionally refuses to comply with the laws may be suspended or dismissed.

Microbiology - Pathogenic organisms must never be used for experimentation. Students should adhere to the following rules at all times when working with microorganisms to avoid accidental contamination:

1. Treat all microorganisms as if they were pathogenic.
2. Maintain sterile conditions at all times

If you are taking a national level exam you should check the Department of Education for your state for safety procedures. You will want to know what your state expects of you not only for the test but also for performance in the classroom and for the welfare of your students.

COMPETENCY 37.0 THE TEACHER UNDERSTANDS THE CORRECT USE OF TOOLS, MATERIALS, EQUIPMENT, AND TECHNOLOGIES.

Skill 37.1 **Selects and safely uses appropriate tools, technologies, materials, and equipment needed for instructional activities.**

Some of the most common laboratory techniques are: dissections, preserving, staining and mounting microscopic specimens, and preparing laboratory solutions.

1. Dissections

Animals that are not obtained from recognized sources should not be used. Decaying animals or those of unknown origin may harbor pathogens and/or parasites. Specimens should be rinsed before handling. Latex gloves are desirable. If gloves are not available, students with sores or scratches should be excused from the activity. Formaldehyde is a carcinogenic and should be avoided or disposed of according to district regulations. Students objecting to dissections for moral reasons should be given an alternative assignment.

No dissections may be performed on living mammalian vertebrates or birds. Lower order life and invertebrates may be used. Biological experiments may be done with all animals except mammalian vertebrates or birds. No physiological harm may result to the animal. All animals housed and cared for in the school must be handled in a safe and humane manner. Animals are not to remain on school premises during extended vacations unless adequate care is provided. Many state laws state that any instructor who intentionally refuses to comply with the laws may be suspended or dismissed. Interactive dissections are available online or from software companies for those students who object to performing dissections. There should be no penalty for those students who refuse to physically perform a dissection.

2. Staining:

Specimens have to be stained because they are mostly transparent (except plant cells which are green) under the microscope and are difficult to be seen under microscope against a white background. The stains add color to the picture, making the image much easier to see. The stains actually work by fixing themselves to various structures on or in the cell. The exact structure determines the staining process used.

It is amazing to know that the variety of stains available are numerous, and are a vital tool to determine what the cellular components are made of.. starch, protein and even nucleic acids can be brought out using special stains.

Some common stains used in laboratories are: methylene blue, chlorazol black, lignin pink, and gentian violet.

3. Mounting of specimens:

In order to observe microscopic specimens or minute parts, mounting them on a microscope slide is essential. There are two different ways of mounting. One kind of procedure is adapted for keeping mounted slides for a long time to be used again. The second type of procedure is for temporary slides. We will discus about temporary mounting since 12th Grade students are mostly concerned with the temporary mounting. Their work does not require permanent mounting.

Water is a very common mounting medium in High school laboratories since it is cheap and best suited for temporary mounting. One problem with water mounting is water evaporates.

Glycerin is also used for mounting. One advantage with glycerin is that it is non-toxic and is stable for years. It provides good contrast to the specimens under microscopic examination. The only problem with glycerin as a medium is it supports mold formation.

3a. Care of microscopes:

Light microscopes are commonly used in high school laboratory experiments. Total magnification is determined by multiplying the ocular (usually 10X) and the objective (usually 10X on low, 40X on high) lenses. A few steps should be followed to properly care for this equipment.

-Clean all lenses with lens paper only.
-Carry microscopes with two hands, one on the arm and one on the base.
-Always begin focusing on low power, then switch to high power.
-Store microscopes with the low power objective down.
-Always use a cover slip when viewing wet mount slides.
-Bring the objective down to its lowest position then focus moving up to avoid the slide from breaking or scratching.

4. Preparation of laboratory solutions:

This is a critical skill needed for any experimental success. The procedure for making solutions must be followed to get maximum accuracy.

i)   weigh out the required amount of each solute
ii)   dissolve the solute in less than the total desired volume (about 75%)
iii) add enough solvent to get the desired volume

Solute?
Solvent?

4a. Weight/volume:

Usually expressed as mg/ml for small amounts of chemicals and other specialized biological solutions. e.g. 100 mg/ml ampicillin = 100 mg. of ampicillin dissolved in 1 ml of water.

4b. Molarity: moles of solute dissolved/ liter of solution

Mole = 6.02 times 10^23 atoms = Avagadro's number
Mole = gram formula weight (FW) or gram molecular weight (MW)

* These values are usually found on the labels or in Periodic Table.
e.g. Na_2SO_4

2 sodium atoms - 2 times 22.99g = 45.98 g
1 sulfur atom   - 1 times 32.06g = 32.06 g
4 oxygen atoms – 4 times16.00g = 64.00 g
  Total   = 142.04g

1M = 1 mole/liter, 1 mM = 1 millimole/liter, 1 uM = 1 umole/liter

* How much sodium is needed to make 1L of 1M solution?
Formula weight of sodium sulfate = 142.04g
Dissolve 142.04g of sodium sulfate in about 750mL of water, dissolve sodium sulfate thoroughly and make up the volume to 1liter (L)

Skill 37.2   Understands concepts of precision, accuracy, and error with regard to reading and recording numerical data from a scientific instrument.

Accuracy and precision

Accuracy is the degree of conformity of a measured, calculated quantity to its actual (true) value. Precision also called reproducibility or repeatability and is the degree to which further measurements or calculations will show the same or similar results.

Accuracy is the degree of veracity while precision is the degree of reproducibility.

The best analogy to explain accuracy and precision is the target comparison.

Repeated measurements are compared to arrows that are fired at a target. Accuracy describes the closeness of arrows to the bull's eye at the target center. Arrows that strike closer to the bull's eye are considered more accurate.

Systematic and random error

All experimental uncertainty is due to either random errors or systematic errors.

Random errors are statistical fluctuations in the measured data due to the precision limitations of the measurement device. Random errors usually result from the experimenter's inability to take the same measurement in exactly the same way to get exactly the same number.

Systematic errors, by contrast, are reproducible inaccuracies that are consistently in the same direction. Systematic errors are often due to a problem, which persists throughout the entire experiment.

Systematic and random errors refer to problems associated with making measurements. Mistakes made in the calculations or in reading the instrument are not considered in error analysis.

Skill 37.3   Understands how to gather, organize, display, and communicate data in a variety of ways (e.g., charts, tables, graphs, diagrams, written reports, oral presentations).

Graphing is an important skill to visually display collected data for analysis. The two types of graphs most commonly used are the **line graph** and the **bar graph** (histogram). Line graphs are set up to show two variables represented by one point on the graph. The X axis is the horizontal axis and represents the dependent variable. Dependent variables are those that would be present independently of the experiment. A common example of a dependent variable is time. Time proceeds regardless of anything else occurring. The Y axis is the vertical axis and represents the independent variable. Independent variables are manipulated by the experiment, such as the amount of light, or the height of a plant. Graphs should be calibrated at equal intervals. If one space represents one day, the next space may not represent ten days. A "best fit" line is drawn to join the points and may not include all the points in the data. Axes must always be labeled, for the graph to be meaningful. A good title will describe both the dependent and the independent variable. Bar graphs are set up similarly in regards to axes, but points are not plotted. Instead, the dependent variable is set up as a bar where the X axis intersects with the Y axis. Each bar is a separate item of data and is not joined by a continuous line.

Classifying is grouping items according to their similarities. It is important for students to realize relationships and similarity as well as differences to reach a reasonable conclusion in a lab experience.

Normally, knowledge is integrated in the form of a **lab report**. A report has many sections. It should include a specific **title** and tell exactly what is being studied. The **abstract** is a summary of the report written at the beginning of the paper. The **purpose** should always be defined and will state the problem. The purpose should include the **hypothesis** (educated guess) of what is expected from the outcome of the experiment. The entire experiment should relate to this problem. It is important to describe exactly what was done to prove or disprove a hypothesis. A **control** is necessary to prove that the results occurred from the changed conditions and would not have happened normally. Only one variable should be manipulated at a time. **Observations** and **results** of the experiment should be recorded including all results from data. Drawings, graphs and illustrations should be included to support information. Observations are objective, whereas analysis and interpretation is subjective. A **conclusion** should explain why the results of the experiment either proved or disproved the hypothesis.

A scientific theory is an explanation of a set of related observations based on a proven hypothesis. A scientific law usually lasts longer than a scientific theory and has more experimental data to support it.

Skill 37.4 Understands the international system of measurement (i.e., metric system) and performs unit conversions within measurement systems.

Science may be defined as a body of knowledge that is systematically derived from study, observations and experimentation. Its goal is to identify and establish principles and theories that may be applied to solve problems. Pseudoscience, on the other hand, is a belief that is not warranted. There is no scientific methodology or application. Some of the more classic examples of pseudoscience include witchcraft, alien encounters, or any topics that are explained by hearsay.

Science uses the metric system as it is accepted worldwide and allows easier comparison among experiments done by scientists around the world. Learn the following basic units and prefixes:

meter - measure of length
liter - measure of volume
gram - measure of mass

deca-(meter, liter, gram)= 10X the base unit   **deci** = 1/10 the base unit
hecto-(meter, liter, gram)= 100X the base unit   **centi** = 1/100 the base unit
kilo-(meter, liter, gram) = 1000X the base unit   **milli** = 1/1000 the base unit

COMPETENCY 38.0 THE TEACHER UNDERSTANDS THE PROCESS OF SCIENTIFIC INQUIRY AND THE HISTORY AND NATURE OF SCIENCE.

Skill 38.1   Understands the characteristics of various types of scientific investigations (e.g., descriptive studies, controlled experiments, comparative data analysis).

Most research in the scientific field is conducted using the scientific method to discover the answer to a scientific problem. The scientific method is the process of thinking through possible solutions to a problem and testing each possibility to find the best solution. The scientific method generally involves the following steps: forming a hypothesis, choosing a method and design, conducting experimentation (collecting data), analyzing data, drawing a conclusion, and reporting the findings. Depending on the hypothesis and data to be collected and analyzed, different types of scientific investigation may be used.

Descriptive studies are often the first form of investigation used in new areas of scientific inquiry. The most important element in descriptive reporting is a specific, clear, and measurable definition of the disease, condition, or factor in question. Descriptive studies always address the five W's: who, what, when, where, and why. They also add an additional "so what?" Descriptive studies include case reports, case-series reports, cross-sectional students, surveillance studies with individuals, and correlational studies with populations. Descriptive studies are used primarily for trend analysis, health-care planning, and hypothesis generation.

A **controlled experiment** is a form of scientific investigation in which one variable, the independent or control variable, is manipulated to reveal the effect on another variable, the dependent (experimental) variable, while are other variables in the system remain fixed. The control group is virtually identical to the dependent variable except for the one aspect whose effect is being tested. Testing the effects of bleach water on a growing plant, the plant receiving bleach water would be the dependent group, while the plant receiving plain water would be the control group. It is good practice to have several replicate samples for the experiment being performed, which allows for results to be averaged or obvious discrepancies to be discarded.

Comparative data analysis is a statistical form of investigation that allows the researcher to gain new or unexpected insight into data based primarily on graphic representation. Comparative data analysis, whether within the research of an individual project or a meta-analysis, allows the researcher to maximize the understanding of the particular data set, uncover underlying structural similarities between research, extract important variables, test underlying assumptions, and detect outliers and anomalies. Most comparative data analysis techniques are graphical in nature with a few quantitative techniques. The use of graphics to compare data allows the researcher to explore the data open-mindedly.

Skill 38.2   Understands how to design, conduct, and communicate the results of a variety of scientific investigations.

Posing a question
Although many discoveries happen by chance, the standard thought process of a scientist begins with forming a question to research. The more limited the question, the easier it is to set up an experiment to answer it.

Form a hypothesis
Once the question is formulated take an educated guess about the answer to the problem or question. This 'best guess' is your hypothesis.

Conducting a test
To make a test fair, data from an experiment must have a **variable** or any condition that can be changed such as temperature or mass. A good test will try to manipulate as few variables as possible so as to see which variable is responsible for the result. This requires a second example of a **control**. A control is an extra setup in which all the conditions are the same except for the variable being tested.

Observe and record the data
Reporting of the data should state specifics of how the measurements were calculated. A graduated cylinder needs to be read with proper procedures. As beginning students, technique must be part of the instructional process so as to give validity to the data.

Drawing a conclusion
After recording data, you compare your data with that of other groups. A conclusion is the judgment derived from the data results.

Graphing data
Graphing utilizes numbers to demonstrate patterns. The patterns offer a visual representation, making it easier to draw conclusions.

Skill 38.3   Understands the historical development of science and the contributions that diverse cultures and individuals of both genders have made to scientific knowledge.

The history of biology traces mans' understanding of the living world from the earliest recorded history to modern times. Though the concept of biology as a field of science arose only in the 19th century, the origin of biological sciences could be traced back to ancient Greeks (Galen and Aristotle).

During the Renaissance and Age of Discovery, renewed interest in the rapidly increasing number of known organisms generated lot of interest in biology.

Andreas Vesalius (1514-1564), a Belgian anatomist and physician whose dissections of human body and descriptions of his findings helped to correct the misconceptions of science. The books Vesalius wrote on anatomy were the most accurate and comprehensive anatomical texts to date.

Anton van Leeuwenhoek is known as the father of microscopy. In the 1650s, Leeuwenhoek began making tiny lenses that gave magnifications up to 300x. He was the first to see and describe bacteria, yeast plants, and the microscopic life found in water. Over the years, light microscopes have advanced to produce greater clarity and magnification. The scanning electron microscope (SEM) was developed in the 1950s. Instead of light, a beam of electrons passes through the specimen. Scanning electron microscopes have a resolution about one thousand times greater than light microscopes. The disadvantage of the SEM is that the chemical and physical methods used to prepare the sample result in the death of the specimen.

Robert Hooke (1635-1703) was a renowned inventor, a natural philosopher, astronomer, experimenter and a cell biologist. He deserves more recognition than he had, but he is remembered mainly for his law, the Hooke's law an equation describing elasticity that is still used today. He was the type of scientist that was then called a "virtuoso"- able to contribute findings of major importance in any field of science. Hooke published *Micrographia* in 1665. Hooke devised the compound microscope and illumination system, one of the best such microscopes of his time, and used it in his demonstrations at the Royal Society's meetings. With it he observed organisms as diverse as insects, sponges, bryozoans, foraminifera, and bird feathers. Micrographia is an accurate and detailed record of his observations, illustrated with magnificent drawings.

Carl Von Linnaeus (1707-1778), a Swedish botanist, physician and zoologist is well known for his contributions in ecology and taxonomy. Linnaeus is famous for his binomial system of nomenclature in which each living organism has two names, a genus and a species name. He is considered as the father of modern ecology and taxonomy.

In the late 1800s, Pasteur discovered the role of microorganisms in the cause of disease, pasteurization, and the rabies vaccine. Koch took this observations one step further by formulating that specific diseases were caused by specific pathogens. **Koch's postulates** are still used as guidelines in the field of microbiology. They state that the same pathogen must be found in every diseased person, the pathogen must be isolated and grown in culture, the disease is induced in experimental animals from the culture, and the same pathogen must be isolated from the experimental animal.

Mattias Schleiden, a German botanist is famous for his cell theory. He observed plant cells microscopically and concluded that cell is the common structural unit of plants. He proposed the cell theory along with Schwann, a zoologist, who observed cells in animals.

In the 18th century, many fields of science like botany, zoology and geology began to evolve as scientific disciplines in the modern sense.

In the 20th century, the rediscovery of Mendel's work led to the rapid development of genetics by Thomas Hunt Morgan and his students.

DNA structure was another key event in biological study. In the 1950s, James Watson and Francis Crick discovered the structure of a DNA molecule as that of a double helix. This structure made it possible to explain DNA's ability to replicate and to control the synthesis of proteins.

Francois Jacob and Jacques Monod contributed greatly to the field of lysogeny and bacterial reproduction by conjugation and both of them won Nobel Prize for their contributions.

Following the cracking of the genetic code biology has largely split between organismal biology consisting of ecology, ethology, systematics, paleontology, and evolutionary biology, developmental biology, and other disciplines that deal with whole organisms or group of organisms and the disciplines related to molecular biology - including cell biology, biophysics, biochemistry, neuroscience, immunology, and many other overlapping subjects.

The use of animals in biological research has expedited many scientific discoveries. Animal research has allowed scientists to learn more about animal biological systems, including the circulatory and reproductive systems. One significant use of animals is for the testing of drugs, vaccines, and other products (such as perfumes and shampoos) before use or consumption by humans. Along with the pros of animal research, the cons are also very significant. The debate about the ethical treatment of animals has been ongoing since the introduction of animals in research. Many people believe the use of animals in research is cruel and unnecessary. Animal use is federally and locally regulated. The purpose of the Institutional Animal Care and Use Committee (IACUC) is to oversee and evaluate all aspects of an institution's animal care and use program.

Skill 38.4   Understands the roles that logical reasoning, verifiable evidence, prediction, and peer review play in the process of generating and evaluating scientific knowledge.

Observations, however general they may seem, lead scientists to create a viable question and an educated guess (hypothesis) about what to expect. While scientists often have laboratories set up to study a specific thing, it is likely that along the way they will find an unexpected result. It is always important to be open-minded and to look at all of the information. An open-minded approach to science provides room for more questioning, and, hence, more learning.

A central concept in science is that all evidence is empirical. This means that all evidence must be is observed by the five senses. He study phenomenon must be both observable and measurable, with reproducible results. The question stage of scientific inquiry involves repetition. By repeating the experiment you can discover whether or not you have reproducibility. If results are reproducible, the hypothesis is valid. If the results are not reproducible, one has more questions to ask.

With confidence in the proposed explanations, the students need to identify what would be required to reject the proposed explanations. Based upon their experience, they should develop new questions to promote further inquiry.

Science is a process of checks and balances. It is expected that scientific findings will be challenged, and in many cases re-tested. Often one experiment will be the beginning point for another. While bias does exist, the use of controlled experiments, logical reasoning, and awareness on the part of the scientist, can go far in ensuring a sound experiment. Even if the science is well done, it may still be questioned. It is through this continual search that hypotheses are made into theories, and sometimes become laws. It is also through this search that new information is discovered.

Skill 38.5   Understands principles of scientific ethics.

To understand scientific ethics, we need to have a clear understanding of ethics. Ethics is defined as a system of public, general rules for guiding human conduct (Gert, 1988). The rules are general in that they are supposed to all people at all times and they are public in that they are not secret codes or practices.

Scientists are expected to show good conduct in their scientific pursuits. Conduct here refers to all aspects of scientific activity including experimentation, testing, education, data evaluation, data analysis, data storing, peer review, government funding, the staff, etc.

The following are some of the guiding principles of scientific ethics:

1 Scientific Honesty: not to fraud, fabricate ,or misinterpret data for personal gain
2 Caution: to avoid errors and sloppiness in all scientific experimentation
3 Credit: give credit where credit is due and not to copy
4 Responsibility: only to report reliable information to public and not to mislead in the name of science
5 Freedom: freedom to criticize old ideas, question new research and freedom to research

Many more principles could be added to this list. Though these principles seem straightforward and clear, it is very difficult to put them into practice since they could be interpreted in more ways than one. Nevertheless, it is not an excuse for scientists to overlook these guiding principles.

To discuss scientific ethics, we can look at natural phenomena like rain. Rain in the normal sense is extremely useful to us and it is absolutely important that there is water cycle. When rain gets polluted with acid, it becomes acid rain. Here lies the ethical issue of releasing all these pollutants into the atmosphere. Should the scientists communicate the whole truth about acid rain or withhold some information because it may alarm the public? There are many issues like this. Whatever may be the case, scientists are expected to be honest and forthright with the public.

Skill 38.6   Develops, analyzes, and evaluates different explanations for a given scientific result.

Armed with knowledge of the subject matter, students can effectively conduct investigations. They need to learn to think critically and logically to connect evidence with explanations. This includes deciding what evidence should be used and accounting for unusual data. Based upon data collected during experimentation, basic statistical analysis, and measures of probability can be used to make predictions and develop interpretations.

Students, with appropriate direction from you (the teacher), should be able to review the data, summarize, and form a logical argument about the cause-and-effect relationships. It is important to differentiate between causes and effects and determine when causality is uncertain.

When developing proposed explanations, the students should be able to express their level of confidence in the proposed explanations and point out possible sources of uncertainty and error. When formulating explanations, it is important to distinguish between error and unanticipated results. Possible sources of error would include assumptions of models and measuring techniques or devices.

Skill 38.7   Demonstrates an understanding of potential sources of error in inquiry-based investigation.

Unavoidable experimental error is the random error inherent in scientific experiments regardless of the methods used. One source of unavoidable error is measurement and the use of measurement devices. Using measurement devices is an imprecise process because it is often impossible to accurately read measurements. For example, when using a ruler to measure the length of an object, if the length falls between markings on the ruler, we must estimate the true value. Another source of unavoidable error is the randomness of population sampling and the behavior of any random variable. For example, when sampling a population we cannot guarantee that our sample is completely representative of the larger population. In addition, because we cannot constantly monitor the behavior of a random variable, any observations necessarily contain some level of unavoidable error.

Statistical variability is the deviation of an individual in a population from the mean of the population. Variability is inherent in biology because living things are innately unique. For example, the individual weights of humans vary greatly from the mean weight of the population. Thus, when conducting experiments involving the study of living things, we must control for innate variability. Control groups are identical to the experimental group in every way with the exception of the variable being studied. Comparing the experimental group to the control group allows us to determine the effects of the manipulated variable in relation to statistical variability.

Skill 38.8   Demonstrates an understanding of how to communicate and defend the results of an inquiry-based investigation.

It is the responsibility of the scientists to share the knowledge they obtain through their research. After the conclusion is drawn, the final step is communication. In this age, much emphasis is put on the way and the method of communication. The conclusions must be communicated by clearly describing the information using accurate data, visual presentation and other appropriate media such as a power point presentation. Examples of visual presentations are graphs (bar/line/pie), tables/charts, diagrams, and artwork. Modern technology must be used whenever necessary. The method of communication must be suitable to the audience.

Written communication is as important as oral communication. This is essential for submitting research papers to scientific journals, newspapers, other magazines etc.

COMPETENCY 39.0 THE TEACHER UNDERSTANDS HOW SCIENCE IMPACTS THE DAILY LIVES OF STUDENTS AND INTERACTS WITH AND INFLUENCES PERSONAL AND SOCIETAL DECISIONS.

Skill 39.1 **Understands that decisions about the use of science are based on factors such as ethical standards, economics, and personal and societal needs.**

Scientific and technological breakthroughs greatly influence other fields of study and the job market. All academic disciplines utilize computer and information technology to simplify research and information sharing. In addition, advances in science and technology influence the types of available jobs and the desired work skills. For example, machines and computers continue to replace unskilled laborers and computer and technological literacy is now a requirement for many jobs and careers. Finally, science and technology continue to change the very nature of careers. Because of science and technology's great influence on all areas of the economy, and the continuing scientific and technological breakthroughs, careers are far less stable than in past eras. Workers can thus expect to change jobs and companies much more often than in the past.

Local, state, national, and global governments and organizations must increasingly consider policy issues related to science and technology. For example, local and state governments must analyze the impact of proposed development and growth on the environment. Governments and communities must balance the demands of an expanding human population with the local ecology to ensure sustainable growth.

In addition, advances in science and technology create challenges and ethical dilemmas that national governments and global organizations must attempt to solve. Genetic research and manipulation, antibiotic resistance, stem cell research, and cloning are but a few of the issues facing national governments and global organizations.

In all cases, policy makers must analyze all sides of an issue and attempt to find a solution that protects society while limiting scientific inquiry as little as possible. For example, policy makers must weigh the potential benefits of stem cell research, genetic engineering, and cloning (e.g. medical treatments) against the ethical and scientific concerns surrounding these practices. Also, governments must tackle problems like antibiotic resistance, which can result from the indiscriminate use of medical technology (i.e. antibiotics), to prevent medical treatments from becoming obsolete.

Skill 39.2 Applies scientific principles and the theory of probability to analyze the advantages of, disadvantages of, or alternatives to a given decision or course of action.

While technology and technological design can provide solutions to problems faced by humans, technology must exist within nature and cannot contradict physical or biological principles. In addition, technological solutions are temporary and new technologies typically provide better solutions in the future. Monetary costs, available materials, time, and available tools also limit the scope of scientific and technological design and solutions. Finally, solutions must have intended benefits and no expected consequences. Scientists must attempt to predict the unintended consequences and minimize any negative impact on nature or society.

The problems and needs, ranging from very simple to highly complex, that technological design can solve are nearly limitless. Disposal of toxic waste, routing of rainwater, crop irrigation, and energy creation are but a few examples of real-world problems that scientists address or attempt to address with technology.

The technological design process consists of identifying a problem, proposing designs and choosing between alternative solutions, implementing the proposed solution, evaluating the solution and its consequences, and reporting the results

After the identification of a problem, the scientist must propose several designs and choose between the alternatives. In evaluating and choosing between potential solutions to a design problem, scientists utilize modeling, simulation, and experimentation techniques. Small-scale modeling and simulation help test the effectiveness and unexpected consequences of proposed solutions while limiting the initial costs. Modeling and simulation may also reveal potential problems that scientists can address prior to full-scale implementation of the solution. Experimentation allows for evaluation of proposed solutions in a controlled environment where scientists can manipulate and test specific variables.

Implementation of the chosen solution involves the use of various tools depending on the problem, solution, and technology. Scientists may use both physical tools and objects and computer software. After implementation of the solution, scientists evaluate the success or failure of the solution against pre-determined criteria. In evaluating the solution, scientists must consider the negative consequences as well as the planned benefits.

Finally, scientists must communicate results in different ways – orally, written, models, diagrams, and demonstrations.

Skill 39.3 **Applies scientific principles and processes to analyze factors that influence personal choices concerning fitness and health, including physiological and psychological effects and risks associated with the use of substances and substance abuse.**

While genetics plays an important role in health, human behaviors can greatly affect short- and long-term health both positively and negatively. Behaviors that negatively affect health include smoking, excessive alcohol consumption, substance abuse, and poor eating habits. Behaviors that positively affect health include good nutrition and regular exercise.

Smoking negatively affects health in many ways. First, smoking decreases lung capacity, causes persistent coughing, and limits the ability to engage in strenuous physical activity. In addition, the long-term affects are even more damaging. Long-term smoking can cause lung cancer, heart disease, and emphysema (a lung disease).

Alcohol is the most abused legal drug. Excessive alcohol consumption has both short- and long-term negative effects. Drunkenness can lead to reckless behavior and distorted judgment that can cause injury or death. In addition, extreme alcohol abuse can cause alcohol poisoning that can result in immediate death. Long-term alcohol abuse is also extremely hazardous. The potential effects of long-term alcohol abuse include liver cirrhosis, heart problems, high blood pressure, stomach ulcers, and cancer.

The abuse of illegal substances can also negatively affect health. Commonly abused drugs include cocaine, heroin, opiates, methamphetamines, and marijuana. Drug abuse can cause immediate death or injury and, if used for a long time, can cause many physical and psychological health problems.

A healthy diet and regular exercise are the cornerstones of a healthy lifestyle. A diet rich in whole grains, fruits, vegetables, polyunsaturated fats, and lean protein and low in saturated fat and sugar, can positively affect overall health. Such diets can reduce cholesterol levels, lower blood pressure, and help manage body weight. Conversely, diets high in saturated fat and sugar can contribute to weight gain, heart disease, strokes, and cancer.

Finally, regular exercise has both short- and long-term health benefits. Exercise increases physical fitness, improving energy levels, overall body function, and mental well-being. Long-term, exercise helps protect against chronic diseases, maintains healthy bones and muscles, helps maintain a healthy body weight, and strengthens the body's immune system.

Skill 39.4 **Understands concepts, characteristics, and issues related to changes in populations and human population growth.**

Populations change over time due to evolution. Evolution occurs very slowly over the course of time through changes in genetics. Certain factors increase the chances of variability in a population, thus leading to evolution. Items that increase variability include mutations, sexual reproduction, immigration, and large population. Items that decrease variation would be natural selection, emigration, small population, and random mating.

Sexual selection - Genes that happen to come together determine the makeup of the gene pool. Animals that use mating behaviors may be successful or unsuccessful. An animal that lacks attractive plumage or has a weak mating call will not attract the female, thereby eventually limiting that gene in the gene pool. Mechanical isolation, where sex organs do not fit the female, has an obvious disadvantage.

Darwin defined the theory of Natural Selection in the mid-1800's. Through the study of finches on the Galapagos Islands, Darwin theorized that nature selects the traits that are advantageous to the organism. Those that do not possess the desirable trait die and do not pass on their genes. Those more fit to survive reproduce, thus increasing that gene in the population. Darwin listed four principles to define natural selection:

1. The individuals in a certain species vary from generation to generation.
2. Some of the variations are determined by the genetic makeup of the species.
3. More individuals are produced than will survive.
4. Some genes allow for better survival of an animal.

Human population increased slowly until 1650. Since 1650, the human population has grown almost exponentially, reaching its current population of over 6 billion. Factors that have led to this increased growth rate include improved nutrition, sanitation, and health care. In addition, advances in technology, agriculture, and scientific knowledge have made the use of resources more efficient and increased their availability.

While the Earth's ultimate carrying capacity for humans is uncertain, some factors that may limit growth are the availability of food, water, space, and fossil fuels. There is a finite amount of land on Earth available for food production. In addition, providing clean, potable water for a growing human population is a real concern. Finally, fossil fuels, important energy sources for human technology, are scarce. The inevitable shortage of energy in the Earth's future will require the development of alternative energy sources to maintain or increase human population growth.

Skill 39.5   Understands the types and uses of natural resources and the effects of human consumption on the renewal and depletion of resources.

Humans have a tremendous impact on the world's natural resources. The world's natural water supplies are affected by human use. Waterways are major sources for recreation and freight transportation. Oil and wastes from boats and cargo ships pollute the aquatic environment. The aquatic plant and animal life is affected by this contamination.

A **renewable resource** is one that is replaced naturally. Living renewable resources would be plants and animals. Plants are renewable because they grow and reproduce. Sometimes renewal of the resource doesn't keep up with the demand. Such is the case with trees.   Since the housing industry uses lumber for frames and homebuilding they are often cut down faster than new trees can grow. Now there are specific tree farms. Special methods allow trees to grow faster.

A second renewable resource is animals. They renew by the process of reproduction. Some wild animals need protection on refuges. As the population of humans increases resources are used faster. Cattle are used for their hides and for food. Some animals like deer are killed for sport. Each state has an environmental protection agency with divisions of forest management and wildlife management.

Non-living renewable resources would be water, air, and soil. Water is renewed in a natural cycle called the water cycle. Air is a mixture of gases. Oxygen is given off by plants and taken in by animals that in turn expel the carbon dioxide that the plants need. Soil is another renewable resource. Fertile soil is rich in minerals. When plants grow they remove the minerals and make the soil less fertile. Chemical treatments are one way or renewing the composition. It is also accomplished naturally when the plants decay back into the soil. The plant material is used to make compost to mix with the soil.

Nonrenewable resources are not easily replaced in a timely fashion. Minerals are nonrenewable resources. Quartz, mica, salt and sulfur are some examples. Mining depletes these resources so society may benefit. Glass is made from quartz, electronic equipment from mica, and salt has many uses. Sulfur is used in medicine, fertilizers, paper, and matches.

Metals are among the most widely used nonrenewable resource. Metals must be separated from the ore. Iron is our most important ore. Gold, silver and copper are often found in a more pure form called native metals.

Skill 39.6   Understands the role science can play in helping resolve personal, societal, and global challenges.

Science can play many important roles in helping resolve personal, societal, and global challenges. Scientific research and advances in technology help solve many problems. In this section, we will discuss just a few of the many roles of science. On a personal level, science can help individuals with medical issues, nutrition, and general health. On the societal level, science can help resolve problems of waste disposal, disease prevention, security, and environmental protection. Finally, on the global level, science can help address the challenges of resource allocation, energy production, food production, and global security.

Science greatly affects our personal lives, improving our quality of life and increasing longevity. Advances in medicine have lessened the impact of many diseases and medical conditions and increased the average life expectancy. Scientific research has helped establish lifestyle guidelines for diet and exercise that increase awareness of fitness and the health-related benefits of regular exercise and proper nutrition.

On the societal level, science helps solve many logistical problems related to the management of a large number of people in a limited space. Science tells us how development will affect the natural environment and helps us build and develop in an environmentally friendly manner. Science can also help develop strategies and technologies for efficient waste disposal and disease prevention. Finally, many products and technologies related to security and defense derive from scientific research.

Science is, and will continue to be, a very important factor in the security and continued viability of the planet. On the global level, science must attempt to resolve the challenges related to natural resource allocation, energy production, and food production. These challenges have an obvious affect on the ecological viability of the planet; however, they also have a pronounced affect on global security. Availability and use of resources, food production, global health, and the economic impact of these factors lays the foundation for global conflict and terrorism. Third World poverty and resource deficiencies create global unrest and an unstable global environment. Scientific and technological advances have the potential to alleviate these problems and increase global security and stability.

COMPETENCY 40.0 THE TEACHER KNOWS AND UNDERSTANDS THE UNIFYING CONCEPTS AND PROCESSES THAT ARE COMMON TO ALL SCIENCES.

Skill 40.1   Understands how the following concepts and processes provide a unifying explanatory framework across the science disciplines: systems, order, and organization; evidence, models, and explanation; change, constancy, and measurements; evolution and equilibrium; and form and function.

The following are the concepts and processes generally recognized as common to all scientific disciplines:

- Systems, order, and organization
- Evidence, models, and explanation
- Constancy, change, and measurement
- Evolution and equilibrium
- Form and function

Systems, order, and organization

Because the natural world is so complex, the study of science involves the **organization** of items into smaller groups based on interaction or interdependence. These groups are called **systems**. Examples of organization are the periodic table of elements and the five-kingdom classification scheme for living organisms. Examples of systems are the solar system, cardiovascular system, Newton's laws of force and motion, and the laws of conservation.

Order refers to the behavior and measurability of organisms and events in nature. The arrangement of planets in the solar system and the life cycle of bacterial cells are examples of order.

Evidence, models, and explanations

Scientists use **evidence** and **models** to form **explanations** of natural events. Models are miniaturized representations of a larger event or system. Evidence is anything that furnishes proof.

Constancy, change, and measurement

Constancy and **change** describe the observable properties of natural organisms and events. Scientists use different systems of **measurement** to observe change and constancy. For example, the freezing and melting points of given substances and the speed of sound are constant under constant conditions. Growth, decay, and erosion are all examples of natural change.

Evolution and equilibrium:

Evolution is the process of change over a long period of time. While biological evolution is the most common example, one can also classify technological advancement, changes in the universe, and changes in the environment as evolution.

Equilibrium is the state of balance between opposing forces of change. Homeostasis and ecological balance are examples of equilibrium.

Form and function

Form and **function** are properties of organisms and systems that are closely related. The function of an object usually dictates its form and the form of an object usually facilitates its function. For example, the form of the heart (e.g. muscle, valves) allows it to perform its function of circulating blood through the body.

Skill 40.2   Demonstrates an understanding of how patterns in observations and data can be used to make explanations and predictions.

Identifying patterns in data and observations and using these patterns to make explanations and predictions is a fundamental scientific skill. One of the main goals of scientific study and research is to explain natural events. Identifying patterns and trends helps us determine cause and effect relationships. In addition, defining relationships between variables allows us to predict how natural systems will behave in the future.

Consider the following example. Suppose we gather data on the amount of edible spinach harvested from a garden over a ten-year period and the local rainfall amounts during each spinach-growing season. The following table shows the amount of spinach harvested and the rainfall totals for each growing season.

Year	1	2	3	4	5	6	7	8	9	10
Spinach Harvested (pounds)	57	40	16	38	65	21	15	58	45	48
Seasonal Rainfall (inches)	12.1	8.3	20.1	6.5	12.6	2.1	19.8	12.2	8.9	10.1

What can we say about the effect of rainfall totals on spinach production? Studying the data, we can determine that unusually high or low amounts of rain hurt spinach production (see years 3, 6, and 7). We also note that, within a certain range, increased rainfall leads to increased spinach production. Thus, we can conclude that spinach production increases as the amount of rain increases, to a point. We can use this conclusion to predict future spinach production based on measured rainfall. For example, if in year 11 the seasonal rainfall is 8.5 inches, we can predict that the garden will produce approximately 40 to 45 pounds of spinach.

In addition, we can attempt to explain the reasons for our observations. Drawing on our knowledge of plants and microorganisms, we can theorize that the decrease in spinach production associated with extremely high amounts of rain is attributable to increased prevalence of disease and bacterial infection. On the other hand, the decrease in spinach production associated with extremely low amounts of rain may be attributable to a lack of photosynthesis. Overexposure to heat and light will also affect the harvest.

Skill 40.3   Analyzes interactions and interrelationships between systems and subsystems.

Students identify and analyze systems and the ways their components work together or affect each other. Topics can range from a variety of scientific concepts directly into environmental and community related concepts. Some examples could include the following:

Multicultural, Politics, Computers, Cities, Government, Transportation, Manufacturing, Communication, Climate, Stock Market, Agriculture, Machines, Conservation

Any of these examples can be put into clearer context as follows:
Biological (e.g., ecosystems)
Physical (e.g., electrical)
Social (e.g., manufacturing)

Students in the Elementary areas should adequately demonstrate the following concepts between systems and subsystems.

Recognize things that work together.
Identify components of a system.
Communicate functions of a system.
Classify systems based on functions or properties.
Distinguish between systems and subsystems and describe interactions between them.
Analyze how the properties of the components of a system affect their function.
Investigate system feedback and self-regulation.
Create a system.

Students in the Middle School areas should also demonstrate the following concepts:

 Investigate and illustrate a system; identify its components and interrelationships with other systems.
Demonstrate how a single system can have multiple functions and applications.
Investigate the role of energy flow in systems.
Evaluate the effects of subsystems and their components on a system.
Design a new system or modify an existing one.

Skill 40.4   Analyzes unifying concepts to explore similarities in a variety of natural phenomena.

Students will be asked to relate the process of scientific inquiry and understand the variety of natural phenomena that take place in the science world. Teachers will be expected to teach and model for students the following frameworks:

- Analyzing all processes by which hypotheses and scientific knowledge are generated
- Analyzing ethical issues related to the process of science and scientific experiments
- Evaluating the appropriateness of specified experiment and design a test to relate to the given hypothesis
- Recognize the role of communication between scientists, public, and educational realms.

Science is a way of learning about the natural world. Students must know how science has built a model for increasing knowledge by understanding described by physical, mathematical, and conceptual models. Students must also understand that these concepts don't answer all of science questions. Students must to understand that investigations are used to depict the events of the natural world. Methods and models are used to build, explain, and attempt to investigate. They help us to draw conclusions that serve as observations and increase our understanding of how the systems of the natural world work.

Skill 40.5   Understands how properties and patterns of systems can be described in terms of space, time, energy, and matter.

Students must know that patterns and properties can be observed and measured in many differing ways. Objects are made up of many different types of materials (e.g., cloth, paper, wood, metal) and have many different observable properties (e.g., color, size, shape, weight). Things can be done to materials to change some of their properties, and this should be demonstrated in the laboratory. Objects can be classified according to their properties (e.g., magnetism, conductivity, density, solubility).

Materials may be composed of parts that are too small to be seen without magnification (microscopic). Properties such as length, weight, temperature, and volume must be measured using appropriate tools (e.g., rulers, balances, thermometers, graduated cylinders). Materials have different states (solid, liquid, gas), and some common materials such as water can be changed from one state to another by heating or cooling. The mass of a material remains constant whether it is together, in parts, or in a different state.

Matter is made up of tiny particles called atoms, and different arrangements of atoms into groups compose all substances. Atoms are in constant, random motion and often combine to form a molecule (or crystal), the smallest particle of a substance that retains its properties. Substances that contain only one kind of atom are pure elements, and over 100 different kinds of elements exist. Elements do not break down by normal laboratory reactions (e.g., heating, exposure to electric current, reaction with acids). Many elements can be grouped according to similar properties (e.g., highly reactive metals, less-reactive metals, highly reactive nonmetals, almost completely nonreactive gases). Substances react chemically in characteristic ways with other substances to form new substances (compounds) with different characteristic properties. The conservation of matter occurs regardless of physical and chemical change. No matter how substances within a closed system interact with one another, or how they combine or break apart, the total weight of the system remains the same; the same number of atoms weighs the same, no matter how the atoms are arranged. Common methods used to separate mixtures into their component parts include boiling, filtering, chromatography, and screening. Factors that influence reaction rates are the types of substances involved, temperature, concentration, and surface area. Oxidation involves the combining of oxygen with another substance and is commonly seen as burning or rusting.

Models of the atomic structure of matter have changed over time. Atoms created quite a controversy in the Greek forum. Two opinions existed; those who believed that matter was continuous followed Aristotle and Plato, and those who believed that matter was not continuous followed Leucippetius. Aristotle and Plato had reputations for being very wise and knowledgeable men, so most people believed them. Aristotle did not like the randomness of Leucippetius' and Democritus' ideas. He preferred a more ordered matter. Therefore, the idea of atoms and those who believed in their existence had to go underground. The existence of fundamental units of matter called atoms of different types called elements was proposed by ancient philosophers without any evidence to support the belief. Modern atomic theory is credited to the work of John Dalton published in 1803-1807. Prior to the late 1800s, atoms, following Dalton's ideas, were thought to be small, spherical and indivisible particles that made up matter. However, with the discovery of electricity and the investigations that followed, this view of the atom changed. Joseph John Thomson was the first to examine the substructure of an atom. Thomson's model of the atom was a uniformly positive particle with electrons contained in the interior. This has been called the "plum-pudding" model of the atom where the pudding represents the uniform sphere of positive electricity and the bits of plum represent electrons. Planck, Rutherford, and Bohr expanded upon the atomic research and the result is our current model of the atom, a nucleus that includes both protons and neutrons, and the nucleus is surrounded by orbits containing electrons.

Skill 40.6   Understands how change and constancy occur in systems.

Constancy and change describe the observable properties of natural organisms and events. Constancy refers to a lack of change, and change obviously means something is altered. Scientists use different systems of measurement to observe change and constancy. For example, the freezing and melting points of given substances and the speed of sound are constant. Growth, decay, and erosion are all examples of natural change.

Homeostasis is a great example. It is defined as the property of an open system, especially living organisms, to regulate its internal environment to maintain a stable, constant condition, by means of multiple adjustments (changes), controlled by interrelated regulation mechanisms.

Skill 40.7   Understands the complementary nature of form and function in a given system.

The structure of the cell is often related to the cell's function. Root hair cells differ from flower stamens or leaf epidermal cells. They all have different functions. Structure and function dictates behavior and aids in the identification of prokaryotic organisms. Important structural and functional aspects of prokaryotes are morphology, motility, reproduction and growth, and metabolic diversity.

Morphology refers to the shape of a cell. The three main shapes of prokaryotic cells are spheres (cocci), rods (bacilli), and spirals (spirilla). Observation of cell morphology with a microscope can aid in the identification and classification of prokaryotic organisms. The most important aspect of prokaryotic morphology, regardless of the specific shape, is the size of the cells. Small cells allow for rapid exchange of wastes and nutrients across the cell membrane promoting high metabolic and growth rates.

Motility refers to the ability of an organism to move and its mechanism of movement. While some prokaryotes glide along solid surfaces or use gas vesicles to move in water, the vast majority of prokaryotes move by means of flagella. Motility allows organisms to reach different parts of its environment in the search for favorable conditions. Flagellar structure allows differentiation of Archaea and Bacteria as the two classes of prokaryotes have very different flagella. In addition, different types of bacteria have flagella positioned in different locations on the cell. The locations of flagella are on the ends (polar), all around (peritrichous), or in a tuft at one end of the cell (lophotrichous).

Most prokaryotes reproduce by binary fission, the growth of a single cell until it divides in two. Because of their small size, most prokaryotes have high growth rates under optimal conditions. Environmental factors greatly influence prokaryotic growth rate. Scientists identify and classify prokaryotes based on their ability or inability to survive and grow in certain conditions. Temperature, pH, water availability, and oxygen levels differentially influence the growth of prokaryotes. For example, certain types of prokaryotes can survive and grow at extremely hot or cold temperatures while most cannot.

Prokaryotes display great metabolic diversity. Autotrophic prokaryotes use carbon dioxide as the sole carbon source in energy metabolism, while heterotrophic prokaryotes require organic carbon sources. More specifically, chemoautotrophs use carbon dioxide as a carbon source and inorganic compounds as an energy source, while chemoheterotrophs use organic compounds as a source of energy and carbon. Photoautotrophs require only light energy and carbon dioxide, while photoheterotrophs require an organic carbon source along with light energy. Examining an unknown organism's metabolism aids in the identification process.

Skill 40.8 **Understands how models are used to represent the natural world and how to evaluate the strengths and limitations of a variety of scientific models (e.g., physical, conceptual, mathematical).**

Once data has been collected and analyzed, it is useful to generalize the information by creating a model. A model is a conceptual representation of a phenomenon. Models are useful in that they clarify relationships, helping us to understand the phenomenon and make predictions about future outcomes. The natural sciences and social sciences employ modeling for this purpose.

Many scientific models are mathematical in nature and contain a set of variables linked by logical and quantitative relationships. These mathematical models may include functions, tables, formulas, graphs, and etc. Typically, such mathematical models include assumptions that restrict them to very specific situations. Often this means they can only provide an *approximate* description of what occurs in the natural world. These assumptions, however, prevent the model from become overly complicated. For a mathematical model to fully explain a natural or social phenomenon, it would have to contain many variables and could become too cumbersome to use. Accordingly, it is critical that assumptions be carefully chosen and thoroughly defined.

Certain models are abstract and simply contain sets of logical principles rather than relying on mathematics. These types of models are generally more vague and are more useful for discovering and understanding new ideas. Abstract models can also include actual physical models built to make concepts more tangible. Abstract models, to an even greater extent than mathematical models, make assumptions and simplify actual phenomena.

Proper scientific models must be able to be tested and verified using experimental data. Often these experimental results are necessary to demonstrate the superiority of a model when two or more conflicting models seek to explain the same phenomenon. Computer simulations are increasingly used in both testing and developing mathematical and even abstract models. These types of simulations are especially useful in situations, such as ecology or manufacturing, where experiments are not feasible or variables are not fully under control.

COMPETENCY 41.0 THE TEACHER UNDERSTANDS FORCES AND MOTION AND THEIR RELATIONSHIPS.

Skill 41.1   Demonstrates an understanding of properties of universal forces (e.g., gravitational, electrical, magnetic).

Dynamics is the study of the relationship between motion and the forces affecting motion. **Force** causes motion.

Mass and weight are not the same quantities. An object's **mass** gives it a reluctance to change its current state of motion. It is also the measure of an object's resistance to acceleration. The force that the earth's gravity exerts on an object with a specific mass is called the object's weight on earth. Weight is a force that is measured in Newtons. Weight (W) = mass times acceleration due to gravity (**W = mg**). To illustrate the difference between mass and weight, picture two rocks of equal mass on a balance scale. If the scale is balanced in one place, it will be balanced everywhere, regardless of the gravitational field. However, the weight of the stones would vary on a spring scale, depending upon the gravitational field. In other words, the stones would be balanced both on earth and on the moon. However, the weight of the stones would be greater on earth than on the moon.

Newton's laws of motion:

Newton's first law of motion is also called the law of inertia. It states that an object at rest will remain at rest and an object in motion will remain in motion at a constant velocity unless acted upon by an external force.

Newton's second law of motion states that if a net force acts on an object, it will cause the acceleration of the object. The relationship between force and motion is Force equals mass times acceleration. **(F = ma).**

Newton's third law states that for every action there is an equal and opposite reaction. Therefore, if an object exerts a force on another object, that second object exerts an equal and opposite force on the first.

Surfaces that touch each other have a certain resistance to motion. This resistance is **friction.**

When an object moves in a circular path, a force must be directed toward the center of the circle in order to keep the motion going. This constraining force is called **centripetal force**. Gravity is the centripetal force that keeps a satellite circling the earth.

Magnets have a north pole and a south pole. Like poles repel and opposing poles attract. A **magnetic field** is the space around a magnet where its force will affect objects. The closer you are to a magnet, the stronger the force. As you move away, the force becomes weaker.

Weight is the measure of the force of the earth's pull or gravity on an object. Gravity causes approximately the same acceleration on all falling bodies close to earth's surface. (It is only "approximately" because there are very small variations in the strength of earth's gravitational field.) More massive bodies continue to accelerate at this rate for longer, before their air resistance is great enough to cause terminal velocity. Bodies on different parts of the planet move in different directions (always toward the center of mass of earth).

Gravity acts over tremendous distances in space (theoretically, infinite distance, though certainly at least as far as any astronaut has traveled). However, gravitational force is inversely proportional to distance squared from a massive body. This means that when an astronaut is in space, s/he is far enough from the center of mass of any planet that the gravitational force is very small, and s/he feels 'weightless'.

Skill 41.2   Understands how to measure, graph, and describe changes in motion using concepts of displacement, velocity, and acceleration.

The science of describing the motion of bodies is known as **kinematics**. The motion of bodies is described using words, diagrams, numbers, graphs, and equations.

The following words are used to describe motion: distance, displacement, speed, velocity, and acceleration.

Distance is a scalar quantity that refers to how much ground an object has covered while moving. **Displacement** is a vector quantity that refers to the object's change in position.

Example:

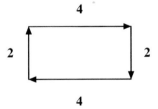

Jamie walked 2 miles north, 4 miles east, 2 miles south, and then 4 miles west. In terms of distance, she walked 12 miles. However, there is no displacement because the directions cancelled each other out, and she returned to her starting position.

Speed is a scalar quantity that refers to how fast an object is moving (ex. the car was traveling 60 mi./hr). **Velocity** is a vector quantity that refers to the rate at which an object changes its position. In other words, velocity is speed with direction (ex. the car was traveling 60 mi./hr east).

$$\text{Average speed} = \frac{\text{Distance traveled}}{\text{Time of travel}}$$

$$v = \frac{d}{t}$$

$$\text{Average velocity} = \frac{\Delta\text{position}}{\text{time}} = \frac{\text{displacement}}{\text{time}}$$

Instantaneous Speed - speed at any given instant in time.

Average Speed - average of all instantaneous speeds, found simply by a distance/time ratio.

Acceleration is a vector quantity defined as the rate at which an object changes its velocity.

$$a = \frac{\Delta velocity}{time} = \frac{v_f - v_i}{t}$$

where *f* represents the final velocity and *i* represents the initial velocity

Since acceleration is a vector quantity, it always has a direction associated with it. The direction of the acceleration vector depends on

1. whether the object is speeding up or slowing down
2. whether the object is moving in the positive or negative direction.

Skill 41.3 Understands the vector nature of force.

The two categories of mathematical quantities that are used to describe the motion of objects are scalars and vectors. **Scalars** are quantities that are fully described by magnitude alone. Examples of scalars are 5m and 20 degrees Celsius. **Vectors** are quantities that are fully described by magnitude and direction. Examples of vectors are 30m/sec, and 5 miles north.

Newton's Three Laws of Motion:

First Law: An object at rest tends to stay at rest and an object in motion tends to stay in motion with the same speed and in the same direction unless acted upon by an unbalanced force, for example, when riding on a descending elevator that suddenly stops, blood rushes from your head to your feet. **Inertia** is the resistance an object has to a change in its state of motion.

Second Law: The acceleration of an object depends directly upon the net force acting upon the object, and inversely upon the mass of the object. As the net force increases, so will the object's acceleration. However, as the mass of the object increases, its acceleration will decrease.

$$F_{net} = m * a$$

Third Law: For every action, there is an equal and opposite reaction, for example, when a bird is flying, the motion of its wings pushes air downward; the air reacts by pushing the bird upward.

Skill 41.4   Identifies the forces acting on a object and applies Newton's laws to describe the motion of an object.

Dynamics is the study of the relationship between motion and the forces affecting motion. **Force** causes motion.

Mass and weight are not the same quantities. An object's **mass** gives it a reluctance to change its current state of motion. It is also the measure of an object's resistance to acceleration. The force that the earth's gravity exerts on an object with a specific mass is called the object's weight on earth. Weight is a force that is measured in Newtons. Weight (W) = mass times acceleration due to gravity (**W = mg**). To illustrate the difference between mass and weight, picture two rocks of equal mass on a balance scale. If the scale is balanced in one place, it will be balanced everywhere, regardless of the gravitational field. However, the weight of the stones would vary on a spring scale, depending upon the gravitational field. In other words, the stones would be balanced both on earth and on the moon. However, the weight of the stones would be greater on earth than on the moon.

Surfaces that touch each other have a certain resistance to motion. This resistance is **friction.**

1. The materials that make up the surfaces will determine the magnitude of the frictional force.
2. The frictional force is independent of the area of contact between the two surfaces.
3. The direction of the frictional force is opposite to the direction of motion.
4. The frictional force is proportional to the normal force between the two surfaces in contact.

Static friction describes the force of friction of two surfaces that are in contact but do not have any motion relative to each other, such as a block sitting on an inclined plane. **Kinetic friction** describes the force of friction of two surfaces in contact with each other when there is relative motion between the surfaces.

When an object moves in a circular path, a force must be directed toward the center of the circle in order to keep the motion going. This constraining force is called **centripetal force**. Gravity is the centripetal force that keeps a satellite circling the earth.

Skill 41.5   Analyzes the relationship between force and motion in a variety of situations (e.g., simple machines, blood flow, geologic processes).

Simple machines include the following:

1. Inclined plane
2. Lever
3. Wheel and axle
4. Pulley

Each one makes work easier to accomplish by providing some trade-off between the force applied and the distance over which the force is applied. In simple machines, force is applied in only one direction.

According to the Kinetic Molecular Theory, ions, atoms, or molecules in all forms of matter (gases, liquids, or solids) are in constant motion. These particles collide with each other or the walls of their container as they move. The collisions produce a measurable force known as pressure.

Pressure is a measurement of the force per unit area. Since a fluid is a liquid or a gas, its pressure applies in all directions. Fluid pressure can be in an enclosed container or due to gravity or motion.

Pressure plays an important part in the fluids inside the human body. Blood flowing through the arteries exerts pressure against the walls of the arteries. If there is a reduction in the diameter of the arteries due to plaque or disease, the pressure called systemic vascular resistance (SVR) is increased. For example, if arteries have a 20% occlusion (blockage), the volume of blood passing through in a given amount of time will be cut in half and the pressure of that blood flow will be five to seven times as great!

In the geologic convection cell, material becomes heated in the asthenosphere by heat radiating from the Earth's core. When material is heated, particles begin to move more quickly, colliding more frequently, requiring more space and causing material to expand. Because particles of heated material are less tightly packed, the density of the heated material decreases. **Density** is the measure of an object's mass per volume. This heated, less dense material will rise toward the solid lithosphere. Less dense material will rise when surrounded by more dense material because of buoyant force. **Buoyant force** is the upward force exerted by fluid on material of lower density. Fluid pressure increases with depth, and increased pressure is exerted in all directions. Buoyancy results from the unbalanced upward force that is exerted on the bottom of submerged, less dense material, as the fluid pressure is greater below the less dense material than above. When the heated material reaches the solid lithosphere, it can no longer rise and begins to move horizontally, dragging with it the lithosphere and causing movement of the tectonic plates. As the heated material moves, it pushes cooler, denser material in its path. Eventually, the cooler material sinks lower into the mantle where it is heated and rises again, continuing the cycle of the convection cell.

COMPETENCY 42.0 THE TEACHER UNDERSTANDS PHYSICAL PROPERTIES OF AND CHANGES IN MATTER.

Skill 42.1   Describes the physical properties of substances (e.g., density, boiling point, solubility, thermal and electrical conductivity).

Everything in our world is made up of **matter**, whether it is a rock, a building, an animal, or a person. Matter is defined by its characteristics: It takes up space and it has mass.

Mass is a measure of the amount of matter in an object. Two objects of equal mass will balance each other on a simple balance scale no matter where the scale is located. For instance, two rocks with the same amount of mass that are in balance on earth will also be in balance on the moon. They will feel heavier on earth than on the moon because of the gravitational pull of the earth. So, although the two rocks have the same mass, they will have different **weight.**

Weight is the measure of the earth's pull of gravity on an object. It can also be defined as the pull of gravity between other bodies. The units of weight measurement commonly used are the pound (English measure) and the kilogram (metric measure).

In addition to mass, matter also has the property of volume. **Volume** is the amount of cubic space that an object occupies. Volume and mass together give a more exact description of the object. Two objects may have the same volume, but different mass, or the same mass but different volumes, etc. For instance, consider two cubes that are each one cubic centimeter, one made from plastic, one from lead. They have the same volume, but the lead cube has more mass. The measure that we use to describe the cubes takes into consideration both the mass and the volume. **Density** is the mass of a substance contained per unit of volume. If the density of an object is less than the density of a liquid, the object will float in the liquid. If the object is denser than the liquid, then the object will sink.

Density is stated in grams per cubic centimeter (g/cm^3) where the gram is the standard unit of mass. To find an object's density, you must measure its mass and its volume. Then divide the mass by the volume ($D = m/V$).

To discover an object's density, first use a balance to find its mass. Then calculate its volume. If the object is a regular shape, you can find the volume by multiplying the length, width, and height together. However, if it is an irregular shape, you can find the volume by seeing how much water it displaces. Measure the water in the container before and after the object is submerged. The difference will be the volume of the object.

Specific gravity is the ratio of the density of a substance to the density of water. For instance, the specific density of one liter of turpentine is calculated by comparing its mass (0.81 kg) to the mass of one liter of water (1 kg):

$$\frac{\text{mass of 1 L alcohol}}{\text{mass of 1 L water}} = \frac{0.81 \text{ kg}}{1.00 \text{ kg}} = 0.81$$

Physical properties and chemical properties of matter describe the appearance or behavior of a substance. A **physical property** can be observed without changing the identity of a substance. For instance, you can describe the color, mass, shape, and volume of a book. **Chemical properties** describe the ability of a substance to be changed into new substances. Baking powder goes through a chemical change as it changes into carbon dioxide gas during the baking process.

Matter constantly changes. A **physical change** is a change that does not produce a new substance. The freezing and melting of water is an example of physical change. A **chemical change** (or chemical reaction) is any change of a substance into one or more other substances. Burning materials turn into smoke; a seltzer tablet fizzes into gas bubbles.

Conductivity:

Substances can have two variables of conductivity. A conductor is a material that transfers a substance easily. That substance may be thermal or electrical in nature. Metals are known for being good thermal and electrical conductors. Touch your hand to a hot piece of metal and you know it is a good conductor- the heat transfers to your hand and you may be burnt. Materials through which electric charges can easily flow are called electrical **conductors**. Metals that are good electric conductors include silicon and boron. On the other hand, an **insulator** is a material through which electric charges do not move easily, if at all. Examples of electrical insulators would be the nonmetal elements of the periodic table.

Solubility is defined as the amount of substance (referred to as solute) that will dissolve into another substance, called the solvent. The amount that will dissolve can vary according to the conditions, most notably temperature. The process is called solvation.

Melting point refers to the temperature at which a solid becomes a liquid. **Boiling point** refers to the temperature at which a liquid becomes a gas. Melting takes place when there is sufficient energy available to break the intermolecular forces that hold molecules together in a solid. Boiling occurs when there is enough energy available to break the intermolecular forces holding molecules together as a liquid.

Hardness describes how difficult it is to scratch or indent a substance. The hardest natural substance is diamond.

Skill 42.2   Describes the physical properties and molecular structure of solids, liquids, and gases.

The phase of matter (solid, liquid, or gas) is identified by its shape and volume. A solid has a definite shape and volume. A liquid has a definite volume, but no shape. A gas has no shape or volume because it will spread out to occupy the entire space of whatever container it is in.

Energy is the ability to cause change in matter. Applying heat to a frozen liquid changes it from solid back to liquid. Continue heating it and it will boil and give off steam, a gas.

Evaporation is the change in phase from liquid to gas. Condensation is the change in phase from gas to liquid.

According to the molecular theory of matter, molecular motion determines the 'phase' of the matter, and the energy in the matter determines the speed of molecular motion. Solids have vibrating molecules that are in fixed relative positions; liquids have faster molecular motion than their solid forms, and the molecules may move more freely but must still be in contact with one another; gases have even more energy and more molecular motion. (Other phases, such as plasma, are yet more energetic.) At the 'freezing point' or 'boiling point' of a substance, both relevant phases may be present.

Skill 42.3   Describes the relationship between the molecular structure of materials (e.g., metals, crystals, polymers) and their physical properties.

Metals are giant structures of atoms held together by metallic bonds. Most metals are close packed - they fit as many atoms as possible into the available volume. Metals tend to have high melting and boiling points because of the strength of the metallic bond. The strength of the bond varies from metal to metal and depends on the number of electrons that each atom contributes to bonding and on the packing of atoms.

A **crystal** is a regular, repeating arrangement of atoms, ions or molecules. Crystals are well organized structures.

There are two kinds of crystals - i) Solid and ii) Liquid.

i). Solid crystals: In a solid crystal, positive ions attract negative ions to form a cube shaped arrangement like that of sodium chloride. The strong attractive forces between the oppositely charged ions holds them together. This strong attractive force is called an ionic bond.

ii). Liquid crystals: When a solid melts, it crystal lattice disintegrates and its particles lose their three dimensional pattern. However, when some materials called liquid crystals melt, they lose their rigid organization in only one or two dimensions. The inter-particle forces in a liquid crystal are relatively weak and their arrangement is easily disrupted. When the lattice is broken, the crystal flows like a liquid. Liquid Crystal Displays (LCDs) are used in watches, thermometers, calculators and laptop computers because liquid crystals change with varying electric charge.

Characteristics of crystals:

1. Symmetry: Under certain operations, the crystal remains unchanged. The constituent atoms, molecules, or ions, are packed in a regularly ordered, repeating pattern extending in all three spatial dimensions. Crystals form when they undergo a process of solidification. The result of solidification may be a single crystal or a group of crystals, a condition called a polycrystalline solid. The symmetry of crystals is one tool used in the classification of crystals.

2. Crystalline structures are universal: Crystalline structures occur in all classes of materials with ionic and covalent bonding. Sodium chloride is an example of a crystal formed out of ionic bonding. Graphite, diamond, and silica are examples of crystals with covalent bonding.

3. Crystallographic defects: Most crystalline structures have inborn crystallographic defects. These defects have a great effect on the properties of the crystals.

4. Electrical properties: Some crystalline materials may exhibit special electrical properties such as the ferro-electric effect or the piezo-electric effect. Also light passing through a crystal is often bent in different directions, producing an array of colors.

5. Crystal system: the crystal systems are a grouping of crystal structures according to the axial system used to describe their lattice. Each crystal system consists of a set of three axes in a particular geometrical arrangement. There are seven unique crystal systems. The cubic is the most symmetrical. The other six (in decreasing order of symmetry) are - hexagonal, rhombohedral, orthorhombic, monoclinic and triclinic.

Polymers are large organic molecules consisting of repeated units linked by covalent bonds. There are many naturally occurring polymers such as proteins and starches. Additionally, many artificial polymers have been developed. The repeated unit in a polymer is known as a monomer. Thus, the monomer in a protein is an amino acid and the monomer in the manmade polymer polyethene (better known as polyethelyene) is ethene. Copolymers may be created by using two or more different monomers. Both the physical and chemical properties of polymers vary widely and are a function of the monomer, the molecular weight or length of the polymer, and intermolecular forces. Polymers range from low viscosity liquids to extremely hard, crystalline solids and from biologically degradable to nearly inert. The structure of polymers can be changed and this allows very tight control of these physical properties. Therefore, polymers have been used in a large variety of medical, construction, clothing, packaging, and industrial applications. Just a few of the many examples of products made from polymers are: poly-styrene food containers, poly-vinyl-chloride (PVC) pipes, poly-lactic acid (absorbable) sutures, neoprene wetsuits, polyethylene grocery bags, and polytetrafluoro-ethylene lined cooking pans (Teflon).

Skill 42.4   Relates the physical properties of an element to its placement in the periodic table.

The **periodic table of elements** is an arrangement of the elements in rows and columns so that it is easy to locate elements with similar properties. The elements of the modern periodic table are arranged in numerical order by atomic number.

The **periods** are the rows down the left side of the table. They are called first period, second period, etc. The columns of the periodic table are called **groups**, or **families.** Elements in a family have similar properties.

There are three types of elements that are grouped by color: metals, nonmetals, and metalloids.

Element Key
Atomic
Number

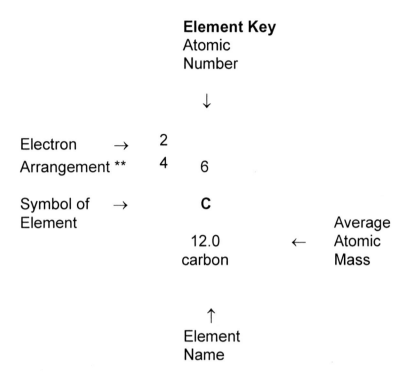

** Number of electrons on each level. Top number represents the innermost level.

The periodic table arranges metals into families with similar properties. The periodic table has its columns marked IA - VIIIA. These are the traditional group numbers. Arabic numbers 1 - 18 are also used, as suggested by the Union of Physicists and Chemists. The Arabic numerals will be used in this text.

Metals:

With the exception of hydrogen, all elements in Group 1 are **alkali metals**. These metals are shiny, softer and less dense than other metals, and are the most chemically active.

Group 2 metals are the **alkaline earth metals.** They are harder, denser, have higher melting points, and are chemically active.

The **transition elements** can be found by finding the periods (rows) from 4 to 7 under the groups (columns) 3 - 12. They are metals that do not show a range of properties as you move across the chart. They are hard and have high melting points. Compounds of these elements are colorful, such as silver, gold, and mercury.

Elements can be combined to make metallic objects. An **alloy** is a mixture of two or more elements having properties of metals. The elements do not have to be all metals. For instance, steel is made up of the metal iron and the non-metal carbon.

Nonmetals:

Nonmetals are not as easy to recognize as metals because they do not always share physical properties. However, in general the properties of nonmetals are the opposite of metals. They are dull, brittle, and are not good conductors of heat and electricity.

Nonmetals include solids, gases, and one liquid (bromine).
Nonmetals have four to eight electrons in their outermost energy levels and tend to attract electrons. As a result, the outer levels are usually filled with eight electrons. This difference in the number of electrons is what caused the differences between metals and nonmetals. The outstanding chemical property of nonmetals is that they react with metals.

The halogens can be found in Group 17. Halogens combine readily with metals to form salts. Table salt, fluoride toothpaste, and bleach all have an element from the halogen family.

The Noble Gases got their name from the fact that they did not react chemically with other elements, much like the nobility did not mix with the masses. These gases (found in Group 18) will only combine with other elements under very specific conditions. They are inert (inactive).

In recent years, scientists have found this to be only generally true, since chemists have been able to prepare compounds of krypton and xenon.

Metalloids:

Metalloids have properties in between metals and nonmetals. They can be found in Groups 13 - 16, but do not occupy the entire group. They are arranged in stair steps across the groups.

Physical Properties:
1. All are solids having the appearance of metals.
2. All are white or gray, but not shiny.
3. They will conduct electricity, but not as well as a metal.

Chemical Properties:
1. Have some characteristics of metals and nonmetals.
2. Properties do not follow patterns like metals and nonmetals. Each must be studied individually.

Boron is the first element in Group 13. It is a poor conductor of electricity at low temperatures. However, increase its temperature and it becomes a good conductor. By comparison, metals, which are good conductors, lose their ability as they are heated. It is because of this property that boron is so useful. Boron is a semiconductor. Semiconductors are used in electrical devices that have to function at temperatures too high for metals.

Silicon is the second element in Group 14. It is also a semiconductor and is found in great abundance in the earth's crust. Sand is made of a silicon compound, silicon dioxide. Silicon is also used in the manufacture of glass and cement.

Skill 42.5 Distinguishes between physical and chemical changes in matter.

A **physical change** does not create a new substance. **Atoms are not rearranged into different compounds**. The material has the same chemical composition as it had before the change. Changes of state as described in the previous section are physical changes. Frozen water or gaseous water is still H_2O. Taking a piece of paper and tearing it up is a physical change. You simply have smaller pieces of paper. A **chemical change** is a chemical reaction. It **converts one substance into another** because atoms are rearranged to form a different compound. Paper undergoes a chemical change when you burn it. You no longer have paper. A chemical change to a pure substance alters its properties.

Skill 42.6 Applies knowledge of physical properties of and changes in matter to processes and situations that occur in life and earth/space science.

Compare these two nails....They are still iron nails, made of iron atoms. The difference is that one is bent while the other is straight. This is a physical change.

An iron nail rusts to form a rusty nail. The rusty nail, however, is not made up of the same iron atoms. It is now composed of iron (III) oxide molecules that form when the iron atoms combine with oxygen molecules during oxidation (rusting).

COMPETENCY 43.0 THE TEACHER UNDERSTANDS CHEMICAL PROPERTIES OF AND CHANGES IN MATTER.

Skill 43.1   Describes the structure and components of the atom.

An atom is the smallest particle of the element that retains the properties of that element. All of the atoms of a particular element are the same. The atoms of each element are different from the atoms of other elements.

The nucleus is the center of the atom. The positive particles inside the nucleus are called protons. The mass of a proton is about 2,000 times that of the mass of an electron. The number of protons in the nucleus of an atom is called the atomic number. All atoms of the same element have the same atomic number.

Neutrons are another type of particle in the nucleus. Neutrons and protons have about the same mass, but neutrons have no charge. Neutrons were discovered because scientists observed that not all atoms in neon gas have the same mass. They had identified isotopes. Isotopes of an element have the same number of protons in the nucleus, but have different masses. Neutrons explain the difference in mass. They have mass but no charge.

The mass of matter is measured against a standard mass such as the gram. Scientists measure the mass of an atom by comparing it to that of a standard atom. The result is relative mass. The relative mass of an atom is its mass expressed in terms of the mass of the standard atom. The isotope of the element carbon is the standard atom. It has six (6) neutrons and is called carbon-12. It is assigned a mass of 12 atomic mass units (amu). Therefore, the atomic mass unit (amu) is the standard unit for measuring the mass of an atom. It is equal to the mass of a carbon atom.

The mass number of an atom is the sum of its protons and neutrons. In any element, there is a mixture of isotopes, some having slightly more or slightly fewer protons and neutrons. The atomic mass of an element is an average of the mass numbers of its atoms.

The following table summarizes the terms used to describe atomic nuclei:

Term	Example	Meaning	Characteristic
Atomic Number	# protons (p)	same for all atoms of a given element	Carbon (C) atomic number = 6 (6p)
Mass number	# protons + # neutrons (p + n)	changes for different isotopes of an element	C-12 (6p + 6n) C-13 (6p + 7n)
Atomic mass	average mass of the atoms of the element	usually not a whole number	atomic mass of carbon equals 12.011

Each atom has an equal number of electrons (negative) and protons (positive). Therefore, atoms are neutral. Electrons orbiting the nucleus occupy energy levels that are arranged in order and the electrons tend to occupy the lowest energy level available. A stable electron arrangement is an atom that has all of its electrons in the lowest possible energy levels.

Each energy level holds a maximum number of electrons. However, an atom with more than one level does not hold more than 8 electrons in its outermost shell.

Level	Name	Max. # of Electrons
First	K shell	2
Second	L shell	8
Third	M shell	18
Fourth	N shell	32

This can help explain why chemical reactions occur. Atoms react with each other when their outer levels are unfilled. When atoms either exchange or share electrons with each other, these energy levels become filled and the atom becomes more stable.

As an electron gains energy, it moves from one energy level to a higher energy level. The electron can not leave one level until it has enough energy to reach the next level. Excited electrons are electrons that have absorbed energy and have moved farther from the nucleus.

Electrons can also lose energy. When they do, they fall to a lower level. However, they can only fall to the lowest level that has room for them. This explains why atoms do not collapse.

Skill 43.2 Distinguishes among elements, mixtures, and compounds and describes their properties.

Elements are assigned an identifying symbol of one or two letters. The symbol for oxygen is O and stands for one atom of oxygen. However, because oxygen atoms in nature are joined together is pairs, the symbol O_2 represents oxygen. This pair of oxygen atoms is a molecule. A molecule is the smallest particle of substance that can exist independently and has all of the properties of that substance. A molecule of most elements is made up of one atom. However, oxygen, hydrogen, nitrogen, and chlorine molecules are made of two atoms each.

A compound is made of two or more elements that have been chemically combined. Atoms join together when elements are chemically combined. The result is that the elements lose their individual identities when they are joined. The compound that they become has different properties.

Substances can combine without a chemical change. A mixture is any combination of two or more substances in which the substances keep their own properties. A fruit salad is a mixture. So is an ice cream sundae, although you might not recognize each part if it is stirred together. Colognes and perfumes are the other examples. You may not readily recognize the individual elements. However, they can be separated.

Compounds and mixtures are similar in that they are made up of two or more substances. However, they have the following opposite characteristics:

Compounds:
1. Made up of one kind of particle
2. Formed during a chemical change
3. Broken down only by chemical changes
4. Properties are different from its parts
5. Has a specific amount of each ingredient.

Mixtures:
1. Made up of two or more particles
2. Not formed by a chemical change
3. Can be separated by physical changes
4. Properties are the same as its parts.
5. Does not have a definite amount of each ingredient.

Common compounds are acids, bases, salts, and oxides and are classified according to their characteristics.

Skill 43.3   Relates the chemical properties of an element to its placement in the periodic table.

The periodic table arranges metals into families with similar properties. The periodic table has its columns marked IA - VIIIA. These are the traditional group numbers. Arabic numbers 1 - 18 are also used, as suggested by the Union of Physicists and Chemists. The Arabic numerals will be used in this text.

Metals:

With the exception of hydrogen, all elements in Group 1 are alkali metals. These metals are shiny, softer and less dense than other metals, and are the most chemically active.

Group 2 metals are the alkaline earth metals. They are harder, denser, have higher melting points, and are chemically active.

The transition elements can be found by finding the periods (rows) from 4 to 7 under the groups (columns) 3 - 12. They are metals that do not show a range of properties as you move across the chart. They are hard and have high melting points. Compounds of these elements are colorful, such as silver, gold, and mercury.

Elements can be combined to make metallic objects. An alloy is a mixture of two or more elements having properties of metals. The elements do not have to be all metals. For instance, steel is made up of the metal iron and the non-metal carbon.

Nonmetals:

Nonmetals are not as easy to recognize as metals because they do not always share physical properties. However, in general the properties of nonmetals are the opposite of metals. They are dull, brittle, and are not good conductors of heat and electricity.

Nonmetals include solids, gases, and one liquid (bromine).

Nonmetals have four to eight electrons in their outermost energy levels and tend to attract electrons. As a result, the outer levels are usually filled with eight electrons. This difference in the number of electrons is what caused the differences between metals and nonmetals. The outstanding chemical property of nonmetals is that they react with metals.

The halogens can be found in Group 17. Halogens combine readily with metals to form salts. Table salt, fluoride toothpaste, and bleach all have an element from the halogen family.

The Noble Gases got their name from the fact that they did not react chemically with other elements, much like the nobility did not mix with the masses. These gases (found in Group 18) will only combine with other elements under very specific conditions. They are inert (inactive).

Skill 43.4   Describes chemical bonds and chemical formulas.

We use a formula to show the elements of a chemical compound. A chemical formula is a shorthand way of showing what is in a compound by using symbols and subscripts. The letter symbols let us know what elements are involved and the number subscript tells how many atoms of each element are involved. No subscript is used if there is only one atom involved. For example, carbon dioxide is made up of one atom of carbon (C) and two atoms of oxygen (O_2), so the formula would be represented as CO_2.

A chemical bond is a force of attraction that holds atoms together. When atoms are bonded chemically, they cease to have their individual properties. For instance, hydrogen and oxygen combine into water and no longer look like hydrogen and oxygen. They look like water.

A covalent bond is formed when two atoms share electrons. Recall that atoms whose outer shells are not filled with electrons are unstable. When they are unstable, they readily combine with other unstable atoms. By combining and sharing electrons, they act as a single unit. Covalent bonding happens among nonmetals. Covalent bonds are always polar between two non-identical atoms.

Covalent compounds are compounds whose atoms are joined by covalent bonds. Table sugar, methane, and ammonia are examples of covalent compounds.

An ionic bond is a bond formed by the transfer of electrons. It happens when metals and nonmetals bond. Before chlorine and sodium combine, the sodium has one valence electron and chlorine has seven. Neither valence shell is filled, but the chlorine's valence shell is almost full. During the reaction, the sodium gives one valence electron to the chlorine atom. Both atoms then have filled shells and are stable. Something else has happened during the bonding. Before the bonding, both atoms were neutral. When one electron was transferred, it upset the balance of protons and electrons in each atom. The chlorine atom took on one extra electron and the sodium atom released one atom. The atoms have now become ions. Ions are atoms with an unequal number of protons and electrons. To determine whether the ion is positive or negative, compare the number of protons (+charge) to the electrons (-charge). If there are more electrons the ion will be negative. If there are more protons, the ion will be positive.

Compounds that result from the transfer of metal atoms to nonmetal atoms are called ionic compounds. Sodium chloride (table salt), sodium hydroxide (drain cleaner), and potassium chloride (salt substitute) are examples of ionic compounds.

We use a formula to show the elements of a chemical compound. A chemical formula is a shorthand way of showing what is in a compound by using symbols and subscripts. The letter symbols let us know what elements are involved and the number subscript tells how many atoms of each element are involved. No subscript is used if there is only one atom involved. For example, carbon dioxide is made up of one atom of carbon (C) and two atoms of oxygen (O_2), so the formula would be represented as CO_2.

Skill 43.5   Analyzes chemical reactions and their associated chemical equations.

There are four kinds of chemical reactions:

In a composition reaction, two or more substances combine to form a compound.

$A + B \rightarrow AB$
i.e. silver and sulfur yield silver dioxide

In a decomposition reaction, a compound breaks down into two or more simpler substances.

$AB \rightarrow A + B$
i.e. water breaks down into hydrogen and oxygen

In a single replacement reaction, a free element replaces an element that is part of a compound.

$A + BX \rightarrow AX + B$
i.e. iron plus copper sulfate yields iron sulfate plus copper

In a double replacement reaction, parts of two compounds replace each other. In this case, the compounds seem to switch partners.

$AX + BY \rightarrow AY + BX$
i.e. sodium chloride plus mercury nitrate yields sodium nitrate plus mercury chloride

Skill 43.6 **Explains the importance of a variety of chemical reactions that occur in daily life (e.g., rusting, burning of fossil fuels, photosynthesis, cell respiration, chemical batteries, digestion of food).**

One of the greatest things about science is that it is directly applicable to everyday life. Students will relate to the lessons and this should facilitate learning. Rusting is a phenomenon that everyone is exposed to through everyday living. Rust occurs when metal is exposed to outdoor elements. During oxidation, the iron atoms of a nail combine with oxygen molecules in the air to form iron (III) oxide molecules. This is what we see when we notice rust.

Common fossil fuels used by humans are coal, petroleum and natural gas, which all form from the remains of dead plants and animals through natural processes after millions of years. Because of their high carbon content, when burnt these substances generate high amounts of energy as well as carbon dioxide, which is released back into the atmosphere increasing global warming. To create electricity, energy from the burning of fossil fuels is harnessed to power a rotary engine called a turbine. Implementation of the use of fossil fuels as an energy source provided for large-scale industrial development.

Cellular respiration is the metabolic pathway in which food (glucose, etc.) is broken down to produce energy in the form of ATP. Both plants and animals utilize respiration to create energy for metabolism. In respiration, energy is released by the transfer of electrons in a process know as an **oxidation-reduction (redox)** reaction. The oxidation phase of this reaction is the loss of an electron and the reduction phase is the gain of an electron. Redox reactions are important for the stages of respiration.

Glycolysis is the first step in respiration. It occurs in the cytoplasm of the cell and does not require oxygen. Each of the ten stages of glycolysis is catalyzed by a specific enzyme. Beginning with pyruvate, which was the end product of glycolysis, the following steps occur before entering the **Krebs cycle**.

1. Pyruvic acid is changed to acetyl-CoA (coenzyme A). This is a three carbon pyruvic acid molecule which has lost one molecule of carbon dioxide (CO_2) to become a two carbon acetyl group. Pyruvic acid loses a hydrogen to NAD^+ which is reduced to NADH.

2. Acetyl CoA enters the Krebs cycle. For each molecule of glucose it started with, two molecules of Acetyl CoA enter the Krebs cycle (one for each molecule of pyruvic acid formed in glycolysis).

The **Krebs cycle** (also known as the citric acid cycle), occurs in four major steps. First, the two-carbon acetyl CoA combines with a four-carbon molecule to form a six-carbon molecule of citric acid. Next, two carbons are lost as carbon dioxide (CO_2) and a four-carbon molecule is formed to become available to join with CoA to form citric acid again. Since we started with two molecules of CoA, two turns of the Krebs cycle are necessary to process the original molecule of glucose. In the third step, eight hydrogen atoms are released and picked up by FAD and NAD (vitamins and electron carriers). Lastly, for each molecule of CoA (remember there were two to start with) you get:

3 molecules of NADH x 2 cycles
1 molecule of $FADH_2$ x 2 cycles
1 molecule of ATP x 2 cycles

Therefore, this completes the breakdown of glucose. At this point, a total of four molecules of ATP have been made; two from glycolysis and one from each of the two turns of the Krebs cycle. Six molecules of carbon dioxide have been released; two prior to entering the Krebs cycle, and two for each of the two turns of the Krebs cycle. Twelve carrier molecules have been made; ten NADH and two $FADH_2$. These carrier molecules will carry electrons to the electron transport chain. ATP is made by substrate level phosphorylation in the Krebs cycle. Notice that the Krebs cycle in itself does not produce much ATP, but functions mostly in the transfer of electrons to be used in the electron transport chain where the most ATP is made.

In the **Electron Transport Chain,** NADH transfers electrons from glycolysis and the Kreb's cycle to the first molecule in the chain of molecules embedded in the inner membrane of the mitochondrion. Most of the molecules in the electron transport chain are proteins. Nonprotein molecules are also part of the chain and are essential for the catalytic functions of certain enzymes. The electron transport chain does not make ATP directly. Instead, it breaks up a large free energy drop into a more manageable amount. The chain uses electrons to pump H^+ across the mitochondrion membrane. The H^+ gradient is used to form ATP synthesis in a process called **chemiosmosis** (oxidative phosphorylation). ATP synthetase and energy generated by the movement of hydrogen ions coming off of NADH and $FADH_2$ builds ATP from ADP on the inner membrane of the mitochondria. Each NADH yields three molecules of ATP (10 x 3) and each $FADH_2$ yields two molecules of ATP (2 x 2). Thus, the electron transport chain and oxidative phosphorylation produces 34 ATP.

So, the net gain from the whole process of respiration is 36 molecules of ATP:
Glycolysis - 4 ATP made, 2 ATP spent = net gain of 2 ATP
Acetyl CoA- 2 ATP used
Krebs cycle - 1 ATP made for each turn of the cycle = net gain of 2 ATP
Electron transport chain - 34 ATP gained

Below is a diagram of the relationship between cellular respiration and photosynthesis.

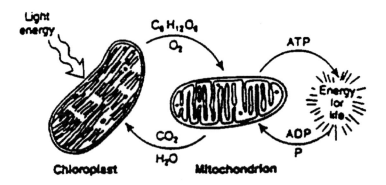

Photosynthesis is an anabolic process that stores energy in the form of a three carbon sugar. We will use glucose as an example for this section. Photosynthesis is done only by organisms that contain chloroplasts (plants, some bacteria, some protists). The **chloroplast** is the site of photosynthesis. It is similar to the mitochondria due to the increased surface area of the thylakoid membrane. It also contains a fluid called stroma between the stacks of thylakoids. The thylakoid membrane contains pigments (chlorophyll) that are capable of capturing light energy.

Photosynthesis reverses the electron flow. Water is split by the chloroplast into hydrogen and oxygen. The oxygen is given off as a waste product as carbon dioxide is reduced to sugar (glucose). This requires the input of energy, which comes from the sun.

Photosynthesis occurs in two stages: the light reactions and the Calvin cycle (dark reactions). The conversion of solar energy to chemical energy occurs in the light reactions. Electrons are transferred by the absorption of light by chlorophyll and cause the water to split, releasing oxygen as a waste product. The chemical energy that is created in the light reaction is in the form of NADPH. ATP is also produced by a process called photophosphorylation. These forms of energy are produced in the thylakoids and are used in the Calvin cycle to produce sugar.

The second stage of photosynthesis is the **Calvin cycle**. Carbon dioxide in the air is incorporated into organic molecules already in the chloroplast. The NADPH produced in the light reaction is used as reducing power for the reduction of the carbon to carbohydrate. ATP from the light reaction is also needed to convert carbon dioxide to carbohydrate (sugar). The process of photosynthesis is made possible by the presence of the sun. The formula for photosynthesis is:

$$CO_2 + H_2O + \text{energy (from sunlight)} \rightarrow C_6H_{12}O_6 + O_2$$

Chemical digestion of food in humans occurs as a series of exothermic reactions. Mechanically speaking, the teeth and saliva begin digestion by breaking food down into smaller pieces and lubricating it so it can be swallowed. The lips, cheeks, and tongue form a bolus or ball of food. It is carried down the pharynx by the process of peristalsis (wave-like contractions) and enters the stomach through the sphincter, which closes to keep food from going back up. In the stomach, pepsinogen and hydrochloric acid form pepsin, the enzyme that hydrolyzes proteins. The food is broken down further by this chemical action and is churned into acid chyme. The pyloric sphincter muscle opens to allow the food to enter the small intestine. Most nutrient absorption occurs in the small intestine. Its large surface area, accomplished by its length and protrusions called villi and microvilli, allow for a great absorptive surface into the bloodstream. Chyme is neutralized after coming from the acidic stomach to allow the enzymes found there to function. Accessory organs function in the production of necessary enzymes and bile. The pancreas makes many enzymes to break down food in the small intestine. The liver makes bile, which breaks down and emulsifies fatty acids. Any food left after the trip through the small intestine enters the large intestine. The large intestine functions to reabsorb water and produce vitamin K. The feces, or remaining waste, are passed out through the anus.

Skill 43.7   Understands applications of chemical properties of matter in physical, life, and earth/space science and technology (e.g., materials science, biochemistry, transportation, medicine, telecommunications).

Materials Science is based on the physics and chemistry of the solid state and embraces all aspects of engineering materials, including metals and their alloys, ceramic materials such as glasses, bricks, and porcelain insulators, polymers such as plastics, and rubbers together with semi-conducting and composite material. Materials Science extends from the extraction of the materials from their mineral sources and their refining and fabrication into finished products. It examines their chemical, crystal, molecular, and electronic structure because structure influences not only a material's magnetic and electronic characteristics but also its mechanical properties such as strength. It studies the degradation of materials in service by wear, corrosion, and oxidation and is concerned with developing methods of combating these; it considers the proper selection of materials for particular applications and the development of new materials for today's sophisticated technology.

Biochemistry is the study of chemical and physiochemical properties of living organisms. The thorough study and understanding of the structure and function of cellular components is based on the knowledge of the chemical properties of matter. An example is the study of cell metabolism. The understanding of processing nutrients is dependent on the understanding of chemical properties of the cell.

Advances have also been made in the field of **transportation** because of the understanding of chemical properties of matter. Scientists have been able to improve the quality of gasoline used in automobiles making it more environmentally friendly. The current research is focusing on the use of biofuels, renewable biological material, primarily plant matter or products derived from plant matter, as a fuel source.

In the **medical** field it was the understanding of the properties of bone and internal tissues of the body that allowed researchers to create magnetic resonance imaging (MRI). Scientists first created the nuclear magnetic machine to determine the structure of chemicals by measuring the vibration of atoms exposed to magnetic fields. They soon realized that this machine, connected to a computer, created the MRI and would allow them to take pictures of bone and internal tissue without the use of radioactivity. Created from an understanding of chemical properties of matter, this invention has also resulted in great strides in the diagnoses of disease and abnormalities.

Telecommunications has become dependent on the study of chemical properties of matter in improving and designing new modes of communication. The chemical properties of matter such as density and percent composition play a large role in the use of fiber optics to transport digital data. The modified chemical vapor deposition process that is used to create the form for optical fibers was created and continues to be refined because of an understanding of the chemical properties of matter.

COMPETENCY 44.0 THE TEACHER UNDERSTANDS ENERGY AND INTERACTIONS BETWEEN MATTER AND ENERGY.

Skill 44.1 Describes concepts of work, power, and potential and kinetic energy.

Work and energy:

Work is done on an object when an applied force moves through a distance.

Power is the work done divided by the amount of time that it took to do it. (Power = Work / time)

Technically, **energy is the ability to do work or supply heat.** Work is the transfer of energy to move an object a certain distance. It is the motion against an opposing force. Lifting a chair into the air is work; the opposing force is gravity. Pushing a chair across the floor is work; the opposing force is friction.

Heat, on the other hand, is not a form of energy but a method of transferring energy.

This energy, according to the First Law of Thermodynamics, is conserved. That means energy is neither created nor destroyed in ordinary physical and chemical processes (non-nuclear). Energy is merely changed from one form to another. Energy in all of its forms must be conserved. In any system, $\Delta E = q + w$ (E = energy, q = heat and w = work).

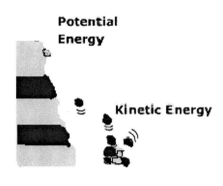

Potential Energy

Kinetic Energy

Energy exists in two basic forms, potential and kinetic. Kinetic energy is the energy of a moving object. Potential energy is the energy stored in matter due to position relative to other objects.

In any object, solid, liquid or gas, the atoms and molecules that make up the object are constantly moving (vibrational, translation and rotational motion) and colliding with each other. They are not stationary.

Due to this motion, the object's particles have varying amounts of kinetic energy. A fast moving atom can push a slower moving atom during a collision, so it has energy. All moving objects have energy and that energy depends on the object's mass and velocity. Kinetic energy is calculated: $K.E. = \frac{1}{2} mv^2$.

The temperature exhibited by an object is proportional to the average kinetic energy of the particles in the substance. Increase the temperature of a substance and its particles move faster so their average kinetic energies increase as well. But temperature is NOT an energy, it is not conserved.

The energy an object has due to its position or arrangement of its parts is called potential energy. Potential energy due to position is equal to the mass of the object times the gravitational pull on the object times the height of the object, or:

$$PE = mgh$$

Where PE = potential energy; m = mass of object; g = gravity; and h = height.

Heat is energy that is transferred between objects caused by differences in their temperatures. Heat passes spontaneously from an object of higher temperature to one of lower temperature. This transfer continues until both objects reach the same temperature. Both kinetic energy and potential energy can be transformed into heat energy. When you step on the brakes in your car, the kinetic energy of the car is changed to heat energy by friction between the brake and the wheels. Other transformations can occur from kinetic to potential as well. Since most of the energy in our world is in a form that is not easily used, man and mother nature has developed some clever ways of changing one form of energy into another form that may be more useful.

Skill 44.2   Understands the concept of heat energy and the difference between heat and temperature.

Heat and temperature are different physical quantities. **Heat** is a measure of energy. **Temperature** is the measure of how hot (or cold) a body is with respect to a standard object.

Two concepts are important in the discussion of temperature changes. Objects are in thermal contact if they can affect each other's temperatures. Set a hot cup of coffee on a desk top. The two objects are in thermal contact with each other and will begin affecting each other's temperatures. The coffee will become cooler and the desktop warmer. Eventually, they will have the same temperature. When this happens, they are in **thermal equilibrium.**

We can not rely on our sense of touch to determine temperature because the heat from a hand may be conducted more efficiently by certain objects, making them feel colder. **Thermometers** are used to measure temperature. A small amount of mercury in a capillary tube will expand when heated. The thermometer and the object whose temperature it is measuring are put in contact long enough for them to reach thermal equilibrium. Then the temperature can be read from the thermometer scale.

Three temperature scales are used:

Celsius: The freezing point of water is set at 0 and the steam (boiling) point is 100. The interval between the two is divided into 100 equal parts called degrees Celsius.

Fahrenheit: The freezing point of water is 32 degrees and the boiling point is 212. The interval between is divided into 180 equal parts called degrees Fahrenheit.

Temperature readings can be converted from one to the other as follows.

Fahrenheit to Celsius	**Celsius to Fahrenheit**
$C = 5/9 \ (F - 32)$	$F = (9/5) \ C + 32$

Kelvin Scale has degrees the same size as the Celsius scale, but the zero point is moved to the triple point of water. Water inside a closed vessel is in thermal equilibrium in all three states (ice, water, and vapor) at 273.15 degrees Kelvin. This temperature is equivalent to .01 degrees Celsius. Because the degrees are the same in the two scales, temperature changes are the same in Celsius and Kelvin.

Temperature readings can be converted from Celsius to Kelvin:

Celsius to Kelvin	**Kelvin to Celsius**
$K = C + 273.15$	$C = K - 273.15$

Heat is a measure of energy. If two objects that have different temperatures come into contact with each other, heat flows from the hotter object to the cooler one.

Heat Capacity of an object is the amount of heat energy that it takes to raise the temperature of the object by one degree.

Heat capacity (C) per unit mass (m) is called **specific heat** (c):

$$c = \frac{C}{m} = \frac{Q/\square}{m}$$

Specific heats for many materials have been calculated and can be found in tables.

There are a number of ways that heat is measured. In each case, the measurement is dependent upon raising the temperature of a specific amount of water by a specific amount. These conversions of heat energy and work are called the **mechanical equivalent of heat**.

The **calorie** is the amount of energy that it takes to raise one gram of water one degree Celsius.

The **kilocalorie** is the amount of energy that it takes to raise one kilogram of water by one degree Celsius. Food calories are kilocalories.

In the International System of Units **(SI),** the calorie is equal to 4.184 **joules**.

A British thermal unit **(BTU)** = 252 calories = 1.054 kJ

Skill 44.3   Understands the principles of electricity and magnetism and their applications (e.g., electric circuits, motors, audio speakers, nerve impulses, lighting).

An electric circuit is a path along which electrons flow. A simple circuit can be created with a dry cell, wire, a bell, or a light bulb. When all are connected, the electrons flow from the negative terminal, through the wire to the device and back to the positive terminal of the dry cell. If there are no breaks in the circuit, the device will work. The circuit is closed. Any break in the flow will create an open circuit and cause the device to shut off.

Air conditioners, vacuum cleaners, and washing machines use electric motors. An electric motor uses an electromagnet to change electric energy into mechanical energy. In a **motor**, electricity is used to create magnetic fields that oppose each other and cause the rotor to move. The wiring loops attached to the rotating shaft have a magnetic field opposing the magnetic field caused by the wiring in the housing of the motor that cannot move. The repelling action of the opposing magnetic fields turns the rotor.

The reflex arc is the simplest nerve response. The brain is bypassed. When a stimulus (like touching a hot stove) occurs, sensors in the hand send the message directly to the spinal cord. This stimulates motor neurons that contract the muscles to move the hand. A nerve impulse strikes a muscle fiber. This causes calcium ions to flood the sarcomere. Calcium ions allow ATP to expend energy. The myosin fibers creep along the actin, causing the muscle to contract. Once the nerve impulse has passed, calcium is pumped out and the contraction ends. Nerve action depends on depolarization and an imbalance of electrical charges across the neuron. A polarized nerve has a positive charge outside the neuron. A depolarized nerve has a negative charge outside the neuron. Neurotransmitters turn off the sodium pump, which results in depolarization of the membrane. This wave of depolarization (as it moves from neuron to neuron) carries an electrical impulse. This is actually a wave of opening and closing gates that allows for the flow of ions across the synapse. Nerves have an action potential. There is a threshold of the level of chemicals that must be met or exceeded in order for muscles to respond. This is called the "all or none" response.

Lightning is a natural phenomena created in electrically charged storm systems. The upper portion of the cloud is positive and the lower portion is negative. When there is a charge separation in a cloud, there is also an electric field that is associated with that separation. Like the cloud, this field is negative in the lower region and positive in the upper region. The strength of the electric field is directly related to the amount of charge built up in the cloud. As atomic collisions occur, the charges at the top and bottom of the cloud increase, and the electric field becomes more intense. The repulsion of electrons causes the earth's surface to acquire a strong positive charge. The strong electric field created on Earth becomes the conductive path for the negative cloud bottom to contact the positive earth surface. The importance of this electric field delineation is that it results in the separation of electrons. The electrons are now free to move much more easily than they could before the separation- the air is considered ionized and allows for electrical flow through the air, sometimes projecting into the atmosphere, and at other times landing on Earth's surface.

Skill 44.4   Applies knowledge of properties of light (e.g., reflection, refraction, dispersion) to describe the function of optical systems and phenomena (e.g., camera, microscope, rainbow, eye).

Shadows illustrate one of the basic properties of light. Light travels in a straight line. If you put your hand between a light source and a wall, you will interrupt the light and produce a shadow.

When light hits a surface, it is reflected. The angle of the incoming light (angle of incidence) is the same as the angle of the reflected light (angle of reflection). It is this reflected light that allows you to see objects. You see the objects when the reflected light reaches your eyes.

Different surfaces reflect light differently. Rough surfaces scatter light in many different directions. A smooth surface reflects the light in one direction. If it is smooth and shiny (like a mirror) you see your image in the surface.

When light enters a different medium, it bends. This bending, or change of speed, is called refraction.

Light can be diffracted, or bent around the edges of an object. Diffraction occurs when light goes through a narrow slit. As light passes through it, the light bends slightly around the edges of the slit. You can demonstrate this by pressing your thumb and forefinger together, making a very thin slit between them. Hold them about 8 cm from your eye and look at a distant source of light. The pattern you observe is caused by the diffraction of light.

Cameras use a convex lens to produce an image on the film. A convex lens is thicker in the middle than at the edges. The image size depends upon the focal length (distance from the focus to the lens). The longer the focal length is, the larger the image. A converging lens produces a real image whenever the object is far enough from the lens so that the rays of light from the object can hit the lens and be focused into a real image on the other side of the lens.

Eyeglasses can help correct deficiencies of sight by changing where the image seen is focused on the retina of the eye. If a person is nearsighted, the lens of his eye focuses images in front of the retina. In this case, the corrective lens placed in the eyeglasses will be concave so that the image will reach the retina. In the case of farsightedness, the lens of the eye focuses the image behind the retina. The correction will call for a convex lens to be fitted into the glass frames so that the image is brought forward into sharper focus.

The most common type of **microscope** is the optical microscope. This is an instrument containing one or more lenses that produce an enlarged image of an object placed in the focal plane of the lens(es). Microscopes can largely be separated into two classes: optical theory microscopes and scanning microscopes. Optical theory microscopes are microscopes which function through lenses to magnify the image generated by the passage of a wave through the sample, this is what one thinks of in the high school classroom. The waves used are either electromagnetic in optical microscopes or electron beams in electron microscopes. Common types are the Compound Light, Stereo, and the electron microscope. Optical microscopes use refractive lenses, typically of glass and occasionally of plastic, to focus light into the eye or another light detector. Typical magnification of a light microscope is up to 1500x. Electron microscopes, which use beams of electrons instead of light, are designed for very high magnification and resolution. The most common of these would be the scanning electron microscopes used in spectroscopy studies.

A **rainbow** is an optical phenomenon. The rainbow's appearance is caused by dispersion of sunlight as it is refracted by raindrops. Hence, rainbows are commonly seen after a rainfall, or near fountains and waterfalls. A rainbow does not actually exist at a specific location in the sky, but rather is an optical phenomenon whose apparent position depends on the observer's location. All raindrops refract and reflect the sunlight in the same way, but only the light from some raindrops will reach the observer's eye. These raindrops create the perceived rainbow (as experienced by that observer).

Skill 44.5   Demonstrates an understanding of the properties, production, and transmission of sound.

Sound waves are produced by a vibrating body. The vibrating object moves forward and compresses the air in front of it, then reverses direction so that the pressure on the air is lessened and expansion of the air molecules occurs. One compression and expansion creates one longitudinal wave. Sound can be transmitted through any gas, liquid, or solid. However, it cannot be transmitted through a vacuum, because there are no particles present to vibrate and bump into their adjacent particles to transmit the wave.

The vibrating air molecules move back and forth parallel to the direction of motion of the wave as they pass the energy from adjacent air molecules (closer to the source) to air molecules farther away from the source.

The **pitch** of a sound depends on the **frequency** that the ear receives. High-pitched sound waves have high frequencies. High notes are produced by an object that is vibrating at a greater number of times per second than one that produces a low note.

The **intensity** of a sound is the amount of energy that crosses a unit of area in a given unit of time. The loudness of the sound is subjective and depends upon the effect on the human ear. Two tones of the same intensity but different pitches may appear to have different loudness. The intensity level of sound is measured in decibels. Normal conversation is about 60 decibels. A power saw is about 110 decibels.

The **amplitude** of a sound wave determines its loudness. Loud sound waves have large amplitudes. The larger the sound wave, the more energy is needed to create the wave.

An oscilloscope is useful in studying waves because it gives a picture of the wave that shows the crest and trough of the wave. **Interference** is the interaction of two or more waves that meet. If the waves interfere constructively, the crest of each one meets the crests of the others. They combine into a crest with greater amplitude. As a result, you hear a louder sound. If the waves interfere destructively, then the crest of one meets the trough of another. They produce a wave with lower amplitude that produces a softer sound.

If you have two tuning forks that produce different pitches, then one will produce sounds of a slightly higher frequency. When you strike the two forks simultaneously, you may hear beats. **Beats** are a series of loud and soft sounds. This is because when the waves meet, the crests combine at some points and produce loud sounds. At other points, they nearly cancel each other out and produce soft sounds.

Skill 44.6 **Applies knowledge of properties and characteristics of waves (e.g., wavelength, frequency, interference) to describe a variety of waves (e.g., water, electromagnetic, sound).**

The electromagnetic spectrum is measured in frequency (f) in hertz and wavelength (λ) in meters. The frequency times the wavelength of every electromagnetic wave equals the speed of light (3.0×10^9 meters/second).

Roughly, the range of wavelengths of the electromagnetic spectrum is:

	f	**λ**
Radio waves	$10^{5} - 10^{-1}$ hertz	$10^{3} - 10^{9}$ meters
Microwaves	$10^{-1} - 10^{-3}$ hertz	$10^{9} - 10^{11}$ meters
Infrared radiation	$10^{-3} - 10^{-6}$ hertz	$10^{11.2} - 10^{14.3}$ meters
Visible light	$10^{-6.2} - 10^{-6.9}$ hertz	$10^{14.3} - 10^{15}$ meters
Ultraviolet radiation	$10^{-7} - 10^{-9}$ hertz	$10^{15} - 10^{17.2}$ meters
X-Rays	$10^{-9} - 10^{-11}$ hertz	$10^{17.2} - 10^{19}$ meters
Gamma Rays	$10^{-11} - 10^{-15}$ hertz	$10^{19} - 10^{23.25}$ meters

Radio waves are used for transmitting data. Common examples are television, cell phones, and wireless computer networks. Microwaves are used to heat food and deliver Wi-Fi service. Infrared waves are utilized in night vision goggles. Visible light we are all familiar with as the human eye is most sensitive to this wavelength range. UV light causes sunburns and would be even more harmful if most of it were not captured in the Earth's ozone layer. X-rays aid us in the medical field and gamma rays are most useful in the field of astronomy.

Sound waves are produced by a vibrating body. The vibrating object moves forward and compresses the air in front of it, then reverses direction so that the pressure on the air is lessened and expansion of the air molecules occurs. The vibrating air molecules move back and forth parallel to the direction of motion of the wave as they pass the energy from adjacent air molecules closer to the source to air molecules farther away from the source.

Sonar is used to measure distances. Sound waves are sent out, and the time is measured for the sound to hit an obstacle and bounce back. By using the known speed of sound, observers (or machines) can calculate the distance to the obstacle.

The movement of ocean water is caused by the wind, the sun's heat energy, the earth's rotation, the moon's gravitational pull on earth, and by underwater earthquakes. Most ocean waves are caused by the impact of winds. Wind blowing over the surface of the ocean transfers energy (friction) to the water and causes waves to form. Waves are also formed by seismic activity on the ocean floor. A wave formed by an earthquake is called a seismic sea wave. These powerful waves can be very destructive, with wave heights increasing to 30 m or more near the shore.

The **crest** of a wave is its highest point. The **trough** of a wave is its lowest point. The distance from wave top to wave top is the **wavelength**. The wave **period** is the time between the passings of two successive waves.

COMPETENCY 045 THE TEACHER UNDERSTANDS ENERGY TRANSFORMATIONS AND THE CONSERVATION OF MATTER AND ENERGY.

Skill 45.1   Describes the processes that generate energy in the sun and other stars.

All stars derive their energy through the thermonuclear fusion of light elements into heavy elements. The minimum temperature required for the fusion of hydgrogen is 5 million degrees. Elements with more protons in their nuclei require higher temperatures. For instance, to fuse Carbon requires a temperature of about 1 billion degrees.

A star that is composed of mostly hydrogen is a young star. As a star gets older its hydrogen is consumed and tremendous energy and light is released through fusion. This is a three-step process: (1) two hydrogen nuclei (protons) fuse to form a heavy hydrogen called deuterium and release an electron and 4.04 MeV energy, (2) the deuterium fuses with another hydrogen nucleus (proton) to form a helium-3 and release a neutron and 3.28 MeV energy, and (3) and the helium-3 fuses with another helium-3 to form a helium-4 and release two hydrogens and 10.28 MeV energy.

In stars with central temperatures greater than 600-700 million degrees, carbon fusion is thought to take over the dominant role rather than hydrogen fusion. Carbon fusions can produce magnesium, sodium, neon, or helium. Some of the reactions release energy and alpha particles or protons.

Skill 45.2   Applies the law of conservation of matter to analyze a variety of situations (e.g., the water cycle, food chains, decomposition, balancing chemical equations).

The law of conservation states that matter can be neither created nor destroyed. In layman's terms, matter is recycled indefinitely. Let's look at the water cycle. In the water cycle, water is recycled through the processes of evaporation and precipitation. Precipitation is part of a continuous process in which water at the Earth's surface evaporates, condenses into clouds, and returns to Earth. The water present now is the water that has been here since our atmosphere formed.

Food chains are linked in nature. Autotrophs produce their own energy, and are consumed by heterotrophs. Herbivores are eaten by carnivores. In most cases, each species has at least one indigenous predator who keeps the size of the population within limits. That predator has its own predator. Where a predator doesn't exist, man has become the hunter, nature has controlled populations through natural catastrophies and succession, or the population becomes too large and individuals eventually out compete one another for resources, while weaker members die.

Decomposition is nature's own compost pile. Over time, all organic matter decomposes, returning vital elements to the soil, increasing its richness for the next generation of growth. There are even specific bacteria and fungi whose aid in this process ensures that nutrients are not lost.

It is important to keep true to the law of conservation when balancing equations. This means that there must be the same number of atoms on both sides of the equation. Remember that the subscript numbers indicate the number of atoms in the elements. If there is no subscript, assume there is only one atom. The quantity of molecules are indicated by the number in front of an element or compound. If no number appears, assume that it is one molecule. Many chemical reactions give off energy. Like matter, energy can change form but it can be neither created nor destroyed during a chemical reaction.

Skill 45.3 Describes sources of electrical energy and processes of energy transformation for human uses (e.g., fossil fuels, solar panels, hydroelectric plants).

Burning of fossil fuels causes a great deal of air pollution as sulfur oxide, unburned hydrocarbons, and carbon monoxide are released into the air. Natural gas burns much cleaner and has the advantage of being able to be pumped through pipes to where it can be used.

Solar energy is radiation from the sun. Solar energy must be stored for use when the sun is not shining. Storage methods include heating water or rocks or converting the sun's rays into electricity using a photoelectric cell. Photoelectric cells are very expensive to make. Enormous amounts of water or rocks must be heated and insulated in storage to make use of the solar energy.

Hydroelectricity is produced by moving water. Building the dam and changing the flow of the stream can be harmful to the environment, can kill fish, and frequently destroys plant life. Hydroelectricity is dependent on the cycle of rain and snow, so heavier rainfall and snowfall in the mountains makes hydroelectricity production more reasonable.

Wood chips and other low-grade wood wastes are one type of biomass fuel. Other common biomass fuel sources are agricultural crop residues and farm animal wastes. Biomass includes gasoline made from corn or soybeans. Biomass is a renewable fuel that can be continuously produced. Since biomass is locally grown and harvested, there are no transportation costs and local jobs are preserved or created. Compared to fossil fuels, biomass fuels are historically lower-priced. Using biomass in place of fossil fuel reduces the atmospheric buildup of greenhouse gases, which cause climate change, and can also reduce the levels of gases that cause acid rain. Particulate emissions are relatively low.

Wind is captured by wind turbines and used to generate electricity. Wind power generation is clean; it doesn't cause air, soil or water pollution. However, wind farms must be located on large tracts of land or along coastlines to capture the greatest wind movement. Devoting those areas to wind power generation sometimes conflicts with other priorities, such as agriculture, urban development, or waterfront views from homes in prime locations.

Heat within the earth is called geothermal energy. Geothermal power plants produce little if any pollution or environmental hazards and can operate continuously for many years.

A nuclear reactor is a device for controlling and using the energy from a nuclear chain reaction. Strict safety regulations must be followed to protect people working in the plant and those in surrounding communities from radiation and the very hot water that is produced. Nuclear energy has some advantages over fossil fuels like coal and oil. Nuclear reactors do not add pollutants to the air. A greater amount of energy can be produced from smaller amounts of nuclear fuels. However, they require enormous amounts of water for cooling and they produce radioactive wastes that must be stored for thousands of years before they lose their radioactivity.

Skill 45.4   Understands exothermic and endothermic chemical reactions and their applications (e.g., hot and cold packs, energy content of food).

Interacting objects in the universe constantly exchange and transform energy. Total energy remains the same, but the form of the energy readily changes. Energy often changes from kinetic (motion) to potential (stored) or potential to kinetic. In reality, available energy, energy that is easily utilized, is rarely conserved in energy transformations. Heat energy is an example of relatively "useless" energy often generated during energy transformations. Exothermic reactions release heat and endothermic reactions require heat energy to proceed. For example, the human body is notoriously inefficient in converting chemical energy from food into mechanical energy. The digestion of food is exothermic and produces substantial heat energy.

Skill 45.5   Applies knowledge of the transfer of energy in a variety of situations (e.g., the production of heat, light, sound, and magnetic effects by electrical energy; the process of photosynthesis; weather processes; food webs; food/energy pyramids).

Thermodynamics is the study of energy and energy transfer. The first law of thermodynamics states the energy of the universe is constant. Thus, interactions involving energy deal with the transfer and transformation of energy, not the creation or destruction of energy.

Electricity is an important source of energy. Ovens and electric heaters convert electrical energy into heat energy. Electrical energy energizes the filament of a light bulb to produce light. Finally, the movement of electrical charges creates magnetic fields. Charges moving in a magnetic field experience a force, which is a transfer of energy.

The process of photosynthesis converts light energy from the sun into chemical energy (sugar). Cellular respiration later converts the sugar into ATP, a major energy source of all living organisms. Plants and certain types of bacteria carry out photosynthesis. The actions of the green pigment chlorophyll allow the conversion of unusable light energy into usable chemical energy.

Energy transfer plays an important role in weather processes. The three main types of heat transfer to the atmosphere are radiation, conduction, and convection. Radiation is the transfer of heat by electromagnetic waves. Sun light is an example of radiation. Conduction is the transfer of energy from one substance to another, or within a substance. Convection is the transfer of heat energy in a fluid. Air in the atmosphere acts as a fluid for the transfer of heat energy. Convection, resulting indirectly from the energy generated by sunlight, is responsible for many weather phenomena including wind and clouds.

Energy transfer is also a key concept in the creation of food webs and food pyramids. Food webs and pyramids show the feeding relationships between organisms in an ecosystem. The primary producers of an ecosystem produce organic compounds from an energy source and inorganic materials. Primary consumers obtain energy by feeding on producers. Finally, secondary consumers obtain energy by feeding on primary consumers.

Skill 45.6 **Applies the law of conservation of energy to analyze a variety of physical phenomena (e.g., specific heat, nuclear reactions, efficiency of simple machines, collisions).**

Heat Capacity of an object is the amount of heat energy that it takes to raise the temperature of the object by one degree.

Heat capacity (C) per unit mass (m) is called **specific heat** (c):

$$c = \frac{C}{m} = \frac{Q / \Delta}{m}$$

Specific heats for many materials have been calculated and can be found in tables.

There are a number of ways that heat is measured. In each case, the measurement is dependent upon raising the temperature of a specific amount of water by a specific amount. These conversions of heat energy and work are called the **mechanical equivalent of heat**. Simple machines make work easier by reducing the energy input required to accomplish the task.

By applying the rules for conservation we discover that simple machines are the ideal tools.

Ideal Machine: Energy input = Energy output

Work input = Force of energy input = Force of energy output = Work output

From this equation we can see that a simple machine is capable of multiplying force. A small input force can accomplish a task requiring a large output force.

The laws of conservation can be applied to nuclear reactions as well. When balancing equations it is important to make sure all reactants and products are accounted for. Generally, we can make the math work, specifically because the mass of electrons are so small. In the universe, though, with millions of ongoing reactions, that small electrical mass is significant and IS conserved. It is conserved in the form of energy. The proton has slightly less mass than the neutron. The mass of the electron makes up for this somewhat, and the difference is energy. Often this is the kinetic energy of the reaction. Therefore, it is crucial to take energy into account when considering reactions.

Skill 45.7   Understands applications of energy transformations and the conservation of matter and energy in life and earth/space science.

The principle of conservation states that certain measurable properties of an isolated system remain constant despite changes in the system. Two important principles of conservation are the conservation of mass and charge.

The principle of conservation of mass states that the total mass of a system is constant. Examples of conservation in mass in nature include the burning of wood, rusting of iron, and phase changes of matter. When wood burns, the total mass of the products, such as soot, ash, and gases, equals the mass of the wood and the oxygen that reacts with it. When iron reacts with oxygen, rust forms. The total mass of the iron-rust complex does not change. Finally, when matter changes phase, mass remains constant. Thus, when a glacier melts due to atmospheric warming, the mass of liquid water formed is equal to the mass of the glacier.

The principle of conservation of charge states that the total electrical charge of a closed system is constant. Thus, in chemical reactions and interactions of charged objects, the total charge does not change. Chemical reactions and the interaction of charged molecules are essential and common processes in living organisms and systems.

COMPETENCY 46.0 THE TEACHER UNDERSTANDS THE STRUCTURE AND FUNCTION OF LIVING THINGS.

Skill 46.1   Describes characteristics of organisms from the major taxonomic groups.

Carolus Linnaeus is termed the father of taxonomy. Taxonomy is the science of classification. Linnaeus based his system on morphology (study of structure). Later on, evolutionary relationships (phylogeny) were also used to sort and group species. The modern classification system uses binomial nomenclature. This consists of a two word name for every species. The genus is the first part of the name and the species is the second part. Notice, in the levels explained below, that Homo sapiens is the scientific name for humans. Starting with the kingdom, the groups get smaller and more alike as one moves down the levels in the classification of humans:

Kingdom: Animalia, Phylum: Chordata, Subphylum: Vertebrata, Class: Mammalia, Order: Primate, Family: Hominidae, Genus: Homo, Species: sapiens

Species are defined by the ability to successfully reproduce with members of their own kind.

Kingdom Monera - bacteria and blue-green algae, prokaryotic, having no true nucleus, unicellular.

Kingdom Protista - eukaryotic, unicellular, some are photosynthetic, some are consumers.

Kingdom Fungi - eukaryotic, multicellular, absorptive consumers, contain a chitin cell wall.

Bacteria are classified according to their morphology (shape). Bacilli are rod shaped, cocci are round, and spirillia are spiral shaped. The gram stain is a staining procedure used to identify bacteria. Gram positive bacteria pick up the stain and turn purple. Gram negative bacteria do not pick up the stain and are pink in color. Microbiologists use methods of locomotion, reproduction, and how the organism obtains its food to classify protista.

Methods of locomotion - Flagellates have a flagellum, ciliates have cilia, and ameboids move through use of pseudopodia.

Methods of reproduction - binary fission is simply dividing in half and is asexual. All new organisms are exact clones of the parent. Sexual modes provide more diversity. Bacteria can reproduce sexually through conjugation, where genetic material is exchanged.

Methods of obtaining nutrition - photosynthetic organisms or producers, convert sunlight to chemical energy, consumers or heterotrophs eat other living things. Saprophytes are consumers that live off dead or decaying material.

Skill 46.2   Analyzes how structure complements function in cells.

Parts of Eukaryotic Cells

1. Nucleus - The brain of the cell. The nucleus contains:

chromosomes- DNA, RNA and proteins tightly coiled to conserve space while providing a large surface area.
chromatin - loose structure of chromosomes. Chromosomes are called chromatin when the cell is not dividing.
nucleoli - where ribosomes are made. These are seen as dark spots in the nucleus.
nuclear membrane - contains pores which let RNA out of the nucleus. The nuclear membrane is continuous with the endoplasmic reticulum which allows the membrane to expand or shrink if needed.

2. Ribosomes - the site of protein synthesis. Ribosomes may be free floating in the cytoplasm or attached to the endoplasmic reticulum. There may be up to a half a million ribosomes in a cell, depending on how much protein is made by the cell.

3. Endoplasmic Reticulum - These are folded and provide a large surface area. They are the "roadway" of the cell and allow for transport of materials. The lumen of the endoplasmic reticulum helps to keep materials out of the cytoplasm and headed in the right direction. The endoplasmic reticulum is capable of building new membrane material. There are two types:

Smooth Endoplasmic Reticulum - contain no ribosomes on their surface.

Rough Endoplasmic Reticulum - contain ribosomes on their surface. This form of ER is abundant in cells that make many proteins, like in the pancreas, which produces many digestive enzymes.

4. Golgi Complex or Golgi Apparatus - This structure is stacked to increase surface area. The Golgi Complex functions to sort, modify and package molecules that are made in other parts of the cell. These molecules are either sent out of the cell or to other organelles within the cell.

5. Lysosomes - found mainly in animal cells. These contain digestive enzymes that break down food, substances not needed, viruses, damaged cell components, and eventually the cell itself. It is believed that lysosomes are responsible for the aging process.

6. Mitochondria - large organelles that make ATP to supply energy to the cell. Muscle cells have many mitochondria because they use a great deal of energy. The folds inside the mitochondria are called cristae. They provide a large surface where the reactions of cellular respiration occur. Mitochondria have their own DNA and are capable of reproducing themselves if a greater demand is made for additional energy. Mitochondria are found only in animal cells.

7. Plastids - found in photosynthetic organisms only. They are similar to the mitochondria due to their double membrane structure. They also have their own DNA and can reproduce if increased capture of sunlight becomes necessary. There are several types of plastids:

> **Chloroplasts** - green, function in photosynthesis. They are capable of trapping sunlight.
> **Chromoplasts** - make and store yellow and orange pigments; they provide color to leaves, flowers and fruits.
> **Amyloplasts** - store starch and are used as a food reserve. They are abundant in roots like potatoes.

8. Cell Wall - found in plant cells only, it is composed of cellulose and fibers. It is thick enough for support and protection, yet porous enough to allow water and dissolved substances to enter. Cell walls are cemented to each other.

9. Vacuoles - hold stored food and pigments. Vacuoles are very large in plants. This is allows them to fill with water in order to provide turgor pressure. Lack of turgor pressure causes a plant to wilt.

10. Cytoskeleton - composed of protein filaments attached to the plasma membrane and organelles. They provide a framework for the cell and aid in cell movement. They constantly change shape and move about. Three types of fibers make up the cytoskeleton:

> **Microtubules** - largest of the three; makes up cilia and flagella for locomotion. Flagella grow from a basal body. Some examples are sperm cells, and tracheal cilia. Centrioles are also composed of microtubules. They form the spindle fibers that pull the cell apart into two cells during cell division. Centrioles are not found in the cells of higher plants.

Intermediate Filaments - they are smaller than microtubules but larger than microfilaments. They help the cell to keep its shape.

Microfilaments - smallest of the three, they are made of actin and small amounts of myosin (like in muscle cells). They function in cell movement such as cytoplasmic streaming, endocytosis, and ameboid movement. This structure pinches the two cells apart after cell division, forming two cells.

Skill 46.3   Analyzes how structure complements function in tissues, organs, organ systems, and organisms.

Structure and function dictates behavior and aids in the identification of prokaryotic organisms. Important structural and functional aspects of prokaryotes are morphology, motility, reproduction and growth, and metabolic diversity.

Morphology refers to the shape of a cell. The three main shapes of prokaryotic cells are spheres (cocci), rods (bacilli), and spirals (spirilla). Observation of cell morphology with a microscope can aid in the identification and classification of prokaryotic organisms. The most important aspect of prokaryotic morphology, regardless of the specific shape, is the size of the cells. Small cells allow for rapid exchange of wastes and nutrients across the cell membrane promoting high metabolic and growth rates.

Motility refers to the ability of an organism to move and its mechanism of movement. While some prokaryotes glide along solid surfaces or use gas vesicles to move in water, the vast majority of prokaryotes move by means of flagella. Motility allows organisms to reach different parts of its environment in the search for favorable conditions. Flagellar structure allows differentiation of Archaea and Bacteria as the two classes of prokaryotes have very different flagella. In addition, different types of bacteria have flagella positioned in different locations on the cell. The locations of flagella are on the ends (polar), all around (peritrichous), or in a tuft at one end of the cell (lophotrichous).

Most prokaryotes reproduce by binary fission, the growth of a single cell until it divides in two. Because of their small size, most prokaryotes have high growth rates under optimal conditions. Environmental factors greatly influence prokaryotic growth rate. Scientists identify and classify prokaryotes based on their ability or inability to survive and grow in certain conditions. Temperature, pH, water availability, and oxygen levels differentially influence the growth of prokaryotes. For example, certain types of prokaryotes can survive and grow at extremely hot or cold temperatures while most cannot.

Prokaryotes display great metabolic diversity. Autotrophic prokaryotes use carbon dioxide as the sole carbon source in energy metabolism, while heterotrophic prokaryotes require organic carbon sources. More specifically, chemoautotrophs use carbon dioxide as a carbon source and inorganic compounds as an energy source, while chemoheterotrophs use organic compounds as a source of energy and carbon. Photoautotrophs require only light energy and carbon dioxide, while photoheterotrophs require an organic carbon source along with light energy. Examining an unknown organism's metabolism aids in the identification process.

Skill 46.4   Identifies human body systems and describes their functions.

Skeletal System - The skeletal system functions in support. Vertebrates have an endoskeleton, with muscles attached to bones. Skeletal proportions are controlled by area to volume relationships. Body size and shape is limited due to the forces of gravity. Surface area is increased to improve efficiency in all organ systems.

Muscular System – Its function is for movement. There are three types of muscle tissue. Skeletal muscle is voluntary. These muscles are attached to bones. Smooth muscle is involuntary. It is found in organs and enable functions such as digestion and respiration. Cardiac muscle is a specialized type of smooth muscle.

Nervous System - The neuron is the basic unit of the nervous system. It consists of an axon, which carries impulses away from the cell body, the dendrite, which carries impulses toward the cell body and the cell body, which contains the nucleus. Synapses are spaces between neurons. Chemicals called neurotransmitters are found close to the synapse. The myelin sheath, composed of Schwann cells, covers the neurons and provides insulation.

Digestive System - The function of the digestive system is to break down food and absorb it into the blood stream where it can be delivered to all cells of the body for use in cellular respiration. As animals evolved, digestive systems changed from simple absorption to a system with a separate mouth and anus, capable of allowing the animal to become independent of a host.

Respiratory System - This system functions in the gas exchange of oxygen (needed) and carbon dioxide (waste). It delivers oxygen to the bloodstream and picks up carbon dioxide for release out of the body. Simple animals diffuse gases from and to their environment. Gills allow aquatic animals to exchange gases in a fluid medium by removing dissolved oxygen from the water. Lungs maintain a fluid environment for gas exchange in terrestrial animals.

Circulatory System - The function of the circulatory system is to carry oxygenated blood and nutrients to all cells of the body and return carbon dioxide waste to be expelled from the lungs. Animals evolved from an open system to a closed system with vessels leading to and from the heart.

Skill 46.5   Describes how organisms obtain and use energy and matter.

All organisms can be classes by the manner in which they obtain energy: chemoautotrophs, photoautotrophs, and heterotrophs.

Chemoautotrophs- These organisms are able to obtain energy via the oxidation of inorganic molecules (i.e., hydrogen gas and hydrogen sufide) or methane. This process is known as chemosynthesis. Most chemoautotrophs are bacteria or archaea that thrive in oxygen-poor environments, such as deep sea vents.

Photoautotrophs- Instead of obtaining energy from simple inorganic compounds like the chemoautotrophs, organisms of this type receive energy from sunlight. They employ the process of photosynthesis to create sugar from light, carbon dioxide and water. Most higher plants and algae as well as some bacteria and protists are photoautotrophs.

Heterotrophs- Any organism that requires organic molecules for as its source of energy is a heterotroph. These organisms are consumers in the food chain and must obtain nutrition from autotrophs or other heterotrophs. All animals are heterotrophs, as are some fungi and bacteria.

Photosynthesis is the process by which plants make carbohydrates from the energy of the sun, carbon dioxide, and water. Oxygen is a waste product. Photosynthesis occurs in the chloroplast where the pigment chlorophyll traps sun energy. It is divided into two major steps:

Light Reactions - Sunlight is trapped, water is split, and oxygen is given off. ATP is made and hydrogens reduce NADP to $NADPH_2$. The light reactions occur in light. The products of the light reactions enter into the dark reactions (Calvin cycle).

Dark Reactions - Carbon dioxide enters during the dark reactions which can occur with or without the presence of light. The energy transferred from $NADPH_2$ and ATP allow for the fixation of carbon into glucose.

Respiration - during times of decreased light, plants break down the products of photosynthesis through cellular respiration. Glucose, with the help of oxygen, breaks down and produces carbon dioxide and water as waste. Approximately fifty percent of the products of photosynthesis are used by the plant for energy.

Transpiration - water travels up the xylem of the plant through the process of transpiration. Water sticks to itself (cohesion) and to the walls of the xylem (adhesion). As it evaporates through the stomata of the leaves, the water is pulled up the column from the roots. Environmental factors such as heat and wind increase the rate of transpiration. High humidity will decrease the rate of transpiration.

Animal respiration takes in oxygen and gives off waste gases. For instance a fish uses its gills to extract oxygen from the water. Bubbles are evidence that waste gasses are expelled. Respiration without oxygen is called anaerobic respiration. Anaerobic respiration in animal cells is also called lactic acid fermentation. The end product is lactic acid.

Animal reproduction can be asexual or sexual. Geese lay eggs. Animals such as bear cubs, deer, and rabbits are born alive. Some animals reproduce frequently while others do not. Some animals only produce one baby yet others produce many (clutch size).

Animal digestion – some animals only eat meat (carnivores) while others only eat plants (herbivores). Many animals do both (omnivores). Nature has created animals with structural adaptations so they may obtain food through sharp teeth or long facial structures. Digestion's purpose is to break down carbohydrates, fats, and proteins. Many organs are needed to digest food. The process begins with the mouth. Certain animals, such as birds, have beaks to puncture wood or allow for large fish to be consumed. The tooth structure of a beaver is designed to cut down trees. Tigers are known for their sharp teeth used to rip hides from their prey. Enzymes are catalysts that help speed up chemical reactions by lowering effective activation energy. Enzyme rate is affected by temperature, pH, and the amount of substrate. Saliva is an enzyme that changes starches into sugars.

Animal circulation – The blood temperature of all mammals stays constant regardless of the outside temperature. This is called warm-blooded, while cold-blooded animals' (amphibians') circulation will vary with the temperature.

Skill 46.6	Applies chemical principles to describe the structure and function of the basic chemical components (e.g., proteins, carbohydrates, lipids, nucleic acids) of living things.

A compound consists of two or more elements. There are four major chemical compounds found in the cells and bodies of living things. These include carbohydrates, lipids, proteins and nucleic acids.

Monomers are the simplest unit of structure. **Monomers** can be combined to form **polymers**, or long chains, making a large variety of molecules possible. Monomers combine through the process of condensation reaction (also called dehydration synthesis). In this process, one molecule of water is removed between each of the adjoining molecules. In order to break the molecules apart in a polymer, water molecules are added between monomers, thus breaking the bonds between them. This is called hydrolysis.

Carbohydrates contain a ratio of two hydrogen atoms for each carbon and oxygen $(CH_2O)_n$. Carbohydrates include sugars and starches. They function in the release of energy. **Monosaccharides** are the simplest sugars and include glucose, fructose, and galactose. They are major nutrients for cells. In cellular respiration, the cells extract the energy in glucose molecules. **Disaccharides** are made by joining two monosaccharides by condensation to form a glycosidic linkage (covalent bond between two monosaccharides). Maltose is formed from the combination of two glucose molecules, lactose is formed from joining glucose and galactose, and sucrose is formed from the combination of glucose and fructose. **Polysaccharides** consist of many monomers joined. They are storage material hydrolyzed as needed to provide sugar for cells or building material for structures protecting the cell. Examples of polysaccharides include starch, glycogen, cellulose and chitin.

> **Starch** - major energy storage molecule in plants. It is a polymer consisting of glucose monomers.
> **Glycogen** - major energy storage molecule in animals. It is made up of many glucose molecules.
> **Cellulose** - found in plant cell walls, its function is structural. Many animals lack the enzymes necessary to hydrolyze cellulose, so it simply adds bulk (fiber) to the diet.
> **Chitin** - found in the exoskeleton of arthropods and fungi. Chitin contains an amino sugar (glycoprotein).

Lipids are composed of glycerol (an alcohol) and three fatty acids. Lipids are **hydrophobic** (water fearing) and will not mix with water. There are three important families of lipids, fats, phospholipids and steroids.

Fats consist of glycerol (alcohol) and three fatty acids. Fatty acids are long carbon skeletons. The nonpolar carbon-hydrogen bonds in the tails of fatty acids are why they are hydrophobic. Fats are solids at room temperature and come from animal sources (butter, lard).

Phospholipids are a vital component in cell membranes. In a phospholipid, one or two fatty acids are replaced by a phosphate group linked to a nitrogen group. They consist of a **polar** (charged) head that is hydrophilic or water loving and a **nonpolar** (uncharged) tail which is hydrophobic or water fearing. This allows the membrane to orient itself with the polar heads facing the interstitial fluid found outside the cell and the internal fluid of the cell.

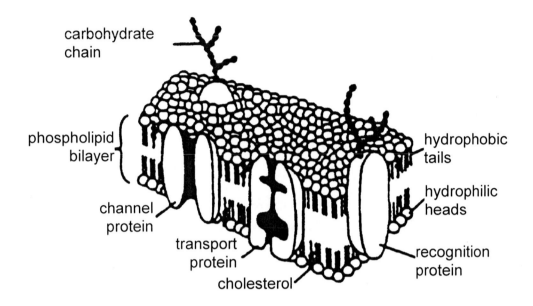

Steroids are insoluble and are composed of a carbon skeleton consisting of four inter-connected rings. An important steroid is cholesterol, which is the precursor from which other steroids are synthesized. Hormones, including cortisone, testosterone, estrogen, and progesterone, are steroids. Their insolubility keeps them from dissolving in body fluids.

Proteins compose about fifty percent of the dry weight of animals and bacteria. Proteins function in structure and aid in support (connective tissue, hair, feathers, quills), storage of amino acids (albumin in eggs, casein in milk), transport of substances (hemoglobin), hormonal to coordinate body activities (insulin), membrane receptor proteins, contraction (muscles, cilia, flagella), body defense (antibodies), and as enzymes to speed up chemical reactions. There are four levels of protein structure: primary, secondary, tertiary, and quaternary.

All proteins are made of twenty **amino acids**. An amino acid contains an amino group and an acid group. The radical group varies and defines the amino acid. Amino acids form through condensation reactions with the removal of water. The bond that is formed between two amino acids is called a peptide bond. Polymers of amino acids are called polypeptide chains. An analogy can be drawn between the twenty amino acids and the alphabet. Millions of words can be formed using an alphabet of only twenty-six letters. This diversity is also possible using only twenty amino acids. This results in the formation of many different proteins, whose structure defines the function.

Nucleic acids consist of DNA (deoxyribonucleic acid) and RNA (ribonucleic acid). Nucleic acids contain the instructions for the amino acid sequence of proteins and the instructions for replicating. The monomer of nucleic acids is called a nucleotide. A nucleotide consists of a 5 carbon sugar, (deoxyribose in DNA, ribose in RNA), a phosphate group, and a nitrogenous base. The base sequence codes for the instructions. There are five bases: adenine, thymine, cytosine, guanine, and uracil. Uracil is found only in RNA and replaces the thymine. A summary of nucleic acid structure can be seen in the table below:

	SUGAR	PHOSPHATE	BASES
DNA	deoxy-ribose	present	adenine, thymine, cytosine, guanine
RNA	ribose	present	adenine, uracil, cytosine, guanine

Due to the molecular structure, adenine will always pair with thymine in DNA or uracil in RNA. Cytosine always pairs with guanine in both DNA and RNA. This allows for the symmetry of the DNA molecule seen below.

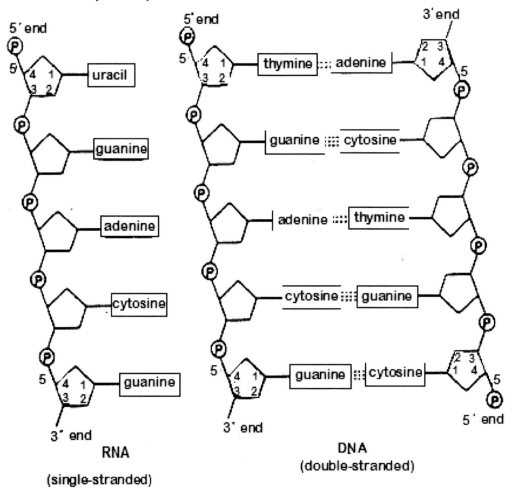

RNA

(single-stranded)

DNA
(double-stranded)

Adenine and thymine (or uracil) are linked by two covalent bonds and cytosine and guanine are linked by three covalent bonds. The guanine and cytosine bonds are harder to break apart than thymine (uracil) and adenine because of the greater number of these bonds. The DNA molecule is called a double helix due to its twisted ladder shape.

COMPETENCY 47.0 THE TEACHER UNDERSTANDS REPRODUCTION AND THE MECHANISMS OF HEREDITY.

Skill 47.1 Compares and contrasts sexual and asexual reproduction.

The obvious advantage of asexual reproduction is that it does not require a partner. This is a huge advantage for organisms, such as the hydra, which do not move around. Not having to move around to reproduce also allows organisms to conserve energy. Asexual reproduction also tends to be faster. There are disadvantages, as in the case of regeneration, in plants if the plant is not in good condition or in the case of spore-producing plants, if the surrounding conditions are not suitable for the spores to grow. As asexual reproduction produces only exact copies of the parent organism, it does not allow for genetic variation, which means that mutations, or weaker qualities, will always be passed on. This can also be detrimental to a species well-adapted to a particular environment when the conditions of that environment change suddenly. On the whole, asexual reproduction is more reliable because it requires fewer steps and less can go wrong.

Sexual reproduction shares genetic information between gametes, thereby producing variety in the species. This can result in a better species with an improved chance of survival. There is the disadvantage that sexual reproduction requires a partner, which in turn with many organisms requires courtship, finding a mate, and mating. Another disadvantage is that sexually reproductive organisms require special mechanisms.

Skill 47.2 Understands the organization of heredity material (e.g., DNA, genes, chromosomes).

DNA and DNA REPLICATION

The modern definition of a gene is a unit of genetic information. DNA makes up genes, which in turn make up the chromosomes. DNA is wound tightly around proteins in order to conserve space. The DNA/protein combination makes up the chromosome. DNA controls the synthesis of proteins, thereby controlling the total cell activity. DNA is capable of making copies of itself.

The purpose of cell division is to provide growth and repair in body (somatic) cells and to replenish or create sex cells for reproduction. There are two forms of cell division. Mitosis is the division of somatic cells and meiosis is the division of sex cells (eggs and sperm). The table below summarizes the major differences between the two processes.

MITOSIS	MEIOSIS
1. Division of somatic cell	1. Division of sex cells
2. Two cells result from each division	2. Four cells or polar bodies result from each division
3. Chromosome number is identical to parent cells.	3. Chromosome number is half the number of parent cells
4. For cell growth and repair	4. Recombinations provide genetic diversity

Some terms to know:

gamete - sex cell or germ cell; eggs and sperm.
chromatin - loose chromosomes; this state is found when the cell is not dividing.
chromosome - tightly coiled, visible chromatin; this state is found when the cell is dividing.
homologues - chromosomes that contain the same information. They are of the same length and contain the same genes.
diploid - 2n number; diploid chromosomes are a pair of chromosomes (somatic cells).
haploid - 1n number; haploid chromosomes are a half of a pair (sex cells).

Review of DNA structure:

1. Made of nucleotides; a five carbon sugar, phosphate group and nitrogen base (either adenine, guanine, cytosine or thymine).

2. Consists of a sugar/phosphate backbone which is covalently bonded. The bases are joined down the center of the molecule and are attached by hydrogen bonds which are easily broken during replication.

3. The amount of adenine equals the amount of thymine and the amount of cytosine equals the amount of guanine.

4. The shape is that of a twisted ladder called a double helix. The sugar/phosphates make up the sides of the ladder and the base pairs make up the rungs of the ladder.

DNA Replication

Enzymes control each step of the replication of DNA. The molecule untwists. The hydrogen bonds between the bases break and serve as a pattern for replication. Free nucleotides found inside the nucleus join on to form a new strand. Two new pieces of DNA are formed which are identical. This is a very accurate process. There is only one mistake for every billion nucleotides added. This is because there are enzymes (polymerases) present that proofread the molecule. In eukaryotes, replication occurs in many places along the DNA at once. The molecule may open up at many places like a broken zipper. In prokaryotic circular plasmids, replication begins at a point on the plasmid and goes in both directions until it meets itself.

Base pairing rules are important in determining a new strand of DNA sequence. For example say our original strand of DNA had the sequence as follows:

1. A T C G G C A A T A G C   This may be called our sense strand as it contains a sequence that makes sense or codes for something. The complementary strand (or other side of the ladder) would follow base pairing rules (A bonds with T and C bonds with G) and would read:

2. T A G C C G T T A T C G   When the molecule opens up and nucleotides join on, the base pairing rules create two new identical strands of DNA

1. A T C G G C A A T A G C   and   A T C G G C A A T A G C
   T A G C C G T T A T C G   2.T A G C C G T T A T C G

Protein Synthesis

It is necessary for cells to manufacture new proteins for growth and repair of the organism. Protein Synthesis is the process that allows the DNA code to be read and carried out of the nucleus into the cytoplasm in the form of RNA. This is where the ribosomes are found, which are the sites of protein synthesis. The protein is then assembled according to the instructions on the DNA. There are several types of RNA. Familiarize yourself with where they are found and their function.

Messenger RNA - (mRNA) copies the code from DNA in the nucleus and takes it to the ribosomes in the cytoplasm.

Transfer RNA - (tRNA) free floating in the cytoplasm. Its job is to carry and position amino acids for assembly on the ribosome.

Ribosomal RNA - (rRNA) found in the ribosomes. They make a place for the proteins to be made. rRNA is believed to have many important functions, so much research is currently being done currently in this area.

Along with enzymes and amino acids, the RNA's function is to assist in the building of proteins. There are two stages of protein synthesis:

Transcription - this phase allows for the assembly of mRNA and occurs in the nucleus where the DNA is found. The DNA splits open and the mRNA reads the code and "transcribes" the sequence onto a single strand of mRNA. For example, if the code on the DNA is T A C C T C G T A C G A , the mRNA will make a complementary strand reading: A U G G A G C A U G C U (Remember that uracil replaces thymine in RNA.) Each group of three bases is called a codon. The codon will eventually code for a specific amino acid to be carried to the ribosome. "Start" codons begin the building of the protein and "stop" codons end transcription. When the stop codon is reached, the mRNA separates from the DNA and leaves the nucleus for the cytoplasm.

Translation - this is the assembly of the amino acids to build the protein and occurs in the cytoplasm. The nucleotide sequence is translated to choose the correct amino acid sequence. As the rRNA translates the code at the ribosome, tRNA's which contain an anticodon seek out the correct amino acid and bring it back to the ribosome. For example, using the codon sequence from the example above:

the mRNA reads A U G / G A G / C A U / G C U
the anticodons are U A C / C U C / G U A / C G A
the amino acid sequence would be: Methionine (start) - Glu - His - Ala.

 *Be sure to note if the table you are given is written according to the codon sequence or the anticodon sequence. It will be specified.

This whole process is accomplished through the assistance of activating enzymes. Each of the twenty amino acids has their own enzyme. The enzyme binds the amino acid to the tRNA. When the amino acids get close to each other on the ribosome, they bond together using peptide bonds. The start and stop codons are called nonsense codons. There is one start codon (AUG) and three stop codons. (UAA, UGA and UAG). Addition mutations will cause the whole code to shift, thereby producing the wrong protein or, at times, no protein at all.

Skill 47.3 **Describes how an inherited trait can be determined by one or many genes and how more than one trait can be influenced by a single gene.**

Gregor Mendel is recognized as the father of genetics. His work in the late 1800's is the basis of our knowledge of genetics. Although unaware of the presence of DNA or genes, Mendel realized there were factors (now known as genes) that were transferred from parents to their offspring. Mendel worked with pea plants and fertilized the plants himself, keeping track of subsequent generations which led to the Mendelian laws of genetics. Mendel found that two "factors" governed each trait, one from each parent. Traits or characteristics came in several forms, known as alleles. For example, the trait of flower color had white alleles and purple alleles. Mendel formed three laws:

Law of dominance - in a pair of alleles, one trait may cover up the allele of the other trait. Example: brown eyes are dominant to blue eyes.

Law of segregation - only one of the two possible alleles from each parent is passed on to the offspring from each parent. (During meiosis, the haploid number insures that half the sex cells get one allele, half get the other).

Law of independent assortment - alleles sort independently of each other. (Many combinations are possible depending on which sperm ends up with which egg. Compare this to the many combinations of hands possible when dealing a deck of cards).

Mutations

Since it's not a perfect world, mistakes happen. Inheritable changes in DNA are called mutations. Mutations may be errors in replication or a spontaneous rearrangement of one or more segments by factors like radioactivity, drugs, or chemicals. The amount of the change is not as critical as where the change is. Mutations may occur on somatic or sex cells. Usually the ones on sex cells are more dangerous since they contain the basis of all information for the developing offspring. Mutations are not always bad. They are the basis of evolution, and if they make a more favorable variation that enhances the organism's survival, then they are beneficial. But, mutations may also lead to abnormalities, birth defects, and even death. There are several types of mutations; let's suppose a normal sequence was as follows:

Normal -   A B C D E F

Duplication - one gene is repeated.   A B C C D E F

Inversion - a segment of the sequence is flipped around.   A E D C B F

Deletion - a gene is left out.   A B C E F

Insertion or Translocation - a segment from another place on the DNA is inserted in the wrong place.   A B C R S D E F

Breakage - a piece is lost.   A B C (DEF is lost)

Nondisjunction – This occurs during meiosis when chromosomes fail to separate properly. One sex cell may get both genes and another may get none. Depending on the chromosomes involved this may or may not be serious. Offspring end up with either an extra chromosome or are missing one. An example of nondisjunction is Down Syndrome, where three of chromosome #21 are present.

Linkage

Genetic linkage is the inheritance of two or more traits together. In general, the transmission of a particular allele is independent of the alleles passed on for other traits. This independent inheritance results from the random sorting of chromosomes during meiosis. Genes found on the same chromosome, however, often remain together during meiosis. Thus, these linked genes have a greater probability of appearing together in offspring.

The phenomenon known as crossing over prevents complete linkage of genes on the same chromosome. During meiosis, paired chromosomes exchange genetic material creating new combinations of DNA. Crossing over is more likely to disrupt linkage when genes are far apart on a chromosome. Greater distance between genes increases the probability that crossing over will occur between the gene loci.

Skill 47.4   Distinguishes between dominant and recessive traits and predicts the probable outcomes of genetic combinations.

Punnet squares - these are used to show the possible ways that genes combine and indicate probability of the occurrence of a certain genotype or phenotype. One parent's genes are put at the top of the box and the other parent at the side of the box. Genes combine on the square just like numbers that are added in addition tables we learned in elementary school.

monohybrid cross - a cross using only one trait. Four possible gene combinations

dihybrid cross - a cross using two traits. Sixteen possible gene combinations

SOME DEFINITIONS TO KNOW

Dominant - the stronger of the two traits. If a dominant gene is present, it will be expressed. Shown by a capital letter.

Recessive - the weaker of the two traits. In order for the recessive gene to be expressed, there must be two recessive genes present. Shown by a lower case letter.

Homozygous - (purebred) having two of the same genes present; an organism may be homozygous dominant with two dominant genes or homozygous recessive with two recessive genes.

Heterozygous - (hybrid) having one dominant gene and one recessive gene. The dominant gene will be expressed due to the Law of Dominance.

Genotype - the genes the organism has. Genes are represented with letters. AA, Bb, and tt are examples of genotypes.

Phenotype - how the trait is expressed in an organism. Blue eyes, brown hair, and red flowers are examples of phenotypes.

Incomplete dominance - neither gene masks the other; a new phenotype is formed. For example, red flowers and white flowers may have equal strength. A heterozygote (Rr) would have pink flowers. If a problem occurs with a third phenotype, incomplete dominance is occurring.

Codominance - genes may form new phenotypes. The ABO blood grouping is an example of co-dominance. A and B are of equal strength and O is recessive. Therefore, type A blood may have the genotypes of AA or AO, type B blood may have the genotypes of BB or BO, type AB blood has the genotype A and B, and type O blood has two recessive O genes.

Linkage - genes that are found on the same chromosome usually appear together unless crossing over has occurred in meiosis. (Example - blue eyes and blonde hair)

Lethal alleles - these are usually recessive due to the early death of the offspring. If a 2:1 ratio of alleles is found in offspring, a lethal gene combination is usually the reason. Some examples of lethal alleles include sickle cell anemia, tay-sachs and cystic fibrosis. Usually the coding for an important protein is affected.

Inborn errors of metabolism - these occur when the protein affected is an enzyme. Examples include PKU (phenylketonuria) and albanism.

Polygenic characters - many alleles code for a phenotype. There may be as many as twenty genes that code for skin color. This is why there is such a variety of skin tones. Another example is height. A couple of medium height may have very tall offspring.

Sex linked traits - the Y chromosome found only in males (XY) carries very little genetic information, whereas the X chromosome found in females (XX) carries very important information. Since men have no second X chromosome to cover up a recessive gene, the recessive trait is expressed more often in men. Women need the recessive gene on both X chromosomes to show the trait. Examples of sex linked traits include hemophilia and color-blindness.

Sex influenced traits - traits are influenced by the sex hormones. Male pattern baldness is an example of a sex influenced trait. Testosterone influences the expression of the gene. Mostly men loose their hair due to this trait.

Skill 47.5   Evaluates the influence of environmental and genetic factors on the traits of an organism.

Environmental factors can influence the structure and expression of genes. For instance, viruses can insert their DNA into the host's genome changing the composition of the host DNA. In addition, mutagenic agents found in the environment cause mutations in DNA and carcinogenic agents promote cancer, often by causing DNA mutations.

Many viruses can insert their DNA into the host genome causing mutations. Many times viral insertion of DNA does not harm the host DNA because of the location of the insertion. Some insertions, however, can have grave consequences for the host. Oncogenes are genes that increase the malignancy of tumor cells. Some viruses carry oncogenes that, when inserted into the host genome, become active and promote cancerous growth. In addition, insertion of other viral DNA into the host genome can stimulate expression of host proto-oncogenes, genes that normally promote cell division. For example, insertion of a strong viral promoter in front of a host proto-oncogene may stimulate expression of the gene and lead to uncontrolled cell growth (i.e. cancer).

In addition to viruses, physical and chemical agents found in the environment can damage gene structure. Mutagenic agents cause mutations in DNA. Examples of mutagenic agents are x-rays, uv light, and ethidium bromide. Carcinogenic agents are any substances that promote cancer. Carcinogens are often, but not always, mutagens. Examples of agents carcinogenic to humans are asbestos, uv light, x-rays, and benzene.

Skill 47.6   Describes current applications of genetic research (e.g., related to cloning, reproduction, health, industry, agriculture).

Research in molecular genetics is highly technical and very useful to society. Because of its use to humanity, molecular genetics is receiving generous funding from various sources and lot of effort from the scientific community.

A major goal of molecular genetics is to correlate the sequence of a gene with its function. The primary objective is to obtain the sequence.

Scientists use a number of techniques to isolate genes. The foremost technique is cDNA cloning, which is very widely used because of its reliability. The aim of many cloning experiments is to obtain a sequence of DNA that directs the production of a specific protein. The principle involved in this cDNA cloning is that an mRNA population isolated from a specific developmental stage should contain mRNAs specific for any protein expressed during that stage. Thus, if the mRNA can be isolated, the gene can be studied. It is not possible to clone mRNA directly , but a DNA, a copy of the mRNA can be cloned. In this method, a single strand of the DNA is copied. The second strand is generated by the DNA polymerase and the result is a double stranded DNA.

The objective of these cloning experiments is to isolate many genes from a wide variety of living organisms.

The application of these isolated genes in genetic engineering are varied.

1. Using the clinically important genes for diagnostic purposes. The gene that encodes for one type of hemophilia has been used for this purpose. This field of research is proving to be of invaluable help to people suffering from various diseases like cancer, diabetes etc. and research in this area hold lot of promise for future generations.
2. The isolated genes could be used to isolate similar genes from other organisms. Thus, it can serve as a heterologous probe.
3. The nucleic acid sequence of the gene can be derived. If a partial or complete sequence of the protein that it encodes is available, the gene can be confirmed in this manner. If the protein product is not known then the sequence of the gene compared with those of the known genes to try to derive a function for that gene. Knowing the function of a gene is very important in clinical diagnostic purposes.
4. Isolating a gene that causes disease in a particular crop, will help the farmers to deal with that disease.

COMPETENCY 48.0 THE TEACHER UNDERSTANDS ADAPTATIONS OF ORGANISMS AND THE THEORY OF EVOLUTION.

Skill 48.1 **Describes similarities and differences among various types of organisms and methods of classifying organisms.**

It is believed that there are probably over ten million different species of living things. Of these, 1.5 million have been named and classified. Systems of classification show similarities and also assist scientists with a world-wide system of organization.

Carolus Linnaeus is termed the father of taxonomy. **Taxonomy** is the science of classification. Linnaeus based his system on morphology (study of structure). Later on, evolutionary relationships (phylogeny) were also used to sort and group species. The modern classification system uses binomial nomenclature. This consists of a two word name for every species. The genus is the first part of the name and the species is the second part. Notice in the levels explained below that Homo sapiens is the scientific name for humans. Starting with the kingdom, the groups get smaller and more alike as one moves down the levels in the classification of humans:

Kingdom: Animalia, Phylum: Chordata, Subphylum: Vertebrata, Class: Mammalia, Order: Primate, Family: Hominidae, Genus: Homo, Species: sapiens

The typical graphic product of a classification is a **phylogenetic tree**, which represents a hypothesis of the relationships based on branching of lineages through time within a group. Every time you see a phylogenetic tree, you should be aware that it is making statements on the degree of similarity between organisms, or the particular pattern in which the various lineages diverged (phylogenetic history).

Cladistics is the study of phylogenetic relationships of organisms by analysis of shared, derived character states. Cladograms are constructed to show evolutionary pathways. Character states are polarized in cladistic analysis to be plesiomorphous (ancestral features), symplesiomorphous (shared ancestral features), apomorphous (derived characteristics), and synapomorphous (shared, derived features).

The current five kingdom system separates prokaryotes from eukaryotes. The prokaryotes belong to the kingdom monera while the eukaryotes belong to either kingdom protista, plantae, fungi, or animalia. Recent comparisons of nucleic acids and proteins between different groups of organisms have led to problems concerning the five kingdom system. Based on these comparisons, alternative kingdom systems have emerged. Six and eight kingdoms as well as a three domain system have been proposed as a more accurate classification system. It is important to note that classification systems evolve as more information regarding characteristics and evolutionary histories of organisms arise.

Species are defined by the ability to successfully reproduce with members of their own kind.

Several different morphological criteria are used to classify organisms:

1. **Ancestral characters** - characteristics that are unchanged after evolution (ie: 5 digits on the hand of an ape).

2. **Derived characters** - characteristics that have evolved more recently (ie: the absence of a tail on an ape).

3. **Conservative characters** - traits that change slowly.

4. **Homologous characters** - characteristics with the same genetic basis but used for a different function. (ie: wing of a bat, arm of a human. The bone structure is the same, but the limbs are used for different purposes).

5. **Analogous characters** – structures that differ, but used for similar purposes (ie- the wing of a bird and the wing of a butterfly).

6. **Convergent evolution** - development of similar adaptations by organisms that are unrelated.

Biological characteristics are also used to classify organisms. Protein comparison, DNA comparison, and analysis of fossilized DNA are powerful comparative methods used to measure evolutionary relationships between species. Taxonomists consider the organism's life history, biochemical (DNA) makeup, behavior, and how the organisms are distributed geographically. The fossil record is also used to show evolutionary relationships.

Skill 48.2 Describes traits in a population or species that enhance its survival and reproductive success.

Anatomical structures and physiological processes that evolve over geological time to increase the overall reproductive success of an organism in its environment are known as biological adaptations. Such evolutionary changes occur through natural selection, the process by which individual organisms with favorable traits survive to reproduce more frequently than those with unfavorable traits. The heritable component of such favorable traits is passed down to offspring during reproduction, increasing the frequency of the favorable trait in a population over many generations.

Adaptations increase long-term reproductive success by making an organism better suited for survival under particular environmental conditions and pressures. These biological changes can increase an organism's ability to obtain air, water, food and nutrients, to cope with environmental variables and to defend themselves. The term adaptation may apply to changes in biological processes that, for example, enable on organism to produce venom or to regulate body temperature, and also to structural adaptations, such as an organisms' skin color and shape. Adaptations can occur in behavioral traits and survival mechanisms as well.

One well-known structural change that demonstrates the concept of adaptation is the development of the primate and human opposable thumb, the first digit of the hand that can be moved around to touch other digits and to grasp objects. The history of the opposable thumb is one of complexly linked structural and behavioral adaptations in response to environmental stressors.

Early apes first appearing in the Tertiary Period were mostly tree dwelling organisms that foraged for food and avoided predators high above the ground. The apes' need to quickly and effectively navigate among branches led to the eventual development of the opposable thumb through the process of natural selection, as apes with more separated thumbs demonstrated higher survival and reproductive rates. This structural adaptation made the ape better suited for its environment, increasing dexterity while climbing trees, moving through the canopy, gathering food and gripping tools such as sticks and branches.

Following the development of the opposable thumb in primates, populations of early human ancestors began to appear in a savannah environment with fewer trees and more open spaces. The need to cross such expanses and to utilize tools led to the development of bipedalism in certain primates and hominids. Bipedalism was both a structural adaptation in the physical changes that occurred in the skull, spine and other parts of the body to accommodate upright walking, as well as a behavioral adaptation that led primates and hominids to walk on only two feet. Freeing of the hands for tool use led, in turn, to other adaptations, and evolutionists attribute the gradual increase in brain size and expansion of motor skills in hominids largely to appearance of the opposable thumb. Thus, the developments of many of the most important adaptations of primates and humans demonstrate closely connected evolutionary histories.

Skill 48.3   Describes how populations and species change through time.

Although evolution is often misunderstood, it occurs via natural selection. Organisms with a life/reproductive advantage will produce more offspring. Giraffes with longer necks are able to reach more leaves, so they eat more and have more babies than other giraffes. Eventually, there are more long-necked giraffes in the population. Over many generations, this changes the proportions of the population. In any case, it is impossible for a stretched neck or a fervent desire to result in a biologically mutated baby. Although there are traits that are naturally selected because of mate attractiveness and fitness, this is not the primary situation.

Skill 48.4   Applies knowledge of the mechanisms and processes of biological evolution (e.g., variation, mutation, environmental factors, natural selection).

Darwin defined the theory of Natural Selection in the mid-1800's. Through the study of finches on the Galapagos Islands, Darwin theorized that nature selects the traits that are advantageous to the organism. Those that do not possess the desirable trait die and do not pass on their genes. Those more fit to survive reproduce, thus increasing that gene in the population. Darwin listed four principles to define natural selection:

1. The individuals in a certain species vary from generation to generation.
2. Some of the variations are determined by the genetic makeup of the species.
3. More individuals are produced than will survive.
4. Some genes allow for better survival of an animal.

Causes of evolution - Certain factors increase the chances of variability in a population, thus leading to evolution. Items that increase variability include mutations, sexual reproduction, immigration, and large population. Items that decrease variation would be natural selection, emigration, small population, and random mating.

Sexual selection - Genes that happen to come together determine the makeup of the gene pool. Animals that use mating behaviors may be successful or unsuccessful. An animal that lacks attractive plumage or has a weak mating call will not attract the female, thereby eventually limiting that gene in the gene pool. Mechanical isolation, where sex organs do not fit the female, has an obvious disadvantage.

Skill 48.5   Describes evidence that supports the theory of evolution of life on Earth.

The wide range of evidence of evolution provides information on the natural processes by which the variety of life on earth developed.

1. **Paleontology**: Paleontology is the study of past life based on fossil records and their relation to different geologic time periods.
When organisms die, they often decompose quickly or are consumed by scavengers, leaving no evidence of their existence. However, occasionally some organisms are preserved. The remains or traces of the organisms from a past geological age embedded in rocks by natural processes are called fossils. They are very important for the understanding the evolutionary history of life on earth as they provide evidence of evolution and detailed information on the ancestry of organisms.

Petrification is the process by which a dead animal gets fossilized. For this to happen, a dead organism must be buried quickly to avoid weathering and decomposition. When the organism is buried, the organic matter decays. The mineral salts from the mud (in which the organism is buried) will infiltrate into the bones and gradually fill up the pores. The bones will harden and be preserved as fossils. If dead organisms are covered by wind- blown sand and if the and is subsequently turned into mud by heavy rain or floods, the same process of mineral infiltration may occur. Besides petrification, the organisms may be well preserved in ice, in hardened resin of coniferous trees (amber), in tar, in anaerobic acidic peat. Fossilization can sometimes be a trace, an impression of a form – e.g., leaves and footprints.

From the horizontal layers of sedimentary rocks (these are formed by silt or mud on top of each other) called strata and each layer consists fossils. The oldest layer is the one at the bottom of the pile and the fossils found in this layer are the oldest and this is how the paleontologists determine the relative ages of these fossils.

Some organisms appear in some layers only indicating that thy lived only during that period and became extinct. A succession of animals and plants can also be seen in fossil records, which supports the theory that organisms ten to progressively increase in complexity.

According to fossil records, some modern species of plants and animals are found to be almost identical to the species that lived in ancient geological ages. They are existing species of ancient lineage that have remained unchanged morphologically and may be physiologically as well. Hence they re called "living fossils". Some examples of living fossils are tuatara, nautilus, horseshoe crab, gingko and metasequoia.

2. Anatomy: Comparative anatomical studies reveal that some structural features are basically similar – e.g., flowers generally have sepals, petals, stigma, style and ovary but the size, color, number of petals, sepals etc., may differ from species to species.

The degree of resemblance between two organisms indicates how closely they are related in evolution.

4   Groups with little in common are supposed to have diverged from a common ancestor much earlier in geological history than groups which have more in common
5   To decide how closely two organisms are, anatomists look for the structures which may serve different purpose in the adult, but are basically similar (homologous)
6   In cases where similar structures serve different functions in adults, it is important to trace their origin and embryonic development

When a group of organisms share a homologous structure, which is specialized, to perform a variety of functions in order to adapt to different environmental conditions are called adaptive radiation. The gradual spreading of organisms with adaptive radiation is known as divergent evolution. Examples of divergent evolution are – pentadactyl limb and insect mouthparts

Under similar environmental conditions, fundamentally different structures in different groups of organisms may undergo modifications to serve similar functions. This is called convergent evolution. The structures, which have no close phylogenetic links but showing adaptation to perform the same functions, are called analogous. Examples are – wings of bats, bird and insects, jointed legs of insects and vertebrates, eyes of vertebrates and cephalopods.

Vestigial organs: Organs that are smaller and simpler in structure than corresponding parts in the ancestral species are called vestigial organs. They are usually degenerated or underdeveloped. These were functional in ancestral species but no have become non functional, e.g., vestigial hind limbs of whales, vestigial leaves of some xerophytes, vestigial wings of flightless birds like ostriches, etc.

3. Geographical distribution: Continental distribution: All organisms are adapted to their environment to a greater or lesser extent. It is generally assumed that the same type of species would be found in a similar habitat in a similar geographic area. An example would be that Africa has short tailed (old world) monkeys, elephants, lions and giraffes. South America has long-tailed monkeys, pumas, jaguars and llamas.

Evidence for migration and isolation: The fossil record shows that evolution of camels started in North America, from which they migrated across the Bering strait into Asia and Africa and through the Isthmus o Panama into south America.

Continental drift: Fossils of the ancient amphibians, arthropods and ferns are found in South America, Africa, India, Australia and Antarctica which can be dated to the Paleozoic Era, at which time they were all in a single landmass called Gondwana.

Oceanic Island distribution: Most small isolated islands only have native species. Plant life in Hawaii could have arrived as airborne spores or as seeds in the droppings of birds. A few large mammals present in remote islands were brought by human settlers.

4. Evidence from comparative embryology:

Comparative embryology shows how embryos start off looking the same. As they develop their similarities slowly decrease until they take the form of their particular class.

Example: Adult vertebrates are diverse, yet their embryos are quite similar at very early stages. Fishlike structures still form in early embryos of reptiles, birds and mammals. In fish embryos, a two-chambered heart, some veins, and parts of arteries develop and persist in adult fishes. The same structures form early in human embryos but do not persist as in adults.

5. Physiology and Biochemistry:

Evolution of widely distributed proteins and molecules: All organisms make use of DNA and/or RNA. ATP is the metabolic currency. Genetic code is same for almost every organism. A piece of RNA in a bacterium cell codes for the same protein as in a human cell.

Comparison of the DNA sequence allows organisms to be grouped by sequence similarity, and the resulting phylogenetic trees are typically consistent with traditional taxonomy, and are often used to strengthen or correct taxonomic classifications. DNA sequence comparison is considered strong enough to b used to correct erroneous assumptions in the phylogenetic tree in cases where other evidence is missing. The sequence of the 168rRNA gene, a vital gene encoding a part of the ribosome was used to find the broad phylogenetic relationships between all life.

The proteomic evidence also supports the universal ancestry of life. Vital proteins such as ribosome, DNA polymerase, and RNA polymerase are found in the most primitive bacteria to the most complex mammals.

Since metabolic processes do not leave fossils, research into the evolution of the basic cellular processes is done largely by comparison of existing organisms.

COMPETENCY 49.0 THE TEACHER UNDERSTANDS REGULATORY MECHANISMS AND BEHAVIOR.

Skill 49.1 Describes how organisms respond to internal and external stimuli.

Behavior - animal behavior is responsible for courtship leading to mating, communication between species, territoriality, aggression between animals, and dominance within a group. Behaviors may include body posture, mating calls, display of feathers/fur, coloration or bearing of teeth and claws.

Innate behavior - behaviors that are inborn or instinctual. An environmental stimulus such as the length of day or temperature results in a behavior. Hibernation among some animals is an innate behavior.

Learned behavior - behavior that is modified due to past experience is called learned behavior.

Response to stimuli is one of the key characteristics of any living thing. Any detectable change in the internal or external environment (the stimulus) may trigger a response in an organism. Just like physical characteristics, organisms' responses to stimuli are adaptations that allow them to better survive. While these responses may be more noticeable in animals that can move quickly, all organisms are actually capable of responding to changes.

Single celled organisms

These organisms are able to respond to basic stimuli such as the presence of light, heat, or food. Changes in the environment are typically sensed via **cell surface receptors**. These organisms may respond to such stimuli by making **changes in internal biochemical pathways or initiating reproduction or phagocytosis**. Those capable of **simple motility**, using flagella for instance, may respond by moving toward food or away from heat.

Plants

Plants typically do not possess sensory organs and so **individual cells recognize stimuli** through a variety of pathways. When **many cells respond to stimuli together**, a response becomes apparent. Logically then, the responses of plants occur on a rather **longer timescale** that those of animals. Plants are capable of **responding to a few basic stimuli including light, water and gravity**. Some common examples include the way plants turn and grow toward the sun, the sprouting of seeds when exposed to warmth and moisture, and the growth of roots in the direction of gravity.

Animals

Lower members of the animal kingdom have responses similar to those seen in single celled organisms. However, higher animals have developed complex systems to detect and respond to stimuli. The **nervous system, sensory organs (eyes, ears, skin, etc), and muscle tissue all allow animals to sense and quickly respond to changes in their environment.**

As in other organisms, many responses to stimuli in animals are **involuntary**. For example, pupils dilate in response to the reduction of light. Such reactions are typically called **reflexes**. However, many animals are also capable of **voluntary response**. In many animal species, voluntary reactions are **instinctual**. For instance, a zebra's response to a lion is a *voluntary* one, but, *instinctually*, it will flee quickly as soon as the lion's presence is sensed. Complex responses, which may or may not be instinctual, are typically termed **behavior**. An example is the annual migration of birds when seasons change. Even more **complex social behavior** is seen in animals that live in large groups.

Skill 49.2   Applies knowledge of structures and physiological processes that maintain stable internal conditions.

All of the body's systems contribute to homeostasis through a complex set of interactions. The following is a discussion of the contribution of different systems to homeostasis.

Skeletal system – Because calcium is an important component of bones, the skeletal system serves as a calcium reserve for the body. Proper levels of calcium are important to many bodily functions. When levels are too low, the body mobilizes calcium from bones to use for other purposes. For example, proper muscle function requires a certain concentration of calcium ions in the blood and body tissue. Thus, the skeletal system acts as a buffer in maintaining calcium homeostasis by absorbing or releasing calcium as needed.

Muscular system – The muscular system contributes to homeostasis in two ways. First, muscle contraction produces heat as a by-product. This heat helps maintain the body's internal temperature. An example of this function is involuntary shivering (i.e. rapid muscle contraction) that occurs when the body temperature drops. Second, the muscular system (in coordination with the skeletal system) allows organisms to move to environments that are more favorable from a homeostatic perspective.

Circulatory system – The circulatory system plays a vital role in homeostasis. The circulatory system delivers nutrients and removes waste from all the body's tissue by pumping blood through blood vessels. Nutrient delivery and waste removal maintains a favorable environment for all the body's cells. In addition, the circulatory system acts in coordination with the integumentary system in the maintenance of body temperature. When the body temperature rises, blood vessels near the skin dilate allowing greater blood flow and greater release of heat from the body. In contrast, when body temperature drops, blood vessels near the skin constrict limiting the amount of heat lost from the skin.

Immune system – The entire function of the immune system is homeostatic in nature. The immune system protects the body's internal environment from invading microorganisms, viruses, and cancerous cells. These actions maintain a favorable environment for cellular function.

Skill 49.3 Demonstrates an understanding of feedback mechanisms that allow organisms to maintain stable internal conditions.

Feedback loops in human systems serve to regulate bodily functions in relation to environmental conditions. Positive feedback loops enhance the body's response to external stimuli and promote processes that involve rapid deviation from the initial state. For example, positive feedback loops function in stress response and the regulation of growth and development. Negative feedback loops help maintain stability in spite of environmental changes and function in homeostasis. For example, negative feedback loops function in the regulation of blood glucose levels and the maintenance of body temperature.

Feedback loops regulate the secretion of classical vertebrate hormones in humans. The pituitary gland and hypothalamus respond to varying levels of hormones by increasing or decreasing production and secretion. High levels of a hormone cause down-regulation of the production and secretion pathways, while low levels of a hormone cause up-regulation of the production and secretion pathways.

"Fight or flight" refers to the human body's response to stress or danger. Briefly, as a response to an environmental stressor, the hypothalamus releases a hormone that acts on the pituitary gland, triggering the release of another hormone, adrenocorticotropin (ACTH), into the bloodstream. ACTH then signals the adrenal glands to release the hormones cortisol, epinephrine, and norepinephrine. These three hormones act to ready the body to respond to a threat by increasing blood pressure and heart rate, speeding reaction time, diverting blood to the muscles, and releasing glucose for use by the muscles and brain. The stress-response hormones also down-regulate growth, development, and other non-essential functions. Finally, cortisol completes the "fight or flight" feedback loop by acting on the hypothalamus to stop hormonal production after the threat has passed.

Skill 49.4 Understands how evolutionary history affects behavior.

Like so many factors affecting behavior, evolutionary history also does affect behavior. Ecology influences the evolutionary behavior. There are two factors that have profound influence on the behavior of animals – one is the phylogenetic characters and the other is the adaptive significance.

The factors that do prevent certain groups of animals from doing certain things, for example, flying, are called phylogenetic constraints. Mammals can't fly, where as birds can. The fact that birds fly and mammals can't fly is no coincidence. The evolutionary history of these characters has helped the birds to fully develop their ability to fly. At the same time, if the birds are not threatened by predators, there is every chance that these same birds may gradually lose their ability to fly. This is evident in New Zealand, where there were no mammals, until the Europeans settled there. There used to be a higher proportion of flightless birds residing there.

Finally, all behavior is subject to natural selection as with the other traits of an animal. This emphasizes the fact that animals that are well adapted sire many offspring compared to those not so organized in their behavioral adaptation.

Evolutionary Stable strategy (ESS) is another driving force in the evolution of behavior. There are two factors that influence animal behavior – one is the optimal behavior, giving maximum benefit to the animal, and the other is the behavior adapted by the population of which it is a member.

It is important to bear in mind that evolution is not only driven by the physical environment of the animal, but also the interaction between other individuals.

COMPETENCY 50.0 THE TEACHER UNDERSTANDS THE RELATIONSHIPS BETWEEN ORGANISMS AND THE ENVIRONMENT.

Skill 50.1   Identifies the abiotic and biotic components of an ecosystem.

Biotic factors - living things in an ecosystem; plants, animals, bacteria, fungi, etc. If one population in a community increases, it affects the ability of another population to succeed by limiting the available amount of food, water, shelter and space.

Abiotic factors - non-living aspects of an ecosystem; soil quality, rainfall, and temperature. Changes in climate and soil can cause effects at the beginning of the food chain, thus limiting or accelerating the growth of populations.

Skill 50.2   Analyzes the interrelationships among producers, consumers, and decomposers in an ecosystem.

Ecosystems are successful primarily because of the interrelationships and recycling that occurs between its three main groups: the producers, the consumers, and the decomposers. The autotrophs produce food, the heterotrophs consume them, and the decomposers clean up any waste left behind, thus keeping the planet tidy and returning essential nutrients to the soil.

Definitions of feeding relationships:

> **Parasitism** - two species that occupy a similar place; the parasite benefits from the relationship, the host is harmed.

> **Commensalism** - two species that occupy a similar place; neither species is harmed or benefits from the relationship.

> **Mutualism (symbiosis)**- two species that occupy a similar place; both species benefit from the relationship.

> **Competition** - two species that occupy the same habitat or eat the same food are said to be in competition with each other.

> **Predation** - animals that eat other animals are called predators. The animals they feed on are called the prey. Population growth depends upon competition for food, water, shelter, and space. The amount of predators determines the amount of prey, which in turn affects the number of predators.

Skill 50.3 Identifies factors that influence the size and growth of population in an ecosystem.

Populations are ultimately limited by their productivity levels. **Carrying Capacity** is the total amount of life a habitat can support. Once the habitat runs out of food, water, shelter, or space, the carrying capacity decreases, and then stabilizes. Growth of a population depends upon the health of the organisms, who depend upon food (among other things), for survival.

A limiting factor is the component of a biological process that determines how quickly or slowly the process proceeds. Photosynthesis is the main biological process determining the rate of ecosystem productivity, the rate at which an ecosystem creates biomass. Thus, in evaluating the productivity of an ecosystem, potential limiting factors are light intensity, gas concentrations, and mineral availability. The Law of the Minimum states that the required factor in a given process that is most scarce controls the rate of the process.

One potential limiting factor of ecosystem productivity is light intensity because photosynthesis requires light energy. Light intensity can limit productivity in two ways. First, too little light limits the rate of photosynthesis because the required energy is not available. Second, too much light can damage the photosynthetic system of plants and microorganisms thus slowing the rate of photosynthesis. Decreased photosynthesis equals decreased productivity.

Another potential limiting factor of ecosystem productivity is gas concentrations. Photosynthesis requires carbon dioxide. Thus, increased concentration of carbon dioxide often results in increased productivity. While carbon dioxide is often not the ultimate limiting factor of productivity, increased concentration can indirectly increase rates of photosynthesis in several ways. First, increased carbon dioxide concentration often increases the rate of nitrogen fixation (available nitrogen is another limiting factor of productivity). Second, increased carbon dioxide concentration can decrease the pH of rain, improving the water source of photosynthetic organisms.

Finally, mineral availability also limits ecosystem productivity. Plants require adequate amounts of nitrogen and phosphorus to build many cellular structures. The availability of the inorganic minerals phosphorus and nitrogen often is the main limiting factor of plant biomass production. In other words, in a natural environment phosphorus and nitrogen availability most often limits ecosystem productivity, rather than carbon dioxide concentration or light intensity.

Skill 50.4   Analyzes adaptive characteristics that result in a population's or species's unique niche in an ecosystem.

The term 'Niche' describes the relational position of a species or population in an ecosystem. Niche includes how a population responds to the abundance of its resources and enemies (e.g., by growing when resources are abundant and predators, parasites and pathogens are scarce).

Niche also indicates the life history of an organism, habitat and place in the food chain. According to the competitive exclusion principle, no two species can occupy the same niche in the same environment for a long time.

The full range of environmental conditions (biological and physical) under which an organism can exist describes its fundamental niche. Because of the pressure from superior competitors, superior are driven to occupy a niche much narrower than their previous niche. This is known as the 'realized niche.'

Examples of niche:

1. Oak trees:
* live in forests
* absorb sunlight by photosynthesis
* provide shelter for many animals
* act as support for creeping plants
* serve as a source of food for animals
* cover their ground with dead leaves in the autumn
If the oak trees were cut down or destroyed by fire or storms they would no longer be doing their job and this would have a disastrous effect on all the other organisms living in the same habitat.

2. Hedgehogs:
* eat a variety of insects and other invertebrates which live underneath the dead leaves and twigs in the garden
* the spines are a superb environment for fleas and ticks
* put the nitrogen back into the soil when they urinate
* eat slugs and protect plants from them
If there were no hedgehogs around, the population of slugs would increase and the nutrients in the dead leaves and twigs would not be recycled.

Skill 50.5   Describes and analyzes energy flow through various types of ecosystems.

Trophic levels are based on the feeding relationships that determine energy flow and chemical cycling.

Autotrophs are the primary producers of the ecosystem. **Producers** mainly consist of plants. **Primary consumers** are the next trophic level. The primary consumers are the herbivores that eat plants or algae. **Secondary consumers** are the carnivores that eat the primary consumers. **Tertiary consumers** eat the secondary consumer. These trophic levels may go higher depending on the ecosystem. **Decomposers** are consumers that feed off animal waste and dead organisms. This pathway of food transfer is known as the food chain.

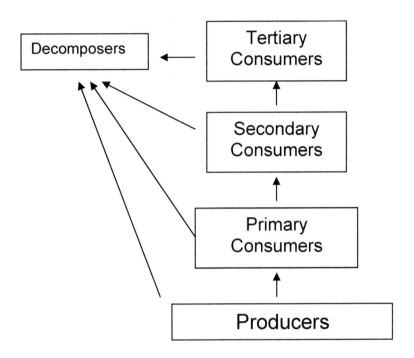

Most food chains are more elaborate, becoming food webs.

Skill 50.6 Knows how populations and species modify and affect ecosystems.

Ecology is the study of organisms, where they live and their interactions with the environment. A **population** is a group of the same species in a specific area. A **community** is a group of populations residing in the same area.

The environment is ever changing because of natural events and the actions of humans, animals, plants, and other organisms. Even the slightest changes in environmental conditions can greatly influence the function and balance of communities, ecosystems, and ecoregions. For example, subtle changes in salinity and temperature of ocean waters over time can greatly influence the range and population of certain species of fish. In addition, a slight increase in average atmospheric temperature can promote tree growth in a forest, but a corresponding increase in the viability of pathogenic bacteria can decrease the overall growth and productivity of the forest.

Another important concept in ecological change is succession. Ecological succession is the transition in the composition of species in an ecosystem, often after an ecological disturbance in the community. Primary succession begins in an environment virtually void of life, such as a volcanic island. Secondary succession occurs when a natural event disrupts an ecosystem, leaving the soil intact. An example of secondary succession is the reestablishment of a forest after destruction by a forest fire.

Factors that drive the process of succession include interspecies competition, environmental conditions, inhibition, and facilitation. In a developing ecosystem, species compete for scarce resources. The species that compete most successfully dominate. Environmental conditions, as previously discussed, influence species viability. Finally, the activities of certain species can inhibit or facilitate the growth and development of other species. Inhibition results from exploitative competition or interference competition. In facilitation, a species or group of species lays the foundation for the establishment of other, more advanced species. For example, the presence of a certain bacterial population can change the pH of the soil, allowing for the growth of different types of plants and trees.

COMPETENCY 51.0 THE TEACHER UNDERSTANDS THE STRUCTURE AND FUNCTION OF EARTH SYSTEMS.

Skill 51.1   Understands the structure of Earth and analyzes constructive and destructive processes that produce geologic change.

Data obtained from many sources led scientists to develop the theory of plate tectonics. This theory is the most current model that explains not only the movement of the continents, but also the changes in the earth's crust caused by internal forces.

Plates are rigid blocks of earth's crust and upper mantle. These rigid solid blocks make up the lithosphere. The earth's lithosphere is broken into nine large sections and several small ones. These moving slabs are called plates. The major plates are named after the continents they are "transporting."

The plates float on and move with a layer of hot, plastic-like rock in the upper mantle. Geologists believe that the heat currents circulating within the mantle cause this plastic zone of rock to slowly flow, carrying along the overlying crustal plates.

Movement of these crustal plates creates areas where the plates diverge as well as areas where the plates converge. A major area of divergence is located in the Mid-Atlantic. Currents of hot mantle rock rise and separate at this point of divergence creating new oceanic crust at the rate of 2 to 10 centimeters per year. Convergence is when the oceanic crust collides with either another oceanic plate or a continental plate. The oceanic crust sinks forming an enormous trench and generating volcanic activity. Convergence also includes continent to continent plate collisions. When two plates slide past one another a transform fault is created.

These movements produce many major features of the earth's surface, such as mountain ranges, volcanoes, and earthquake zones. Most of these features are located at plate boundaries, where the plates interact by spreading apart, pressing together, or sliding past each other. These movements are very slow, averaging only a few centimeters a year.

Boundaries form between spreading plates where the crust is forced apart in a process called rifting. Rifting generally occurs at mid-ocean ridges. Rifting can also take place within a continent, splitting the continent into smaller landmasses that drift away from each other, thereby forming an ocean basin between them. The Red Sea is a product of rifting. As the seafloor spreading takes place, new material is added to the inner edges of the separating plates. In this way the plates grow larger, and the ocean basin widens. This is the process that broke up the super continent Pangaea and created the Atlantic Ocean.

Boundaries between plates that are colliding are zones of intense crustal activity. When a plate of ocean crust collides with a plate of continental crust, the more dense oceanic plate slides under the lighter continental plate and plunges into the mantle. This process is called **subduction**, and the site where it takes place is called a subduction zone. A subduction zone is usually seen on the sea-floor as a deep depression called a trench.

The crustal movement which is identified by plates sliding sideways past each other produces a plate boundary characterized by major faults that are capable of unleashing powerful earth-quakes. The San Andreas Fault forms such a boundary between the Pacific Plate and the North American Plate.

Orogeny is the term given to natural mountain building. A mountain is terrain that has been raised high above the surrounding landscape by volcanic action, or some form of tectonic plate collisions. The plate collisions could be intercontinental or ocean floor collisions with a continental crust (subduction). The physical composition of mountains would include igneous, metamorphic, or sedimentary rocks; some may have rock layers that are tilted or distorted by plate collision forces.

There are many different types of mountains. The physical attributes of a mountain range depends upon the angle at which plate movement thrust layers of rock to the surface. Many mountains (Adirondacks, Southern Rockies) were formed along high angle faults.

Folded mountains (Alps, Himalayas) are produced by the folding of rock layers during their formation. The Himalayas are the highest mountains in the world and contain Mount Everest which rises almost 9 km above sea level. The Himalayas were formed when India collided with Asia. The movement which created this collision is still in process at the rate of a few centimeters per year.

Fault-block mountains (Utah, Arizona, and New Mexico) are created when plate movement produces tension forces instead of compression forces. The area under tension produces normal faults and rock along these faults is displaced upward.

Dome mountains are formed as magma tries to push up through the crust but fails to break the surface. Dome mountains resemble a huge blister on the earth's surface.

Upwarped mountains (such as the Black Hills of South Dakota) are created in association with a broad arching of the crust. They can also be formed by rock thrust upward along high angle faults.

Volcanism is the term given to the movement of magma through the crust and its emergence as lava onto the earth's surface. Volcanic mountains are built up by successive deposits of volcanic materials.

An active volcano is one that is presently erupting or building to an eruption. A dormant volcano is one that is between eruptions but still shows signs of internal activity that might lead to an eruption in the future. An extinct volcano is said to be no longer capable of erupting. Most of the world's active volcanoes are found along the rim of the Pacific Ocean, which is also a major earthquake zone. This curving belt of active faults and volcanoes is often called the Ring of Fire.

The world's best known volcanic mountains include: Mount Etna in Italy and Mount Kilimanjaro in Africa. The Hawaiian Islands are actually the tops of a chain of volcanic mountains that rise from the ocean floor.

There are three types of volcanic mountains: shield volcanoes, cinder cones and composite volcanoes.

Shield Volcanoes are associated with quiet eruptions. Lava emerges from the vent or opening in the crater and flows freely out over the earth's surface until it cools and hardens into a layer of igneous rock. A repeated lava flow builds this type of volcano into the largest volcanic mountain. Mauna Loa found in Hawaii, is the largest volcano on earth.

Cinder Cone Volcanoes are associated with explosive eruptions as lava is hurled high into the air in a spray of droplets of various sizes. These droplets cool and harden into cinders and particles of ash before falling to the ground. The ash and cinder pile up around the vent to form a steep, cone-shaped hill called the cinder cone. Cinder cone volcanoes are relatively small but may form quite rapidly.

Composite Volcanoes are described as being built by both lava flows and layers of ash and cinders. Mount Fuji in Japan, Mount St. Helens in Washington, USA and Mount Vesuvius in Italy are all famous composite volcanoes.

Mechanisms of producing mountains

Mountains are produced by different types of mountain-building processes. Most major mountain ranges are formed by the processes of folding and faulting.

Folded Mountains are produced by the folding of rock layers. Crustal movements may press horizontal layers of sedimentary rock together from the sides, squeezing them into wavelike folds. Up-folded sections of rock are called anticlines; down-folded sections of rock are called synclines. The Appalachian Mountains are an example of folded mountains with long ridges and valleys in a series of anticlines and synclines formed by folded rock layers.

Faults are fractures in the earth's crust which have been created by either tension or compression forces transmitted through the crust. These forces are produced by the movement of separate blocks of crust.

Faultings are categorized on the basis of the relative movement between the blocks on both sides of the fault plane. The movement can be horizontal, vertical or oblique.

A dip-slip fault occurs when the movement of the plates is vertical and opposite. The displacement is in the direction of the inclination, or dip, of the fault. Dip-slip faults are classified as normal faults when the rock above the fault plane moves down relative to the rock below.

Reverse faults are created when the rock above the fault plane moves up relative to the rock below. Reverse faults having a very low angle to the horizontal are also referred to as thrust faults.

Faults in which the dominant displacement is horizontal movement along the trend or strike (length) of the fault are called **strike-slip faults**. When a large strike-slip fault is associated with plate boundaries it is called a **transform fault**. The San Andreas Fault in California is a well-known transform fault.

Faults that have both vertical and horizontal movement are called **oblique-slip faults**.

When lava cools, igneous rock is formed. This formation can occur either above ground or below ground.

Intrusive rock includes any igneous rock that was formed below the earth's surface. Batholiths are the largest structures of intrusive type rock and are composed of near granite materials; they are the core of the Sierra Nevada Mountains.

Extrusive rock includes any igneous rock that was formed at the earth's surface.

Dikes are old lava tubes formed when magma entered a vertical fracture and hardened. Sometimes magma squeezes between two rock layers and hardens into a thin horizontal sheet called a **sill**. A **laccolith** is formed in much the same way as a sill, but the magma that creates a laccolith is very thick and does not flow easily. It pools and forces the overlying strata creating an obvious surface dome.

A **caldera** is normally formed by the collapse of the top of a volcano. This collapse can be caused by a massive explosion that destroys the cone and empties most if not all of the magma chamber below the volcano. The cone collapses into the empty magma chamber forming a caldera.

An inactive volcano may have magma solidified in its pipe. This structure, called a volcanic neck, is resistant to erosion and today may be the only visible evidence of the past presence of an active volcano.

When lava cools, igneous rock is formed. This formation can occur either above ground or below ground.

Glaciation

A continental glacier covered a large part of North America during the most recent ice age. Evidence of this glacial coverage remains as abrasive grooves, large boulders from northern environments dropped in southerly locations, glacial troughs created by the rounding out of steep valleys by glacial scouring, and the remains of glacial sources called **cirques** that were created by frost wedging the rock at the bottom of the glacier. Remains of plants and animals found in warm climate have been discovered in the moraines and out wash plains help to support the theory of periods of warmth during the past ice ages.

The Ice Age began about 2 -3 million years ago. This age saw the advancement and retreat of glacial ice over millions of years. Theories relating to the origin of glacial activity include Plate Tectonics, where it can be demonstrated that some continental masses, now in temperate climates, were at one time blanketed by ice and snow. Another theory involves changes in the earth's orbit around the sun, changes in the angle of the earth's axis, and the wobbling of the earth's axis. Support for the validity of this theory has come from deep ocean research that indicates a correlation between climatic sensitive micro-organisms and the changes in the earth's orbital status.

About 12,000 years ago, a vast sheet of ice covered a large part of the northern United States. This huge, frozen mass had moved southward from the northern regions of Canada as several large bodies of slow-moving ice, or glaciers. A time period in which glaciers advance over a large portion of a continent is called an ice age. A glacier is a large mass of ice that moves or flows over the land in response to gravity. Glaciers form among high mountains and in other cold regions.

There are two main types of glaciers: valley glaciers and continental glaciers. Erosion by valley glaciers is characteristic of U-shaped erosion. They produce sharp peaked mountains such as the Matterhorn in Switzerland. Erosion by continental glaciers often rides over mountains in their paths leaving smoothed, rounded mountains and ridges.

Skill 51.2   Understands the form and function of surface and subsurface water.

World weather patterns are greatly influenced by ocean surface currents in the upper layer of the ocean. These currents continuously move along the ocean surface in specific directions. Ocean currents that flow deep below the surface are called sub-surface currents. These currents are influenced by such factors as the location of landmasses in the current's path and the earth's rotation.

Surface currents are caused by winds and are classified by temperature. Cold currents originate in the Polar regions and flow through surrounding water that is measurably warmer. Those currents with a higher temperature than the surrounding water are called warm currents and can be found near the equator. These currents follow swirling routes around the ocean basins and the equator.

The Gulf Stream and the California Current are the two main surface currents that flow along the coastlines of the United States. The Gulf Stream is a warm current in the Atlantic Ocean that carries warm water from the equator to the northern parts of the Atlantic Ocean. Benjamin Franklin studied and named the Gulf Stream. The California Current is a cold current that originates in the Arctic regions and flows southward along the west coast of the United States.

Differences in water density also create ocean currents. Water found near the bottom of oceans is the coldest and the densest. Water tends to flow from a denser area to a less dense area. Currents that flow because of a difference in the density of the ocean water are called density currents. Water with a higher salinity is denser than water with a lower salinity. Water that has salinity different from the surrounding water may form a density current.

Two percent of all the available water is fixed and held in ice or the bodies of organisms. Available water includes surface water (lakes, ocean, and rivers) and ground water (aquifers, wells). 96% of all available water is from ground water. Water is recycled through the processes of evaporation and precipitation. The water present now is the water that has been here since our atmosphere formed.

Water flows and is collected in a predictable manner. In most situations it runs across land and into small streams that feed larger bodies of water. All of the land that acts like a funnel for water flowing into a single larger body of water is known as a watershed or drainage basin. The watershed includes the streams and rivers that bear the water and the surfaces across which the water runs. Thus, the pollution load and general state of all the land within a watershed has an effect on the health and cleanliness of the body of water to which it drains. Large land features, such as mountains, separate watersheds from one another. However, some portion of water from one watershed may enter the groundwater and ultimately flow towards another, adjacent watershed.

Not all water flows to the streams, rivers, and lakes that comprise the above ground water supply. Some water remains in the soil as ground water. Additionally, underground rivers are found in areas of karst topography, though these are relatively rare. It is more common for water to collect in underground aquifers. Aquifers are layers of permeable rock or loose material (gravel, sand, or silt) that hold water. Aquifers may be either confined or unconfined. Confined aquifers are deep in the ground and below the water table. Unconfined aquifers border on the water table. The water table is the level at which ground water exists and is always equal to atmospheric pressure. To visualize the entire ground water system, we can imagine a hole dug in wet sand at the beach and a small pool of water within the hole. The wet sand corresponds to the aquifer, the hole to a well or lake, and the level of water in the hole to the water table.

In some cases, people have created reservoirs, artificial storage areas that make large amounts of water readily available. Reservoirs are most often created by damming rivers. A dam is built from cement, soil, or rock and the river fills the newly created reservoir. A reservoir may be created by building a dam either across a valley or around the entire perimeter of an artificial lake (a bunded dam). The former technique is more common and relies on natural features to form a watertight reservoir. However, such a feature must exist to allow this type of construction. A fully bunded dam does not require such a natural feature but does necessitate more construction since a waterproof structure must be built all the way around the reservoir. This structure is typically made from clay and/or cement. Since no river feeds such reservoirs, mechanical pumps are used to fill them from nearby water sources. Occasionally, watertight roofs are added to these reservoirs so they can be used to hold treated water. These are known as service reservoirs.

Skill 51.3   Applies knowledge of the composition and structure of the atmosphere and its properties.

Dry air is composed of three basic components; dry gas, water vapor, and solid particles (dust from soil, etc.).

The most abundant dry gases in the atmosphere are:

(N_2) Nitrogen   78.09 % makes up about 4/5 of gases in atmosphere
(O_2) Oxygen   20.95 %
(AR) Argon   0.93 %
(CO_2) Carbon Dioxide 0.03 %

The atmosphere is divided into four main layers based on temperature. These layers are labeled Troposphere, Stratosphere, Mesosphere, Thermosphere.

Troposphere - this layer is the closest to the earth's surface and all weather phenomena occurs here as it is the layer with the most water vapor and dust. Air temperature decreases with increasing altitude. The average thickness of the Troposphere is 7 miles (11 km).

Stratosphere - this layer contains very little water, clouds within this layer are extremely rare. The Ozone layer is located in the upper portions of the stratosphere. Air temperature is fairly constant but does increase somewhat with height due to the absorption of solar energy and ultra violet rays from the ozone layer.

Mesosphere - air temperature again decreases with height in this layer. It is the coldest layer with temperatures in the range of -100^0 C at the top..

Thermosphere - extends upward into space. Oxygen molecules in this layer absorb energy from the sun, causing temperatures to increase with height. The lower part of the thermosphere is called the Ionosphere. Here charged particles or ions and free electrons can be found. When gases in the Ionosphere are excited by solar radiation, the gases give off light and glow in the sky. These glowing lights are called the Aurora Borealis in the Northern Hemisphere and Aurora Australis in Southern Hemisphere. The upper portion of the Thermosphere is called the Exosphere. Gas molecules are very far apart in this layer. Layers of Exosphere are also known as the Van Allen Belts and are held together by earth's magnetic field.

Air masses moving toward or away from the Earth's surface are called air currents. Air moving parallel to Earth's surface is called **wind**. Weather conditions are generated by winds and air currents carrying large amounts of heat and moisture from one part of the atmosphere to another. Wind speeds are measured by instruments called anemometers.

The wind belts in each hemisphere consist of convection cells that encircle Earth like belts. There are three major wind belts on Earth: (1) trade winds (2) prevailing westerlies, and (3) polar easterlies. Wind belt formation depends on the differences in air pressures that develop in the doldrums, the horse latitudes, and the polar regions. The Doldrums surround the equator. Within this belt heated air usually rises straight up into Earth's atmosphere. The Horse latitudes are regions of high barometric pressure with calm and light winds and the Polar regions contain cold dense air that sinks to the Earth's surface.

Skill 51.4   **Demonstrates an understanding of the interactions that occur among the biosphere, geosphere, hydrosphere, and atmosphere.**

While the hydrosphere, lithosphere, and atmosphere can be described and considered separately, they are actually constantly interacting with one another. Energy and matter flows freely between these different spheres. For instance, in the water cycle, water beneath the Earth's surface and in rocks (in the lithosphere) is exchanged with vapor in the atmosphere and liquid water in lakes and the ocean (the hydrosphere). Similarly, significant events in one sphere almost always have effects in the other spheres. The recent increase in greenhouse gases provides an example of this ripple effect. Additional greenhouse gases produced by human activities were released into the atmosphere where they built up and caused widening holes in certain areas of the atmosphere and global warming. These increasing temperatures have had many effects on the hydrosphere: rising sea levels, increasing water temperature, and climate changes. These lead to even more changes in the lithosphere such as glacier retreat and alterations in the patterns of water-rock interaction (run-off, erosion, etc).

Skill 51.5   **Applies knowledge of how human activity and natural processes, both gradual and catastrophic, can alter earth systems.**

An important topic in science is the effect of natural disasters and events on society and the effect human activity has on inducing such events. Naturally occurring geological, weather, and environmental events can greatly affect the lives of humans. In addition, the activities of humans can induce such events that would not normally occur.

Nature-induced hazards include floods, landslides, avalanches, volcanic eruptions, wildfires, earthquakes, hurricanes, tornadoes, droughts, and disease. Such events often occur naturally, because of changing weather patterns or geological conditions. Property damage, resource destruction, and the loss of human life are the possible outcomes of natural hazards. Thus, natural hazards are often extremely costly on both an economic and personal level.

While many nature-induced hazards occur naturally, human activity can often stimulate such events. For example, destructive land use practices such as mining can induce landslides or avalanches if not properly planned and monitored. In addition, human activities can cause other hazards including global warming and waste contamination. Global warming is an increase in the Earth's average temperature resulting, at least in part, from the burning of fuels by humans. Global warming is hazardous because it disrupts the Earth's environmental balance and can negatively affect weather patterns. Ecological and weather pattern changes can promote the natural disasters listed above. Finally, improper hazardous waste disposal by humans can contaminate the environment. One important effect of hazardous waste contamination is the stimulation of disease in human populations. Thus, hazardous waste contamination negatively affects both the environment and the people that live in it.

Skill 51.6   Identifies the sources of energy (e.g., solar, geothermal) in earth systems and describes mechanisms of energy transfer (e.g., convection, radiation).

Energy is transferred in Earth's atmosphere in three ways. Earth gets most of its energy from the sun in the form of waves. This transfer of energy by waves is termed **radiation**. The transfer of thermal energy through matter by actual contact of molecules is called **conduction**. For example, heated rocks and sandy beaches transfer heat to the surrounding air. The transfer of thermal energy due to air density differences is called **convection**. Convection currents circulate in a constant exchange of cold, dense air for less dense warm air.

Carbon Dioxide in the atmosphere absorbs energy from the sun. Carbon Dioxide also blocks the direct escape of energy from the Earth's surface. This process by which heat is trapped by gases, water vapor and other gases in the Earth's atmosphere is called the **Greenhouse Effect**.

Most of the Earth's water is found in the oceans and lakes. Through the **water cycle**, water evaporates into the atmosphere and condenses into clouds. Water then falls to the Earth in the form of precipitation, returning to the oceans and lakes on falling on land. Water on the land may return to the oceans and lakes as runoff or seep from the soil as groundwater.

COMPETENCY 52.0 THE TEACHER UNDERSTANDS CYCLES IN EARTH SYSTEMS.

Skill 52.1 Understands the rock cycle and how rocks, minerals, and soils are formed.

Three major subdivisions of rocks are sedimentary, metamorphic and igneous.

Lithification of sedimentary rocks

When fluid sediments are transformed into solid sedimentary rocks, the process is known as lithification. One very common process affecting sediments is compaction where the weights of overlying materials compress and compact the deeper sediments. The compaction process leads to cementation. Cementation is when sediments are converted to sedimentary rock.

Factors in crystallization of igneous rocks

Igneous rocks can be classified according to their texture, their composition, and the way they formed.

Molten rock is called magma. When molten rock pours out onto the surface of Earth, it is called lava.

As magma cools, the elements and compounds begin to form crystals. The slower the magma cools, the larger the crystals grow. Rocks with large crystals are said to have a coarse-grained texture. Granite is an example of a coarse grained rock. Rocks that cool rapidly before any crystals can form have a glassy texture such as obsidian, also commonly known as volcanic glass.

Metamorphic rocks are formed by high temperatures and great pressures. The process by which the rocks undergo these changes is called metamorphism. The outcome of metamorphic changes include deformation by extreme heat and pressure, compaction, destruction of the original characteristics of the parent rock, bending and folding while in a plastic stage, and the emergence of completely new and different minerals due to chemical reactions with heated water and dissolved minerals.

Metamorphic rocks are classified into two groups, foliated (leaflike) rocks and unfoliated rocks. Foliated rocks consist of compressed, parallel bands of minerals, which give the rocks a striped appearance. Examples of such rocks include slate, schist, and gneiss. Unfoliated rocks are not banded and examples of such include quartzite, marble, and anthracite rocks.

Minerals are natural, non-living solids with a definite chemical composition and a crystalline structure. **Ores** are minerals or rock deposits that can be mined for a profit. **Rocks** are earth materials made of one or more minerals. A **Rock Facies** is a rock group that differs from comparable rocks (as in composition, age or fossil content).

Minerals must adhere to five criteria. They must be (1) non-living, (2) formed in nature, (3) solid in form, (4) their atoms form a crystalline pattern, (5) its chemical composition is fixed within narrow limits.

There are over 3000 minerals in Earth's crust. Minerals are classified by composition. The major groups of minerals are silicates, carbonates, oxides, sulfides, sulfates, and halides. The largest group of minerals is the silicates. Silicates are made of silicon, oxygen, and one or more other elements.

Soils are composed of particles of sand, clay, various minerals, tiny living organisms, and humus, plus the decayed remains of plants and animals. Soils are divided into three classes according to their texture. These classes are sandy soils, clay soils, and loamy soils.

Sandy soils are gritty, and their particles do not bind together firmly. Sandy soils are porous- water passes through them rapidly. Sandy soils do not hold much water.

Clay soils are smooth and greasy, their particles bind together firmly. Clay soils are moist and usually do not allow water to pass through easily.

Loamy soils feel somewhat like velvet and their particles clump together. Loamy soils are made up of sand, clay, and silt. Loamy soils holds water but some water can pass through.

In addition to three main classes, soils are further grouped into three major types based upon their composition. These groups are pedalfers, pedocals, and laterites.

Pedalfers form in the humid, temperate climate of the eastern United States. Pedalfer soils contain large amounts of iron oxide and aluminum-rich clays, making the soil a brown to reddish brown color. This soil supports forest type vegetation.

Pedocals are found in the western United States where the climate is dry and temperate. These soils are rich in calcium carbonate. This type of soil supports grasslands and brush vegetation.

Laterites are found where the climate is wet and tropical. Large amounts of water flows through this soil. Laterites are red-orange soils rich in iron and aluminum oxides. There is little humus and this soil is not very fertile.

Skill 52.2   Understands the water cycle and its relationship to earth systems.

Essential elements are recycled through an ecosystem. The water present now is the water that has been here since our atmosphere formed.

Water cycle - 2% of all the available water is fixed and held in ice or the bodies of organisms. Available water includes surface water (lakes, ocean, and rivers) and ground water (aquifers, wells). 96% of all available water is from ground water. Water is recycled through the processes of evaporation and precipitation.

Water that falls to Earth in the form of rain and snow is called **precipitation.** Precipitation is part of a continuous process in which water at the Earth's surface evaporates, condenses into clouds, and returns to Earth. This process is termed the **water cycle**. The water located below the surface is called groundwater.

The impacts of altitude upon climatic conditions are primarily related to temperature and precipitation. As altitude increases, climatic conditions become increasingly drier and colder. Solar radiation becomes more severe as altitude increases while the effects of convection forces are minimized. Climatic changes as a function of latitude follow a similar pattern (as a reference, latitude moves either north or south from the equator). The climate becomes colder and drier as the distance from the equator increases. Proximity to land or water masses produce climatic conditions based upon the available moisture. Dry and arid climates prevail where moisture is scarce; lush tropical climates can prevail where moisture is abundant. Climate, as described above, depends upon the specific combination of conditions making up an area's environment. Man impacts all environments by producing pollutants in earth, air, and water. It follows then, that man is a major player in world climatic conditions.

Skill 52.3   Understands the nutrient (e.g., carbon, nitrogen) cycle and its relationship to earth systems.

Carbon cycle - Ten percent of all available carbon in the air (from carbon dioxide gas) is fixed by photosynthesis. Plants fix carbon in the form of glucose, animals eat the plants and are able to obtain their source of carbon. When animals release carbon dioxide through respiration, the plants again have a source of carbon to fix.

Nitrogen cycle - Eighty percent of the atmosphere is in the form of nitrogen gas. Nitrogen must be fixed and taken out of the gaseous form to be incorporated into an organism. Only a few genera of bacteria have the correct enzymes to break the triple bond between nitrogen atoms. These bacteria live within the roots of legumes (peas, beans, alfalfa) and add bacteria to the soil so it may be taken up by the plant. Nitrogen is necessary to make amino acids and the nitrogenous bases of DNA.

Phosphorus cycle - Phosphorus exists as a mineral and is not found in the atmosphere. Fungi and plant roots have structures called mycorrhizae that are able to fix insoluble phosphates into useable phosphorus. Urine and decayed matter returns phosphorus to the earth where it can be fixed in the plant. Phosphorus is needed for the backbone of DNA and for the manufacture of ATP.

Skill 52.4   Applies knowledge of how human and natural processes affect earth systems.

An important topic in science is the effect of natural disasters and events on society and the effect human activity has on inducing such events. Naturally occurring geological, weather, and environmental events can greatly affect the lives of humans. In addition, the activities of humans can induce such events that would not normally occur.

Nature-induced hazards include floods, landslides, avalanches, volcanic eruptions, wildfires, earthquakes, hurricanes, tornadoes, droughts, and disease. Such events often occur naturally, because of changing weather patterns or geological conditions. Property damage, resource destruction, and the loss of human life are the possible outcomes of natural hazards. Thus, natural hazards are often extremely costly on both an economic and personal level.

While many nature-induced hazards occur naturally, human activity can often stimulate such events. For example, destructive land use practices such as mining can induce landslides or avalanches if not properly planned and monitored. In addition, human activities can cause other hazards including global warming and waste contamination. Global warming is an increase in the Earth's average temperature resulting, at least in part, from the burning of fuels by humans. Global warming is hazardous because it disrupts the Earth's environmental balance and can negatively affect weather patterns. Ecological and weather pattern changes can promote the natural disasters listed above. Finally, improper hazardous waste disposal by humans can contaminate the environment. One important effect of hazardous waste contamination is the stimulation of disease in human populations. Thus, hazardous waste contamination negatively affects both the environment and the people that live in it.

Skill 52.5   Understands the dynamic interactions that occur among the various cycles in the biosphere, geosphere, hydrosphere, and atmosphere.

While the hydrosphere, lithosphere, and atmosphere can be described and considered separately, they are actually constantly interacting with one another. Energy and matter flows freely between these different spheres. For instance, in the water cycle, water beneath the Earth's surface and in rocks (in the lithosphere) is exchanged with vapor in the atmosphere and liquid water in lakes and the ocean (the hydrosphere). Similarly, significant events in one sphere almost always have effects in the other spheres. The recent increase in greenhouse gases provides an example of this ripple effect. Additional greenhouse gases produced by human activities were released into the atmosphere where they built up and caused widening holes in certain areas of the atmosphere and global warming. These increasing temperatures have had many effects on the hydrosphere: rising sea levels, increasing water temperature, and climate changes. These lead to even more changes in the lithosphere such as glacier retreat and alterations in the patterns of water-rock interaction (run-off, erosion, etc).

COMPETENCY 53.0 THE TEACHER UNDERSTANDS THE ROLE OF ENERGY IN WEATHER AND CLIMATE.

Skill 53.1 Understands the elements of weather (e.g., humidity, wind speed, pressure, temperature) and how they are measured.

Humidity is the amount of water vapor in the air. Humidity may be measured as absolute humidity, relative humidity, and specific humidity. Relative humidity is the most frequently used measurement because it is used in weather forecasts. Relative humidity indicates the likelihood of precipitation, dew, or fog. **Relative humidity** is the actual amount of water vapor in a certain volume of air compared to the maximum amount of water vapor this air could hold at a given temperature. The air temperature at which water vapor begins to condense is called the dew point.

Wind speed is the speed of movement of air relative to a point on Earth. A wind occurs when air moves from one place to the next. High wind speeds can cause destruction, and strong winds are referred to as gales, hurricanes, and typhoons. An **anemometer** measures wind speed and a **wind vane** measures wind direction.

Cyclones are huge air masses of low pressure air. The wind in a low-pressure system blows counterclockwise. Air pressure in a low pressure system is lowest at the center and highest along its outer edges. Air masses of high pressure air are called **anticyclones**. The wind in a high-pressure system blows clockwise. Air pressure is greatest at the center of the air mass and lowest along its outer edge.

Temperature is measured with a thermometer. The scale may be in either degrees Celsius or degrees Fahrenheit. Fahrenheit is common in America, but the worldwide standard is Celsius. The conversions are: [°F] = [°C] (9/5 + 32) and conversely [°C] = ([°F] − 32)(5/9).

Skill 53.2 Compares and contrasts weather and climate.

The weather in a region is called the climate of that region. Unlike the weather, which consists of hourly and daily changes in the atmosphere over a region, climate is the average of all weather conditions in a region over a period of time. Many factors are used to determine the climate of a region including temperature and precipitation. Climate varies from one place to another because of the unequal heating of the Earth's surface. This varied heating of the surface is the result of the unequal distribution of land masses, oceans, and polar ice caps.

Skill 53.3   Analyzes weather charts and data to make weather predictions

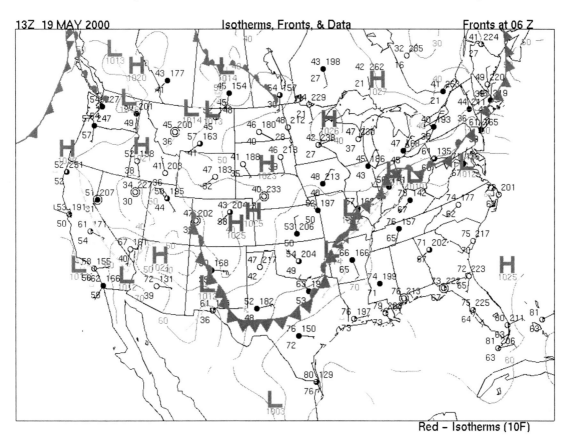

http://www.dnr.sc.gov/climate/sercc/education/saer/aer_summer_00.ht

This map can be used to predict future weather conditions at the weather station in central Arkansas represented by the circle symbol.

This map indicates that a cold front is moving toward the weather station from West to East, as do most weather conditions in the United States. Cold weather fronts occur when a cold air mass of high density pushes under a warm air mass, causing moisture in the warm air to quickly rise, cool, and condense. Heavy precipitation in the near future can thus be predicted for this area.

Additionally, this weather map indicates that a low-pressure system is moving toward the weather station with the approaching cold front. Low-pressure systems allow air to rise and moisture to condense, and are also associated with precipitation.

The cloud coverage symbol of a completely dark circle on this weather map indicates that skies are overcast. This state could be due to the presence of nimbostratus clouds, which form dark sheets that block sunlight and are often responsible for lengthy periods of precipitation.   Therefore, all conditions for Arkansas portrayed on this weather map indicate imminent precipitation.

Skill 53.4   Applies knowledge of how transfers of energy among earth systems affect weather and climate.

Air masses moving toward or away from the Earth's surface are called air currents. Air moving parallel to Earth's surface is called **wind**. Weather conditions are generated by winds and air currents carrying large amounts of heat and moisture from one part of the atmosphere to another. Wind speeds are measured by instruments called anemometers.

The wind belts in each hemisphere consist of convection cells that encircle Earth like belts. There are three major wind belts on Earth: (1) trade winds (2) prevailing westerlies, and (3) polar easterlies. Wind belt formation depends on the differences in air pressures that develop in the doldrums, the horse latitudes, and the polar regions. The Doldrums surround the equator. Within this belt heated air usually rises straight up into Earth's atmosphere. The Horse latitudes are regions of high barometric pressure with calm and light winds and the Polar regions contain cold dense air that sinks to the Earth's surface.

Winds caused by local temperature changes include sea breezes, and land breezes.

Sea breezes are caused by the unequal heating of the land and an adjacent, large body of water. Land heats up faster than water. The movement of cool ocean air toward the land is called a sea breeze. Sea breezes usually begin blowing about mid-morning; ending about sunset.

A breeze that blows from the land to the ocean or a large lake is called a **land breeze.**

Monsoons are huge wind systems that cover large geographic areas and that reverse direction seasonally. The monsoons of India and Asia are examples of these seasonal winds. They alternate wet and dry seasons. As denser cooler air over the ocean moves inland, a steady seasonal wind called a summer or wet monsoon is produced.

Skill 53.5   Analyzes how Earth's position, orientation, and surface features affect weather and climate.

Earth is the third planet away from the sun in our solar system. Earth's numerous types of motion and states of orientation greatly effect global conditions, such as seasons, tides and lunar phases. The Earth orbits the Sun with a period of 365 days. During this orbit, the average distance between the Earth and Sun is 93 million miles. The shape of the Earth's orbit around the Sun deviates from the shape of a circle only slightly. This deviation, known as the Earth's eccentricity, has a very small affect on the Earth's climate. The Earth is closest to the Sun at perihelion, occurring around January 2nd of each year, and farthest from the Sun at aphelion, occurring around July 2nd. Because the Earth is closest to the sun in January, the northern winter is slightly warmer than the southern winter.

Seasons

The rotation axis of the Earth is not perpendicular to the orbital (ecliptic) plane. The axis of the Earth is tilted 23.45° from the perpendicular. The tilt of the Earth's axis is known as the obliquity of the ecliptic, and is mainly responsible for the four seasons of the year by influencing the intensity of solar rays received by the Northern and Southern Hemispheres. The four seasons, spring, summer, fall and winter, are extended periods of characteristic average temperature, rainfall, storm frequency and vegetation growth or dormancy. The effect of the Earth's tilt on climate is best demonstrated at the solstices, the two days of the year when the Sun is farthest from the Earth's equatorial plane. At the Summer Solstice (June Solstice), the Earth's tilt on its axis causes the Northern Hemisphere to the lean toward the Sun, while the southern hemisphere leans away. Consequently, the Northern Hemisphere receives more intense rays from the Sun and experiences summer during this time, while the Southern Hemisphere experiences winter. At the Winter Solstice (December Solstice), it is the Southern Hemisphere that leans toward the sun and thus experiences summer. Spring and fall are produced by varying degrees of the same leaning toward or away from the Sun.

Tides

The orientation of and gravitational interaction between the Earth and the Moon are responsible for the ocean tides that occur on Earth. The term "tide" refers to the cyclic rise and fall of large bodies of water. Gravitational attraction is defined as the force of attraction between all bodies in the universe. At the location on Earth closest to the Moon, the gravitational attraction of the Moon draws seawater toward the Moon in the form of a tidal bulge. On the opposite side of the Earth, another tidal bulge forms in the direction away from the Moon because at this point, the Moon's gravitational pull is the weakest. "Spring tides" are especially strong tides that occur when the Earth, Sun and Moon are in line, allowing both the Sun and the Moon to exert gravitational force on the Earth and increase tidal bulge height. These tides occur during the full moon and the new moon. "Neap tides" are especially weak tides occurring when the gravitational forces of the Moon and the Sun are perpendicular to one another. These tides occur during quarter moons.

COMPETENCY 54.0 THE TEACHER UNDERSTANDS THE CHARACTERISTICS OF THE SOLAR SYSTEM AND THE UNIVERSE.

Skill 54.1 Understands the properties and characteristics of celestial objects.

There are eight established planets in our solar system; Mercury, Venus, Earth, Mars, Jupiter, Saturn, Uranus, and Neptune. Pluto was an established planet in our solar system, but as of Summer 2006, it's status is being reconsidered. The planets are divided into two groups based on distance from the sun. The inner planets include: Mercury, Venus, Earth, and Mars. The outer planets include: Jupiter, Saturn, Uranus, and Neptune.

Planets

Mercury - the closest planet to the sun. Its surface has craters and rocks. The atmosphere is composed of hydrogen, helium and sodium. Mercury was named after the Roman messenger god.

Venus - has a slow rotation when compared to Earth. Venus and Uranus rotate in opposite directions from the other planets. This opposite rotation is called retrograde rotation. The surface of Venus is not visible due to the extensive cloud cover. The atmosphere is composed mostly of carbon dioxide. Sulfuric acid droplets in the dense cloud cover give Venus a yellow appearance. Venus has a greater greenhouse effect than observed on Earth. The dense clouds combined with carbon dioxide trap heat. Venus was named after the Roman goddess of love.

Earth - considered a water planet with 70% of its surface covered by water. Gravity holds the masses of water in place. The different temperatures observed on earth allow for the different states (solid. Liquid, gas) of water to exist. The atmosphere is composed mainly of oxygen and nitrogen. Earth is the only planet that is known to support life.

Mars - the surface of Mars contains numerous craters, active and extinct volcanoes, ridges, and valleys with extremely deep fractures. Iron oxide found in the dusty soil makes the surface seem rust colored and the skies seem pink in color. The atmosphere is composed of carbon dioxide, nitrogen, argon, oxygen and water vapor. Mars has polar regions with ice caps composed of water. Mars has two satellites. Mars was named after the Roman war god.

Jupiter -- largest planet in the solar system. Jupiter has 16 moons. The atmosphere is composed of hydrogen, helium, methane and ammonia. There are white colored bands of clouds indicating rising gas and dark colored bands of clouds indicating descending gases. The gas movement is caused by heat resulting from the energy of Jupiter's core. Jupiter has a Great Red Spot that is thought to be a hurricane type cloud. Jupiter has a strong magnetic field.

Saturn - the second largest planet in the solar system. Saturn has rings of ice, rock, and dust particles circling it. Saturn's atmosphere is composed of hydrogen, helium, methane, and ammonia. Saturn has 20 plus satellites. Saturn was named after the Roman god of agriculture.

Uranus - the second largest planet in the solar system with retrograde revolution. Uranus is a gaseous planet. It has 10 dark rings and 15 satellites. Its atmosphere is composed of hydrogen, helium, and methane. Uranus was named after the Greek god of the heavens.

Neptune - another gaseous planet with an atmosphere consisting of hydrogen, helium, and methane. Neptune has 3 rings and 2 satellites. Neptune was named after the Roman sea god because its atmosphere is the same color as the seas.

Pluto – once considered the smallest planet in the solar system; it's status as a planet is being reconsidered . Pluto's atmosphere probably contains methane, ammonia, and frozen water. Pluto has 1 satellite. Pluto revolves around the sun every 250 years. Pluto was named after the Roman god of the underworld.

Comets, asteroids, and meteors

Astronomers believe that rocky fragments may have been the remains of the birth of the solar system that never formed into a planet. **Asteroids** are found in the region between Mars and Jupiter.

Comets are masses of frozen gases, cosmic dust, and small rocky particles. Astronomers think that most comets originate in a dense comet cloud beyond Pluto. Comet consists of a nucleus, a coma, and a tail. A comet's tail always points away from the sun. The most famous comet, **Halley's Comet,** is named after the person whom first discovered it in 240 B.C. It returns to the skies near earth every 75 to 76 years.

Meteoroids are composed of particles of rock and metal of various sizes. When a meteoroid travels through the earth's atmosphere, friction causes its surface to heat up and it begins to burn. The burning meteoroid falling through the earth's atmosphere is called a **meteor** (also known as a "shooting star").

Meteorites are meteors that strike the earth's surface. A physical example of a meteorite's impact on the earth's surface can be seen in Arizona. The Barringer Crater is a huge meteor crater. There are many other meteor craters throughout the world.

Astronomers use groups or patterns of stars called **constellations** as reference points to locate other stars in the sky. Familiar constellations include: Ursa Major (also known as the big bear) and Ursa Minor (known as the little bear). Within the Ursa Major, the smaller constellation, The Big Dipper is found. Within the Ursa Minor, the smaller constellation, The Little Dipper is found.

Different constellations appear as the earth continues its revolution around the sun with the seasonal changes.

Magnitude stars are 21 of the brightest stars that can be seen from earth. These are the first stars noticed at night. In the Northern Hemisphere there are 15 commonly observed first magnitude stars.

A vast collection of stars are defined as **galaxies**. Galaxies are classified as irregular, elliptical, and spiral. An irregular galaxy has no real structured appearance; most are in their early stages of life. An elliptical galaxy consists of smooth ellipses, containing little dust and gas, but composed of millions or trillion stars. Spiral galaxies are disk-shaped and have extending arms that rotate around its dense center. Earth's galaxy is found in the Milky Way and it is a spiral galaxy.

Terms related to deep space

A **pulsar** is defined as a variable radio source that emits signals in very short, regular bursts; believed to be a rotating neutron star.

A **quasar** is defined as an object that photographs like a star but has an extremely large redshift and a variable energy output; believed to be the active core of a very distant galaxy.

Black holes are defined as an object that has collapsed to such a degree that light can not escape from its surface; light is trapped by the intense gravitational field.

Skill 54.2   Applies knowledge of the earth-moon-sun system and the interactions among them (e.g., seasons, lunar phases, eclipses).

Lunar Phases

The Earth's orientation in respect to the solar system is also responsible for our perception of the phases of the moon. As the Earth orbits the Sun with a period of 365 days, the Moon orbits the Earth every 27 days. As the moon circles the Earth, its shape in the night sky appears to change. The changes in the appearance of the moon from Earth are known as "lunar phases." These phases vary cyclically according to the relative positions of the Moon, the Earth and the Sun. At all times, half of the Moon is facing the Sun and is thus illuminated by reflecting the Sun's light. As the Moon orbits the Earth and the Earth orbits the Sun, the half of the moon that faces the Sun changes. However, the Moon is in synchronous rotation around the Earth, meaning that nearly the same side of the moon faces the Earth at all times. This side is referred to as the near side of the moon. Lunar phases occur as the Earth and Moon orbit the Sun and the fractional illumination of the Moon's near side changes.

When the Sun and Moon are on opposite sides of the Earth, observers on Earth perceive a "full moon," meaning the moon appears circular because the entire illuminated half of the moon is visible. As the Moon orbits the Earth, the Moon "wanes" as the amount of the illuminated half of the Moon that is visible from Earth decreases. A gibbous moon is between a full moon and a half moon, or between a half moon and a full moon. When the Sun and the Moon are on the same side of Earth, the illuminated half of the moon is facing away from Earth, and the moon appears invisible. This lunar phase is known as the "new moon." The time between each full moon is approximately 29.53 days.

A list of all lunar phases includes:

- New Moon: the moon is invisible or the first signs of a crescent appear
- Waxing Crescent: the right crescent of the moon is visible
- First Quarter: the right quarter of the moon is visible
- Waxing Gibbous: only the left crescent is not illuminated
- Full Moon: the entire illuminated half of the moon is visible
- Waning Gibbous: only the right crescent of the moon is not illuminated
- Last Quarter: the left quarter of the moon is illuminated
- Waning Crescent: only the left crescent of the moon is illuminated

Viewing the moon from the Southern Hemisphere would cause these phases to occur in the opposite order.

Eclipses

Eclipses are defined as the passing of one object into the shadow of another object. A **Lunar eclipse** occurs when the moon travels through the shadow of the earth. A **Solar eclipse** occurs when the moon positions itself between the sun and earth.

Skill 54.3   Identifies properties of the components of the solar system.

Cosmic microwave background radiation (CMBR) is the oldest light we can see. It is a snapshot of how the universe looked in its early beginnings. First discovered in 1964, CMBR is composed of photons which we can see because of the atoms that formed when the universe cooled to 3000 K. Prior to that, after the Big Bang, the universe was so hot that the photons were scattered all over the universe, making the universe opaque. The atoms caused the photons to scatter less and the universe to become transparent to radiation. Since cooling to 3000K, the universe has continued to expand and cool.

COBE, launched in 1989, was the first mission to explore slight fluctuations in the background. WMAP, launched in 2001, took a clearer picture of the universe, providing evidence to support the Big Bang Theory and add details to the early conditions of the universe. Based upon this more recent data, scientists believe the universe is about 13.7 billion years old and that there was a period of rapid expansion right after the Big Bang. They have also learned that there were early variations in the density of matter resulting in the formation of the galaxies, the geometry of the universe is flat, and the universe will continue to expand forever.

The **mass of any celestial object** may be determined by using Newton's laws of motion and his law of gravity.

For example, to determine the mass of the Sun, use the following formula:

$$M = \frac{4\pi^2}{G} = \frac{a^3}{P^2}$$

where M = the mass of the Sun, G = a constant measured in laboratory experiments, a = the distance of a celestial body in orbit around the Sun from the Sun, and P = the period of the body's orbit.

In our solar system, measurable objects range in mass from the largest, the Sun, to the smallest, a near-Earth asteroid. (This does not take into account, objects with a mass less than 10^{21} kg.)

The surface temperature of an object depends largely upon its proximity to the Sun. One exception to this, however, is Venus, which is hotter than Mercury because of its cloud layer that holds heat to the planet's surface. The surface temperatures of the planets range from more than 400 degrees on Mercury and Venus to below -200 degrees on the distant planets.

Most minor bodies in the solar system do not have any atmosphere and, therefore, can easily radiate the heat from the Sun. In the case of any celestial object, whether a side is warm or cold depends upon whether it faces the sun or not and the time of rotation. The longer rotation takes, the colder the side facing away from the sun will become, and vice versa.

If the density of an object is less than 1.5 grams per cc, then the object is almost exclusively made of frozen water, ammonia, carbon dioxide, or methane. If the density is less than 1.0, the object must be made of mostly gas. In our solar system, there is only one object with that low a density -- Saturn. If the density is greater than 3.0 grams per cc, then the object is almost exclusively made of rocks; and if the density exceeds 5.0 grams per cc, then there must be a nickel-iron core. Densities between 1.5 and 3.0 indicate a rocky-ice mixture.

The density of planets correlates with their distance from the Sun. The inner planets (Mercury-Mars) are known as the terrestrial planets because they are rocky, and the outer planets (Jupiter and outward) are known as the icy or Jovian (gaslike) planets.

In order for two bodies to interact gravitationally, they must have significant mass. When two bodies in the solar system interact gravitationally, they orbit about a fixed point (the center of mass of the two bodies). This point lies on an imaginary line between the bodies, joining them such that the distances to each body multiplied by each body's mass are equal. The orbits of these bodies will vary slightly over time because of the gravitational interactions.

Skill 54.4   Recognizes characteristics of stars and galaxies and their distribution in the universe.

The **sun** is considered the nearest star to earth that produces solar energy. By the process of nuclear fusion, hydrogen gas is converted to helium gas. Energy flows out of the core to the surface, then radiation escapes into space.

Parts of the sun include: (1) **core:** the inner portion of the sun where fusion takes place, (2) **photosphere:** considered the surface of the sun which produces **sunspots** (cool, dark areas that can be seen on its surface), (3) **chromosphere:** hydrogen gas causes this portion to be red in color (also found here are solar flares (sudden brightness of the chromosphere) and solar prominences (gases that shoot outward from the chromosphere)), and (4) **corona**, the transparent area of sun visible only during a total eclipse.

Solar radiation is energy traveling from the sun that radiates into space. **Solar flares** produce excited protons and electrons that shoot outward from the chromosphere at great speeds reaching earth. These particles disturb radio reception and also affect the magnetic field on earth.

Astronomers use groups or patterns of stars called **constellations** as reference points to locate other stars in the sky. Familiar constellations include: Ursa Major (also known as the big bear) and Ursa Minor (known as the little bear). Within the Ursa Major, the smaller constellation, The Big Dipper is found. Within the Ursa Minor, the smaller constellation, The Little Dipper is found.

Different constellations appear as the earth continues its revolution around the sun with the seasonal changes.

Magnitude stars are 21 of the brightest stars that can be seen from earth. These are the first stars noticed at night. In the Northern Hemisphere there are 15 commonly observed first magnitude stars.

A vast collection of stars are defined as **galaxies**. Galaxies are classified as irregular, elliptical, and spiral. An irregular galaxy has no real structured appearance; most are in their early stages of life. An elliptical galaxy consists of smooth ellipses, containing little dust and gas, but composed of millions or trillion stars. Spiral galaxies are disk-shaped and have extending arms that rotate around its dense center. Earth's galaxy is found in the Milky Way and it is a spiral galaxy.

Skill 54.5   Demonstrates an understanding of scientific theories of the origin of the universe.

Two main hypotheses of the origin of the solar system are: (1) **the tidal hypothesis** and (2) **the condensation hypothesis**.

The tidal hypothesis proposes that the solar system began with a near collision of the sun and a large star. Some astronomers believe that as these two stars passed each other, the great gravitational pull of the large star extracted hot gases out of the sun. The mass from the hot gases started to orbit the sun, which began to cool then condensing into the nine planets. (Few astronomers support this example).

The condensation hypothesis proposes that the solar system began with rotating clouds of dust and gas. Condensation occurred in the center forming the sun and the smaller parts of the cloud formed the nine planets. (This example is widely accepted by many astronomers).

Two main theories to explain the origins of the universe include: (1) **The Big Bang Theory** and (2) **The Steady-State Theory.**

The Big Bang Theory has been widely accepted by many astronomers. It states that the universe originated from a magnificent explosion spreading mass, matter and energy into space. The galaxies formed from this material as it cooled during the next half-billion years.

The Steady-State Theory is the least accepted theory. It states that the universe is a continuously being renewed. Galaxies move outward and new galaxies replace the older galaxies. Astronomers have not found any evidence to prove this theory.

The future of the universe is hypothesized with the Oscillating Universe Hypothesis. It states that the universe will oscillate or expand and contract. Galaxies will move away from one another and will in time slow down and stop. Then a gradual moving toward each other will again activate the explosion or The Big Bang theory.

COMPETENCY 55.0 THE TEACHER UNDERSTANDS THE HISTORY OF THE EARTH SYSTEM.

Skill 55.1 Understands the scope of the geologic time scale and its relationship to geologic processes.

The biological history of the earth is partitioned into four major Eras which are further divided into major periods. The latter periods are refined into groupings called Epochs.

Earth's history extends over more than four billion years and is reckoned in terms of a scale. Paleontologists who study the history of the Earth have divided this huge period of time into four large time units called eons. Eons are divided into smaller units of time called eras. An era refers to a time interval in which particular plants and animals were dominant, or present in great abundance. The end of an era is most often characterized by (1) a general uplifting of the crust, (2) the extinction of the dominant plants or animals, and (3) the appearance of new life-forms.

Each era is divided into several smaller divisions of time called periods. Some periods are divided into smaller time units called epochs.

Methods of geologic dating

Estimates of the Earth's age have been made possible with the discovery of **radioactivity** and the invention of instruments that can measure the amount of radioactivity in rocks. The use of radioactivity to make accurate determinations of Earth's age is called Absolute Dating. This process depends upon comparing the amount of radioactive material in a rock with the amount that has decayed into another element. Studying the radiation given off by atoms of radioactive elements is the most accurate method of measuring the Earth's age. These atoms are unstable and are continuously breaking down or undergoing decay. The radioactive element that decays is called the parent element. The new element that results from the radioactive decay of the parent element is called the daughter element.

The time required for one half of a given amount of a radioactive element to decay is called the half-life of that element or compound.

Geologists commonly use Carbon Dating to calculate the age of a fossil substance.

Infer the history of an area using geologic evidence

The determination of the age of rocks by cataloging their composition has been outmoded since the middle 1800s. Today a sequential history can be determined by the fossil content (principle of fossil succession) of a rock system as well as its superposition within a range of systems. This classification process was termed stratigraphy and permitted the construction of a Geologic Column in which rock systems are arranged in their correct chronological order.

Principles of catastrophism and uniformitarianism

Uniformitarianism - is a fundamental concept in modern geology. It simply states that the physical, chemical, and biological laws that operated in the geologic past operate in the same way today. The forces and processes that we observe presently shaping our planet have been at work for a very long time. This idea is commonly stated as "the present is the key to the past."

Catastrophism - the concept that the earth was shaped by catastrophic events of a short term nature.

Skill 55.2   Demonstrates an understanding of theories about the earth's origin and geologic history.

The dominant scientific theory about the origin of the Universe, and consequently the Earth, is the Big Bang Theory. According to this theory, an atom exploded about 10 to 20 billion years ago throwing matter in all directions. Although this theory has never been proven, and probably never will be, it is supported by the fact that distant galaxies in every direction are moving away from us at great speeds.

Earth, itself, is believed to have been created 4.5 billion years ago as a solidified cloud of gases and dust left over from the creation of the sun. As millions of years passed, radioactive decay released energy that melted some of Earth's components. Over time, the heavier components sank to the center of the Earth and accumulated into the core. As the Earth cooled, a crust formed with natural depressions. Water rising from the interior of the Earth filled these depressions and formed the oceans. Slowly, the Earth acquired the appearance it has today.

The **Heterotroph Hypothesis** supposes that life on Earth evolved from **heterotrophs**, the first cells. According to this hypothesis, life began on Earth about 3.5 billion years ago. Scientists have shown that the basic molecules of life formed from lightning, ultraviolet light, and radioactivity. Over time, these molecules became more complex and developed metabolic processes, thereby becoming heterotrophs. Heterotrophs could not produce their own food and fed off organic materials. However, they released carbon dioxide which allowed for the evolution of **autotrophs**, which could produce their own food through photosynthesis. The autotrophs and heterotrophs became the dominant life forms and evolved into the diverse forms of life we see today.

Proponents of **creationism** believe that the species we currently have were created as recounted in the book of Genesis in the Bible. This retelling asserts that God created all life about 6,000 years ago in one mass creation event. However, scientific evidence casts doubt on creationism.

Evolution

The most significant evidence to support the history of evolution is fossils, which have been used to construct a fossil record. Fossils give clues as to the structure of organisms and the times at which they existed. However, there are limitations to the study of fossils, which leave huge gaps in the fossil record.

Scientists also try to relate two organisms by comparing their internal and external structures. This is called **comparative anatomy**. Comparative anatomy categorizes anatomical structures as **homologous** (features in different species that point to a common ancestor), **analogous** (structures that have superficial similarities because of similar functions, but do not point to a common ancestor), and **vestigial** (structures that have no modern function, indicating that different species diverged and evolved). Through the study of **comparative embryology**, homologous structures that do not appear in mature organisms may be found between different species in their embryological development.

There have been two basic **theories of evolution: Lamarck's and Darwin's**. Lamarck's theory that proposed that an organism can change its structure through use or disuse and that acquired traits can be inherited has been disproved.

Darwin's theory of **natural selection** is the basis of all evolutionary theory. His theory has four basic points:

1. Each species produces more offspring than can survive.
2. The individual organisms that make up a larger population are born with certain variations.
3. The overabundance of offspring creates competition for survival among individual organisms (**survival of the fittest**).
4. Variations are passed down from parent to offspring.

Points 2 and 4 form the genetic basis for evolution.

New species develop from two types of evolution: divergent and convergent. **Divergent evolution**, also known as **speciation**, is the divergence of a new species from a previous form of that species. There are two main ways in which speciation may occur: **allopatric speciation** (resulting from geographical isolation so that species cannot interbreed) and **adaptive radiation** (creation of several new species from a single parent species). **Convergent evolution** is a process whereby different species develop similar traits from inhabiting similar environments, facing similar selection pressures, and/or use parts of their bodies for similar functions. This type of evolution is only superficial. It can never result in two species being able to interbreed.

Skill 55.3 Demonstrates an understanding of how tectonic forces have shaped landforms over time.

Data obtained from many sources led scientists to develop the theory of plate tectonics. This theory is the most current model that explains not only the movement of the continents, but also the changes in the earth's crust caused by internal forces.

Plates are rigid blocks of earth's crust and upper mantle. These rigid solid blocks make up the lithosphere. The earth's lithosphere is broken into nine large sections and several small ones. These moving slabs are called plates. The major plates are named after the continents they are "transporting."

The plates float on and move with a layer of hot, plastic-like rock in the upper mantle. Geologists believe that the heat currents circulating within the mantle cause this plastic zone of rock to slowly flow, carrying along the overlying crustal plates.

Movement of these crustal plates creates areas where the plates diverge as well as areas where the plates converge. A major area of divergence is located in the Mid-Atlantic. Currents of hot mantle rock rise and separate at this point of divergence creating new oceanic crust at the rate of 2 to 10 centimeters per year. Convergence is when the oceanic crust collides with either another oceanic plate or a continental plate. The oceanic crust sinks forming an enormous trench and generating volcanic activity. Convergence also includes continent to continent plate collisions. When two plates slide past one another a transform fault is created.

These movements produce many major features of the earth's surface, such as mountain ranges, volcanoes, and earthquake zones. Most of these features are located at plate boundaries, where the plates interact by spreading apart, pressing together, or sliding past each other. These movements are very slow, averaging only a few centimeters a year.

Boundaries form between spreading plates where the crust is forced apart in a process called rifting. Rifting generally occurs at mid-ocean ridges. Rifting can also take place within a continent, splitting the continent into smaller landmasses that drift away from each other, thereby forming an ocean basin between them. The Red Sea is a product of rifting. As the seafloor spreading takes place, new material is added to the inner edges of the separating plates. In this way the plates grow larger, and the ocean basin widens. This is the process that broke up the super continent Pangaea and created the Atlantic Ocean.

Boundaries between plates that are colliding are zones of intense crustal activity. When a plate of ocean crust collides with a plate of continental crust, the more dense oceanic plate slides under the lighter continental plate and plunges into the mantle. This process is called **subduction**, and the site where it takes place is called a subduction zone. A subduction zone is usually seen on the sea-floor as a deep depression called a trench.

The crustal movement which is identified by plates sliding sideways past each other produces a plate boundary characterized by major faults that are capable of unleashing powerful earth-quakes. The San Andreas Fault forms such a boundary between the Pacific Plate and the North American Plate.

Skill 55.4 Understands the formation of fossils and the importance of the fossil record in explaining the earth's history.

A fossil is the remains or trace of an ancient organism that has been preserved naturally in the Earth's crust. Sedimentary rocks usually are rich sources of fossil remains. Those fossils found in layers of sediment were embedded in the slowly forming sedimentary rock strata. The oldest fossils known are the traces of 3.5 billion year old bacteria found in sedimentary rocks. Few fossils are found in metamorphic rock and virtually none found in igneous rocks. The magma is so hot that any organism trapped in the magma is destroyed.

The fossil remains of a woolly mammoth embedded in ice were found by a group of Russian explorers. However, the best-preserved animal remains have been discovered in natural tar pits. When an animal accidentally fell into the tar, it became trapped sinking to the bottom. Preserved bones of the saber-toothed cat have been found in tar pits.

Prehistoric insects have been found trapped in ancient amber or fossil resin that was excreted by some extinct species of pine trees.

Fossil molds are the hollow spaces in a rock previously occupied by bones or shells. A fossil cast is a fossil mold that fills with sediments or minerals that later hardens forming a cast.

Fossil tracks are the imprints in hardened mud left behind by birds or animals.

COMPETENCY 56.0 THE TEACHER HAS THEORETICAL AND PRACTICAL KNOWLEDGE ABOUT TEACHING SCIENCE AND ABOUT HOW STUDENTS LEARN SCIENCE.

Skill 56.1 Understands how the developmental characteristics, prior knowledge and experience, and attitudes of students influence science learning.

Learning styles refers to the ways in which individuals learn best. Physical settings, instructional arrangements, materials available, techniques, and individual preferences are all factors in the teacher's choice of instructional strategies and materials. Information about the student's preference can be done through a direct interview or a Likert-style checklist where the student rates his preferences.

Physical Settings

A. **Noise**: Students vary in the degree of quiet that they need and the amount of background noise or talking that they can tolerate without getting distracted or frustrated.

B. **Temperature and Lighting**: Students also vary in their preference for lighter or darker areas of the room, tolerance for coolness or heat, and ability to see the chalkboard, screen, or other areas of the room.

C. **Physical Factors**: This refers to the student's need for workspace and preference for type of work area, such as desk, table, or learning center. Proximity factors such as closeness to other students, the teacher or high traffic areas such as doorways or pencil sharpeners, may help the student to feel secure and stay on task, or may serve as distractions, depending on the individual.

Instructional Arrangements
Some students work well in large groups; others prefer small groups or one-to-one instruction with the teacher, aide or volunteer. Instructional arrangements also involve peer-tutoring situations with the student as tutor or tutee. The teacher also needs to consider how well the student works independently with seatwork.

Instructional Techniques
Consideration of the following factors will affect the teacher's choice of instructional techniques, as well as selecting optimal times to schedule certain types of assignments. Some of these factors are listed below:

- How much time the student needs to complete work
- Time of day the student works best
- How student functions under timed conditions

- How much teacher demonstration and attention is needed for the task
- The student's willingness to approach new tasks
- Student's willingness to give up
- Student's preference for verbal or written instruction
- Student's frustration tolerance when faced with difficulty
- Number of prompts, cues, and attention needed for the student to maintain expected behavior

Material and Textbook Preferences

Students vary in their ability to respond and learn with different techniques of lesson presentation. They likewise vary in their preference and ability to learn with different types of materials. Depending on the student's preference and success, the teacher can choose from among these types of instructional materials:

- Self-correcting materials
- Worksheets wit or without visual cues
- Worksheets with a reduced number of items or lots of writing space
- Manipulative materials
- Flash cards, commercial or student-prepared
- Computers
- Commercial materials
- Teacher-made materials
- Games, board or card
- Student-made instructional materials

Learning Styles

Students also display preferences for certain learning styles and these differences are also factors in the teacher's choice of presentation and materials.

A) **Visual:** Students who are visual may enjoy working with and remember best from books, films, pictures, pictures, modeling, overheads, demonstrating and writing.

B) **Auditory:** Students who are auditory may enjoy working with and remember best from hearing records of tapes, auditory directions, listening to people, radio, read-aloud stories, and lectures.

C) **Tactile:** Indicators are drawing, tracing, manipulating and working with materials such as clay or paints.

Kinesthetic: Indicators include learning through writing, experiments, operating machines, such as typewriters or calculators, motor activities and games, and taking pictures.

Skill 56.2   Selects and adapts science curricula, content, instructional materials, and activities to meet the interests, knowledge, understanding, abilities, experiences, and needs of all students, including English Language Learners.

Teaching students of diverse backgrounds is very challenging and must be handled very carefully since the teacher must be politically correct, when handling such students. Apart from that, from a humanitarian point of view, the teacher needs to be compassionate and empathetic, since it is a challenge to settle in a different country and call it home.

The lesson plans must reflect the teachers understanding and respect towards the diverse students.

One of the things is to incorporate the different cultural practices into the lessons and connect with science. For example, studying the contributions to science made by the Latino scientists, the African American scientists, the native American scientists, the Asian scientists etc. In February, we can study about famous scientists of African American origin. Same thing goes with other cultures. When this is done, the students feel very happy and appreciate the effort and thought of their teacher, who took time to recognize their heritage.

Decorating the classroom using ethnic material would be interesting and also creates an atmosphere of being at home. Incorporating the cultural and linking them to science needs a little bit of time and ingenuity, which will go a long way in establishing good relationships with students and their families.

Skill 56.3   Understands how to use situations from students' daily lives to develop instructional materials that investigate how science can be used to make informed decisions.

Before the teacher begins instruction, he or she should choose activities that are at the appropriate level of student difficulty, are meaningful, and relevant. Because biology is the study of living things, we can easily apply the knowledge of biology to daily life and personal decision-making. For example, biology greatly influences the health decisions humans make everyday. What foods to eat, when and how to exercise, and how often to bathe are just three of the many decisions we make everyday that are based on our knowledge of biology. Other areas of daily life where biology affects decision-making are parenting, interpersonal relationships, family planning, and consumer spending.

Skill 56.4   Understands common misconceptions in science and effective ways to address these misconceptions.

There are many common misconceptions about science. The following are a few scientific misconceptions that are or have been common in the past:

* The Earth is the center of the solar system.
* The Earth is the largest object in the solar system
* Rain comes from the holes in the clouds
* Acquired characters can be inherited
* The eye receives upright images
* Energy is a thing
* Heat is not energy

Some strategies to uncover and dispel misconceptions include:

1. Planning appropriate activities, so that the students will see for themselves where there are misconceptions.

2. Web search is a very useful tool to dispel misconceptions. Students need to be guided in how to look for answers on the Web, and if necessary the teacher should explain scientific literature to help the students understand it.

3. Science journals are a great source of information. Recent research is highly beneficial for the senior science students.

4. Critical thinking and reasoning are two important skills that the students should be encouraged to use to discover facts – for example, that heat is a form of energy. Here, the students have to be challenged to use their critical thinking skills to reason that heat can cause change – for example, causing water to boil – and so it is not a thing but a form of energy, since only energy can cause change.

Skill 56.5   Understands the rationale for the use of active learning and inquiry processes for students.

The purpose of practice is to help the student move through the acquisition of learning a skill (initial learning), to maintenance (remembering how to do the skill), to generalization (applying the skill to new or different situations),

During guided or semi-independent practice, the teacher should provide specific directions and model the procedure on the practice materials while the student follows along. Gradually, the teacher prompts, and modeling will fade out as the student becomes more proficient. The teacher should apply positive and corrective feedback at this stage.

During independent practice, the teacher's role is to monitor the students and provide individual attention and modeling as necessary. The student should be encouraged to "think aloud" so the teacher can monitor what strategies and problem-solving skills are being used to answer questions. Again, positive and/or corrective feedback with praise should be used for achievement.

Transfer of learning occurs when experience with one task influences performance on another task. Positive transfer occurs when the required responses are about the same and the stimuli are similar, such as moving from baseball, handball, to racquetball, or field hockey to soccer. Negative transfer occurs when the stimuli remain similar, but the required responses change, such as shifting from soccer to football, tennis to racquetball, and boxing to sports karate. Instructional procedures should stress the similar features between the activities and the dimensions that are transferable. Specific information should emphasize when stimuli in the old and new situations are the same as or similar, and when responses used in the old situation apply to the new.

To facilitate learning, instructional objectives should be arranged in order according to their patterns of similarity. Objectives involving similar responses should be closely sequenced; thus, the possibility for positive transfer is stressed. Likewise, learning objectives that involve different responses should be programmed within instructional procedures in the most appropriate way possible. For example, students should have little difficulty transferring handwriting instruction to writing in other areas; however, there might be some negative transfer when moving from manuscript to cursive writing. By using transitional methods and focusing upon the similarities between manuscript and cursive writing, negative transfer can be reduced.

Generalization is the occurrence of a learned behavior in the presence of a stimulus other than the one that produced the initial response (e.g. novel stimulus). It is the expansion of a student's performance beyond conditions initially anticipated. Students must be able to generalize what is learned to other settings.

Generalization may be enhanced by the following:

1. Use many examples in teaching to deepen application of learned skills.
2. Use consistency in initial teaching situations, and later introduce variety in format, procedure, and use of examples.
3. Have the same information presented by different teachers, in different settings, and under varying conditions.
4. Include a continuous reinforcement schedule at first, later changing to delayed, and intermittent schedules as instruction progresses.

5. Teach students to record instances of generalization and to reward themselves at that time.
6. Associate naturally occurring stimuli when possible.

Skill 56.6 Understands questioning strategies designed to elicit higher-level thinking and how to use them to move students from concrete to more abstract understanding.

Inquiry learning provides opportunities for students to experience and acquire thought processes through which they can gather information about the world. This requires a higher level of interaction among the learner, the teacher, the area of study, available resources, and the learning environment. Students become actively involved in the learning process as they :

1. Act upon their curiosity and interests
2. Develop questions that are relevant
3. Think their way through controversies or dilemmas
4. Analyze problems
5. Develop, clarify, and test hypotheses
6. Draw conclusions
7. Find possible solutions

The most important element in inquiry-based learning is questioning. Students must ask relevant questions and develop ways to search for answers and generate explanations. High order thinking is encouraged.
Here are some **inquiry strategies**:

1. Deductive inquiry: The main goal of this strategy is moving the student from a generalized principle to specific instances. The process of testing general assumptions, applying them, and exploring the relationships between specific elements is stressed. The teacher coordinates the information and presents important principles, themes, or hypotheses. Students are actively engaged in testing generalizations, gathering information, and applying it to specific examples.

2. Inductive inquiry: The information-seeking process of the inductive inquiry method helps students to establish facts, determine relevant questions, and develop ways to pursue these questions and build explanations. Students are encouraged to develop and support their own hypotheses. Through inductive inquiry, students experience the thought processes which require them to move from specific facts and observations to inferences.

3. Interactive instruction: This strategy relies heavily on discussion and sharing among participants. Students develop social skills, learning from teacher and peers. They also learn organizational skills. Examples are debates, brainstorming, discussion, laboratory groups, etc.

4. Direct instruction strategy: This is highly teacher-oriented and is among the most commonly used strategies. It is effective for providing information or developing step-by-step skills. Examples are lecture, demonstrations, explicit teaching, etc.

5. Indirect instruction: This is mainly student-centered. Direct and indirect instruction strategies can compliment each other. Indirect instruction seeks a high level of student involvement such as observing, investigating, drawing inferences from data, or forming hypotheses. In this strategy, the role of the teacher shifts from that of teacher/lecturer to that of facilitator, supporter, and resource person.
Examples are problem solving, inquiry, concept formation, etc.

6. Independent study: Independent study refers to the range of instructional methods that are purposely provided to foster the development of individual student initiative, self reliance, and self improvement. Examples are research projects, homework, etc.

The above mentioned strategies promote higher-level thinking skills such as problem solving, synthesizing (hypothesizing), designing (identifying the problem), analyzing (analyzing data in an experiment), and connecting (logical thinking).

Skill 56.7   Understands the importance of planning activities that are inclusive and accommodate the needs of all students.

The term diversity is defined as the presence of a wide range of variation in the qualities or attributes under discussion.

In the human context, particularly in a social context, the term diversity refers to the presence in one population of a variety of cultures, ethnic groups, languages, physical features, socio-economic backgrounds, religious faiths, sexuality, gender identity and neurology.

At the international level, diversity refers to the existence of many peoples contributing their unique experiences to humanity's culture.

In a class, there may be students from different ethnicities, cultures, nationalities etc. The teacher as an adult, is responsible for recognizing the diversity of the students, respect their cultures and to plan lessons keeping in mind the various students who are diverse and for some of them, their first language is not English.

Skill 56.8   Understands how to sequence learning activities in a way that allows students to build upon their prior knowledge and challenges them to expand their understanding of science.

Subject matter should be presented in a fashion that helps students <u>organize, understand,</u> and <u>remember</u> important information. Advance organizers and other instructional devices can help students to:

- Connect information to what is already known
- Make abstract ideas more concrete
- Capture students' interest in the material
- Help students to organize the information and visualize the relationships.

Organizers can be visual aids such as diagrams, tables, charts, guides or verbal cues that alert students to the nature and content of the lesson. Organizers may be used:

- **Before the lesson** to alert the student the student to the main point of the lesson, establish a rationale for learning, and activate background information.
- **During the lesson** to help students organize information, keep focused on important points, and aid comprehension.
- **At the close of the lesson** to summarize and remember important points.

Examples of organizers include:
- Question and graphic-oriented study guide.
- Concept diagramming: students brainstorm a concept and organize information into three lists (always present, sometimes present, and never present).
- Semantic feature analysis: students construct a table with examples of the concept in one column and important features or characteristics in the other column opposite.
- Semantic webbing: The concept is placed in the middle of the chart or chalkboard and relevant information is placed around it. Lines show the relationships.
- Memory (mnemonic) devices. Diagrams charts and tables

COMPETENCY 57.0 THE TEACHER UNDERSTANDS THE PROCESS OF SCIENTIFIC INQUIRY AND ITS ROLE IN SCIENCE INSTRUCTION.

Skill 57.1 Plans and implements instruction that provides opportunities for all students to engage in non-experimental and experimental inquiry investigations.

Individual teaching should be the method for exceptional students and those who need more attention than the regular student. A few minutes of explaining the lesson or the task on hand will be very helpful. In the case of pair share or collaborative pairs, a small assignment could be given and a time frame set, at the end of which students will share as a class what they have learned. This is very good if an exceptional student and a bright student are paired. A small group is very productive since there are many things involved in that situation, such as sharing information, waiting for one's turn, listening to other's ideas, views, and suggestions, and taking responsibility for doing a job in the group (writing/presenting/drawing etc.) which also teach basic manners. Teaching as a class involves traditional and modern methods such as lecture, lecture/demonstration, pause and lecture, etc. The same applies for experimental, field and nonexperimental work.

Today's learning, especially science, is largely inquiry-based. Sometimes it becomes part of teaching to encourage the students to ask questions. Sufficient time must be given to students to ask these questions.

As a teacher, one must be a good manager of not only the classroom but also of time, resources, and space. The teacher needs to plan how much time should be given to exceptional students, bright students, regular students, and disruptive students. The exceptional and the disruptive students must get more of the teacher's time. Next will be the regular and last the bright students, since they are a few steps ahead of the rest. If they finish work quickly, however, bright students need to be engaged, so some extra work must be available. In terms of space the same things apply. Resources must be shared equally as far as possible, since everybody has the right to have equal opportunity. However, there must be modification of resources suitable for the exceptional students, if required.

One thing is most important - a teacher must use logic and be able to think laterally since all the answers are not in books. The best teaching is part original thinking and part innovation and ingenuity.

Skill 57.2 **Focuses inquiry-based instruction on questions and issues relevant to students and uses strategies to assist students with generating, refining, and focusing scientific questions and hypotheses.**

Scientific questions are very important because they are the starting point for learning. Students need to be encouraged, provoked and challenged to ask questions. The questions need not necessarily make sense at the beginning, but as the time goes by, these questions begin to make lot of sense.

The first and foremost thing is to encourage the students to ask **questions**. They need to learn to frame questions.

There are a few ways in which the students can be encouraged to ask questions:
1. Brainstorming the topic under study
2. Discussing it in the class and inviting students to ask questions
3. By letting students discuss in small groups and come up with questions - this is extremely useful to students who are introverts and shy by nature.

There can be other ways as well besides those mentioned above. The teacher must realize that questioning is an important tool in teaching and it can be an effective in learning as well. It must be mentioned here that not all students are curious and inquisitive. Not all parents encourage their children to ask questions. In such cases the teacher needs to show lot of patience in encouraging the students to be inquisitive and curious. This takes time and with time, this could be achieved to a large extent.

The next step in this process of teaching students to question is, **refining** questions. By now the students have learned to ask questions. These questions may not be completely relevant to the topic under discussion, but still the students have a set of questions. It is the responsibility of the teacher to take these questions and to convert them to "How" and "Why" type of open ended questions. Many times the students may end up asking questions such as: Who landed on the moon? These sorts of questions are not really knowledge generating questions. They are not thought provoking questions. The teacher can modify this question to " what did the missions to moon accomplish? With this type of question, a lot of discussion will be generated. Who landed on the moon first, as well as the weather of the moon, moon rock samples, etc.

The next step is **focusing**. The questions need to be focused on the topic under discussion or investigation. Focusing is absolutely important because it is very easy to be carried away and to be side tracked. The students need to be made aware of being able to focus on a topic understand and not to deviating from it, however tempting it may be.

The last step in this is **testing scientific questions and hypotheses.** All questions can not be tested. Some questions can answered by research. Like the question that was cited above regarding the moon, can not be tested, but on the other hand, can be answered by research. A wealth of information could be discovered and most of the questions will be answered.

However, some questions can be tested and answers could be found. For example, "which fertilizer is best for rose cuttings? This kind of questions will be best answered by experimentation.

Skill 57.3   Instructs students in the safe and proper use of a variety of grade-appropriate tools, equipment, resources, technology, and techniques to access, gather, store, retrieve, organize, and analyze data.

Some of the most common laboratory techniques are: dissections, preserving, staining and mounting microscopic specimens, and preparing laboratory solutions.

1. Dissections

Animals that are not obtained from recognized sources should not be used. Decaying animals or those of unknown origin may harbor pathogens and/or parasites. Specimens should be rinsed before handling. Latex gloves are desirable. If gloves are not available, students with sores or scratches should be excused from the activity. Formaldehyde is a carcinogenic and should be avoided or disposed of according to district regulations. Students objecting to dissections for moral reasons should be given an alternative assignment.

Live specimens - No dissections may be performed on living mammalian vertebrates or birds. Lower order life and invertebrates may be used. Biological experiments may be done with all animals except mammalian vertebrates or birds. No physiological harm may result to the animal. All animals housed and cared for in the school must be handled in a safe and humane manner. Animals are not to remain on school premises during extended vacations unless adequate care is provided. Many state laws state that any instructor who intentionally refuses to comply with the laws may be suspended or dismissed. Interactive dissections are available online or from software companies for those students who object to performing dissections. There should be no penalty for those students who refuse to physically perform a dissection.

2. Staining

Specimens have to be stained because they are mostly transparent (except plant cells which are green) under the microscope and are difficult to be seen under microscope against a white background. The stains add color to the picture, making the image much easier to see. The stains actually work by fixing themselves to various structures on or in the cell. The exact structure determines the staining process used.

It is amazing to know that the variety of stains available are numerous, and are a vital tool to determine what the cellular components are made of starch, protein and even nucleic acids can be brought out using special stains.

Some common stains used in the laboratories are methylene blue, chlorazol black, lignin pink, gentian violet, etc.

3. Mounting of specimens

In order to observe microscopic specimens or minute parts, mounting them on a microscope slide is essential. There are two different ways of mounting. One kind of procedure is adapted for keeping mounted slides for a long time to be used again. The second type of procedure is for temporary slides. We will discus about temporary mounting since 12th Grade students are mostly concerned with the temporary mounting. Their work does not require permanent mounting.

Water is a very common mounting medium in High school laboratories since it is cheap and best suited for temporary mounting. One problem with water mounting is water evaporates.

Glycerin is also used for mounting. One advantage with glycerin is that it is non-toxic and is stable for years. It provides good contrast to the specimens under microscopic examination. The only problem with glycerin as a medium is it supports mold formation.

3a. Care of microscopes

Light microscopes are commonly used in high school laboratory experiments. Total magnification is determined by multiplying the ocular (usually 10X) and the objective (usually 10X on low, 40X on high) lenses. A few steps should be followed to properly care for this equipment.

-Clean all lenses with lens paper only.
-Carry microscopes with two hands, one on the arm and one on the base.
-Always begin focusing on low power, then switch to high power.
-Store microscopes with the low power objective down.
-Always use a cover slip when viewing wet mount slides.
-Bring the objective down to its lowest position then focus moving up to avoid the slide from breaking or scratching.

4. Preparation of laboratory solutions

This is a critical skill needed for any experimental success. The procedure for making solutions must be followed to get maximum accuracy.

    A. weigh out the required amount of each solute
    B. dissolve the solute in less than the total desired volume (about 75%)
    C. add enough solvent to get the desired volume

1. Weight/volume:

Usually expressed as mg/ml for small amounts of chemicals and other specialized biological solutions. e.g. 100 mg/ml ampicillin = 100 mg. of ampicillin dissolved in 1 ml of water.

2. Molarity: moles of solute dissolved/ liter of solution

    Mole = 6.02 times 10^23 atoms = Avagadro's number
    Mole = gram formula weight (FW) or gram molecular weight (MW)

* These values are usually found on the labels or in Periodic Table.
e.g. Na2SO4

2 sodium atoms - 2 times 22.99g = 45.98 g
1 sulfur atom   - 1 times 32.06g = 32.06 g
4 oxygen atoms – 4 times16.00g = 64.00 g
    Total   = 142.04g

1M = 1 mole/liter, 1 mM = 1 millimole/liter, 1 uM = 1 umole/liter

* How much sodium is needed to make 1L of 1M solution?
Formula weight of sodium sulfate = 142.04g
Dissolve 142.04g of sodium sulfate in about 750mL of water, dissolve sodium sulfate thoroughly and make up the volume to 1liter (L)

Skill 57.4   Knows how to guide students in making systematic observations and measurements.

The starting point for any science is systematic observation. Systematic observation is observing and recording the occurrence of certain specific (naturally occurring) behaviors.

There are four descriptive observation methods:

1. Naturalistic observation: observers record occurrence of naturally occurring behavior.

2. Systematic observation: observers record the occurrence of certain specific (naturally occurring) behaviors.

3. Case study: gather detailed information about one individual.

4. Archival research: use existing behavior to establish occurrence of behavior. With each type of approach, there are potential problems and limitations. Systematic observation emphasizes gathering quantitative data on certain specific behaviors. The researcher is interested in a limited set of behaviors. This allows them to study and test specific hypotheses.

The first step is to develop a coding system. The coding system is a description of behaviors and how they will be recorded. The key idea is to delimit the range of behaviors that are observed. The operational definitions of each behavior that will be recorded are defined, and occurrence of each behavior and its duration is recorded.

For example, consider the recording of animal behavior. Potential problems that can occur during the observation include:

1. Remaining vigilant: Following an animal in its natural habitat is difficult, especially when human presence is required. Recording devices (audio, video) are used to deal with this problem.

2. Reactivity: Humans and animals often change their behavior when they are being observed. The observer must take steps to remain unobtrusive or become a participant observer.

3. Reliability: Ensuring that the coding of behavior is accurate (two or more observers are used consistently and their results compared). This is known as inter-rater or inter-observer reliability.

4. Sampling: Setting up a schedule of observation intervals, using multiple observations over a range of time. This measures the behavior of an animal over a period of time and is considered to be reliable.

It is the responsibility of the teacher to introduce the process of systematic observation to students in a meaningful way. It is also the responsibility of the teacher to instruct students on how to take correct scientific measurements.

Measurements in science

In science the system of measurements is called the SI or Standard International system of units, or Systeme Internacionale in French. This method is a refined version of the Metric system used in France. This method is unique in that all the measurements are in multiples of tens, which makes it very easy to do basic mathematical operations such as multiplication and division.

SI prefixes:

kilo - k - 1000
hecto - h -   100
deka - da -   10
deci - d   -   0.1 (1/10)
centi - c   -   0.01 (1/100)
milli - m -   0.001 (1/1000)

Length: The SI units of length are millimeter, centimeter, meter and kilometer.
10 millimeters make 1 centimeter
100 centimeters make 1 meter
1000 meters make 1 kilometer

Mass and weight:
The SI units of mass and weight are milligrams and kilograms
1000 milligrams make 1 kilogram

Volume:
The SI units of volume are milliliters and liters.
There are 1000 milliliters in a liter.

Time:
This is the same in any system of measurement.

Temperature:
The SI scale for measuring temperature is Kelvin (K). Scientists also use Celsius for temperature measurement.

Skill 57.5   Knows how to promote the use of critical-thinking skills, logical reasoning, and scientific problem solving to reach conclusions based on evidence.

It is imperative that teachers are able to teach students to use the skills necessary to evaluate scientific principles and ideas, as well as lead students to their own discoveries. This promotes a better understanding of science and its topics of study. Critical-thinking skills are a necessity for a student to adequately understand all processes of science. For example, students must be able to apply the principles of sciences to the question being considered. It requires a higher level thinking in students, rather than just a repeat of terms or facts found in the text. A good example of a higher level thinking or critical-thinking question would be as follows.

If five appliances are all in place in a parallel circuit and all separately connected to the voltage source, and there is a microwave plugged in at the beginning of the circuit, will all the appliances still operate? Why or why not?

Asking such questions force student to think about the answer rather than just define a vocabulary term. Using logical reasoning skills are equally as important for students' understanding. Logical reasoning skills involve comprehending what the scientific possibilities are and how the possibilities may occur. For example, when studying earthquakes and natural disasters, students should be able to reason that fault lines which normally have some movement, and have not moved in the past ten years, would be expected within the next few years to produce major movements resulting in an earthquake.

Finally, scientific problem solving will lead students to a greater understanding of scientific tools and processes. Scientific problem solving involves inquiry, assessment, lastly solving or drawing conclusions. This can be observed in each step of The Scientific Method. Students should be given the opportunity to test problem solving during a display of their scientific knowledge. An excellent opportunity for this display is during a science fair or an engineering fair. Students should build, develop, and display their findings.

Skill 57.6   Knows how to teach students to develop, analyze, and evaluate different explanations for a given scientific result.

Testing of scientific questions can be carried out by the using scientific method. This is a process consisting of a series of steps, designed to solve a problem. This method is designed is designed in such a way that most of our bias / prejudices are eliminated.

This method consists of the following steps:

1. Question / problem: any investigation, big or small has a beginning as a question / problem. It is important to begin with a well-defined problem. The problem needs to be stated in simple and clear language. Any body who reads the problem should be able to understand it.

2. Gathering information: It is very important that relevant information is gathered for a better understanding of the problem.

3. Forming a hypothesis: Hypothesis is otherwise known as an educated guess. It is based on information and knowledge and that is the reason why it is called an educated guess.
Again, hypothesis needs to be simple and put in clear language for any body to understand.

4. The fourth step is **designing an experiment**. This involves identifying control / standard, the constants and the variables. There has to be a control /standard for any experiment to compare the results with at the end of the experiment. Some things have to be kept constant through out the experiment. The more constants an experiment has, the better the experiment. Variables are of two types - the first one, independent variables that the experimenter changes, and the dependent variable, which is the factor that is measured in an experiment. Independent variables are the ones that are tested in an experiment. These should not be more than four in an ideal experiment. If there are more independent variables, the experiment gets complicated and tedious usually resulting in the experimenter losing interest. There should be only one dependent variable. More than one dependent veritable complicates an experiment at the High School level. Students need to be educated to do quality science experiments and get good results than doing complicated and lengthy experiments. All experiments must be repeated twice, which means there are three sets of data, since reliability of results is absolutely important science experiments.

5. Analyzing data: The data collected must well presented by graphing and in tables and analyzed for any patterns that may be. The numbers are important, but the students must be trained to recognize patterns and trends, which are very important.

6. Conclusion: Drawing conclusions is very important because those are the answers for the question the students started with. Conclusions are very important. The conclusion tells us whether the hypothesis is proved or disproved. If the hypothesis is disproved after experimentation, the hypothesis needs to be modified.

The teacher must emphasize one important thing - data must be recorded truthfully and that calls for honesty and integrity.

Skill 57.7   Knows how to teach students to demonstrate an understanding of potential sources of error in inquiry-based investigation.

Students should be taught that there are many ways in which errors could creep in measurements. Errors in measurements could occur because of:

1. Improper use of instruments used for measuring – weighing etc.
2. Parallax error – not positioning the eyes during reading of measurements
3. Not using same instruments and methods of measurement during an experiment
4. Not using the same source of materials, resulting in the content of a certain compound used for experimentation

Besides these mentioned above, there could be other possible sources of error as well. When erroneous results are used for interpreting data, the conclusions are not reliable. An experiment is valid only when all the constants (time, place, method of measurement, etc.) are strictly controlled. Students should be aware of this when conducting investigations.

Skill 57.8 Knows how to teach students to demonstrate an understanding of how to communicate and defend the results of an inquiry-based investigation.

Conclusions must be communicated by clearly describing the information using accurate data, visual presentation and other appropriate media such as a power point presentation. Examples of visual presentations are graphs (bar/line/pie), tables/charts, diagrams, and artwork. Modern technology must be used whenever necessary. The method of communication must be suitable to the audience. Written communication is as important as oral communication. The scientist's strongest ally is a solid set of reproducible data.

COMPETENCY 58.0 THE TEACHER KNOWS THE VARIED AND APPROPRIATE ASSESSMENTS AND ASSESSMENT PRACTICES TO MONITOR SCIENCE LEARNING IN LABORATORY, FIELD, AND CLASSROOM SETTINGS.

Skill 58.1 Understands the relationships among science curriculum, assessment, and instruction and bases instruction on information gathered through assessment of students' strengths and needs.

All children enrolled in our educational system will experience testing throughout their schooling, whether it is preschool sensory screenings, teacher-made quizzes, or annual standardized assessments. Assessment is continuous, and occurs on a regular basis. There are a variety of assessment instruments: standardized, criterion-referenced, curriculum-based, and teacher-made. Teachers in the field should possess sufficient knowledge to be able to determine quantitative dimensions such as the validity and reliability of tests, to recognize sound test content, and to choose appropriate tests for specific purposes. Continuous assessment allows the teacher to direct, and sometimes redirect, resources appropriately.

Skill 58.2 Understands the importance of monitoring and assessing students' understanding of science concepts and skills on an ongoing basis.

Much of science is based on past research. Because the concepts build upon one another it is vital that the student understands all previous concepts. For instance, a child who does not sufficiently grasp the difference between chemical and physical properties will be unable to make the leap towards understanding chemical reactions, nor would s/he then understand the law of conservation of matter. For this reason, assessment should occur regularly. Where a student or students is/are not proficient, the subject matter should be covered again to enhance understanding.

Skill 58.3 Understands the importance of carefully selecting or designing formative and summative assessments for the specific decisions they are intended to inform.

Formative assessment is the sum of all activities undertaken by teachers and by their students that provide information. That information can be considered feedback, and the teacher should modify the teaching and learning activities in response.

Teachers are responsible for assessment. They are required to give a report on each student's progress to both parents and administrators, as well as above and beyond regular administrators (often state mandates require a report as well). These reports inform parents, other teachers, officials, and also serve accountability purposes. In addition, other teachers are informed in regards to placement and teaching skills necessary for students to be successful. Teachers must take on multiple roles and must use formative assessment to help support and enhance student learning. The teacher ultimately decides the future for most students and must make summative judgments about a student's achievement at a specific point in time for purposes of placement, grading, accountability, and informing parents and future teachers about student performance. Teachers have special skills and observe students on a daily basis therefore giving them the power to use their perspective and knowledge to make recommendations for students in the future. Teachers are able to observe and assess over a period of time. This assessment may conflict with other performances and a teacher may be able to make better recommendations for students. Teachers must also remember that assessment-based judgments must be adjusted and reexamined over long periods of time to insure that conclusions are accurate.

Summative assessments are typically used to evaluate instructional programs and services. Typically these take place at the end of each school year. The overall goal of summative assessments is to make a judgment of student competency after an instructional phase is complete, in an attempt to see what has been learned or mastered by the students. Summative evaluations are used to determine if students have mastered specific competencies and to identify instructional areas that need additional attention. Some formative and summative assessments that are common in K-12 schools are listed below:

Formative Assessments	Summative Assessments
Anecdotal records	Final Exams
Quizzes and essays	State wide tests
Diagnostic tests	National tests
Lab reports	Entrance exams (SAT & ACT)

Skill 58.4   Selects or designs and administers a variety of appropriate assessment methods (e.g., performance assessment, self-assessment, formal/informal, formative/summative) to monitor students understanding and progress.

Some assessment methods can be both formal and informal tools. For example, observation may incorporate structured observation instruments as well as other informal observation procedures, including professional judgment. When evaluating a child's developmental level, a professional may use a formal adaptive rating scale while simultaneously using professional judgment to assess the child's motivation and behavior during the evaluation process.

Curriculum-Based Assessment—Assessment of an individual's performance of objectives of a curriculum, such as a reading, math, or science program. The individual's performance is measured in terms of what objectives were mastered. This type of testing be verbal, written, or demonstration based. Its general structure may include such factors as how much time to complete, amount to complete, and group or individual testing. The level of response may be multiple choice, essay, or recall of facts.

Momentary time sampling—This is a technique used for measuring behaviors of a group of individuals or several behaviors from the same individual. Time samples are usually brief, and may be conducted at fixed or variable intervals. The advantage of using variable intervals is increased reliability, as the students will not be able to predict when the time sample will be taken.

Multiple Baseline Design—This may be used to test the effectiveness of an intervention in a skill performance or to determine if the intervention accounted for the observed changes in a target behavior. First, the initial baseline data is collected, followed by the data during the intervention period. To get the second baseline, the intervention is removed for a period of time and data is collected again. The intervention is then reapplied, and data collected on the target behavior. An example of a multiple baseline design might be ignoring a child who calls out in class without raising his hand. Initially, the baseline could involve counting the number of times the child calls out before applying interventions. During the time the teacher ignores the child's call-outs, data is collected. For the second baseline, the teacher would resume the response to the child's call-outs in the way she did before ignoring. The child's call-outs would probably increase again, if ignoring actually accounted for the decrease. If the teacher reapplies the ignoring strategy, the child's call-outs would probably decrease again.

Group Tests And Individual Tests

The obvious distinction between a group test and in individual test is that individual tests must be administered to only one person at a time, whereas group tests are administered to several people simultaneously, or can be administered individually. However, there are several other subtle differences.

When administering an individual test, the tester has the opportunity to observe the individual's responses and to determine how such things as problem solving are accomplished. Within limits, the tester is able to control the pace and tempo of the testing session, and to rephrase and probe responses in order to elicit the individual's best performance. If the child becomes tired, the examiner can break between sub tests of end the test; if he loses his place on the test, the tester can help him to regain it; if he dawdles or loses interest, the tester can encourage or redirect him. If the child lacks self-confidence, the examiner can reinforce his efforts. In short, individual tests allow the examiner to encourage best efforts, and to observe how a student uses his skills to answer questions. Thus, individual tests provide for the gathering of both quantitative and qualitative information. On the other hand, with a group test, the examiner may provide oral directions for younger children, but beyond the fourth grade, directions are usually written. The children write or mark their own responses, and the examiner monitors the progress of several students at the same time. He cannot rephrase questions, or probe or prompt responses. Even when a group test is administered to only one child, qualitative information is very difficult, if not impossible, to obtain.

The choice between group and individual testing should be primarily determined by purpose and efficiency. When testing for program evaluation, screening, and some types of program planning (such as tracking), group tests are appropriate. Individual tests could be used but are impractical in terms of time and expense. Special consideration may need to be given if there are any motivational, personalities, linguistic, or physically disabling factors that might impair the examinee's performance on group tests.

Skill 58.5   **Uses formal and informal assessments of student performance and products (e.g., projects, lab journals, rubrics, portfolios, student profiles, checklists) to evaluate student participation in and understanding of the inquiry process.**

It is vital for teachers to track students' performances through a variety of methods. Teachers should be able to asses students on a daily basis using informal assessments such as monitoring during work time, class discussions, and note taking. Often these assessments are a great way to determine whether or not students are "on track" learning selected objectives. Generally teachers can assess students just by class discussion and often this is a great time to give participation points, especially to those students who have special needs and participate well in class but may struggle with alternative assignments. More formal assessments are necessary to ensure students are fully understanding selected objectives. Regular grading using selected performance skills is necessary, however teachers should develop personal ways of grading using a variety of assessment tools. For example, students could keep a "Science Journal" and track progress of ongoing assignments, projects, and labs. Another great tool for observing and evaluating students is the use of rubrics and checklists. Student profiles and checklists are a great way to quickly determine if students are meeting selected objectives. These are useful during monitoring time for teachers. It is easy for a teacher to check off students who are meeting objectives using a checklist while monitoring students' work done in class. See example below:

Student Name	Objective #1	Objective #2	On task
Joe Student	X	X	X
Jon Student		X	X

Checklists provide an easy way for teachers to track students and quickly see who is behind or needs a lesson or objective reviewed.

Skill 58.6   **Understands the importance of sharing evaluation criteria and assessment results with students.**

Effective teachers:
- offer students a safe and supportive learning environment, including clearly expressed and reasonable expectations for behavior;
- create learning environments that encourage self-advocacy and developmentally appropriate independence; and
- offer learning environments that promote active participation in independent or group activities.

Such an environment is an excellent foundation for building rapport and trust with students, and communicating a teacher's respect for and expectation that they take a measure of responsibility for their educational development. Ideally, mutual trust and respect will afford teachers opportunities to learn of and engage students' ideas, preferences and abilities.

Teacher behaviors that motivate students include:

- Maintain Success Expectations through teaching, goal setting, establishing connections between effort and outcome, and self-appraisal and reinforcement.
- Have a supply of intrinsic incentives such as rewards, appropriate competition between students, and the value of the academic activities.
- Focus on students' intrinsic motivation through adapting the tasks to students' interests, providing opportunities for active response, including a variety of tasks, providing rapid feedback, incorporating games into the lesson, allowing students the opportunity to make choices, create, and interact with peers.
- Stimulate students' learning by modeling positive expectations and attributions. Project enthusiasm and personalize abstract concepts. Students will be better motivated if they know what they will be learning about. The teacher should also model problem-solving and task-related thinking so students can see how the process is done.

For adolescents, motivation strategies are usually aimed at getting the student actively involved in the learning process. Since the adolescent has the opportunity to get involved in a wider range of activities outside the classroom (job, car, being with friends), stimulating motivation may be the focus even more than academics. Motivation may be achieved through extrinsic reinforcers or intrinsic reinforcers. This is accomplished by allowing the student a degree of choice in what is being taught or how it will be taught. The teacher will, if possible, obtain a commitment either through a verbal or written contract between the student and the teacher. Adolescents also respond to regular feedback, especially when that feedback shows that they are making progress. Motivation is a key component in learning.

Sample Test: Science

DIRECTIONS: Read each item and select the best response.

1. **Chemicals should be stored**
    (Easy) (Skill 36.2)

    A. in the principal's office.
    B. in a dark room.
    C. in an off-site research facility.
    D. according to their reactivity with other substances.

2. **When measuring the volume of water in a graduated cylinder, where does one read the measurement?**
    (Average Rigor) (Skill 37.2)

    A. At the highest point of the liquid.
    B. At the bottom of the meniscus curve.
    C. At the closest mark to the top of the liquid
    D. At the top of the plastic safety ring.

3. **When is a hypothesis formed?**
    (Easy) (Skill 38.2)

    A. Before the data is taken.
    B. After the data is taken.
    C. After the data is analyzed.
    D. Concurrent with graphing the data.

4. **Which of the following is the most accurate definition of a non-renewable resource?**
    (Average Rigor) (Skill 39.5)

    A. A nonrenewable resource is never replaced once used.
    B. A nonrenewable resource is replaced on a timescale that is very long relative to human life-spans.
    C. A nonrenewable resource is a resource that can only be manufactured by humans.
    D. A nonrenewable resource is a species that has already become extinct.

5. A scientist exposes mice to cigarette smoke, and notes that their lungs develop tumors. Mice that were not exposed to the smoke do not develop as many tumors. Which of the following conclusions may be drawn from these results?:

I. Cigarette smoke causes lung tumors.
II. Cigarette smoke exposure has a positive correlation with lung tumors in mice.
III. Some mice are predisposed to develop lung tumors.
IV. Cigarette smoke exposure has a positive correlation with lung tumors in humans.

(Rigorous) (Skill 40.2)

A. I and II only.
B. II only.
C. I , II, III and IV.
D. II and IV only.

6. Which of the following is a correct explanation for an astronaut's 'weightlessness'?
(Average Rigor) (Skill 41.1)

A. Astronauts continue to feel the pull of gravity in space, but they are so far from planets that the force is small.
B. Astronauts continue to feel the pull of gravity in space, but spacecraft have such powerful engines that those forces dominate, reducing effective weight.
C. Astronauts do not feel the pull of gravity in space, because space is a vacuum.
D. The cumulative gravitational forces, that the astronaut is experiencing, from all sources in the solar system equal out to a net gravitational force of zero.

7. Physical properties are observable characteristics of a substance in its natural state. Which of the following are considered physical properties.

I Color
II Density
III Specific gravity
IV Melting Point
(Rigorous) (Skill 42.1)

A. I only
B. I and II only
C. I, II, and III only
D. III and IV only

8. The change in phase from liquid to gas is called:
    (Rigorous) (Skill 42.2)

    A. Evaporation.
    B. Condensation.
    C. Vaporization.
    D. Boiling.

9. Which of the following statements is true of all transition elements?
    (Rigorous) (Skill 43.3)

    A. They are all hard solids at room temperature.
    B. They tend to form salts when reacted with Halogens.
    C. They all have a silvery appearance in their pure state.
    D. All of the Above

10. A boulder sitting on the edge of a cliff has which type of energy?
    (Easy) (Skill 44.1)

    A. Kinetic energy
    B. Latent Energy
    C. No energy
    D. Potential Energy

11. A converging lens produces a real image
    _____.
    (Rigorous) (Skill 44.4)

    A. always.
    B. never.
    C. when the object is within one focal length of the lens.
    D. when the object is further than one focal length from the lens.

12. Which of the following is not a factor in how different materials will conduct seismic waves?
    (Average Rigor) (Skill 44.6)

    A. Density
    B. Incompressiblity
    C. Rigidty
    D. Tensile strength

13. The Law of Conservation of Energy states that
    _____.
    (Average Rigor) (Skill 45.2)

    A. There must be the same number of products and reactants in any chemical equation.
    B. Mass and energy can be interchanged.
    C. Energy is neither created nor destroyed, but may change form.
    D. One form energy must remain intact (or conserved) in all reactions

14. When you step out of the shower, the floor feels colder on your feet than the bathmat. Which of the following is the correct explanation for this phenomenon?
(Rigorous) (Skill 45.5)

A. The floor is colder than the bathmat.
B. The bathmat being smaller that the floor quickly reaches equilibrium with your body temperature.
C. Heat is conducted more easily into the floor.
D. Water is absorbed from your feet into the bathmat so it doesn't evaporate as quickly as it does off the floor thus not cooling the bathmat as quickly.

15. Identify the correct sequence of organization of living things from lower to higher order:
(Average Rigor) (Skill 46.3)

A. Cell, Organelle, Organ, Tissue, System, Organism.
B. Cell, Tissue, Organ, Organelle, System, Organism.
C. Organelle, Cell, Tissue, Organ, System, Organism.
D. Organelle, Tissue, Cell, Organ, System, Organism.

16. Catalysts assist reactions by _____ .
(Easy) (Skill 46.5)

A. lowering required activation energy.
B. maintaining precise pH levels.
C. keeping systems at equilibrium.
D. changing the starting amounts of reactants.

17. Which process result in a haploid chromosome number?
(Rigorous) (Skill 47.2)

A. Mitosis.
B. Meiosis I.
C. Meiosis II.
D. Neither mitosis nor meiosis.

18. A carrier of a genetic disorder is heterozygous for a disorder that is recessive in nature. Hemophilia is a sex-linked disorder. This means that:
(Easy) (Skill 47.4)

A. Only females can be carriers
B. Only males can be carriers.
C. Both males and females can be carriers.
D. Neither females nor males can be carriers.

19. Which of the following is a correct explanation for scientific biological adaptation?
(Average Rigor) (Skill 48.2)

   A. Giraffes need to reach higher for leaves to eat, so their necks stretch. The giraffe babies are then born with longer necks. Eventually, there are more long-necked giraffes in the population.
   B. Giraffes with longer necks are able to reach more leaves, so they eat more and have more babies than other giraffes. Eventually, there are more long-necked giraffes in the population.
   C. Giraffes want to reach higher for leaves to eat, so they release enzymes into their bloodstream, which in turn causes fetal development of longer-necked giraffes. Eventually, there are more long-necked giraffes in the population.
   D. Giraffes with long necks are more attractive to other giraffes, so they get the best mating partners and have more babies. Eventually, there are more long-necked giraffes in the population.

20. An animal choosing its mate because of attractive plumage or a strong mating call is an example of:
(Average Rigor) (Skill 48.4)

   A. Sexual Selection.
   B. Natural Selection.
   C. Mechanical Isolation.
   D. Linkage

21. Many male birds sing long complicated songs that describe thier identity and the area of land that they claim. Which of the answers below is the best decription of this behavior?
(Rigorous) (Skill 49.1)

   A. Innate territorial behavior
   B. Learned competitve behavior
   C. Innate mating behavior
   D. Learned territorial behavior

22. A wrasse (fish) cleans the teeth of other fish by eating away plaque. This is an example of _____ between the fish.
(Average Rigor) (Skill 50.2)

   A. parasitism.
   B. symbiosis (mutualism).
   C. competition.
   D. predation.

23. **Which of the following causes the aurora borealis?** *(Rigorous) (Skill 51.3)*

    A. gases escaping from earth
    B. particles from the sun
    C. particles from the moon
    D. electromagnetic discharges from the North pole.

24. **The transfer of heat from the earth's surface to the atmosphere is called** *(Average Rigor) (Skill 51.6)*

    A. Convection
    B. Radiation
    C. Conduction
    D. Advection

25. **What is the most accurate description of the Water Cycle?** *(Rigorous) (Skill 52.2)*

    A. Rain comes from clouds, filling the ocean. The water then evaporates and becomes clouds again.
    B. Water circulates from rivers into groundwater and back, while water vapor circulates in the atmosphere.
    C. Water is conserved except for chemical or nuclear reactions, and any drop of water could circulate through clouds, rain, ground-water, and surface-water.
    D. Water flows toward the oceans, where it evaporates and forms clouds, which causes rain, which in turn flow back to the oceans after it falls.

26. **What makes up the largest abiotic portion of the Nitrogen Cycle?** *(Average Rigor) (Skill 52.3)*

    A. Nitrogen Fixing Bacteria.
    B. Nitrates.
    C. Decomposers.
    D. Atomsphere.

27. What are the most significant and prevalent elements in the biosphere?
(Easy) (Skill 52.5)

A. Carbon, Hydrogen, Oxygen, Nitrogen, Phosphorus.
B. Carbon, Hydrogen, Sodium, Iron, Calcium.
C. Carbon, Oxygen, Sulfur, Manganese, Iron.
D. Carbon, Hydrogen, Oxygen, Nickel, Sodium, Nitrogen.

28. "Neap Tides" are especially weak tides that occur when the Sun and Moon are in a perpindicular arrangment to the Earth, and "Spring Tides" are espically strong tides that occur when the Sun and Moon are in line. At which combination of lunar phases do these tides occur (respectively)?
(Rigorous) (Skill 53.5)

A. Half Moon, and Full Moon
B. Quarter Moon, and New Moon
C. Gibbous Moon, and Quarter Moon
D. Full Moon and New Moon

29. The planet with true retrograde rotation is:
(Rigorous) (Skill 54.1)

A. Pluto
B. Neptune
C. Venus
D. Saturn

30. The phases of the moon are the result of its _____ in relation to the sun.
(Average Rigor) (Skill 54.2)

A. revolution
B. rotation
C. position
D. inclination

31. The end of a geologic era is most often characterized by?
(Average Rigor) (Skill 55.1)

A. A general uplifting of the crust.
B. The extinction of the dominant plants and animals
C. The appearance of new life forms.
D. All of the above.

32. The best preserved animal remains have been discovered in?
(Rigorous) (Skill 55.4)

A. Resin
B. Fossil Mold
C. Tar pits
D. Glacial Ice

33. **Which type of student activity is most likely to expose a student's misconceptions about science?**
(Average Rigor) (Skill 56.4)

A. Multiple-Choice and fill-in-the-blank worksheets.
B. Laboratory activities, where the lab is laid out step by step with no active thought on the part of the student.
C. Teacher- lead demonstrations.
D. Laboratories in which the student are forced to critically consider the steps taken and the results.

34. **In an experiment measuring the inhibition effect of different antibiotic discs on bacteria grown in Petri dishes, what are the independent and dependent variables respectively?**
(Rigorous) (Skill 57.6)

A. Number of bacterial colonies and the antibiotic type.
B. Antibiotic type and the distance between antibiotic and the closest colony.
C. Antibiotic type and the number of bacterial colonies.
D. Presence of bacterial colonies and the antibiotic type.

Answer Key: Science

1.	D	10.	D	19.	B	28.	B
2.	B	11.	D	20.	A	29.	C
3.	A	12.	D	21.	D	30.	C
4.	B	13.	C	22.	B	31.	D
5.	B	14.	C	23.	A	32.	C
6.	A	15.	C	24.	C	33.	D
7.	C	16.	A	25.	C	34.	B
8.	A	17.	C	26.	D		
9.	B	18.	A	27.	A		

Rigor Table: Science

	Easy %20	Average Rigor %40	Rigorous %40
Question #	1, 3, 10, 16, 18, 27	2, 4, 6, 12, 13, 15, 19, 20, 22, 24, 26, 30, 31, 33	5, 7, 8, 9, 11, 14, 17, 21, 23, 25, 28, 29, 32, 34

Rationales with Sample Questions: Science

1. **Chemicals should be stored**
   (Easy) (Skill 36.2)

   A. in the principal's office.
   B. in a dark room.
   C. in an off-site research facility.
   D. according to their reactivity with other substances.

Answer: D. According to their reactivity with other substances.

Chemicals should be stored with other chemicals of similar properties (e.g. acids with other acids), to reduce the potential for either hazardous reactions in the store-room, or mistakes in reagent use. Certainly, chemicals should not be stored in anyone's office, and the light intensity of the room is not very important because light-sensitive chemicals are usually stored in dark containers. In fact, good lighting is desirable in a store-room, so that labels can be read easily. Chemicals may be stored off-site, but that makes their use inconvenient. Therefore, the best answer is (D).

2. **When measuring the volume of water in a graduated cylinder, where does one read the measurement?**
   (Average Rigor) (Skill 37.2)

   A. At the highest point of the liquid.
   B. At the bottom of the meniscus curve.
   C. At the closest mark to the top of the liquid
   D. At the top of the plastic safety ring.

Answer: B. At the bottom of the meniscus curve.

To measure water in glass, you must look at the top surface at eye-level, and ascertain the location of the bottom of the meniscus (the curved surface at the top of the water). The meniscus forms because water molecules adhere to the sides of the glass, which is a slightly stronger force than their cohesion to each other. This leads to a U-shaped top of the liquid column, the bottom of which gives the most accurate volume measurement. (Other liquids have different forces, e.g. mercury in glass, which has a convex meniscus.) This is consistent only with answer (B).

3.   **When is a hypothesis formed?**
       (Easy) (Skill 38.2)

  A. Before the data is taken.
  B. After the data is taken.
  C. After the data is analyzed.
  D. Concurrent with graphing the data.

Answer: A. Before the data is taken.

A hypothesis is an educated guess, made before undertaking an experiment. The hypothesis is then evaluated based on the observed data. Therefore, the hypothesis must be formed before the data is taken, not during or after the experiment. This is consistent only with answer (A).

4.   **Which of the following is the most accurate definition of a non-renewable resource?**
       (Average Rigor) (Skill 39.5)

  A. A nonrenewable resource is never replaced once used.
  B. A nonrenewable resource is replaced on a timescale that is very long relative to human life-spans.
  C. A nonrenewable resource is a resource that can only be manufactured by humans.
  D. A nonrenewable resource is a species that has already become extinct.

Answer: B. A nonrenewable resource is replaced on a timescale that is very long relative to human life-spans.

Renewable resources are those that are renewed, or replaced, in time for humans to use more of them. Examples include fast-growing plants, animals, or oxygen gas. (Note that while sunlight is often considered a renewable resource, it is actually a nonrenewable but extremely abundant resource.) Nonrenewable resources are those that renew themselves only on very long timescales, usually geologic timescales. Examples include minerals, metals, or fossil fuels. Therefore, the correct answer is (B).

5.	A scientist exposes mice to cigarette smoke, and notes that their lungs develop tumors. Mice that were not exposed to the smoke do not develop as many tumors. Which of the following conclusions may be drawn from these results?:

I.	Cigarette smoke causes lung tumors.
II.	Cigarette smoke exposure has a positive correlation with lung tumors in mice.
III.	Some mice are predisposed to develop lung tumors.
IV.	Cigarette smoke exposure has a positive correlation with lung tumors in humans.

(Rigorous) (Skill 40.2)

A.	I and II only.
B.	II only.
C.	I , II, III and IV.
D.	II and IV only.

Answer: B. II only.

Although cigarette smoke has been found to cause lung tumors (and many other problems), this particular experiment shows only that there is a positive correlation between smoke exposure and tumor development in these mice. It may be true that some mice are more likely to develop tumors than others, which is why a control group of identical mice should have been used for comparison. Mice are often used to model human reactions, but this is as much due to their low financial and emotional cost as it is due to their being a "good model" for humans, and thus this scientist cannot make the conclusion that cigarette smoke exposure has a positive correlation with lung tumors in humans based on this data alone. Therefore, the answer must be (B).

6.   **Which of the following is a correct explanation for an astronaut's 'weightlessness'?**
     (Average Rigor) (Skill 41.1)

   A. Astronauts continue to feel the pull of gravity in space, but they are so far from planets that the force is small.
   B. Astronauts continue to feel the pull of gravity in space, but spacecraft have such powerful engines that those forces dominate, reducing effective weight.
   C. Astronauts do not feel the pull of gravity in space, because space is a vacuum.
   D. The cumulative gravitational forces, that the astronaut is experiencing, from all sources in the solar system equal out to a net gravitational force of zero.

Answer: A. Astronauts continue to feel the pull of gravity in space, but they are so far from planets that the force is small.

Gravity acts over tremendous distances in space (theoretically, infinite distance, though certainly at least as far as any astronaut has traveled). However, gravitational force is inversely proportional to distance squared from a massive body. This means that when an astronaut is in space, s/he is far enough from the center of mass of any planet that the gravitational force is very small, and s/he feels 'weightless'. Space is mostly empty (i.e. vacuum), and spacecraft do have powerful engines. However, none of these has the effect attributed to it in the incorrect answer choices (B), or (C). Although, theoretically there is a point in space where the cumulative gravitational forces of sources within the solar system would equal a net force of zero, that point would be in constant motion and difficult to find, making answer D unlikely at best and but more accurately near impossible to keep an astronaught at this point. The answer to this question must therefore be (A).

7. **Physical properties are observable characteristics of a substance in its natural state. Which of the following are considered physical properties.**

   I   **Color**
   II **Density**
   III **Specific gravity**
   IV **Melting Point**
   (Rigorous) (Skill 42.1)

   A. I only
   B. I and II only
   C. I, II, and III only
   D. III and IV only

Answer: C. I, II, and III only

Of the possibilities only the melting point of a substance cannot be found without altering the substance itself. Color is readily observable. Density can be measured without changing a substances form or structure, and specific gravity is a ratio based on density, so once one is know the other can be calculated. Thus answer (C) is the only possible answer.

8. **The change in phase from liquid to gas is called:**
   (Rigorous) (Skill 42.2)

   A. Evaporation.
   B. Condensation.
   C. Vaporization.
   D. Boiling.

Answer: A. Evaporation.

Condensation is the change in phase from a gas to a liquid; Vaporization is the conversion of matter to vapor- not all gases are vapors. Boiling is one method of inducing the change from a liquid to a gas; the process is evaporation. The answer is (A).

9. **Which of the following statements is true of all transition elements?**
   (Rigorous) (Skill 43.3)

   A. They are all hard solids at room temperature.
   B. They tend to form salts when reacted with Halogens.
   C. They all have a silvery appearance in their pure state.
   D. All of the Above

Answer: B. They tend to form salts when reacted with Halogens.

Answer (A) is incorrect because of Mercury which has a low melting point is thus a liquid at room temperature. Answer (C) is incorrect because Copper and Gold do not have a silvery appearance in the natural states. Since answers (A) and (C) are not correct then answer (D) cannot be correct either. This leaves only answer (B).

10. **A boulder sitting on the edge of a cliff has which type of energy?**
    (Easy) (Skill 44.1)

    A. Kinetic energy
    B. Latent Energy
    C. No energy
    D. Potential Energy

Answer: D. Potential Energy

Answer (A) would be true if the boulder fell off the cliff and started falling. Answer (C) would be a difficult condition to find since it would mean that no outside forces where operating on an object, and gravity is difficult to avoid. Answer (B) might be a good description of answer (D) which is the correct energy. The boulder has potential energy is imparted from the force of gravity.

11. A converging lens produces a real image _____.
    (Rigorous) (Skill 44.4)

    A. always.
    B. never.
    C. when the object is within one focal length of the lens.
    D. when the object is further than one focal length from the lens.

Answer: D. When the object is further than one focal length from the lens.

A converging lens produces a real image whenever the object is far enough from the lens (outside one focal length) so that the rays of light from the object can hit the lens and be focused into a real image on the other side of the lens. When the object is closer than one focal length from the lens, rays of light do not converge on the other side; they diverge. This means that only a virtual image can be formed, i.e. the theoretical place where those diverging rays would have converged if they had originated behind the object. Thus, the correct answer is (D).

12. Which of the following is not a factor in how different materials will conduct seismic waves?
    (Average Rigor) (Skill 44.6)

    A. Density
    B. Incompressiblity
    C. Rigidty
    D. Tensile strength

Answer: D. Tensile strength

Density affects the speed at which seismic waves travel through the material. Incompressibilty has to do with how quickly a material compresses and rebounds as the waves hit it. The more compressable a material (and thus the slower the rebound) the slower the wave travels trhough the material. Seismic waves create a shearing force as they travel through a material, rigidity is the measure of the material's resistance to that shearing force. Tensile strength measures how far something can be stretched before breaking. Since seismic waves compress materials and are not stretching them that makes answer (D) the correct answer.

13. The Law of Conservation of Energy states that _____.
(Average Rigor) (Skill 45.2)

A. There must be the same number of products and reactants in any chemical equation.
B. Mass and energy can be interchanged.
C. Energy is neither created nor destroyed, but may change form.
D. One form energy must remain intact (or conserved) in all reactions

Answer: C. Energy is neither created nor destroyed, but may change form.

Answer (C) is a summary of the Law of Conservation of Energy (for non-nuclear reactions). In other words, energy can be transformed into various forms such as kinetic, potential, electric, or heat energy, but the total amount of energy remains constant. Answer (A) is untrue, as demonstrated by many synthesis and decomposition reactions. Answers (B) and (D) may be sensible, but they are not relevant in this case. Therefore, the answer is (C).

14.   **When you step out of the shower, the floor feels colder on your feet than the bathmat. Which of the following is the correct explanation for this phenomenon?**
(Rigorous) (Skill 45.5)

     A. The floor is colder than the bathmat.
     B. The bathmat being smaller that the floor quickly reaches equilibrium with your body temperature.
     C. Heat is conducted more easily into the floor.
     D. Water is absorbed from your feet into the bathmat so it doesn't evaporate as quickly as it does off the floor thus not cooling the bathmat as quickly.

Answer: C. Heat is conducted more easily into the floor.

When you step out of the shower and onto a surface, the surface is most likely at room temperature, regardless of its composition (eliminating answer (A)). The bathmat is likely a good insulator and is unlikely to reach equilibrium with your body temperature after a short exposure so answer (B) is incorrect. Although evaporation does have a cooling effect, it the short time it takes you to step from the bathmat to the floor, it is unlikely to have a significant effect on the floor temperature (eliminating answer (D)). Your feet feel cold when heat is transferred from them to the surface, which happens more easily on a hard floor than a soft bathmat. This is because of differences in specific heat (the energy required to change temperature, which varies by material). Therefore, the answer must be (C), i.e. heat is conducted more easily into the floor from your feet.

15. **Identify the correct sequence of organization of living things from lower to higher order:**
(Average Rigor) (Skill 46.3)

    A. Cell, Organelle, Organ, Tissue, System, Organism.
    B. Cell, Tissue, Organ, Organelle, System, Organism.
    C. Organelle, Cell, Tissue, Organ, System, Organism.
    D. Organelle, Tissue, Cell, Organ, System, Organism.

Answer: C. Organelle, Cell, Tissue, Organ, System, Organism.

Organelles are parts of the cell; cells make up tissue, which makes up organs. Organs work together in systems (e.g. the respiratory system), and the organism is the living thing as a whole. Therefore, the answer must be (C).

16. **Catalysts assist reactions by _____ .**
(Easy) (Skill 46.5)

    A. lowering required activation energy.
    B. maintaining precise pH levels.
    C. keeping systems at equilibrium.
    D. changing the starting amounts of reactants.

Answer: A. Lowering required activation energy.

Chemical reactions can be enhanced or accelerated by catalysts, which are present both with reactants and with products. They induce the formation of activated complexes, thereby lowering the required activation energy—so that less energy is necessary for the reaction to begin. Catalysts may require a well maintained pH to operate effectively, however they do not do this themselves. A catalyst, by lowering activation energy, may change a reaction's equilibrium point however it does not maintain a system at equilibrium. The starting level of reactants is controlled separately from the addition of the catalyst, and has no direct correlation. Thus the correct answer is (A).

17.   Which process result in a haploid chromosome number?
      (Rigorous) (Skill 47.2)

      A. Mitosis.
      B. Meiosis I.
      C. Meiosis II.
      D. Neither mitosis nor meiosis.

Answer: C. Meiosis II.

Meiosis is the division of sex cells. The resulting chromosome number is half the number of parent cells, i.e. a 'haploid chromosome number'. Meiosis I mirrors Mitosis, resulting in diploid cells. It is only during Meiosis II that the number of chromosomesx is halved. Mitosis, however, is the division of other cells, in which the chromosome number is the same as the parent cell chromosome number. Therefore, the answer is (B).

18.   A carrier of a genetic disorder is heterozygous for a disorder that is recessive in nature. Hemophilia is a sex-linked disorder. This means that:
      (Easy) (Skill 47.4)

      A. Only females can be carriers
      B. Only males can be carriers.
      C. Both males and females can be carriers.
      D. Neither females nor males can be carriers.

Answer: A. Only females can be carriers

Since Hemophilia is a sex-linked disorder the gene only appears on the X chromosome, with no counterpart on the Y chromosome. Since males are XY they cannot be heterozygous for the trait, what ever is on the single X chromosome will be expressed. Females being XX can be heterozygous. Answer (C) would describe a genetic disorder that is recessive and expressed on one of the somatic chromosomes (not sex-linked). Answer (D) would describe a genetic disorder that is dominant and expressed on any of the chromosomes. An example of answer (C) is sickle cell anemia. An example of answer (D) is Achondroplasia (the most common type of short-limbed dwarfism), in fact for this condition people that are Homozygous dominant for the gene that creates the disorde rusually have severe health problems if they live past infancy, so almost all individuals with this disorder are carriers.

19. **Which of the following is a correct explanation for scientific biological adaptation?**
    (Average Rigor) (Skill 48.2)

    A. Giraffes need to reach higher for leaves to eat, so their necks stretch. The giraffe babies are then born with longer necks. Eventually, there are more long-necked giraffes in the population.
    B. Giraffes with longer necks are able to reach more leaves, so they eat more and have more babies than other giraffes. Eventually, there are more long-necked giraffes in the population.
    C. Giraffes want to reach higher for leaves to eat, so they release enzymes into their bloodstream, which in turn causes fetal development of longer-necked giraffes. Eventually, there are more long-necked giraffes in the population.
    D. Giraffes with long necks are more attractive to other giraffes, so they get the best mating partners and have more babies. Eventually, there are more long-necked giraffes in the population.

Answer: B. Giraffes with longer necks are able to reach more leaves, so they eat more and have more babies than other giraffes. Eventually, there are more long-necked giraffes in the population.

Although evolution is often misunderstood, it occurs via natural selection. Organisms with a life/reproductive advantage will produce more offspring. Over many generations, this changes the proportions of the population. In any case, it is impossible for a stretched neck (A) or a fervent desire (C) to result in a biologically mutated baby. Although there are traits that are naturally selected because of mate attractiveness and fitness (D), this is not the primary situation here, so answer (B) is the best choice.

20. **An animal choosing its mate because of attractive plumage or a strong mating call is an example of:**
    (Average Rigor) (Skill 48.4)

    A. Sexual Selection.
    B. Natural Selection.
    C. Mechanical Isolation.
    D. Linkage

Answer: A. Sexual Selection.

The coming together of genes determines the makeup of the gene pool. Sexual selection, the act of choosing a mate, allows animals to have some choice in the breeding of its offspring. The answer is (A).

21. **Many male birds sing long complicated songs that describe thier identity and the area of land that they claim. Which of the answers below is the best decription of this behavior?**
    (Rigorous) (Skill 49.1)

    A. Innate territorial behavior
    B. Learned competitve behavior
    C. Innate mating behavior
    D. Learned territorial behavior

Answer: D. Learned territorial behavior

Birds often learn their songs, through a combination of trial and error, and listening to the songs of other members of their species (in some cases other species, this is called mimicry). Thus answers (A) and (C) are not correct. Typically a male bird will use a short song to impress a mate, the longer song is territorial because it is trying to convey to other males both identity, and the territory that it claims.

22. **A wrasse (fish) cleans the teeth of other fish by eating away plaque. This is an example of _____ between the fish.**
(Average Rigor) (Skill 50.2)

    A. parasitism.
    B. symbiosis (mutualism).
    C. competition.
    D. predation.

Answer: B. Symbiosis (mutualism).

When both species benefit from their interaction in their habitat, this is called 'symbiosis', or 'mutualism'. In this example, the wrasse benefits from having a source of food, and the other fish benefit by having healthier teeth. Note that 'parasitism' is when one species benefits at the expense of the other, 'competition' is when two species compete with one another for the same habitat or food, and 'predation' is when one species feeds on another. Therefore, the answer is (B).

23. **Which of the following causes the aurora borealis?**
(Rigorous) (Skill 51.3)

    A. gases escaping from earth
    B. particles from the sun
    C. particles from the moon
    D. electromagnetic discharges from the North pole.

Answer: A. particles from the sun

Aurora Borealis is a phenomenon caused by particles escaping from the sun. The particles escaping from the sun include a mixture of gases, electrons and protons, and are sent out at a force that scientists call solar wind. Together, we have the Earth's magnetosphere and the solar wind squeezing the magnetosphere and charged particles everywhere in the field. When conditions are right, the build-up of pressure from the solar wind creates an electric voltage that pushes electrons into the ionosphere. Here they collide with gas atoms, causing them to release both light and more electrons.

24.   The transfer of heat from the earth's surface to the atmosphere is
        called
        (Average Rigor) (Skill 51.6)

        A. Convection
        B. Radiation
        C. Conduction
        D. Advection

Answer: C. Conduction

Radiation is the process of warming through rays or waves of energy, such as
the Sun warms earth. The Earth returns heat to the atmosphere through
conduction. This is the transfer of heat through matter, such that areas of greater
heat move to areas of less heat in an attempt to balance temperature.

25.   What is the most accurate description of the Water Cycle?
        (Rigorous) (Skill 52.2)

        A. Rain comes from clouds, filling the ocean. The water then evaporates
           and becomes clouds again.
        B. Water circulates from rivers into groundwater and back, while water
           vapor circulates in the atmosphere.
        C. Water is conserved except for chemical or nuclear reactions, and any
           drop of water could circulate through clouds, rain, ground-water, and
           surface-water.
        D. Water flows toward the oceans, where it evaporates and forms clouds,
           which causes rain, which in turn flow back to the oceans after it falls.

**Answer: C. Water is conserved except for chemical or nuclear reactions,
        and any drop of water could circulate through clouds, rain,
        ground-water, and surface-water.**

All natural chemical cycles, including the Water Cycle, depend on the principle of
Conservation of Mass. (For water, unlike for elements such as Nitrogen,
chemical reactions may cause sources or sinks of water molecules.)
Any drop of water may circulate through the hydrologic system, ending up in a
cloud, as rain, or as surface- or ground-water. Although answers (A), (B) and (D)
describe parts of the water cycle, the most comprehensive and correct answer is
(C).

26. **What makes up the largest abiotic portion of the Nitrogen Cycle?**
   (Average Rigor) (Skill 52.3)

   A. Nitrogen Fixing Bacteria.
   B. Nitrates.
   C. Decomposers.
   D. Atomsphere.

Answer: D. Atomsphere.

Since answers (A) and (C) are both examples of living organisms they are biotic components of the nitrogen cycle. Nitrates are one type of nitrogen compond, (making it abiotic) that can be found in soil and in living organisms, however it makes up a small portion of the avaible nitrogen. The atmosphere being 78% Nitrogen gas (an abiotic component) makes up the largest source available to the Nitrogen Cycle.

27. **What are the most significant and prevalent elements in the biosphere?**
   (Easy) (Skill 52.5)

   A. Carbon, Hydrogen, Oxygen, Nitrogen, Phosphorus.
   B. Carbon, Hydrogen, Sodium, Iron, Calcium.
   C. Carbon, Oxygen, Sulfur, Manganese, Iron.
   D. Carbon, Hydrogen, Oxygen, Nickel, Sodium, Nitrogen.

Answer: A. Carbon, Hydrogen, Oxygen, Nitrogen, Phosphorus.

Organic matter (and life as we know it) is based on Carbon atoms, bonded to Hydrogen and Oxygen. Nitrogen and Phosphorus are the next most significant elements, followed by Sulfur and then trace nutrients such as Iron, Sodium, Calcium, and others. Therefore, the answer is (A). If you know that the formula for any carbohydrate contains Carbon, Hydrogen, and Oxygen, that will help you narrow the choices to (A) and (D) in any case.

28.   "Neap Tides" are especially weak tides that occur when the Sun and Moon are in a perpindicular arrangment to the Earth, and "Spring Tides" are espically strong tides that occur when the Sun and Moon are in line. At which combination of lunar phases do these tides occur (respectively)?
       (Rigorous) (Skill 53.5)

       A. Half Moon, and Full Moon
       B. Quarter Moon, and New Moon
       C. Gibbous Moon, and Quarter Moon
       D. Full Moon and New Moon

Answer: B. Quarter Moon, and New Moon

"Spring tides" are especially strong tides that occur when the Earth, Sun and Moon are in line, allowing both the Sun and the Moon to exert gravitational force on the Earth and increase tidal bulge height. These tides occur during the full moon and the new moon. "Neap tides" occur during quarter moons, when the sun is illuminating half of the Moon's surface, (the term quarter is used to refer to the fact that the Moon has traveled 1/2 of it's way there its cycle, not the amount of the surface illuminated by the Sun.) A Gibbous Moon describes the Moon between Full and Quarter.

29.   The planet with true retrograde rotation is:
       (Rigorous) (Skill 54.1)

       A. Pluto
       B. Neptune
       C. Venus
       D. Saturn

Answer: C. Venus

Venus has an axial tilt of only 3 degrees and a very slow rotation. It spins in the direction opposite of its counterparts (who spin in the same direction as the Sun). Uranus is also tilted and orbits on its side. However, this is thought to be the consequence of an impact that left the previously prograde rotating planet tilted in such a manner.

30.   The phases of the moon are the result of its _____ in relation to the sun.
       (Average Rigor) (Skill 54.2)

A. revolution
B. rotation
C. position
D. inclination

Answer: C. Position

The moon is visible in varying amounts during its orbit around the earth. One half of the moon's surface is always illuminated by the Sun (appears bright), but the amount observed can vary from full moon to none

31.   The end of a geologic era is most often characterized by?
       (Average Rigor) (Skill 55.1)

A. A general uplifting of the crust.
B. The extinction of the dominant plants and animals
C. The appearance of new life forms.
D. All of the above.

Answer: D. All of the above.

Any of these things can be used to characterize the end of a geologic era, and often a combination of factors are applied to determining the end of an era.

32. **The best preserved animal remains have been discovered in?**
    (Rigorous) (Skill 55.4)

    A. Resin
    B. Fossil Mold
    C. Tar pits
    D. Glacial Ice

Answer: C. tar pits.

Tar pits provide a wealth of information when it comes to fossils. Tar pits are oozing areas of asphalt, which were so sticky as to trap animals. These animals, without a way out, would die of starvation or be preyed upon. Their bones would remain in the tar pits, and be covered by the continued oozing of asphalt. Because the asphalt deposits were continuously added, the bones were not exposed to much weathering, and we have found some of the most complete and unchanged fossils from these areas, including mammoths and saber toothed cats.

33. **Which type of student activity is most likely to expose a student's misconceptions about science?**
    (Average Rigor) (Skill 56.4)

    A. Multiple-Choice and fill-in-the-blank worksheets.
    B. Laboratory activities, where the lab is laid out step by step with no active thought on the part of the student.
    C. Teacher- lead demonstrations.
    D. Laboratories in which the student are forced to critically consider the steps taken and the results.

Answer: D. Laboratories in which the student are forced to critically consider the steps taken and the results.

Answer (A) is a typical retain and repeate exercise, where a student just needs to remember the answer and doesn't need to understand it. Answer (B), is often called a cookie cutter lab because everything fit to a specific plan. Students are often able to geuss the right answer without understanding the process. Teacher lead demonstrations can be interesting for the students, and my challenge a students misconceptions. A student's misconceptions are often firmly routed and will require critical thought and reflection by the student for it to change, often an attempt to illuminate a student's misconception doesn't get rid of it, but gets incorporated into their inaccurate understanding of the universe. Answer (D) requires active mental participation on the behalf of the student and thus is most likely to alter their personally understanding. These types of labs are often refered to as guided discovery laboratories.

34. **In an experiment measuring the inhibition effect of different antibiotic discs on bacteria grown in Petri dishes, what are the independent and dependent variables respectively?**
(Rigorous) (Skill 57.6)

   A. Number of bacterial colonies and the antibiotic type.
   B. Antibiotic type and the distance between antibiotic and the closest colony.
   C. Antibiotic type and the number of bacterial colonies.
   D. Presence of bacterial colonies and the antibiotic type.

Answer: B. Antibiotic type and the distance between antibiotic and the closest colony.

To answer this question, recall that the independent variable in an experiment is the entity that is changed by the scientist, in order to observe the effects the dependent variable. In this experiment, antibiotic used is purposely changed so it is the independent variable. Answers A and D list antibiotic type as the dependent variable and thus cannot be the answer, leaving answers B and C as the only two viable choices. The best answer is B, because it measures at what concentration of the antibiotic the bacteria are able to grow at, (as you move from the source of the antibiotic the concentration decreases). Answer C is not as effective because it could be interpreted that that a plate that shows a large number of colonies a greater distance from the antibiotic is a less effective antibiotic than a plate a smaller number of colonies in close proximity to the antibiotic disc, which is reverse of the actually result.

Sample Essays: Science

1. Using your accumulated knowledge, discuss the components of biogeochemical cycles.

Best:

Essential elements are recycled through an ecosystem. At times, the element needs to be made available in a useable form. Cycles are dependent on plants, algae and bacteria to fix nutrients for use by animals. The four main cycles are: water, carbon, nitrogen, and phosphorous.

Two percent of all the water is fixed in ice or the bodies of organisms, rendering it unavailable. Available water includes surface water (lakes, ocean, and rivers) and ground water (aquifers, wells). The majority (96%) of all available water is from ground water. Water is recycled through the processes of evaporation and precipitation. The water present now is the water that has been here since our atmosphere was formed.

Ten percent of all available carbon in the air (in the form of carbon dioxide gas) is fixed by photosynthesis. Plants fix carbon in the form of glucose, animals eat the plants and are able to obtain the carbon necessary to sustain themselves. When animals release carbon dioxide through respiration, the cycle begins again as plants recycle the carbon through photosynthesis.

Eighty percent of the atmosphere is in the form of nitrogen gas. Nitrogen must be fixed and taken out of the gaseous form to be incorporated into an organism. Only a few genera of bacteria have the correct enzymes to break the strong triple bond between nitrogen atoms. These special bacteria live within the roots of legumes (peas, beans, alfalfa) and add bacteria to the soil so it may be taken-up by the plant. Nitrogen is necessary in the building of amino acids and the nitrogenous bases of DNA.

Phosphorus exists as a mineral and is not found in the atmosphere. Fungi and plant roots have structures called mycorrhizae that are able to fix insoluble phosphates into useable phosphorus. Urine and decayed matter returns phosphorus to the earth where it can be fixed in the plant. Phosphorus is needed for the backbone of DNA and for the manufacture of ATP.

The four biogeochemical cycles are present concurrently. Water is continually recycled, and is utilized by organisms to sustain life. Carbon is also a necessary component for life. Both water and carbon can be found in the air and on the ground. Nitrogen and phosphorous are commonly found in the ground. Special organisms, called decomposers, help to make these elements available in the environment. Plants use the recycled materials for energy and when they are consumed, the cycle begins again.

Better:

Essential elements are recycled through an ecosystem. Cycles are dependent on plants, algae and bacteria to make nutrients available for use by animals. The four main cycles are: water, carbon, nitrogen, and phosphorous. Water is typically available as surface water (large bodies of water) or ground water. Water is recycled through the states of gas, liquid (rain), and solid (ice or snow). Carbon is necessary for life as it is the basis for organic matter. It is a byproduct of photosynthesis and is found in the air as carbon dioxide gas. Nitrogen is the largest component of the atmosphere. It is also necessary for the creation of amino acids and the nitrogenous bases of DNA. Phosphorous is another elemental cycle. Phosphorous is found in the soil and is made available by decomposition. It is then converted for use in the manufacture of DNA and ATP.

Basic:

Elements are recycled through an ecosystem. This occurs through cycles. These important cycles are called biogeochemical cycles. The water cycle consists of water moving from bodies of water into the air and back again as precipitation. The carbon cycle includes all organisms, as mammals breathe out carbon dioxide and are made of carbon molecules. Nitrogen is an amino building block and is found in soil. As things are broken down phosphorous is added to the earth, enriching the soil.

2. Examine the components of a eukaryotic cell.

Best:

The cell is the basic unit of all living things. Eukaryotic cells are found in protists, fungi, plants, and animals. Eukaryotic cells are organized. They contain many organelles, which are membrane bound areas for specific functions. Their cytoplasm contains a cytoskeleton that provides a protein framework for the cell. The cytoplasm also supports the organelles and contains the ions and molecules necessary for cell function. The cytoplasm is contained by the plasma membrane. The plasma membrane allows molecules to pass in and out of the cell. The membrane can bud inward to engulf outside material in a process called endocytosis. Exocytosis is a secretory mechanism, the reverse of endocytosis.

Eukaryotes have a nucleus. The nucleus is the brain of the cell that contains all of the cell's genetic information. The genetic information is contained on chromosomes that consist of chromatin, which is a complex of DNA and proteins. The chromosomes are tightly coiled to conserve space while providing a large surface area. The nucleus is the site of transcription of the DNA into RNA. The nucleolus is where ribosomes are made. There is at least one of these dark-staining bodies inside the nucleus of most eukaryotes. The nuclear envelope is two membranes separated by a narrow space. The envelope contains many pores that let RNA out of the nucleus.

Ribosomes are the site for protein synthesis. They may be free floating in the cytoplasm or attached to the endoplasmic reticulum. There may be up to a half a million ribosomes in a cell, depending on how much protein is made by the cell.

The endoplasmic reticulum (ER) is folded and provides a large surface area. It is the "roadway" of the cell and allows for transport of materials through and out of the cell. There are two types of ER. Smooth endoplasmic reticulum contains no ribosomes on their surface. This is the site of lipid synthesis. Rough endoplasmic reticulum has ribosomes on its surfaces. They aid in the synthesis of proteins that are membrane bound or destined for secretion.

Many of the products made in the ER proceed on to the Golgi apparatus. The Golgi apparatus functions to sort, modify, and package molecules that are made in the other parts of the cell. These molecules are either sent out of the cell or to other organelles within the cell. The Golgi apparatus is a stacked structure to increase the surface area.

Lysosomes are found mainly in animal cells. These contain digestive enzymes that break down food, substances not needed, viruses, damaged cell components and eventually the cell itself. It is believed that lysomomes are responsible for the aging process.

Mitochondria are large organelles that are the site of cellular respiration, where ATP is made to supply energy to the cell. Muscle cells have many mitochondria because they use a great deal of energy. Mitochondria have their own DNA, RNA, and ribosomes and are capable of reproducing by binary fission if there is a greater demand for additional energy. Mitochondria have two membranes: a smooth outer membrane and a folded inner membrane. The folds inside the mitochondria are called cristae. They provide a large surface area for cellular respiration to occur.

Plastids are found only in photosynthetic organisms. They are similar to the mitochondira due to the double membrane structure. They also have their own DNA, RNA, and ribosomes and can reproduce if the need for the increased capture of sunlight becomes necessary. There are several types of plastids. Chloroplasts are the sight of photosynthesis. The stroma is the chloroplast's inner membrane space. The stoma encloses sacs called thylakoids that contain the photosynthetic pigment chlorophyll. The chlorophyll traps sunlight inside the thylakoid to generate ATP which is used in the stroma to produce carbohydrates and other products. The chromoplasts make and store yellow and orange pigments. They provide color to leaves, flowers, and fruits. The amyloplasts store starch and are used as a food reserve. They are abundant in roots like potatoes.

The Endosymbiotic Theory states that mitochondria and chloroplasts were once free living and possibly evolved from prokaryotic cells. At some point in our evolutionary history, they entered the eukaryotic cell and maintained a symbiotic relationship with the cell, with both the cell and organelle benefiting from the relationship. The fact that they both have their own DNA, RNA, ribosomes, and are capable of reproduction helps to confirm this theory.

Found in plant cells only, the cell wall is composed of cellulose and fibers. It is thick enough for support and protection, yet porous enough to allow water and dissolved substances to enter. Vacuoles are found mostly in plant cells. They hold stored food and pigments. Their large size allows them to fill with water in order to provide turgor pressure. Lack of turgor pressure causes a plant to wilt.

The cytoskeleton, found in both animal and plant cells, is composed of protein filaments attached to the plasma membrane and organelles. They provide a framework for the cell and aid in cell movement. They constantly change shape and move about. Three types of fibers make up the cytoskeleton:

1. Microtubules – the largest of the three, they make up cilia and flagella for locomotion. Some examples are sperm cells, cilia that line the fallopian tubes, and tracheal cilia. Centrioles are also composed of microtubules. They aid in cell division to form the spindle fibers that pull the cell apart into two new cells. Centrioles are not found in the cells of higher plants.

2. Intermediate filaments – intermediate in size, they are smaller than microtubules but larger than microfilaments. They help the cell to keep its shape.

3. Microfilaments – smallest of the three, they are made of actin and small amounts of myosin (like in muscle tissue). They function in cell movement like cytoplasmic streaming, endocytosis, and ameboid movement. This structure pinches the two cells apart after cell division, forming two new cells.

Better:

The cell is the basic unit of all living things. Eukaryotic cells are found in protists, fungi, plants, and animals. Eukaryotic cells are organized. Their cytoplasm contains a cytoskeleton that provides a protein framework for the cell. The cytoplasm is contained by the plasma membrane. The plasma membrane allows molecules to pass in and out of the cell.

Eukaryotes have a nucleus. The nucleus is the brain of the cell that contains all of the cell's genetic information. The chromosomes house genetic information and are tightly coiled to conserve space while providing a large surface area. The nucleus is the site of transcription of the DNA into RNA. The nucleolus is where ribosomes are made.

Ribosomes are the site for protein synthesis. There may be up to a half a million ribosomes in a cell, depending on how much protein is made by the cell.

The endoplasmic reticulum (ER) is folded and provides a large surface area. It is the "roadway" of the cell and allows for transport of materials through and out of the cell. It may be smooth or rough.

Many of the products made in the ER proceed on to the Golgi apparatus. The Golgi apparatus functions to sort, modify, and package molecules that are made in the other parts of the cell.

Mitochondria are large organelles that are the site of cellular respiration, where ATP is made to supply energy to the cell. Mitochondria have their own DNA, RNA, and ribosomes and are capable of reproducing by binary fission if there is a greater demand for additional energy.

Plastids are found only in photosynthetic organisms. They are similar to the mitochondira. They also have their own DNA, RNA, and ribosomes and can reproduce if the need for the increased capture of sunlight becomes necessary.

Found in plant cells only, the cell wall is composed of cellulose and fibers. It is thick enough for support and protection, yet porous enough to allow water and dissolved substances to enter.

The cytoskeleton, found in both animal and plant cells, is composed of protein filaments attached to the plasma membrane and organelles. They provide a framework for the cell and aid in cell movement. They constantly change shape and move about. Three types of fibers make up the cytoskeleton (in order of size: largest-smallest): microtubules, intermediate filaments, microfilaments.

Basic:

The cell is the basic unit of all living things. Eukaryotic cells contain many organelles. Eukaryotes have a nucleus. The nucleus is the brain of the cell that contains all of the cell's genetic information. The nucleus is the site of DNA transcription. There is at least one nucleolus inside the nucleus of most eukaryotes. Ribosomes are the site for protein synthesis and can be found on the endoplasmic reticulum (ER). The Golgi apparatus functions to sort, modify, and package molecules that are made in the other parts of the cell. Mitochondria are large organelles that are the site of cellular respiration, where ATP is made to supply energy to the cell.

In plant cells, the cell wall is composed of cellulose and fibers. The cytoskeleton, found in both animal and plant cells, is composed of protein filaments. The three types of fibers differ in size and help the cell to keep its shape and aid in movement.

3. Discuss the scientific process.

Best:

Science may be defined as a body of knowledge that is systematically derived from study, observations, and experimentation. Its goal is to identify and establish principles and theories that may be applied to solve problems. Pseudoscience, on the other hand, is a belief that is not warranted. There is no scientific methodology or application. Some of the more classic examples of pseudoscience include witchcraft, alien encounters or any topic that is explained by hearsay.

Scientific theory and experimentation must be repeatable. It is also possible to be disproved and is capable of change. Science depends on communication, agreement, and disagreement among scientists. It is composed of theories, laws, and hypotheses.

theory - the formation of principles or relationships which have been verified and accepted.

law - an explanation of events that occur with uniformity under the same conditions (laws of nature, law of gravitation).

hypothesis - an unproved theory or educated guess followed by research to best explain a phenomena. A theory is a proven hypothesis.

Science is limited by the available technology. An example of this would be the relationship of the discovery of the cell and the invention of the microscope. As our technology improves, more hypotheses will become theories and possibly laws. Science is also limited by the data that is able to be collected. Data may be interpreted differently on different occasions. Science limitations cause explanations to be changeable as new technologies emerge.

The first step in scientific inquiry is posing a question to be answered. Next, a hypothesis is formed to provide a plausible explanation. An experiment is then proposed and performed to test this hypothesis. A comparison between the predicted and observed results is the next step. Conclusions are then formed and it is determined whether the hypothesis is correct or incorrect. If incorrect, the next step is to form a new hypothesis and the process is repeated.

Better:

Science is derived from study, observations, and experimentation. Its goal is to identify and establish principles and theories that may be applied to solve problems. Scientific theory and experimentation must be repeatable. It is also possible to disprove or change a theory. Science depends on communication, agreement, and disagreement among scientists. It is composed of theories, laws, and hypotheses. A theory is a principle or relationship that has been verified and accepted through experiments. A law is an explanation of events that occur with uniformity under the same conditions. A hypothesis is an educated guess followed by research. A theory is a proven hypothesis.

Science is limited by the available technology. An example of this would be the relationship of the discovery of the cell and the invention of the microscope. The first step in scientific inquiry is posing a question to be answered. Next, a hypothesis is formed to provide a plausible explanation. An experiment is then proposed and performed to test this hypothesis. A comparison between the predicted and observed results is the next step. Conclusions are then formed and it is determined whether the hypothesis is correct or incorrect. If incorrect, the next step is to form a new hypothesis and the process is repeated.

Basic:

Science is composed of theories, laws, and hypotheses. The first step in scientific inquiry is posing a question to be answered. Next, a hypothesis is formed to provide a plausible explanation. An experiment is then proposed and performed to test this hypothesis. A comparison between the predicted and observed results is the next step. Conclusions are then formed and it is determined whether the hypothesis is correct or incorrect. If incorrect, the next step is to form a new hypothesis and the process is repeated. Science is always limited by the available technology.

XAMonline, INC. 21 Orient Ave. Melrose, MA 02176
Toll Free number 800-509-4128
TO ORDER Fax 781-662-9268 OR www.XAMonline.com

TEXAS EXAMINATION OF EDUCATOR STANDARD-EXAMINATION FOR THE CERTIFICATION OF EDUCATORS   - TEXES/EXCET - 2008

PO#   Store/School:

Address 1:

Address 2 (Ship to other):

City, State Zip

Credit card number_____-_____-_____-_____   expiration_____

EMAIL _____

PHONE   FAX

ISBN	TITLE	Qty	Retail	Total
978-1-58197-925-1	ExCET ART SAMPLE TEST (ALL-LEVEL-SECONDARY) 005 006			
978-1-58197-926-8	ExCET FRENCH SAMPLE TEST (SECONDARY) 048			
978-1-58197-927-5	ExCET SPANISH (SECONDARY) 047			
978-1-58197-580-2	TExES PRINCIPAL 068			
978-1-58197-929-9	TExES PEDAGOGY AND PROFESSIONAL RESPONSIBILITIES 4-8 110			
978-1-58197-899-5	TExES PEDAGOGY AND PROFESSIONAL RESPONSIBILITIES EC-4 100			
978-1-58197-271-9	TExES GENERALIST 4-8 111			
978-1-58197-945-9	TExES GENERALIST EC-4 101			
978-1-58197-948-0	TExES MATHEMATICS-SCIENCE 4-8 114			
978-1-58197-295-5	TExES MATHEMATICS 4-8 114-115			
978-1-58197-297-9	TExES SCIENCE 4-8 116			
978-1-58197-931-2	TExES SCIENCE 8-12 136			
978-1-58197-772-7	TExES ENGLISH LANG-ARTS AND READING 4-8 117			
978-1-58197-771-4	TExES ENGLISH LANG-ARTS AND READING 8-12 131			
978-1-58197-661-8	TExES SOCIAL STUDIES 4-8 118			
978-1-58197-621-2	TExES SOCIAL STUDIES 8-12 132			
978-1-58197-339-6	TExES MATHEMATICS 8-12 135			
978-1-58197-618-2	TExES LIFE SCIENCE 8-12 138			
978-1-58197-949-7	TExES CHEMISTRY 8-12 140			
978-1-58197-939-8	TExES MATHEMATICS-PHYSICS 8-12 143			
978-1-58197-940-4	TExES SCHOOL LIBRARIAN 150			
978-1-58197-941-1	TExES READING SPECIALIST 151			
978-1-58197-942-8	TExES SCHOOL COUNSELOR 152			
978-1-58197-620-5	TExES PHYSICAL EDUCATION EC-12 158			
978-1-58197-262-7	TExES SPECIAL EDUCATION EC-12 161			
978-1-58197-606-9	THEA TEXAS HIGHER EDUCATOR ASSESSMENT			
			SUBTOTAL	
			Ship	$8.25
			TOTAL	

LaVergne, TN USA
25 March 2011
221681LV00001B/7/P